THE GARDEN PROBLEM SOLVER

Reader's Digest

THE READER'S DIGEST ASSOCIATION, INC.
Pleasantville, New York/Montreal

THE GARDEN PROBLEM SOLVER

STAFF

Project Senior Editor
Delilah Smittle

Project Design Director
Sandra Berinstein

Senior Editor
Don Earnest

Senior Designer
Carol Nehring

Editorial Assistant
Donna Gataletto

Special Thanks
Carolyn T. Chubet
Jim Cozby
Diane Hoffman
Barbara Lapic
Tomaso Milian
Nancy Shuker
Robert Steimle
Susan Welt

**Editorial Director,
Gardening Books**
David Schiff

READER'S DIGEST GENERAL BOOKS

Editor-in-Chief
Christopher Cavanaugh

Art Director
Joan Mazzeo

CONTRIBUTORS

Consulting Editor
Rosemary C. Rennicke

Writers
Trevor Cole
Jeff Day
Terri Dunn
Natalia Hamill
Jacqueline Murphy
Pam Pierce
Barbara Pleasant
Kathleen Pyle
Sally Roth

Picture Research
by Carousel Research, Inc.

Picture Editor
Laurie Platt Winfrey

Picture Researcher
J. Christopher Deegan

Picture Research Assistant
Van Bucher

Copy Editors
Nancy Wallace Humes
Kathryn Phelps Summers
Nancy Stabile

Proofreaders
Elizabeth P. Stell
Ann Snyder

Illustrator
Mavis Augustine Torke

Indexer
Lina Burton

Editorial Development
by Storey Communications, Inc.

Deborah Burns
Dan Callahan
Laurie Figary
Catherine Gee Graney
Betty Kodela
Cindy McFarland
Giles Prett
Marie Salter
Charles W. G. Smith
Jana Stone

CONSULTANTS

Ronald D. Gardner,
Senior Extension Associate,
Cornell University

Guy Sternberg,
Star Hill Forest Arboretum

Elizabeth P. Stell

Henry A. Art,
Professor of Biology,
Williams College

Copyright © 1999 The Reader's Digest Association, Inc.
Copyright © 1999 The Reader's Digest Association (Canada) Ltd.
Copyright © 1999 Reader's Digest Association Far East Ltd.
Philippine Copyright 1999 Reader's Digest Association Far East Ltd.

All rights reserved. Unauthorized reproduction, in any manner, is prohibited.

Library of Congress Cataloging in Publication Data

The garden problem solver
         p.   cm.
      Includes index.
      ISBN 0-7621-0140-7 (alk. paper)
      1. Gardening.   I. Reader's Digest Association.
SB453.G2733 1999
635—dc21   98-47125

Address any comments about
THE GARDEN PROBLEM SOLVER to

Editor-in-Chief
U.S. General Books
Reader's Digest
Reader's Digest Road
Pleasantville, NY 10570

To order additional copies of
THE GARDEN PROBLEM SOLVER, call
1-800-846-2100

You can also visit us on the
World Wide Web at
http://www.readersdigest.com

INTRODUCTION

Colorful flower beds and lush groundcovers, fragrant herbs, a bountiful vegetable garden, productive fruit trees and berry bushes, and a velvety green lawn—these are the goals of every gardener. Keeping plants healthy and beautiful is not a matter of luck, but of skill and knowledge. In fact, pests and diseases are the best garden teachers, and dealing with problems successfully is the best way that a gardener can master the craft.

This book is designed to give you the knowledge and skills required to overcome garden problems. It will help you diagnose the cause of trouble and apply solutions, plant by plant, in order to create and maintain a thriving community of plants in your yard and garden. Included, too, are Quick Troubleshooting Guides for diagnosing problems common to various groups of plants, a calendar of preventive garden maintenance tasks that will help you establish a healthy garden and avoid problems in the future, and detailed information on pesticides. The following pages present suggestions on using this book effectively, along with an important overview of how to use pesticides safely and responsibly.

Equipped with this book, you can look at your garden, note the condition of plants, and ask yourself these questions. Are the plants thriving or failing? Is a plant strong and sturdy or weak and drooping? Is one plant growing more slowly than others or so quickly that it will soon outgrow its space? Is the plant's foliage vigorous, or does it have spots, holes, or poor color? Are insects present? Is the plant progressing through its life cycle, blossoming and setting seeds or fruits as expected? Are flowers plentiful and of adequate size? Are fruits and vegetables of expected size, quantity, and flavor? Observing your plants closely is part of the process of being a gardener and, more than any books or classes or professional advice, will make you wise and knowledgeable about the innermost workings of your garden.

—The Editors

ABOUT THIS BOOK

PART ONE

Solving plant problems

What do you do if your flowering tree does not flower? What if your lettuce leaves are brown at the edges? Turn to the relevant chapter on trees or vegetables to find out. Look up the name of the plant and check the descriptions and photographs until you find an entry that describes and shows a problem that matches your plant's troubles.

You can do the same for more than 1,000 other garden problems in this comprehensive guide to solving problems of flowers, vegetables, herbs, ornamental grasses and ground covers, shrubs and vines, trees, and fruits and nuts. For each plant, you'll find detailed descriptions of problems that commonly affect it and explanations of the causes of the problems. Each problem is followed by a solution, which gives you remedies for treating the plant as well as preventative tips and long-term garden techniques for discouraging the problem in the future.

The solution may recommend the use of a specific product, such as a floating fabric row cover or a sticky trap. These products are commonly available from garden centers or mail-order garden catalogs. If a home remedy, such as baking-soda solution, is recommended, you can refer to the recipes in the Home Remedies appendix (pp.392–93). If an organic or synthetic pesticide is recommended, you can refer to the Organic Treatments appendix (pp.394–95) or to the Synthetic Treatments appendix (pp.396–99).

Plant identification information

Each plant entry begins with an identification box—a thumbnail description of the plant's primary growing requirements. The box includes the following:

- **Common name.** Plants have two names: the common name, by which the plant is popularly known, and the botanical name, which is recognized worldwide as the scientific designation. To make this book accessible to all gardeners, the plants in Part One

are organized alphabetically by common name. If you are having a problem with sunflowers, for instance, you won't need to know that their botanical name is *Helianthus annuus* to find them.

- **Botanical name.** These Latin names are necessary to identify a plant precisely, because different plants often share the same common name or a single plant may have more than one common name. A plant's botanical name, however, is unique. Botanical names are easy to understand. For example, *erectus* denotes an upright growth habit; *robustus* means stout or strong. Once you become familiar with them, you will find it easier to select exactly the specimen you want from a nursery or catalog.

  A plant's scientific botanical name usually has three parts: the genus (first); species (second), both set in italics; and the variety or cultivar (a variety is italicized; a cultivar, or cultivated variety, is enclosed in single quotation marks). If an entry covers more than one species in the same genus, the identification box will have the abbreviation "spp.," denoting several species. If it covers different varieties, they will be listed as "vars." If the symbol "×" appears in a name, it indicates that the plant is a hybrid—the offspring between the listed species and another plant of dissimilar parentage.

- **Light.** All plants need light to survive. How much light they need, however, varies from plant to plant. In this book, full sun means at least six hours of light a day, partial shade means two to six hours, and shade means two hours or less.

- **Soil.** The term soil describes the types of earth in which plants grow. Depending on where you live, the soil might be sandy and well drained or clay and soggy, rich and fertile or thin and infertile. While some plants tolerate a range of soils, others require a specific type of soil in order to thrive. Another factor that affects the soil is pH, which is a soil's level of acidity or alkalinity measured on a scale from 0 to 14. A pH between 0 and 6.9 is acidic, while a pH between 7.1 and 14 is alkaline; a perfectly balanced, neutral pH is 7.0.

- *Moisture.* As with light and soil, each plant requires a different level of moisture during the growing season. There are four moisture categories used in the identification box: wet means more than 1 inch of water per week, moist means 1 inch of water per week, seasonally dry is 0 to 1 inch per week, and dry is consistently less than 1 inch of water per week. (For how to measure water, see p.386.)

- *Hardiness.* This indicates the range of temperatures a perennial plant will tolerate. The U.S. Department of Agriculture has divided North America into 11 hardiness zones, each determined by plotting the average winter minimum temperatures; the higher the zone number, the milder the winter climate. While a plant hardiness rating indicates how much cold a plant can endure, it also includes such factors as heat and humidity. For this reason, each plant in this book is assigned a lower and an upper zone limit. For example, mountain laurel (*Kalmia latifolia*) is hardy in zones 4 to 9. This means that it performs best in areas whose minimum temperatures are between –20° and 30°F. Refer to the zone map on the last page of this book to find the zone in which your garden is located. Every plant that you grow outdoors should be hardy to that zone. If a plant is designated as a tender annual, it can be grown anywhere during the summer growing season. And a cold-hardy annual may be grown during the cool spring and fall (and overwinter in mild-winter areas) as well as summer. Annuals, unlike perennials, set seeds and die within a year. Biennials complete their growth cycle in two years.

Special features

Part One also offers other unique and valuable features:

- *Quick Troubleshooting Guides* at the beginning of each chapter give descriptions and photographs of pests and diseases common to many plants in that chapter.

- *Time-Tested Techniques* boxes explain tried-and-true gardening skills, such as dividing perennials, pruning roses, and digging and storing tender bulbs.

- *Wise Choices* boxes list plant varieties selected for their tolerance to insects or diseases, their suitability for use in problem sites, or some other notable feature.

- *Regional Focus* side columns throughout each chapter cover problems specific to a particular plant growing in the East, Southeast, Southwest, Northwest, or Central region of the country.

- *Did You Know?* side columns provide interesting tips and tidbits to help you grow plants more successfully.

PART TWO

Solving yard, garden, and landscape problems

In addition to covering specific pests and diseases, this book includes information on solving more general problems in the yard and garden, such as growing plants on difficult sites, improving the soil, making perfect compost, choosing a lawn grass, and making the most of your landscape.

- *Chapter 8, Soil and Compost,* tells you what those numbers on a fertilizer label mean, along with down-to-earth advice on amending your soil to suit your plants, making and using compost, and correcting soil problems, such as poor drainage.

- *Chapter 9, Lawns,* explains how to improve poor lawn growth, plant the lawn that suits your climate, and overcome lawn damage, weeds, insects, and diseases.

- *Chapter 10, In the Landscape,* discusses how to use plants effectively in your yard and helps you solve environmental and design problems, such as growing plants in the dry shade under trees, screening unattractive views, and concealing the foundation at the front of your house.

- *Chapter 11, Maintenance,* is a handy guide to preventive care, providing a calendar that outlines essential tasks in the garden from late winter, through spring and summer, into fall.

APPENDICES

Other important information appears in the appendices at the end of the book. These sections will help you understand how pesticides work, so that you can choose and use organic and synthetic pesticides effectively. They also give you simple recipes for mixing economical and environmentally friendly home remedies, and will help you understand the gardening terms used in this book.

● ***Understanding Pesticides*** gives a detailed explanation of pesticide classifications and uses. Pesticides include a wide range of products used to control insects and diseases, and selecting the right product and using it properly can be confusing. Before reaching for any recommended pesticide, be sure to read How to Use Pesticides Safely (box, right).

● ***Home Remedies*** gives recipes for some easy-to-make preventatives and treatments, such as disease-inhibiting compost tea and fungicidal baking-soda solution. These remedies are an effective control for many common garden problems and are generally much safer for you and your garden than other treatments. They are recommended in this book as your first recourse whenever appropriate.

● ***Organic Treatments*** provides information on specific organically acceptable treatments, which range from insecticidal soap to predatory insects to mineral treatments. Organic treatments are generally less harmful to the environment than synthetic pesticides. But you should read their descriptions before using them. Some are powerful pesticides that can harm birds, fish, and other wildlife.

● ***Synthetic Treatments*** gives details on specific manufactured active ingredients used in pesticides designed to control pests and diseases. Each pesticide entry tells how the chemical works and whether there are health or environmental concerns associated with it.

● ***Glossary*** provides definitions of gardening terms used in this book. Most are easy to understand or self-explanatory, but if you do come across a word that is new to you, this appendix can help you.

● ***U.S. Climate Zone Map*** is a map published by the U.S. Department of Agriculture that divides the U.S. into 11 plant-hardiness zones. It will help you understand which plants will thrive in your area.

Before You Spray

Before using any pesticide, make sure that you are treating an identifiable pest or disease and not a condition caused by a soil imbalance, an inappropriate site, or bad weather. Use the descriptions and photographs in this book to guide you. Sometimes the solution will be as simple as fertilizing, pruning, changing the plant's location, planting at a different time, or using some other gardening technique.

Try Organic Treatments First

When a treatment more aggressive than good garden sanitation is called for, turn first to organically acceptable controls. These treatments, called simply organic controls in this book, include:

■ insecticidal soap

■ biological controls, such as predatory insects and naturally occurring diseases that target pests

■ plant-derived botanical controls, such as the insecticide pyrethrin

■ mineral treatments, such as fungicidal copper and sulfur

■ petroleum-based, insecticidal horticultural oils.

Use these controls as recommended in the book, timing their application to the proper season, as needed. Repeat as suggested on product labels or in the entry.

Save Strong Chemicals for Severe Problems

When all else fails, you may want to turn to synthetic pesticides. Before buying any commercial pesticide, read the label. Make sure it is labeled (registered) for use on the pest and plant you wish to treat. Do not use a pesticide on a plant or a pest for which it is not registered. Also, note the signal word indicating the pesticide's toxicity:

■ CAUTION is least toxic.

■ WARNING is moderately toxic.

■ DANGER is most toxic (and not sold to home gardeners).

Use Common-Sense Precautions

The product label also gives guidelines about protective clothing and application; what the best season, time of day, and

HOW TO USE PESTICIDES SAFELY

weather conditions are for application, and how long you should wait before you reenter the area.

Before applying pesticides, walk around the area to be treated. Make sure the pesticides will be applied only to the targeted plant or area. Watch the weather. Do not apply pesticides when it is windy or rainy or when the temperature is above 85°F. Make sure weather conditions match the label recommendations to avoid damaging leaves, flowers, or beneficial insects.

- Apply pesticides on a calm, dry day with a moderate temperature (65° to 85°F) and low humidity.

- Keep children, pets, and adults away from the area where pesticides are being applied until the pesticide has dried or settled completely. (Check the labels for recommendations for individual products).

- Inform neighbors that you are going to spray and when.

- Cover as much of your skin as possible when you spray—wear rubber gloves, a long-sleeved shirt, long pants (or disposable coveralls made for this purpose, which are available at hardware stores), and nonporous rubber shoes. Cover your hair with a hat, wear goggles to protect your eyes, and do not wear soft contact lenses, which can absorb pesticides and transfer them to your eyes. Fasten a respirator mask (available at hardware stores) over your nose and mouth.

- Measure and mix chemicals as directed on the product label in a well-ventilated area. Keep separate utensils for each chemical and lock them up along with the product. Don't use these utensils for mixing or applying other pesticides. Calibrate your equipment to deliver the appropriate amount of pesticide. Applying more than the recommended amount is not only wasteful but also illegal.

- Do not eat, drink, smoke, or touch your face while applying pesticides.

- Clean all equipment carefully after each application. Wash your hands and face with soap and warm water and shower, using soap. Dispose of clothing, or

launder it as a separate washing-machine load and store along with pesticides and sprayers. Wash rubber gloves and boots with soap and water.

- For pesticides with the signal word CAUTION on the label, wait 12 hours before reentering the treated area. For pesticides with the signal word WARNING, wait 24 hours. For pesticides with the signal word DANGER (that you hire a licensed professional to apply), wait 48 hours. For organophosphate pesticides with the signal word DANGER that have applied outdoors in arid climates (less than 25 inches of annual rainfall), wait 72 hours.

- Consult a physician before spraying to be sure you have no medical conditions that should prevent your using these products. Hire a professional licensed applicator if you are in doubt about your ability to apply pesticides.

Store and Dispose of Products Safely

To minimize storage and disposal problems, buy only the amount of pesticide you will need for an immediate problem. Store pesticides in their original containers in a locked, cool, dry place. Temperatures should not exceed 90°F or drop below 40°F. Mark the storage area with a sign that reads "Poison—Keep Out," or "Keep Out—Pesticide Storage." The letters should be large enough to read from 20 feet away, so that emergency personnel, such as firefighters, who may enter the area can read them. Store herbicides away from pesticides to keep the vapors from combining. Purchase only enough to use in one season, and write the date of purchase on the label.

Requirements for the safe and proper disposal of pesticides vary in different regions of the country. To determine the proper method of pesticide disposal in your community, contact your local sanitation department or your state environmental protection agency.

When Accidents Happen

Pesticide poisoning, which occurs through ingestion, inhalation, or skin contact, can be serious. Symptoms include nausea, headache, blurred vision, and weakness. If you suspect pesticide poisoning, consult

the product label for appropriate first-aid action. Also, call 911, a physician, or a poison-control center (the number is listed in the front of your telephone book) immediately. Have the pesticide product label handy so that you can read the active ingredient and any other necessary information to the medical personnel.

To clean up a minor pesticide spill in the garden or on the lawn, remove soil from the area and dispose of it as directed by your local government agency or regional pesticide regulatory agency. On a paved surface, cover the pesticide with kitty litter, sweep it up and dispose of it as directed by the appropriate agency.

Assess the Results

After applying a pesticide, watch the plant closely to see if the problem is controlled. In some cases, you may need to reapply the treatment at regular intervals. If the plant does not respond to your efforts, try another solution listed in the book. If a second solution fails, consider replacing the plant with a resistant species or variety.

Long-term Treatments

Ultimately, good gardening techniques, called cultural practices, or good garden sanitation, are the most effective way to manage pests. By improving your gardening techniques, you can address the core problem, as opposed to treating the symptoms with pesticides and perpetuating the environmental conditions that encourage pest infestation. Using pesticides too frequently can actually exacerbate the problem by killing beneficial insects that prey on pests, and can cause pests to develop immunities to pesticides.

Even when you do use a pesticide to treat a severe problem, it is wise to use techniques, such as improving the soil, moving the plant to a healthier location, or watering more effectively. These good garden sanitation techniques are described throughout this book; consult the index for specific references.

For more on using pesticides and more information on specific pesticides, see pages 390 through 399.

CONTENTS

PART TWO

CHAPTER ONE

FLOWERS

AS A GARDENER, YOU CHERISH the color, fragrance, and beauty that flowers bring to your garden in every season. Daffodils in spring, roses in summer, chrysanthemums in fall, snowdrops in winter— all have their moment on center stage. Sometimes, however, with all that beauty comes trouble. If you decide to design a garden from scratch, you can discourage problems by choosing pest- and disease-resistant flowering plants. But most gardeners have established flower gardens and may well have plants that are not so resilient. In any case, it is the rare garden that isn't vulnerable to some degree.

This chapter outlines common symptoms of ailing flowers, causes, and reliable solutions. As a rule, when you discover unwanted visitors or the signs of disease, take the most environmentally friendly approaches, as we list them, first. For more on careful use of organic and chemical treatments, see pages 9 and 390 through 399.

Quick Troubleshooting Guide

SEEDLINGS

SEEDS DO NOT SPROUT

Cause: Old seeds, improper timing or planting depth, dehydration, seeds washed away

Solution: Use fresh seeds. Follow seed-package directions for proper timing and planting depth. Keep soil evenly moist during germination. Water seeds gently, or bottom water. Resow if garden seeds wash away in heavy rain.

SEEDLING ROTS AT BASE AND FALLS OVER

Cause: Damping off disease

Solution: To combat this fungal disease, discard diseased seedlings. Indoors, sow in sterile seed-starting mix. Outdoors, sprinkle milled peat moss or clean sand over seeds to discourage fungi.

HEALTHY SEEDLINGS DISAPPEAR OVERNIGHT

Cause: Cutworm, slug, or snail

Solution: Cut the bottoms from paper or plastic cups, and set cups over seedlings to keep cutworms from chewing through stems. Handpick pests at night by flashlight, or drown them in saucers of beer or commercial traps set on the soil. Remove decaying vegetation and other debris to eliminate daytime hiding places for the pests.

SEEDLING FAILS TO THRIVE OR DIES AFTER BEING PLANTED IN THE GARDEN

Cause: Transplant shock

Solution: Transplant when the weather is cool and overcast. Disturb roots and soil as little as possible. If the plant is potbound, gently straighten the roots. If the top growth is overly developed, trim one third of the foliage.

SEEDLINGS ARE INVASIVE

Cause: Plant self-sows freely

Solution: Dig up unwanted seedlings; be sure to remove the entire root system. Remove spent flowers from the parent plant before they can set seeds.

BULBS AND CORMS

BULB IS SOFT, DECAYED, OR CHALKY

Cause: Bulb rot

Solution: Dig up and discard diseased bulbs. Inspect bulbs before planting, and discard those with symptoms. Before storing, air dry bulbs and dust them with the organic fungicide sulfur. Do not plant healthy bulbs where diseased bulbs previously grew.

PLANT ROTS AT TOP OF BULB OR RHIZOME

Cause: Crown rot

Solution: Dig up and destroy diseased bulbs or rhizomes, and the surrounding 6 inches of soil. Divide overcrowded plantings. In the future, solarize the soil before planting, or plant in disease-free, well-drained soil.

BULBS ROT OR PRODUCE LITTLE GROWTH

Cause: Bulb mite, bulb fly

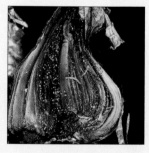

Solution: Remove yellowing foliage. Inspect the base of the plant for soft spots. Dig and destroy rotting bulbs, or bulbs that are infested with maggots. Inspect bulbs before planting and discard those with symptoms. Plant healthy bulbs in a different location.

BULBS HAVE KNOT-LIKE SWELLINGS; LEAVES ARE YELLOW AND STUNTED

Cause: Root-knot nematode

Solution: Try to revive plants with water and fertilizer. Dig and discard damaged bulbs. Introduce beneficial soil organisms by incorporating compost into soil. Solarize soil before replanting the area.

FLOWERS

BLOSSOMS AND BUDS ARE CHEWED

Cause: Snail, slug, caterpillar, beetle

Solution: Handpick and destroy pests in the morning. Spray caterpillars with the biological insecticide B; spray beetles with the botanical insecticide neem, as directed. Trap slugs and snails in shallow containers of beer, or commercial traps set on soil.

BUDS FALL OFF NEW PLANT

Cause: Transplant shock

Solution: Transplant when the weather is cool and overcast. Handle root system carefully, disturbing roots and soil as little as possible. If the plant is potbound, gently straighten the roots before planting. If the top growth is overly developed, trim one third of the foliage.

PLANT STOPS FLOWERING IN SUMMER

Cause: Heat stress

Solution: Irrigate deeply when the soil is dry 1 inch below the surface. Spread a 3-inch-thick layer of mulch under the plant to help retain soil moisture. Move affected plant where it will receive shade at midday. Select heat- and drought-tolerant varieties.

HEALTHY PLANT PRODUCES FEW, OR NO FLOWERS

Cause: Cold temperature, insufficient light, excess nitrogen

Solution: Site a plant that needs heat and full sun in a location with proper growing conditions. Apply low-nitrogen fertilizer, such as a 5-10-10 formulation.

BUDS AND BLOSSOMS HAVE FUZZY GRAY GROWTH

Cause: Botrytis blight

Solution: Discard and destroy diseased plant. Drench the soil with disease-fighting compost tea in humid conditions when temperature is around 60°F. Space plants widely for good air circulation. Divide overcrowded clumps. Remove plant debris and mulch lightly to create a barrier between plants and soilborne disease spores.

NEW PLANT PRODUCES NO FLOWERS

Cause: Immature biennial or perennial, potbound plant

Solution: Do not expect bloom the first year from biennials, which flower in their second year. Let a young perennial become established for a season before expecting bloom. Select small, vigorous plants from the nursery; avoid those with roots emerging from the drain holes of pots and those in flower. Untangle roots before planting.

PLANT PRODUCES FEW OR SMALL FLOWERS

Cause: Insufficient light or nutrients, overcrowding, failure to deadhead, disease

Solution: Site plant in a location with sufficient sun. Apply low-nitrogen fertilizer, such as 5-10-10 , in spring. Divide perennials every three years. Remove spent flowers, called deadheading, regularly. Identify and treat disease.

PETALS HAVE WHITE OR BROWN STREAKS

Cause: Thrips

Solution: Set out yellow sticky traps to monitor for pests. As soon as thrips appear, spray flowers, buds, and leaves with insecticidal soap, or the botanical insecticide neem. Remove weeds and grass to eliminate host plants.

HEALTHY PLANT PRODUCES MANY SMALL FLOWERS

Cause: Failure to disbud

Solution: Some plants, such as chrysanthemum, must have most of their buds removed to stimulate production of large flowers. Pinch out the side buds, leaving a bud at the end of the main stem.

ABNORMAL STREAKS OF COLOR MAR FLOWERS

Cause: Viral disease

Solution: Viral diseases are incurable. They are spread from plant to plant by sucking insects. Remove and destroy infected plants. Control insects by spraying insecticidal soap. Select plants without symptoms.

LEAVES

LEAVES ARE MOTTLED OR YELLOWED, DISTURBED INSECTS MOVE RAPIDLY

Cause: Whitefly, leafhopper

Solution: Set out yellow sticky traps to monitor for whiteflies. Spray both insects with insecticidal soap, or the botanical insecticide neem as soon as they appear.

LEAVES LOOK DULL AND ARE STIPPLED

Cause: Spider mites

Solution: Dislodge mites with a strong stream of water from a hose. In severe infestations, spray foliage with insecticidal soap. Coat both leaf surfaces. Keep plant well watered and mist foliage during dry spells.

LEAVES ARE CURLED, DISTORTED, OR YELLOWED

Cause: Aphids

Solution: Dislodge aphids with a strong stream of water from a hose. In severe infestations, spray foliage with insecticidal soap. Grow alyssum and dill to attract beneficial insects that prey on aphids.

LEAVES HAVE SPOTS OR BLOTCHES

Cause: Bacterial or fungal leaf spot, sun damage

Solution: Clip off affected leaves. Discard a severely damaged plant. Remove plant debris. Water at ground level to keep leaves dry. Move sunburned plant to a shaded site. Thin or space plants widely to promote air circulation.

LEAVES ARE MOTTLED, YELLOWED, OR DEFORMED

Cause: Viral disease

Solution: Incurable viral diseases are spread from plant to plant by sucking insects. Remove and destroy infected plants and weeds. Control insects by spraying insecticidal soap. Select plants with no symptoms.

LEAVES ARE YELLOW WITH BROWN, CRISP EDGES

Cause: Insufficient water, salt accumulation, sun damage

Solution: Supplement rainfall with water sufficient to prevent wilting. In arid regions, water deeply to flush salts out of the soil. Move sun-sensitive plant to a shaded location.

LEAVES TURN YELLOW AND PLANT ROTS

Cause: Excess water

Solution: Remove damaged plant parts or rotting plants. Add organic matter to the soil to improve drainage. Allow soil to dry between waterings. If the soil is soggy, move plant to a well-drained site, raised bed, or container.

LEAVES YELLOW AND MAY DROP

Cause: Nutrient deficiency

Solution: Spray foliage with nutrient-rich kelp solution or compost tea. Have the soil tested, and correct soil acidity or add minerals as directed. Mulch with compost. Fertilize in spring with a balanced fertilizer, such as 10-10-10.

LEAVES ARE CHEWED AND HAVE RAGGED HOLES

Cause: Japanese beetle, slug, snail, caterpillar

Solution: Handpick and destroy pests. Spray caterpillars when small with the biological insecticide BT. Spray Japanese beetles with the botanical insecticide neem. Follow label directions.

LEAVES ARE MARRED WITH WINDING TRAILS

Cause: Leafminers

Solution: Destroy infested leaves. Apply the biological control beneficial nematodes. Mulch with plastic sheets to keep larvae from maturing in soil. In fall, cut plant to the ground and destroy debris.

WHITE FOAM APPEARS BETWEEN LEAVES

Cause: Spittlebug

Solution: Spray plant with a strong stream of water from a hose to dislodge pests and foam. If infestation is large, spray the plant with insecticidal soap as needed.

A WHITE, POWDERY COATING COVERS LEAVES

Cause: Powdery mildew

Solution: Destroy infected foliage. Rinse spores off foliage. Thin plants to increase air circulation. Spray baking-soda solution. Cut plants back after blooming to promote healthy foliage.

LEAVES DEVELOP RUST-COLORED SPOTS

Cause: Rust

Solution: Remove diseased foliage. Thin plants to increase air circulation. Spray plant with organic fungicide sulfur. Water at ground level with a soaker hose or drip irrigation. In fall, remove weeds and debris from the garden.

WHOLE PLANT

PLANT YELLOWS, WILTS, AND DIES

Cause: Bacterial wilt, fungal wilt disease

Solution: Dig up and destroy infected plant. Wash hands and sterilize tools after handling diseased plants. Do not replant in contaminated soil.

PLANT BLOOMS, THEN YELLOWS AND DIES BACK

Cause: Natural dormancy

Solution: Water as needed to keep top growth vigorous until dormancy. When dormant, trim foliage and fill empty garden space with annuals; take care not to disturb dormant plant's roots.

PLANT YELLOWS AND WILTS, SOIL IS DRY

Cause: Insufficient moisture

Solution: Supplement rainfall with water sufficient to keep plant from wilting. Amend soil with compost or other organic matter to increase moisture retention. Spread an organic mulch to slow evaporation from the soil.

PLANT YELLOWS AND WILTS, SOIL IS MOIST

Cause: Stem and root rot, root-knot nematode

Solution: Remove damaged plant parts or severely damaged plant. Let soil dry between waterings. Add organic matter to soil to improve drainage. If nematodes are present, remove plants and solarize the soil.

PERENNIAL PLANT FAILS TO EMERGE IN SPRING

Cause: Improper growing conditions, extreme winter weather, lack of hardiness

Solution: Select a site that meets the plant's sun and soil requirements. Mulch plant after fall's first freeze to protect it from winter damage. Select plants hardy for your region.

PLANT WILTS, BUT LEAVES STAY GREEN

Cause: Heat or wind stress, root damage

Solution: Water to keep soil moist when weather is dry, or windy. Shade plant in hot climates. Cultivate around plants carefully to avoid damaging roots. Protect plants from animals with wire fence.

PLANT GROWS POORLY

Cause: Cool weather, improper timing, nutrient deficiency

Solution: Do not expect growth from heat-loving plants until spring weather warms. Wait to set out tender annuals until soil feels warm to the touch. Fertilize with compost tea or fast-acting, soluble fertilizer to promote growth. Apply compost mulch after soil warms.

Ageratum
Ageratum houstonianum

LIGHT: Full sun to partial shade

SOIL: Average; pH 5.0 to 6.0

MOISTURE: Moist

HARDINESS: Tender annual

Leaves are pale and stippled

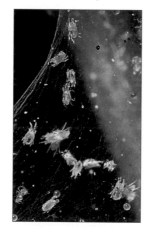

Problem: Foliage fades to pale green, and yellow spots appear. Leaves and growing tips are sometimes covered with webbing.

Cause: Spider mites are minute, sap-sucking spider relatives. They are particularly active in hot, dry weather and can seriously weaken a plant.

Solution: Hose off mites, apply pesticide and repellent, and keep plant healthy.

- Hose plant with a strong stream of water once or twice a week to knock off mites.
- Spray with insecticidal soap or a synthetic pesticide registered for ageratums that contains the active ingredient malathion. Follow label directions carefully.
- Spray leaves with garlic oil, an organic repellent.
- Keep the plant vigorous so that it is less appealing to mites. Once a week, feed plant with an organic fertilizer, such as kelp or fish emulsion. Or apply a balanced synthetic fertilizer, such as a 10-10-10 formulation (p.324), once a month during the growing season.
- Water the plant when the soil is dry 1 inch below the surface.

White powdery patches appear on leaves

Problem: Patches of a white powdery substance, which cannot be rubbed off, develop on leaves. They appear first on older leaves but may spread to younger ones as well.

Cause: Powdery mildew is a fungal disease that is most severe in warm, humid weather. While it makes leaves unsightly, it usually does not seriously affect a plant's health.

Solution: Practice good garden sanitation, spray, and increase air circulation.

- If the infection is light, pick off and dispose of infected leaves. Cut back a severely infected plant to the ground to encourage healthy regrowth. Clean up plant debris.
- Spray foliage with baking-soda solution (p.392) to limit the spread of disease.
- Thin existing plants or space new plants according to nursery directions to promote good air circulation.

Plant stops flowering

Problem: The plant seems healthy but produces few flowers. It may have bloomed well for weeks, then suddenly stops flowering.

Cause: Hot, sunny weather combined with dry soil stresses plants. Like many flowering plants, ageratums may react to stressful conditions by stopping production of flower buds.

Solution: Provide proper growing conditions.

- Water whenever the soil is dry 1 inch below the surface. Water early in the day so that the sun does not evaporate the water.
- Add a 3-inch layer of organic mulch, such as shredded bark, buckwheat hulls, or compost, around the base of the plant to reduce water evaporation from the soil.
- Fertilize with a water-soluble, balanced fertilizer, such as a 10-10-10 formulation (p.324), at half-strength once weekly.
- In areas with hot summers, plant ageratums in a location that receives shade from late morning to early afternoon.

Allium
Allium spp.

LIGHT: Full sun

SOIL: Well drained; pH 6.0 to 7.5

MOISTURE: Moist to dry

HARDINESS: Zones 3 to 8

Leaves wither after flowering

Problem: Foliage withers and turns yellow or brown. Leaves then die, resulting in bare spots in the garden.

Cause: It is normal for the leaves of some species to turn yellow and die once the flowers fade. They will reemerge next spring.

Solution: Remove affected leaves and use other plants to hide bare spots.

- Remove leaves once they turn brown.
- Fill bare spots with flowering annuals.
- Next year, move tall alliums behind or between tall, bushy plants. As allium leaves die, the surrounding plants will hide the bare spots.

Plant rots at the base; white mold is present

Problem: The flower stalk does not develop, and the plant begins to rot at the base. The leaf shoots and bulb are covered with fluffy white mold and small black dots. The roots of the plant may rot.

Cause: White rot is a fungal disease that attacks all onion-family members. It is most common in heavy, poorly drained, soggy soil or during long periods of wet weather.

Solution: Remove infected plants. Provide good growing conditions. Select healthy bulbs. Don't reuse an infected site.

- Dig up the infected plant and dispose of it in the trash. Don't compost it to avoid returning the fungus to the garden.
- Provide proper moisture for the particular species. For early-blooming allium, keep the soil moist while they are growing and blooming; let the soil dry once the leaves wither and the plants begin to go dormant in summer. For late-blooming types, water as needed so that the plant receives about 1 inch of water per week until blooms begin to fade, then let the soil dry.
- Buy healthy bulbs that show no sign of disease. Before buying new bulbs, check them for discoloration or soft spots.
- Plant allium in warm, well-drained soil with a near-neutral pH (p.329) that has been amended with organic matter, such as compost or leaf mold.
- Do not plant allium in soil where diseased plants were grown previously.

Allium seedlings invade other plant beds

Problem: Allium seedlings begin spreading into other plantings where you do not want them.

Cause: Most alliums self-sow, or produce offspring from seeds they shed. Some, including garlic chives and drumstick allium, are so prolific that they can become invasive, taking over spaces occupied by other plants.

Solution: Practice good garden maintenance to prevent seeding and regrowth.

- Deadhead, or remove old flower blossoms, before plants go to seed.
- If seedlings appear where they are unwanted, dig up the entire plant, including the bulb. If the foliage is removed, but the bulb remains, the seedling may reappear.

Alyssum, Sweet
Lobularia maritima

LIGHT: Full sun to partial shade

SOIL: Rich; pH 6.0 to 7.0

MOISTURE: Moist

HARDINESS: Hardy annual

Plant is chewed, and a shiny slime trail is present

Problem: Plant is ragged and chewed. Slimy silver trails appear on the plant or surrounding soil.

Cause: Slugs and snails are mollusks that feed on tender plants at night and hide in debris by day. Moist soil, cool weather, and humidity encourage their activity.

Solution: Remove the pests, use traps and repellents, and clean up garden debris.

- Handpick slugs and snails, and squash them or drop them in a jar of salty water. Work by flashlight at night if necessary.
- Set shallow containers in the ground and fill them with an inch of stale beer. Slugs and snails will crawl in and drown.
- Use other traps and repellents to control slugs and snails (p.49).
- Keep the garden free of decaying vegetation and other debris to eliminate daytime hiding places for the pests.

Plant produces few flowers

Problem: The plant begins flowering well, but blooms decrease in late summer. Foliage appears pale to dark green.

Cause: Sweet alyssum flowers best when it is grown in full sun and consistently moist soil. A plant grown in dry soil will become pale and produce a decreasing number of blooms. Similarly, a plant grown in shade produces fewer flowers than one that gets full sun.

Solution: Provide proper growing conditions.

- Plant sweet alyssum in soil amended with compost or other organic matter.
- Keep the soil consistently moist throughout the growing season.
- In the future, plant in a location that receives full sun.

Plant base rots and dies

Problem: Lower leaves yellow, and plant wilts in warm weather. The roots and crown are rotted and eventually die. White, threadlike fungal strands appear on stems at soil level.

Cause: Crown rot, or Southern blight, is caused by several fungi that thrive in warm, moist weather and poorly drained soil. The disease can persist in the soil for years.

Solution: Remove the infected plant and soil. Apply fertilizer, fungicide, and a soil drench. Plant only in healthy, well-drained soil.

- Remove and destroy diseased plants. Also discard the surrounding 6 inches of soil.
- Treat soil where the plant grew with ammonium nitrate, a high-nitrogen fertilizer.
- If the disease is severe, treat the soil with a synthetic fungicide registered for sweet alyssums that contains the active ingredient PCNB. Follow label directions carefully.
- When weather conditions favor the disease, drench the soil with compost tea (p.392).
- Do not plant in infected soil. Amend planting area with compost to promote drainage.

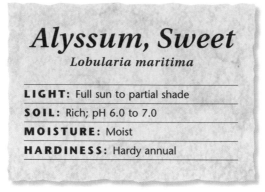

Aster
Aster spp.

LIGHT: Full sun to light shade

SOIL: Well drained; pH 5.5 to 7.5

MOISTURE: Moist

HARDINESS: Zones 3 to 8

Foliage has a white, powdery coating that won't rub off

Problem: Foliage, and sometimes flowers, are covered with a white, feltlike dust that can't be rubbed off. Lower leaves are usually the most severely affected. The plant rarely dies, but leaves may be distorted and drop off.

Cause: Powdery mildew is a fungal disease whose spores are carried by wind and splashing water. While the disease can develop in dry weather, the spores need a droplet of water on foliage in which to germinate. It is most prevalent in mid- to late summer.

Solution: Remove infected foliage, spray with fungicide, and increase air circulation.

- Remove infected plant parts and debris that have fallen to the ground.
- Spray plant with an antifungal home remedy (p.392): baking-soda solution, compost tea, or summer oil. To avoid burning the foliage, do not spray in direct sunlight.
- If problems persist, apply an organic sulfur fungicide. Or use a synthetic fungicide registered for asters that contains the active ingredient mancozeb. Follow label directions carefully.
- Thin existing plants or space new plants according to nursery directions to promote good air circulation.

Lower leaves yellow and drop

Problem: A tall aster variety loses its lower leaves in hot weather.

Cause: Inconsistent soil moisture causes lower leaves to dehydrate, turn yellow, and drop.

Solution: Provide good growing conditions and use other plants to hide the leaf loss.

- Water asters when the soil is dry 1 inch beneath the surface. Water early in the day so that leaves can dry before sundown.
- Cover the soil with 2 to 3 inches of organic mulch to slow evaporation.
- Plant taller varieties at the back of the border to hide any damaged leaves.

Leaf tissue is chewed, leaving only veins

Problem: Leaf tissue is eaten away between the veins, and only the veins remain. Succulent new foliage is damaged first.

Cause: Japanese beetles feed on asters in masses when temperatures are between 80° and 95°F. The adult beetles have metallic-green heads and copper-colored wing covers. The larvae are grayish white grubs that overwinter in the soil under grass.

Solution: Handpick pests. Use insecticide and biological controls.

- Handpick beetles and drop them in a bucket of hot, soapy water. For large infestations, place a sheet under the plant and shake the plant lightly so that beetles drop onto the sheet. Do this in the morning, when insects are sluggish.
- If problems persist, spray with the organic insecticide neem. Or use a synthetic insecticide registered for asters that contains the active ingredient carbaryl. Follow label directions carefully.
- Control grubs by applying milky-spore disease to the lawn at the first sign of beetles. Apply again the following spring and fall, when grubs are active.

Growth is stunted, leaves yellow, and branches proliferate

Problem: Leaf veins turn pale and clear. Leaves yellow, and edges may turn brown. Plants are stunted, and multiple branches develop. Flowers are green, dwarfed, or absent.

Cause: Aster yellows is caused by a bacterialike organism transmitted by feeding aster leafhoppers, also called six-spotted leafhoppers. There is no cure.

Solution: Remove infected plant, clean up weeds, and control aster leafhoppers.

- Remove and destroy diseased plant.
- Remove nearby weeds that may harbor the disease or aster leafhoppers.
- Control aster leafhoppers (entry, below).

Leaves are bleached or stippled; tiny bugs are present

Problem: Leaves lose color, turn whitish, and often have a stippled pattern. Plant becomes less vigorous, and its growth is stunted. Leaves and stems may be deformed.

Cause: Aster leafhoppers, also called six-spotted leafhoppers, are very small insects, about ⅛-inch long, with greenish-yellow, wedge-shaped bodies and six black spots. They feed on leaf undersides, extracting plant juices, and may transmit diseases, such as aster yellows (entry, above). Because they are small and fast moving, they are difficult to control.

Solution: Tolerate light damage or use insecticide. Keep the garden free of weeds and encourage beneficial insects.

- If the problem is not too severe, tolerate a light infestation.
- If an infestation is severe, spray the plant with insecticidal soap, repeating the application every 7 to 10 days as needed. Or spray with the botanical insecticide neem or with a refined horticultural oil. Follow label directions carefully.
- If problems persist, spray with a synthetic insecticide registered for asters that contains the active ingredient carbaryl or malathion. Follow label directions carefully.
- Keep the garden free of weeds, especially dandelions and plantains. Clean up all garden debris in fall to eliminate overwintering sites for eggs.
- Grow small-flowered nectar plants, such as sweet alyssum and scabiosa, nearby to attract beneficial insects, including lacewings (p.103), which prey on leafhoppers.

Leaf undersides develop orange spots; leaves yellow

Problem: Small yellow spots form on leaf undersides. The spots are filled with bright orange-yellow, powdery-looking spores resembling blisters. Leaves turn yellow.

Cause: Rust is a fungal disease that develops in damp conditions. It spreads when spores are blown onto moist leaves and overwinters on infected leaves.

Solution: Remove infected foliage and apply fungicide. Water properly, practice good garden sanitation, and provide good growing conditions. Apply a preventive spray.

- Remove and destroy leaves at the first sign of infection.
- If the rust infection is severe, apply an organic sulfur fungicide. Follow label directions carefully.
- Water at ground level using a soaker hose or drip irrigation. Water early in the day so that leaves dry before sundown.
- Clean up leaf debris during the season and after it ends.
- If problems persist, move the plant to a site with full sun and good air circulation.
- Discourage future problems by spraying the plant early in the growing season with an antitranspirant, a waxy or plastic coating that limits moisture loss from leaves and helps prevent fungal growth. Follow label directions carefully.

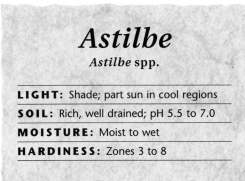

Astilbe
Astilbe spp.

LIGHT: Shade; part sun in cool regions

SOIL: Rich, well drained; pH 5.5 to 7.0

MOISTURE: Moist to wet

HARDINESS: Zones 3 to 8

Leaves turn yellow; leaf edges are chewed

Problem: Foliage yellows in spring. Later in the season, the leaf edges are chewed and are marred with ragged holes.

Cause: Larvae of the black vine weevil are small white grubs that have a yellowish brown head. They feed on roots and plant crowns, or bases, in spring, causing the leaves to yellow. Adults emerge in late spring as small black beetles, chew round holes in foliage, and lay eggs near the plant crowns.

Solution: Handpick adults. Use insecticide, traps, and biological controls. Select planting location to avoid host plants.

- Remove insects from plant in the evening, when they are active. Squash or drop them in a jar of hot, soapy water.
- Spray adults with the botanical insecticide neem. Follow label directions carefully. There is no chemical control for grubs.
- Apply a commercial yellow sticky trap (p.52) around plant stems to capture adults before they can lay eggs.
- In spring, apply beneficial nematodes (p.126) to the soil to attack the grubs. Apply again in late summer.
- Plant astilbe away from needle evergreens, such as yew and hemlock, and broad-leaf evergreens, such as rhododendron, which are host plants for the pest.

Leaves dry out, curl, and have white powdery deposits

Problem: Foliage is covered with a white, feltlike dust that cannot be rubbed off. Lower leaves are usually the most severely affected. The leaves may dry out and curl.

Cause: Powdery mildew is a fungal disease most prevalent when plants are grown in areas with poor air circulation. Outbreaks occur mostly in mid- to late summer. Although unsightly, powdery mildew is seldom fatal.

Solution: Remove infected foliage and treat with fungicide. Water properly and increase air circulation.

- Remove and dispose of infected plant parts and plant debris on the ground.
- Spray the plant with an antifungal home remedy (p.392): baking-soda solution, compost tea, or summer oil. To avoid burning foliage, don't spray in direct sunlight.
- If problems persist, spray with an organic sulfur fungicide. Or use a synthetic fungicide registered for astilbes that contains the active ingredient mancozeb or thiophanate-methyl. Follow label directions carefully.
- Water at ground level with a soaker hose or drip irrigation. Water early in the day to let leaves dry before sunset.
- Thin existing plants or space new plants according to nursery directions to promote good air circulation.

Plant doesn't flower

Problem: The plant is generally healthy but doesn't produce blooms.

Cause: Astilbes require nutrient-rich soil and supplemental fertilizer to flower well. Older plants don't produce as many blooms as younger plants do.

Solution: Provide good growing conditions and divide older plants.

- Work compost or other organic matter into the soil around an established plant.

- Before planting new astilbes, amend the soil with a 4-inch layer of compost or other organic matter.
- In early spring and midsummer, apply a complete granular fertilizer, such as 10-10-10 formulation (p.324).
- Divide astilbe (p.29) every three to four years. In the South, divide in fall; in the North, divide in early spring.

Leaves develop brown edges and wither

Problem: Leaf edges turn brown; whole leaves wither and die. The flower plumes are stunted or drooping.

Cause: Lack of soil moisture can damage and eventually kill an astilbe, which requires consistent moisture.

Solution: Provide good growing conditions and select drought-tolerant varieties.

- Supplement rainfall as needed to provide at least 1 inch of water per week.
- Mulch around the plant with 3 inches of organic matter to retain soil moisture.
- Move the plant to a location that receives at least partial shade.
- Before planting, prepare the hole with one part compost or other organic matter to two parts soil.
- If problems persist, plant a drought-tolerant variety, such as *A. chinensis* 'Pumila' or *A. chinensis* var. *taquetii* 'Superba'.

Plant appears stunted, leaves yellow, and roots have swellings

Problem: Plant growth is stunted. Leaves may yellow and curl. If you pull the plant out of the ground, the root system is shorter than normal, with small bumps or knots.

Cause: Root-knot nematodes are tiny soil-dwelling worms that feed on plant roots. Their damage limits the plant's ability to take up water and nutrients, slowly killing it. Root-knot nematodes are common in areas with moist, sandy loam soil.

Solution: Remove infested plant, amend the soil, and fumigate soil before planting.

- Remove and destroy the infested plant and soil around the roots.
- Add compost to garden beds to introduce nematode-fighting beneficial soil organisms.
- Solarize the soil. During summer's hottest days, empty the bed and cover the soil with clear-plastic sheeting. Leave it in place for 6 to 8 weeks to allow the sun's heat to kill most insects and diseases in the soil.

WISE CHOICES

No perennial is perfect, but easy-to-grow astilbes come close. Try these.

Astilbe × arendsii 'Avalanche' is tall, with linen white blossoms on its 3-foot-long floral plumes. 'Bridal Veil' is similar.

A. thunbergii 'Ostrich Plume' is graceful, with slender 3½-foot-tall stems topped with gently drooping pink flowers.

A. × rosea 'Peach Blossom' has soft peach-pink flowers that turn white tightly massed atop strong 2-foot-tall stems.

Plant wilts, yellows, and dies; watering does not revive it

Problem: Leaves turn yellow from the bottom up and wilt. Watering does not revive the plant, which dies. If you pull the plant up, its root system is smaller than normal.

Cause: Fusarium wilt is a soilborne fungal disease common in warm, wet climates. It thrives in wet soil and enters plant roots through openings or wounds, such as those caused by root-knot nematodes (entry, left). There is no cure for this disease.

Solution: Remove infected plant, water carefully, improve drainage, and clean tools well.

- Remove and destroy infected plant immediately. Do not replant astilbes in soil where infected plants have grown previously.
- Do not overwater plant.
- Before planting, work 2 to 4 inches of compost or other organic matter into the soil to promote good drainage.
- After working around an infected plant, wash hands and garden tools thoroughly, sterilizing pruners (p.310).

Baby's Breath

Gypsophila paniculata

LIGHT: Full sun

SOIL: Deep, well drained; pH 7.0 to 7.5

MOISTURE: Seasonally dry

HARDINESS: Zones 3 to 8

Plant fails to thrive or dies in moist areas

Problem: Plant does not grow well the first year it is planted. It yellows and dies in moist soil or a rainy climate.

Cause: Baby's breath has a deep taproot that needs to become established, and the plant takes two years to produce new top growth. It requires good drainage and slightly alkaline soil to grow well. It does not tolerate wet roots, especially in winter.

Solution: Provide good growing conditions.

- Prepare the planting bed to provide a deep, loose, crumbly growing medium. Dig the hole to a depth of 18 inches and amend the soil with 4 to 6 inches of compost or other organic matter.
- Test the soil pH (p.329) and add dolomitic lime to increase the pH to the proper level. Also test for calcium and magnesium and adjust as needed.

WISE CHOICES

Baby's breath is a great garden plant with many choices.

- Baby's breath (*Gypsophilia elegans*) 'Covent Garden' is an airy, fast-growing annual.
- Baby's breath (*G. paniculata*) 'Perfecta' is a tall perennial with large flowers. 'Double Snowflake' is also nice.
- Creeping gypsophilia (*G. repens* var. *rosea*) is a cascading perennial dotted with bright pink buds.
- Cushion gypsophilia (*G. muralis*) 'Garden Bride' is an annual that blossoms abundantly from late spring to frost.

Gray spots appear on foliage

Problem: Flower buds and stems turn gray. Stem tips die.

Cause: Gray mold is a fungal disease that occurs in wet weather, when temperatures are around 60°F. The spores are spread by water and wind. They infect plants growing in low areas and where nights are cool and damp.

Solution: Remove diseased plant parts, apply fungicide, practice good garden sanitation, and locate new plants carefully.

- Remove and destroy infected plant parts.
- Drench soil with compost tea (p.392).
- If problems persist, spray with the organic fungicide Bordeaux mixture. Start when plants are 6 inches high and continue every 10 to 14 days until flowering. Follow label directions carefully.
- Or apply a synthetic fungicide registered for baby's breath that contains the active ingredient mancozeb. Follow label directions carefully.
- Clean debris from around plant in fall and mulch lightly with wood chips.
- Water at ground level early in the day.
- Avoid planting in shade, low spots, and areas with poor air circulation. Space plants as nursery suggests.

Small insects on leaves hop away quickly when disturbed

Problem: Small insects cluster on leaves hop away when disturbed. Leaves are small, with yellow or red tips. Multiple shoots form. Flowers are yellow-green instead of normal color. Leaf veins may turn clear.

Cause: Aster yellows is caused by a bacteria-like organism transmitted by aster leaf-hoppers, also called six-spotted leafhoppers. There is no cure for this disease.

Solution: Remove infected plant, destroy weeds, and control aster leafhoppers.

- Remove and destroy the diseased plant.
- Remove weeds, which attract leafhoppers.
- Control aster leafhoppers (p.22).

Begonia
Begonia spp.

LIGHT: Partial shade to shade
SOIL: Rich; pH 6.0 to 7.0
MOISTURE: Moist
HARDINESS: Tender annual

Water-soaked spots appear on leaves

Problem: Leaves develop water-soaked brown spots. As the infection spreads, the leaves turn yellow and drop prematurely. In severe cases, the disease rots the stems.

Cause: Xanthomonas leaf spot is a bacterial disease that is most troublesome in wet, crowded conditions. It is spread by splashing water.

Solution: Remove affected leaves and spray. Water and space plants properly. Grow resistant varieties.

- At the first sign of infection, remove and dispose of affected leaves and clean up all leaf debris.
- Spray healthy foliage with organic copper sulfate, a fungicide with antibacterial properties. Follow label directions carefully.
- Water plant at ground level with a soaker hose or drip irrigation. Water early in the morning so that the foliage can dry before sundown. Let soil dry between waterings and avoid working among wet plants.
- Thin existing plants and space new plants according to nursery directions to promote good air circulation.
- In the future, select Rex begonias (*B. rex*), such as 'Duarten', 'Peace', and 'Vesuvius', which show some resistance to this disease.

Leaves and flowers are eaten and show slime trails

Problem: Foliage is ragged and chewed; lower leaves are usually eaten first. Shiny slime trails appear on the plant or the ground.

Cause: Slugs and snails are mollusks that feed on plants at night and hide in debris by day. Cool weather, moist soil, and humidity encourage their activity.

Solution: Remove the pests, use traps and repellents, and clean up garden debris.

- Handpick slugs and snails. Squash them or drop them in a jar of salty water.
- Set shallow containers in the ground and fill them with an inch of stale beer. Slugs and snails will crawl in and drown.
- Consider other traps and repellents for slugs and snails (p.49).
- Keep the garden free of debris to eliminate daytime hiding places for the pests.

Leaves have pale stippling

Problem: Leaves have tiny pale dots and may be encased in fine webbing.

Cause: Spider mites are tiny, eight-legged pests related to spiders that suck sap from plants. They are especially common when plants are underwatered or dusty. To check for mites, tap leaves over a sheet of white paper. Use a magnifying glass to look for insects.

Solution: Remove affected foliage. Hose off mites. Water the plant regularly.

- Clip off and destroy infested plant material.
- Hose the foliage weekly to knock off mites.
- Water the plant whenever the soil is dry 1 inch below the surface.

Bellflower
Campanula spp.

LIGHT: Full sun to partial shade

SOIL: Very well drained; pH 6.5 to 7.5

MOISTURE: Moist to seasonally dry

HARDINESS: Zones 3 to 8

Leaves rot at ground level; plant dies back or topples over

Problem: Leaves rot around the plant base. White, thread-like fungal strands are found on stems at soil level. Small, round, tan or yellowish structures can be seen in the soil around stems.

Cause: Crown rot, also called Southern blight, is a persistent soil fungus. It is most prevalent in hot, humid midsummer weather and attacks plants that are deficient in nitrogen.

Solution: Remove infected plants and soil. Apply fertilizer and a soil drench. Provide good growing conditions.

- Remove and destroy the infected plant at the first sign of disease. Also discard the surrounding 6 inches of soil by placing it on a sheet and carrying it away from the plant.

- Treat the soil where the plant once grew with ammonium nitrate, a high-nitrogen fertilizer. Follow label directions carefully.

- If the disease is severe and widespread, drench the soil with a synthetic fungicide registered for bellflowers that contains the active ingredient PCNB. Follow label directions carefully.

- In midsummer, when conditions favor the disease, drench the infected soil with compost tea (p.392).

- In the future, plant bellflowers in well-drained soil that has been amended with compost or other organic matter.

Leaves are silvery streaked and infested with minute insects

Problem: Buds turn brown and fail to open. Petals and leaves are mottled and streaked with silver.

Cause: Thrips are small, winged insects that attack plant tissue and suck out sap. They are most active in spring and early summer and can increase rapidly during a drought.

Solution: Remove infested plant parts. Apply insecticide. Water and mulch plant.

- At the first sign of damage, remove and destroy all affected plant parts. Also remove weeds and debris.

- Spray the plant with a synthetic insecticide registered for bellflowers that contains the active ingredient acephate, carbaryl, diazinon, or malathion. Follow label directions carefully. Spray the plant again in 10 days if the pests are still a problem.

- Water the plant when the soil is dry 1 inch below the surface. Add 2 inches of mulch to retain soil moisture.

REGIONAL FOCUS
SOUTHEAST

Bellflowers generally do not thrive where night temperatures are higher than 70°F. In a cooler microclimate, at a higher elevation, or with an eastern exposure, you can try a heat-resistant variety, such as clustered bellflower (*Campanula glomerata*) or Dalmatian bellflower (*C. portenschlagiana*). Site plants in part shade, water frequently, and mulch the soil with 3 inches of organic matter.

WISE CHOICES

There are some 300 species of bellflowers, more than 20 of which are commonly grown and beloved for their blue or white bell-shaped blooms. Select a variety that suits your needs.

Campanula carpatica, C. garganica, C. portenschlagiana, and *C. poscharskyana* are sprawling or spreading types that grow between 4 and 8 inches tall. They are suitable for bed edges and for rock gardens.

C. glomerata, C. persicifolia, and *C. rotundifolia* reach between 1 and 3 feet tall and are graceful, colorful additions to a perennial border.

C. latifolia and *C. medium* are among the tallest types, growing about 4 feet high. They are best at the back of a border.

Black-Eyed Susan

Rudbeckia spp.

LIGHT: Full sun to light shade

SOIL: Well drained; pH 6.0 to 7.5

MOISTURE: Moist to seasonally dry

HARDINESS: Zones 3 to 8

New growth is deformed

Problem: Various plant parts are covered with small, pear-shaped insects. New growth may be stunted or deformed, and the plant may wilt.

Cause: Brown ambrosia aphids are bright red sapsucking insects with long legs. They can transmit harmful diseases.

Solution: Hose off pests and apply insecticide.

- Spray with a strong stream of water from the hose every other day to dislodge pests.
- Spray with insecticidal soap every three to five days. Follow label directions carefully.
- If problems persist, spray with a synthetic insecticide registered for black-eyed Susans that contains the active ingredient malathion or acephate. Follow label directions carefully.

Leaves rot at ground level; plant dies back

Problem: Leaves rot around the plant base. White, threadlike fungal strands are found on stems at soil level. Small, round, tan or yellowish structures can be seen in the soil around stems.

Cause: Crown rot, also called Southern blight, is a persistent soil fungus. It is most prevalent in hot, humid midsummer weather and attacks plants that are deficient in nitrogen.

Solution: Remove infected plants and soil. Apply fertilizer and a soil drench.

- Remove and destroy the infected plant at the first sign of disease. Also discard the surrounding 6 inches of soil by placing it on a sheet and carrying it away.
- Treat the soil where the plant grew with ammonium nitrate, a high-nitrogen fertilizer. Follow label directions carefully.
- If the disease is severe and widespread, drench the soil with a synthetic fungicide registered for black-eyed Susans that contains the active ingredient PCNB. Follow label directions carefully.
- In midsummer, when conditions most favor the disease, drench the soil with compost tea (p.392).

Leaves are covered with a powdery white coating

Problem: Foliage and flowers are covered with a white, feltlike dust that can't be rubbed off. The lower leaves are usually the most severely affected.

Cause: Powdery mildew is a fungal disease that is most prevalent in mid- to late summer. The disease is spread by spores carried on wind and splashing water.

Solution: Remove affected plant parts and spray with fungicide. Water carefully.

- Remove infected foliage and blooms at the first sign of disease.
- Spray the plant with an antifungal home remedy (p.392): baking-soda solution, compost tea, or ultrafine horticultural oil.
- If problems persist, spray with an organic sulfur fungicide. Or use a synthetic fungicide registered for black-eyed Susans that contains the active ingredient thiophanate-methyl. Follow label directions carefully.
- Water plants at ground level to avoid splashing water and spreading spores.

⚜ TIME-TESTED TECHNIQUES ⚜

DIVIDING PERENNIALS

Division is a method of propagating plants that involves separating an overgrown cluster of plants into many individuals. In addition to increasing garden stock, division is used to remove older, weakened plants and to thin and control invasive plants.

HOW TO TELL IF A PLANT NEEDS TO BE DIVIDED

Many perennials benefit from division every three to five years. A clump of plants should be divided if it is not flowering as well as in the past, if bare spots appear in the center of the clump, if plants in the clump flop over, or if plants spread to the point of becoming invasive.

WHEN TO DIVIDE

Divide most perennials in early spring when the foliage is about 3 inches high. There are three exceptions.

- Divide perennials with fleshy roots, such as peony (*Paeonia* spp.), Oriental poppy (*Papaver orientale*), and Siberian iris (*Iris sibirica*), in fall, approximately one month before the first frost.

- Divide perennials that bloom in early spring, such as basket-of-gold (*Aurinia saxatilis*) and moss phlox (*Phlox subulata*), right after flowering.

- Divide bearded iris in late summer, a few weeks after blooming (p.62).

HOW TO DIVIDE

Remove the entire clump from the ground using a flat-edged spade or garden fork. Begin digging 12 inches away from the outside edge of the clump and work inward to ensure that you get most of the root system. Keep the root ball moist and shaded while it is out of the ground; dividing on a cloudy day is ideal.

Divide the clump so that each new piece has three to five growth buds, or eyes; this will ensure larger plants with better flowers the first year. Discard the old, woody center of the clump and any damaged or broken plant parts.

Rinse soil off the plant so that you can see its base. Divide plants with fine, fibrous roots, such as aster (*Aster* spp.) and bee balm (*Monarda* spp.), by pulling plantlets apart by hand.

For large clumps, such as daylilies (*Hemerocallis* spp.), insert two garden forks back to back and pry the clump apart. Use a sturdy knife for creating smaller divisions.

PLANTING THE DIVISIONS

Put a shovelful of compost or other organic matter into the soil at the base of the planting hole, so you can set the plant at its former depth. Spread the roots over the compost, fill the hole with soil, firm, and water well. Use a burlap screen to protect the plant from sun and wind until it is established. To test, tug gently; if the plant resists, it is established.

Bleeding Heart
Dicentra spp.

LIGHT:	Partial to full shade
SOIL:	Rich, moist; pH 5.0 to 7.5
MOISTURE:	Moist
HARDINESS:	Zones 2 to 9

Plant wilts suddenly and dies

Problem: The plant wilts suddenly, and stems rot. A white ring is visible around the plant at soil level. Round, tan, pinhead-sized growths resembling mustard seeds may be present in the soil around the plant.

Cause: Stem rot is a fungal disease that occurs when summer temperatures reach 85° to 95°F.

Solution: Remove the infected plant. Keep others healthy with compost tea and fertilizer.

- Dig out and destroy the infected plant along with 6 inches of surrounding soil.
- Drench healthy plants with compost tea (p.392) in midsummer. Also apply ammonium nitrate, a high-nitrogen fertilizer (p.324). Follow label directions carefully.

Leaves and flowers are eaten; foliage has shiny streaks

Problem: Foliage is ragged and chewed or has holes in it. The damage occurs overnight, and lower leaves are usually eaten first. Shiny slime trails appear on the plant or ground.

Cause: Slugs and snails are mollusks that feed on plants at night and hide in debris by day. Cool weather, moist soil, and high humidity encourage their activity.

Solution: Remove the pests, use traps, and clean up garden debris.

- Handpick slugs and snails and squash them or drop them in a jar of salty water.
- Place shallow containers in the ground and fill them with an inch of stale beer. The pests will crawl in and drown. Consider other traps and repellents (p.49).
- Keep the garden free of debris.

Foliage yellows and dies back

Problem: Leaves turn yellow as the weather warms. Foliage dies to the ground, leaving bare spots.

Cause: Common bleeding heart (*D. spectabilis*) goes dormant in summer. This process is hastened if the weather or soil is dry or if the plant gets too much sun. Because the plant can reach 18 to 36 inches tall and 18 to 24 inches wide, a large gap is left in the garden.

Solution: Provide good growing conditions and design the garden carefully.

- Keep the soil evenly moist. Incorporate compost or other organic matter into the soil at planting time to help retain moisture. Water when the soil is dry 1 inch beneath the surface. Apply a 2- to 3-inch layer of organic mulch to slow evaporation.
- Locate a new plant where it will receive part to full shade.
- Also locate a new plant near large hostas or other spreading plants that will at least partially cover the bare spot left by the dormant bleeding heart.

Chrysanthemum
Dendranthema × grandiflorum

LIGHT: Full sun

SOIL: Rich, moist; pH 6.0 to 7.5

MOISTURE: Moist

HARDINESS: Zones 5 to 10

Leaves are disfigured, stunted and infested with small insects

Problem: Leaves turn yellow or brown and may be puckered or distorted. The plant may wilt. Small, pear-shaped insects are visible.

Cause: Aphids are small, soft-bodied, pinhead-sized insects that may be green, yellow, brown, or black. They are found clustered on leaf undersides or at the shoot tips. If infestations are large enough, a sticky secretion produced by the aphids, called honeydew, is noticeable on the plant.

Solution: Hose off insects, spray with insecticide, and encourage natural predators.

- Spray the plant with a strong stream of water from the hose every other day to knock off the aphids.
- Spray the foliage with insecticidal soap every three to five days. Follow label directions carefully.
- If problems persist, spray the plant with a synthetic insecticide registered for chrysanthemums that contains the active ingredient malathion or acephate. Follow label directions carefully.
- Plant small-flowered nectar plants, such as yarrow and dill, nearby to attract ladybugs, lacewings, and other beneficial insects that prey on aphids.

Plant doesn't grow back in the spring

Problem: A plant that grew vigorously during the previous year does not emerge in spring.

Cause: Many chrysanthemum varieties are not cold hardy. Wet soil in winter will rot plant roots.

Solution: Protect plant from cold and provide proper growing conditions.

- Grow the plant where it will be sheltered from drying winter wind.
- Plant in well-drained soil. Keep the soil moist through mid-October.
- In early winter, mulch the plant with 3 inches of compost or other organic matter.
- Leave the foliage on the plant over winter. Wait until spring to remove the previous year's growth.

Flowers or leaves have silvery streaks that turn brown

Problem: Young leaves and flowers develop silvery white flecks or streaks. Flowers and leaves may be distorted and brown. A gummy residue may be present on the leaf surfaces.

Cause: Thrips are tiny insects that scrape plant tissue with their mouth parts, leaving silver-white streaks or flecks. To test for the pests, shake a damaged flower over white paper and look for dark specks with a magnifying glass.

Solution: Hose off pests and spray.

- Spray with a strong stream of water from a hose to dislodge pests.
- Set out yellow sticky traps (p.52) near the plant to monitor for thrips. At the first sign of them, spray with insecticidal soap. Repeat every three days for up to two weeks or until pests are gone.
- If problems persist, apply the botanical insecticide neem. Follow label directions carefully.

Leaves are spotted and bleached

Problem: Upper surfaces of leaves have small yellow or brown spots. The leaves eventually lose color and look bleached out. Leaf undersides are covered with a brown, sticky substance.

Cause: Chrysanthemum lace bugs are small, flat insects, about ⅛-inch long, with lacy, transparent wings. They suck sap from leaf undersides and excrete a dark, varnishlike waste.

Solution: Remove affected leaves and spray plant with insecticide.

- Prune and destroy infested leaves.
- Spray with insecticidal soap every three to five days. Follow label directions carefully.
- If problems persist, spray with a synthetic insecticide registered for chrysanthemums that contains the active ingredient malathion. Follow label directions carefully.

Leaves and stems have pale, winding trails

Problem: Squiggly tan, milky white, or yellow trails form on leaves and stems. In a severe infestation, leaves may turn brown and hang from the plant.

Cause: Leafminers are small insects that tunnel into leaf tissue and feed between the upper and lower surfaces. They often pupate and overwinter in the soil.

Solution: Use good garden sanitation, spray with insecticide, and use biological controls.

- Cut off infested leaves and throw them away or burn them.
- Spray the plant with a synthetic insecticide registered for chrysanthemums that contains the active ingredient malathion. Follow label directions carefully.

- Spread plastic sheeting under the affected plant to prevent larvae from reaching the soil; top the plastic with organic mulch.
- In fall, cut the plant back to the ground and destroy plant debris.
- Apply beneficial nematodes (p.126) to soil to kill overwintering pests before spring growth starts or before planting new mums.

Flowers turn brown or black

Problem: Petals turn brown, beginning at the base and moving to the tip, and wither. The flower base and upper part of the stem turn black. Buds may not open.

Cause: Ray blight is a fungal disease that causes buds and flowers to blacken. It is most common when humidity and moisture are high and plants are spaced close together.

Solution: Destroy affected plant. Water and space plants properly. Apply fungicide.

- Remove and destroy the diseased plant.
- Water at ground level using a soaker hose or drip irrigation. Water early in the day so that the foliage dries before sunset.
- Thin existing plants and space new plants according to nursery directions to increase air circulation.
- If the problem persists, apply an organic sulfur fungicide. Or use a synthetic fungicide registered for chrysanthemums that contains the active ingredient mancozeb. Follow label directions carefully.

TIME-TESTED TECHNIQUES

PINCHING MUMS

When a chrysanthemum reaches about 6 inches tall, begin pinching out the growing tips to stimulate bushiness and formation of flower buds. Keep pinching until mid-July, when flower buds begin forming. For larger flowers, pinch out all but two buds per cluster.

Cockscomb
Celosia argentea

LIGHT: Full sun to partial shade

SOIL: Average; pH 6.0 to 7.0

MOISTURE: Moist

HARDINESS: Warm-season annual

Plant is small, with few or deformed flowers

Problem: A newly purchased starter plant does not thrive after planting. It may quickly produce small, sometimes deformed flowers. It often weakens and dies before summer.

Cause: A plant that was potbound, or became too large for its container, will often grow poorly and produce disappointing flowers.

Solution: Select a healthy plant and provide good growing conditions.

- In spring, purchase a small plant that does not have flower buds. Avoid a plant that has roots growing from the drainage holes at the base of the container.
- After planting, keep the soil moist until the plant begins to bloom.
- Feed the plant with a water-soluble fertilizer at half strength every two weeks from planting until flowering.

Leaves are pale green with yellow specks

Problem: Leaves are marked with tiny yellow spots and have a pale green color. Leaf undersides and growing tips are often covered with a fine webbing.

Cause: Spider mites are small relatives of spiders that suck sap from plants. Their feeding robs the leaves of their green color and weakens the plant. They reproduce quickly in hot, dry conditions.

Solution: Destroy the plant. Or hose off mites, spray, and keep plant well watered.

- Pull up and destroy any plant that is severely infested with mites.
- At the first sign of the pests, spray the plant with a strong stream of water from a hose.
- Spray the foliage with insecticidal soap. Or use a synthetic insecticide registered for cockscombs that contains the active ingredient malathion, methoxychlor, or diazinon. Follow label directions carefully.
- Water the plant whenever the soil is dry 1 inch below the surface.

Leaves have tan or brown spots

Problem: Leaves are covered with tiny yellow or tan spots. As the disease progresses, the spots enlarge, often forming concentric rings in different shades of tan or brown. In severe infections, the entire leaf turns brown and the plant weakens.

Cause: Leaf spot is a disease that can be caused by several different fungi, and the symptoms for all of them are similar. The treatments are also the same. The disease is most noticeable during periods of wet weather. The spores of the fungi are carried by splashing water and by plant debris.

Solution: Apply fungicide. Water plants properly. Keep the garden free of plant debris.

- Spray the plant with an organic sulfur fungicide. Or use a synthetic fungicide registered for cockscombs that contains the active ingredient thiophanate-methyl. Follow label directions carefully.
- Water at ground level with a soaker hose or drip irrigation. Water early in the morning so that leaves can dry before sundown.
- In fall, clean up and remove all plant debris from the garden.

Columbine
Aquilegia spp.

LIGHT: Full sun to partial shade

SOIL: Rich, moist; pH 5.5 to 7.0

MOISTURE: Moist to wet

HARDINESS: Zones 3 to 8

Leaves have spots with purple or yellow-green margins

Problem: Leaves have circular or oval spots that are reddish-brown or black. Purple or yellow-green borders develop around the spots. Older leaves are often affected first.

Cause: Fungal leaf spot is caused by a variety of fungi and develops in wet or humid weather. The spores are spread by splashing water and overwinter in infected leaves and garden debris.

Solution: Remove affected leaves, water and space plants properly, apply fungicide, and practice good garden sanitation.

- Remove and discard diseased leaves at the first sign of infection.

- Water at ground level with a soaker hose or drip irrigation. Water early in the day so that the foliage can dry rapidly.

- Thin existing plants or space new plants according to nursery directions to allow for good air circulation.

- Spray with organic sulfur fungicide. Or use a synthetic fungicide registered for columbines that contains the active ingredient mancozeb. Follow label directions carefully.

- Collect and destroy all fallen leaves and other debris at the end of the growing season.

Leaves are disfigured by squiggly lines

Problem: Leaves are marked by squiggly, milky white or yellow trails. Tiny black specks are sometimes visible in the trails.

Cause: Columbine leaf miners, which are the larvae of small flies, feed between upper and lower leaf surfaces, leaving distinct tan, winding tunnels. They often pupate and overwinter in the soil. Their damage is disfiguring but rarely fatal.

Solution: Remove infested leaves and treat with insecticide.

- Cut off infested leaves and throw them away or burn them.

- Spray plant with a synthetic insecticide registered for columbines that contains the active ingredient malathion. Follow label directions carefully.

- Place a plastic sheet under the plant to prevent larvae from reaching the soil; place a layer of organic mulch on top of the plastic.

- In fall, cut the plant to the ground and destroy plant debris.

WISE CHOICES

With their nodding heads and spurred blooms in many colors, columbines are long-time garden favorites. They are, however, short-lived, and although they self-sow freely, the offspring are not always true. If you have planted hybrids (*Aquilegia* × *hybrida*), you will need to replace them about every three years to guarantee getting the exact plant. You can let species columbines, such as *A. caerulea* or *A. canadensis*, self-sow, as they will reproduce replicas of the parent plants.

Coneflower, Purple

Echinacea purpurea

LIGHT: Full sun to partial shade

SOIL: Well drained; pH 5.5 to 7.0

MOISTURE: Moist to seasonally dry

HARDINESS: Zones 3 to 9

Brown spots develop on foliage

Problem: Leaves are marked with spots, which may have a yellowish or dark margin. Leaf tissue between the spots turns yellow. Leaves eventually turn dry and brittle.

Cause: Leaf spots are caused by various fungi, which are favored by warm, wet weather. The spores are spread by splashing water and overwinter in garden debris.

Solution: Practice good garden sanitation.

- Remove and destroy infected foliage. Also clean up garden debris.
- Spray plant with fermented compost tea (p.392) at the first sign of infection.
- Water at ground level using a soaker hose or drip irrigation. Water early in the day so foliage can dry before sundown.

Leaves have yellow patterns

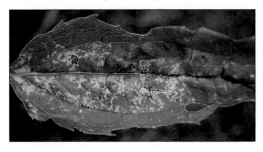

Problem: Leaves develop greenish yellow patterns and may be malformed. Leaf veins are yellow, but the surrounding tissue is green. The flowers develop unusual color streaks or bleached spots.

Cause: Mosaic virus is a viral disease that is transmitted by feeding insects and tools. There is no cure.

Solution: Control insects and practice good garden sanitation.

- When insects appear, spray the plant with insecticidal soap. Be sure to cover both leaf surfaces thoroughly.
- Keep the garden free of weeds to eliminate hiding areas for insects and clean up debris.
- Disinfect tools (p.310) after working among diseased plants.

Leaves are chewed and a shiny slime trail is present

Problem: Foliage is ragged and chewed. Slimy silver trails appear on the plant or the surrounding soil.

Cause: Slugs and snails are mollusks that feed on tender foliage at night and hide in debris by day. Moist soil, cool weather, and humidity encourage their activity.

Solution: Remove the pests, use traps to reduce further infestations, and clean up garden debris.

- Handpick slugs and snails and dispose of them. Begin hunting for them about an hour after sunset, using a flashlight.
- Set beer traps and use other methods of controlling slugs and snails (p.49).
- Keep the garden free of decaying vegetation and other debris to eliminate daytime hiding places for the pests.

Coralbells
Heuchera spp.

LIGHT: Part shade
SOIL: Rich, well drained; pH 5.5 to 7.0
MOISTURE: Moist
HARDINESS: Zones 4 to 9

Leaves turn brown at the edges and curl

Problem: Leaves turn brown and curl along the edges, then shrivel.

Cause: Plants that are grown in full sun or are not sufficiently shaded in warm climates can develop leaf scorch, or sunburn. Unlike sun-tolerant coralbells with green leaves, newer varieties with purple or variegated leaves need shade and evenly moist soil to grow well.

Solution: Prune and adjust conditions.

- Prune scorched leaves and move the plant to a shady, cool, moist location. Keep the soil moist; healthy new growth should emerge in a few weeks.
- Coralbells prefer slightly acidic soil. Test soil pH (p.329) and acidify if needed with sulfur according to package directions. Mulch with acidic chopped oak leaves, pine needles, or peat moss. Recheck soil pH yearly and amend as needed.
- Before planting new coralbells, incorporate a 3-inch layer of organic matter, such as compost or leaf mold, into the soil to help retain moisture and provide nutrients.

Leaves have dark spots or pale blotches

Problem: Brown or whitish spots surrounded by a darker margin appear on leaves. Spots may become numerous and grow together to form large dead areas.

Cause: Many kinds of fungi cause leaf spot disease. Spores are spread by splashing water and overwinter in garden debris.

Solution: Remove infected leaves and debris. Apply compost tea and fungicide. Water properly and add mulch.

- Pick off and destroy infected leaves, and remove plant debris from the garden. Dispose of all leaf litter and plant debris at the end of the growing season.
- Spray the plant and drench the soil with disease-inhibiting compost tea (p.392).
- For severe infections, spray with an organic sulfur fungicide. Or use a synthetic fungicide registered for coralbells that contains the active ingredient thiophanate-methyl. Follow label directions carefully.
- Water at ground level with a soaker hose or drip irrigation. Water early in the day so that leaves can dry before sundown.
- Mulch plant to prevent spore-laden debris on the soil from splashing onto leaves.

Leaves develop white, powdery patches that won't rub off

Problem: Foliage is covered with a white, feltlike dust that cannot be rubbed off. Lower leaves are usually the most severely affected. Leaves may dry and curl.

Cause: Powdery mildew is a fungal disease most prevalent when plants are grown in areas with poor air circulation. Outbreaks occur mostly in mid- to late summer, when warm days are followed by cool nights. Although unsightly, powdery mildew is seldom fatal.

Solution: Remove and destroy infected plant parts and garden debris. Apply a fungicide.

- Remove and dispose of infected plant parts and plant debris on the ground.
- Spray infected foliage with summer oil or an antifungal home remedy (p.392): baking-soda solution or compost tea. To avoid burning foliage, don't spray plants in direct sun.
- If problems persist, spray with an organic sulfur fungicide. Or use a synthetic fungicide registered for coralbells that contains the active ingredient mancozeb. Follow label directions carefully.

Stems darken at the base and die; the plant may die

Problem: Leaf stems turn dark at the base and die from the bottom up. A white, cottony substance forms at stem bases. If you cut a stem open, a white growth that later turns black is visible. Plants collapse, fall to the ground, and die.

Cause: Stem rot is a fungal disease that develops in warm, moist conditions. Poor soil drainage encourages the disease.

Solution: Remove affected foliage, use fungicide, and provide good growing conditions.

- Remove and discard infected stems and badly infected plants.
- Treat with an organic sulfur fungicide. Follow label directions carefully.
- Pull mulch away from the base of the plant to promote air circulation. Allow the soil to dry between waterings.
- Incorporate compost or other organic matter into the soil to improve drainage, or move the plant to a new location with well-drained soil.

White larvae infest soil near the plant; plant weakens

Problem: Growth is stunted. Leaves are bunched together and chewed; they turn black and die. If you dig the plant out of the ground, you will find damage to the plant base and roots.

Cause: Strawberry root weevils are black, ¼-inch-long insects with short, blunt snouts. Adults feed on foliage at night beginning in early summer. The larvae are white, curved grubs that feed on roots and the base of plants in early spring. Grubs overwinter in soil; adults overwinter in debris and the plant bases.

Solution: Destroy weevils, remove infested plant parts, apply insecticide, and introduce beneficial insects.

- Look for adult weevils after dark by flashlight. Handpick and destroy them.
- Remove and destroy infested plant parts. Dig up and remove badly infested plants and the surrounding, grub-infested soil.
- Treat serious infestations with the botanical insecticide pyrethrum or rotenone. Apply in evening. Follow label directions carefully.
- Or introduce the biological control beneficial nematodes (p.126), which attack larvae. Apply in midspring and again in late summer according to package directions.

WISE CHOICES

In addition to traditional coralbells with green leaves, try some of the handsome new varieties with colored foliage.

Purple foliage: *Heuchera americana* 'Purpurea', *H. micrantha* 'Palace Purple', *H.* × 'Plum Pudding', *H.* × 'Velvet Night'

Silver foliage: *H. micrantha* 'Pewter Veil', *H.* × 'Can-Can', *H.* × 'Mint Frost'

White-variegated foliage: *H. sanguinea* 'Frosty', *H.* × 'Splish Splash'

Coreopsis
Coreopsis spp.

LIGHT: Full sun

SOIL: Well drained; pH 5.5 to 7.5

MOISTURE: Moist to seasonally dry

HARDINESS: Zones 3 to 9

Leaves develop white, powdery spots that won't rub off

Problem: Foliage is covered with a white, felt-like dust that cannot be rubbed off. Lower leaves are the most severely affected. Diseased leaves may dry out and curl.

Cause: Powdery mildew is a fungal disease that is most prevalent when plants are grown in areas with poor air circulation. Outbreaks occur mostly in mid- to late summer, when warm days are followed by cool nights. Although it is unsightly, powdery mildew is seldom fatal.

Solution: Remove affected plant material, increase air circulation, and apply fungicide.

- Remove and dispose of infected plant parts and plant debris on the ground.
- Thin existing plants or space new plants according to nursery directions to allow for good air circulation.
- Spray infected leaves with an antifungal home remedy (p.392): baking-soda solution, compost tea, or summer oil. To avoid burning the foliage, do not spray a plant in direct sunlight; spray before the sun is overhead.
- If problems persist, spray with the organic sulfur fungicide. Or use a synthetic fungicide registered for coreopsis that contains the active ingredient mancozeb. Follow label directions carefully.

Plant stops flowering

Problem: The plant stops flowering after the first flush of bloom or in midseason.

Cause: A plant will fail to bloom if it is not pruned regularly or if it receives too much nitrogen. Also, many types of coreopsis stop blooming in the hot weather of late summer.

Solution: Deadhead plants regularly and select fertilizer carefully.

- Remove spent flowers regularly. Cut back the stems of tickseed coreopsis (*C. grandiflora*) to two younger, opposing flower buds or flowering stalks. Cut back threadleaf coreopsis (*C. verticillata*) in the same manner, then shear the plant to the ground in August; keep the soil moist until new flowering growth appears.
- Do not use high-nitrogen fertilizer, which will stimulate green growth but not flowers. Instead, use a fertilizer high in phosphorus, such as 5-10-10 (p.324).

Leaves are chewed, and a shiny slime trail is present

Problem: Foliage is ragged and chewed. Slimy silver trails appear on the plant or the surrounding soil.

Cause: Slugs and snails are mollusks that feed on tender foliage at night and hide in garden debris by day. Moist soil, cool weather, and humidity encourage their activity.

Solution: Remove the pests, use traps to reduce further infestations, and clean up plant debris in the garden.

- Handpick and destroy slugs and snails. Using a flashlight, hunt them at night.
- Set beer traps in the garden. Slugs and snails will crawl in and drown. Or try other traps and repellents for slugs and snails (p.49).
- Keep the garden free of decaying vegetation and other debris, such as overturned pots and rocks, to eliminate daytime hiding places for the pests.

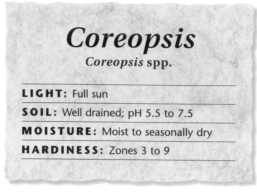

Cosmos
Cosmos spp.

LIGHT: Full sun

SOIL: Average; pH 5.0 to 7.0

MOISTURE: Moist

HARDINESS: Tender annual

Leaves and flowers are chewed off or have ragged holes

Problem: Petals and leaves are marred with small, ragged holes or are chewed off. Small, greenish yellow beetles with 12 black spots are feeding on plants, which may become weakened.

Cause: The spotted cucumber beetle is a common garden pest. It feeds first on flowers and pollen parts, then moves on to leaves. Adult beetles lay their eggs in the ground, and the brown-headed white larvae feed on roots. Besides chewing damage, spotted cucumber beetles can transmit viral diseases as they feed.

Solution: Remove pests, use insecticide, and introduce beneficial insects.

- Handpick and destroy beetles.
- Dust the affected plant with pyrethrum or rotenone, which are botanical insecticides. Apply in the morning, when leaves are damp and insects are inactive.
- If problems persist, spray with a synthetic insecticide registered for cosmos that contains the active ingredient carbaryl. Follow label directions carefully.
- Or introduce the biological control beneficial nematodes (p.126), which attack the larvae. Apply in midspring and again in late summer, following label directions.

Dark lesions appear on stems

Problem: Dark brown, irregularly shaped spots appear on stems at leaf joints. The spots enlarge, often girdling stems, which wilt and die.

Cause: Stem canker is a fungal disease that can be transmitted by contaminated seeds, leaves, and other plant parts. It most often appears after plants begin to flower.

Solution: Remove and destroy infected plant material. Clean up plant debris. Space plants.

- Remove and destroy infected plant parts.
- In fall, clean up the garden thoroughly and remove all plant debris.
- Thin plants or space new plants far apart to promote air circulation.

Leaves have sunken, circular spots and are distorted

Problem: Small, sunken, yellow or brownish spots mar leaves, beginning when weather warms in the spring. Leaves and flowers may be distorted, and stem tips may wilt. Bright, yellow-striped insects are feeding on the plant.

Cause: Fourlined plant bugs suck sap, leaving small, sunken craters in leaves. The adults are easily recognized by the black and bright yellow stripes on their back.

Solution: Remove pests, use insecticide, and clean up garden debris.

- Handpick bugs early in the morning when they are sluggish; destroy them.
- Spray the plant with insecticidal soap every three days until pests are gone. Alternatively, spray with a synthetic insecticide registered for cosmos that contains the active ingredient malathion. Follow label directions carefully.
- Keep the garden free of plant debris.

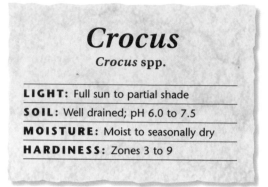

Crocus
Crocus spp.

LIGHT: Full sun to partial shade

SOIL: Well drained; pH 6.0 to 7.5

MOISTURE: Moist to seasonally dry

HARDINESS: Zones 3 to 9

Corms are infested with tiny, white pests; plant doesn't bloom

Problem: Leaves turn yellow and may be oddly shaped. Flowers don't form or shatter quickly after opening. Corms have corky brown spots that turn dry and crumbly.

Cause: Bulb mites are tiny white pests that suck juices from corms and transmit diseases. To verify their presence, dig up corms and use a magnifying glass to look for small, eight-legged, spiderlike pests.

Solution: Treat infested corms, destroy badly infested corms, and purchase healthy corms.

- If a corm is mildly infested, dip it in hot (120°F) water for three minutes to kill the mites. Let it dry in a dimly lit, ventilated area for several days before replanting.

- If a corm is severely infested, remove and discard it, along with 6 inches of surrounding soil. Don't plant new corms in soil that has been previously infested.

- Before buying new corms, inspect them closely for corky brown spots. Purchase only those corms that do not have spots.

Flowers don't open, or foliage doesn't emerge in spring

Problem: Foliage emerges in spring, but flowers don't open. Or neither foliage nor flowers appear in spring.

Cause: Corms will produce only leaves, but not flowers, if the leaves were cut just after flowering the previous year. Neither foliage nor flowers will appear if corms are grown in wet soil or are eaten by rodents, such as squirrels, mice, voles, or gophers.

Solution: Cut back crocus at the right time. Use a physical barrier to protect corms. Provide proper growing conditions.

- Before cutting the foliage back, wait until it yellows and dies back naturally, usually six to eight weeks after flowering.

- If you suspect that rodents are eating the corms, plant groups of them in hardware cloth or chicken wire to discourage animals.

- Plant corms in well-drained soil. Dig the hole 6 inches deep and incorporate 2 inches of organic matter, such as compost or peat moss, into the base of the hole.

- Test the soil pH (p.329) and add lime if it is too acidic.

- In fall, feed with a potassium-rich fertilizer, such as 5-10-20 (p.324).

Plants yellow and die; corms rot

Problem: Plants turn yellow and die prematurely. Corms in the ground rot; those in storage have small red specks with elevated borders. These spots eventually darken and become larger.

Cause: Dry rot is caused by a persistent soil-borne fungus that is active in cold, wet weather. Corms are susceptible if they are planted in cold, soggy soil or stored in a site that is too moist.

Solution: Discard infected corms. Buy healthy corms. Plant and store corms properly.

- Destroy infected corms.

- Purchase disease-free corms without lesions.

- Plant corms in sunny, well-drained soil.

- Dig up corms before the weather becomes cold and wet. Let corms dry, then store them in a dry location.

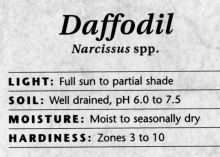

Daffodil

Narcissus spp.

LIGHT: Full sun to partial shade

SOIL: Well drained, pH 6.0 to 7.5

MOISTURE: Moist to seasonally dry

HARDINESS: Zones 3 to 10

Bulb develops black spots; emerging leaves are distorted

Problem: Plant produces deformed foliage, with leaves sticking together. Leaves rot at base and fall over. When bulb is dug up, black spots and rot are evident. Stored bulbs have black spots and decay.

Cause: Bulb and neck rot of this type, also known as botrytis blight, is caused by a fungus that thrives in damp soil and weather. There is no cure for this disease.

Solution: Follow preventative measures.

- Inspect new bulbs carefully for black spots and signs of decay. Discard affected bulbs.
- After digging up healthy bulbs, dust them with an organic sulfur fungicide before storing them. Follow label directions carefully.
- Store bulbs in a cool, dry, well-ventilated location where temperatures will not fall below freezing or rise above 70°F.
- Prepare the planting bed by working compost or other organic matter into the soil to create a fast-draining growing medium. Alternatively, plant in a raised bed.
- Avoid planting when the weather is especially damp.

Leaf tips are damaged

Problem: The top 2 or 3 inches of the leaf tip is brown, with a yellow margin separating it from the healthy green tissue. After the tip browns, the lower part of the leaf develops yellow spots that become raised, scabby, and reddish brown.

Cause: Leaf scorch is caused by a fungus that resides at the top of bulb scales; it infects leaf tips as they emerge from the bulb. It is especially prevalent on the West Coast and in the East.

Solution: Discard infected plant parts. Apply fungicide and compost tea. Purchase new bulbs carefully.

- Remove and destroy infected leaves and spent flowers immediately. Also remove foliage that has turned brown and finished maturing. Do not compost infected plant material.
- Spray the plant with Bordeaux mixture, a combination of copper sulfate and hydrated lime. Follow label directions carefully.
- In wet or humid spring weather, drench the soil with compost tea (p.392).

WISE CHOICES

Some narcissus will naturalize, or spread without assistance. Among the best naturalizers are:

Large-cupped narcissus (*Narcissus* spp.): 'Accent', 'Flower Record', 'Gigantic Star', 'Salome'

Poeticus narcissus (*N. poeticus*): 'Actaea', 'Pheasant's eye'

Cyclamineus narcissus (*N. cyclamineus*): 'Foundling', 'Tête-à-Tête'

Tazetta narcissus (*N. tazetta*): 'Minnow'

Triandrus narcissus (*N. triandrus*): 'Hawara', 'Petrel', 'Quail', 'Thalia'

DIVIDING DAFFODILS

Every three to four years, daffodils may show signs of overcrowding, such as reduced flowering, and would benefit from division. The clumps should be divided about six weeks after flowers have finished blooming, once the foliage has turned yellow or brown.

1. Use a spading fork to dig up whole clumps. Insert the fork in the ground all the way around a clump and gently rock it back and forth to loosen the soil so that you can lift the bulbs more easily.

2. Wash the soil off the bulbs and pull them apart. Cut away the remaining foliage. Discard dead bulbs and any that show signs of damage or disease.

3. Separate large mother bulbs from their offsets by gently pulling them apart with your hands. Discard the mother bulbs.

4. Replant the offsets in soil that has been dug or tilled 10 inches deep. Incorporate 2 inches of organic matter, such as compost or peat moss, into the planting hole and add lime if the soil is acidic (p.329). Also mix in some greensand, which is a natural source of potassium, or a high-potassium fertilizer, such as 5-10-20 (p.324), to encourage bloom. Be sure to set the bulbs at the proper depth for the variety.

Bleached streaks mar leaves; flowers are streaked or spotted

Problem: Leaves are streaked with pale lines, then become completely yellow, wilt, and fall over prematurely. Flowers are smaller than normal and may be streaked or spotted.

Cause: Several viral diseases can affect daffodils. The viruses are spread by sucking insects, like aphids, and by contaminated garden tools. There is no cure for viral infections.

Solution: Remove infected plants, control aphids, and disinfect tools.

- Dig up and discard infected plants.
- Dislodge aphids with a strong stream of water from the hose. Alternatively, spray plant with insecticidal soap.
- Disinfect tools (p.310) and wash your hands well after working around infected bulbs.

Flowers are sparse

Problem: The plant blooms well the first year but poorly the second year. Or, after flowering well for many years, the plant produces fewer and fewer blooms.

Cause: Several factors affect blooming. A daffodil planted in heavy shade will flower the first year, but the bulb will not be able to manufacture enough food to produce good flowers and foliage the second year. Also, daffodil bulbs multiply yearly, producing larger stands each spring. As the clumps become overcrowded, flowering is gradually reduced.

Solution: Locate bulbs carefully, remove foliage at the proper time, divide clumps, and provide good growing conditions.

- If the bulb is planted in deep shade, move it after it blooms and the foliage has turned yellow or brown. Replant immediately in a location that receives sunlight for at least half the day.
- Leave the foliage on the plant until it has turned yellow or brown, usually six to eight weeks after flowering. After the foliage has withered and matured completely, clip it off at ground level. If you find the yellowing foliage unsightly, plant daffodils among

daylilies, whose emerging leaves will hide those of the daffodil.

- If plants are overcrowded, divide clumps (facing page) after the plants have bloomed and the foliage has turned yellow or brown.

- Before planting new bulbs, prepare the bed with well-drained soil. Dig the soil to a depth of 10 inches and incorporate 2 inches of compost or other organic matter into the hole. Add greensand or a potassium-rich fertilizer, such as 5-10-20 (p.324). Also add lime if the soil is acidic (p.329). If the soil is particularly soggy, plant bulbs in a raised bed.

- In fall, feed bulbs with a high-potassium fertilizer, such as 5-10-20 (p.324).

Plant is stunted; bulb base is soft and brown

Problem: The bottom of the bulb, or basal bulb plate, turns soft and brown. If you cut the bulb in half, you see inner leaf scales that are dark brown, and white or pink fungal growth. Infected bulbs produce dwarfed plants with malformed flowers or fail to produce growth in spring.

Cause: Narcissus basal rot is a persistent soil-borne fungal disease that infects both planted and stored bulbs. Infection is spread by contaminated soil, bulbs, and tools and is most active in warm weather, when soil temperatures are between 60° and 75°F.

Solution: Discard infected plants. Select bulbs carefully. Treat stored bulbs.

- Dig up and discard diseased bulbs and the surrounding 6 inches of soil. Do not replant healthy bulbs in the same location.

- Purchase only healthy-looking, firm bulbs.

- Before storing bulbs, dust them with an organic sulfur fungicide. Follow label directions carefully. Store bulbs in a cool, well-ventilated location.

- Before planting stored bulbs, inspect the bases for signs of infection. Discard all bulbs that appear rotted or feel soft.

Bulb fails to grow and has few leaves

Problem: A newly planted bulb fails to grow or produces only a few spindly leaves. The bulb is soft and has brown scars on the outer scales. Maggots and their waste may be visible.

Cause: Two types of narcissus bulb flies infest daffodils: the bulb fly and the lesser bulb fly. Both resemble small bumblebees and lay eggs at the base of the foliage and on the surrounding soil. The larvae are gray to brown grubs that bore into bulbs to feed; their damage may cause rotting.

Solution: Firm the soil. Select the planting site and bulbs carefully.

- Firm the soil around the neck of the bulb as the foliage dies down to discourage adults from laying eggs at the plant base.

- Before planting new bulbs, select a cool, open location, because bulb flies prefer a warm, protected area for laying eggs.

- Inspect new and stored bulbs for signs of infestation. Do not buy or plant any bulb that feels soft or spongy.

A new bulb doesn't flower

Problem: Plant does not produce blooms the first year after planting.

Cause: A newly planted bulb that has been exposed to temperatures above 80°F will not bloom, because the flowering structure inside the bulb has been killed.

Solution: Time planting carefully and store bulbs properly.

- In the future, plant bulbs after the soil temperature has dropped to 60°F.

- Store bulbs in a cool, dry location, with temperatures between 50° and 60°F and with good air circulation. A dark basement or refrigerator works well. However, do not store bulbs in the same refrigerator as ripening fruit, which emits a natural aging agent that kills bulbs. If the bulbs are stored in a bag, open the bag so that the air can circulate freely.

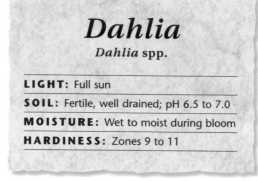

Dahlia
Dahlia spp.

LIGHT: Full sun

SOIL: Fertile, well drained; pH 6.5 to 7.0

MOISTURE: Wet to moist during bloom

HARDINESS: Zones 9 to 11

Flowers and leaves are chewed

Problem: Foliage is ragged and chewed; lower leaves are usually eaten first. Shiny slime trails appear on the plant or ground.

Cause: Slugs and snails are mollusks that feed on plants at night and hide in debris by day. Cool weather, moist soil, and humidity encourage their activity.

Solution: Remove the pests, use traps, and clean up garden debris.

- Handpick slugs and snails at night, using a flashlight, and destroy them.
- Set beer traps and use other methods of control (p.49).
- Place a copper strip, or edging, around the plant. The pests will receive a mild electric shock when they touch the metal.
- Keep the garden free of debris, including fallen leaves, stones, and old pots, to eliminate daytime hiding places for the pests.

Plant is tall and spindly, with few blooms

Problem: The plant grows tall and leggy, producing only one or a few flowers.

Cause: Dahlias must be topped, or pinched back, to stimulate the production of multiple flowers per plant. Although dahlias are heavy feeders, applying too much nitrogen fertilizer causes them to produce leafy growth at the expense of flowers.

Solution: Pinch the plant back regularly. Provide proper growing conditions. Stake flopping plants.

- After the plant has two to four sets of leaves, carefully pinch off the new top growth above the second set of leaves.
- Several weeks before planting, amend the soil with well-rotted manure. After tubers are in the ground, fertilize once with a formula high in phosphorus and potassium, such as 5-10-10 or 10-20-20 (p.324). After the plant grows 12 inches high, mulch with a 1-inch layer of rotted manure or compost; keep the mulch away from the plant's stem to prevent burning.
- To support the plant, drive a bamboo stake next to the stem. Wrap soft green string around the stake, then loosely around the plant stem and tie.

Leaves are chewed between the veins; flowers have holes

Problem: Leaf tissue is eaten away, leaving only the veins. Flowers are partially or completely eaten. Succulent new foliage is damaged first.

Cause: Japanese beetles feed on dahlias in masses when temperatures are between 80° and 95°F. The adults have metallic-green heads and coppery wing covers. The larvae are grayish white grubs that overwinter in the soil and eat grass roots in spring.

Solution: Handpick beetles. Use insecticide and biological control.

- Handpick and destroy beetles. For large infestations, place a sheet under the plant and shake the plant lightly until the beetles drop onto the sheet. Do this in the early morning, when insects are sluggish. Destroy the beetles.

- If problems persist, spray with the biological insecticide neem. Or use a synthetic insecticide registered for dahlias that contains the active ingredient carbaryl. Follow label directions carefully.

- Control grubs by applying the biological control milky-spore disease (p.348) to the lawn at the first sign of them in early spring and again in fall. Apply the following spring, when grubs are active.

Leaves are twisted and have yellow patches

Problem: Leaves are distorted, sometimes blistered, and often twisted. Small yellow spots with irregular edges are present, especially along the midribs and large leaf veins. In some varieties, leaves turn yellow and leaf margins roll upward. In other varieties, the plant may be abnormally short and bushy with stunted flower stems.

Cause: Numerous viruses can distort leaves. The diseases are transmitted by sap-sucking insects, such as leafhoppers and aphids.

Solution: Remove the infected plant and control pests. Clean up debris. There is no cure for viral disease.

- Remove and dispose of the infected plant and tuber at the first sign of disease.

- Spray the plant with a strong stream of water from the hose every other day to dislodge leafhoppers and aphids. Or, spray insecticidal soap every three to five days.

- For severe infestations, apply a synthetic insecticide registered for dahlias that contains the active ingredient malathion or acephate. Follow label directions carefully.

- Keep the garden free of weeds and plant debris, which often harbor viruses.

Foliage develops white, powdery patches that don't rub off

Problem: Leaves and stems are covered with a white, feltlike dust that cannot be rubbed off. Lower leaves are the most severely affected. These leaves may dry out and curl up.

Cause: Powdery mildew is a fungal disease most prevalent when plants are grown in areas with poor air circulation. Outbreaks occur mostly in mid- to late summer when warm days are followed by cool nights. Although unsightly, powdery mildew is seldom fatal.

Solution: Remove infected plant parts and spray plants with fungicide.

- Remove and dispose of infected plant parts and plant debris on the ground.

- Spray infected foliage with summer oil or an antifungal home remedy (p.392): baking-soda solution or compost tea. To avoid burning foliage, don't spray in direct sunlight.

- If problems persist, spray with an organic sulfur fungicide. Or use a synthetic fungicide registered for dahlias that contains the active ingredient mancozeb. Follow label

TIME-TESTED TECHNIQUES

DIGGING UP DAHLIAS

Dahlias have tender tubers, which must be overwintered indoors in cold-winter areas. After the first frost kills the top growth, dig up the tubers, shake off excess soil, and let them dry in the sun for several hours. Once the roots dry, cut off the foliage. Store tubers in sand in a cool, dry, dark location. Check several times through the winter for signs of disease, and discard any tubers that show decay. If tubers begin to sprout, they are getting too much heat or light.

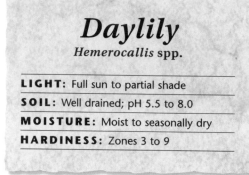

Daylily

Hemerocallis spp.

LIGHT: Full sun to partial shade

SOIL: Well drained; pH 5.5 to 8.0

MOISTURE: Moist to seasonally dry

HARDINESS: Zones 3 to 9

Leaves have small pale spots

Problem: Tiny bleached spots develop on the top surface of leaves; leaves turn progressively ashen green to brown as they die. Leaf undersides have a fine webbing and a coating of dustlike brownish grit.

Cause: Spider mites are tiny spider relatives that attack daylilies in hot, dry weather, sucking juices from leaf undersides. By the time damage is evident, mite populations are frequently very high.

Solution: Hose off mites and use insecticide.

- Dislodge mites by spraying the plant with a strong stream of water from the hose; be sure to spray leaf undersides. Also keep the soil moist during droughts.

- Spray with insecticidal soap at the first sign of infestation. In areas where spider mites are a persistent problem, spray the plant as soon as it leafs out. Repeat treatments at one-week intervals through the summer. Follow label directions carefully.

- If problems persist, spray with a synthetic insecticide registered for daylilies that contains the active ingredient malathion. Follow label directions carefully. Make sure to cover both leaf surfaces, especially the underside.

Plant has few or no blooms

Problem: Foliage growth is healthy and thick, but the plant produces few blooms.

Cause: Several factors affect flowering. A plant will bloom sparsely if it is receiving too little sunlight or too much nitrogen, if it is growing in poor soil, or if it is overcrowded.

Solution: Provide good growing conditions and divide plants as needed.

- Move plants to a location that receives at least six hours of sunlight daily.

- Before planting, work a 3- to 4- inch layer of compost or other organic matter into the bed to provide moist, well-drained soil.

- In spring or early summer, feed plants with a balanced granular fertilizer, such as a 5-10-10 or 5-10-5 formulation (p.324). Later in the season, feed with a low-nitrogen fertilizer, such as 3-12-12 or 4-8-12.

- Divide overcrowded plants (p.29) immediately. In the future, divide plants every three to five years or when flowering decreases in a clump of daylilies.

WISE CHOICES

Daylilies have been called the perfect perennial, but not all are created equal in terms of hardiness. They are divided into three major hardiness categories:

Dormant
These varieties are the most hardy, thriving across most of the northern states and southern Canada. They do not do well in areas where the ground does not freeze in winter. The foliage dies back to the ground each fall.

Evergreen
These types thrive in warm regions and need winter protection to survive in cooler climates. In zones 5 to 7, lay a generous mulch of coarse straw over the plants after the first hard freeze of fall to protect the roots when the soil alternately freezes and thaws.

Semievergreen
A cross between dormant and evergreen types, these varieties can be as tender as evergreens or as hardy as dormants. Unless the hardiness of a semievergreen variety is known, do not plant it in areas that freeze.

Small bumps appear on leaves or flower buds

Problem: Flower buds develop small, warty bumps. Leaves may be bumpy or distorted, and the plant may lose vigor.

Cause: Daylily aphids are tiny, pear-shaped green, sap-sucking insects that feed in groups on buds or in leaf fans. A shiny, sticky aphid excretion, called honeydew, may be present at the base of leaves. The pests are most active in cool spring and fall weather.

Solution: Hose off aphids and use insecticide.

- Spray plants with a stream of water to dislodge aphids. Or spray insecticidal soap as needed, coating the base of leaf fans.
- If problems persist, spray with horticultural oil or with a synthetic insecticide registered for daylilies that contains the active ingredient chlorpyrifos or bifenthrin. Follow label directions carefully.

Flower buds may die; stems have corky lesions

Problem: Buds drop without opening. Flower stalks are bent and can be twisted. Flower stems develop some brown, corky areas. Pale streaks or speckles are sometimes visible on plant leaves and flowers.

Cause: Several species of thrips attack daylilies. Thrips are very small, slender insects that are difficult to detect without a magnifying glass. They feed deep inside petal folds and leaf crevices, scraping tissue with their mouth parts and leaving characteristic silver-white streaks.

Solution: Use traps and insecticide. Eliminate potential host plants.

- Set yellow sticky traps (p.52). Spray plants with insecticidal soap as soon as thrips appear on the traps. Continue to spray every three days for up to two weeks or until insects are gone.
- Spray with the botanical insecticide neem. Or apply a synthetic insecticide registered for daylilies that contains the active ingredient malathion, chlorpyrifos, or diazinon. Follow label directions carefully.
- Remove weeds from around the garden to eliminate alternate homes for the insects.

Leaves and flowers turn mushy and smell rotten

Problem: Leaves turn yellow and mushy, decay, and die. Flowers become water soaked and mushy. Affected plant parts have a foul, rotten odor.

Cause: Bacterial soft rot thrives in warm, wet weather and heavy, poorly drained soil. The bacteria are spread by infected plants and contaminated garden tools. The disease spreads rapidly, and there is no cure.

Solution: Remove diseased plants, provide good growing conditions, and disinfect tools.

- Dig up and discard infected plants. Clean up all garden debris.
- Work a 2- to 4-inch layer of compost or other organic matter into soil to improve drainage. Or grow plants in a raised bed.
- After working around infected plants, wash your hands and tools thoroughly, disinfecting pruning tools (p.310).

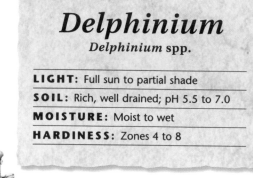

Delphinium
Delphinium spp.

LIGHT: Full sun to partial shade
SOIL: Rich, well drained; pH 5.5 to 7.0
MOISTURE: Moist to wet
HARDINESS: Zones 4 to 8

Plant dies during winter

Problem: The plant does not reemerge in spring. The growth point at the plant base, or crown, turns black. A smelly substance oozes from the rotten parts of the plant.

Cause: Crown rot is the name for both a soilborne fungal and bacterial disease common to delphinium. Both organisms produce similar symptoms that usually occur in poorly drained, wet soils. The disease enters the plant when flower stems break off below the soil line or the crown is otherwise damaged.

Solution: Discard diseased plants. Protect plants from injury. Water properly and provide good growing conditions.

- Dig up and discard an infected plant at the first sign of disease.

- Stake flower stems to prevent breakage. Cut off the stems well above the soil line when blooming is finished.

- Avoid injuring the crown when cultivating the soil around plants.

- Water at ground level with a soaker hose or drip irrigation. Water early in the day so that foliage can dry before sundown to discourage fungal infections.

- Add organic matter, such as compost, to soil for a well-drained growing medium.

Leaves and flowers are eaten; slime trails are present

Problem: The foliage is eaten and ragged. The lower leaves are usually affected first. Damage often occurs overnight. Shiny slime trails appear on the plant or on the soil.

Cause: Slugs and snails are land-dwelling mollusks that feed on plants at night and hide in debris by day. Cool weather, moist soil, and high humidity encourage their nighttime plant-eating activity.

Solution: Remove the pests, use traps and barriers, and clean up garden debris.

- Handpick and destroy slugs and snails. Use a flashlight and look for them after dark, beginning about an hour after sunset.

- Set beer traps and use other tried-and-true means of controlling slugs and snails (box, facing page).

Leaves develop black spots that may run together

Problem: Irregular, shiny, tarlike spots form on the top surfaces of leaves. The leaf undersides have brown spots. The small spots may merge to form larger black areas or become holes. Lower leaves are affected first.

Cause: Bacterial black spot is a disease that attacks primarily leaves but may also affect flowers and stems. It spreads in cool, damp conditions and overwinters on garden debris.

Solution: Remove infected plant parts. Water properly. Practice good garden sanitation. Apply fungicide.

- Remove and discard diseased foliage.
- Water at ground level with a soaker hose or drip irrigation. Water early in the day so leaves can dry before sundown.
- Don't work around plants in wet weather or when plants have wet foliage.
- Spray with an organic copper-sulfate fungicide. Follow label directions carefully.
- Cut and burn old stalks at the end of the season to eliminate overwintering sites.

Flower stems have small holes; plant wilts

Problem: Buds, flowers, and leaves become distorted and turn brown. Affected flowering tips have small holes. You may see a light-colored, sawdust material (frass) around the holes. Plants wilt from the top down. Stems break and fall over.

Cause: Common stalk borers are moth larvae. Adult moths lay eggs near the flowering tips of delphinium plants. Eggs hatch, and the larvae feed on tender buds, flowers, and leaves, causing them to turn brown. Tips usually die, and then the larvae move down through the stalk, causing the plant to wilt. Larvae overwinter in the plant stalks of many species, including corn and weeds.

Solution: Dispose of infested stems, kill borers by hand, or use a biological insecticide. Keep the garden free of weeds and debris.

- Cut off and discard infested plant parts.
- Insert a wire into stems to kill borers. Or inject beneficial nematodes (p.126), a biological control, into the holes.
- Spray or dust with the biological control BT before borers enter plant stems.
- Control weeds and do a thorough cleanup of plant debris in the winter to eliminate plant stalks, where borers overwinter.

TIME-TESTED TECHNIQUES

SEVEN TIPS FOR CONTROLLING SLUGS AND SNAILS

Slugs and snails are mollusks with voracious appetites for many types of plants, and they are prolific, making them a serious threat to gardens. Follow the suggestions below to prevent these pests from doing major damage.

1. Keep gardens free of decaying vegetation, rocks, pots, and other debris to eliminate daytime hiding places.

2. Mulch makes a perfect home for slugs and snails. Don't spread it until plants are well established and daytime temperatures consistently reach 70°F. Make sure the mulch is not more than than 3 inches thick.

3. Slugs and snails don't like to crawl over rough surfaces. Spread sawdust, wood ashes, or crumbled egg shells around plant bases to deter the pests. Another effective material is diatomaceous earth, which is the finely ground, sharp-edged fossil remains of marine creatures. However, these substances work only if they are dry, so reapply as needed after rain.

4. Set a trap. Place an overturned flowerpot on the ground on the shady side of a plant to provide a cool, dark hiding place for slugs and snails. Prop up one edge slightly so that the pests can crawl under. Because slugs and snails like citrus, you can use inverted grapefruit and orange halves with the fruit removed in the same way. Place pots or rinds in the garden in the evening and check under them daily; if pests are present, discard them; put out fresh citrus rinds. Squash pests or drop them into a jar of salty water.

5. Beer is a tried-and-true bait. Place shallow containers, such as small margarine tubs, in the garden so that the rims are just at soil level. Pour stale beer into the containers to a depth of 1 inch. Slugs and snails crawl in and drown. Empty and refill every two days.

6. Spray slugs and snails with a lethal solution of equal parts vinegar and water.

7. Slugs and snails won't crawl across copper, which gives them a slight electrical shock on contact. However, copper is only effective if the pests are not already in the garden bed. To construct a barrier, attach 3-inch-wide copper strips, available at hardware stores or through mail-order sources, to stakes placed around beds or planters. Keep foliage within the barrier.

Flowering Tobacco

Nicotiana alata

LIGHT: Full sun to partial shade

SOIL: Average; pH 6.0 to 7.0

MOISTURE: Moist

HARDINESS: Tender annual

Leaves are marred with tiny holes or are chewed

Problem: Leaves have holes or are chewed, as are stems and flowers. Plants are partially or totally defoliated. Spotted red or yellow grubs or yellow beetles with 10 black stripes are on plants. Clusters of yellow-orange eggs are found on leaf undersides.

Cause: Colorado potato beetles and their plump, black-headed red larvae ravage not only the leaves of potatoes, but also those of the related flowering tobacco. Adults overwinter in the soil and emerge in midspring to lay more than 500 eggs per insect.

Solution: Destroy adults, larvae, and eggs. Spray with biological insecticide.

- Handpick adults and larvae as soon as they are evident, and destroy them.
- Scrape eggs from leaf undersides and crush them.
- Spray or dust plants with the biological control BTSD to kill the grubs.

New leaves are deformed and streaked with yellow or tan

Problem: Leaf margins may be stiff, dry, and crinkled. New leaves are small, crinkled, and mottled. Plant becomes stunted and may wilt.

Cause: Tobacco mosaic virus is a disease that affects ornamental tobacco and its relatives. The virus is carried in smoking tobacco and can be spread by smoking in the garden and touching plants or tools after smoking; it can also be spread from plant to plant by feeding grasshoppers. The incurable disease persists in dead plants for up to 50 years.

Solution: Destroy diseased plants. Rotate crops. Wash hands and avoid smoking.

- Remove and destroy infected plants.
- Do not replant the area with flowering tobacco or other susceptible plants.
- Avoid smoking in the garden; wash hands before handling plants or garden tools.

Tiny insects swarm on plant

Problem: Clusters of small insects appear on flowers and leaves. The foliage is gradually stippled with yellow spots.

Cause: Aphids are small, pear-shaped, soft-bodied insects that suck plant juices. They can be green, yellow, brown, or black.

Solution: Hose off pests and use insecticide.

- Knock aphids off plants with a strong stream of water from a hose every few days.
- If problems persist, spray with the botanical insecticide neem. Or use a synthetic insecticide registered for flowering tobacco that contains the active ingredient carbaryl or acephate. Follow label directions carefully.

Foxglove
Digitalis purpurea

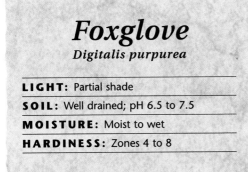

LIGHT: Partial shade

SOIL: Well drained; pH 6.5 to 7.5

MOISTURE: Moist to wet

HARDINESS: Zones 4 to 8

Plant wilts on one side

Problem: Plant first wilts at midday, but recovers by nightfall. Then it wilts for longer periods of time. The wilting may be confined to one side of the plant. The plant does not respond to watering.

Cause: Verticillium wilt is a fungal disease that enters damaged roots. Fungal colonies build up in roots and stems, blocking the flow of water and nutrients, which causes wilting. It is common when conditions are moist and the temperature is around 70°F.

Solution: Apply fertilizer; drench the soil; remove a severely infected plant.

- Stimulate growth by applying fast-acting liquid fertilizer. Make several applications, following label directions.
- Drench the soil with compost tea (p.392).
- Remove and discard badly infected plants.

Leaves have brown spots

Problem: Irregular brown spots with reddish borders form on lower leaves, then spread. Foliage may have a white, moldy appearance.

Cause: Foxglove leaf spot is a fungal disease that usually develops in late summer.

Solution: Remove infected foliage and debris, and drench the soil.

- Remove and destroy infected leaves. Also remove all plant debris from the garden.

- Spray infected plants with disease-inhibiting compost tea (p.392) to help control the spread of disease.
- If leaf spot has been a problem in your area but is not yet present, drench the soil with compost tea as a preventive.

Minute insects cluster on discolored leaves or flowers

Problem: Flowers and leaves have glistening silver or light gray streaks. The flowers are discolored and spotted, and may fail to open. Leaves turn brown and dry out.

Cause: Thrips are very small, brown, winged insects that feed on flowers and foliage, scraping tissue away with their mouth parts. They look like slender, crawling spots and are difficult to see without a magnifying glass.

Solution: Remove affected plant parts, spray with insecticide, and eliminate host plants.

- Prune and destroy infested flowers and leaves.
- Set out yellow sticky traps (p.52) to monitor for pests, and spray with insecticidal soap at the first sign of them. Spray every three days for up to two weeks or until pests are gone. Follow label directions carefully.
- If problems persist, spray with the botanical insecticide neem. Or use a synthetic insecticide registered for foxglove that contains the active ingredient malathion or carbaryl. Follow label directions carefully.
- Remove weeds from the garden to eliminate alternate host plants for the pests.

Plant dies after a season

Problem: Plant flowers one season and dies.

Cause: Foxglove may be either perennial or biennial, dying after its second year.

Solution: Allow plant to self-sow, or select perennial species.

- Allow seed heads to release seed.
- Grow perennial yellow foxglove (*D. grandiflora*), Grecian foxglove (*D. lanata*), or strawberry foxglove (*D. × mertonensis*).

REGIONAL FOCUS
NORTHWEST

Common foxglove (*Digitalis purpurea*) can become an invasive pest in the Pacific Northwest. To prevent seedlings from taking over, remove flower stalks after two-thirds of the blooms have opened. This way, you can enjoy the flowers, but they will not produce viable seeds before the flower stalk is removed.

Fuchsia

Fuchsia spp.

LIGHT: Full sun to partial shade

SOIL: Fertile, well drained; pH 6.0 to 7.0

MOISTURE: Consistently moist

HARDINESS: Tender perennial

Tiny white insects appear on leaf undersides

Problem: Leaf undersides are crawling with small white insects. Leaves may turn yellow. When the leaves are disturbed, clouds of the insects fly up from the plant. A black, sooty mold may develop on foliage where the insects feed.

Cause: Whiteflies are tiny, winged insects common on greenhouse-grown plants and in hot, still summer weather. They suck plant juices, and their secretion, called honeydew, provides a breeding ground for sooty mold. Whiteflies are killed by freezing temperatures.

Solution: Use sticky traps and insecticide, provide good growing conditions, and purchase healthy plants.

- Set out yellow sticky traps (see left) at plant level to monitor for whiteflies. At the first sign of the pests, spray the plant with insecticidal soap or with a synthetic insecticide registered for fuchsias that contains the active ingredient malathion. Be sure to coat leaf undersides thoroughly. Follow label directions carefully.
- Grow fuchsia in a cool, moist location with moderate air circulation, and partial shade in the South.
- When purchasing a new plant, inspect leaf undersides for whiteflies or lightly touch foliage to see if insects rise from the plant.

Leaves and shoots are distorted

Problem: A formerly healthy plant becomes increasingly debilitated. Leaves and new shoots become misshapen.

Cause: Fuchsia gall mites are tiny spider relatives that are a serious pest in mild climates.

Solution: Remove infested foliage and treat the plant with insecticide.

- Remove and destroy affected plant parts at the first sign of infestation.
- Spray the plant with a synthetic insecticide registered for fuchsias that contains the active ingredient carbaryl or endosulfan. Spray again two weeks later. Follow label directions carefully.

Leaves have red or red-ringed spots; growth is stunted

Problem: Leaves have red or red-ringed spots on the top and brown spore pustules on the underside. Plant grows slowly and is stunted.

Cause: Rust is a fungal disease spread by wind. The spores thrive in warm, moist conditions and germinate on damp leaves. The disease overwinters on plant debris.

Solution: Remove affected foliage, water plants properly, increase air circulation, and clean up garden debris.

- Remove and destroy diseased foliage.
- Water plants carefully at ground level to avoid wetting leaves. Water early in the day so that leaves can dry before sundown.
- Space plants far enough apart to keep them from touching to ensure air circulation.
- In fall, remove garden debris and weeds.

Geranium, Annual

Pelargonium spp.

LIGHT: Full sun to partial shade

SOIL: Well drained; pH 6.0 to 7.0

MOISTURE: Moist to seasonally dry

HARDINESS: Tender perennial

Leaf undersides have dark spots

Problem: Small, round, yellow spots mar leaf surfaces. Reddish brown spores develop in concentric rings on the leaf undersides, opposite the the surface spots. Affected leaves yellow and drop.

Cause: Pelargonium rust is a fungal disease that develops when the weather is moist, days are warm, and nights are cool. The spores are spread by wind, and they germinate on damp leaves. The disease overwinters on plant debris.

Solution: Remove diseased foliage, apply fungicide, practice good garden sanitation, and consider transplanting.

- Remove and destroy infected leaves.
- If the fungal infection is severe, apply an organic sulfur fungicide. Follow label directions carefully.
- Water at ground level to avoid wet leaves. Water during the day so leaves dry rapidly.
- Clean up leaf debris all through the season.
- If problems persist, move plants to a location with full sun and good air circulation.

Plant is swarming with tiny, pear-shaped insects

Problem: Small insects cluster on buds, flowers, and foliage. New growth may be stunted. Buds and shoots may be deformed.

Cause: Geranium aphids and green peach aphids are soft-bodied insects that suck plant juices. They can transmit diseases from plant to plant as they feed.

Solution: Hose pests off plant, use insecticide, and encourage beneficial insects.

- Knock aphids off plants with a strong stream of water from a hose as needed.
- Spray the foliage with insecticidal soap every three to five days. Follow label directions carefully.
- Grow small-flowered nectar plants, such as sweet alyssum and scabiosa, to attract lacewings and parasitic wasps to prey on aphids.

Foliage has gray mold

Problem: Leaves, stems or flowers turn yellow, develop gray, fuzzy mold, and begin to rot. Symptoms are worse in humid weather conditions.

Cause: Gray mold, which is also called botrytis blight, is a fungal disease that is prevalent in cool, moist weather. The spores travel from plant to plant on wind.

Solution: Remove diseased plant parts, and improve soil drainage and air circulation.

- Prune and discard infected plant parts.
- Allow soil to dry between waterings, incorporate compost or sand to improve drainage, or replant in a raised bed.
- Thin or space plants widely for maximum air circulation.

Geranium, Perennial

Geranium spp.

LIGHT: Partial shade

SOIL: Well drained; pH 5.5 to 7.0

MOISTURE: Moist

HARDINESS: Zones 4 to 7

Stems and leaves are infested with small, pear-shaped insects

Problem: Yellow spots appear on foliage. Leaves may be misshapen or deformed.

Cause: Aphids are small, soft-bodied insects that suck plant juices, causing leaf spotting. Their secretion, called honeydew, leaves clear, sticky spots on foliage. Aphids often feed in clusters on growing tips or leaf undersides.

Solution: Hose aphids off plant, spray with insecticide, and encourage beneficial insects.

- Dislodge aphids with a strong stream of water from the hose every other day.
- If problems persist, spray insecticidal soap every third day. Spray both sides of leaves. Follow label directions carefully.
- Or spray with a synthetic insecticide registered for geraniums that contains the active ingredient malathion. Follow label directions carefully.
- Grow small-flowered nectar plants, such as yarrow and scabiosa, to attract beneficial insects that prey on aphids.

Black-and-yellow bugs feed on leaves, causing yellow spots

Problem: Rows of small, dark, and depressed spots appear on leaves. Foliage and flowers are deformed.

Cause: Fourlined plant bugs are yellow-green insects with four black lines on their wings. They suck plant juices, causing spots to develop around the wounds. The insects feed for about six weeks in early summer. Their eggs overwinter in plant debris.

Solution: Destroy pests, spray with insecticide, and clean up garden debris.

- Handpick and dispose of the bugs.
- Spray plants with insecticidal soap or a synthetic insecticide registered for geraniums that contains the active ingredient malathion or acephate. Follow label directions carefully.
- Remove plant debris in fall and again in spring to eliminate overwintering sites.

Leaves develop brown spots, turn yellow, and drop

Problem: Leaves develop irregular, brown, sunken spots that grow larger. Affected leaves turn yellow and drop.

Cause: Bacterial leaf spot is a disease that is spread by splashing water. It is most severe in spring and is seldom fatal.

Solution: Remove infected leaves or plants, water properly, and increase air circulation.

- Remove and destroy infected leaves. Pull up and discard severely diseased plants.
- Water at ground level, early in the day so that leaves can dry before sundown.
- Thin existing plants or space new plants far enough apart to promote air circulation.

Gladiolus
Gladiolus spp.

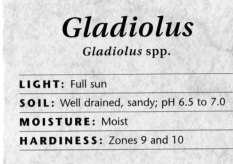

LIGHT: Full sun

SOIL: Well drained, sandy; pH 6.5 to 7.0

MOISTURE: Moist

HARDINESS: Zones 9 and 10

Flowers have silver streaks

Problem: Flowers and leaves have silver or light gray streaks, or are spotted and discolored. Leaves turn brown and dry. Stored corms turn brown and develop a corky texture.

Cause: Thrips are minute, brown, winged insects that feed by scraping plant tissue and consuming the sap that flows from the wounds. Thrips hide between leaves or deep within flower petals. They overwinter in plant debris in mild climates and on stored corms in cold climates.

Solution: Monitor plants and treat with insecticide. Store and plant healthy corms. Eliminate host plants.

- Set out yellow sticky traps (p.52) to monitor for pests. When you see thrips stuck to the traps, spray the plants with insecticidal soap. Follow label directions carefully.
- For a severe infestation, spray the plants with a synthetic insecticide registered for gladiolus that contains the active ingredient acephate or methoxychlor. Follow label directions carefully.
- Before storing corms, soak them in hot water, at 120°F, for 30 minutes to kill thrips. Air dry corms for several days and store them in a cool, dry place.
- Before planting, check corms for thrips.
- Remove weeds and grass from the garden to eliminate alternate homes for the pests.

Flowers and leaves are streaked or spotted

Problem: Flowers and leaves have white streaks, reddish blotches, or other abnormal coloration. Leaves turn yellow or thicken, and flower buds may open partially, then quickly fade. The flower spike or plant may be dwarfed.

Cause: Viral infections disfigure and weaken gladiolus. The diseases are spread by aphids and other sucking insects.

Solution: Destroy plant and control pests.

- Dig up and destroy entire diseased plant, including top growth, corm, and roots.
- Spray healthy plants with a strong stream of water from the hose every other day to dislodge sucking insects.
- If insects persist, spray with insecticidal soap every three days. Or use horticultural oil. Follow label directions carefully.

Foliage yellows and dies

Problem: Foliage may not emerge in spring. Leaves that do emerge yellow and die early in the season. Corms may rot in storage or in the ground.

Cause: Bulb mites are small, white, beadlike spider relatives that feed on corms. They transmit diseases, causing corms to rot. They are found in colonies on rotting tissue and spread to healthy corms.

Solution: Discard damaged corms. Soak in hot water. Encourage beneficial predators.

- Check corms and discard any rotting ones.
- Before planting, soak corms in hot water, at 120°F, for 30 minutes to kill any pests.
- Plant small-flowered nectar plants, such as alyssum and scabiosa, to attract beneficial insects that prey on mites.

REGIONAL FOCUS
NORTHWEST

Botrytis blight is a fungal disease that thrives in cool, moist climates. It causes spotting on foliage and flowers, which turn brown and slimy in wet weather. Destroy any plant, including the corm, that develops symptoms. In fall, dig up healthy corms and air-dry them for several days before storing them in a cool, dry place. Plant corms in well-drained soil and mulch with compost to discourage disease.

Stems rot at the soil line; stems and leaves turn brown

Problem: Leaf bases are brittle, shredded, and tan in color. Small, black, slightly sunken spots appear together at the leaf bases. Clusters of plants rot at the soil line and die. Corm husks or corms become soft and are rotten.

Cause: Basal rot is a persistent, soil-borne fungal disease that enters plants through wounds. Corms are susceptible if they are stored in rooms that are too moist, or are planted in cold, wet soil. The disease can live in the soil for years.

Solution: Destroy diseased plants. Cure and store fungicide-treated corms properly. Provide good growing conditions.

- In fall, dig up and destroy the infected plant and corm.
- Dig up healthy corms (box, below) before cool, wet fall weather begins. Air-dry, then store in a dry, well-ventilated place. If basal rot has been a problem, dust corms with an organic sulfur fungicide before storing. Follow label directions carefully.
- When planting in spring, choose a site with warm, quick-draining soil, or plant corms in a raised bed of healthy soil. Do not plant where an infected corm has grown.

Corm has galls or swellings

Problem: Plant growth is stunted. Foliage wilts, turns yellow, and may die. Dug-up corms have galls, or swellings.

Cause: Root-knot nematodes are minute, soil-dwelling worms that attack roots and corms, which develop knotty swellings where the pests enter.

Solution: Remove an infested plant and discard damaged corms. Select a new planting location or solarize the soil.

- Dig and destroy a severely damaged plant.
- Do not store corms that have galls; discard them instead.
- In spring, plant corms in a different site. Or solarize (p.117) the soil in the existing planting area before planting.

Flower stems have small holes and break

Problem: Leaves wilt, and flowering stems have small holes with a saw-dustlike material at the openings. The stems may fall over or break. Buds, flowers, and leaves may become distorted.

Cause: Borers, including the common stalk borer, feed on gladiolus. Moths lay eggs near the flowering tips. The larvae feed on buds, flowers, and leaves; then the larvae move down through the stem, causing the plant to wilt. Larvae overwinter in other plants, including corn debris and weeds.

Solution: Discard infested stems, kill borers, apply insecticide, and remove weeds.

- Cut off and destroy infested stems.
- Insert a wire into the holes to spear and remove the borers.
- Apply the biological control BT before borers enter the stems.
- Remove garden weeds and plant debris.

TIME-TESTED TECHNIQUES

DIGGING AND STORING GLADIOLUS CORMS

In cold climates, gladiolus corms must be dug up and stored in winter.

1. Lift the corms with a garden fork when foliage begins dying.
2. Cut foliage back to 1 inch above each corm. Shake off loose soil and let corm air-dry a few days. Break off and discard old corm, keeping new corm and small offsets, or cormels.
3. Dust them with an organic sulfur or copper fungicide. Store in a cool (35° to 45°F), dry, airy place.

Hollyhock
Alcea rosea

LIGHT: Full sun to light shade

SOIL: Well drained; pH 6.0 to 7.5

MOISTURE: Moist to seasonally dry

HARDINESS: Zones 4 to 8

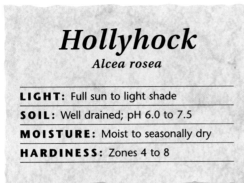

Leaves have yellow or orange spots

Problem: Bright yellow or orange spots develop on the surface of leaves. Brown, pinhead-sized blisters develop on leaf undersides. The spots may eventually merge and destroy large portions of the leaf. In severe cases, leaves dry out and hang from stems.

Cause: Hollyhock rust is a fungal disease that starts early, disfiguring the plant by mid-season. It is most active when humidity is high and temperatures are just above 70°F.

Solution: Remove infected leaves, spray with fungicide, practice good garden sanitation, and select a better planting location.

- Remove and destroy infected leaves at the first sign of symptoms.
- Spray with an organic sulfur fungicide. Or use a synthetic fungicide registered for hollyhocks that contains the active ingredient mancozeb. Follow label directions carefully. If rust has been a problem earlier, start spraying early in the season as a preventive.
- Water at ground level with a soaker hose or drip irrigation. Water early in the day.
- In fall, clean up debris and mulch lightly to create a barrier between plants and spores on the soil.
- Before planting next spring, select a location with full sun and good air circulation.

Leaf tissue is chewed; only leaf veins remain

Problem: Leaves may be skeletonized until only the leaf veins remain. Flowers are chewed or completely consumed.

Cause: Japanese beetles feed on flowers and foliage in masses. The adults have metallic-green heads and copper-colored wing covers. Their larvae are whitish grubs that develop in the soil and feed on grass roots in spring.

Solution: Destroy adults and spray with insecticide. Control grubs.

- Handpick and destroy beetles.
- In severe infestations, spread a sheet under the plant and shake it. Collect and destroy beetles that drop onto the sheet. Do this early in the morning, when beetles are sluggish.
- If problems persist, apply the botanical insecticide neem. Or use a synthetic insecticide registered for hollyhocks that contains the active ingredient carbaryl. Follow label directions carefully. Spray after sunset, when honeybees are less active; carbaryl is toxic to bees.
- In early spring, sprinkle milky-spore disease on the lawn to control beetle grubs.

Leaves have angular spots of various colors

Problem: Leaves develop angular, circular, or irregularly shaped spots in a variety of colors.

Cause: Leaf spot is a disease that can be caused by fungi or bacteria. The disease occurs most often in wet or humid weather. Splashing water carries spores from plant to plant. The disease overwinters on plant debris.

Solution: Remove infected foliage and severely infected plants, spray with fungicide, practice good garden sanitation, and provide healthy growing conditions.

- Immediately prune and discard diseased leaves. Pull up and dispose of severely damaged plants.

- If problems persist, spray the infected plant with an organic sulfur fungicide. Or use a synthetic fungicide registered for hollyhocks that contains the active ingredient thiophanate-methyl. Follow label directions carefully.

- Water at ground level with a soaker hose or drip irrigation. Water early in the day so that leaves dry before sundown.

- After working among infected plants, wash tools, sterilizing cutting tools (p.310).

- Move healthy plants to a location with morning sun and good air circulation.

- In fall, collect and destroy garden debris.

Leaves wither and turn brown

Problem: Dark, ragged blotches with black edges form on leaves, stems, and roots. Leaves may wither, darken, and cling to dying stems. Flower petals may not develop properly. Seedlings are also susceptible.

Cause: Anthracnose is a fungal disease that is carried on seeds, plant parts, debris, wind, and splashing water. It is common in humid climates with plentiful summer rainfall.

Solution: Remove infected plant parts and debris, apply fungicide, and water properly. Clean up debris and mulch.

- Remove and destroy diseased foliage at the first sign of infection. Remove and discard a severely infected plant.

- When conditions favor the disease, spray the plant with the organic fungicide Bordeaux mix. Or spray with a synthetic fungicide registered for hollyhocks that contains the active ingredient mancozeb. Follow label directions carefully.

- Water at ground level, early in the day, so that foliage can dry before sundown.

- In fall, remove garden debris. Lightly mulch to keep soilborne spores off plants.

≈ TIME-TESTED TECHNIQUES ≈

GROWING GOOD-LOOKING HOLLYHOCKS

Hollyhocks are tall, stately plants, up to 9 feet high, that need a little help to look their best. Although perennial, they are often short-lived and benefit from extra care.

Water and fertilize hollyhocks regularly. Supplement rainfall so that plants receive 1 inch of water per week (p386). Water at ground level with a soaker hose or drip irrigation early in the day. Scratch a balanced fertilizer, such as 12-12-12 (p.324), into the soil around plants when new foliage is 2 inches high. From late spring to midsummer, spray the foliage with a water-soluble food high in phosphorous, such as 10-30-20, once a week.

Stake tall varieties about one month after growth starts. Or cut them back by half in May and again in mid-June. Plants will be about half the normal height and flower several weeks later.

Hollyhocks can look scruffy by the middle of the growing season. Tidy them up by removing old foliage. Prune off a flower stalk when there are more seed heads on it than flowers; cut it just above two younger opposing flower buds or flowering stalks (lateral buds). If you want plants to reseed, leave a few ripe flower stalks in place. Also remove leaves that have yellowed or have been damaged by pests or disease.

After plants have finished flowering, remove all old flowering stems and old foliage around the plant base. Water and fertilize plants to encourage new growth. Plants will regrow and may even rebloom in early autumn.

Impatiens
Impatiens spp.

LIGHT: Part to full shade

SOIL: Well drained; pH 6.0 to 7.5

MOISTURE: Moist

HARDINESS: Tender perennial

Moldy spots disfigure leaves

Problem: Leaves, stems, or flowers are marked with gray blotches or brown spots.

Cause: Gray mold, also called bud and flower blight, is a fungus that is active in cool, humid weather.

Solution: Remove infected plant material and debris. Use fungicide.

- Prune and discard infected foliage and flowers. Remove plant debris when you see it.
- In severe cases, spray the plant with a synthetic fungicide registered for impatiens that contains the active ingredient benomyl or captan. Follow label directions carefully.

Plant turns yellow and wilts; stem rots

Problem: The plant wilts, and watering does not revive it. The stem darkens at the base, and the plant turns yellow and dies. If the stem is cut, it oozes a yellow substance.

Cause: Stem rot is a fungal disease that is active in warm weather and often attacks plants growing in poorly drained soil. It infects plants through wounds and can cause both roots and stems to rot.

Solution: Remove diseased plant and soil, add compost, provide good growing conditions, and remove debris.

- Dig up and remove the infected plant and soil around the roots. Fill the hole with disease-inhibiting compost.
- Space plants widely to encourage air circulation, and allow soil to dry between waterings.
- Remove all plant debris.
- Add compost to the soil every fall.

Foliage is stippled and faded

Problem: Leaves may have webbing. They develop many tiny spots, then fade and fall off. Growth is stunted, and plant may die.

Cause: Spider mites are tiny spider relatives that pierce foliage and suck plant juices. The webs hide eggs and young mites. The pests are most active in hot, dry weather.

Solution: Remove damaged leaves, hose mites off plant, water, and spray with insecticide.

- Prune and destroy damaged leaves.
- Spray plants daily with a strong stream of water from the hose to dislodge mites.
- Water to keep the soil evenly moist.
- If problems persist, spray the plant with insecticidal soap. Or use a synthetic insecticide registered for impatiens that contains the active ingredient diazinon. Follow label directions carefully.

Iris

Iris spp.

LIGHT: Full sun to partial shade

SOIL: Average; pH 5.5 to 8.0

MOISTURE: Moist to seasonally dry

HARDINESS: Zones 3 to 8

Leaves have brown spots

Problem: Tiny brown spots appear on foliage. The spots enlarge and vary in size. They are often surrounded by water-soaked areas that turn yellow. The symptoms become more serious after the iris plant blooms.

Cause: Leaf spot is a fungal disease that is most active in wet weather and is frequently found in areas with alkaline soil. The fungus does not infect rhizomes but may kill foliage to the point that rhizomes weaken and die after a few years. Spores are spread by wind and splashing water. Leaf spot overwinters on old leaves.

Solution: Remove and destroy infected foliage, apply fungicide, water properly, and acidify the soil.

- At the first sign of infection, prune and dispose of diseased foliage. Cut below damaged areas. Sterilize pruners (p.310) between cuts.

- Spray the plant with a synthetic fungicide registered for irises that contains the active ingredient mancozeb or thiophanate-methyl. Follow label directions carefully.

- To keep leaves dry, water at ground level with a soaker hose or drip irrigation, and water early in the day.

- Test the soil pH (p.329). If the soil is alkaline, add garden sulfur to achieve a neutral (7.0) or slightly acidic pH.

Dark powdery spots appear on leaves and stems

Problem: Powdery, brown or brownish red oval spots appear on the leaves and stems of iris from early spring to summer. The spots sometimes have yellow margins. As the spots spread and become more numerous, the iris plant grows progressively weaker.

Cause: Iris rust attacks bulbous iris, such as Dutch iris (*I.* × *hollandica*), as well as many other iris species. The disease thrives in hot, humid summer weather and is most serious in the Southeast.

Solution: Remove infected leaves or a severely infected plant, water properly, and grow disease-resistant varieties.

- Remove and destroy the infected foliage. Sterilize the pruners after each cut (p.310). If the symptoms are severe, remove and destroy the plant.

- To keep leaves dry, water at ground level with a soaker hose early in the day.

- Plant a variety of Dutch iris that resists rust, such as 'Early Blue', Gold and Silver', 'Golden West', 'Imperator', 'Lemon Queen', or 'Texas Gold'.

Leaves turn yellow and die

Problem: Leaves die from the top down, gradually turning completely yellow. The bases of leaves are dry and brown. White, threadlike fungal strands are visible on lower leaves of an infected plant. Round, pinhead-sized fungal structures are often found in the soil around the plant bases.

Cause: Crown rot is a persistent soilborne fungal disease that is most active in hot weather and in areas where air circulation is poor and plants are overcrowded.

Solution: Remove the infected plant and soil. Apply fertilizer, fungicide, and a soil drench. Space plants properly and acidify the soil.

- Remove and destroy the diseased plant and surrounding 6 inches of soil.

- Treat the soil where the plant grew with ammonium nitrate, a high-nitrogen fertilizer. Follow label directions carefully.

- In severe cases, treat the soil with a synthetic fungicide registered for irises that contains the active ingredient PCNB. Follow label directions carefully.

- In midsummer, when conditions favor the disease, drench the soil with disease-fighting compost tea (p.392).

- When planting, space plants far apart to promote good air circulation.

- Test the soil pH (p.329). If it is above 7.5, add garden sulfur following label directions to lower it to between 5.5 and 7.0. Mulch with acidifying oak leaves or pine needles.

WISE CHOICES

Different types of iris may look similar, but some require special growing conditions to thrive. Match the species to the location to encourage healthy plants.

- Blue flag (*Iris versicolor*), copper iris (*I. fulva*), Virginia iris (*I. virginica*), and yellow flag (*I. pseudacorus*) are bog and water plants, and require wet soil.

- Japanese iris (*I. ensata*) and rabbitear iris (*I. laevigata*) prefer damp and marshy soil that is not wet.

- Crested iris (*I. cristata*), roof iris (*I. tectorum*), and Siberian iris (*I. siberica*) need moist but not damp soil.

- Bearded iris cultivars and Pacific Coast hybrid irises require well-drained soil.

- Crested iris, Japanese iris, and Siberian iris do best in acidic soil.

- Louisiana hybrid irises tolerate a hot, humid climate.

- Arctic iris (*I. setosa*), dwarf bearded iris (*I. pumila*), German iris (*I. germanica*), and Rocky Mountain iris (*I. missouriensis*) are exceptionally cold hardy.

Leaves are chewed; plant rots and collapses

Problem: Leaf margins are chewed. Irregular tunnels appear near leaf bases, and pinholes dot foliage a few inches above the ground. Leaves may have dark streaks and be wilted or rotten. Plants may collapse.

Cause: Iris borers are serious pests that damage plants directly and create entry points for bacterial soft rot disease (p.62). Their eggs hatch in spring, when the foliage is 5 to 6 inches high. Larvae burrow into leaves and rhizomes, then exit and develop in soil. Borer eggs overwinter on plant debris.

Solution: Remove damaged plant parts and pests. Apply insecticide. Clean up debris.

- Remove and destroy infested foliage and a severely infested rhizome.

- If damage is slight, dig up the rhizome and spear borers with a piece of wire threaded into their tunnels. Dust damaged tissue with organic sulfur fungicide and replant.

- Apply the biological control beneficial nematodes (p.126) to the soil.

- In fall, clean up and remove plant debris.

- Next spring, spray the plants with a synthetic insecticide registered for irises that contains the active ingredient dimethoate when leaves are 4 inches high. Follow label directions carefully.

Small spots or streaks appear on foliage or flowers

Problem: Brown or silvery streaks, or small, rough, brownish spots appear on foliage. Leaves become sooty and black. Flower buds

---

REGIONAL FOCUS
SOUTHWEST

A disease called iris scorch is a problem in the Southwest and in some central states. The first symptom is browning of the leaf tips. The reddish brown discoloration quickly advances down the leaf and into the roots, killing the entire fan and the rhizome within a few days. The cause of the disease is unknown. The only control is to remove and destroy the infected plant at the first sign of this incurable disease.

turn black. Growth is stunted, and plant tops die out. Roots in older clumps die.

Cause: Iris thrips are very small, slender insects that are difficult to see without a magnifying glass. The black-bodied adults are sometimes visible around leaf bases, but the pests generally hide deep within leaf shoots and flower petals. When feeding, thrips rasp plant tissue so that they can suck plant juices, causing the spots and streaks.

Solution: Hose pests off plant, spray with insecticide, pull weeds, and attract predators.

- Spray plant with a strong stream of water from a hose to dislodge the pests. Be sure to spray crevices between leaves and petals.

- Set out yellow sticky traps (p.52) to monitor for pests. Spray with insecticidal soap at the first sign of thrips. Continue to spray every three days for up to two weeks or until the insects are gone.

- If problems persist, spray the plant with the botanical insecticide neem. Or use a synthetic insecticide registered for irises that contains the active ingredient malathion. Follow label directions carefully.

- Remove weeds from the garden to eliminate alternate homes for thrips.

- Grow small-flowered nectar plants, such as yarrow and alyssum, nearby to attract beneficial insects that prey on thrips.

⚜ TIME-TESTED TECHNIQUES ⚜

DIGGING, DIVIDING, AND PLANTING IRIS

For maximum flowering, divide rhizomatous iris every three or four years. Divide a month after flowering, or in early fall, to allow rhizomes time to store food. Plant divisions in full sun and well-drained soil. If planting a rhizome that was stored, soak it for a few hours in a solution of ½ cup of household bleach and 1 quart of water to inhibit disease; rinse and air-dry before planting.

1. Dig up the clump with a garden fork. Shake off excess soil or wash off soil with a hose to expose the rhizome.

2. Using a clean, sharp knife, cut off and discard any old, damaged, or diseased rhizome part. Save only firm, swollen rhizomes attached to foliage fans.

3. Cut back foliage to 6 inches from the rhizome and let the plant dry in the sun for a few hours.

4. Mound soil in a hole and top it with the rhizome, spreading its roots over the mound. In average soil, top rhizome with 1 inch of soil. In heavy soil, expose slightly.

Leaves are streaked; rhizome is wet and rotten

Problem: Leaves turn yellow from the tip down and have water-soaked streaks that spread outward until the foliage rots and falls over. The rhizome is rotten and foul smelling.

Cause: Bacterial soft rot is a soil-borne disease that enters the plant through wounds, such as those caused by iris borers (p.61). The disease is spread by splashing water and contaminated tools.

Solution: Remove damaged foliage and rhizomes, control borers, and provide good growing conditions.

- Prune infected leaves below the damaged area to prevent bacteria from traveling down to the rhizome. Sterilize pruners (p.310) after each cut and wash your hands.

- If the disease spreads, dig up and destroy infected rhizomes.

- Control iris borers (p.61).

- Next season, plant iris in well-drained soil and full sun. Cover rhizomes partially with soil so that sunlight can discourage the growth of bacteria.

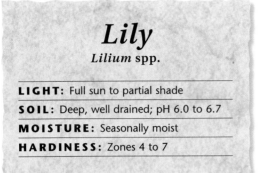

Lily

Lilium spp.

LIGHT: Full sun to partial shade

SOIL: Deep, well drained; pH 6.0 to 6.7

MOISTURE: Seasonally moist

HARDINESS: Zones 4 to 7

Small, pear-shaped insects infest foliage and flowers

Problem: Buds, flowers, and foliage are covered with clusters of small, soft-bodied insects. New growth may be stunted; buds and shoots may be deformed. A clear, sticky substance or sooty, black areas may be present.

Cause: Several species of aphid attack lilies. All suck plant juices and can transmit harmful viral or bacterial diseases. If infestations are large enough, a sticky aphid secretion, called honeydew, is noticeable. Sooty mold is a fungus that often develops on honeydew.

Solution: Hose aphids off plants, spray with insecticide, and attract beneficial insects.

- Knock aphids off the plant with a stream of water from the hose every other day. Place one hand behind the stem to support it.
- Spray with insecticidal soap every three to five days. Be sure to spray leaf undersides.
- If problems persist, spray the plant with a synthetic insecticide registered for lilies that contains the active ingredient malathion or acephate. Follow label directions carefully.
- Grow small-flowered nectar plants, such as sweet alyssum and yarrow, to attract lacewings, ladybugs, and other beneficial insects that prey on aphids.

Bulbs are soft and moldy

Problem: Stored or purchased bulbs are decayed, with sunken brown lesions. In severe cases, the bulb is soft and covered with a fuzzy, blue-gray mold.

Cause: Blue mold rot is caused by a fungus that is active in damp conditions. It enters the bulb through wounds.

Solution: Discard infected bulbs. Use fungicide. Store bulbs properly.

- At planting time, discard bulbs that have bruises, wounds, or other signs of disease.
- Store lily bulbs in a cool, dry location with good air circulation.
- Before planting, inspect bulbs carefully and plant only those that are firm and healthy.
- If rot has been a problem, treat healthy bulbs with organic sulfur or with a synthetic fungicide containing benomyl before planting. Follow label directions carefully.

Flies appear on plants; growth is weakened

Problem: Bulb produces weak growth and turns into a soft brown mass. The bulb feels light in weight and softer than normal.

Cause: Narcissus bulb flies are yellow and black pests that lay eggs at the base of a plant. Fat, yellowish grubs emerge and bore into bulbs, causing great damage.

Solution: Firm the soil. Discard infested bulbs and select a new planting location.

- After blooming, firm the soil around the neck of the bulb as the foliage dies to discourage flies from laying eggs there.
- Discard infested or soft bulbs.
- Plant lilies in the open; flies prefer plants in protected areas.

REGIONAL FOCUS
NORTHEAST

The red lily leaf beetle is a serious pest of lilies along the East Coast. Adults have a long, scarlet body and black head. They lay orange-red eggs on leaf undersides; the eggs hatch in 7 to 10 days. The larvae, which eat large holes in leaves, look like slugs, with orange, brown, yellowish, or greenish bodies and black heads.

If only a few plants are infested, handpick the pests. Otherwise use the botanical insecticide neem to kill larvae and repel adults. Follow label directions carefully.

Lupine

Lupinus spp.

LIGHT: Full sun to light shade

SOIL: Fertile, well drained; pH 5.5 to 7.0

MOISTURE: Wet

HARDINESS: Zones 3 to 8

Dark spots are on leaf tops; undersides have orange spots

Problem: Tops of leaves have dark or yellowish spots. The undersides have powdery orange or yellowish spots opposite the spots on the leaf tops. Plants may be stunted.

Cause: Rust is a fungal disease that is most prevalent in moist or humid weather. The spores travel from plant to plant in splashing water or on the wind. Spores overwinter in infected plant debris.

Solution: Use a fungicide, water properly, and practice garden sanitation to control rust.

- At the first sign of the disease, spray plants with an organic sulfur fungicide. Follow label directions carefully.
- Water plants at ground level with a soaker hose or sprinkler to avoid wetting leaves. Water early in the day so leaves can dry before sundown.
- Remove and destroy infected leaves. Pick up leaf litter and other garden debris throughout the season and especially in fall to remove overwintering sites for the disease.
- In moist climates, space new plants far apart to promote good air circulation to keep spores from germinating on damp leaves.

Foliage is ragged and chewed

Problem: Silver trails appear on the plant. Leaves are ragged and chewed or have holes.

Cause: Slugs and snails can devastate lupine. Cool weather, moist soil, and humidity encourage slug and snail activity. Leaf litter and debris provide them with daytime shelter.

Solution: Handpick. Use garden sanitation, traps, and barriers to limit the damage.

- Handpick and destroy slugs and snails.
- Eliminate debris to remove hiding places. Use beer traps, wood ash, copper barriers, or other time-tested remedies (p.49).

Leaves develop white, powdery areas that won't rub off

Problem: Foliage and stems are covered with a white, feltlike dust that can not be rubbed off. Lower leaves are the most severely affected. Leaves may dry out and curl.

Cause: Powdery mildew is a fungal disease most prevalent when plants are grown in areas with poor air circulation and low light. Outbreaks occur mostly in mid- to late summer, when warm days are followed by cool nights. Although unsightly, powdery mildew seldom kills plants.

Solution: Numerous garden techniques and fungicidal sprays can slow the spread of powdery mildew.

- Remove and dispose of infected plant parts and plant debris on the ground.
- Wash down leaves with water from a hose to dislodge spores. Do this early in the day so foliage has time to dry before nightfall.

● Spray with summer oil or an antifungal home remedy (p.392): baking soda solution or compost tea, to reduce the severity of powdery mildew. To avoid burning foliage, do not spray in direct sunlight; instead spray in the morning before the sun is overhead. Although compost tea won't eliminate powdery mildew once it has started, it can slow its spread.

● If the problem persists, spray with an organic sulfur fungicide. Or use a synthetic fungicide registered for lupines that contains the active chemical ingredient mancozeb. Follow label directions carefully.

● In new plantings, select a sunny site. Increase air circulation by spacing plants far apart and by avoiding low-lying planting sites where the air is still.

Leaves have gray fuzz

Problem: Leaves and flowers become discolored and a gray furry growth forms. Plant parts turn to mush. If flowers are attacked, they turn brown, droop, and rot.

Cause: Downy mildew is a fungal disease that occurs in the spring when temperatures are cool (between 45° and 55°F) and moisture is plentiful. It requires low light and high humidity to germinate and spread. After downy mildew strikes, plant growth slows and, in severe cases, plants die. Spores overwinter in weeds and plant debris.

Solution: Pick infected leaves, and practice good gardening techniques.

● Remove infected leaves. If leaf removal is followed by several days of dry weather, you have a good chance of significantly slowing the spread of the fungus.

● Thin plants to allow sunlight and air into plantings, and reduce watering to create unfavorable conditions for the disease.

● If downy mildew is a persistent problem, move plants to a location where they get full sun and excellent air circulation.

Disfigured leaves have yellow spots

Problem: The leaves turn yellow or brown and may be puckered or distorted. The plant may wilt.

Cause: Aphids are pear-shaped, soft-bodied insects. They are found clustered together on the undersides of leaves and on tender new growth. If infestations are large, a sticky, clear aphid secretion, called honeydew, is present.

Solution: Control aphids by crushing them, hosing them off, or spraying them with an insecticide.

● If aphid populations are not large, crush the insects between your fingers.

● Use a strong steam of water from a hose to knock the insects off the foliage as often as needed.

● Spray the infested leaves with insecticidal soap every three to five days. If problems persist, spray with a synthetic insecticide registered for lupines that contains the active ingredient malathion. Follow label directions carefully.

Plant dies after one season

Problem: Although the plant appears healthy, it dies after one season, especially when grown in a region with warm summers.

Cause: These short-lived perennials grow best where summers are not hot and dry.

Solution: Treat lupines as annuals in warm regions. Provide optimal growing conditions.

● Grow lupine as an annual in warm regions. Remove the spent flowers before seeds are released.

● In cool climates, keep the soil moist and place plants in afternoon shade. After the first flush of flowering, cut the plant back to the point where new leaves develop at the base. Apply a winter mulch.

● Fertilize in spring with a formula that is high in phosphorus and potassium, such as a 5-10-10 formulation (p.324).

Marigold
Tagetes spp.

LIGHT: Full sun to partial shade

SOIL: Fertile; pH 6.0 to 7.0

MOISTURE: Moist to seasonally dry

HARDINESS: Warm-season annual

Leaves are greenish gray and have tiny yellow spots

Problem: The foliage is greenish gray with fine webbing and small dots. The problem is most severe during periods of hot, dry weather and on dwarf types of marigold.

Cause: Spider mites are tiny relatives of spiders that suck sap. Chlorophyll, the substance that gives plants their green color, is destroyed as the mites feed, causing pale spots on leaves. Mites feed in masses, and by the time damage is noticed plants can be seriously weakened.

Solution: Spray water and apply a mite repellent or an insecticide. In the future, grow tall varieties that are less susceptible to mites.

- Knock mites from the infested plant with a strong stream of water from a hose; keep the soil moist during dry periods.

- If problems continue, spray with insecticidal soap as needed. Or use a synthetic insecticide registered for marigolds that contains the active ingredient malathion. Follow label directions carefully.

- Repel mites from healthy plants by applying garlic oil to marigold leaves.

- To avoid problems next season, consider resistant varieties, such as those in the Antigua Series, Discovery Series, Galore Series, Jubilee Series, and Lady Series.

Gray mold appears on flowers

Problem: Flowers are covered with a disfiguring gray mold. The stem is weakened and may collapse.

Cause: Botrytis blight is a fungal disease that is a common problem on marigold. It is most common during periods of moist and cool weather.

Solution: Control the disease with a fungicide. Use proper garden sanitation, air circulation, watering, and mulching techniques to discourage botrytis in the future.

- Spray the plant with a synthetic fungicide registered for marigolds that contains the active ingredient mancozeb. Follow label directions carefully.

- Water at ground level to keep leaves dry. When blossoms begin to fade, remove them from the plants to prevent reinfection.

- Mulch with compost to keep spore-laden soil from splashing onto plants.

- When planting new marigolds, space plants far apart to allow good air circulation.

Leaves have large holes; flowers are chewed

Problem: Large, ragged holes appear in leaves and flowers, or scalloped holes are chewed into their edges.

Cause: Caterpillars of various butterflies and moths feed on marigolds throughout the growing season.

Solution: Handpick, use biological insecticide, and practice good garden techniques.

- Handpick and dispose of caterpillars. Hunt for them early in the morning, when cool temperatures make them sluggish.
- Spray caterpillars with the biological insecticide BT. It works best on small, young pests.
- Remove weeds and debris from the garden to eliminate alternate shelters and sources of food for caterpillars.
- Grow nectar plants, such as scabiosa, yarrow, and alyssum to attract beneficial insects that prey on caterpillars.

Leaves and flowers are discolored or deformed

Problem: Plants become less vigorous and have stunted growth. Leaves and stems may be deformed.

Cause: Aster yellows is an incurable viral disease that is spread by sap-sucking insects called leafhoppers. As the name implies, leafhoppers jump quickly when disturbed. These insects feed on the undersides of marigold leaves, extracting plant juices and causing leaf tips, then margins, to brown. Viral symptoms may follow.

Solution: Remove diseased plants. If populations of leafhoppers become high, use insecticides and encourage beneficial insects. Keep the garden free of weeds.

- Remove diseased plants from the garden to prevent the spread of aster yellows.
- Make repeated applications of insecticidal soap. Follow label directions carefully.
- Spray with the botanical insecticide neem or with refined horticultural oil to protect leaves and to smother remaining leafhoppers. Follow label directions carefully.
- If problem persists, spray with a synthetic insecticide registered for marigolds that contains the active ingredient malathion. Follow label directions carefully.
- Grow small-flowered nectar plants, such as sweet alyssum and scabiosa to attract beneficial insects such as assassin bugs and lacewings, which prey on leafhoppers.
- Remove weeds in fall to eliminate overwintering sites for leafhopper eggs.

Leaves and flowers are chewed ragged; slime trails remain

Problem: Foliage is ragged and chewed or has holes in it. The damage occurs overnight; lower leaves are usually eaten first. Although the culprits are never seen during the day, silver-gray slimy trails appear on the plant or on the ground.

Cause: Slugs and snails feed on plants at night. Cool weather, moist soil, and humidity encourage slug and snail activity. Leaf litter and debris, such as boards and pots, left around the garden, provide daytime shelters.

Solution: Remove these pests when you see them. Use traps to reduce further infestations, and remove garden debris.

- Handpick and remove slugs and snails. Hunt at night with a flashlight, beginning about an hour after sunset.
- Make beer traps and use other techniques (p.49) for controlling slugs and snails.
- Keep your garden free of decaying vegetation and other debris to eliminate daytime hiding places for the pests.

Plant rots at the base

Problem: The plant grows slowly or not at all from the time of transplanting; it rots at the base before flowering.

Cause: Dwarf varieties are very sensitive to overwatering and quickly rot in sodden soil.

Solution: Water carefully; improve drainage. Grow tall types.

- Water the soil, then allow it to dry out completely before watering again.
- Before planting, amend heavy soil with compost or sand to improve drainage.
- Consider growing tall varieties of marigolds.

Nasturtium
Tropaeolum majus

LIGHT: Full sun to partial shade

SOIL: Well drained, average; pH 6.0 to 7.0

MOISTURE: Moist

HARDINESS: Hardy annual

Leaves are marred by winding, narrow trails

Problem: Narrow, squiggly trails in tan, milky white, or yellow are found on some of the leaves. These leaves may eventually brown and hang from the plant.

Cause: Serpentine leafminers are the larvae of tiny yellow-and-black flies that lay eggs on leaf undersides. The larvae tunnel into leaves, feeding on tissue between the upper and lower leaf surfaces, leaving winding trails. The larvae drop to the soil to mature. While unsightly, leafminer damage is seldom fatal.

Solution: Remove infested leaves, introduce beneficial predators, apply insecticide, and erect barriers. Practice good garden sanitation.

- Cut off infested leaves and discard them or burn them.
- Introduce the biological control beneficial nematodes, which prey on leafminers.
- Or spray the plant with a synthetic insecticide registered for nasturtiums that contains the active ingredient carbaryl. Follow label directions carefully.
- Place plastic sheeting under plants to prevent pests from maturing in the soil. Cover sheeting with an organic mulch.
- In fall, cut the plants back to the ground and destroy all plant debris in the garden.

Small insects cluster on leaves

Problem: Leaf undersides are covered with tiny insects. Leaves turn pale yellow-green. The plant doesn't grow well and may wilt.

Cause: Aphids are tiny, pear-shaped insects that suck sap, giving foliage a pale color. The most common type that feeds on nasturtium is the dark-green to black bean aphid.

Solution: Hose off aphids. Apply insecticide and a repellent.

- Every other day, knock aphids off plants with a stream of water from a hose.
- If problems persist, spray with insecticidal soap or with the botanical insecticide neem or pyrethrin. Coat all leaf surfaces thoroughly. Follow label directions carefully.
- Or spray with a synthetic insecticide registered for nasturtiums that contains the active ingredient malathion. Follow label directions carefully.
- As a preventative, spray plants with commercial garlic oil to repel aphids.

Leaves develop yellow spots and eventually die

Problem: Leaves become spotted with yellow, then turn yellow completely and die.

Cause: Various fungi cause leaf spot. They become active in mild, wet weather, and the disease is common in areas with hot, humid summers.

Solution: Remove affected foliage and debris. Apply fungicide. Water properly.

- Prune and discard diseased foliage. Clean up all debris around plantings.
- Spray plant with an organic copper-sulfate fungicide. Follow label directions carefully.
- Water at ground level or early in the day so that leaves can dry before sundown.

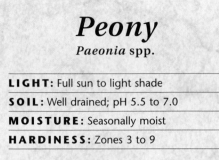

Peony
Paeonia spp.

LIGHT: Full sun to light shade

SOIL: Well drained; pH 5.5 to 7.0

MOISTURE: Seasonally moist

HARDINESS: Zones 3 to 9

Ants overrun flowers and stems

Problem: Buds, flowers, and stems are covered with ants.

Cause: Ants are attracted to the sweet, sticky secretion found on the buds.

Solution: Tolerate infestation. Spray plant with water.

- Tolerate the ants. Because the ants do no harm, they do not need to be removed.
- Spray water gently to wash ants off blossoms you wish to bring indoors.

Flower buds fail to form

Problem: Foliage is healthy, but flower buds do not form.

Cause: Several factors can affect bud formation. First, the plant may be too immature for buds to develop. Second, the roots may be planted too deeply. Third, excessive shade can prevent flowering. Fourth, competition from other plants can rob moisture and nutrients from the plant. Fifth, excess nitrogen causes foliage growth at the expense of flowers. And finally, overcrowding can inhibit blooming.

Solution: Provide proper growing conditions.

- If the plant is young, it may need to mature three to five years before producing flowers.
- If it may have been planted too deeply, dig up the root in fall and replant it with the buds, or eyes, 1 inch below soil level. Do not add more than 1 inch of mulch.
- If a plant is shaded, dig it in fall and replant in a sunny location, as described above.

- If the plant is close to trees or shrubs, either move it to a more open location or give it additional water and fertilizer. Use a fertilizer that is low in nitrogen and high in phosphorus, such as 5-10-10 (p.324).
- If the soil is rich or you have been fertilizing heavily, stop fertilizing.
- If the plant is old and overcrowded, dig it up and divide it (p.29) in late summer. Make sure each division has three to five eyes, and replant divisions 3 feet apart.

Flower buds do not open

Problem: Buds are green or brown and pea-size. They may turn black and die or may partially open, then turn brown and fall off.

Causes: There may be one or several causes. Late spring frost can kill buds, while hot spring weather can prevent them from opening. Partly opened buds waterlogged by excessive rain won't open. Nearby trees and shrubs rob moisture and nutrients, preventing flowering. Buds can be killed in early spring by botrytis blight, a fungal disease common in cold, wet weather.

Solution: Select carefully; protect buds; provide water and nutrients; treat disease.

- If spring frosts repeatedly kill buds, ask a nursery for a late-blooming variety.
- If hot weather keeps buds from opening, plant early-blooming varieties recommended by your local nursery.
- If weather is wet when buds form, tie a plastic bag around each bud to keep them dry.
- If the plant is near trees or shrubs, move it or give it additional water and a fertilizer formulation low in nitrogen, such as 5-10-10 (p.324).
- If it has botrytis blight, remove infected parts and mulch. Allow soil to dry. Drench the soil with compost tea (p.392). Burn plant debris.

REGIONAL FOCUS
SOUTHEAST

Peonies need a period of winter chilling to grow and flower properly. Their dormancy requirement is met when the soil temperature stays near 40°F for a few weeks. While peonies can also be raised in warmer areas, they will grow over winter and gradually be exhausted. In a warm climate, place the plant in partial shade. And select an early or midseason bloomer, such as 'Red Glory', 'America', or 'Red Charm'. Or grow a single-flowered or Japanese-type peony.

Flowers have silvery streaks; petals turn brown

Problem: Flowers develop silvery white flecks or streaks. Flower buds may not open, or flowers may be distorted with brown edges.

Cause: Flower thrips are very small, slender, bright yellow or orange, winged insects that are difficult to detect without a magnifying glass. They hide deep within petal folds and scrape plant tissue with their mouth parts to suck juices, leaving silver-white streaks or flecks.

Solution: Remove affected blooms. Treat with insecticide. Eliminate potential host plants.

- Clip off and destroy infested flowers.

- Set out sticky traps (p.52) to monitor thrips. Spray with insecticidal soap as soon as thrips appear. Spray every three days for up to two weeks or until insects are gone.

- If problems persist, spray with the botanical insecticide neem. Or use a synthetic insecticide registered for peonies that contains the active ingredient malathion. Follow label directions carefully.

- Remove weeds from around the garden to eliminate alternate homes for the insects.

Leaf tissue is chewed; only leaf veins remain

Problem: In early summer leaves are skeletonized until only veins remain. Flowers are also eaten. Beetles are present on the plant.

Cause: Japanese beetles feed on flowers and foliage, especially when the temperature is between 80° and 95°F. The adults have metallic-green heads and copper-colored wing covers. The larvae are grayish white grubs that develop in the soil under the lawn and feed on grass roots in spring.

Solution: Destroy adults and control grubs.

- Handpick and destroy adults. For a large infestation, place a sheet under the plant and shake the plant gently; do this early in the morning, when pests are sluggish. Destroy beetles that drop onto the sheet.

- If problems persist, spray the plant with the botanical insecticide neem. Follow label directions carefully.

- In early spring, apply milky-spore disease (p.394), a biological grub control, to the lawn. Apply again in fall.

⚘ TIME-TESTED TECHNIQUES ⚘

STAKING PEONIES

Peonies produce voluptuous blossoms on relatively slender stems, which sometimes cannot support the heavy flower heads. Even moderate rainfall or wind can bow the stems to the ground or snap them.

　　To protect flower stems, select a site that is sheltered from wind. And begin staking early, before the buds form, so that the foliage will grow up to cover the supports. For a single plant, which grows about 3 feet tall and wide, use a circular metal support; some are manufactured as half-circles that can be linked together to form a ring of the desired size. Alternatively, drive bamboo stakes at intervals around the plant, being careful not to injure the fleshy roots. Encircle the stakes with green yarn or twine at one-third the plant's height, then at two-thirds.

　　For a mass planting, drive stakes around the perimeter of the group of plants and surround the stakes with twine. If peonies are lined up against a wall, drive stakes at the ends and at intervals along the row, and connect the stakes with twine.

Petunia
Petunia spp.

LIGHT: Full sun

SOIL: Rich, well drained; pH 6.5 to 7.5

MOISTURE: Moist

HARDINESS: Tender annual

Leaves and flowers are chewed

Problem: Ragged holes are chewed in buds or in flowers and leaves, especially around the margins. Dark pellets of insect waste, or frass, are on leaves. Caterpillars may be present.

Cause: Several caterpillars feed on petunias. The tomato hornworm and tobacco hornworm are large and green. The former has eight white stripes and a green-and-black horn at the rear; the latter has seven white stripes and a red horn. The tobacco budworm is smaller and rust colored or green striped. The adults of all these pests are moths that emerge in spring and can be seen hovering over petunias at dusk.

Solution: Destroy caterpillars, use insecticide, and encourage natural predators.

- Handpick and destroy caterpillars.
- Treat the plant with the biological control BT as soon as the pests appear. Or spray with a synthetic insecticide registered for petunias that contains the active ingredient acephate. Follow label directions carefully. Continue treating once a week until the problem is under control.
- Grow nectar plants, such as yarrow, dill, and daisy, to attract parasitic wasps that prey on caterpillars.

Foliage has white patches

Problem: Foliage is covered with a white, feltlike dust. Lower leaves are the most severely affected. Leaves may dry and curl.

Cause: Powdery mildew is a fungal disease prevalent in sites with poor air circulation and hot, humid days in mid- to late summer. While unsightly, it is seldom fatal.

Solution: Prune foliage. Use fungicide.

- Clip off and dispose of infected plant parts and plant debris on the ground.
- Spray with summer oil or an antifungal home remedy (p.392): baking-soda solution or compost tea. Do not spray in direct sun.
- If problems persist, spray with an sulfur organic fungicide. Or use a synthetic fungicide registered for petunias that contains the active ingredient mancozeb. Follow label directions carefully.

Flowers and leaves have holes

Problem: Plant is eaten and ragged. The damage occurs overnight; lower leaves are usually eaten first. Silver-gray slime trails appear on the plant or the ground.

Cause: Slugs and snails are mollusks that hide in debris by day and feed on petunia foliage and flowers at night. Moist soil, cool weather, and humidity encourage activity.

Solution: Remove the pests, use traps and other controls, and clean up garden debris.

- Handpick and destroy pests. Hunt them after dark, using a flashlight.
- Set beer traps and use other means of controlling slugs and snails (p.49).
- Keep the garden free of decaying vegetation and other debris where slugs and snails can hide during the day.

Phlox

Phlox spp.

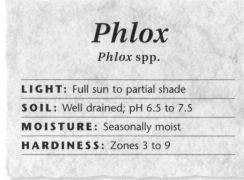

LIGHT: Full sun to partial shade

SOIL: Well drained; pH 6.5 to 7.5

MOISTURE: Seasonally moist

HARDINESS: Zones 3 to 9

White, powdery coating covers foliage

Problem: Foliage, and sometimes flowers, are covered with a white, feltlike growth. Lower leaves are usually the most severely affected. The leaves may become distorted and drop off.

Cause: Powdery mildew is a fungal disease most prevalent on plants grown in areas with poor air circulation. Outbreaks frequently occur in mid- to late summer, when warm days are followed by cool nights.

Solution: Spray with fungicide, grow resistant varieties, and provide good air circulation.

- Spray with an antifungal home remedy (p.392): baking soda solution, compost tea, or ultrafine horticultural oil.

- If problems persist, spray with an organic sulfur fungicide. Or use a synthetic fungicide registered for phlox that contains the active ingredient thiophanate-methyl. Follow label directions carefully. Don't apply sulfur when temperature exceeds 80°F.

- Select mildew-resistant varieties, such as *P. paniculata* 'David' and 'Franz Schubert'; *P. maculata* 'Alpha', 'Natasha', and 'Omega'; and *P. carolina* 'Miss Lingard'.

- To control future outbreaks, space plants apart for good air circulation. Spray with compost tea in midsummer.

Plants yellow, dry up, and die

Problem: Plants blacken at the bottom of stems, wilt, turn yellow, dry out, and die.

Cause: Stem rot, or root rot, is a persistent, soilborne fungal disease that enters stems or roots through wounds. It is most common in poorly drained soil.

Solution: Destroy badly infected plants. Grow healthy plants in disease-free soil.

- Remove and destroy the diseased plants.

- Plant healthy plants in well-drained soil where no phlox previously grew.

- As a preventive, in midsummer, when conditions favor the disease, drench the soil around plants with compost tea (p.392).

- Improve soil drainage by working in 2 to 4 inches of compost, or plant in a raised bed.

Leaves are stippled with specks

Problem: Leaves are stippled with yellow specks. Gradually, they turn pale or yellow. Tiny red specks or fine webs are visible on leaf undersides.

Cause: Spider mites are small relatives of spiders that suck sap from plants. They are commonly found during hot, dry weather. By the time damage is evident, mite populations are often high.

Solution: Hose off mites and spray.

- Dislodge mites with a strong stream of water every two or three days.

- For severe infestations, spray the plant with a synthetic insecticide registered for phlox that contains the active ingredient malathion. Follow label directions carefully.

- To prevent mites, spray healthy plants with insecticidal soap as soon as they leaf out, especially when the weather is hot and dry.

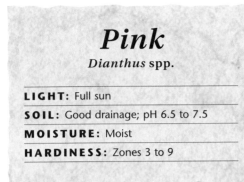

Pink
Dianthus spp.

LIGHT: Full sun

SOIL: Good drainage; pH 6.5 to 7.5

MOISTURE: Moist

HARDINESS: Zones 3 to 9

Portions of plant turn yellow and wilt

Problem: Stems turn yellow from the bottom up and wilt, or patches of the plant turn brown and wilt. If you pull the plant out of the ground, its root system is significantly smaller than normal and the stem is rotted.

Cause: Three types of fusarium fungi attack pinks, each with slightly different symptoms. Carnation bud rot turns flower buds brown. The inside of the infected buds are often pink and infested with tiny grass mites. Stem rot erodes the basal stem and roots, producing reddish brown spots at the stem base. Carnation wilt turns shoots yellow.

Solution: Remove the plant and spray the surrounding area with an insecticide. Plant pinks in an airy location and do not overcrowd. Handpick and destroy diseased buds.

- Destroy the infected plant and disinfect the soil with a 10 percent bleach solution before replanting.
- Prevent insects from spreading disease to healthy plants by spraying nearby grass areas with an insecticide registered for lawns that contains the active ingredient malathion. Follow label directions carefully. Do not overwater healthy plants.

Seedlings are cut off at base of stems

Problem: Newly planted seedlings are severed at base of the stems and fall to the ground.

Cause: Cutworms are small grayish or brown caterpillars. They take a few bites from each plant, then move on to the next, so they can easily kill many plants in a few days.

Solution: Handpick the pests and protect new seedlings with a physical barrier.

- Handpick cutworms late in the evening. Use a flashlight and search for caterpillars around the seedlings. Drop them in a can, seal it tight, and dispose of it.
- When transplanting seedlings, surround each with a protective collar made from a paper cup with the bottom punched out.

Flowering is unsatisfactory

Problem: Plant stops flowering, the flowers become smaller late in season, or the plant doesn't flower until the second year.

Cause: Pinks often stop flowering in summer heat or when they get old and woody. Heat can also cause flowers to become smaller in size. Perennial pinks often don't flower well until the second year. In addition, some pinks are biennial, so by nature they put energy into producing foliage the first year and flowers the second.

Solution: Give new plants a chance, replace old woody plants, and provide shade.

- If a newly placed plant doesn't flower but looks healthy, be patient and look forward to flowers in the second season.
- Replace old, woody plants that have stopped flowering with new plants.
- To reduce heat stress, plant new pinks in a location that receives midday shade.

Plant falls over or flops apart

Problem: Flower stems do not stay upright. The foliage may flop apart in the middle of the planting, leaving a bare spot in the center of the clump of pinks.

Cause: The natural growth habit of many types of pinks, especially older varieties, is to become leggy, with flower stems protruding from the plant at all different angles. Excessive heat can also cause pinks to stretch. Also, if the plant is grown in a shady location, the stems will grow toward the light and into an unattractive heap.

Solution: Careful plant placement, trimming, relocation to a sunnier spot, and regular watering can help prevent flopping problems.

- Grow tall, flopping pinks near other garden plants with sturdy stalks so that the stems of the pinks are supported.

- If the plant splits apart, leaving bare stems in the center, give it a good shearing in mid-April, then again two weeks later. To determine how much to cut back, take a handful of foliage and cut it level with the top of your fist.

- If too much shade causes a plant to flop, move it to a sunnier part of the garden.

- If hot weather causes a plant to stop blooming and stretch, there's no good solution except to keep adequate moisture in the soil and wait until temperatures drop.

White, bubbly foam appears on leaves and stems

Problem: Globs of foamy, white bubbles are lodged between stems and leaves. If you remove the bubbles, you will see small, green insects.

Cause: Leafhoppers, also called cuckoo spit, are soft-bodied insects that cover themselves with a protective layer of bubbles while they suck sap from plants. The brown-winged adults lay eggs on plants in fall, and the young emerge to feed in spring. The damage they cause is mostly cosmetic, although large numbers can stunt growth.

Solution: Hose off insects, and spray.

- If populations are not large, wash the insects off leaves with a forceful spray of water from a hose whenever you see them.

- Spray foliage with insecticidal soap every three to five days or until the insects are gone. Follow label directions carefully.

TIME-TESTED TECHNIQUES

PROPAGATION BY STEM CUTTINGS

For an easy and inexpensive way to grow new pinks, try propagating them by stem cuttings. It's a technique that also works with many other perennials and annuals. The cuttings will root easily and should be ready for potting in two to four weeks. Don't replant them outdoors if frost is expected within three weeks.

1. Take 4-inch-long tip cuttings in midsummer from nonblooming stems. Cut ¼ inch below the last pair of leaves. Remove all but the top two leaves and growing tip.

2. Insert the cuttings halfway into moist perlite or vermiculite mixed with coarse sand. Shelter planted cuttings from direct sunlight; keep the medium moist and warm.

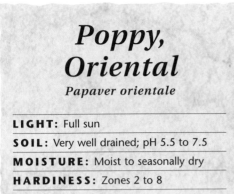

Poppy, Oriental
Papaver orientale

LIGHT: Full sun

SOIL: Very well drained; pH 5.5 to 7.5

MOISTURE: Moist to seasonally dry

HARDINESS: Zones 2 to 8

Plant does not thrive

Problem: Plant either dies or grows poorly.

Cause: Poppies need very good drainage and do not tolerate waterlogged soil. Plant poppies in fall for maximum spring growth. Although hardy to zone 8, Oriental poppies often grow poorly in warm-winter areas.

Solution: Practice good garden techniques. Plant a different species of poppy.

- Plant Oriental poppies in full sun. Incorporate a 3-inch-thick layer of organic matter, such as compost, to improve drainage.
- For best growth, plant in fall, when poppies are dormant. Prepare the soil to a depth of 12 inches to accommodate the taproots.
- Try planting Icelandic poppy (*P. nudicaule*) instead in zones 8 or warmer. Icelandic poppies are not perennial, but seeds can be planted in fall and put on a great show the following spring in warm regions.

Leaves and flowers have pale spots and yellow-striped bugs

Problem: Leaves and flowers have rows of small, dark, depressed spots and become distorted. Small yellow bugs are present. Young stem tips wilt.

Cause: Four-lined plant bugs are greenish yellow insects with black lines on their backs. They pierce leaves in numerous places, causing characteristic round spots.

Solution: Spray and attract natural predators.

- Spray with insecticidal soap every three to five days or until the pests are gone. Follow label directions carefully.
- Or use the botanical insecticide rotenone. Follow label directions carefully.
- Grow small-flowered nectar plants, such as sweet alyssum and scabiosa, to attract beneficial predator insects, such as lacewings.

Foliage dies after flowering

Problem: After blooming, the foliage turns brown and dies back to the ground, leaving gaps in mixed plantings.

Cause: Oriental poppies bloom in late spring and naturally go dormant in early summer. They will re-emerge and bloom the following spring. But their dormancy leaves gaps in the garden all summer.

Solution: Plant them by themselves or with bushy plants that can hide the gaps.

- Grow poppies in a single stand so they won't leave a large hole in a mixed border.
- If you place Oriental poppies in a mixed border, surround them with top-spreading perennials, such as boltonia, baby's breath, or German statice, which can fill the gaps.

Plant turns black

Problem: Leaves, stems, flowers, and seedpods develop water-soaked yellow to brown spots, which later turn black.

Cause: Xanthomonas blight is a bacterial disease; it strikes in wet, crowded conditions.

Solution: Destroy infected plant parts, spray, and keep foliage dry.

- Remove and destroy infected plant parts.
- Spray with an organic copper-hydroxide fungicide, which has antibiotic properties. Follow label directions carefully.
- To prevent reinfection, water in the morning to give leaves time to dry in the sun.

REGIONAL FOCUS
SOUTHEAST

In very hot, humid weather, salvias may grow leggy and bloom sparsely. When this happens, cut back the top growth by half to stimulate new growth. You can also prolong blooming by pinching out the main flower head after it is spent to encourage side shoots. Water when the soil is dry 1 inch below the surface and spread mulch to keep roots cool.

Salvia
Salvia spp.

LIGHT: Full sun
SOIL: Rich, well drained; pH 6.0 to 7.0
MOISTURE: Moist
HARDINESS: Tender annual

Leaves yellow and wilt; the plant dies

Problem: Plant first wilts at midday, then stays wilted for longer periods of time. Watering does not revive the plant. Leaves and stems have yellow or brown spots. There may be white fungal strands at the base of the plant.

Cause: Stem rot is a fungal disease that enters damaged tissue. Fungal colonies build up in roots and stems, inhibiting the flow of water and nutrients and causing wilting. Groups of plants may die. The disease is common in moist weather and poorly drained soil.

Solution: Remove infected plant and soil, apply fertilizer, and use a soil drench.

- Pull out and discard a severely infected plant and the soil its roots touched.
- Encourage the plant to outgrow the disease by applying fast-acting liquid fertilizer at the first sign of disease. Make several applications. Follow label directions carefully.
- As a preventive, drench the soil with compost tea (p.392) when conditions favor the disease.

Seedlings collapse from rot at base of stem

Problem: Brown discoloration appears at the base of a seedling stem, which then collapses.

Cause: Damping-off is a fungal disease that is most common on seedlings grown in warm, moist environments.

Solution: Spray and practice good sanitation.

- When symptoms appear, treat the soil around the plant with a synthetic fungicide registered for salvias that contains the active ingredient metalaxyl or etridiazole. Follow label directions carefully.
- Before sowing seed again, disinfect all tools with a bleach solution (p.392).

Small, white insects are on leaf undersides

Problem: Small, white, winged insects cover leaf undersides. A black, sooty mold may develop.

Cause: Whiteflies are small insects whose larvae suck sap from plants, which weakens them. The insects exude a sticky substance that promotes the growth of sooty mold. They fly up in a cloudlike group when disturbed.

Solution: Use yellow sticky traps. Spray with pesticide and repellent.

- Set out yellow sticky traps (p.52) just above the foliage. Check the traps every other day for signs of infestation.
- In severe infestations, spray with the botanical insecticide neem or pyrethrum. Or use a synthetic insecticide registered for salvias that contains the active ingredient acephate, diazinon, or methoxychlor. Follow label directions carefully.
- Spray with garlic oil as a repellent.

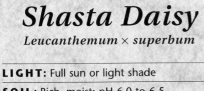

Shasta Daisy

Leucanthemum × superbum

LIGHT: Full sun or light shade

SOIL: Rich, moist; pH 6.0 to 6.5

MOISTURE: Seasonally moist

HARDINESS: Zones 5 to 9

Plant is weak or dies quickly

Problem: Plant blooms vigorously, then becomes weak or dies. The following spring, the plant develops a woody center and produces a few tufts of fresh growth.

Cause: Shasta daisies are short-lived plants that usually display weak growth after two or three years.

Solution: Let plant self-sow. Divide plant. Add new plant.

- Let flower heads ripen on plant and drop seed so that seedlings develop next spring.
- Divide the plant (p.29) every other spring, replanting the vigorous new growth.
- Sow seeds or purchase starter plant. Replace a few older specimens each year so that the planting does not die out all at once.

WISE CHOICES

To keep a Shasta daisy planting productive, select a single-flowered form, such as 'White Knight' or 'Snowcap', which lives longer than double-flowered types. Other varieties that have good durability include 'Becky' and 'Polaris'.

To ensure that self-sown seed is true, grow a variety that produces offspring nearly identical to the parent, such as 'Alaska' or 'Snow Lady'.

Petals and leaves are streaked and distorted

Problem: Leaves are flecked and deformed. Buds turn brown and fail to open. Flower petals have white or silver streaks. The damage is more severe during dry spells.

Cause: Thrips are small, slender insects that scrape plant tissue with their mouth parts and suck out sap.

Solution: Remove damaged plant parts. Treat with insecticide.

- Remove and destroy infested foliage and flowers. If the infestation is severe, destroy the plant and surrounding debris.
- Spray insecticidal soap or a synthetic insecticide registered for Shasta daisies that contains the active ingredient diazinon or malathion. Follow label directions carefully.

Flowers and leaves are chewed

Problem: Leaves are skeletonized, and flowers are eaten and have ragged holes.

Cause: Rose chafers are small beetles with brown bodies and long legs. The damage they cause looks similar to that caused by Japanese beetles. The larvae overwinter in lawns, and adults emerge from the soil in late May and early June.

Solution: Handpick adults, use insecticide, and cultivate the soil.

- Handpick and destroy chafers.
- If infestation is severe, spray the botanical insecticide neem or a synthetic insecticide registered for Shasta daisies that contains the active ingredient carbaryl. Follow label directions carefully.
- Keep garden soil cultivated through early June to eliminate pupae in the soil.

Warm, humid weather, with night temperatures around 50°F and days around 75°F, is the perfect climate for the fungal disease snapdragon rust (entry, right). Southern gardeners should select rust-resistant varieties, such as 'Double Sweetheart Mixed', 'Little Darling Mixed', or 'Royal Carpet Mixed' hybrids.

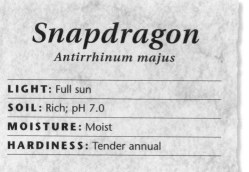

Snapdragon
Antirrhinum majus

LIGHT: Full sun

SOIL: Rich; pH 7.0

MOISTURE: Moist

HARDINESS: Tender annual

Flower head decays

Problem: Flower spike wilts and base of flower stem turns brown. Stem breaks, and plant topples. Stem develops tan cankers and becomes girdled. Leaves may develop gray or light brown fuzzy patches.

Cause: Gray mold is a fungal disease that is active in wet weather when temperatures are around 60°F. It is carried by water and wind. The disease spreads quickly among plants growing in low areas and where nights are cool and damp. Spores overwinter on plant debris.

Solution: Prune plant, apply a soil drench, mulch, use fungicide, practice good garden sanitation, and plant properly.

● Remove and destroy infected plant parts. Clean all debris from around plants.

  ● Drench the soil with compost tea (p.392) Mulch with compost to keep spores from splashing onto plants.

  ● If problems persist, spray with the organic fungicide Bordeaux mixture, starting when plants are 6 inches high and repeating every 10 to 14 days until flowering occurs. Follow label directions carefully.

● When planting next year, avoid placing plants too closely together, in low spots and in areas with poor air circulation.

Foliage is covered with bumps

Problem: Small swellings arranged in concentric patterns on leaves and stems appear on leaves and stems. The bumps on leaf undersides are dark brown, while those on upper leaf surfaces are yellowish.

Cause: Snapdragon rust is a serious fungal disease in warm weather. The spores are spread by wind and germinate on wet leaves, infecting a plant within six hours of exposure.

Solution: Spray with fungicide. Water properly to avoid spreading spores.

● At the first sign of disease, spray with a synthetic fungicide registered for snapdragons that contains the active ingredient mancozeb. Follow label directions carefully.

● Water at ground level early in the day so that foliage can dry before sundown.

Leaves or flowers are chewed

Problem: Leaves and sometimes flowers have scalloped edges or are chewed ragged. Caterpillars may be present on plants.

Cause: A variety of caterpillars, the larvae of moths and butterflies, including the tobacco budworm, feed on snapdragons.

Solution: Handpick, apply biological insecticide, and use proper garden techniques.

● Handpick and destroy caterpillars. Look for them early in the morning when they are sluggish and easy to catch.

● Spray with the biological insecticide BTK when caterpillars are feeding.

● Control weeds throughout the season. In fall, clean up all weeds and debris, to remove hiding places for caterpillars.

● Cultivate the soil in fall to expose caterpillars to freezing temperatures.

Sunflower
Helianthus annuus

LIGHT: Full sun

SOIL: Rich; pH 5.0 to 7.0

MOISTURE: Moist to seasonally dry

HARDINESS: Tender annual

Foliage and flowers have white, powdery splotches

Problem: Foliage and flowers are covered with a white, feltlike dust that cannot be rubbed off. Lower leaves are the most severely affected. Leaves may dry out and curl.

Cause: Powdery mildew is a fungal disease most prevalent in areas with poor air circulation and hot, humid conditions, typical of late summer. Spores overwinter on plant debris and weeds. Although unsightly, it is seldom fatal.

Solution: Remove infected plant material. Use fungicide. Provide proper growing conditions.

● Prune and dispose of infected plant parts and plant debris on the ground.

● Spray with an antifungal home remedy (p.392): baking-soda solution, compost tea, or summer oil. To avoid burning foliage, do not spray in sunlight.

● If problems persist, spray with an organic sulfur fungicide. Or use a synthetic fungicide registered for sunflowers that contains the active ingredient mancozeb. Follow label directions carefully.

● Clean up and remove all weeds and debris.

● When planting next season, select a location in full sun and space plants far apart, or thin them, to promote air circulation.

Stalk is weakened or broken

Problem: The flower stalk grows weak and may collapse. It produces no flowers, or flowers are misshapen.

Cause: The stalk borer is a gray or purple caterpillar that burrows into a stem to feed, weakening it. The pests overwinter as eggs on grasses and weeds.

Solution: Remove infested plant. Destroy pests. Apply insecticide. Clean up debris.

● Pull up and destroy the damaged plant.

● Cut a slit in the stem to locate borer; destroy it.

● Spray remaining plants with a synthetic insecticide registered for sunflowers that contains the active ingredient carbaryl. Follow label directions carefully.

● Clear away weeds and debris to remove places for the pests to overwinter.

Buds rot; flowers are moldy

Problem: Buds rot and may not develop. Buds and open flower heads are coated with dusty gray or blue-gray mold.

Cause: Gray mold is a fungal disease that thrives in cool, humid conditions. Spores are spread by wind and splashing water.

Solution: Remove diseased plants and debris. Water properly. Increase air circulation.

● Remove faded or infected flowers. Dig up and discard severely infected plants. Clean up all debris.

● Water at ground level to keep foliage dry. Water early in the day so that foliage dries before sundown.

● Space or thin plants for air circulation.

Sweet Pea

Lathyrus odoratus

LIGHT: Full sun

SOIL: Rich; pH 6.0 to 7.0

MOISTURE: Moist

HARDINESS: Cool-season annual

Leaves or flowers have bleached or brown areas

Problem: Flower petals have bleached-out spots or streaks that later turn brown. Leaves may also be affected. Plant growth may be stunted.

Cause: Western flower thrips and onion thrips are tiny insects that vary in color from yellow to dark brown. They suck plant juices, leaving characteristic white streaks. They can transmit the virus of spotted wilt disease.

Solution: Monitor pests and spray. Eliminate host plants.

- Set yellow sticky traps (p.52) to monitor pests. Spray with insecticidal soap as soon as thrips appear. Repeat every three days for up to two weeks, or until insects are gone.
- If problems persist, apply the botanical insecticide neem. Follow label directions carefully.
- Remove weeds to eliminate alternate homes for the insects.

WISE CHOICES

Many varieties of sweet pea have been bred to produce attractive flowers at the expense of their legendary fragrance. In most cases, small-flowered sweet peas will be much more fragrant than large-flowered types. Some richly fragrant varieties to consider include 'Old Spice', 'Marion', 'Firecrest', 'Maggie May', 'North Shore', 'Wings', 'Cream Southbourne', and 'White Supreme'.

Leaves have squiggly white lines

Problem: Leaves develop twisted white tunnels. The problem is most common after sweet pea begins to flower.

Cause: Leafminers are the larvae of a tiny fly. The little worms can mangle a leaf in short order. Minor infestations only produce cosmetic damage. Larger populations can weaken plants, resulting in poor growth and reduced flowering.

Solution: Spray with insecticide and repellent. Don't grow sweet peas near garden peas.

- Spray with the botanical insecticide neem. Or use a synthetic insecticide registered for sweet peas that contains the active ingredient malathion or malathion plus methoxychlor. Follow label directions carefully.
- To repel leafminers, spray healthy plants with garlic oil throughout growing season.
- Avoid attracting leafminers by growing sweet peas away from a vegetable patch where garden peas are grown.

Flower buds drop prematurely

Problem: Flower buds don't open and fall. In severe cases, nearly every flower bud drops. The leaves may have green veins.

Cause: Bud drop is caused by poor growing conditions, such as insufficient light or deficiencies of potassium or phosphorous.

Solution: Site plant in full sun and fertilize.

- Locate or relocate the plant in full sun.
- Feed with a balanced, water-soluble fertilizer such as 10-10-10 (p.324) monthly during growing season. Begin when plants are about 4 to 6 inches tall. Keep the soil consistently moist.
- If a plant in full sun has pale leaves, use a high-phosphorous, high-potassium fertilizer such as 10-30-20 or 15-17-17.
- A plant with dark green leaves and few flower buds may have too much nitrogen. Excess nitrogen also promotes bud drop. Water the soil around the plant when it is dry 1 inch beneath the surface.

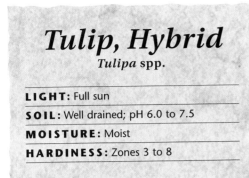

Tulip, Hybrid
Tulipa spp.

LIGHT: Full sun

SOIL: Well drained; pH 6.0 to 7.5

MOISTURE: Moist

HARDINESS: Zones 3 to 8

Plant fails to come up in spring

Problem: A tulip that was planted in fall doesn't emerge the following spring.

Cause: There are two common reasons for a tulip's failure to grow. If you live in a very cold region, bulbs will freeze and die if they are not planted deep enough. Another possibility is that squirrels or voles ate the bulbs after you planted them.

Solution: Plant bulbs before the soil freezes. Use barriers to keep animals from bulb.

- To avoid freezing, plant bulbs at least six weeks before the ground freezes so that they have time to become established.

- If squirrels or voles are a problem, line the planting hole with a wire mesh, such as hardware cloth, to prevent rodents from getting to the bulb. Roots and shoots will grow through the hardware cloth.

- Or deter rodents by sprinkling sharp-edged pea gravel under and around bulbs as you plant them.

Blooms are small; plant slowly disappears

Problem: Flowers are glorious the first year but become smaller and smaller in successive years. The plant eventually disappears.

Cause: Hybrid tulips need cool summer temperatures to regenerate reliable blooms. High temperatures prevent the bulb from storing food reserves, resulting in small flowers in following seasons. Tulips also need a chilling period through winter months. Winter temperatures in southern regions are often too warm to meet this need, causing plants with short flower stems and small flowers.

Solution: Treat hybrid tulips as annuals. Or, for reliable perennials, grow species tulips.

- In all but the coolest regions, grow tulips for only one year. Dig up and discard bulbs after bloom, and plant new bulbs in fall for the best floral show.

- Consider species tulips instead of hybrid tulips if you want plants that return every year. Species tulips are smaller and shorter than hybrids but much tougher. They are truly perennial, multiplying and naturalizing freely if grown in lean soil that dries out quickly after rains. Like all tulips, they require excellent drainage in winter. *T. acuminata, T. batalinii, T. praestans,* and *T. tarda* are good species to try. Also consider *T. clusiana* and *T. saxatilis,* which are excellent in warm summer gardens.

Leaves are distorted; the plant may die

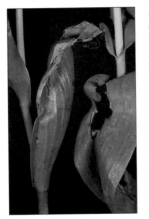

Problem: Leaves are distorted. They may turn yellow or red and die. The bulbs are mushy and rotten, or hard and dotted with small, dark, round objects. The tulip plant may die.

Cause: Tulip basal rot, also called root rot, is caused by soilborne fungi. The disease proliferates in soggy soil and attacks damaged bulbs. If a bulb becomes infected in storage, it can rot in the ground without producing foliage. The hard, round objects are fungal fruiting bodies that can survive for years in soil, waiting for a plant to infect.

Solution: Destroy infected plants and bulbs. Inspect bulbs and avoid injuring them. Treat bulbs with fungicide before storing.

- Dig up and destroy infected plants and the surrounding soil.

- Take care not to damage bulbs when planting and cultivating. Discard damaged bulbs.

- When digging bulbs for storage, air-dry them for a week and dust with an organic sulfur fungicide before storing. Pack prepared bulbs in paper bags of peat moss or vermiculite and store in a cool, dry place.

SELECTING HEALTHY BULBS

Selecting healthy bulbs is the most important step toward having a beautiful display of flowers in your garden. Whether the plants grow from true bulbs, tubers, corms, or rhizomes (all loosely called bulbs), the buying tips are the same. If you buy at a store, look for the largest bulbs available. These will have the greatest food reserves and will produce more flowers of a larger size than their smaller counterparts.

1. Select plump, firm bulbs. The bottom of the bulb should be hard. Avoid bulbs that are soft or withered.

2. The brown, papery covering around a bulb is called a tunic. It's all right to buy bulbs if the tunic is flaking or missing, but discard any bulb that has bruises or other damage to its tip or base.

3. Completely dormant bulbs will establish best, so buy bulbs that show no signs of root or shoot growth.

Leaves or flowers are streaked or may be deformed

Problem: New leaves are small and crinkled or mottled and streaked. Flower petals may be streaked or spotted. Plant size and vigor may be reduced.

Cause: Several viral diseases are spread to tulips by aphids. Double-flowered varieties are generally more susceptible than singles.

Solution: Use good garden techniques and aphid control to prevent virus.

- Remove and destroy infected plants.
- Knock aphids off with a strong stream of water from a hose every other day.
- Spray the foliage with insecticidal soap every three to five days. Follow label directions carefully.
- Grow small-flowered nectar plants, such as sweet alyssum, to attract aphid-eating insects such as lacewings and parasitic flies.
- Don't plant tulips near virus-prone plants such as lilies, gladiolus, and cucumbers.

Leaves and flower have gray or brown mold

Problem: A few deformed leaves and shoots appear, along with light patches that resemble frost damage. Later small white spots emerge on colored flowers, and brown spots are visible on white flowers; patches of fuzzy gray mold are also present.

Cause: Botrytis blight, also called gray mold, is common during rainy spring weather. Spores are easily splashed from infected plant debris to healthy plants.

Solution: Destroy infected plant parts, use fungicide, practice good garden sanitation, buy healthy bulbs, and plant properly.

- Remove and destroy infected plant parts as soon as you notice them. Place infected material in a paper bag and dispose of it immediately. Do not carry infected foliage or flowers around the garden.
- To prevent the disease from spreading, drench the soil with compost tea (p.392). Or use a synthetic fungicide registered for tulips that contains the active ingredient mancozeb or thiophanate-methyl. Follow label directions carefully.
- Discourage future problems by removing all fading flowers from the plant before the petals fall. Cut off mature, yellow foliage at ground level and pick up any leftover plant debris in the garden.
- Before purchasing new bulbs, inspect them closely for signs of infection. Don't buy or plant any bulbs with black lesions. Also consider selecting bulbs that have been treated with fungicide.
- When it is time to plant, place tulips where there is adequate air circulation; do not overcrowd the bulbs. If possible, rotate (p.115) tulip plantings to different locations on a three-year cycle.

Verbena

Verbena × hybrida

LIGHT: Full sun

SOIL: Rich, well drained; pH 6.0 to 7.0

MOISTURE: Moist

HARDINESS: Warm-season annual

Silvery areas mar leaves

Problem: Leaves and flower petals have silvery streaks or bleached areas that later turn brown. The plant may be stunted.

Cause: Thrips are minute insects that hide deep within the folds of petals and leaf joints, where they rasp away the tissue and suck sap, leaving the translucent, silvery streaks. Feeding in mass, they can stunt plant growth.

Solution: Monitor pests and spray insecticide. Eliminate host plants.

- Use yellow sticky traps (p.52) to monitor the pests. Spray the plant with insecticidal soap as soon as thrips appear on the traps. Spray plants every three days for up two weeks, or until thrips are gone. Follow label directions carefully.

- For severe infestations, spray with the botanical insecticide neem. Follow label directions carefully.

- Remove nearby weeds to eliminate alternate feeding and overwintering sites for thrips.

Leaves turn yellow and fall

Problem: A healthy plant begins to develop yellowing foliage. Individual leaves may drop when they turn completely yellow.

Cause: Leaf drop is most often caused by abrupt changes in soil moisture, by unfavorable light conditions, or by a plant being moved from place to place.

Solution: Maintain stable moisture. Provide adequate sunlight. Fertilize for new foliage.

- If leaf drop is due to excessive dryness, water the plant deeply and keep the soil consistently moist.

- If leaf drop is the result of low light or frequent plant relocation, place the plant in bright, indirect light.

- If extensive defoliation has occurred, fertilize the plant with a balanced, water-soluble fertilizer (half strength), such as a 15-15-15 formulation (p.324), once every two weeks until new foliage emerges.

Growing tips have clusters of small insects

Problem: Small insects are clustered along growing tips or on leaves. New leaves are distorted.

Cause: Aphids are small, soft-bodied insects that suck sap from plants. Their feeding can weaken the plant, making it more susceptible to other insects and diseases.

Solution: Hose aphids off plants and apply insecticides.

- Knock aphids off plant with a strong stream of water from a hose.

- When aphids appear, spray plant foliage with insecticidal soap or the botanical insecticide neem or pyrethrum. Follow label directions carefully.

- Or apply a synthetic insecticide registered for verbenas that contains the active ingredient malathion, acephate, or carbaryl. Follow label directions carefully.

Viola and Pansy
Viola spp.

LIGHT: Full sun to partial shade

SOIL: Rich, well drained; pH 5.5 to 7.0

MOISTURE: Seasonally moist

HARDINESS: Zones 5 to 8

Plant is leggy with few flowers

Problem: Leaf and flower stems elongate, causing the plant to flop. Flowers are sparse.

Cause: Pansies (*Viola* × *wittrockiana*), including the popular blue- and yellow-flowered varieties, are usually grown as a cool-season annual and can survive spring frosts. But a plant grows leggy and stops flowering if it is grown in too much shade, if temperatures are too high, or if spent flowers are not removed. Pansies can be killed by extreme cold or heat.

Solution: Deadhead regularly and provide good growing conditions.

- Replant in sun if it is in shade. In warm climates, plant in afternoon shade.

- Keep the soil moist and spread a 3-inch layer of mulch to retain moisture and keep roots cool.

- Remove spent flowers to promote more blooms.

- In early summer, cut back a leggy plant to 2 inches. Keep it well watered, and fertilize weekly for three weeks with a balanced, water-soluble fertilizer, such as a 12-12-12 formulation (p.324), half-strength.

Leaves are brown or blotched

Problem: Leaves develop circular dead spots with black margins. Petals are spotted or not fully developed. The plant is weakened and may die.

Cause: Anthracnose is a fungal disease that develops in humid weather.

Solution: Remove a diseased plant and plant debris from the garden. Spray with fungicide.

- Remove and destroy an infected plant. Clean up debris from around the plant.

- As a preventive in wet weather, spray healthy plants with a synthetic fungicide registered for violas and pansies that contains the active ingredient mancozeb. Follow label directions carefully.

Leaves and flowers are eaten; foliage has shiny streaks

Problem: Leaves and flowers are ragged and look chewed, or they have holes. The damage occurs overnight. Lower leaves are usually eaten first. Silver-gray slime trails appear on the plant or on the nearby soil.

Cause: Slugs and snails are ground-dwelling mollusks that climb onto plants at night to eat foliage and hide in debris on the soil by day. Moist soil, cool weather, and humidity encourage their activity.

Solution: Remove the pests, use traps, and clean up garden debris.

- Handpick and destroy slugs and snails. Hunt them after dark, beginning an hour after sundown, using a flashlight.

- Set beer traps and use other techniques (p.49) for controlling slugs and snails.

- Keep the garden free of decaying vegetation and other debris to eliminate daytime hiding places for the pests.

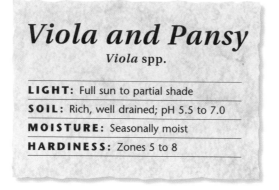

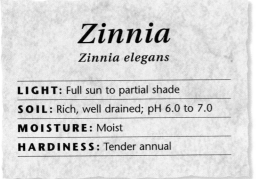

Zinnia
Zinnia elegans

LIGHT: Full sun to partial shade

SOIL: Rich, well drained; pH 6.0 to 7.0

MOISTURE: Moist

HARDINESS: Tender annual

Leaves or flowers are splotched with a powdery substance

Problem: Foliage and flowers are covered with a white, feltlike dust that cannot be rubbed off. Lower leaves are the most severely affected. Leaves may dry out and curl.

Cause: Powdery mildew is a fungal disease prevalent when plants are grown in areas with poor air circulation or in hot, humid daytime conditions with cooler nights. It occurs most in mid- to late summer.

Solution: Remove diseased plant parts. Use fungicide. Provide good growing conditions.

- Remove and dispose of infected plant material and plant debris on the ground.
- Spray plants with summer oil or an antifungal home remedy (p.392): baking-soda solution or compost tea. To prevent burned foliage, do not spray in direct sunlight.
- If problems persist, spray with an organic sulfur fungicide. Or use a synthetic fungicide registered for zinnias that contains the active chemical ingredient mancozeb. Follow label directions carefully.
- Clean up and remove all weeds and debris at the end of the season.
- When planting next season, select a location in full sun, thin plants, and space them far apart to increase air circulation.

Tan or grayish spots appear on leaves

Problem: Round spots develop on leaves, then enlarge into an irregular shape. The spots have tan to gray centers with reddish purple borders.

Cause: Alternaria leaf spot is a fungal disease active in warm, moist conditions. The spores overwinter on debris.

Solution: Remove affected foliage and plants. Use fungicide. Water properly.

- Prune and dispose of infected foliage. Discard badly infected plants. Clean up debris.
- Spray the plants with a synthetic fungicide registered for zinnias that contains the active ingredient maneb or mancozeb. Repeat every two weeks as needed. Follow label directions carefully.
- Water at ground level with a soaker hose or drip irrigation. Water early in the day so that the plants can dry before sundown.

Holes mar leaves and flowers

Problem: Leaves and flowers are riddled with holes. Large beetles are on plant.

Cause: Japanese beetles feed on flowers and foliage, leaving ragged holes.

Solution: Handpick, spray, and site plants well.

- Handpick beetles in the morning, when the insects are sluggish and dispose of them.
- If problems persist, spray with the botanical insecticide neem. Or use a synthetic insecticide registered for zinnias that contains the active ingredient malathion or carbaryl. Follow label directions carefully.
- Next season, plant in partial shade because Japanese beetles prefer to feed in full sun.

CHAPTER TWO

VEGETABLES

NOTHING IS AS SATISFYING AS the first bite of a ripe, red tomato right off the vine, brimming with flavor, and not available at any store for any price. Growing your own vegetables—whether it's a pot of cherry tomatoes and a trough of lettuce on the terrace or a garden big enough for tall sweet corn and sprawling melons—has many rewards. No other produce will be as fresh or nutritious as your own. You can grow varieties that never make it to the market. You can literally pick your dinner while the water is coming to a boil on the stove. And you get prime vegetable pickings for pennies.

But, like all gardens, the vegetable patch has its unwelcome guests. This chapter will help you avoid many problems and tell you how to reliably manage others. For safe use of commercial treatments for insects and diseases in the vegetable garden, see page 9 and pages 390 to 399.

Quick Troubleshooting Guide

SEEDLINGS

SEEDS DO NOT SPROUT

Cause: Old seeds, improper planting, poor timing

Solution: Sprout ten seeds on a damp paper towel to test for viability and sow extra seeds to compensate for percentage of duds, or use new seeds. Cover seeds to the depth recommended on package. Plant seeds outdoors after the predicted last frost date, when soil is warmer.

SEEDLINGS ROT BEFORE OR JUST AFTER EMERGING FROM SOIL

Cause: Damping off disease

Solution: To combat this soil-borne fungal disease, plant seeds indoors in sterile commercial seed-starting mix. When sowing seeds outdoors, sprinkle milled peat moss or clean sand on the soil's surface after sowing the seeds to discourage fungi.

SEEDLINGS SEEM HEALTHY, THEN FALL OVER OR DISAPPEAR OVERNIGHT

Cause: Cutworm, slug, or snail

Solution: Cut the bottoms from paper or plastic cups, and set cups over seedlings, pushing them slightly into the soil to keep cutworms from chewing through stems. Handpick slugs and snails after dark, or drown them in saucers of beer or commercial traps set on the soil.

FRUITS

FRUIT HAS DARK, SUNKEN, OR ROTTED AREAS

Cause: Anthracnose

Solution: Clean up plant debris so this fungal disease is not harbored; avoid splashing plant when watering. Spray organic Bordeaux mixture in spring. Pick fruits when ripe. Practice crop rotation.

FRUITS ARE SPOTTED WITH GRAY FUZZ AND ARE BEGINNING TO DECAY

Cause: Gray mold, also called botrytis mold

Solution: To discourage this fungal disease, pick and dispose of rotten or fallen fruits and foliage. Avoid splashing plants when watering; drench soil with compost tea. Space plants widely for air circulation. Rotate plantings.

BLEACHED, BROWN, SCABBY, OR SUNKEN AREAS MAR FRUITS

Cause: Sunscald

Solution: Tender-skinned vegetables, such as peppers, that grow in full sun can be sunburned when temperatures top 80°F. Shade fruiting plants from the midday sun in hot climates or plant a few extra plants in partial shade as insurance against sunscald.

PODS AND FRUITS HAVE WATER-SOAKED SPOTS

Cause: Bacterial soft rot

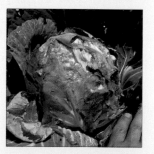

Solution: This disease is easily spread, so pick and discard affected fruits and remove debris from the ground. Water at ground level. Sterilize tools. Plant healthy seeds. Rotate crops.

PODS AND FRUITS ARE DEFORMED, WARTY OR HAVE WHITE SPOTS UNDER THE SKIN

Cause: Stink bug

Solution: Handpick and destroy adult beetles. Remove and compost plant debris. Spray insecticidal soap or the botanical insecticide pyrethrum before fruits develop. Follow label directions. Remove weeds.

FRUITS HAVE POOR TASTE AND ARE SMALL IN SIZE; THERE IS A LOW YIELD

Cause: Poor soil, moisture fluctuations, hot weather

Solution: Plant in fertile, well-drained soil. Keep soil evenly moist. Mulch to preserve soil moisture. Grow in cooler weather or shelter the crop from the blazing midday sun.

ROOTS AND TUBERS

ROOT CROPS ARE DEFORMED

Cause: Poor growing conditions

Solution: Incorporate compost into the soil to improve its drainage and water retention. Water plants frequently during droughts. Mulch the bed to retain soil moisture.

SMALL ROUND HOLES APPEAR IN ROOT CROPS

Cause: Wireworm

Solution: These beetle larvae feed when the soil is cool in spring and fall, burrowing deep into soil in summer to escape the heat. Wait to plant root crops until soil is warm. Cultivate soil frequently.

BULBS ARE MUSHY AND HAVE BROWN TUNNELS

Cause: Onion maggots

Solution: In late spring, apply beneficial nematodes, a biological control, to the bed. Cover new crops with floating row covers. Keep crops free of plant debris and weeds. Turn soil in fall to kill larvae. Rotate.

ROOT CROPS SPLIT OR CRACK

Cause: Irregular watering

Solution: Water consistently and evenly, whenever the soil is dry an inch below the surface. Mulch to conserve soil moisture. Harvest promptly, as soon as the roots are plump and ripe.

LEAVES

SILVERY SPECKLING OR STREAKS ARE ON LEAVES

Cause: Thrips

Solution: These tiny, sap-sucking insects feed in warm weather. Spray plants with insecticidal soap as often as needed until pests are gone. In fall, remove and discard all plant debris.

PALE LEAVES ARE STIPPLED WITH WHITE

Cause: Spider mite

Solution: These minute, sap-sucking pests multiply in dry conditions. Knock them off plants with a forceful spray of water. Water plants frequently and mulch to conserve moisture. Spray insecticidal soap as needed to eradicate mites.

LEAVES HAVE WHITE OR GRAY DUSTY SPOTS

Cause: Powdery mildew

Solution: Spray with baking soda solution or dust with organic fungicide sulfur. Pick and destroy affected leaves. Remove plant debris. Grow varieties labeled resistant to this fungal disease.

LEAVES HAVE YELLOW SPOTS AND FURRY UNDERSIDES

Cause: Downy mildew

Solution: Spray with baking soda solution. Pick off afflicted leaves and clean area of plant debris. Water at ground level to keep leaves dry, preventing spores from germinating. Thin bed for air circulation.

LEAVES ARE CURLED, PUCKERED, OR STICKY

Cause: Aphid

Solution: Aphids are small, pear-shaped insects that leave a sticky deposit when sucking juices from leaves and stems. Knock them off plants with a forceful spray of water or apply insecticidal soap.

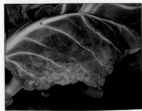

LEAVES HAVE PURPLE SPLOTCHES; UNDERSIDES ARE FURRY

Cause: Potato late blight

Solution: Destroy affected leaves on plants and ground; mound up soil over plant bases so fungal disease spores don't reach tubers. Dig tubers in dry weather. Rotate crops; plant resistant varieties.

FOLIAGE HAS ROUND YELLOW SPOTS OR WATER-SOAKED MARKINGS

Cause: Fungal leaf spot disease

Solution: Clip out and discard affected leaves and those that have fallen. Spread mulch at base of plants to prevent soil-borne spores from splashing them. Water at plant base to keep leaves dry. Clean up debris in fall. Grow resistant varieties; rotate crops.

LEAVES DISCOLOR AND DROP; FRUIT ENDS ROT

Cause: Nutrient deficiency

Solution: Fertilize the struggling plants. Nitrogen will help yellow leaves turn green; potassium will prevent browning and curling; magnesium will prevent fruit rot and orange leaf veins. Use organic fertilizers such as fish emulsion or cottonseed meal (nitrogen), wood ash (potassium), dolomitic limestone or Epsom salts (magnesium), or synthetic formulations.

LEAVES ARE MOTTLED SHADES OF GREEN AND YELLOW

Cause: Mosaic virus

Solution: This disease enters plants through injuries. Control sucking insects, such as aphids, that spread the disease by rinsing plants with water or spraying insecticidal soap. Buy resistant varieties. Remove plant debris and weeds, which harbor pests.

LEAVES HAVE WINDING WHITE TUNNELS

Cause: Leafminer

Solution: To control fly larvae called leafminers, cover plants with insect-excluding floating row covers in spring. Destroy damaged leaves. Use botanical insecticide neem as directed; mulch to keep miners from maturing in soil.

LEAVES WILT; SMALL HOLES ARE IN STEMS

Cause: Borer

Solution: Cover young plants with floating row cover to keep adults from laying eggs; uncover plants when flowering for pollination. Spray plant bases with botanical insecticide pyrethrum as directed. Slit stems to remove borers; mound soil over injury to encourage rooting.

LEAVES HAVE RAGGED EDGES OR HOLES

Cause: Beetle, caterpillar, grasshopper, slug, or snail

Solution: Handpick. Spray with insecticidal soap or the botanical insecticide pyrethrum, as directed. Drown slugs and snails in saucers of beer or commercial traps placed on the ground.

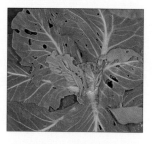

LEAVES ARE SPOTTED AND GROW IRREGULARLY

Cause: Pesticide damage

Solution: Remove damaged leaves. Flush the soil with water. In future, shield plants you are not spraying. Always follow herbicide label directions. Never spray on a windy or hot (over 80°F) day.

LEAVES TURN DARK BROWN, THEN DIE

Cause: Salt damage

Solution: Dilute and wash away excess salt in soil with extra irrigation. Saturate the soil in the affected area, but don't flood it. When plants revive, fertilize. Or, move plants away from salt source.

LEAVES TURN SILVER OR GRAY AND FALL OFF

Cause: Frost damage

Solution: On nights when frost is predicted, lay plastic sheeting, insulating fabric floating row covers, or sheets over the vulnerable plants. Or sprinkle plants with water before the sun rises. Don't plant too early in the season. Avoid planting in low areas, where cold air pools.

WHOLE PLANT

PLANT HAS SLOW GROWTH, PALE COLOR, FEW FRUITS

Cause: Poor soil, excess water, insufficient light, cool weather

Solution: Improve soil fertility: apply fish emulsion, kelp solution, or a balanced synthetic fertilizer. Plant in a spot that receives six to eight hours of sun a day. Incorporate compost into soil to improve drainage. Plant after the last frost date in warm soil.

DIMINISHED CROP ON FULL PLANTS

Cause: Overcrowding

Solution: Divide perennial crops, such as asparagus and rhubarb, when they become overcrowded and less productive. Dig and separate plants. Replant divisions with generous spacing. Thin seedlings.

PLANT SUDDENLY BLOOMS, GOES TO SEED, AND DIES

Cause: Bolting

Solution: Plant earlier or later in the season, provide shade during the hottest days, or do both. Stagger plantings and harvest as soon as crops ripen, so that you always have some part of the crop at its peak. Grow bolt-resistant varieties of vegetables.

PLANT WILTS BUT RECOVERS WHEN WATERED

Cause: Dry soil, insufficient rain

Solution: Set up a regular watering schedule. Water deeply when soil is dry 1 inch below the surface. Apply a 3-inch-thick layer of mulch to help preserve soil moisture. At year's end, improve soil texture by digging in compost.

PLANT WILTS; LEAVES CURL AND YELLOW; FEW FRUITS FORM

Cause: Fungal wilt disease

Solution: Dispose of dying plants and discard garden plant debris. Allow soil to dry between waterings. Disinfect tools. Test soil; add lime to raise alkalinity as needed. Grow resistant varieties.

PLANT WILTS AND SETS FEW FRUITS

Cause: Root and stem rot; southern blight

Solution: Tear out and discard affected plants so disease doesn't spread. Water at soil level and let soil dry out between waterings. Thin plants to improve air circulation. Grow resistant varieties.

PLANT WILTS IN HOT WEATHER, REVIVES AT NIGHT

Cause: Nematodes

Solution: Examine the roots for "knots" and discard affected ones. Allow soil to dry between waterings. Dig compost into the bed to introduce beneficial soil organisms. Solarize soil before planting.

PLANTS OR FRUITS ARE CHEWED OR EATEN

Cause: Birds, rodents, deer

Solution: Cover seedlings with fabric floating row cover or hardware-cloth cages. Cover fruiting plants with bird netting. Or fence the garden from small animals with 2-foot-tall fine-mesh, burying the edges. Hang bars of soap near plants to repel deer or use a commercial repellent.

Asparagus is a hardy perennial that grows best where the top 2 to 3 inches of soil freeze in winter. If winters are mild and summers dry, choose a variety, such as 'UC 157', that is bred for these conditions. Water plants deeply throughout the summer whenever the first 1 to 2 inches of soil are dry. Withhold water in fall to encourage dormancy.

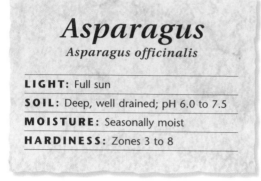

Asparagus
Asparagus officinalis

LIGHT: Full sun

SOIL: Deep, well drained; pH 6.0 to 7.5

MOISTURE: Seasonally moist

HARDINESS: Zones 3 to 8

Holes are chewed in spears

Problem: The spear tips are pitted and chewed and have brown blemishes. There may be tiny gray larvae, which look similar to slugs, or adult beetles on spears. A plant may be entirely stripped of its leaves.

Cause: Two insects cause this kind of damage. Asparagus beetles are small insects with black wing covers. Both adults and their plump grayish larvae feed on the leaves and stems. The spotted asparagus beetle is red with black spots. The adults feed on leaves, and their orange larvae eat asparagus berries.

Solution: Handpick beetles and protect spears. Spray with insecticide and eliminate overwintering sites. Plant berryless varieties.

- Handpick and crush all beetles and larvae, or hose them off plants with water.
- At harvest time, cover asparagus with an insect-excluding fabric floating row cover. Harvest daily, so that eggs can't hatch.
- After harvest, treat plants with a synthetic insecticide registered for asparagus that contains the active ingredient carbaryl, malathion, or methoxychlor. Follow label directions carefully.
- To discourage future infestations, remove asparagus berries and old foliage. In late fall, clean up plant debris.
- Grow berryless all-male varieties, such as 'Jersey Giant' and 'Jersey King'. These plants are less attractive to spotted beetles.

Stem has rusty brown spots

Problem: Rust-colored blisters on stems release a fine powder when touched. Later, black blisters form. The plant turns yellow, then brown.

Cause: Asparagus rust is a fungal disease spread by powdery spores that are red in summer and black in winter. It spreads rapidly in warm or wet weather and can kill the plants.

Solution: Remove affected stems, water well, and use a fungicide. Plant resistant varieties.

- Cut and discard stems with rust symptoms.
- Water well when the soil is dry 1 inch below the surface.
- To prevent recurrence, dust plants with sulfur, an organic fungicide, three weeks and seven weeks after harvest. Or apply a synthetic fungicide registered for asparagus that contains the active ingredient mancozeb. Follow label directions carefully.
- Plant rust-resistant varieties, such as 'Jersey King', 'Jersey Giant', and 'California 500'.

Spears are thin and few

Problem: Spears are small, thin, and few.

Cause: In a mature planting, more than three years old, a shortage of spears may be due to low soil fertility, poor drainage, weed competition, or overharvesting.

Solution: Improve growing conditions. Wait until the third season to harvest.

- If a site is wet or weedy, dig roots after tops die in fall; replant in a well-drained bed.
- For new beds, use a fertilizer rich in phosphorus and potassium, such as a 5-10-10 formulation (p.324).
- Harvest sparingly—for two weeks the third year, four the fourth year, eight thereafter.

Bean
Phaseolus vulgaris

LIGHT: Full sun

SOIL: Well drained; pH 5.5 to 6.5

MOISTURE: Moist

HARDINESS: Warm-season annual

Leaves are chewed and lacy

Problem: Leaves are eaten between the veins until they resemble lace. Copper-colored beetles with black spots and their small, spined, yellowish orange larvae are feeding on the leaves, pods, and stems. Yellow egg masses are also often present on the backs of leaves.

Cause: The Mexican bean beetle is common east of the Rocky Mountains and is sometimes found in the West. Its damage can be severe, reducing crops and even killing plants.

Solution: Destroy pests by hand or with insecticides. Remove plant debris from the garden in fall. Introduce beetle parasites.

- Pick and crush eggs, larvae, and adults.

- Apply neem, a botanical insecticide, every 7 to 10 days until the pests are gone. Follow label directions carefully.

- For a severe infestation, use a synthetic insecticide registered for beans that contains acephate, carbaryl, dimethoate, or malathion. Follow label directions carefully. Don't apply dimethoate to blooming plants. After using acephate or dimethoate, don't fertilize plants for three to four weeks.

- Remove plant debris to limit overwintering by the pests.

- In the future, buy Mexican bean beetle parasites (available from garden catalogs) and release according to directions.

Plant grows few pods

Problem: The plant blooms, but pods are few and may be poorly filled out. Pod production may stop altogether.

Cause: Blossoms will drop prematurely and fail to produce pods when the temperature rises above 90°F or dips below 50°F. They will also drop when irrigation is uneven.

Solution: Pay careful attention to watering. Choose bean varieties suited to your climate and time the plantings properly.

- Water when the soil is dry 1 to 2 inches beneath the surface. In hot, dry weather, spread a 3- to 4-inch straw or leaf mulch.

- In hot areas, plant in early spring or late summer, in well-drained, humus-rich soil. Select adapted varieties such as 'Blue Coco' and 'Genuine Cornfield'. In an arid climate, try yard-long, or asparagus, beans (*Vigna unguiculata* spp. *sesquipedalis*).

- Where it's cool, try scarlet runner beans (*P. coccineus*), which set pods in cool weather, or a cool-weather-blooming pole variety.

Pods, leaves, or stems have dark brown spots

Problem: Small lesions appear on the pods. They are dark brown with a red margin, and in moist weather they ooze a salmon-colored substance. Reddish brown streaks may also appear on stems and on the undersides of leaves.

Cause: Bean anthracnose is a fungal disease that is most common in the East and Southeast, but it occurs as far west as the Rockies. Outbreaks most often occur during cool, rainy summers. The disease spores can be spread by infected seeds or splashing water.

Solution: Use a fungicide and practice good garden sanitation. Grow resistant varieties from healthy seeds. Rotate crops.

- If outbreaks are severe, spray with Bordeaux mixture, an organic fungicide, as plants bud and again at peak bloom. Follow label directions; to avoid damaging leaves, don't spray when temperatures are above 80°F.

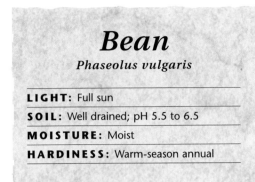

- Remove potentially infected plant debris from the garden.
- To keep from spreading spores, water at ground level to avoid splashing leaves and don't work among wet bean plants.
- Because anthracnose spores can remain in the soil over winter, rotate (p.115) beans with unrelated plants, waiting three years before planting again in the same site.
- For future plantings, seek resistant varieties, and buy certified disease-free seeds.

Leaves and pods have yellow-and-red spots

Problem: Pale yellow spots, with red powder in the center, appear on bean leaves. Symptoms appear in midsummer in the North but can develop in early spring in the South. The leaves may turn yellow and drop.

Cause: Bean rust is a fungal disease that is most serious in humid weather when nights are cool and daytime temperatures are around 75°F. New spores are produced every 10 days in summer. They are transported by the wind and overwinter in plant debris.

Solution: Use a fungicide. Practice good garden sanitation. Rotate crops and plant resistant bean varieties.

- Apply sulfur, an organic fungicide, to bean leaves; repeat weekly until symptoms disappear. Follow label directions. If fungicide gets on the pods, rinse them at harvest.
- Remove infected plant debris often and avoid working among wet beans.
- If rust occurs on pole beans, use new poles the next season.
- Rotate (p.115) beans with other crops every three to four years.
- Consider planting resistant varieties, such as 'Kentucky Blue' and 'Kentucky Wonder' pole beans or 'Butter Crisp', 'Goldkist', and 'Jade' bush beans.

Leaves or pods have brown spots

Problem: Brown spots, sometimes ringed in yellow, disfigure the bean leaves or pods. Reddish brown streaks may also appear on the pods and stems. The affected leaves may become ragged or die.

Cause: Bean common blight and bean halo blight are two diseases with similar symptoms caused by different bacteria. The bacteria live on seeds and in plant debris. New plants grown from infected seeds show symptoms. Older plants can be infected when the bacteria are carried to them by splashing water or by a gardener working among wet plants.

Solution: To control, practice garden sanitation, purchase healthy seeds, and rotate crops.

- To avoid spreading the disease, water at ground level to keep from wetting leaves. Don't work among wet plants.
- After harvest, remove plants and debris.
- Don't save seeds from diseased plantings. Buy seeds that are certified disease free.
- When you replant, rotate (p.115) beans with other crops every two to three years.

WISE CHOICES

To get the most from your bean patch, try growing some of the varieties listed below. All produce high yields of very flavorful beans in diverse growing conditions, from coastal regions to the mountains.

Bush Beans
- 'Atlantic' is an early variety with long, slim pods.
- 'Bush Blue Lake' produces pods of excellent quality.
- 'Eagle' provides very large yields of tasty beans.
- 'Opus' is resistant to rust and bears attractive pods.
- 'Provider' produces large yields of great-tasting pods.

Pole Beans
- 'Dade' is rust resistant and bears uniform, delicious pods.
- 'White Seeded Kentucky Wonder' is a vigorous climber.

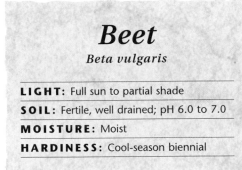

Beet

Beta vulgaris

LIGHT: Full sun to partial shade

SOIL: Fertile, well drained; pH 6.0 to 7.0

MOISTURE: Moist

HARDINESS: Cool-season biennial

Root has hard, dark, rough-textured areas

Problem: The mature beet root has dark areas on both the surface and inside and may be cracked and uneven. The plant may also be small, and young leaves may turn dark and die.

Cause: Beet black, also called brown heart, is most often caused by a shortage of the trace element boron in the soil but can also be caused by a phosphorus deficiency. It's most common in arid climates with sandy, alkaline soil high in potassium or calcium.

Solution: Test soil fertility and amend with boron and fertilizer as needed. Test and adjust soil pH as needed. Water regularly.

- Have the soil tested (p.329) to determine any mineral deficiencies.
- To provide boron, spray leaves with a liquid seaweed solution. Or water the soil with a solution of household borax (p.400).
- Apply a balanced synthetic fertilizer, such as a 10-10-10 (p.324) formulation; don't exceed the recommended amount. In arid areas, water before and after applying fertilizer to inhibit a buildup of fertilizer salts.
- Check the soil pH (p.329). Add amendments to achieve a pH of 6.5, which is ideal for beet growth and boron uptake.
- Discourage any problems among healthy plants by watering when the soil is dry 1 inch below the surface.

Leaves have pale spots with dark borders

Problem: Tan or gray spots with dark red-brown borders appear on leaves, usually in mid- to late summer. Often the centers of the spots fall out, leaving ragged holes.

Cause: Cercospora beet leaf spot is a fungal disease most common in warm (75° to 80°F), humid weather. Spores are carried by wind, splashing water, and insects.

Solution: Remove infected leaves and practice good garden sanitation to discourage a recurrence. Plant healthy seeds and rotate crops.

- Remove infected leaves from the garden.
- Mulch soil under plants and avoid wetting leaves to keep from spreading spores.
- At season's end, remove all plant debris.
- Before replanting, obtain certified disease-free seeds. Select disease-tolerant varieties, such as 'Big Red' and 'Red Ace'.
- Rotate (p.115) beets every three years.

Root has tan, corky scabs

Problem: The root exhibits rough tan or brown patches. New leaves are deformed, and the plant may be stunted.

Cause: Scab, a soilborne fungal disease that lives in acidic soil, causes roots to develop corky areas and fuzzy feeder roots.

Solution: Adjust soil pH to near neutral, add compost, and rotate crops.

- Apply garden lime to raise the soil pH to between 6.0 and 7.0.
- Mulch with compost (p.334), which suppresses disease.
- Rotate (p.115) beets with unrelated crops.

REGIONAL FOCUS
SOUTHWEST

West of the Continental Divide, beets may be infected by curly top, a viral disease that causes leaves to curl and develop small warts on their undersides. The disease is spread by an insect known as the beet leafhopper.

To avoid curly top, plant in early spring or late summer so plants are not in the ground when leafhoppers are most active.

Broccoli
Brassica oleracea

LIGHT: Full sun to partial shade

SOIL: Fertile, well drained; pH 6.0 to 6.8

MOISTURE: Moist

HARDINESS: Cool-season biennial

Plant wilts; larvae appear at base of plant

Problem: Even though the soil is moist, the plant wilts and is stunted. Later, it turns yellow and dies.

Cause: Cabbage maggots, which are about the size and shape of rice grains, are the larvae of a small fly. In early spring, when the weather is cool, the maggots eat into the lower stem and upper roots of the plant. The maggots mature in the soil, then emerge as flies.

Solution: Create barriers against egg-laying flies, practice good sanitation, use biological controls, time plantings, and rotate crops.

- Wrap the stems of transplants in brown paper, extending the paper 1 inch above and below the soil. Or, during the first few weeks, grow seedlings under an insect-excluding floating row cover; tuck the edges firmly under the soil.

- Remove infested plants from the garden, and clean up all plant debris after harvest.

- In spring, apply beneficial nematodes (p.126), a biological control, to the soil.

- As a preventive, sprinkle diatomaceous earth (DE), an abrasive dust that discourages these soft-bodied pests, on the soil around seedlings at planting time.

- Where spring is long and cool, plant early so that the plants can grow enough by April to withstand infestations. Or plant in June or later.

- Rotate (p.115) with nonsusceptible crops, such as peas or beans, every two years.

Small, slow-moving insects infest broccoli head

Problem: Small insects cling to the stems and florets of the plant. The insects may infest the broccoli head from the inside.

Cause: Several kinds of aphids infest broccoli. The most common of these small, pear-shaped, soft-bodied insects are the gray cabbage aphid and the green peach aphid. These sap-sucking pests cause the leaves to curl but do their worst damage within the broccoli heads.

Solution: Hose aphids off plants. Treat infested plants with organic insecticides. Remove infested heads. Cultivate aphid parasites.

- Check for aphids from planting time onward and dislodge any you find with a strong stream of water. Early control reduces the chances of an infestation.

- For partial to complete control, apply insecticidal soap or neem, a biological insecticide, to infested plants, including heads. Follow label directions carefully.

- Before cooking harvested heads, soak them in a mild solution of water and table salt to dislodge any insects.

TIME-TESTED TECHNIQUES

KEEPING BIRDS AT BAY

For generations, the scarecrow has served as guardian of the vegetable patch. Lately, however, this traditional sentinel has some new company.

One device is an inflatable ball with colorful eye-shaped designs. When wind stirs the ball, which can be hung from a pole, the eyes pan the garden, like those of a giant predator. Another innovation is reflective tape, which is hung over plants. When it flutters in the breeze, it casts light across the garden.

Both the ball and the reflecting tape are available at garden centers or from mail-order garden-supply companies.

- If your variety forms side sprouts, remove the first infested heads, treat the plant, and wait for new, insect-free heads to grow.
- For long-term control, grow small-flowered nectar plants nearby to attract predators. Sweet alyssum and yarrow attract a minute wasp that parasitizes aphids.

A small central head forms on an immature plant

Problem: A young broccoli plant forms a head before it has fully matured. The stem is narrow, and the head is too small.

Cause: Cold weather causes young broccoli plants to produce small heads. Other possible causes are dry soil, lack of nutrients in the soil, overcrowding, or damage to the roots. Pot-bound seedlings may also produce small heads as a result of a lack of nutrients and room for roots to expand.

Solution: Meet broccoli's water and nutrient needs, control diseases and insects, acclimate young plants to cold, and time plantings.

- Don't let the soil dry out; water when the soil is dry 1 inch below the surface. Use an organic mulch to reduce evaporation.
- Check for signs of disease or insect damage (facing page).
- Acclimate your seedlings, hardening them off by gradual exposure to the cold. Transplant them before they are seven weeks old, but when it's not likely to stay below 50°F for 10 days or more. Space your variety as the seed packet directs. Fertilize seedlings according to packet directions.
- To prepare for future plantings, add 3 to 4 inches of organic matter to the soil.
- In mild-winter areas, plant a crop in late summer or early fall so plants can mature before cool weather causes head growth.

No broccoli head forms

Problem: A plant growing in summer has plenty of healthy-looking leaves but no head.

Cause: Broccoli is sensitive to high temperatures. A broccoli head may not form when the temperature rises above 85°F in the daytime or 77°F at night.

Solution: Time plantings to avoid having plants mature in the hottest part of the year.

- If the summers are hot in your area, plant as early as spring temperatures allow, selecting varieties that are labeled early maturing and heat resistant (see entry below).
- If summers are long, plant a second early-maturing variety in late summer.

Plant makes tall flower stalks

Problem: The main stem of the plant produces elongated stalks filled with flowers. Harvested florets taste bitter.

Cause: Hot weather causes bolting, which means that flower buds produce seed stalks and set seed prematurely. The buds develop when the young plant is exposed to temperatures below 50°F for several days in a row, but the buds remain dormant until hot weather arrives. Once bolting has begun, it can't be reversed.

Solution: Remove bolting plants. Time planting and harvesting carefully. Select early-maturing varieties.

- Cut and compost bolting plants. Trimming the stalks won't produce new heads with improved flavor.
- Set out a second crop in late summer or early fall. A late-season crop rarely bolts.
- Next spring, plant an early-maturing heat-tolerant variety, such as 'Arcadia', 'Big Sur', or 'Saga'. Harvest heads promptly, before hot weather causes plants to bolt.
- Plant when it's not likely to stay below 50°F for 10 days or more. If there is a cold snap, use a fabric floating row cover to keep plants warm.

REGIONAL FOCUS
NORTHWEST

The long, cool autumns and mild winters of the Northwest allow slow-maturing types of broccoli to grow successfully, even over winter. Here are varieties to plant in summer for crops from late fall to early spring.

- 'Purple Sprouting' has a large number of small purple heads.
- 'Romanesco' produces huge chartreuse heads with exceptional texture and flavor.
- 'Minaret' is a 'Romanesco' type with small, 4- to 5-inch heads.
- 'Shogun' has large, compact, dark green heads that are followed by smaller side heads after harvest.
- 'White Sprouting' is similar to 'Purple Sprouting', but the heads are light green.

REGIONAL FOCUS
CENTRAL

The long growing season that Brussels sprouts require can be a special problem in the Midwest. To speed head formation, twist off the top of each plant when at least seven whorls of leaves have formed sprouts.

If winter threatens to cut the harvest short, dig up whole plants before continuous cold sets in, bury their roots in a container of moist soil, and place the pots in a root cellar. This will help to keep the plants alive while the sprouts mature.

Brussels Sprouts
Brassica oleracea

LIGHT: Full sun to partial shade
SOIL: Fertile, well drained; pH 6.0 to 6.8
MOISTURE: Moist
HARDINESS: Cool-season biennial

Heads are loose and open; insects are present

Problem: The heads are loose and may burst open before they reach full size, revealing small, gray, slow-moving insects; the heads also taste bitter.

Cause: Brussels sprouts need cool weather to develop firm, well-flavored heads. When it's too warm, they rush toward flowering. If they continue to open, flower stems emerge from the heads. Aphids, which are small, sucking insects, often feed in the open heads.

Solution: Discard spoiled sprouts and dislodge aphids. Keep plants watered and harvest early. Time plantings for cool-weather harvest.

- Remove infested sprouts from the garden. Dislodge minor infestations of aphids with a strong spray of water.
  - Water plants well when the soil is dry 1 inch below the surface.
  - Harvest sprouts before they open, even if small.
    - Time future plantings by counting back from the last frost-free date (see next entry).
    - In mild-winter areas, a crop started in late winter might succeed, but it is best to time planting so that sprouts ripen as weather cools.

Heads don't form before cold weather hits

Problem: The plant grows large, but the heads haven't formed by the time cold weather causes the plant to die.

Cause: Late-maturing varieties of Brussels sprouts may not have time to develop in climates with short summers and cold winters.

Solution: Choose a variety adapted to your climate, and time planting so that heads can develop before the weather turns cold.

- Grow a fast-maturing variety, which will take about 90 days to mature, such as 'Oliver' or 'Prince Marvel'.
- To determine the planting date, subtract the time your variety takes to mature from the expected date of the first frost. For example, if a variety takes 90 days to mature and the first frost is expected September 30, set out transplants on June 30. Sow seeds six weeks earlier, on May 15.

Leaves have ragged holes

Problem: In spring, seedlings may be entirely eaten. From early summer to early fall, leaves develop ragged holes or are chewed away.

Cause: Two kinds of caterpillars eat the foliage. Imported cabbageworms, the larvae of cabbage white butterflies, are green caterpillars with yellow stripes that feed in summer. In late summer and early fall, dark caterpillars called fall armyworms eat seedlings and leaves of mature sprouts. Damage from the caterpillars decreases with cool fall temperatures.

Solution: Remove caterpillars, apply biological controls, and protect seedlings.

- Handpick and dispose of caterpillars.
- When caterpillars are small, apply BTK, a biological insecticide that is harmless to most beneficial insects. Follow label directions carefully.
- Next season, protect new seedlings with an insect-excluding fabric floating row cover.

Cabbage
Brassica oleracea

LIGHT: Full sun to partial shade

SOIL: Fertile, well drained; pH 6.0 to 6.8

MOISTURE: Moist

HARDINESS: Cool-season biennial

Leaves have V-shaped, wet, discolored areas near edges

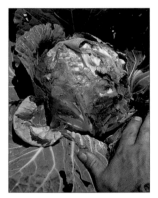

Problem: Leaf edges yellow, then the damage moves inward, creating yellow and then brown, mushy triangles at the leaf edges. A young plant may be stunted or lopsided. An older one may lose lower leaves until only a stalk remains. If you cut open the stem of an infected plant, you'll see a black ring.

Cause: Black rot of cabbage is caused by a bacterium that is carried on seeds and infected plant debris as well as in soil, in water, and on infected tools.

Solution: Practice good garden sanitation to discourage the disease and to keep it from spreading. Buy healthy seeds and select varieties resistant to black rot. Rotate crops.

- Remove infected plants and destroy any plant debris that has fallen from them.
- Avoid splashing plants when watering.
- At season's end, discard any cabbage plant debris that remains in the garden.
- For future crops, obtain seeds that are certified disease free. Grow varieties that resist black rot, such as 'Stonehead' and 'Tasty'.
- In future plantings, space plants at least 12 to 24 inches apart, depending on variety, so that they can dry out quickly.
- Rotate (p.115) cabbage with unrelated crops every three years.

Cabbage head splits open

Problem: Cracks appear in a cabbage head.

Cause: When cabbage is exposed to sudden increases in soil moisture, inner leaves grow faster than outer ones. The outer leaves split, exposing the interior to insects and diseases.

Solution: Keep the soil evenly moist, harvest heads promptly, and plant resistant varieties.

- Water when the soil is dry 1 to 2 inches beneath the surface. Apply an organic mulch, such as compost or grass clippings, to reduce moisture loss from the soil.
- Harvest cabbages as they mature. To delay harvest, give plants a quarter twist. This damages some roots, reducing water intake and splitting.
- In the future, use split-resistant varieties such as 'Dynamo', 'Julius', and 'Super Red 80'.

Leaves are pale and wilted and have a sticky residue

Problem: Leaves and stems, especially the tender foliage of immature cabbages, begin to wilt, droop, and develop yellowing areas. The foliage may also have sticky clear spots or fuzzy black patches.

Cause: Cabbage aphids are small, slow-moving, pear-shaped green insects. Feeding in clusters that sometimes entirely cover tender new growth, these sap-sucking insects weaken cabbage plants and can transmit diseases.

Solution: Knock insects off plants and create barriers to exclude them.

- Knock these fragile insects off plants with a blast of hose water as needed.
- Protect seedlings with an insect-excluding fabric floating row cover; remove the covering when plants begin to form heads.

REGIONAL FOCUS
SOUTHWEST

Many types of whitefly can infest cabbage, but a particularly problematic species, the silverleaf whitefly, is common only in the Southwest.

The silverleaf whitefly sucks sap from plants, stunting them and reducing yields. The best way to control this pest is to spray the plants with insecticidal soap. Follow label directions carefully.

To lessen future infestations, don't plant cabbage or other cabbage-family crops near melons, which are also susceptible. And cover young plants with an insect-excluding fabric floating row cover.

Leaves have large ragged holes

Problem: A young plant may be entirely devoured. An older one may have holes in the leaves. Holes may also be eaten into the developing cabbage head.

Cause: Several moths and butterflies lay eggs on cabbage, a food source for their caterpillars. Imported cabbageworms are green with yellow stripes. Cabbage loopers are also green, but move like inchworms. Smaller diamondback moth caterpillars eat leaf undersides.

Solution: Remove caterpillars; spray insecticide. Protect seedlings; buy resistant varieties.

- Handpick and destroy caterpillars; crush eggs found on the undersides of leaves.
- If caterpillars are still small, spray the plant, including the head, with BT, a biological insecticide. If they are mature, use neem, a botanical insecticide. Follow label directions carefully.
- Grow transplants under an insect-excluding fabric floating row cover.
- Select resistant varieties such as 'Mammoth Red Rock', 'Savoy Chieftain', and 'Savoy Perfection Drumhead'.

Base of stem darkens

Problem: Plant is stunted, wilted, and yellowing and has brown spots, or cankers, at the base of the main stem and on the leaves. Black specks are within the larger brown spots. Plant may die, but leaves don't drop.

Cause: Blackleg is a fungal disease. Spores travel on seeds, debris, and splashing water and spread quickly among wet leaves.

Solution: There is no cure. Destroy infected plants. Protect healthy plants with good garden sanitation, insect control, and crop rotation. Buy healthy seeds.

- Dig up infected plants and dispose of any plant debris that is lying on the ground.
- Mulch and water at ground level to prevent disease spores from splashing onto plants.
- Control cabbage maggots (facing page), which can spread blackleg.
- Rotate (p.115) with crops that are not susceptible, such as peas, every four years.
- Obtain seeds that are certified disease free or are pretreated with fungicide.

Roots are abnormally thick

Problem: The plant wilts even though the soil is moist; the leaves yellow. Roots are thickened, especially near the soil surface, and large swellings may fuse some together.

Cause: Clubroot is a fungal disease carried by cabbage relatives and infected transplants. When an infected plant dies, spores spread into the soil, where they live up to 10 years.

Solution: There's no cure. Destroy infected plants and treat soil with fungicide. To protect healthy plants, practice garden sanitation and crop rotation. Start cabbage from seed and avoid conditions that foster clubroot.

- As soon as fungus appears, remove the diseased plant, roots, and surrounding soil.
- For a serious infection, treat the soil with a synthetic fungicide registered for cabbage that contains the active ingredient PCNB. Follow label directions carefully.
- Destroy carrier cabbage-family weeds such as wild radish, wild mustard, pennycress, peppergrass, and shepherd's purse. Don't plant alyssum, stock, candytuft, or wallflower, which are also hosts.
- Add lime to raise the soil pH (p.329) to 7.2, making it unfavorable for the fungus.
- Plant cabbage in well-drained soil. Avoid growing cabbage-related crops where infected plants grew for 7 to 10 years.
- Always obtain transplants that are certified disease free, or grow your own from seed.

GETTING A SECOND CABBAGE CROP FROM THE SAME PLANTS

Instead of planting a second crop, you can often extend the cabbage harvest by encouraging plants to produce a second, smaller batch of heads.

• Harvest the first crop, as usual, when the cabbage head is firm. But instead of cutting the stem at soil level, as is customary, cut it just below the head without removing the leaves.

• Water well when the soil is dry 1 inch below the surface, and give plants an application of compost or a balanced fertilizer, such as 10-10-10 (p.324).

• Smaller heads should develop on the stem near the base of the leaves.

Plant wilts, yellows, and dies; larvae appear at the base

Problem: The plant wilts in warm weather even though the soil is moist. The plant may also be stunted, and it eventually yellows and dies. Small white larvae are visible at the base of the plant.

Cause: Cabbage maggots, which are about the size and shape of rice grains, are the larvae of a small fly. In early spring, when the weather is cool, the maggots eat into the lower stem and upper roots of the plant. They mature in the soil, then emerge as flies.

Solution: Protect plants by creating barriers to the egg-laying flies, using biological controls on the soil, and timing plantings.

● Wrap the stems of transplants in brown paper, extending the paper 1 inch above and below the soil. Or, during the first few weeks, grow seedlings under a fabric floating row cover to exclude insects; tuck the edges firmly under the soil.

● Remove infested plants from the garden, and clean up debris after the harvest.

● In spring, kill overwintering maggots by applying beneficial nematodes (p.126), a biological control, to the soil where you plan to grow cabbage.

● Rotate (p.115) cabbage with nonsusceptible crops, such as peas, every two years to starve overwintering pupae.

● In areas with long, cool springs, plant early so that the transplants are large enough by April to withstand infestations. If it remains too cold to plant before the flies have laid their eggs, set transplants out in June for fall harvest.

Plant has dull, greenish yellow leaves

Problem: The plant has a sickly, yellowish cast that is more pronounced on one side than on the other. The lower leaves are twisted and curled; they turn yellow, then brown before dropping. The woody tissue inside the stem is brown.

Cause: Fusarium yellows of cabbage is a serious fungal disease that prevents moisture and nutrients from reaching the leaves. The damage is most serious in warm weather. The spores of this disease can survive in the soil for many years.

Solution: There is no cure for this disease. Destroy infected plants, rotate crops regularly, and grow resistant varieties.

● Remove and destroy infected plants, which will rarely recover if left in the soil.

● Rotate (p.115) cabbage with unrelated crops every three years.

● For future plantings, buy seeds or seedlings that are certified disease free. Sow seeds in sterile planting mix.

● Buy resistant cabbage varieties such as 'Early Jersey Wakefield', 'Red Acre', 'Stonehead', and 'Tasty'.

Carrot

Daucus carota

LIGHT: Full sun

SOIL: Well drained, rock free; pH 6.0 to 7.5

MOISTURE: Moist

HARDINESS: Cool-season biennial

Leaves have brown areas

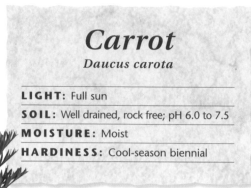

Problem: Circular or irregular splotches form on the leaves and leaf stems.

Cause: Two kinds of blight, early and late, are both major fungal diseases of carrots. Early blight usually appears early in the season, affects young leaves first, and forms gray to dark brown, round spots on the leaves that eventually merge. Late blight often appears as weather cools at the end of the growing season, forming dark, irregular lesions on older leaves, and sometimes kills the entire top of the plant.

Solution: Use good garden sanitation and fungicides to control blight. Water carefully. Rotate crops and grow resistant varieties.

- At the first sign of blight, remove and dispose of the affected leaves.

- Treat the leaves and crowns with an organically acceptable fungicide containing copper. Follow label directions carefully.

- When watering, use drip irrigation or a soaker hose to avoid wetting leaves; disease spores are spread by splashing water.

- Rotate (p.115) carrots with other crops every three years.

- Obtain certified disease-free seeds or packaged seeds that have been pretreated with a fungicide. Also try blight-tolerant varieties, such as 'Bolero', 'Chantenay', 'Navajo', 'Nevis', and 'Red Cored Chantenay'.

Seedlings fail to emerge

Problem: Several weeks after carrot seeds are sown, there are still no seedlings visible.

Cause: Carrot seedlings take two weeks or longer to emerge from the soil. Sometimes the small seedlings don't emerge because they can't push aside soil that is crusted and dry. Also, in very hot, dry weather, carrot seeds won't germinate at all. Since carrots do not transplant well, they must be sown in place.

Solution: Meet the needs of germinating carrot seeds by keeping the soil moist, sowing carrots with other plants, and timing plantings appropriately.

- When sowing, cover carrot seeds with a strip of fabric floating row cover to help the soil retain moisture and to prevent a crust from forming.

- At the time of sowing, mix some radish seeds in with the carrot seeds. The fast-germinating radishes will break the soil surface, making it easier for carrot seeds to sprout. The radishes will also remind you where you planted the carrots.

- In areas with very hot summers, plan to grow carrots either before or after the heat of midsummer.

Carrot roots are misshapen

Problem: Roots are twisted, lumpy, or forked.

Cause: Carrots that are otherwise healthy and edible will develop deformed roots if they are overcrowded or grown in rocky or heavy clay soil. Fresh manure in the soil can also cause forking, as can the microscopic worms called root-knot nematodes.

Solution: Sow carrots in soft, loose soil; space and thin them properly. If symptoms appear, solarize the soil, or resow in sterile soil.

- Before planting, prepare the seedbed well. Remove rocks and, if necessary, sift the soil through a hardware-cloth screen. Alternatively, grow carrots in a raised bed of loose soil. Add plenty of organic matter to clay soil. However, never add fresh manure.

- When carrots are about 2 inches tall, thin them to stand 1 to 1½ inches apart.
- Before planting again, place clear plastic sheeting over nematode-infested soil for four weeks to solarize the soil (p.117) and kill the nematodes. Or grow carrots in raised beds or containers of sterile soil.

Carrot root has holes

Problem: Carrot roots have surface tunnels or deep holes. The roots may also be partially decayed. Small, legless white larvae are present in the tunnels.

Cause: Several insects tunnel into carrot roots. The carrot weevil larva bores into roots and stems. Similarly, the carrot rust fly larva eats into roots, leaving rusty red debris in them; this pest is especially common in the Northeast and West. Also the wireworm, the larva of the click beetle can dig deep holes in roots, often leaving before the harvest.

Solution: Remove affected plants and use insecticides. Clean up debris, protect crops with barriers, and use biological controls. Harvest early in the season, when damage is less.

- Once you notice damage, remove the injured plants or damaged root parts.
- To control carrot weevil, spray the plant with pyrethrum, a botanical insecticide, when the pests become active. To control wireworms, treat the soil with a synthetic insecticide registered for carrots that contains the active ingredient diazinon. Follow label directions carefully.
- In late fall, clean up weeds and debris in which carrot weevils can overwinter.
- Sow seeds as early as possible for your climate. Grow seedlings under a fabric floating row cover to protect crops from frost and to exclude egg-laying insects.
- If maggot damage to roots is a problem year after year, treat the soil with beneficial nematodes (p.126), a biological control, as soon as the soil warms in spring.

Middle leaves are yellow and twisted

Problem: Young leaves at the center of the plant are pale yellow. As more leaves form, they remain small and misshapen. Carrots are small, bitter, and woody and are covered with many short roots.

Cause: Aster yellows is a disease caused by a virus-like organism, which is spread by the six-spotted, or aster, leafhopper.

Solution: There is no cure for aster yellows. Practice good garden sanitation to prevent spreading the disease, and use insecticides. Prevent future outbreaks by keeping leafhoppers from feeding on the plants.

- Remove from the garden any plant that shows aster yellows symptoms. Clean up plant debris that may also be infected.
- If leafhoppers are present, dislodge them with a strong stream of water or apply neem, a botanical insecticide. If the insects persist, use a synthetic insecticide registered for carrots that contains the active ingredient carbaryl or malathion. Follow label directions carefully.
- Grow young plants under a fabric floating row cover or cone-shaped paper protectors to exclude insects.

WISE CHOICES

To ensure well-formed carrots, even in heavy or rocky soil, select a variety that develops short or round roots. Look for compact "baby" or "mini" types or the globelike "ball" type, such as those listed here.

- 'Danvers Half Long' produces a tapering, red-cored root about 6 inches long.
- 'Little Finger', a crisp, blunt-tipped carrot, can be pulled at 4 inches.
- 'Minicor' has a tender orange root that will reach 6 inches but can be harvested as a "baby" at 3 inches.
- 'Parmex' is a crunchy, smooth-skinned, nearly round carrot that matures quickly.
- 'Thumbelina' grows to a sweet, round nugget 2 inches in diameter.

Cauliflower
Brassica oleracea

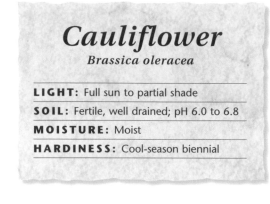

LIGHT: Full sun to partial shade

SOIL: Fertile, well drained; pH 6.0 to 6.8

MOISTURE: Moist

HARDINESS: Cool-season biennial

Leaves have yellow blotches with fuzzy mold

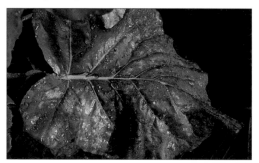

Problem: Both sides of leaves have pale patches that develop gray, fuzzy mold. Heads may have dark gray mold between the curds.

Cause: Downy mildew is a fungal disease that strikes most often in damp conditions, especially when days are warm and nights are cool. Spores live in weeds and overwinter on plant debris left in the garden.

Solution: Use good garden sanitation and proper growing techniques to discourage this disease.

- Remove fallen leaves and plant debris from the garden, as well as nearby weeds.
- Thin plants to increase air circulation.
- Harvest heads as they ripen. Trim off discolored portions before preparing for the table.
- Mulch plants to keep spore-laden soil from splashing onto them.
- In future seasons, plant cauliflower in soil of nearly neutral acidity (7.0), or pH (p.329).

Head forms leaves or has uneven surface

Problem: The cauliflower head is interrupted by small leaves. Or the head isn't smooth; it may be granular or "hairy" in appearance.

Cause: When heads form in hot weather, various problems can occur. Leaves may form amid the curds, the curds may not be compact and smooth, or the heads may not form at all.

Solution: Use a variety suited to your climate.

- In areas with hot summers, plant early-maturing varieties, such as 'Cashmere Hybrid' and 'Snow Crown', as soon as spring temperatures allow.
- In areas with long summers, plant early-maturing varieties in mid- to late summer.

Cauliflower head is discolored

Problem: Rather than being the expected snowy white color, the cauliflower head is tinged purple, green, or yellow.

Cause: If the curd of a white-headed variety is exposed to direct sunlight, it discolors.

Solution: To ensure a white head, tie leaves over curds or grow self-blanching varieties.

- When the head is about 1 inch in diameter, tie the outer leaves over its top with string.
- For next year, consider self-blanching varieties, such as 'Avalanche' and 'Fremont', which grow leaves that cover heads. They are best grown in cool weather; in warm areas, the leaves may not cover adequately.

Corn
Zea mays

LIGHT: Full sun

SOIL: Fertile, well drained; pH 6.0 to 6.8

MOISTURE: Moist

HARDINESS: Warm-season annual

Ear is poorly filled out

Problem: Not all of the kernels have formed properly. Gaps may occur throughout the ear or only at the top.

Cause: Poor kernel formation can have several causes, including poor pollination, inadequate moisture or nutrients, and improper plant spacing. Additionally, corn earworms may eat the silks, which are necessary for pollination.

Solution: Use proper growing techniques and control earworms with insecticides.

- Water corn well when the silks and tassels are opening. Also water whenever the soil is dry 1 inch beneath the surface.

- Control earworms with BT, a biological insecticide. Apply around ears as soon as the silks emerge from the husks; repeat every few days until silks turn brown. For severe infestations, use a synthetic pesticide registered for corn that contains the active ingredient carbaryl or esfenvalerate. Follow label directions.

- Before next season, fertilize average soil with a 10-10-10 formulation (p.324). Use 20-20-20 for moist soil.

- Sow corn in a block, with a minimum of 4 feet on a side. This will ensure that the wind blows the pollen onto as many silks as possible. Follow packet recommendations for the proper seed spacing.

Plants have silver-gray growths

Problem: Swollen growths, called galls, start out green, become gray to white, and then burst open, releasing a blackish powder. Galls may be on the ears, tassels, stalk, or leaves.

Cause: Corn smut is a fungal disease that causes these galls. The galls release black spores that remain alive for up to seven years in manure, soil, and crop debris. The spores are transported by wind and splashing water, and they germinate on corn in moist conditions but can sometimes strike during very hot, dry summers. Infection is most likely to occur when plants have been injured by hail, blowing sand, or cultivating tools; when the soil is very high in nitrogen; or during periods of hot, dry weather.

Solution: There is no cure for corn smut. Remove galls, practice good garden sanitation, and feed plants. Select resistant varieties.

- For immediate control, remove and dispose of galls as they appear and before they release spores.

- Avoid damaging healthy plants when cultivating around them.

- After sowing, fertilize once a month until the tassels form. Apply a low-nitrogen organic fertilizer, such as fish emulsion or well-composted manure.

- After harvest, clean up and remove all plant debris from the garden.

- Next season, plant varieties resistant to the disease (box, right).

WISE CHOICES

Certain varieties of corn are bred to be resistant to common problems.

Varieties with tight husks that resist entry by earworms include 'Breeder's Choice', 'Country Gentleman', 'Golden Security', 'Silvergent', and 'Staygold'.

Smut-resistant varieties include 'Apache', 'Aztec', 'Brave SE', 'Candy Store SH-2', 'Capitan', 'Comanche', 'Comet', 'Country Gentleman', 'Merit', 'Quick silver', and 'Seneca'.

Ear contains one caterpillar near tip

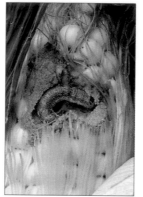

Problem: A single striped, brownish green caterpillar is at the tip of the ear. It is eating silks and corn kernels and leaving a mealy mess.

Cause: The corn earworm is a moth larva that feeds on corn leaves and ears. Early feeding can damage the silks, preventing kernels from forming; later feeding damages the kernels. The insect may also transmit fungal disease to the corn.

Solution: Control earworms by handpicking or with insecticide. Avoid future problems with preventive measures.

- Handpick and destroy the pests. Or cut off the infested ear tips; the rest of the ear is still edible.

- For severe infestations, apply a synthetic insecticide registered for corn that contains the active ingredient carbaryl or esfenvalerate. Follow label directions. Note that carbaryl is toxic to bees; apply when evenings are dry to minimize its effect on them.

- As a preventive measure, apply BT, a biological insecticide, as soon as silks emerge from husks; repeat every few days until silks turn brown. Follow label directions. BT is most effective when the larvae are small.

- Turn off outdoor lights at night. Light attracts the night-flying moth that is the adult stage of the corn earworm.

- In the South, where earworms overwinter in the soil, till the soil in fall to kill them.

Seedlings and small plants are damaged or chewed

Problem: Seedlings are damaged or disappear. The roots of young plants are chewed.

Cause: Wireworms, the slender, dark brown larvae of click beetles, attack corn roots. They are easily detected during soil cultivation.

Solution: Use insecticides and appropriate gardening techniques. Rotate crops.

- As soon as damage occurs, treat the soil with a synthetic insecticide registered for corn that contains the active ingredient

diazinon or chlorpyrifos. Follow label directions carefully.

- After harvesting ears, till the soil to a depth of 6 to 12 inches to kill the larvae.

- Before planting the following season, solarize the soil (p.117) by laying a clear plastic sheet over the prepared bed for three to four weeks to kill wireworms with heat.

- Rotate (p.115) corn with wireworm-resistant crops, such as spinach, squash, or peas.

Leaves have small holes; stalks are bent

Problem: Small holes mar leaves of a young plant. Leaves and stalks break. At the breaking point is a hole and a sawdustlike substance. Pinkish gray caterpillars with dotted segments and dark heads are boring into the leaves, stems, and ears.

Cause: European corn borers, the larvae of a night-flying moth, are a serious corn pest east of the Rocky Mountains. They overwinter in corn and other plant stalks and mature in spring. Adult moths lay masses of eggs that look like fish scales on leaf undersides.

Solution: Handpick caterpillars, apply insecticides, practice good garden sanitation, and time new crops carefully to avoid infestation.

- Handpick and dispose of caterpillars.

- While caterpillars are small, apply BTK, a biological insecticide, to stalks, ears, and leaves, including the undersides. Follow label directions carefully.

- If BTK is ineffective, use neem, a botanical insecticide, or spray with a synthetic insecticide registered for corn that contains the active ingredient esfenvalerate. Follow label directions carefully.

- Remove weeds, which can host the pests, during the growing season. At season's end, remove from the garden all corn debris and weeds in which larvae could overwinter.

- Ask the staff at a local garden center when corn should be planted in your area to avoid damage by European corn borers.

Cucumber

Cucumis sativus

LIGHT:	Full sun
SOIL:	Fertile, well drained; pH 6.0 to 7.0
MOISTURE:	Moist
HARDINESS:	Warm-season annual

Holes are chewed in leaves

Problem: Ragged holes appear in the leaves. Small striped or spotted beetles are chewing leaves and may also be chewing fruits.

Cause: Striped, spotted, and banded cucumber beetles are most troublesome to small plants. The striped beetle does the most damage; its larvae chew on plant roots as well as on foliage. All three can spread diseases, including cucumber mosaic virus (right) and bacterial wilt (p.108), as they feed.

Solution: Handpick; control beetles with insecticides. Protect young plants with barriers and select resistant varieties.

- As soon as damage is apparent, handpick beetles, drop them into a container of soapy water, and dispose of it. Continue picking until the infestation subsides.

- If seedlings are emerging, or recently transplanted, spray with neem, a botanical insecticide, or with a synthetic insecticide registered for cucumbers that contains the active ingredient carbaryl. Follow label directions. Carbaryl is toxic to bees; to protect bees, do not spray blooming plants.

- Grow seedlings and transplants under a fabric floating row cover or cone-shaped paper protectors to exclude insects.

- For future plantings, choose resistant varieties (box, p.108).

Fruits taste bitter

Problem: Cucumbers look normal but have a bitter taste.

Cause: Bitter flavor is due to a combination of inadequate growing conditions and the bitter tendency of some varieties. Bitterness most often occurs when cucumbers are grown in soil that is inconsistently watered or deficient in nutrients.

Solution: Provide proper growing conditions and select varieties described as nonbitter.

- Water cucumbers whenever the soil is dry 1 inch beneath the surface. Be particularly careful about watering while fruits are forming.

- Before eating cucumbers, remove the skin and stem end, where bitterness is often located.

- Before planting next year, work compost or a balanced fertilizer, such as 10-10-10 (p.324), into the soil.

Young leaves are mottled, fruits may be mottled or misshapen

Problem: The youngest leaves become mottled with light green and yellow splotches. The leaves are also thick and wrinkled, with down-curled edges. The fruits may be mottled with yellow, misshapen, and covered with warts.

Cause: Cucumber mosaic virus is a disease spread by sap-sucking insects such as aphids. The disease overwinters on some perennial weeds, including ground cherry, milkweed, and pokeweed.

Solution: There is no cure. Pull out and discard affected plants, control feeding insects, and grow resistant varieties.

- Remove infected plants and fruits from the garden as soon as you notice them.

- As a preventive, hose insects off plants with a strong stream of water. Alternatively, spray plants completely with insecticidal soap or with neem, a botanical insecticide. Follow label directions carefully.

- Destroy nearby weeds on which aphids and other insects are present or might feed.
- Grow cucumber plants under a fabric floating row cover to exclude insects.
- To avoid future problems, select cucumber varieties that are resistant to cucumber mosaic virus (box, below right).

Angular spots and holes appear on leaves

Problem: Dark, angular spots appear on leaf undersides. The tissue eventually disintegrates, leaving ragged holes in the leaves. A white crust develops on fruits, which later start to rot.

Cause: Angular leaf spot is caused by a bacterium that lives on seeds and infected plant debris. The disease is most prevalent in warm, moist weather. It is spread by wind, splashing water, and gardeners working among wet crops.

Solution: Use fungicides with antiobiotic properties to control severe outbreaks. Practice good garden sanitation. Select resistant varieties and rotate crops.

- Alternate applications of an organic copper-based fungicide with a synthetic fungicide. Use a synthetic fungicide registered for cucumbers that contains the active ingredient maneb. Water plants thoroughly before application, use the most dilute solution recommended, and spray only when the sky is overcast and the temperature is below 80°F to prevent leaf damage. Follow label directions carefully.
- Discourage angular leaf spot from spreading to healthy plants by keeping foliage dry when watering. Water at ground level, using drip irrigation or a soaker hose. Also avoid working among plants when the leaves are wet.
- After harvesting cucumbers, remove plant debris from the garden.
- In future years, select cucumber varieties that are noted for resistance to the disease (box, right).
- Rotate (p.115) cucumbers with other crops every two years.

Plant wilts and then dies a few days later

Problem: The plant looks healthy, except for several dull green, wilted areas on the leaves. Within a few days, part of the plant wilts, then the whole plant wilts and dies.

Cause: Bacterial wilt is spread from plant to plant by spotted cucumber beetles and other insects.

Solution: Test for the disease, practice good garden sanitation, control insects with pesticides, and use insect barriers to protect plants.

- First test for the disease by cutting a section from an affected plant. Squeeze sap from the stem ends, press the ends together for 10 to 15 seconds, and then pull them apart slowly. A string of white ooze between them indicates that the disease is present.
- Remove and dispose of infected plants.
- Treat young plants with insecticide as recommended for cucumber beetles (p.107).
- Use a fabric floating row cover or cone-shaped paper protectors to protect seedlings or transplants from insects.

WISE CHOICES

Common cucumber problems can often be avoided by growing resistant varieties. Check your local garden center or mail-order catalogs for these and others:

Varieties that show resistance to disease include 'Fanfare', 'Little Leaf', and 'Sweet Slice', which are not susceptible to the bacterial disease angular leaf spot. Those that resist cucumber mosaic virus include 'Early Set', 'Green Star', 'Marketmore 76', 'Marketmore 80', and 'Pacer'.

'Marketmore 80' also offers resistance to cucumber beetles, which spread diseases as well as damage plants.

Bitter-free varieties include 'Aria', 'Jazzer', 'Marketmore 80', 'Slicemaster Select', and 'Sweet Slice'.

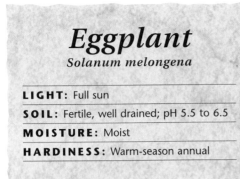

Eggplant
Solanum melongena

LIGHT: Full sun

SOIL: Fertile, well drained; pH 5.5 to 6.5

MOISTURE: Moist

HARDINESS: Warm-season annual

Fruits have sunken rotten spots

Problem: Tan to brown spots appear on the lower leaves, and tiny black dots may develop within the spots. Dark brown spots with gray centers develop on stems, weakening them until the plant falls over. Fruits have pale, sunken spots that begin rotting.

Cause: Phomopsis blight is a fungal disease of eggplants. The spores are carried on seeds and overwinter in soil and plant debris. Hot, wet weather encourages the disease, which is most common in the Southeast.

Solution: There is no effective remedy for the disease. Practice good garden sanitation and treat with a fungicide. Water properly and rotate crops. Select resistant varieties.

- Remove infected plants. Clean up and dispose of any plant debris.
- Spray the eggplant foliage with an organic copper-based fungicide. Follow label directions carefully.
- Avoid overwatering the soil where seedlings are growing. Water when the soil is dry 1 inch beneath the surface.
- Rotate (p.115) eggplant with other crops every four years.
- If you garden in the Southeast, select varieties resistant to phomopsis blight, such as 'Florida Beauty' and 'Florida Market'.

Leaves have tiny holes and spots

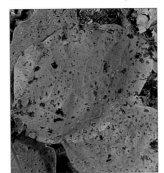

Problem: The leaves have small holes and tan dots and may shrivel and die. Tiny brown or black insects are seen hopping away.

Cause: Flea beetles eat leaves and seedlings. Their larvae eat roots, which stunts plants.

Solution: Treat with a pesticide, protect young plants with barriers, remove debris, and introduce insect predators.

- Spray with insecticidal soap or a synthetic insecticide registered for eggplants with the active ingredient methoxychlor. Follow label directions.
- Grow young plants under a fabric floating row cover to exclude insects.
- Weed regularly and clean up debris in fall.
- Next year, add beneficial nematodes (p.126), a biological control, to the soil.

Leaves yellow and drop, plants are stunted

Problem: Seedlings grow slowly and die. New leaves on young plants are small, and mature leaves yellow, shrivel, and drop.

Cause: Verticillium wilt is a soilborne fungal disease that is most prevalent in the Midwest.

Solution: Destroy affected plants and use proper growing techniques.

- Pull up and dispose of infected plants.
- When setting out plants, space them 2 to 3 feet apart to ensure good air circulation.
- Mulch with compost to keep spore-laden soil from splashing on plants.

Gardeners in warm climates may encounter the vegetable weevil, which feeds on lettuce and other vegetables. This beetle, which has a downturned snout, feeds mostly at night. Adults and their green, legless larvae eat leaves and roots. Look for both stages hiding in debris on the soil during the day. Because the pest can't fly, you can control them by handpicking, and the infestations usually spread slowly.

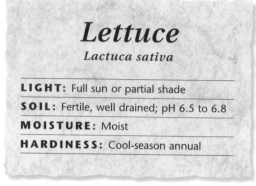

Lettuce

Lactuca sativa

LIGHT: Full sun or partial shade
SOIL: Fertile, well drained; pH 6.5 to 6.8
MOISTURE: Moist
HARDINESS: Cool-season annual

Stem rots; plant collapses

Problem: Decay spreads to the roots and bottom leaves from a wet, decaying area on the stem at the soil line. The entire plant wilts, collapses, and rots. In humid conditions, a cottony white mold forms over the plant. Small black particles appear in the mold.

Cause: Lettuce drop is caused by a soilborne fungus. The fungus remains alive in the soil for many years, releasing spores that are carried by wind. It is most active when the weather is cool and humid.

Solution: Practice good garden sanitation and growing techniques. Treat infected plants and soil with a fungicide. Rotate crops.

- Remove infected plants immediately.
- Avoid overwatering. Water only when the soil is dry 1 inch beneath the surface.
- Remove lettuce debris at season's end.
- Grow new plants on ridges of soil or in raised beds (p.328) to improve drainage and air circulation; space at least 1 foot apart.
- If lettuce drop has been a problem in the past, apply a synthetic fungicide registered for lettuce that contains the active ingredient vinclozolin to leaves. Do not cultivate the soil after applying the fungicide. Follow label directions carefully.
- Rotate (p.115) lettuce with nonsusceptible crops, such as corn, every three years.

Plant suddenly grows tall and has bitter-tasting leaves

Problem: The leaves taste bitter and are tough in texture. The central leaves are small, and the plant may develop a tall stem with blossoms at the top.

Cause: Lettuce becomes bitter and tough when the weather is too warm. It grows best around 60°F. If warm weather sets in and continues, especially in spring, lettuce will bloom prematurely and set seed, a process called bolting.

Solution: Provide cool growing conditions, plant often, and grow bolt-resistant varieties.

- Plant lettuce as early as possible for your climate, about two weeks before the last expected frost date; protect plants with a fabric floating row cover if frost threatens.
- In areas with warm springs, plant lettuce where it will get afternoon shade, or grow it under commercial shade cloth.
- Plant small amounts every two weeks, depending on your consumption, and harvest regularly, before plants begin to bolt.
- Select bolt-resistant varieties, such as 'Buttercrunch', 'Green Ice', 'Mighty Red Oak', 'Red Sails', 'Royal Oak Leaf', 'Simpson Elite', and 'Sangria.'

Leaf edges are brown and dry

Problem: Small brown spots appear at leaf edges. The leaves may become black and slimy.

Cause: Tipburn occurs when lettuce plants do not receive enough water, which prevents the soluble nutrient calcium from reaching leaf tips. Later, bacteria may enter damaged tissue and cause decay.

Solution: Provide adequate water and mulch. Time plantings. Grow resistant varieties.

- Water deeply when the soil is dry 1 inch beneath the surface. Mulch with a 3-inch layer of compost to retain soil moisture.

- Plant in spring or late summer, so that lettuce will not mature in hot, dry weather.

- Select resistant varieties, such as butterhead varieties 'Divina', 'Optima', or 'Sangria'; iceberg types 'Ithaca', 'Great Lakes Mesa 659', or 'Salinas'; Batavian types 'Nevada' and 'Sierra'; and the romaine lettuce 'Parris Island Cos'.

Leaf veins are wide and pale

Problem: The leaf veins are very wide and pale. Leaves are puckered and may be more upright than usual.

Cause: Big vein is caused by a virus or similar organism that has not yet been identified. The disease, which is most severe in cool weather, is spread by an otherwise harmless soilborne fungus that survives in soil for many years.

Solution: There is no cure for big vein. Use proper gardening techniques to minimize it.

- Remove infected plants from the garden.

- Don't overwater, especially when the weather is cool, to discourage onset of the disease. Water lettuce when the soil is dry 1 inch beneath the surface.

- Avoid growing lettuce in poorly drained soil or where infected plants have been grown. Crop rotation is not effective against big vein.

Lower leaves brown and decay

Problem: Brown spots and streaks develop on the leaf veins and the lower leaves, which decay and become dark and slimy. The lettuce head may become dry and mummified.

Cause: Bottom rot is caused by a soilborne fungus and is spread through infected soil. It kills seedlings and can infect plants as the heads begin to form. Bottom rot is most likely to develop in wet weather or saturated soil.

Solution: Destroy affected plants and use proper gardening techniques. Rotate crops and choose plants carefully.

- Remove infected plants immediately.

- To protect crops, water when the soil is dry, 1 inch beneath the surface, and leave room between plants for air to circulate.

- Remove lettuce plant debris at season's end.

- Rotate (p.115) lettuce with other crops, such as corn or onions, every two years.

- In the future, grow resistant varieties, such as 'Nevada' and 'Sierra'.

Rotate (p.115)

DID YOU KNOW?

Your best defense against slugs and snails may be in your toolbox. Surround lettuce with strips of gritty sandpaper to protect it from slugs and snails. Although lettuce is their favorite menu item, these soft-bodied mollusks will turn away from the scratchy barrier rather than crawl across it to reach the salad bar.

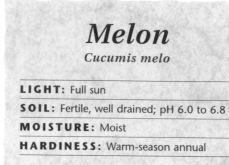

Melon
Cucumis melo

LIGHT: Full sun

SOIL: Fertile, well drained; pH 6.0 to 6.8

MOISTURE: Moist

HARDINESS: Warm-season annual

Powdery white substance covers leaves

Problem: Round areas of a white powdery substance appear on some older leaves. Soon these white areas merge, coating both sides of the leaves. The white material, which cannot be rubbed off, spreads to younger leaves, and all the affected leaves turn dry and brown.

Cause: Powdery mildew is a fungal disease. Infected leaf surfaces release spores that are spread by the wind. The spores germinate in warm weather and don't need moist conditions to grow. In mild-winter areas, spores overwinter on plant debris. Plants infected with powdery mildew often produce low yields and poor-tasting fruit.

Solution: Garden sanitation discourages the disease and fungicides can stop its spread, but fungicides can't cure infected leaves. Selecting resistant varieties offers the best protection.

- At the first sign of disease, pick and dispose of infected leaves and other plant debris.
- To dislodge spores, spray both sides of leaves with a stream of water. Spray early in the day so that leaves will dry quickly; this will discourage other kinds of fungi.
- To curb the spread of the disease, spray a fungicidal baking soda solution (p.392) on both sides of leaves at weekly intervals until harvest.
- As an alternative, apply an organic sulfur fungicide to leaves. Avoid application when temperatures are above 85°F, to prevent damage to foliage. Or apply a systemic synthetic fungicide registered for melons that contains the active ingredient benomyl. Follow label directions carefully.
- Next season, use varieties resistant to powdery mildew, such as 'Ambrosia', 'Burpee Hybrid', 'Hale's Best Jumbo', 'Luscious Plus', 'Savor Charantais', and 'Solid Gold'.

Plant wilts in midday and dies soon after

Problem: A branch begins to droop, and the leaves turn brown, starting with the oldest ones. There may be a dark brown streak on one side of the stem, extending from the soil line up 1 to 2 feet. If you cut a stem at the base, you'll see a yellow, orange, or brown discoloration inside.

Cause: Fusarium wilt is a common fungal disease that remains active in the soil for several years. It can also be carried on seeds, infected vines, and garden tools.

Solution: Use good gardening techniques, proper soil pH, healthy seeds, and crop rotation to discourage fusarium wilt.

- Remove infected plants and plant debris that could harbor disease.
- Add lime to raise the soil pH (p. 329) to 6.5 to 7.5 to discourage the growth of soil fungi.

- Buy certified disease-free seeds. Plant resistant varieties, such as 'Alaska', 'Pancha', 'Savor Charantais', and 'Solid Gold'.
- Rotate (p.115) crops. Wait 5 years before planting resistant varieties in the same place; wait 15 years for susceptible varieties.

Tan areas spread on leaves

Problem: The leaves develop spreading tan lesions that eventually fall away, creating a ragged look. Elongated tan streaks mar stems. Young, infected fruits may blacken and shrivel. Larger infected melons have water-soaked spots that turn dark green to brown.

Cause: Anthracnose is a fungal disease carried on seeds and released from lesions on infected plants. Spores overwinter in crop residue and related weeds. Wet soil and warm, humid conditions favor this disease. Its spores are spread by wind and by splashing water.

Solution: Spray and use good garden sanitation. Rotate crops and buy healthy seeds.

- Spray infected leaves with a synthetic fungicide registered for melons that contains the active ingredient mancozeb or maneb. In some regions, sprays containing benomyl, copper, or thiophanate-methyl are also available; make sure the active ingredient is labeled for use on melons. Follow label directions carefully.
- Destroy infected plants and plant debris.
- Protect healthy plants by watering at ground level to keep leaves dry.
- In the future, rotate crops (p.115). Wait four years before planting melons and related crops in the same area.
- Alternatively, plant melons in raised beds filled with uninfected soil.
- Buy seeds and seedlings that are certified disease free. Consider a resistant melon variety, such as 'Saticoy'.

Melon has poor flavor

Problem: The fruit does not taste sweet.

Cause: Poorly flavored fruits most often result from inadequate growing conditions or premature harvest. Sweetness does not improve after harvest. In potassium-deficient soil, melons develop gritty, bitter flesh. Long periods of cool, cloudy, or rainy weather may cause fruits to lack sweetness. Very cool summers may not be sufficient to ripen any melon.

Solution: Pick melons when ripe, improve growing conditions, and select sweet varieties.

- Harvest only fully ripe melons. Some, such as cantaloupe, are ripe when a crack develops between the stem and fruit and fruit comes off easily. Others, such as honeydew, undergo a final color change and yield slightly when you press the blossom end.
- Before planting, work a high-potassium fertilizer, such as a 15-10-30 or 15-11-29 formulation (p.324), into the soil.
- In the future, consider growing high-sugar, super-sweet varieties, such as the cantaloupe 'Primo' or the honeydew 'Passport'.

Leaves curl and become mottled with yellow

Problem: The leaves begin to develop yellow splotches between the veins and curl along the edges. New growth may be stunted.

Cause: Several types of mosaic virus can attack melons at any stage during their development. Infection is usually much more severe on young plants than on fully formed ones, frequently stunting an immature plant's growth and causing it to die. Mosaic viruses may overwinter in weeds and are spread by feeding insects and infected seeds.

Solution: There is no cure. Remove infected plants and control insect pests and weeds.

- Remove and destroy infected plants and clean up plant debris in the garden.
- Cover healthy plants with a fabric floating row cover to keep insects away.
- Pull up any weeds growing near melons.

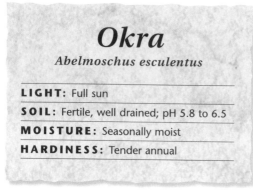

Okra

Abelmoschus esculentus

LIGHT: Full sun

SOIL: Fertile, well drained; pH 5.8 to 6.5

MOISTURE: Seasonally moist

HARDINESS: Tender annual

Pods and leaves have holes

Problem: Small holes are chewed in pods; leaves have large, ragged holes or may be almost completely eaten.

Cause: Corn earworms are destructive pests that feed on a number of crops, including okra. The brown or greenish caterpillars, which have striped backs, hatch, eat the fruits and leaves, fall to the ground to mature, and emerge as gray moths, ready to lay thousands more eggs.

Solution: Control infestations by handpicking or applying insecticide. Practice good garden sanitation.

- If caterpillars are visible, handpick and destroy them. You can also apply neem, a botanical insecticide, to control pests found on leaves or outside the pods. Follow label directions carefully.

- If caterpillars are already inside the pods, contact insecticides will not be effective. Instead, use BTK, a biological control. Follow label directions carefully.

- From Virginia southward, where earworms can survive winters, remove plant debris and cultivate the soil in fall and spring to expose overwintering pupae to predators. North of Virginia, cultivate in spring if the winter was unusually mild and dry.

Flowers and pods decay

Problem: White, brown, and purple spots develop on pods and flowers.

Cause: Choanephora rot, or pod rot, is a fungal disease that is encouraged by moist conditions. Its spores are spread by insects, by wind, and by splashing water.

Solution: Practice good garden sanitation, and apply fungicide to inhibit the disease. Water plants carefully.

- Remove all decaying flowers and pods from the garden immediately.

- Limit infections by applying sulfur, an organic fungicide. Follow label directions.

- Water plants at ground level, with a soaker hose or drip irrigation, to prevent water from splashing onto foliage.

Few flowers form, or flowers drop off plant

Problem: The plant is healthy looking but forms few flowers. Alternatively, flowers form, but they drop from the plant.

Cause: Lush foliage but poor bloom formation is caused by overfertilization, especially too much nitrogen. Blossom drop occurs below 64°F or above 95°F or if plants grow in poorly drained soil.

Solution: Fertilize properly and use appropriate techniques to meet okra's growing requirements. Time planting and select a variety suited to the climate.

- Fertilize in spring with rotted manure or a granular 5-10-5 fertilizer (p.324).

- In areas with short summers, select a protected location for okra and warm the soil with black or clear plastic mulch before planting. Select an early-maturing variety, such as 'North and South' or 'Green Best', and time planting so that okra matures in warm weather.

- In areas with long, hot summers, plant okra so that it matures before the hottest days are expected to arrive.

CROP ROTATION

Closely related plants often share pest and disease problems. Crop rotation simply means growing your vegetables in different locations in the garden from year to year so that it becomes more difficult for pests and diseases to find the plants they favor. The families of plants that are commonly rotated are shown below.

To rotate plants, grow crops of the same family together in one part of the garden. The following year, swap them with another group grown in a different section of the garden. A full rotation should take four years.

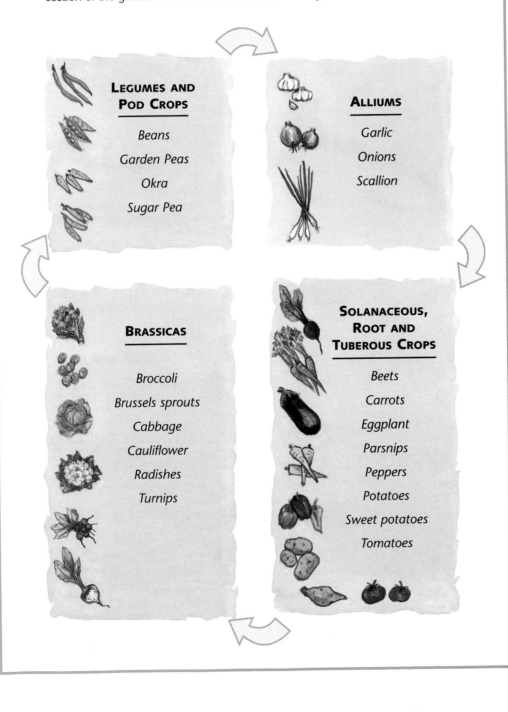

LEGUMES AND POD CROPS

Beans

Garden Peas

Okra

Sugar Pea

ALLIUMS

Garlic

Onions

Scallion

BRASSICAS

Broccoli

Brussels sprouts

Cabbage

Cauliflower

Radishes

Turnips

SOLANACEOUS, ROOT AND TUBEROUS CROPS

Beets

Carrots

Eggplant

Parsnips

Peppers

Potatoes

Sweet potatoes

Tomatoes

Onion, Garlic, and Scallion

Allium spp.

LIGHT: Full sun

SOIL: Fertile, well drained; pH 6.0 to 7.0

MOISTURE: Seasonally moist

HARDINESS: Cool-season perennials

Roots are pinkish brown; leaves turn yellow

Problem: The plant grows very slowly, roots are pinkish brown, leaves yellow, and bulbs are too small.

Cause: Onion pink root is a fungal disease that is carried in infected starter plants and transplants. Its spores can live in the soil indefinitely, infecting plants in the onion family. It is most pervasive when the temperature is between 60° and 85°F.

Solution: There is no cure. Good gardening practices will help keep it out of the garden.

- Remove and dispose of infected plants.
- Weed and provide plants with fertile, moist soil to increase their resistance.
- Control the pathogen by solarizing the soil (p.117).
- Start new onions from certified, disease-free seeds, starter plants, or sets. Do not plant grocery-store bulbs.
- Grow onion varieties that show resistance to pink root disease, such as 'Crystal Wax Pickling', 'Early Supreme', 'Early Yellow Globe', 'Evergreen White Bunching', 'Fiesta', and 'Granex'.

Bulb rots and develops a mat of white growth

Problem: The oldest leaves turn yellow and die, then the bulb decays. Eventually, a mat of white fungal tissue forms on the bulb or soil, and small black dots develop in it.

Cause: White rot of onion and garlic is a fatal fungal disease. The spores, which are carried in infected starter plants and soil, can survive in the soil for up to 20 years.

Solution: Remove any diseased plants. Keep from introducing this disease by treating garlic cloves before planting and by obtaining healthy starter plants, or sets.

- If infection appears, remove and dispose of infected plants, and do not grow onion-family crops in that soil again.
- Dip garlic cloves in 115°F water before planting. Watch the temperature carefully, because water only a few degrees hotter will kill garlic.
- Grow only certified disease-free sets of onion and garlic rather than grocery-store bulbs, and consider planting the resistant onion variety 'Festival'.

Leaves yellow and wilt; larvae are just under the soil

Problem: The plant may appear stunted before yellowing and dying. Small, legless white larvae are in the soil, lower stem, and upper roots.

Cause: Onion root maggots are fly larvae that feed on onion-family plants. The fly lays eggs at the base of the plant. Larvae hatch and bore into the base. Hot weather kills the eggs, so this is mainly a cool-weather pest. The pupae overwinter in the soil.

Solution: Biological controls are the best remedy. Garden sanitation and crop rotation will protect healthy crops.

- In late spring, apply beneficial nematodes (p.126), a biological control, to the soil around onion family crops to kill maggots. You may need to make a second application in midsummer for later generations.

- Control nearby weeds, especially those related to onions, to reduce cover for the flies and to avoid attracting them.

- After the growing season, in fall, turn the soil to kill overwintering pupae.

- Rotate (p.115) onion family crops with unrelated crops, such as lettuce, peppers, or cucumbers, using a two-year rotation.

- If onion root maggots continue to be a problem year after year, grow red onions, which are the least susceptible to the pests. Avoid white onions, which are the most susceptible (yellow varieties fall in between red and white).

Leaves develop white spots

Problem: Small white spots become large purplish blotches surrounded by orange and yellow bands. The leaves turn yellow and brown.

Cause: Purple blotch is a fungal disease that is most common in areas where plants are irrigated and in the South. The spores, which are spread by splashing water, overwinter in crop refuse and germinate in moist conditions.

Solution: Use a fungicide to control this disease. To discourage purple blotch, remove crop debris and avoid growing in wet soil.

- Spray plants with garden sulfur, an organic fungicide, at the first sign of the disease, and repeat according to package directions.

- If sulfur is ineffective, remove the infected plant. At the end of the season, make sure no plant debris, where the spores can overwinter, remains in the garden.

- Discourage the disease by growing future onion-family crops in well-drained soil and spacing plants to allow for air circulation.

Onion bulbs are small

Problem: The plant seems healthy, and leaves die back normally, but the bulbs are small.

Cause: Onion varieties are categorized as either long-day or short-day. Long-day varieties grown in the South will never form bulbs. Short-day varieties grown in the North will form only small bulbs.

Solution: Plant the correct type of onion for your region.

- North of 35° latitude, grow varieties of onions adapted to long days, such as 'Copra' and 'Walla Walla Sweet'.

- South of 35° latitude, grow onions adapted to short days, such as 'Granex' and 'White Bermuda'.

☙ TIME-TESTED TECHNIQUES ☙

SOLARIZING SOIL

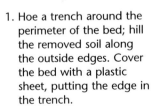

Solarization uses the sun's energy to heat and cleanse the top few inches of soil of many weeds, pests, and diseases. All you need is a rake, a hoe, a garden fork, a trowel, and a sheet of clear, 4-mil plastic (available at home or garden centers). Solarizing is most effective during the hottest days of summer.

Before you start, remove any existing plants from the bed and loosen the soil with a garden fork. Then rake the bed smooth and water the soil well.

1. Hoe a trench around the perimeter of the bed; hill the removed soil along the outside edges. Cover the bed with a plastic sheet, putting the edge in the trench.

2. Cover the edges of the plastic sheet with soil to hold it in place. Leave the plastic for four to eight weeks to allow time for the sun to heat up the soil.

Parsnip
Pastinaca sativa

LIGHT: Full sun

SOIL: Fertile, well drained; pH 6.0 to 7.0

MOISTURE: Moist

HARDINESS: Cool-season biennial

Parsnip seeds fail to grow

Problem: The seedbed remains bare, or only a few parsnip seedlings appear.

Cause: Parsnip seeds require three to four weeks to emerge after sowing. If watering is uneven during this period, or if the soil crusts over, seeds may not germinate. In addition, a high proportion of parsnip seeds are infertile and are not capable of developing for more than two years after harvesting.

Solution: Water evenly, prevent evaporation and soil crusting, and sow extra seeds.

- After sowing, keep the seedbed moist, and cover it with a fabric floating row cover to preserve moisture.
- Sow radish seeds with parsnip seeds; the fast-growing radishes will remind you where the parsnips are, and they will also break the soil surface, making it easier for the parsnips to emerge.
- To compensate for the naturally low germination rate of parsnips, sow seeds thickly, and thin as needed.

Roots have many small holes

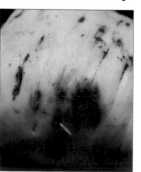

Problem: The plant stops making new leaves, the mature leaves turn pale and droop. Inspecting the roots reveals numerous small tunnels with rust-colored openings.

Cause: Carrot rust fly larvae, hatched from eggs laid by flies that look like small houseflies, burrow into roots, leaving holes.

Solution: Prevent flies from laying eggs on seedlings with a barrier. Rotate crops.

- Cover seedlings with an insect-excluding fabric floating row cover.
- In future seasons, rotate (p.115) parsnips with other plants—except carrots, which are also susceptible to carrot rust flies.

Root has large dark cankers

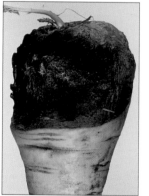

Problem: The root develops dry, dark brown cankers, usually near the top. Leaves have silvery spots that turn brown and have dark borders. The plant may lose the affected leaves.

Cause: Parsnip canker, also known as parsnip leaf blight, is a fungal disease found mostly in the Northeast.

Solution: Discard infected parsnip plants and protect healthy ones with a soil barrier. Provide good soil drainage and rotate parsnips with unrelated vegetable crops to discourage the onset of this disease.

- Remove infected parsnip plants from the garden as soon as they show symptoms.
- Mound soil lightly around the base of healthy plants, so that the shoulders of the roots are fully covered.
- Avoid planting new parsnips in poorly drained soil. Grow them in a 1-foot-deep raised bed (p.328) if necessary.
- Rotate (p.115) parsnips with other vegetable crops on a two-year cycle.

Root shrivels in spring

Problem: Parsnips left in the ground over winter form a flower stem when the weather warms. The root shrivels and toughens.

Cause: Parsnip is a biennial, and cold stimulates it to bloom and set seeds. Flowering is most likely in cold-winter climates.

Solution: Time harvest to avoid the problem.

- Dig up overwintered parsnips and eat them before the onset of warm weather.
- If a parsnip begins to bloom, harvest it while the flower stem is still short.

Pea, garden
Pea, sugar
Pisum sativum

LIGHT: Full sun

MOISTURE: Moist

SOIL: Well drained; pH 5.8 to 6.8

HARDINESS: Cool-season annual

Leaves turn yellow and wilt, and the plant is stunted

Problem: The plant does not reach full height. The edges of leaflets curl under. After the lower leaves turn yellow and wilt, the entire plant wilts for increasing periods, eventually not recovering. The stem may be slightly swollen and brittle at the soil line; if you cut it open, you'll see yellow, orange, or brick red discoloration inside.

Cause: Fusarium wilt of peas is a fungal disease. The spores are carried on seeds, and they persist in the soil for up to 10 years.

Solution: No fungicides are effective. Prevent the spread of the disease by destroying infected plants and by taking care in soil preparation, crop rotation, and seed selection.

- Remove and destroy any infected plant as soon as you discover it.
- Prepare the soil for new pea crops by adding plenty of compost or other organic matter. Avoid sowing pea seeds in low spots where water will puddle on the ground.
- Rotate (p.115) peas on a three- to four-year cycle. If fusarium wilt appears, don't plant peas in the infected soil for 5 to 10 years.
- Obtain certified disease-free seeds. Try resistant varieties, such as shelling peas 'Green Arrow', 'Little Marvel', and 'New Era'; snap pea 'Sugar Snap'; and snow peas 'Mammoth Melting Sugar' and 'Oregon Giant'.

Plant is stunted; roots rot

Problem: The plant is small and yellowish. Some roots are rotted and black. The lower stems may also be discolored.

Cause: Root rot is a fungal disease encouraged by poor drainage. The spores can survive in the soil for several years.

Solution: Dig and destroy infected plants. Amend the soil to improve drainage, rotate crops, and use treated seeds.

- Remove and destroy any infected plant as soon as you discover it.
- Prepare the soil by adding plenty of compost or other organic matter. Avoid sowing seeds in low spots where water will puddle.
- Rotate (p.115) peas with other crops on a three- to four-year cycle.
- No peas resist root rot. Obtain seeds treated with a synthetic fungicide containing the active ingredient metalaxyl or thiram, which protects against most root rot fungi.

Leaves and pods are distorted or mottled

Problem: The leaves curl and have pale spots and blisterlike growths. Pods may also have blisters and be purple, misshapen, or split.

Cause: Peas are subject to several viruses, including pea enation mosaic virus, which are spread by feeding insects or by infected seeds.

Solution: There are no cures for pea viruses. Prevent their spread by removing infected plants, controlling insects on peas and related

Gardeners in the Northwest, and occasionally in other regions, may encounter the pea leaf weevil. This small insect damages pea plants by notching the edges of leaves. The damage is most serious on seedlings.

Rotating (p.115) peas each season protects them from a buildup of this pest. As an extra precaution, make sure the young pea plants receive a fast-acting fertilizer, such as ammonium sulfate, so that they can quickly grow past the point when the damage can be most devastating.

plants, and selecting disease-free seeds and resistant varieties.

- Remove and dispose of virus-infected pea plants and plant debris from the garden as soon as symptoms appear.
- If aphids or other feeding insects are on healthy plants, dislodge them with a strong spray of water.
- If insects continue to be a problem, spray with neem, a botanical insecticide, or with a commercially available mixture of soap blended with the botanical insecticide pyrethrum. Follow label directions carefully.
- Control aphids with water or insecticidal soap on related plants, such as beans, broad beans, sweet peas, alfalfa, and clover, or segregate pea plants from these plants, which can harbor the same viruses.
- For a long-term solution, grow small-flowered nectar plants, such as coreopsis, sweet alyssum, and yarrow; they attract beneficial insects that feed on aphids.
- Obtain pea seeds that are certified disease free. Select varieties that resist viruses, such as the shelling peas 'Knight', 'Maestro', 'Oregon Pioneer', and 'Oregon Trail'; the snap peas 'Cascadia' and 'Sugar Daddy'; and the snow pea 'Oregon Giant'.

White powdery coating covers leaves

Problem: The leaves and pods develop a white coating. The leaves may also curl and dry out.

Cause: Powdery mildew is a fungal disease spread by airborne spores. Its spores can grow in warmer, drier weather than those of most fungi, and the disease can kill pea plants.

Solution: Practice good garden sanitation. Use fungicidal sprays to slow the spread of the disease. Time your planting to minimize the risk, and select mildew-resistant varieties.

- Dispose of affected leaves and pods.
- At the first sign of powdery mildew, spray the leaves and stem with a baking soda solution (p.392), or use an organic sulfur fungicide. Repeat at 7- to 10-day intervals.

Sulfur won't kill fungus that's already growing, but it will prevent spores from germinating on more leaves.

- When planting new pea crops, sow early enough in spring so that the weather will still be cool when the peas are maturing. In mild-winter areas, plant in early to midfall.
- If powdery mildew persists, try resistant varieties, such as the shelling peas 'Knight', 'Maestro', and 'Bounty'; the snap peas 'Cascadia' and 'Sugar Bon'; and the snow pea 'Oregon Giant'.

Pale, winding trails mar leaves

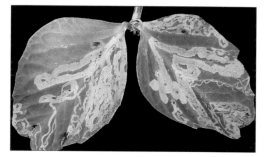

Problem: Light-colored winding trails appear on the leaves. Holding a leaf up to the light reveals dark shadows of insects in tunnels between the leaf surfaces.

Cause: Pea leafminers are the larvae of small flies that feed on the insides of leaves, leaving disfiguring trails. The damage is usually not serious unless the plant is still small or the insects are numerous.

Solution: Remove damaged leaves and cover seedlings. Spray damaged plants with insecticide. Attract wasps that parasitize the larvae.

- If the infestation is mild, pick off the leaves with leafminer trails and discard them outside of the garden.
- Protect young plants from further leafminer damage by covering them with an insect-excluding fabric floating row cover. To allow pollination by insects, remove the covering when peas bloom.
- If damage is severe, spray the leaves with neem, a botanical insecticide. Make sure to follow label directions carefully.
- To attract minute parasitic wasps, which help to control leafminers, grow nectar plants, such as baby-blue-eyes, catnip, and sweet alyssum.

Pepper

Capsicum annuum

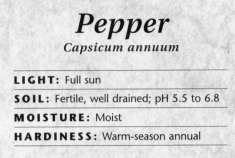

LIGHT: Full sun

SOIL: Fertile, well drained; pH 5.5 to 6.8

MOISTURE: Moist

HARDINESS: Warm-season annual

Fruits are mottled, leaves are curled, and plant is stunted

Problem: Fruits and leaf surfaces may be mottled with yellow or pale green. Leaf edges curl up. The plant may become stunted and die.

Cause: Peppers are susceptible to several viral diseases, including tobacco mosaic virus, alfalfa mosaic virus, curly top, tomato spotted wilt virus, and cucumber mosaic virus. Viruses are most problematic in dry weather. They are spread by feeding insects, such as leafhoppers, aphids, and thrips, and by contact with infected plants. Tobacco mosaic virus is spread by cigarette tobacco.

Solution: There is no effective treatment for viruses. Destroy infected plants before the disease spreads and weed regularly. Select resistant varieties and control feeding insects.

- Remove and destroy any pepper plant that shows symptoms.

- Keep weeds under control; they often harbor viral diseases and the insects that spread them.

- Avoid smoking when in the garden.

- In future years, plant varieties (p.123) that resist tobacco mosaic virus—no pepper varieties are resistant to cucumber mosaic virus and some other viruses.

- Cover seedlings with an insect-excluding fabric floating row cover. To allow pollination and fruit set, remove the covering when plants begin to bloom.

Spots appear on leaves; corky areas develop on fruits

Problem: Small spots appear on the leaves. They are initially yellowish green, later turning tan with dark edges. Fruit spots are brown, corky, and raised. Blossoms and leaves may drop, and infected fruits may decay.

Cause: Bacterial leaf spot is common on peppers everywhere, except in regions with dry summers. Humid, rainy, warm weather allows the disease to spread rapidly.

Solution: Practice good garden sanitation and nourish plants to discourage the disease. Even though leaf spot is bacterial, fungicide may slow its spread. Management is less effective if the weather is wet. Rotating crops also helps.

- Remove all infected parts of the plant as soon as you detect leaf spot, and pick up fallen leaves and flowers.

- When damage is discovered, apply a fertilizer with a 5-10-10 formulation (p.324) to help plants recover. Spray with a copper-based organic fungicide, repeating as often as label directions suggest.

- If spraying has no effect on a badly infected plant, remove the entire plant from the garden.

- Water peppers at soil level to avoid wetting the leaves, because the spores develop in wet areas. To avoid spreading the disease, don't work among wet plants.

- Rotate (p.115) peppers with other crops, planting new peppers in the same location only once every three to four years.

Fruits in full sun develop pale, sunken areas

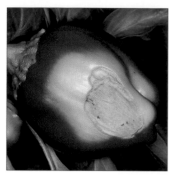

Problem: Areas on the top or one side of the fruit become pale and soft, then sunken and papery. Black mold may grow on the lesions.

Cause: Sunscald mars peppers when the sunlight is strong and the leaves don't provide enough cover to shade the fruit. Some varieties just don't have enough leaf cover, but the condition can also occur when disease causes the leaves to fall off. The mold that often grows on the lesions doesn't cause the problem; it's encouraged by the damage.

Solution: Shade susceptible plants, check for disease, and consider growing a leafier variety.

- If sunlight is particularly harsh, shade peppers with a commercial shade cloth or a light-filtering fabric floating row cover.

- Check for a disease that causes leaf loss, such as a tobacco mosaic or other viral infection (p.121), bacterial leaf spot (p.121), or fungal leaf spot (below).

- When planting new peppers, choose varieties that develop good leaf cover to shade the fruits, including the sweet pepper 'Admiral Hybrid' and the hot peppers 'Anaheim TMR' and 'Valencia'.

Pale spots appear on leaves

Problem: Pepper leaves and stems develop circular or oval spots of varying sizes. The spots are pale with dark brown edges. The leaves gradually turn yellow and fall. The fruits may rot at the stem.

Cause: Pepper leaf spot, or frog-eye leaf spot, is a fungal disease. Its spores are carried on seeds, in soil and plant debris, and by wind. This disease is most common in the Southeast, especially during rainy summers.

Solution: Remove infected parts, spray plants with fungicide, and protect exposed fruits. Rotate plants to prevent spore buildup.

- Remove and discard all infected plant parts.

- Spray infected leaves with a copper-based organic fungicide registered for use on pepper plants. Follow label directions carefully.

- To prevent sunscald (left), shade the fruits of plants that lose many leaves.

- Rotate (p.115) plantings every two years.

Dark spots disfigure fruits

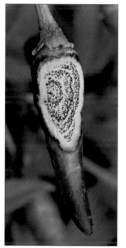

Problem: Dark areas with concentric rings appear on both green and ripe fruits. There may also be small dark spots on leaves and stems.

Cause: Pepper anthracnose is a fungal disease. Anthracnose spores are carried on pepper seeds, on tomato-family weeds, and by infected pepper plants and debris. The disease develops in moist, hot weather.

Solution: Spray with a fungicide to control the disease. Discourage it with good garden sanitation, by harvesting fruits in a timely manner, and by rotating crops.

- At the first sign of disease, apply a synthetic fungicide registered for peppers that contains the active ingredient maneb. Follow label directions carefully.

- If the fungicide is not effective, remove and dispose of infected fruits, don't compost.

- Water peppers at soil level to avoid wetting the leaves, because the spores develop in water. To avoid spreading the disease, don't work among wet plants.

- Pick fruit as soon as it matures.

- At the end of the season, remove infected plants from the garden and destroy them.

- To discourage future outbreaks, rotate (p.115) peppers with other crops on a three-year schedule.

- Before you plant, make sure you obtain seeds or seedlings that are certified disease free. Seedlings grown from infected seeds won't show symptoms until they set fruit.

Black beetles with long snouts are on plants, fruits are spoiled

Problem: Buds and young fruits turn yellow and fall from the plant. Flowers that do open are misshapen. Some fruits have small entrance holes and yellow or red blotches. You may find black beetles on the plant or legless white larvae feeding in peppers.

Cause: Pepper weevils are dark brown or black beetles with long, downturned snouts. They are a serious problem in the Southwest and Southeast. Adults feed primarily on flower buds and fruits, while larvae bore into the buds and fruits and feed inside. Adults overwinter in debris and on weeds.

Solution: Remove infected parts and plant debris to reduce damage to present and future crops. An insecticide may help.

- Remove infested buds or fruits, including fallen ones.

- As a preventive measure, spray with the botanical insecticide neem, following label directions carefully. This will reduce populations of adult weevils but won't kill larvae within buds or fruits.

- At the end of the season, remove pepper plants and weed debris from the garden.

Plant appears healthy, but no fruits form

Problem: The plant has good color and flowers form, but they fall off without making fruits. Or the plant is bushy and deep green but has few or no flowers.

Cause: Peppers will not set fruit if the soil is too dry or if temperatures are too high or too low. All peppers drop blossoms below 60°F, and sweet peppers also shed flowers at temperatures above 90°F. Hot pepper varieties may continue to bear fruits in hotter weather than do sweet or bell varieties. Also, a plant that receives excess nitrogen fertilizer will form few or no blossoms.

Solution: Improve growing conditions and choose varieties and planting times suitable for your location.

- Water deeply anytime the soil is dry 1 to 2 inches beneath the surface.

- In midsummer in a hot area, provide afternoon shade with a shade cloth or a light-filtering fabric floating row cover.

- Where summer nights are cool, plant pepper varieties that are described in seed catalogs as setting fruits well in cool weather.

- In a hot area, time the planting of sweet peppers so that they mature either before or after the hottest days of summer.

- Transplant pepper plants when small (about 4 inches tall). Peppers are sensitive to transplanting; larger plants often drop flowers and immature fruits after being moved.

- When planting, use a fertilizer that contains more phosphorus than nitrogen, such as a 5-10-10 formulation (p.324). Follow the label directions for fertilizing peppers if they are listed.

WISE CHOICES

Pepper plants are susceptible to tobacco mosaic virus (p.121), an incurable disease, which is spread by sap-sucking insects and by a gardener smoking tobacco in the pepper patch. Controlling insects and refraining from smoking while gardening will discourage the spread of this disease, as will planting resistant varieties and types. The following peppers—and others labeled "TMV" in catalogs and at nurseries—tolerate the disease.

Sweet Pepper
'Bell Boy Hybrid', 'Big Berth', 'Golden Summer Hybrid', 'Lilac Hybrid', 'Park's Early Thickset', 'Ultra Set', and 'Valencia'

Banana Pepper
'Sweet Banana'

Pimento Pepper
'Pimento Perfection' and 'Pimento Select'

Hot Pepper
'Anaheim TMR', 'Delicias Hybrid', 'Flash Hybrid', 'Garden Salsa Hybrid', 'Hungarian Hot Wax', Jalapeno, Poblano 'Jaloro', 'Sonora', and 'Super Cayenne'.

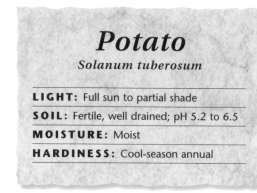

Potato
Solanum tuberosum

LIGHT: Full sun to partial shade

SOIL: Fertile, well drained; pH 5.2 to 6.5

MOISTURE: Moist

HARDINESS: Cool-season annual

Leaves are chewed or eaten by orange beetles

Problem: The leaves of potato plants are chewed or eaten. Rounded, yellow-and-black-striped beetles and orange-red larvae may both be visible on foliage.

Cause: Both adults and larvae of the Colorado potato beetle eat foliage. Adults, larvae, and the yellow-orange eggs may all be visible on leaves or leaf undersides at the same time. Adult beetles overwinter in the soil.

Solution: To control pests, handpick and spray. To deter them, practice good garden sanitation, mulch, attract natural predators, and grow resistant varieties.

● Crush eggs. Handpick beetles and larvae.

● From late spring to midsummer, control the first generation of larvae by applying either BTSD, a biological insecticide, or neem, a botanical insecticide. Control larvae discovered after midsummer by applying BTSD. Follow label directions carefully.

● Control adults by alternately using a synthetic insecticide containing the active ingredient methoxychlor and one containing the active ingredient carbaryl. Use formulations registered for potatoes and follow label directions carefully.

● Mulch plants with straw as a deterrent.

● Cut foliage 1 inch below the soil surface 10 to 14 days before harvest and discard.

● Turn soil in fall to kill overwintering adults.

● Discourage future infestations by growing nectar plants, such as yarrow, dill, and sunflower, to attract ladybugs and lacewings, which will feed on beetle eggs.

● Plant resistant varieties, such as 'Katahdin' and 'Sequoia'.

Leaves and stems have lesions

Problem: Areas on the leaves and stems are dark brown. A downy white fungal growth appears in moist weather, mainly on leaf undersides. Rotten blotches develop on tubers.

Cause: Potato late blight is caused by the same fungus that causes late blight of tomatoes (p.135). Disease spores are carried by wind and water from infected leaves to tubers that are near the soil surface. Humid or foggy weather, or heavy dew favors the disease. The disease overwinters in decaying plants and in harvested and stored tubers.

Solution: To protect tubers, mound soil and spray. Also, practice good garden sanitation, select resistant varieties, and rotate crops.

● If blight occurs, mound soil over bases of plants so that spores can't fall onto tubers.

● In moist weather, protect healthy plants by spraying a synthetic fungicide registered for potatoes that contains the active ingredient mancozeb. Apply every 5 to 10 days or as needed for control. Follow label directions. Don't use a fungicide containing metalaxyl; some strains of fungus are resistant to it.

● Water plants at ground level, using drip irrigation or a soaker hose, to keep the foliage dry, since spores mature in moisture.

● After the foliage dies back, wait a week before harvesting the tubers. After harvest, remove and destroy all plant debris.

● Rotate (p.115) potatoes yearly.

● Next season, plant resistant varieties (box, facing page). Or select certified disease-free starter potatoes.

Pinkish white caterpillars tunnel into tubers and stems

Problem: As the plant grows, new shoots and young leaves wilt and shrivel. If you cut away damaged parts, you may find small pinkish white caterpillars inside the stems. When you dig the potato out of the ground, you find narrow tunnels in it. There may also be insect debris at the tunnel openings.

Cause: Potato tuberworms are the larvae of a small moth that lays eggs on potato plants and tubers. Early in the season, caterpillars feed on stems and leaves; later generations feed on tubers. They overwinter in cocoons in stored potatoes or in debris left in the garden.

Solution: Discard infested plants and tubers. Protect plants with mounded soil and mulch. Practice good garden sanitation. Rotate crops.

- Before digging the tubers, remove infested plants from the garden. Also discard any infested tubers, and do not leave healthy tubers exposed to egg-laying moths.

- Protect healthy plants by making a barrier with soil and mulch. Hill up a 2-inch layer of soil around the plants and cover it well with an organic mulch.

- Amend the soil with compost or other organic matter to minimize soil cracking and make it more difficult for pests to reach the tubers.

- Clean up plant debris in fall and remove all potato-family weeds, such as wild night-shades. Also remove any volunteer potato plants that may have sprouted from last year's leftovers; they could be carrying last year's tuberworms.

- Rotate (p.115) potato-family plants with other crops every two years.

- In future years, do not plant seed pieces from potentially infested potatoes.

Tubers have scabby, raised, or sunken patches

Problem: Patches of dark, corky scabs cover most of the potato skin. Other parts of the tuber have sunken, rotted spots.

Cause: Potato scab is a fungal disease that affects potato skins. Although the fungus lives in many soils, scab is

---

WISE CHOICES

A number of potato varieties are resistant to different diseases. Here are some varieties that resist problems listed here or in the troubleshooting guide (p.88).

Brown-skinned Varieties
- 'Butte': scab
- 'Frontier Russet': late blight, scab, fusarium dry rot, verticillium wilt
- 'Kennebec': late blight, mosaic virus
- 'Norgold M': heat resistant

Red-skinned Varieties
- 'Bison': late blight, scab
- 'Buffalo': late blight, scab, verticillium wilt
- 'Red Cloud': early blight, scab

Yellow-fleshed Variety
- 'Island Sunshine': late blight

prevalent in soil that is soggy and rich in decaying organic matter; it persist for years. The disease is most active when the soil pH is between 5.7 and 7.5 and temperatures are between 70° to 85°F.

Solution: Test the soil pH and adjust it if necessary. Provide good growing conditions, rotate crops, and plant disease-free seed pieces from resistant potato varieties.

- If potato scab is a problem, acidify the soil to achieve a pH between 5.2 and 5.5. Test the pH (p.329) and add aluminum sulfate as needed, according to package directions.

- Make sure that the soil is well drained and do not overwater. Water only when the soil is dry 1 to 2 inches beneath the surface.

- Rotate (p.115) potatoes with nonsusceptible crops every three to four years, or rotate with the cover crops rye or oats. Crops that are susceptible include beets, carrots, spinach, turnips, parsnips, and radishes.

- Avoid planting in soil that has recently been limed or amended with alkaline wood ashes. Also, wait at least one month before planting in soil to which manure has been added, as it favors the disease.

- Plant only certified disease-free seed pieces. Never plant potentially infected potatoes from the grocery store.

- Grow varieties with rough, reddish brown, or "russeted," skin; these resist potato scab better than smooth-skinned types do. Or select other resistant varieties (p.125).

TIME-TESTED TECHNIQUES

USING BENEFICIAL NEMATODES

Nematodes are microscopic worms that live in soils all over the world. Beneficial nematodes (*Steinernema* spp.) prey on a wide range of plant pests, from maggots and grubs to ants and cutworms. Nematodes enter the bodies of their prey and kill them in a day or two. As the nematodes reproduce, their young seek out more pests to parasitize.

Beneficial nematodes are safe and easy to use. They are available from garden centers or mail-order suppliers. Mix the product with water and apply to the soil with a watering can. Reapply as needed every three to six weeks.

Lower leaves develop brown spots ringed with tan

Problem: Brown spots appear on the leaves, usually just after flowering has occurred. The spots may enlarge and merge. The tuber has slightly sunken dark spots, and there may also be shallow areas of dark, dry rot under the surface spots. The tuber spots may not develop until the potatoes are in storage.

Cause: Potato early blight is a fungal disease that affects potato leaves and tomato leaves similarly. The spores are carried by infected tomato seeds and potato tubers, wind, splashing water, and sometimes insect flea beetles. The disease develops in warm, moist weather; 85°F is optimal. It survives in soil on decaying infected plant material and in tubers.

Solution: Protect tubers with mounded soil and a fungicide. Use proper gardening and harvesting techniques, and plant healthy, disease-resistant seed potatoes.

- If early blight appears, mound soil around the plants to keep the disease spores from falling onto the tubers.

- For severe outbreaks, use a synthetic fungicide registered for potatoes that contains the active ingredient maneb or mancozeb every 5 to 10 days, after symptoms appear. Follow label directions carefully.

- Keep plant leaves dry. Water only at ground level, using a soaker hose or drip irrigation. Grow potatoes in full sun.

- Wait until plant tops die before you dig up the tubers, so they can develop tough skins. Do not store tubers showing symptoms.

- Clean up all plant debris after harvest.

- Grow only certified, disease-free starter plants. Do not plant potentially infected potatoes from the grocery store.

- Select resistant varieties (p.125).

Radish
Raphanus sativus

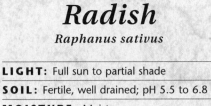

LIGHT: Full sun to partial shade

SOIL: Fertile, well drained; pH 5.5 to 6.8

MOISTURE: Moist

HARDINESS: Cool-season annual

Healthy root splits open

Problem: When you pull up a radish, you find that the root has split but is otherwise healthy.

Cause: Uneven moisture levels can cause radish roots to crack open, especially when a sudden supply of water causes the inside of the root to grow more quickly than the outside.

Solution: Make sure radishes receive a consistent supply of water while they are growing and harvest promptly.

- Water whenever the soil is dry 1 inch beneath the surface. A heavy rain may still cause some roots to split, but if watering has been consistent and adequate, fewer cracks are likely to develop.

- Pull up radishes as soon as they are plump and ripe and the root skin is well colored.

Discolored areas appear in root

Problem: The radish root is riddled with slimy tunnels that contain small, white, legless larvae. Young plants may wilt on warm days.

Cause: Cabbage maggots are the larvae of a small fly and burrow into radish roots. Their tunneling may merely make the roots unappetizing, or it may kill the plants.

Solution: To control infestations, use predators, insecticides, and pest barriers. Time plantings to limit the problem.

- To kill maggots, apply beneficial nematodes (facing page), a biological control, to the soil when pests are active.

- For persistent infestations, apply to the soil at planting time a synthetic insecticide registered for radishes that contains the active ingredient diazinon. Follow label directions carefully.

- Grow young plants under a fabric floating row cover to exclude insects. Make sure plants do not overheat as the weather warms.

- Spread diatomaceous earth, an abrasive dust, around plants.

- In mild-winter areas, grow radishes in fall through early spring, when maggots are inactive.

Root does not enlarge

Problem: The plant forms leafy growth, but the root stays narrow, not forming the expected radish.

Cause: Radish roots may not enlarge properly if the plants receive excess nitrogen or if the temperature rises above 85°F. The problem can also result from inadequate thinning.

Solution: Provide proper growing conditions and time plantings.

- Do not overfertilize. Radishes should not require fertilizer when grown in average garden soil. However, if your soil is poor, fertilize with a 5-10-10 formulation (p.324) two to three days before sowing seeds.

- Thin radish seedlings to 1 to 2 inches when they have four true leaves.

- Plan to plant when temperatures are cool. In spring, sow seeds three to four weeks before the last expected frost date for your region. In fall, sow two to three weeks before the first expected frost date.

The mild winters in the Gulf Coast region challenge rhubarb, which grows best where the ground freezes. In addition, rhubarb is likely to die from disease during hot, humid summers.

In areas with such summers, you're most likely to succeed if you grow rhubarb as a winter annual. Start seeds of the variety 'Victoria' in pots in September for planting in November.

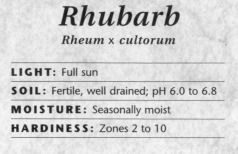

Rhubarb
Rheum x *cultorum*

LIGHT: Full sun

SOIL: Fertile, well drained; pH 6.0 to 6.8

MOISTURE: Seasonally moist

HARDINESS: Zones 2 to 10

Plant wilts and collapses; leaves or stems turn yellow or brown

Problem: Leaf stems have sunken, yellow-brown spots. The discoloration spreads until the leaves wilt and the leaf bases rot; the decay ultimately moves into the roots.

Cause: Phytophthora crown rot, or foot rot, is a fungal disease that affects rhubarb in central and eastern states. Spores live in the soil and germinate in warm, moist conditions. Continued infection kills rhubarb plants.

Solution: Use a fungicide to control the disease, but discard severely damaged plants. Rotate plantings and water carefully.

- For minor infections, spray the base of the plant (called the crown) with an organic copper-sulfate fungicide. Follow label directions carefully.

- In a severe case, remove the diseased plant from the garden.

- Buy plants that are certified disease free.

- Rotate crops (p.115), planting them in a different part of the garden, in well-drained soil or in a raised bed (p.328). Water only when the soil is dry 1 inch below the surface.

Stems have small holes

Problem: Small holes or dark spots appear on leaf stems. You may see small beetles with downturned snouts on the plant.

Cause: Rhubarb curculios are black beetles that feed on the leaf stems and lay eggs in them. Damage is usually minor; curculios feed mainly on curly-dock weeds.

Solution: Handpick the beetles. Give special attention to weeding, fertilizing, and watering to improve growing conditions.

- Remove and crush rhubarb curculios when you see them.

- Remove curly dock from your garden; it is a weed that attracts beetles.

- Fertilize rhubarb with a half cup of 5-10-10 fertilizer (p.324) per plant in early spring and again after the main harvest.

- During summer dry spells, water deeply once a week—healthy plants repel insects.

Plant has thin stems

Problem: A once-vigorous rhubarb plant now produces only spindly leaf stems.

Cause: Plants are overcrowded. Like other perennials, rhubarb grows new plants from the base, or crown, each season. After a few years, overcrowding causes thin leaf stems.

Solution: Divide and replant rhubarb plants every three to four years.

- Dig plants in early spring (or autumn in mild climates). Cut roots into sections, each with at least one leaf bud, and replant with ample space between sections.

- Or, leave the plant in the ground, and dig the soil away from one side. Cut through and remove part of the roots and new buds to give the original plant room to spread.

Spinach
Spinacia oleracea

LIGHT: Full sun to partial shade

SOIL: Well drained; pH 6.0 to 7.0

MOISTURE: Moist

HARDINESS: Cool-season annual

Leaves are pale and moldy

Problem: Patches of yellow or pale green appear on leaves. Under humid conditions, gray fuzz develops on leaf undersides.

Cause: Spinach downy mildew, or blue mold, is a fungal disease. Spores splash up from the soil and germinate on the leaves in cool, moist weather. The disease spreads quickly, killing entire plantings.

Solution: Remove infected leaves, practice good garden sanitation, grow resistant varieties, and rotate crops.

- Remove and destroy infected leaves.
- Avoid wetting spinach leaves, and thin plants to improve air circulation.
- Rotate (p.115) spinach with other crops on a two- to three-year cycle.

Leaves have tan, winding lines

Problem: Some leaves have pale, winding lines.

Cause: Spinach leafminers are the larvae of a small fly. The larvae tunnel through leaves before dropping to the soil to mature.

Solution: Discard infested leaves, and mulch to disrupt the egg-laying cycle. Put a protective cover over seedlings.

- Pick and dispose of infested leaves.
- Mulch crop with plastic sheeting to keep maggots from dropping to the soil.
- Cover seedlings with a floating row cover.

Leaves yellow and curl

Problem: Leaves are yellow, curled, puckered, or mottled. Inner leaves are affected first. Plants become stunted.

Cause: Spinach blight is an incurable virus, usually cucumber mosaic virus. Viruses are spread by sap-sucking insects like aphids.

Solution: Remove infected plants and control aphids and weeds. Select different varieties.

- Remove any plant with symptoms.
- Knock aphids off plants with a strong spray of water from a hose. In severe cases, spray insecticidal soap or the botanical insecticide neem, following label directions.
- Remove weeds, which can harbor viruses.
- Grow smooth-leaf or resistant varieties (box, below).

WISE CHOICES

These varieties resist problems listed here or in the troubleshooting guide (p.88).

Crinkled-leaf (savoyed) Spinach
- 'Grandstand': downy mildew, cucumber mosaic virus, bolting
- 'Longstanding Savoy #653': bolting
- 'Marathon': bolting
- 'Melody': downy mildew, cucumber mosaic virus

Smooth-leaf Spinach
- 'Hector': downy mildew, bolting
- 'Nordic IV': downy mildew
- 'Olympia': downy mildew, bolting
- 'Space': downy mildew, bolting

DID YOU KNOW?

Long, hot days can cause spinach to "bolt"—to flower before maturing. To prevent this, plant for an early or late harvest and select a bolt-resistant variety (box, below). If afternoons are torrid, shade your plants with fabric, or plant spinach in a shady area.

Squash and Pumpkin

Cucurbita spp.

LIGHT: Full sun

SOIL: Fertile, well drained; pH 6.0 to 6.5

MOISTURE: Moist

HARDINESS: Warm-season annuals

Fruits or blossoms develop gray fuzz

Problem: The flowers or fruits decay, and the area behind them is rotten. They have a white, gray, or purple mold, and small black dots may form on the moldy growth.

Cause: Several fungi cause squash fruits to rot. Choanephora decays blossoms and fruits of squashes and pumpkins, and the black dots are spores that spread the disease. Botrytis gray mold infects many kinds of plants. Its spores are medium gray. Both fungi thrive in moist weather.

Solution: Discard infected plant parts. To discourage disease spread, keep fruits and foliage dry, and leave space between plants.

- Remove any infected flowers and fruits from the garden as soon as you see them. Check other garden plants for signs of disease, and attend to them as well.
- Protect healthy squashes and pumpkins by watering at ground level. Also, water early in the day to give foliage time to dry. If fruits get wet, set them on rocks or flowerpots to keep them off the moist ground.
- Don't overcrowd the plants. Space squashes and pumpkins at least 3 feet apart to allow adequate air circulation.

Irregular yellow spots appear on leaves

Problem: Yellow splotches appear on the tops of leaves. The undersides of leaves have brown spots, sometimes covered with a purplish or gray downy mildew. The damage often begins on leaves nearest the center of the hill and spreads outward to other leaves. Entire leaves may shrivel and die, and infected fruits shrivel and have poor flavor.

Cause: Downy mildew is a fungal disease that thrives in warm, damp weather and is often at its worst in July and August. The spores are spread by wind and feeding insects, particularly cucumber beetles.

Solution: Remove infected plants, control insects, and practice good garden sanitation.

- Dispose of infected plants.
- Handpick beetles and destroy them.
- Apply compost tea (p.392), which has disease-fighting organisms, to the soil around plants, and mulch with a 3-inch-thick layer of compost to discourage future infection.
- At the end of the season, clean up and compost all squash plants and fallen debris.
- In the future, cover squash seedlings with an insect-excluding fabric floating row cover. To ensure pollination, remove the covering when plants begin to bloom.

Leaves and vines suddenly wilt

Problem: All or parts of squash or pumpkin vines wilt on warm days. Holes appear in the stems above wilted branches, with a greenish yellow sawdustlike material at the openings.

Cause: Squash vine borers are the larvae of a moth with a metallic green body and transparent wings. Their favorite plant is squash, but they also damage pumpkins. The wrinkled white caterpillars eat the insides of stems; later, they may feed on fruits as well. They overwinter in the soil as pupae.

Solution: Remove pests from stems. Discourage future problems with good sanitation, crop rotation, timing, and plant selection.

- Slit an infested stem with a razor blade and remove the insect. Mound soil over the damaged stem area to encourage new roots.
- Protect new plantings with an insect-excluding fabric floating row cover. Remove the cover as the plants come into bloom, so that pollination can occur.
- Turn the soil in fall and again in spring to kill overwintering pupae. If the problem persists, rotate (p.115) squash-family plants to a different location next year.
- Sow new plants as early as possible, so that they are large and robust by the time borer eggs begin to hatch in late June and July. Grow resistant varieties (box, above right).

Insects cause leaves to develop pale patches that blacken

Problem: The leaves develop light green spots that turn black and crisp. There are many insects, especially under leaves. The largest are dark brown. There may also be smaller gray insects and tiny green-and-red ones. Young plants may die, while older ones lose runners.

Cause: Anasa wilt is caused by squash bugs. Adult squash bugs and smaller immature ones injure squashes and pumpkins by sucking out plant sap. As they feed, they inject a poison that causes leaves to turn black and die. Adults overwinter in garden debris or under boards and rocks.

Solution: Handpicking, insecticides, garden cleanup, and crop rotation discourage infestations.

- Handpick and crush squash bugs when you detect

WISE CHOICES

Squash vine borers and squash bugs (both left) weaken and damage squash plants by feeding on them. But these insects find some varieties of squash more palatable than others.

Varieties somewhat resistant to squash borers include the winter squashes 'Butternut' and 'Green Striped Cushaw'.

Varieties of squash resistant to squash bugs include 'Butternut', 'Early Summer Crookneck', 'Improved Green Hubbard', and 'Royal Acorn'.

them. When crushed, they emit an unpleasant odor but are harmless.

- To capture groups of bugs, lay a board on the ground near squash plants; in the early morning you'll find bugs hiding under it.
- If an infestation is severe or on young plants, use a synthetic insecticide registered for squashes or pumpkins that contains the active ingredient carbaryl. Follow label directions carefully. Apply the insecticide at dusk to avoid killing honeybees.
- To avert problems the following year, clean up plant debris in the garden at the end of the season. Rotate (p.115) squash-family plants with other plants every year.
- Grow resistant varieties (box, above).

A healthy plant flowers but develops no fruit

Problem: A healthy-looking young plant has many flowers but no fruits.

Cause: Squash plants have two types of flowers: male and female. Male flowers, which produce pollen but no fruits, open before the female flowers. About a week later, the fertile female flowers open. Female flowers can be distinguished by a squash-shaped bulge at the base of the flower.

Solution: Provide good growing conditions and wait for both flowers to develop.

- Plant squash seeds in warm, rich garden soil. When plants emerge, apply a low-nitrogen fertilizer, such as 5-10-10 (p.324), according to package directions. Mulch with compost, and irrigate to keep the soil moist 1 inch beneath the surface.

- Look for slender-stemmed male flowers to open first. Wait another week for the bulbous-based female flowers to open before looking for small squashes to develop.

Tan or grayish, angular spots develop on leaves

Problem: Tan or gray, bleached-looking spots appear on the leaves, often developing first between the veins. The spots dry out over time and may turn into holes. Infected fruits develop small sunken spots, and the entire fruit then quickly rots.

Cause: Angular leaf spot is a bacterial disease that overwinters in plant debris and can be transmitted by infected seeds.

Solution: Practice good garden sanitation and buy healthy seeds. Plant in disease-free soil.

- When symptoms appear, remove and destroy infected plants.

- To keep healthy plants disease free, remove plant debris frequently from the garden, especially in the fall to prevent the disease from overwintering.

- Mulch squash and pumpkin plants with a 3-inch-thick layer of compost, which has disease-inhibiting organisms, and periodically drench the soil with disease-inhibiting compost tea (p.392).

- In the future, do not save seeds from potentially infected plants. Buy certified disease-free seeds from a garden center or mail-order source.

- If the disease has been a problem in the past, plant squashes and pumpkins where they have not previously grown, or grow them in raised beds of disease-free soil.

Fruits are shriveled or fail to develop

Problem: The plant looks healthy and has blossoms, but the fruits turn yellow and shrivel. Fruits may not form at all.

Cause: Lack of pollination causes female blossoms to drop without forming fruits. Incomplete pollination produces fruits that start to enlarge but then shrivel. The reason for poor pollination is often a lack of bee activity, which may be the result of cold, wet weather; the use of pesticides; or the presence of an insect-excluding floating row cover to protect young plants. Also, pumpkin and squash plants can support only a limited number of fruits and then may abort new ones as they begin to develop.

Solution: Supplement the work of bees by hand-pollinating. Use pesticides with care. Encourage new fruits by early harvesting.

- Hand-pollinate. Pick a male flower that has released its pollen, and use it to spread pollen onto the yellow cushion in the middle of a female flower.

- Spray pesticides wisely. If you must use an insecticide that is toxic to bees, spray in the evening, when bees are inactive. Use an insecticide registered for squashes or pumpkins and follow label directions carefully.

- To promote more fruit growth, harvest summer squash while the fruits are small. This method won't work for winter squash, which produces its fruits all at once.

Sweet Potato
Ipomoea batatas

LIGHT: Full sun

SOIL: Sandy loam; pH 5.5 to 6.5

MOISTURE: Seasonally dry

HARDINESS: Tender annual

Roots have furrows with larvae in them

Problem: Narrow channels or holes are chewed into tubers. Larvae are present. The leaf edges have rounded notches.

Cause: White-fringed beetles are a serious pest in the East and Southeast. Major damage is caused by the larvae, or grubs, which feed on tubers. The brownish gray beetles don't fly; they infest localized areas and colonize wider areas slowly. Larvae are spread by tools or other objects that contact infested soil.

Solution: Spray with insecticide, destroy host weeds, limit watering, rotate crops, and select resistant varieties.

- Spray plants thoroughly with a synthetic insecticide registered for sweet potatoes that contains the active ingredient carbaryl. Follow label directions carefully. Repeat every two weeks until four weeks before harvest. Results may take a year because the grubs in the soil may survive spraying.
- Keep whitefringed beetles away from healthy plants by removing nearby broadleaf weeds.
- Don't overwater as tubers begin to develop in summer. Allow the soil to dry out between waterings.
- In future seasons, rotate (p.115) plantings of sweet potatoes with corn.
- Before planting next year, select varieties that are less prone to injury from beetles, such as 'Beauregard', 'Regal', and 'Resisto'.

White larvae tunnel into tubers

Problem: Tubers are peppered with small, deep holes that may contain white wormlike larvae. Antlike creatures swarm on the ground.

Cause: Sweet potato weevils are a serious problem east of the Mississippi. Often mistaken for ants, the blue-black beetles are ¼ inch long. They burrow into tubers, leaving small black holes.

Solution: Destroy infested plants, remove host plants, and buy healthy starter plants.

- If you see beetles, inspect the tubers for holes. Dig up and remove infested ones.
- Weed to remove plants that harbor pests.
- In future seasons, buy slips (starter plants) that are certified weevil free.

Dark spots appear on tubers

Problem: Harvested tubers have brown or blackened areas. The spots may peel off the surface or may be deeper and have a greenish, bitter-tasting area just beneath them.

Cause: Two fungal diseases may be the cause. Scurf produces grayish brown to black areas that are skin deep and may peel off. Black rot causes deeper, more damaging lesions. Spores of both fungi are carried in seeds and soil.

Solution: Select disease-free and resistant varieties of starter plants, and rotate crops.

- Obtain slips (starter plants) that are certified disease free. Grow them in a raised bed (p.328), in sterile soil mix in containers, or in soil never used before for sweet potatoes.
- Select a variety, such as 'Jasper', resistant to scurf, or 'Allgold', resistant to black rot.
- Rotate (p.115) sweet potatoes with other crops on a three- to four-year cycle.

REGIONAL FOCUS
CENTRAL

Sweet potatoes require a long, warm summer to develop well. And temperatures below 50°F can damage them. If your area of the Midwest receives at least 90 days of warm weather, try early varieties such as 'Centennial' and 'Georgia Jet'. Grow them in a raised bed (p.328), using a black plastic mulch to warm the soil. Tuck the edges of the plastic firmly in the soil, and cut slits in the plastic through which to insert the plants.

Tomato
Lycopersicon esculentum

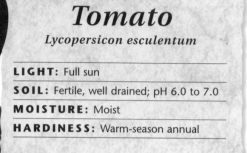

LIGHT: Full sun

SOIL: Fertile, well drained; pH 6.0 to 7.0

MOISTURE: Moist

HARDINESS: Warm-season annual

Green caterpillars eat large holes in fruits and leaves

Problem: Damage usually starts in the middle of the plant, where leaves are chewed or eaten completely. Holes may also be eaten in the fruits. Close inspection reveals a green caterpillar with a large rear prong that looks like a horn.

Cause: Tomato hornworms are the larvae of sphinx moths. They are green with white markings. Each hornworm can do substantial damage to tomato plantings.

Solution: Handpick and apply insecticides to control this pest. Attract natural predators.

● Handpick and dispose of caterpillars. But if you see hornworms that have white cocoons on their backs, leave them in the garden. The cocoons nurture parasitic wasp pupae that will soon emerge to kill these and other hornworms.

● If the problem persists, spray small hornworms with varieties of the biological insecticide BTK or BTA. Spray large hornworms with neem, a botanical insecticide. Follow label directions carefully.

● Plant small-flowered nectar plants such as dill, sweet alyssum, and scabious, allowing them to flower to attract beneficial insects.

Fruits have holes in stem ends

Problem: Holes appear in the tops of fruits; leaves may be eaten. You may find green- or brown-striped caterpillars.

Cause: Tomato fruitworms are caterpillars that move from plant to plant, eating into fruits and leaves. From Virginia south, pupae overwinter in the soil.

Solution: Handpick fruitworms or spray them with an insecticide. Prevent overwintering.

● If you see only a few caterpillars, handpick and destroy them and the damaged fruits.

● If an infestation is severe, spray the plants. For small fruitworms, use a variety of the biological insecticide BTK or BTA. Spray large ones with neem, a botanical insecticide. Follow label directions carefully.

● In mild-winter areas, turn the soil in late fall to prevent pupae from overwintering.

Lower leaves have brown spots with rings

Problem: Irregularly shaped brown spots with a subtle bull's-eye pattern appear on the lower leaves, then gradually move higher. Badly infected leaves turn yellow and drop off. Fruits have dark, sunken blemishes. Seedlings may have a spot on the stem.

Cause: Early blight (alternaria blight) is a fungal disease most active in warm, moist weather. Spores are spread by wind, splashing water, and seeds. They overwinter in plant debris left in the garden and on tomato-family weeds, such as wild nightshades.

Solution: Spray, use good garden sanitation, rotate crops, and buy healthy, resistant seeds.

● Apply a synthetic fungicide registered for tomatoes that contains the active ingredi-

ent maneb, or mancozeb. Follow label
directions carefully.

- If sprays don't work, remove the infected
  plants and fallen debris from the garden.
- To avoid spreading blight, water at ground
  level. Don't work among wet plants.
- Rotate (p.115) tomatoes and related crops
  with others on a two- to three-year cycle.
- Obtain seeds that are certified disease free.
  Select blight-resistant varieties (box, right).

Leaves and stems have dark blotches

Problem: Dark green or brown patches appear
on leaves and stems. In humid weather, leaf
undersides develop gray fuzz. The stem ends
of fruits have slick brown areas. Badly infected leaves drop. The plant often dies.

Cause: Tomato late blight is a fungal disease.
Its spores germinate in humid weather when
days are moderately warm and nights are
cool. They are carried by wind, water, and
tools. The fungus overwinters in potatoes left
in the ground and on tomato-family weeds.

Solution: To discourage the disease, spray,
avoid crowding, and practice good sanitation.

- At the first sign of infection, apply a synthetic fungicide registered for tomatoes
  that contains the active ingredient maneb,
  or mancozeb. Follow label directions. Don't
  use a fungicide containing metalaxyl; many
  late-blight strains are resistant to it.
- Remove and destroy badly infected plants.
- Water plants at ground level. Leave space
  between plants for adequate air circulation.
- Remove all tomato-family plants, such as
  potatoes, eggplants, and weeds, including
  nightshade, after harvest and throughout
  winter. Destroy volunteer potato plants.

Fruits crack and split open

Problem: Cracks
circle the stem
end of ripening
fruits or stretch
down from the
stem end. They
can be long and
deep, causing the
fruits to rot.

Cause: A growth
spurt caused by a
sudden increase in
soil moisture after
a prolonged drought causes the skins to split.

Solution: Provide adequate water and grow
resistant varieties to avoid cracked tomatoes.

- Water as needed to keep soil evenly moist.
- If droughts are common in your area, select
  a crack-resistant variety (box, below).

WISE CHOICES

The varieties below resist tomato disorders discussed
here or in the Quick Troubleshooter (p.88). As in catalogs, the initials after the variety name indicate kinds of
resistance. Double initials signal resistance to more
than one strain of a disease.

V = verticillium wilt	T = tobacco mosaic virus
F = fusarium wilt	A = alternaria (early blight)
N = nematodes	

Large Red Varieties
- 'Celebrity': VFFNTA
- 'Early Girl': VFF
- 'Early Pick': VF, cold tolerant
- 'Floramerica': VFFA, catface resistant
- 'Hawaiian': VFNT, heat tolerant
- 'Homestead 24': F, heat and catface resistant
- 'Mountain Spring': VFF, resistant to cracking and
  blossom-end rot
- 'Solar Set': VFF, heat resistant
- 'Stupice': cold tolerant

Pear Tomato Varieties
- 'Classica': VFFNA, blossom-end rot resistant
- 'Viva Italia': VFFNA, bacterial spot resistant

Small-fruited Varieties
- 'Sweet Chelsea': VFNT, resists 15 different diseases
- 'Sweet Million': FNT, crack tolerant

Yellow Varieties
- 'Lemon Boy': VFN
- 'Mountain Gold': VFF, crack resistant

REGIONAL FOCUS
SOUTHEAST

Spider mites (p.88) can infest tomatoes anywhere in the United States, but a related species, tomato russet mite, is a particular problem in the Southwest, where the feeding mites turn leaves a dirty bronze-yellow color.

If you suspect these mites have been active in previous years but have not yet appeared this year, apply an organic sulfur spray to full-size plants. Apply it again in a month if the mites do turn up. This schedule of sulfur applications kills the tomato russet mites but spares predatory mites that help you to control the pests.

Bottoms of tomatoes have brown sunken areas

Problem: Brown, sunken, watery areas appear on the bottom, or blossom end, of the ripening tomato fruits. Later, these areas become black, dry, and leathery or develop mold.

Cause: Blossom-end rot is caused by a shortage of the soluble nutrient calcium, which is in the soil but often unavailable to plants as a result of uneven watering.

Solution: Salvage fruits. Watch watering and growing techniques. Grow resistant varieties.

- Harvest affected fruits; they are edible if you cut away the damage.
- Water tomatoes deeply when the soil is dry 1 to 2 inches beneath the surface.
- Spread a 3-inch-deep layer of water-conserving organic mulch at the base of plants.
- Select rot-resistant varieties (box, p.135).

Leaves are misshapen or mottled

Problem: Leaves are curled or very skinny ("shoe-stringed") and may be mottled with pale green or yellow. Fruits may be discolored.

Cause: Several viruses can infect tomatoes. Most are spread by insects, tools, and handling. The virulent tobacco mosaic virus is spread on seeds and by contact—not by insects. Smokers also spread it, because it is often present in cigarette tobacco. It infects all tomato-family crops as well as spinach and many weeds. Cucumber mosaic virus and tomato spotted wilt virus also infect tomatoes.

Solution: Remove the infected plants, practice good sanitation, and plant resistant varieties.

- Remove virus-infected plants from garden.
- Wash your hands before handling plants. After removing an infected plant, wash tools and launder your clothes.
- Rotate (p.115) crops on a two-year cycle.
- Grow virus-resistant varieties (box, p.135).

Blossoms form, but few or no fruits develop

Problem: The plant develops flowers, but they fall off without forming fruits.

Cause: Tomato blossoms fall prematurely when it's very cool or hot, or the soil is dry.

Solution: Improve growing conditions. Select appropriate varieties and planting times.

- In cool weather, mulch with black plastic, or wrap clear plastic on stakes around plant to form an open-topped mini-greenhouse.
- In summer, shade plants with a commercial shade cloth or other light-filtering fabric.
- Water plants when the soil is dry 1 to 2 inches beneath the surface.
- Grow long-blooming indeterminate, or tall, varieties, which are likely to bloom in favorable weather.
- Buy climate-suited varieties (box, p.135).

Bottoms of fruits are distorted

Problem: The stem ends of fruits have bulges and crevices bordered by "zipper" lines.

Cause: Catfacing is caused by anything that damages the fruit as it begins to develop within the flower—including cold, heat, low soil moisture, or too much nitrogen fertilizer.

Solution: Provide sufficient water and low-nitrogen fertilizer. Plant resistant varieties.

- Water soil if dry 1 inch below the surface.
- Use fertilizer from transplanting to harvest that provides more phosphorus than nitrogen, such as a 5-10-10 formulation (p.324).
- Select resistant varieties (box, p.135).

Turnip
Brassica rapa

LIGHT: Full sun to partial shade

SOIL: Fertile, well drained; pH 5.5 to 6.8

MOISTURE: Moist

HARDINESS: Cool-season biennial

Tiny holes appear in leaves

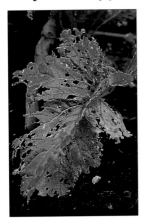

Problem: The leaves are covered with many small, round holes. You may see tiny black or brown jumping flea-like insects.

Cause: Several different kinds of flea beetles damage the leaves of turnips. The pests can kill seedlings, but older plants are rarely seriously damaged. The insects are most active in spring, with both larvae and adults chewing holes in leaves. Flea beetles may be hard to see, because they quickly jump when disturbed. Adults overwinter in weeds and debris.

Solution: Spray with insecticide. To discourage the beetles, protect susceptible young plants, destroy weed hosts, use beneficial predators, and plant later in the season.

- Spray infested plants with an insecticide registered for turnips that contains the active ingredient carbaryl. Follow label directions carefully.
- Protect seedlings with an insect-excluding floating row cover. Tuck edges under soil.
- Discourage infestations by removing cabbage-family weeds, such as wild turnip and wild radish, which harbor flea beetles.
- Apply beneficial nematodes (p.126), a biological control, to the soil in spring when the pests are active, to reduce larvae.
- Try planting in late summer when flea beetles are less numerous. (Turnips also grow well in cool fall weather.)

Root is tough and tastes bitter

Problem: The turnip root is fibrous and small and has a strong, bitter taste.

Cause: Warm weather causes turnips to produce roots of low quality. Poorly cared for or overmature roots may also taste bitter.

Solution: Time plantings to grow and mature in cool weather, provide good growing conditions, and harvest early.

- Where summers are long and hot, plant turnips in mid- to late summer. In mild-winter areas, plant again in late winter.
- Plant turnips in fertile garden soil. Water when the soil is dry 1 to 2 inches beneath the surface, so plants will mature quickly.
- Harvest mature turnips as early as possible.

Leaves have pale yellow spots with white or gray fuzz

Problem: Leaves develop pale green spots that turn pale yellow, then develop a fuzzy growth. Roots may be partially or completely blackened.

Cause: Downy mildew is a fungal disease most likely to develop in crowded plantings and in moist weather. The disease especially prefers warm days followed by cool nights.

Solution: Destroy infected plant parts or plants. Thin turnips, practice good sanitation, and control weeds. Grow tolerant varieties.

- Remove and destroy infected plant parts and badly infected plants. After harvest, clean up and destroy crop debris.
- Thin turnips so that air can circulate freely among them. Water at ground level to avoid wetting leaves.
- Remove cabbage-family weeds, such as wild turnip and wild radish, which may host the downy mildew fungus.
- For future plantings, select varieties of turnips that show resistance to downy mildew, such as 'Crawford' and 'Scarlet Queen'. Avoid seeding too thickly, and thin seedlings.

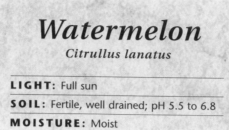

Watermelon

Citrullus lanatus

LIGHT: Full sun

SOIL: Fertile, well drained; pH 5.5 to 6.8

MOISTURE: Moist

HARDINESS: Warm-season annual

Fruit has dark green, fast-spreading blotches

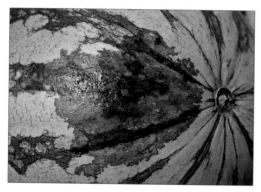

Problem: Dark, olive green stains about the size of a quarter appear on the upper surface of the watermelons. The spots enlarge, and a week or so later, most of the fruits are stained. The rinds crack open, and a sticky, clear amber substance oozes out. Leaves have dark brown, somewhat angular spots. Infected seedlings show brown spots on the undersides of the young leaves.

Cause: Watermelon fruit blotch is a bacterial disease that may destroy an entire crop if not controlled. It is spread by splashing water and is carried on crop residue, seeds, and tools.

Solution: Remove infected plants and debris, spray plants, and practice good garden sanitation. Buy healthy seeds and seedlings and rotate crops in future seasons.

- Remove infected plants and fallen debris as soon as you discover them.
- If the disease spreads, spray with an organic copper spray fungicide to control the disease. Follow label directions carefully. Be aware that the spray may injure leaves.
- Water at ground level and avoid working among wet leaves to prevent transmission.
- Sterilize tools (p.310) after each use.
- Buy watermelon seeds and seedlings that are certified disease free. Don't save seeds.
- Rotate (p.115) watermelons with other plants on a three-year cycle.

Ends of fruits turn brown

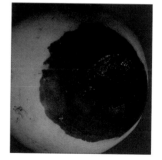

Problem: Fruits may wither or show a brown discoloration at the blossom end (the melon end opposite the stem). Rot follows, progressing up the fruit toward the stem.

Cause: Blossom-end rot is a fungal disease often found in the South and Southwest, especially during periods of drought. It is most severe when the soil is allowed to dry out between waterings or stay dry for long periods. Blossom-end rot is also common in regions with acidic soils.

Solution: To control this problem, water and fertilize regularly and prepare the soil well.

- Keep the soil consistently moist throughout the growing season.
- Apply a balanced fertilizer with a 10-10-10 formulation (p.324) regularly and before planting a new crop.
- Before planting, test the soil's pH (p.329). Add lime to raise it to 6.8.
- Also add organic matter, such as compost or leaf mold, to neutralize the soil.

TIME-TESTED TECHNIQUES

USE MYCORRHIZAE FOR HEALTHY PLANTS

Healthy plants give better yields and fend off pests and diseases more successfully than unhealthy ones do. Mycorrhizae are tiny fungi that help plants use the nutrients in the soil more effectively. Although mycorrhizae are present in many soils, most plants need a specific type of mycorrhizae for best growth.

Purchase mycorrhizae for vegetables at a local nursery or from a mail-order company. Simply mix them with water and apply to the soil at planting time, following label directions. Mycorrhizae work best in soil that is well drained and contains lots of compost but doesn't stay wet or dry for long periods.

Plant wilts under midday sun

Problem: Drooping begins on warm days, often starting in one branch of a vine, and then the entire plant wilts and dies. A white cottony growth sometimes forms on dying vines. If you cut the stem base, you will see a yellow, orange, or brown discoloration inside.

Cause: Watermelon fusarium wilt is a fungal disease. The spores are carried by seeds and persist in the soil for 15 to 18 years. Wind, water, and tools carry the infection to new plants, and warm temperatures allow the fungus to spread quickly. The disease can attack plants at any time during the growing season.

Solution: Spray and remove infected debris. Select resistant seeds, and rotate crops.

- To prevent serious damage, spray as the fruit begins to develop. Use a synthetic fungicide registered for watermelons that contains the active ingredient maneb or mancozeb. Follow label directions carefully.

- Remove any plants that die of the disease to slow the spread of the fungus.

- Carefully clean up plant debris at season's end to discourage future problems.

- Buy seeds that are certified disease free and grow resistant varieties (box, right).

- Rotate (p.115) crops; wait five years before growing watermelons in the same place.

Fruit has pale flesh and lacks flavor

Problem: The flesh of harvested watermelon fruits is pale in color and is not very sweet.

Cause: Watermelon fruits will not taste sweet when they are picked before they ripen. The melons may also not ripen completely and lack flavor when the plants are grown in cool, wet conditions.

Solution: Harvest fully ripened fruit. In cool-summer areas, plant early-maturing varieties.

- Make sure a melon is ripe before picking. Check the bottom for a color change from white to cream; check the body for dark stripes that turn from glossy to dull. It should make a dull (not ringing) sound when thumped. Browning tendrils are not a foolproof sign; they can be caused by drought and occur early in some varieties.

- If you live in a cool or short-summer area, grow varieties that ripen early in the season, such as 'Earliqueen' or 'Garden Baby'. But be aware that no watermelon variety will ripen well during a very cool season.

WISE CHOICES

Here are some varieties that resist or tolerate watermelon diseases. Select ones that resist the problems most common in your area. The symptoms (and treatments) for anthracnose, powdery mildew, and mosaic virus are similar to those for melon (p.112).

- 'Charleston Gray': anthracnose, fusarium wilt
- 'Crimson Sweet': anthracnose, fusarium wilt
- 'Fiesta': alternaria, fusarium wilt
- 'Hybrid Jade Star': fusarium wilt
- 'Mini-Jubilee Hybrid': powdery mildew, mosaic virus
- 'Tiger Baby': fusarium wilt

CHAPTER THREE

HERBS

WHEN YOU ARE GARDENING, you can relish the aromatic presence of herbs among your other plantings. You also can capitalize on the fact that the tiny, nectar-filled flowers of the parsley family members caraway, dill, fennel, and parsley and the mint family members basil, bee balm, catnip, lavender, rosemary, sage, and thyme attract beneficial insects that prey on pests. What's more, you can pick some fresh herbs and add them to nearly every dish you make. Still other herbs, such as yellow or orange pot marigold, are pretty in the garden and excellent for use in bouquets.

One of the nicest things about herbs is that, when properly sited, they require little care and have few pests. However, problems can arise, and this chapter will help you deal with them. Remember to try environmentally friendly solutions first. For the safe use of commercial treatments, see page 9 and pages 390 to 399.

Quick Troubleshooting Guide

SEEDLINGS

SEEDLING IS CHEWED OR SHEARED OFF

Cause: Cutworm, earwig, grasshopper, slug, snail, bird, rabbit

Solution: Cover seedlings with a floating row cover or fine-mesh screen; bury edges in soil. Handpick and dispose of pests. Control cutworms with biological control BT.

SEEDLING FAILS TO SPROUT

Cause: Old seeds, improper planting, or poor timing

Solution: Use only fresh seeds. Sow seeds at the time, rate, and depth recommended on the package. If in doubt about a seed package's age, sprout 10 seeds on a damp paper towel to test viability, and sow seeds more densely to compensate. Plant seeds outdoors after the predicted last frost date, when soil warms.

SEEDLING WILTS AND DIES

Cause: Damping-off disease

Solution: To combat this soil-borne fungal disease, plant seeds indoors in sterile commercial seed-starting mix. When sowing seeds outdoors, sprinkle milled peat moss or clean sand on the soil's surface after sowing the seeds to discourage fungi.

LEAVES

LEAVES ARE CHEWED AND HAVE RAGGED HOLES

Cause: Slug and snail

Solution: Handpick and crush pests. Trap slugs and snails in saucers of beer or commercial traps. Sprinkle sharp-edged granules of diatomaceous earth (ground fossilized crustaceans) on ground around plants after each rain.

LEAVES HAVE POWDERY WHITE SPOTS

Cause: Powdery mildew

Solution: Cut off and destroy fungal-disease-affected foliage and plant debris. Cut back a severely diseased plant after flowering. Spray plant with compost tea or baking-soda solution. Thin or plant widely to encourage air circulation.

LEAVES ARE DISTORTED, YELLOWING, OR STICKY

Cause: Aphid

Solution: Spray plant with a strong stream of water from the hose to dislodge pests. Grow small-flowered nectar plants, such as dill, fennel, or alyssum, nearby to attract ladybugs and other beneficial insects that prey on aphids.

LEAVES HAVE FUZZY GRAY SPOTS

Cause: Botrytis

Solution: Prune fungal-disease-affected foliage and remove debris. Remove and destroy severely infected plants. Drench soil with compost tea. Avoid overhead watering to keep leaves dry. Spread organic mulch to keep soil-borne spores from splashing plant. Move plant into full sun and good air circulation.

LEAVES HAVE BROWN OR DARK SPOTS

Cause: Leaf-spot disease

Solution: Remove and discard fungal-disease-affected foliage and badly infected plants. Spray with compost tea. Avoid overhead watering to keep leaves dry. Move plant to a location with full sun and good air circulation.

LEAVES ARE STIPPLED AND WEBBED

Cause: Spider mite

Solution: Knock pests off plant with a strong stream of water from a hose. Keep plant well watered and spray foliage with water during dry spells. Spray plant with garlic oil as a repellent.

LEAVES ARE PALE OR YELLOW AND MAY DROP

Cause: Nutrient deficiency

Solution: Make sure that plant is receiving sufficient nitrogen. Spray foliage and water soil with compost tea, fish emulsion, liquid kelp, or other water-soluble fertilizer that is high in nitrogen.

LEAVES HAVE WAXY BUMPS AND STICKY DEPOSITS

Cause: Scale

Solution: Prune off infested foliage. Scrape scale from plant with a scouring pad. Grow small-flowered nectar plants, such as dill, fennel, or alyssum, nearby to attract lacewings and other beneficial insects that prey on scale.

LEAVES ARE DEVOURED OR HAVE LARGE HOLES

Cause: Caterpillar or other chewing insect

Solution: Handpick and destroy pests in early morning, when they are sluggish. Cover plants in the spring with insect-excluding floating row covers.

WHOLE PLANT

PLANT BASE TURNS BROWN AND DECAYS

Cause: Soft rot

Solution: Dig up and destroy diseased plant. Cultivate around healthy plants carefully to prevent injury. Avoid overhead watering. Grow plants in a location with good drainage and air circulation.

PLANT WILTS AND COLLAPSES

Cause: Soil is too wet.

Solution: Allow soil to dry between waterings. Improve drainage by incorporating compost or sand into soil. Transplant into a raised bed or container.

PLANT WILTS AND DROPS LEAVES; ROOTS ROT

Cause: Fungal infection

Solution: Remove infected plant and surrounding 6 inches of soil. Improve soil drainage, incorporate compost, or grow plant in a raised bed. Water when the soil is dry 1 to 2 inches below the soil's surface.

PLANT WILTS, STEMS ROT

Cause: Stem rot

Solution: Dig up and remove fungal-disease-infected plant and surrounding 6 inches of soil. Clean up plant debris. Water at ground level with a soaker hose or drip irrigation to keep spores from germinating. Water when the soil is dry 1 to 2 inches below the surface. Rotate crops.

PLANT IS STUNTED WITH MOTTLED LEAVES

Cause: Mosaic virus, aster yellows

Solution: Dig up and destroy diseased plant and nearby disease-host weeds. Control the sucking insects that spread disease by spraying plant with a strong stream of hose water.

PLANT IS STUNTED, WITH SPARSE OR PALE FOLIAGE

Cause: Overcrowding, insufficient water or nutrients

Solution: Thin seedlings or space plants according to seed package or nursery directions. Water when soil is dry 1 inch below surface. Fertilize in spring with a balanced, slow-release fertilizer.

Basil

Ocimum basilicum

LIGHT: Full sun

SOIL: Fertile, well drained; pH 5.0 to 8.0

MOISTURE: Moist

HARDINESS: Tender annual

Large holes appear in leaves

Problem: Leaves are chewed and riddled with large holes. There also may be shiny slime trails on the leaves or soil.

Cause: Slugs and snails are mollusks that feed on plants at night. During the day, these pests hide in moist, dark places, such as cracks in the soil. Snails also hide on dry, smooth surfaces that don't receive much light. In summer, both pests lay small, white, spherical eggs just under the soil's surface.

Solution: Remove and destroy the pests, apply repellent, and erect barriers.

- Handpick and dispose of slugs or snails. Hunt them at night by flashlight.
- Apply commercial garlic oil to leaves to act as a repellent.
- Place a copper strip around the plant or bed to repel them. Slugs and snails receive a mild electric shock when their moist skin touches copper.
- Or sprinkle the soil around plant with diatomaceous earth, an abrasive organic substance that injures these soft-skinned pests on contact.
- Protect seedbeds and transplanted seedlings by covering with fabric floating row covers to exclude slugs and snails.

Plant has many flowers but few leaves

Problem: The plant is covered with flowers but bears relatively few large leaves. Lower leaves are yellow.

Cause: Basil is an annual that flowers quickly, sets seed, and dies. Blooms are edible, but not desirable if basil is grown for leaves.

Solution: Prevent flowering and prolong leaf growth with proper maintenance and harvest techniques.

- When the plant is 6 to 8 inches tall, harvest the top one or two pairs of leaves by pinching through the stem above a pair of leaves.
- As basil grows, continue pinching out the tips of stems that have several pairs of large leaves to prevent flowering.
- Snip or pinch off flower stalks. Discard the flowers or use them to flavor vinegar, salads or sauces.

Leaves are severely chewed

Problem: Leaves are eaten, sometimes completely. On sunny days, shiny beetles are seen feeding.

Cause: Japanese beetles can severely damage basil. These ½-inch-long, copper-and-metallic-green insects feed in summer, preferring plants in full sun. They lay eggs in fall. Their larvae, or grubs, feed on grass roots in spring.

Solution: Destroy adults and control grubs.

- Handpick beetles and dispose of them.
- In severe infestations, spray with neem, a botanical insecticide, to repel and kill the beetles. Follow label directions carefully. Alternatively, apply garlic powder or commercial garlic oil as a repellent.
- To kill grubs, treat lawns with a biological control, such as beneficial nematodes or milky spore disease, as directed.

Bay
Laurus nobilis

LIGHT: Full sun or partial shade

SOIL: Average, well drained; pH 4.5 to 8.0

MOISTURE: Seasonally moist

HARDINESS: Zones 8 to 11

Leaf edges have red or brown galls or curl

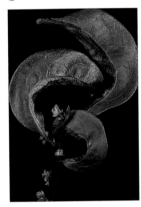

Problem: Leaf edges curl in and are marked with swollen red areas called galls. The galls turn brown.

Cause: Laurel psyllids are small, sap-sucking insects that cause gall formations where they feed. The pale-yellow-and-orange young, called nymphs, are covered by long, white, waxy strands. Adults, which resemble cicadas, overwinter amid plant leaves and stems, then lay eggs on or near buds in spring.

Solution: Treat with insecticide, attract natural predators, and grow a resistant variety.

- If psyllids are present in spring, spray the plant with either summer oil or pyrethrum, a botanical insecticide. Follow label directions. Repeat in several weeks if needed.
- Grow yarrow, coreopsis, or other small-flowered nectar plants nearby to encourage colonization of beneficial insect predators.
- Grow 'Saratoga', a variety of bay that resists attacks of laurel psyllids.

Plant has small, sticky bumps on leaves or stems

Problem: The plant does not thrive, and some branches die or decline. Leaves and stems may be sticky and coated with a dark gray powder.

Cause: Scales are sucking insects that attach to leaves or the bark of a stem to feed. Because of their brown color, they can be difficult to detect. Young scale crawl briefly, then develop a soft, waxy shield, and become stationary.

Solution: Spray plant with water and treat with an insecticide. Remove scale.

- Squirt the plant with a strong stream of water from a hose to remove the insect's sticky waste product and the dark gray, sooty mold that can grow on it.
- When the plant is dry, spray it with summer oil, covering both sides of the leaves and branch joints. Follow label directions carefully and reapply as instructed. Avoid spraying when temperatures are hot, as the oil can damage foliage then. Alternatively, spray with pyrethrum, a botanical insecticide. Follow label directions carefully.
- Scrape off dead scale with a dish scrubber or an old toothbrush. Dislodge remaining debris with water from a hose.

REGIONAL FOCUS
SOUTHEAST

Thread blight, a fungal disease that infects many kinds of ornamental and fruit trees in the Southeast, may also damage bay. On an infected plant, groups of leaves will be intergrown with fungal threads that resemble spider webs. Later, white or buff patches will appear on the foliage. To halt this disease, cut out any affected leaves or branches and dispose of fallen leaves.

TIME-TESTED TECHNIQUES

REPOTTING BAY

Bay is a slow-growing, tender perennial that is an ideal container plant in cool climates. Grow it as a houseplant in winter and set it outside in summer. Repot container-grown bay plants every three to four years, according to the following steps:

1. In spring, remove the plant from the pot and trim ¼ inch of the roots from the sides and bottom of the root ball.
2. Add a 2-inch layer of moist potting soil to the bottom of a clean pot that is about 2 inches wider than the old pot.
3. Place the plant in the center of the pot and fill with moist potting soil. Water well.

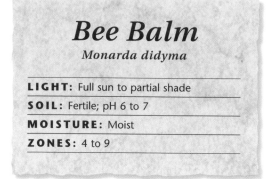

Bee Balm

Monarda didyma

LIGHT: Full sun to partial shade

SOIL: Fertile; pH 6 to 7

MOISTURE: Moist

ZONES: 4 to 9

Plant dies out in the center or becomes invasive

Problem: A large, established clump shows vigorous growth at the edges but no new growth in the center. New stems appear in other parts of the garden, where they are not desired.

Cause: Bee balm is a vigorous perennial whose roots will spread rapidly in moist, fertile soil. Its natural growth habit is to send out suckers, or new underground stems, from the outer edge of the clump and to die out in the center.

Solution: Remove suckers. Divide the plant to rejuvenate it and control its spread. Divide the clump every two years, or when it begins producing fewer blooms and the center of the clump dies back.

WISE CHOICES

Colorful, fragrant, and attractive to hummingbirds, bee balm is also notoriously susceptible to powdery mildew disease (entry, right). Resistant varieties are the best bet for plants whose beauty won't be lost under a powdery shroud.

• 'Jacob Cline' offers brilliant red blooms and superb mildew resistance.

• 'Marshall's Delight' and 'Raspberry Wine' are pink and deep rose-pink resistant varieties.

• *M. fistulosa* is a related species with pale lavender flowers that is less prone to mildew and, like bee balm, it makes a delicious tea.

● If stems are becoming invasive, drive a sharp spade forcefully into soil around the perimeter of the clump to chop off the suckering shoots. Pull up the severed stems and remove them from the garden.

● To divide bee balm, dig up the clump in spring and use a knife or sharp spade to cut the actively growing edges into several sections. Discard the center portion. Trim off any wayward suckers from the divisions and replant as desired.

Leaves have patches of a white, powdery substance

Problem: The leaves have a white or gray powdery coating that you cannot rub off. As the problem progresses, the leaves may also turn yellow.

Cause: Powdery mildew is a fungal disease that can be active when conditions are either cool and damp or hot and humid; it is generally worse in late summer. The spores are carried by wind and can spread through a planting quickly. Dry soil and poor air circulation also contribute to the disease.

Solution: Practice good garden sanitation. Treat with fungicide. Keep soil moist. Space plants properly.

● Cut back an infected plant to within 6 inches of the soil after it blooms. Remove plant debris, which is a potential overwintering site for the disease, from the garden.

● Slow the spread of disease by applying baking soda spray (p.392) from early summer through frost.

● Keep the soil evenly moist. Water at ground level with a soaker hose or drip irrigation and water early in the day so that leaves can dry before sundown.

● Space plants 18 to 24 inches apart. Divide clumps (p.29) every two years in spring, and replant using the same spacing to encourage air circulation.

Caraway
Carum carvi

LIGHT: Full sun

SOIL: Average, well drained; pH 6 to 7.5

MOISTURE: Moist to seasonally dry

ZONES: 4 to 9

Plant grows large but does not develop flowers

Problem: The plant produces ample foliage but does not form flower stems or seeds.

Cause: Although some herbs grow as annuals, caraway is typically a biennial. This means that it sends up foliage the first year but does not produce flower stalks and seeds until early summer of the second year.

Solution: Time plantings carefully and provide good growing conditions.

- In cold climates, sow seeds as soon as the soil can be worked in spring. In warm climates, sow seeds in late summer or fall. Plant a new crop every season or every other season.

- Where the soil freezes, insulate plants with a 6-inch-thick mulch in late fall to ensure flowers and a good crop of seeds.

Small green insects swarm on the plant

Problem: Small, pear-shaped, green insects are seen moving slowly on stems and leaves. The infested plant is sticky, and new leaves are yellow.

Cause: Aphids are sap-sucking insects especially attracted to tender new leaves, where they gather to feed.

Solution: Spray with water and treat with insecticide or repellent. Site plant carefully.

- Dislodge aphids by spraying plant with a strong stream of water from the hose. While spraying, place one hand behind delicate leaves and stems to support them. Spray both sides of leaves.

- Control severe infestations by treating an infested plant with the botanical insecticide pyrethrum or neem. Follow label directions carefully.

- Discourage future infestations by spraying the plant with commercial hot pepper wax or garlic oil.

- In the future, plant caraway as far away as possible from willows, which are a host to the species of aphid that attacks caraway.

Roots have rust-colored tunnels

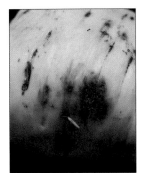

Problem: A plant has yellowing or wilted leaves and may be stunted. When you pull a plant up, you find tunnels in the roots.

Cause: Carrot rust flies attack not only carrots but also caraway. The small flies lay eggs near the base of plants. The resulting 1/3-inch-long maggots tunnel into the soil, then into plant roots, leaving small, rust-colored holes.

Solution: Apply an organic remedy, treat with insecticide. Erect physical barriers, use a biological pest control. Remove any severely infested plants.

- Treat a plant that has suffered minor damage with compost tea (p.392) or a liquid seaweed solution to help it recover.

- Spray the leaves of a heavily infested plant with pyrethrum, a botanical insecticide. Follow label directions carefully.

- Remove a badly damaged plant from the garden and do not compost it.

- Before replanting, treat the soil where caraway will be grown with beneficial nematodes, a biological control. Renew the treatment in spring.

- Cover seedbeds with a fabric floating row cover, tucking edges into soil to exclude egg-laying flies. Remove the cover when plants are tall enough to touch it.

Catnip
Nepeta cataria

LIGHT: Full sun to partial shade

SOIL: Average, well drained; pH 5.0 to 7.5

MOISTURE: Moist

HARDINESS: Zones 4 to 11

Leaves have dark spots

Problem: Leaves develop gray or brown spots, which may be surrounded by yellow areas. The leaves may eventually fall off.

Cause: Catnip is susceptible to several types of leaf spot disease caused by fungi. The diseases are spread by wind and splashing water and can also enter the garden on new plants.

Solution: Remove infected leaves or plants. Apply compost tea. Water carefully. Provide good growing conditions. Rotate.

- Immediately remove and discard infected leaves. Also remove badly diseased plants.
- Spray plant with disease-fighting compost tea (p.392) at the first sign of infection.
- Try to keep foliage dry when watering. Water early in the day so leaves can dry out.
- Rotate (p.115) catnip, planting in a different part of the garden next year. Plant in full sun and space at least 18 inches apart.

TIME-TESTED TECHNIQUES

CONTROLLING CATNIP

Pretty when young, catnip can grow leggy and self-sow to the point of invasiveness. Shear stems to 6 inches above ground after flowering for shapely new growth and a second flowering in late summer. Remove seeds to stop spread.

Leaves are marked with twisting tan lines

Problem: Tan or translucent tunnels, sometimes filled with tiny black specks, are seen on leaves. Tan blotches may also appear.

Cause: Leaf miners are the larvae of various insects that tunnel between the two leaf surfaces to feed. While they disfigure and damage individual leaves, they seldom kill the entire plant.

Solution: Remove affected leaves and apply insecticide. Interrupt life cycle of the pest.

- Handpick and destroy any leaves with trails.
- Spray the plant with the botanical insecticide pyrethrum or neem. Follow label directions carefully.
- Lay black plastic mulch around plant to prevent pests from dropping onto the soil and maturing.

Leaves are mottled with yellow and may be distorted

Problem: Leaves have yellow mottling or streaks. They may be smaller than normal, and leaf edges may curl and become brittle.

Cause: Cucumber mosaic virus is an incurable disease spread by insect aphids as they feed.

Solution: Remove infected plants, control aphids, and practice good garden sanitation.

- Remove and destroy infected plants as soon as you see the symptoms.
- Knock aphids off with water from a hose.
- Keep the garden and surrounding areas free of weeds to eliminate overwintering sites for the disease and the insects that spread it.

Chamomile, German

Matricaria recutita

LIGHT: Full sun

SOIL: Sandy, well drained; pH 5.0 to 8.0

MOISTURE: Seasonally moist

HARDINESS: Cool-season annual

Leaves have gray or white spots that won't rub off

Problem: Foliage and stems are covered with a white, feltlike dust that cannot be rubbed off; lower leaves are the most severely affected. Leaves may dry out and curl.

Cause: Powdery mildew is a fungal disease encouraged by poor air circulation and humid weather conditions. It is seldom fatal.

Solution: Remove diseased tissue and use a spray to slow disease. Promote better air circulation. Prune back plant.

- Remove and dispose of infected plant parts and plant debris that falls to the ground.
- Spray plant with baking-soda solution (p.392), compost tea (p.392), or summer oil. Do not spray in direct sunlight.
- Thin plants to about 12 inches apart to improve air circulation.
- Shear badly infected plant to a few inches above the ground for healthy regrowth.

Seeds fail to sprout

Problem: Few or no chamomile plants appear after sowing seeds.

Cause: Seeds require light to germinate. In addition, 30 percent of the seeds in a packet won't sprout at all, and this percentage rises when seeds are more than one year old.

Solution: Prepare seeds correctly when sowing; use fresh seeds. Allow plants to self-sow.

- In spring or fall, prepare a seed bed in full sun and rake smooth. Scatter fresh seeds on the soil surface. Do not cover, but lightly press seeds against the soil. Keep the soil moist until the seedlings emerge.
- After flowering, allow some seeds to ripen on the plant and fall in the garden.

WISE CHOICES

German chamomile has a Mediterranean cousin, known as Roman chamomile (*Chamaemelum nobile*). While both are apple-scented herbs with daisylike blooms that can be brewed for tea, they have different uses in the landscape. German chamomile is an annual that forms an open, ferny plant about 2 to 3 feet tall; it works best in an herb garden or border. Roman chamomile is a perennial that grows into a thick, resilient, 9-inch-tall clump that can tolerate foot traffic and clipping. It performs well as an edging, a fragrant filler between paving stones, and even as a lawn.

Plant has few flowers

Problem: The plant grows tall and leggy or is leafy but produces few flowers.

Cause: German chamomile is an annual that performs best if it starts growing in cool weather; warm weather causes it to grow tall and bolt (bloom prematurely), resulting in few blooms. The plant also grows best when sown in place; transplanted specimens may bloom early due to shock. Too much fertilizer stimulates leaves at the expense of flowers.

Solution: Provide proper growing conditions.

- In cold climates, sow seed in the garden in early spring. In warm regions, sow in fall.
- If you must transplant, do it before seedlings are 1 inch tall.
- Sow in an area that has not received high-nitrogen (p.324) fertilizer within a year.

Dill

Anethum graveolens

LIGHT: Full sun

SOIL: Fertile, well drained; pH 5 to 7

MOISTURE: Moist

HARDINESS: Cool-season annual

Plant is infested with yellowish or green insects

Problem: Small, slow-moving, pear-shaped insects are crawling over the stems and leaves. The plant may be sticky.

Cause: Aphids are sap-sucking insects that feed on dill in summer. The species most likely to be found on dill are honeysuckle and parsnip aphids, which are yellowish, and also willow aphids, which are green.

Solution: Dislodge aphids with water. Spray with insecticide and repellent. Treat host plants nearby.

● Knock aphids off the plant with a strong stream of water from a hose. Place one hand behind delicate foliage while spraying to provide support.

● For a severe infestation, spray plant with insecticidal soap or the botanical insecticide pyrethrum or neem. Follow label directions carefully.

● Prevent aphids from returning by spraying plants with garlic oil.

● In winter or early spring, apply a dormant oil spray to trunks and branches of nearby plants that can harbor aphids, such as honeysuckle and willow.

Plant is small with yellowed, deformed leaves

Problem: The plant grows slowly, and the leaves are not normal in shape or color.

Cause: Dill is susceptible to viral diseases including mosaic virus, and to aster yellows, which is caused by an organism that produces virus-like symptoms. The diseases are spread from plant to plant by feeding insects, such as aphids and leafhoppers.

Solution: Remove the infected plant and control insect carriers. There is no cure.

● Remove and destroy the infected plant.

● Control aphids (entry, left).

● Dislodge leafhoppers from the plant with a strong stream of water from the hose. Place one hand behind delicate foliage while spraying to provide support.

● If leafhoppers are numerous, treat plant with neem, a botanical insecticide. Follow label directions carefully.

Plant is small, with few leaves

Problem: A plant doesn't grow tall and starts blooming when it has only a few leaves.

Cause: Overcrowding will stunt a plant's growth.

Solution: Thin seedlings, time plantings, and select a variety with abundant foliage growth.

● Avoid overcrowding by thinning seedlings to at least 4 inches apart. The tender thinnings are edible.

● Sow dill seeds in the garden as early as possible in spring and again in midsummer for a second crop.

● Select a variety bred for abundant foliage, such as 'Dukat'.

Fennel
Foeniculum vulgare

LIGHT: Full sun

SOIL: Average, well drained; pH 7 to 8.5

MOISTURE: Moist to seasonally dry

ZONES: 5 to 11

Soft brown decay is found near the base of plant

Problem: Part of the fleshy base of the plant decays. The decayed area is brown, wet, and foul smelling.

Cause: Soft rot is a bacterial disease. The bacteria live in the soil and enter a plant through injuries. In moist conditions, they can spread rapidly in splashing water and can kill the plant.

Solution: Dispose of infected plants. Space plants well; water properly; handle plants carefully to avoid injury.

- Remove and dispose of infected plants.
- Space or thin plants 10 to 12 inches apart.
- Water at ground level with a soaker hose or drip irrigation. Water early in the day so that leaves can dry before sundown.
- Avoid injuring plants when cultivating.

Plant wilts and stems rot

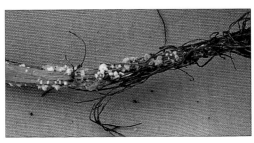

Problem: Fennel leaves wilt and yellow, and the plant collapses. In moist conditions, white fungal threads form on the stems.

Cause: Fennel stem rot is caused by fungi. Symptoms include a white fungal mat forming on the stems. The black spores that spread the disease, called sclerotia, are often visible in stem cracks or appear in lumps on the stems of fennel plants.

Solution: Remove the infected plant and surrounding soil. Avoid overwatering. Plant future crops elsewhere.

- Dig up the infected plant and remove any debris around it that might harbor the fungal spores. Also remove and discard any soil that touched the infected roots.
- Water the remaining fennel plants only when the soil is dry 1 inch below the surface.
- Next season, plant fennel on fresh ground.

Large, striped caterpillars are eating foliage

Problem: Smooth-skinned, light green caterpillars with black and yellow markings are feeding on the plant leaves.

Cause: Parsley-worms are 2-inch-long caterpillars common east of the Rocky Mountains, although they are rarely numerous enough to do much harm. They are the larvae of a pretty butterfly, the black swallowtail. In California, a similar caterpillar, the larva of the western parsley swallowtail, also feeds on fennel. Both caterpillars give off a sickeningly sweet odor when disturbed.

Solution: For minor infestations, leave the caterpillars alone, or relocate them. Treat larger infestations with insecticide.

- Let the caterpillar feed if it is not causing too much damage. Alternatively, move it from garden fennel to a wild relative, such as Queen Anne's lace.
- If caterpillars become numerous, spray with the botanical insecticides pyrethrum or neem. Follow label directions carefully.

Lavender

Lavandula spp.

LIGHT: Full sun

SOIL: Light, well drained; pH 6 to 8.3

MOISTURE: Moist to seasonally dry

HARDINESS: Zones 5 to 7

Small mounds of white foam collect on leaves and stems

Problem: Some leaves and the points at which leaves emerge from stems develop small mounds of a white, frothy material.

Cause: Several species of sap-sucking insects called froghoppers, or spittlebugs, feed on lavender. The brown or black adults are winged insects with froglike heads. Immature froghoppers are wingless, yellow-green miniatures of the adults. They settle into leaf joints where they cover themselves with a protective covering of frothy white bubbles and feed. Adults lay eggs and feed on nearby grasses and weeds. These pests are more unsightly than damaging, although feeding in large numbers can stunt plant growth.

Solution: Control adults, encourage beneficials, and keep the garden weed free.

- Wash foam and immature froghoppers off plants with a strong stream of water.
- Grow small-flowered nectar plants, such as alyssum and scabiosa to attract beneficial insects that prey on froghoppers.
- Cover crop with fabric floating row cover late summer to fall to prevent egg laying.
- Remove weeds, which harbor froghoppers.

Leaves have dark, ringed spots

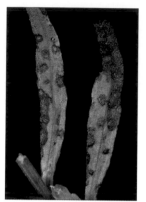

Problem: The leaves develop tiny yellow spots that enlarge, becoming brown, gray, or reddish, often with yellow halos. Some spots have black dots in the centers.

Cause: Septoria leaf spot is a fungal disease that is transmitted on infected seeds, or the spores are carried to mature plants on wind and in splashing water. The disease is deadly to seedlings and severely disfiguring to older plants. Spores overwinter in plant debris and weeds.

Solution: Use good garden sanitation and spray compost solution as controls.

- Remove and destroy badly infected plants.
- Remove plant debris and weeds, the potential overwintering sites of the disease.
- Spray healthy plants early in the season with disease-fighting compost tea (p.392) as a preventive.

Plant has gray fuzzy mold

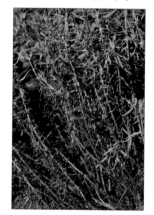

Problem: A gray fuzzy mold forms on leaves and stems.

Cause: Botrytis mold is a fungus whose spores are spread by wind and splashing water. They germinate in cool, moist conditions.

Solution: Prune affected plant parts or remove plant. Water and site plant properly. Select varieties carefully.

- Cut out and destroy infected stems. Remove a severely infected plant.
- Water at ground level with a soaker hose or drip irrigation. Water early in the day.
- Locate lavender in full sun.
- Select a tall, open variety that is less likely to retain moisture in the center. Avoid planting compact varieties such as 'Munstead Dwarf' or 'Hidcote'.

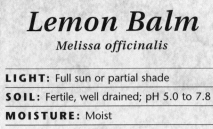

Lemon Balm

Melissa officinalis

LIGHT: Full sun or partial shade

SOIL: Fertile, well drained; pH 5.0 to 7.8

MOISTURE: Moist

HARDINESS: Zones 5 to 11

Leaves have large holes and shiny streaks

Problem: Large ragged holes are chewed in the leaves. Lower leaves are usually damaged first. Shiny, slimy trails are visible on the plant and surrounding soil.

Cause: Slugs and snails are mollusks that feed on plants at night. Moist soil, cool weather, and humidity encourage their activity.

Solution: Remove the pests by hand, use traps and barriers to reduce further infestations, and clean up garden debris.

- Handpick and dispose of slugs and snails at night by flashlight.
- Set homemade traps in the ground baited with beer (p.49), or use commercial traps. Slugs and snails will crawl in and drown.
- Lay copper strips around the plant or bed. The pests are repelled by receiving a mild electric shock when they contact the metal.
- Sprinkle diatomaceous earth around plants. This abrasive natural substance injures slugs and snails on contact.
- Keep the garden free of decaying vegetation and other debris to eliminate daytime hiding places for these pests.

The plant is pale and spindly

Problem: The plant has sparse, open stems and pale, yellowish green leaves.

Cause: A plant that lacks adequate water and nutrients grows pale and sparse. If left unharvested, it then grows leggy.

Solution: Provide proper growing conditions. Harvest regularly or prune it.

- Water deeply when the soil is dry 1 inch below the surface.
- In spring, fertilize with a balanced formula, such as 5-10-5 (p.324).
- Harvest the plant before it blooms by cutting stems to 2 inches above the ground.
- Shear plants back by a third, two or three times per growing season.
- In late spring, cut overgrown plants back by half and dig them up. Mix organic matter into the bed and replant immediately.

Leaves have dark spots

Problem: Rounded brown spots appear on the leaves.

Cause: Leaf spot is a fungal disease. The fungal spores are carried by wind and splashing water. It is most active in humid weather. The spores overwinter on diseased plant debris in the garden.

Solution: Remove affected leaves and debris, water carefully, and improve air circulation.

- Snip out affected leaves or stems and remove them from the garden.
- Keep leaves dry by watering at soil level. Water early in the day.
- Prune out enough stems to promote good air circulation.
- Remove plant debris from the garden.

REGIONAL FOCUS
NORTHEAST

Lemon verbena can grow to 5 feet. If you have no room to over-winter this tender plant indoors, you can save just the roots. Cut the plant to 6 inches above ground in fall and dig it up. Plant the roots in a pot of moist soil and store the pot in a cool, dark place, moistening every few weeks. Plant it outdoors after the last spring frost.

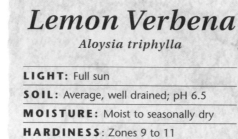

Lemon Verbena
Aloysia triphylla

LIGHT: Full sun

SOIL: Average, well drained; pH 6.5

MOISTURE: Moist to seasonally dry

HARDINESS: Zones 9 to 11

Leaves wilt and turn brown

Problem: Part or all of the branches of a plant develop brown, wilted leaves. The plant often dies within a week or two of showing symptoms.

Cause: Root rot is a fungal disease. It is especially a problem in areas of the Southwest with mild winters and alkaline soil. The disease flourishes in waterlogged, poorly drained soil and left untreated can kill a plant quickly.

Solution: Improve soil drainage and increase soil acidity. Remove severely diseased plants. Water carefully. Rotate crops.

- Dig up the affected plant and allow the roots to dry. Incorporate compost into the soil when replanting to improve drainage around the roots.
- Test soil pH (p.329) and add sulfur to reduce level to 6.5.
- Dig up and discard a severely diseased plant and the surrounding 6 inches of soil. Do not replant lemon verbena in the same location.
- Do not overwater. Water only when the soil is dry 1 inch below the surface.
- Start new plants in a different location or in pots of sterile soil.

Leaves yellow and drop prematurely; growth is spindly

Problem: Leaves turn yellow from tip to stem. Lower leaves yellow first, and yellowing progresses upward. Leaves drop off, and growth may be weak.

Cause: Lemon verbena is a heavy feeder and responds to lack of nitrogen (p.324) by yellowing and dropping leaves. This is especially pronounced in plants that are grown in pots.

Solution: Fertilize plants. Refresh potted soil.

- Fertilize with a water-soluble fertilizer, such as 10-20-10 (p.324), at half the recommended strength and twice as often as recommended. Alternately, use fish emulsion according to label directions.
- Remove the top 2 inches of soil in a pot each spring. Replace with fresh potting mix.

Leaves have pale stippling

Problem: Leaves have tiny pale dots and may be encased in fine webbing.

Cause: Spider mites are tiny, eight-legged pests related to spiders that suck sap from plants. Feeding in mass, these pests are especially damaging during dry periods, when plants are underwatered or dusty. Left untreated, they can quickly kill plants.

Solution: Remove affected foliage. Water the soil and rinse the plant off regularly.

- Clip off and destroy infested foliage.
- Water plants when the soil is dry 1 inch below the surface.
- Hose off the foliage of an outdoor plant weekly. Mist or rinse the leaves of an indoor plant with tepid water weekly.

Mint

Mentha spp.

LIGHT: Full sun or partial shade

SOIL: Fertile, well drained; pH 6.0 to 8.0

MOISTURE: Moist

HARDINESS: Zones 5 to 11

Leaves have spots and webbing

Problem: Leaves have pale stippling, a bronze discoloration, and fine webbing.

Cause: Spider mites are tiny, eight-legged pests related to spiders that suck leaf juices. The pests are encouraged by dry, dusty conditions and multiply rapidly in warm weather.

Solution: Treat with water and insecticide.

- Every two days spray foliage with a strong stream of water to dislodge mites.
- Spray with the botanical insecticide pyrethrum or neem, following directions.
- In severe cases, use a synthetic insecticide containing the active ingredient malathion. Use a formulation registered for mint and follow label directions carefully.
- Water well when the soil is dry 1 inch below the surface.

Leaves have raised yellow or brown spots

Problem: Leaves are disfigured by spots on stems, stalks, and veins; spots may be light yellow to chocolate brown. Leaves dry and may become less aromatic.

Cause: At least two strains of rust can infect mint. Wet, humid conditions encourage this fungal disease, which often appears in late summer and overwinters in plant debris.

Solution: Remove infected stems and avoid wetting leaves. Harvest early. Fertilize annually, practice good garden sanitation, and select new plants carefully.

- Clip out and discard infected plant parts.
- Keep leaves dry. Water at ground level with a soaker hose or drip irrigation. Water early in the day so leaves can dry rapidly.
- Harvest mint leaves early in the season before the symptoms develop.
- After the spring harvest, cut back an infected plant to 2 inches above the ground and remove cuttings from the garden.
- In the fall, apply a fertilizer, such as 5-10-5 formulation (p.324) Use a formulation registered for mint and follow label directions carefully.
- At the end of the season, cut plants back to the soil and remove all debris.
- Inspect new plants for signs of rust and prune before planting.

Leaves have many small spots

Problem: Leaves or flowers have small, clustered pale or dark spots.

Cause: Four-lined plant bugs are greenish bugs with four black lines on each wing. Adults and their red-and-black spotted young suck sap from plants from May through midsummer, causing mostly cosmetic damage. Eggs overwinter in debris.

Solution: Handpicking and good garden sanitation will control these pests.

- Handpick and dispose of adults.
- Remove plant debris and weeds, which are overwintering sites, from the garden.

REGIONAL FOCUS
SOUTHEAST

While oregano thrives in the West, with its mild winters and dry summers, it may die out quickly in areas that have mild winters and wet summers, such as the Southeast. In such areas, grow oregano-flavored plants that are often used as replacements in tropical climates. Flavorful oregano substitutes include Mexican oregano *(Lippia graveolens)* and Spanish thyme *(Plectranthus amboinicus).*

Oregano
Origanum spp.

LIGHT: Full sun

SOIL: Average, well drained; pH 6.0 to 8.0

MOISTURE: Moist to seasonally dry

HARDINESS: Zones 5 to 11

Leaves have webs and insects

Problem: Leaves have tiny yellowish spots and may be curled or covered with fine webbing.

Cause: Spider mites are tiny, eight-legged, sap-sucking pests related to spiders. Spider mites are especially common on and most damaging to dry or dusty plants.

Solution: Spray infested plants with water and insecticide. Water plants often and use a mite repellent.

- At the first sign of infestation, dislodge insects from plants by rinsing leaves with a strong stream of water from a garden hose. Repeat every few days until symptoms subside.
- Spray foliage with pyrethrum, a botanical insecticide. Repeat applications until the infestation subsides. Follow label directions carefully.
- Water plants well when the soil is dry 2 to 3 inches beneath the surface.
- Spray with commercial garlic oil, as needed, to repel the pests.

Flavor is poor

Problem: Leaves have little flavor, or the flavor is not as expected.

Cause: Several factors can affect the flavor of this herb. Oregano will have a weak aroma and taste when it is grown in rich, moist soil. Seed-grown plants are likely

to vary in flavor. Also, certain species or varieties of oregano are less flavorful than others. Golden oregano *(O. vulgare* 'Aureum'), for example, is grown more for its attractive yellow-green leaves than its mild flavor.

Solution: Grow oregano from transplants and select culinary, rather than ornamental, varieties. Provide proper growing conditions.

- Do not grow oregano from seeds. Instead, purchase labeled, rooted plants. Rub a leaf between your fingers and check for a strong scent before buying a plant.
- Select varieties that are strongly flavored and suitable for cooking. Greek oregano *(O. heracleoticum)* has the strongest aroma and taste. Sicilian oregano *(O. vulgare* ssp. *hirtum)* and Italian oregano *(O. onites)* are also full flavored.
- Grow oregano in full sun and in soil that is only moderately fertile (p.324). Allow soil to dry out somewhat between waterings.

Leaves have winding, tan lines

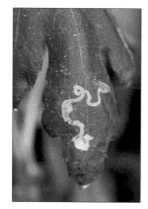

Problem: Narrow tan trails or small tan blotches appear on the leaves.

Cause: Leafminers are the larvae of small flies. The larvae, or maggots, hatch from eggs laid on the leaves and feed between the leaf surfaces. While the feeding of leafminers creates unattractive patterns and may kill individual leaves, it rarely kills the entire plant.

Solution: Remove infested leaves. Spray plants with insecticide. Erect barriers.

- Pinch off and dispose of leaves at the first sign of infestation.
- Spray foliage with the botanical insecticide pyrethrum or neem. Follow label carefully.
- Spread black plastic mulch around the plant to prevent maggots from dropping onto the soil, where they develop into adults.
- Cover plant with a fabric floating row cover to keep flies from laying eggs on leaves.

Parsley
Petroselinum crispum

LIGHT: Full sun to partial shade

SOIL: Fertile, well drained; pH 6.0 to 8.0

MOISTURE: Moist

HARDINESS: Cool-season biennial

Plant blooms early and dies

Problem: The plant sends up a flower stalk, blooms, sets seeds, and dies. Once the plant begins to flower, it produces few leaves.

Cause: Parsley is a biennial, so after being exposed to cold weather, it naturally bolts, or blooms and dies. This can happen to a plant that has overwintered and is returning the following spring, or it may happen to a plant that has been transplanted into the garden in spring when the weather is still cold.

Solution: Time parsley plantings well. Where the climate permits, start new plants more than once a year.

● Plant parsley in early spring. If spring nights are cool, expect some plants to bolt. Plant more parsley in late spring as a backup.

● In mild areas, plant more parsley in late summer for fall harvest. If the plant survives the winter, harvest leaves while the plant is still leafy but has not bloomed.

Plant develops white foam on leaves and is distorted

Problem: Small bunches of white bubbles appear on leaves and in leaf joints, especially in the center of the plant. Nearby leaves are a darker green and may be twisted or stunted.

Cause: Frog-hoppers, also called spittlebugs, are sap-sucking insects. The immature insects, or nymphs, secrete spittlelike foam to protect themselves while they are feeding. Their feeding causes leaves to become stunted and deformed.

Solution: Remove pests and rinse foliage thoroughly. Apply insecticide and keep the garden free of weeds that harbor insects.

● At the first sign of infestation, spray with a strong stream of water from the hose. Continue to wash foam from the affected plant every two to three days as needed.

● Spray plant with pyrethrum, a botanical insecticide, or a synthetic insecticide containing the active ingredient carbaryl. Use a formulation registered for parsley and follow label directions carefully.

● Cut down weedy grasses and plow under crop stubble in fall to destroy overwintering insect eggs.

Leaves are devoured by large, striped caterpillars

Problem: Smooth-skinned, light green caterpillars with black and yellow markings are chewing parsley leaves.

Cause: Parsleyworms are the larvae of a pretty butterfly, the black swallowtail. They grow to a length of 2 inches and can strip a plant of its leaves when feeding. However, they are rarely numerous enough to harm entire plantings. In California, a similar caterpillar, the larva of the western parsley swallowtail, feeds on parsley. Both give off a sickeningly sweet odor when disturbed.

Solution: Tolerate minor damage. Grow a larger crop to allow for damage. Treat large infestations with insecticide.

● Let caterpillars feed, or move them to a wild relative, such as Queen Anne's lace or wild fennel, far from your garden.

● Consider growing extra plants so that the caterpillars can feed and grow into butterflies while leaving enough leaves to harvest.

● If caterpillars are numerous and destructive, spray with the botanical insecticid pyrethrum or neem, following label directions.

- In severe infestations, spray a synthetic insecticide containing the active ingredient malathion. Use a formulation registered for parsley and follow label directions carefully.

Plant has yellow leaves, and maggots infest roots

Problem: A plant fails to thrive, and some of the leaves are yellowing. There are small white maggots visible in the roots.

Cause: The legless white larvae of the carrot weevil and the carrot rust fly often infest parsley, eating holes in roots. The larva of the carrot weevil, a small brown beetle present east of the Rocky Mountains, tunnels into the top of roots. The larva of the carrot rust fly, a tiny green-and-yellow fly common in the Northeast and the West, creates rust-colored channels as it tunnels into the middle to lower portions of roots. The leaves of a parsley plant with minor root damage are edible.

Solution: Apply fertilizer. Remove seriously affected plants. Use pesticides. Practice good garden sanitation.

- Remove the yellowed leaves from a slightly injured plant and fertilize the plant with liquid seaweed to restore vigor.
- Remove a badly infested plant from the garden and discard.
- If carrot weevil or carrot rust fly adults are present, spray with pyrethrum, a botanical insecticide. Follow label directions carefully.
- At the end of the growing season, clean up weeds and debris in which carrot weevil adults can overwinter.
- To prevent infestations the following year, treat the soil in spring with beneficial nematodes, a biological control, as soon as the soil temperature reaches 55°F.

Seeds don't sprout or seedlings die

Problem: No plants appear several weeks after seeds are sown. Or, seedlings come up but then wilt and die.

Cause: Parsley seeds are slow to germinate, requiring up to six weeks. The seedlings are susceptible to damping-off, a fungal disease, which can kill them as they begin to grow.

Solution: Prepare seeds. Start seeds indoors and transplant seedlings while they are still small. Provide good growing conditions.

- Before sowing, soak seeds overnight in warm water to soften the outer shell.
- Sow seeds in a sterile pot and potting mix about 10 weeks before the first frost-free date in spring. Keep the soil mix barely moist while seedlings are in pots.
- As soon as seedlings appear, move the pot to a sunny, cool location. If you live in a humid climate, provide air circulation with an electric fan. Thin seedlings by clipping out extra ones rather than pulling them.
- Transplant seedlings outdoors two to three weeks before the first frost-free date.

Plant leaves and stems yellow, and the plant may collapse

Problem: Leaves wilt and turn yellow, and the plant collapses. Watering does not revive it.

Cause: These symptoms can be caused by fungal disease. One commonly encountered problem, fusarium wilt, also called root rot, is a soil-borne fungal disease that causes roots to rot and plants to wilt and die.

Solution: Use seaweed remedy, or remove the plant. Rotate crops, use a protective covering.

- Water with seaweed solution; follow label.
- Discard unrevived plants and adjacent soil.
- Rotate parsley (p.115) with unrelated plants.
- Mulch to keep spore-laden soil from splashing on to plants.

Pot Marigold
Calendula officinalis

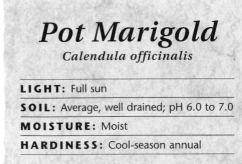

LIGHT: Full sun

SOIL: Average, well drained; pH 6.0 to 7.0

MOISTURE: Moist

HARDINESS: Cool-season annual

Leaves are coated with a white, powdery substance

Problem: Leaves develop a white or light gray coating that won't rub off. The plant is unsightly and may grow poorly.

Cause: Two types of powdery mildew infect pot marigolds: one species that also infects peas and beans, and one that also infects zinnias. Powdery mildew often strikes in mid- to late summer. It can develop in humid or dry weather. In cold regions, spores do not overwinter, but in mild areas they overwinter in infected plants and plant debris.

Solution: Remove infected leaves. Treat plants with water and baking-soda solution. Remove severely affected plants. Avoid wetting leaves when irrigating.

- Pick off and dispose of infected leaves.
- Spray both sides of leaves with water to wash off the spores. Spray early in the day, so foliage can dry quickly.
- If problems persist, spray with baking soda solution (p.392).
- Remove a badly infected plant from the garden. In mild areas, don't add it to the compost pile.
- Keep leaves of plants as dry as possible. Water at ground level, using only a soaker hose or drip irrigation. Water early in the day so that the leaves have time to dry before sundown, since spores germinate more rapidly on cool, damp leaves.

Flowering decreases

Problem: A plant blooms freely for a while, then blooms decrease. In some cases, the plant may bloom poorly from the outset.

Cause: If seedheads form, blooms will decrease. Hot weather stresses plants, reducing the number of flowers.

Solution: Remove spent blooms. Time plantings for cool weather.

- Remove spent blooms, or deadhead, regularly.
- In cold climates, plant in early spring so that plants mature in cool weather. In warm regions, plant in fall or late winter.

Plant is stunted and yellowish

Problem: Plant is yellow-green and grows poorly. Leaves may have yellowish dots.

Cause: Leafhoppers suck out leaf juices, creating yellowish spots. Aster leafhoppers also spread the fatal disease aster yellows, which causes stunted plants and discolored leaves.

Solution: Spray with water and insecticide. Remove infected plants.

- If leafhoppers are visible, dislodge them with a strong stream of hose water.
- Apply insecticidal soap or pyrethrum botanical insecticide. Follow label directions.
- Discard plants with disease symptoms.

REGIONAL FOCUS
NORTHEAST

Rosemary is a tender herb native to the Mediterranean that will not survive hard freezes. In cold climates, grow it as an annual, or as a potted plant and overwinter it indoors. Also try 'Arp', a variety hardy to zone 7. Plant it in a protected spot and mulch with 6 inches of straw or other loose, organic mulch in fall.

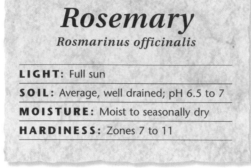

Rosemary
Rosmarinus officinalis

LIGHT: Full sun

SOIL: Average, well drained; pH 6.5 to 7

MOISTURE: Moist to seasonally dry

HARDINESS: Zones 7 to 11

A gray fuzzy substance forms on leaves and flowers

Problem: Small brown or orange blotches appear on leaves and flowers. Soon after, a thick gray fuzz develops.

Cause: Botrytis, or gray mold, is a soilborne fungus that develops on plants in moist conditions. The gray fuzz contains its spores.

Solution: Remove affected plant parts. Water properly. Mulch plants. Site plant properly.

- Clip out damaged plant parts. Remove and discard stems and flowers that exhibit either spots or gray fuzz.

- Keep foliage as dry as possible. Water at ground level only, using a soaker hose or drip irrigation. Water early in the day so that the plant can dry before sundown.

- Spread an organic mulch around the bases of plants to prevent spore-laden soil from splashing up and onto the foliage.

- Grow rosemary in full sun. In regions with rainy summer weather, locate plants against a south-facing wall under a high overhang. There they will receive the maximum amount of sunlight, and some protection from rain.

Leaves appear bleached and may be covered in fine webs

Problem: Tiny pale spots develop on leaf tops. Foliage turns progressively ashen to brown as it dies. Fine webbing and dustlike brownish grit may be found on leaf undersides.

Cause: Spider mites attack plants in hot, dry weather. They suck plant juices from leaf undersides and spin webs.

Solution: Remove affected foliage. Spray with water. Encourage natural predators.

- Prune out and destroy badly affected stems.

- At the first sign of infestation, dislodge mites with a strong stream of water from a hose. Repeat daily until mites are gone.

- Grow small-flowered nectar plants, such as Queen Anne's lace, sweet alyssum, and yarrow, nearby to attract beneficial insects, including green lacewings, which kill mites.

A white powder coats leaves

Problem: A white or pale gray powdery coating that will not rub off covers the foliage.

Cause: Powdery mildew is a fungal disease that thrives in high humidity. Poor air circulation and shady areas also favor powdery mildew disease.

Solution: Remove affected plant parts, keep foliage dry, and improve circulation and sun.

- Cut back an infected plant after it blooms and remove all debris from the garden.

- Keep foliage dry by watering only at ground level. Water early in the day so that leaves that become damp can dry rapidly.

- Thin out interior stems, sterilizing pruners between cuts (p.310). Space plants widely to promote good air circulation.

- Move plants from shade into full sunlight.

Sage
Salvia officinalis

LIGHT: Full sun

SOIL: Average, well drained; pH 6.0 to 7.0

MOISTURE: Moist

HARDINESS: Zones 2 to 11

Plant dies and roots are rotten

Problem: A plant wilts or loses leaves despite being adequately watered. When the plant dies, you discover that the roots are dark and rotten. There may be a white or tan fungal mat present on the soil surface.

Cause: Sage grows best in areas with low rainfall. When the soil is too wet, the plant becomes susceptible to several root-rot fungi. In addition, sage is susceptible to several soil fungi that infect plants whether or not they are overwatered. Sage can be infected with fusarium or verticillium wilt, Southern blight, and Texas root rot; all are potentially lethal diseases.

Solution: Water and locate plant properly to minimize problems. Grow resistant varieties. Time plantings.

- Water sage deeply only when the soil is dry 2 to 3 inches beneath the surface.

- If the garden soil is often soggy, transplant sage to a raised bed or container filled with loose, well-drained soil.

- In very rainy climates, grow sage under a south-facing overhang. This location will allow maximum sunlight to reach the plant and will also keep the soil drier than the surrounding area.

- In the South, grow the dwarf sage variety 'Compacta', which tolerates warm, moist summer weather better than the species.

- In the muggy climate of central and southern Florida and southern Texas, grow sage plants as annuals in winter.

Sage grown from seeds varies in flavor and appearance

Problem: Leaf flavor varies, with some seed-grown plants having better flavor than others.

Cause: Sage seeds do not produce uniformly flavored or colored plants.

Solution: Purchase named varieties at a nursery. Take stem cuttings from desirable plants.

- Select a nursery-grown, named variety with strongly scented leaves. Rub a leaf between your fingers to release the aroma. Then check its scent by sniffing the leaf.

- To start your own new plants, in spring root 4-inch stem-cuttings taken from plants with superior flavor.

White powdery spots spread and cover leaves

Problem: Sage leaves develop white powdery spots that cannot be rubbed off.

Cause: Powdery mildew is a fungal disease. Spores spread in wind and splashing water, and develop on leaves. In mild climates, spores overwinter on infected plants and plant debris.

Solution: Discard affected leaves and plant debris, apply baking-soda spray, and prune badly infected plants.

- Pick off and dispose of infected leaves.

- Spray baking-soda solution (p.392) on both sides of leaves at the first sign and once a week thereafter, until symptoms are gone.

- Cut badly infected plants to 4 inches to promote healthy new growth.

- In fall remove plant debris.

REGIONAL FOCUS

SOUTHEAST

French tarragon requires a dormant period in winter and may die if it receives less than two months of chilling. In mild-winter areas, substitute Mexican mint marigold *(Tagetes lucida)*, which has a similar flavor. Also called winter tarragon, this half-hardy perennial (zones 8 to 10) grows easily from seeds and can be harvested most of the year in warm climates.

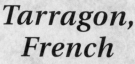

Tarragon, French

Artemisia dracunculus

LIGHT: Full sun

SOIL: Fertile, well drained; pH 6.5 to 7.5

MOISTURE: Moist

HARDINESS: Zones 3 to 9

Leaves are covered with a white, powdery coating

Problem: Foliage and stems have a white coating that won't rub off.

Cause: Powdery mildew is a fungal disease most prevalent when plants have poor air circulation and low light. The outbreaks occur mostly during mid- to late summer when cool nights follow warm days. It strikes in dry and moist air. While unsightly, powdery mildew is seldom fatal, and unaffected leaves can be harvested.

Solution: Spray plants with water and fungicide. Provide proper sanitation and growing conditions.

● Dislodge spores with a strong stream of water from a hose. Spray early in the day so that foliage dries before sundown.

● To slow the spread, spray plants with baking-soda solution (p.392), compost tea (p.392), or summer oil. Do not spray plants in direct sunlight, when sprays can damage leaves. Wait to spray until plants are shaded, or early in the day, before the sun is fully up.

● Remove and dispose of infected plant parts and other plant debris. Thin plants so that they do not touch, to allow adequate air circulation.

Plant dies suddenly or fails to return in spring

Problem: Plant dies in the summer; when you dig it up, you see that the roots are rotten. Or, the plant may disappear over winter, failing to emerge again in spring.

Cause: French tarragon requires well-drained soil that has a chance to dry briefly between waterings. Soggy soil favors the soilborne bacteria and fungi that cause root rot. In warm climates, French tarragon may go dormant in summer, and die over winter, as it requires two months of cold weather to thrive.

Solution: Provide proper growing conditions or grow French tarragon as an annual.

● Plant French tarragon in sandy, well-drained soil, ideally in a raised bed.

● In warm climates, water and fertilize French tarragon plants in midsummer to stimulate new growth. If a plant fails to emerge the following spring, replace it, and grow it as an annual from then on.

● In cold climates, shear back the top growth to ground level after the first killing frost in fall, and apply a 6-inch layer of loose mulch, such as straw, after soil freezes solid.

Leaves have a gray coating

Problem: A gray, dusty covering develops on the leaf undersides.

Cause: French tarragon can develop a particular form of downy mildew. Spores of this fungal disease spread and develop in moist conditions.

Solution: Dispose of infected leaves. Spray plants with fungicide, prune infected plants, and water properly.

● Pick off and discard infected leaves.

● Control the spread of the disease by spraying plants with baking-soda solution (p.392) until symptoms subside.

● If damage is serious, cut the plant back to a few inches above the ground so that it can produce new, healthy leaves.

● Water at ground level with a soaker hose or drip irrigation. Water early in the day so that leaves can dry before sundown.

Thyme
Thymus spp.

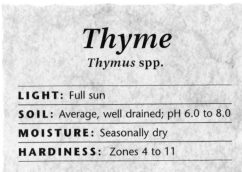

LIGHT: Full sun

SOIL: Average, well drained; pH 6.0 to 8.0

MOISTURE: Seasonally dry

HARDINESS: Zones 4 to 11

Leaves have a white coating

Problem: Leaves develop white areas that cannot be rubbed off.

Cause: Powdery mildew is a fungal disease that often strikes in late summer, when days are warm and nights are cool and damp. It spreads quickly in low-lying areas. Splashing water and wind spread the spores, which overwinter on plant debris.

Solution: Remove infected plant parts and practice good garden sanitation. Keep leaves dry, improve air circulation, or move plants.

- Remove and destroy infected foliage. Avoid wetting leaves when irrigating.
- If plants look bedraggled, cut them back to near the soil and allow healthy regrowth.
- In fall, clean up all plant debris.
- Space plants widely for good air circulation.
- If problems continue, replant in disease-free, well-drained soil, or raised beds.

TIME-TESTED TECHNIQUES

BANISHING BEES
Bees make a beeline for thyme flowers. To keep these busy pollinators from overrunning the garden, snip off blossoms before they open in summer. Or, plant a patch of thyme in a quiet corner of the garden, where the bees are unlikely to be disturbed.

Thyme lacks expected scent and flavor

Problem: The plant has a weak or unexpected scent or taste.

Cause: There are many species and varieties of thyme available. Some are preferred for culinary uses, and others for ornamental uses.

Solution: Select plant varieties carefully. Read plant labels and sniff plants before buying. Rub a leaf between your fingers to determine the scent.

- For culinary use, choose common, or English, thyme (*T. vulgaris*), the species used most in cooking; lemon thyme (*T.* x *citriodorus*), which has a lemon flavor; or caraway thyme (*T. herba-barona*), which has a spicy flavor.
- Plants with milder scents to use as ground covers include mother-of-thyme (*T. praecox* ssp. *arcticus*), woolly thyme (*T. pseudolanuginosus*), and wild thyme (*T. serpyllum*).

Plant wilts and dies; roots are decayed

Problem: The plant dies. When you dig it up, it has decayed roots. A cottony white mat may appear on soil and lower leaves.

Cause: Thyme growing in wet soil is susceptible to root-rot fungi. These cause decay and may also cause a white mat to form on the plant base and soil surface. Spores can live in the soil for years.

Solution: Destroy infected plants. Water properly. Provide well-drained soil. Rotate crops.

- Dig up and dispose of an infected plant.
- Water soil when it is dry 2 inches below the surface.
- Add compost or other organic matter to the soil to improve drainage. Alternatively, plant thyme in a container or raised bed.
- Locate new plants in a part of the garden where thyme has not grown previously.

DID YOU KNOW?

Time is not on thyme's side. Even with the best care, it lives only a few years. To keep the foliage lush, harvest leaves, cutting back the stems just as they start to bloom. Replace one or two plants yearly so that the patch doesn't die out all at once.

CHAPTER FOUR

ORNAMENTAL GRASSES AND GROUNDCOVERS

ORNAMENTAL GRASSES AND sturdy groundcovers bring welcome texture and movement to the garden. These tough, resilient plants require little maintenance, so they are ideal for massing on slopes or under trees or for filling awkward spots. You can partner statuesque grasses with tall flowers or underplant groundcovers with petite spring-flowering bulbs to charming effect.

At season's end, prune brown grasses to within one foot of the ground to make way for the new foliage and provide some fertilizer in spring, and they should enjoy a long, healthy life. For groundcovers, simply remove dead and damaged foliage each spring. If the occasional insect or disease problem does arise, turn to this chapter for well-tested solutions. For the safe use of commercial treatments, see page 9 and pages 390 to 399.

Quick Troubleshooting Guide

FLOWERS

POOR FLOWERING

Cause: Lack of sun, nutritional deficiency, excess nitrogen, cold temperatures

Solution: Transplant reluctant bloomers into a sunnier spot or prune overhead trees to admit more sunlight. Fertilize annually, but avoid use of high-nitrogen fertilizers. Pick plants suited to your hardiness zone.

LEAVES

ANGULAR DARK SPOTS ON LEAVES; BLACKENED STEMS

Cause: Bacterial leaf spot/twig blight

Solution: Remove and discard diseased foliage and stems. Apply an organic sulfur fungicide as directed. Prune in cool weather to avoid spreading the infection; sterilize pruners between cuts. Water at ground level to keep foliage dry. Plant resistant varieties.

RAGGED HOLES IN LEAVES; STEMS EATEN

Cause: Slugs, snails

Solution: Handpick and dispose of slugs and snails in the evening. Trap slugs and snails in saucers of beer or commercial traps set on the soil; spray plants with garlic-oil repellent.

DUSTY WHITE OR YELLOW SPOTS ON LEAF UNDERSIDES

Cause: Powdery mildew; rust

Solution: Remove and dispose of fungal-infected leaves and garden debris. Treat powdery mildew and rust with organic sulfur fungicide or baking soda solution. Water plants at ground level to prevent spreading spores. Site plants for air circulation and sun.

LEAVES STIPPLED WITH WHITE; YELLOW FOLIAGE

Cause: Spider mite

Solution: Spray plants, including leaf undersides, with insecticidal soap. Prevent mite buildup with regular watering and fertilizing. Hose plants off frequently during hot weather. Treat serious infestations with botanical insecticide pyrethrum, as directed.

WAXY OR CRUSTY BUMPS ON LEAVES

Cause: Scale

Solution: Spray the crawling stage of these insects with insecticidal soap as needed to control them. Apply dormant oil spray in early spring to smother overwintering adults. Site new plants away from those prone to scale.

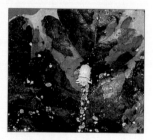

BROWN OR DEAD LEAF EDGES AND TIPS

Cause: Damage from sun, freezing winds, or salt

Solution: Soil moisture can prevent scorching and wash away soil salts. Water well when soil is dry 1 inch below the surface. Add organic matter to the soil to improve moisture retention. Apply mulch for winter protection.

BROWN BLOTCHES ON LEAVES; STEM TIPS SHRIVEL; NEARBY PLANTS TURN BROWN AND DIE

Cause: Leaf blight

Solution: Remove and discard infected plant parts. Mulch to prevent soilborne fungal spores from splashing onto the plants. Boost plant resistance with regular fertilizing and watering. Spray a fungicide labeled for plant species.

LEAVES DEVELOP SPOTS, TURN YELLOW, AND DIE

Cause: Leaf spot

Solution: Remove and dispose of fungal-diseased leaves. Thin out overgrown plants to improve air circulation. Water plants near the ground to avoid splashing the fungal spores onto plants.

DISTORTED, YELLOWING, STICKY LEAVES

Cause: Aphids

Solution: Dislodge insects from plant leaves with a strong stream of water from a hose as often as needed. Spray plants with insecticidal soap as directed.

BROWN OR BLACK SPOTS OR FUZZY MOLD

Cause: Fungal mold

Solution: Treat mold-prone plants with an organic lime-sulfur fungicide or a synthetic fungicide labeled for plant. Space plants widely. Use a 3-inch-thick layer of mulch to protect leaves from soil-borne spores. Remove disease-harboring weeds and plant debris.

YELLOWING LEAVES; SLOW PLANT GROWTH

Cause: Excessive sunlight

Solution: Relocate shade-loving groundcovers to an area protected from afternoon sun. In spring, work organic matter into the soil to improve moisture retention and fertility. Water deeply when soil is dry 1 inch under the surface.

WHOLE PLANT

BROWN GROWING TIPS; BLACKENED PLANT; PLANT DIES

Cause: Dieback

Solution: Remove and discard fungal-infected stems or branches. Thin out growth to improve air circulation. Spray infected plants with an organic copper-based fungicide.

PLANT FLOPS OVER

Cause: Overfertilization, lack of sunlight

Solution: Avoid fertilizing grasses the first season after planting unless they're grown in sandy, porous soil. Transplant young plants to a sunnier location in early spring. Divide old clumps into small sections and discard the central portion of the clump.

YELLOW WILTED LEAVES; FOLIAGE BLACKENS AND ROTS AT PLANT BASE

Cause: Root, stem, or crown rot

Solution: Where fungal infection is serious, remove diseased plant and the surrounding 6 inches of soil. Improve soil drainage by digging in organic matter and by moving mulch a few inches away from plant crown. Plant in raised beds if soil drainage is poor. Allow top 2 inches of soil to dry between waterings.

GROUNDCOVER INVADES OTHER GARDEN AREAS

Cause: Invasive plant in too small an area

Solution: Use mulch, weed barrier cloth, and edgings to contain vigorously spreading plants. A shadier location will slow their growth. Prune frequently in the summer to prevent unwanted rooting. Promptly remove rooted runners or seedlings before they become established.

NO NEW GROWTH IN SPRING

Cause: Cold-weather damage

Solution: Prevent winter kill by planting species suited to your climate or grow tender groundcovers and grasses as annuals. In cold-winter areas, protect plants with mulches and burlap wraps. Tender plants can also be sheltered in a garage or shed insulated from hard freezes.

English Ivy
Hedera helix

LIGHT: Partial to full shade

SOIL: Any, well drained; pH 3.7 to 7

MOISTURE: Moist

HARDINESS: Zones 4 to 9

Leaves appear bleached

Problem: Leaves appear pale and dry, and close examination reveals the presence of countless tiny white or yellow specks. Leaf undersides may be covered with fine webs and minute red or brown insects.

Cause: Spider mites are widespread pests related to spiders. Mites overwinter in leaf litter and other debris and are most active during hot, dry weather. To confirm their presence, tap an affected leaf over a sheet of white paper and look for the tiny, moving insects. Feeding in masses and left untreated, spider mites can swiftly kill a plant.

Solution: Keep soil and leaves moist; apply insecticide at the first sign of infestation.

- Water when the soil is dry 1 inch beneath the surface. Hose off plants frequently.
- Thoroughly spray an infested plant with insecticidal soap, being sure to coat the undersides of the leaves. Repeat according to label directions until pests are gone.
- In severe cases, treat plant alternately with light horticultural oil and insecticidal soap. You can also use pyrethrum, a botanical insecticide, or a synthetic insecticide registered for English ivy that contains the active ingredient acephate. Follow label directions carefully.

Leaves droop in summer

Problem: In hot weather, new leaves appear slightly wilted, even though the roots have adequate water. Leaves may yellow and drop. Tiny dark bumps appear on new growth.

Cause: Black scale are tiny, stationary insects that suck juices from the stems and leaf undersides of plants. The species that attacks ivy is most prevalent in warm climates and can kill a planting in a single season.

Solution: Treat plants with appropriate insecticidal sprays.

- Spray infested plants with light horticultural oil to smother scale, following directions.
- If the plant continues to show damage during the summer, spray oil again in winter to kill overwintering scale.
- In early summer, thoroughly coat the plant with insecticidal soap or use pyrethrum, a botanical insecticide, to kill new hatchlings. Follow label directions carefully.

Leaves have angular dark spots; stems blacken

Problem: Following the appearance of angular brown or black leaf spots, ivy stems blacken and die. Major leafy stems, rather than a few scattered leaves, exhibit symptoms.

Cause: Bacterial leaf spot is most common when the weather is warm and humid. The bacteria enter ivy through pruning cuts or other injuries and can be spread from plant to plant by splashing water. When this disease infects stems, it is often called twig blight.

Solution: Remove diseased growth. Use fungicides to treat the infection. Fertilize and prune plants regularly to remove damaged or diseased stems. Water properly and select resistant varieties.

- Prune and dispose of diseased growth.
- Treat infected plants with a organic sulfur fungicide. Follow label directions carefully.
- Fertilize ivy in early spring with a slow-release, low-nitrogen fertilizer, such as 5-10-10 (p.324).
- Avoid wetting the foliage when watering. Use a soaker hose or drip irrigation and water early in the morning so that leaves can dry during the day.
- Prune in cool weather. Disinfect pruners (p.310) with rubbing alcohol between cuts to keep from spreading disease.
- For future plantings, select a resistant variety, such as 'Gold Dust'.

New leaves are stunted and yellowing

Problem: As new growth emerges in spring, the growing tips appear distorted and wilted. Tiny, pear-shaped insects cling to young stems and undersides of new leaves.

Cause: Aphids are soft-bodied insects that damage ivy by sucking sap.

Solution: Dislodge aphids, apply an insecticide, and attract natural predators.

- Knock the aphids from the new growth with a strong stream of water.
- If problems persist, apply pyrethrum, a botanical insecticide. Or use a synthetic insecticide registered for English ivy that contains the active ingredient acephate. Follow label directions carefully.
- Grow small-flowered nectar plants nearby, such as yarrow, dill, or scabiosa, to attract beneficial insects, including ladybugs, lacewings, and predatory wasps.

Leaves have brown spots

Problem: Brown or tan spots mar the leaves, especially near the margins.

Cause: Several types of fungi cause leaf spots on ivy. The most common is amerosporium leaf spot, which usually infects leaves from winter through early spring.

Solution: Remove diseased foliage, keep leaves dry, and apply fungicide.

- Pick off affected leaves to reduce the number of spores present in a planting.
- Avoid overhead watering to keep leaves dry.
- Apply a synthetic fungicide registered for English ivy that contains the active ingredient chlorothalonil or iprodione. Follow label directions carefully.

Yellow-orange, stringy growth covers plant

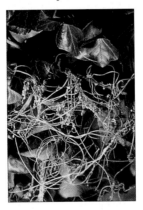

Problem: A planting suddenly becomes covered with what appears to be a yellow-orange mass of tangled yarn.

Cause: Dodder, a parasitic weed that lacks chlorophyll and belongs to the morning glory family, can infest ivy rapidly in summer. If allowed to grow, dodder produces small white flowers and seeds that grow into plants the following season.

Solution: Remove dodder and keep the garden free of materials that can harbor seeds. Apply a pre-emergent herbicide.

- Pull dodder by hand and dispose of it.
- Avoid hay or straw mulch, as it can harbor dodder seeds.
- In spring, apply DCPA, a synthetic pre-emergent herbicide. Use a formulation registered for English ivy and follow label directions carefully.

**REGIONAL FOCUS
SOUTHEAST**

In the warm, humid climate of the coastal Southeast, a soilborne fungal disease called Rhizoctonia root rot can infect English ivy, causing it to wither and die. To discourage the fungus, grow plants in well-drained soil or raised beds amended with compost, which contains disease-fighting organisms. Or grow Algerian ivy (*Hedera algeriensis*), a species better adapted to hot, humid conditions.

REGIONAL FOCUS
SOUTHEAST

Ornamental grasses are easy-care plants in most parts of the country. The majority are cold hardy, and there is usually no need to supplement with soil amendments, fertilizer, or water.

Southern gardeners, however, may find that grasses suffer from root rot where it's hot and humid and the soil drains poorly. If these conditions exist in your garden, improve soil drainage (p.331) before planting, or plant ornamental grasses in raised beds or containers.

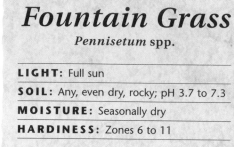

Fountain Grass
Pennisetum spp.

LIGHT: Full sun

SOIL: Any, even dry, rocky; pH 3.7 to 7.3

MOISTURE: Seasonally dry

HARDINESS: Zones 6 to 11

Leaves have small yellow spots

Problem: From midsummer to fall, the leaf undersides exhibit small, oblong, yellow spots or streaks with powdery orange deposits.

Cause: Rust is a fungal disease. Its spores are carried from plant to plant by wind or splashing water. Damp weather encourages rust.

Solution: Remove infected leaves and keep foliage dry. Site plants carefully and prune them back in fall. There is no fungicide registered for rust on fountain grass.

● Cut out and dispose of leaves that show signs of infection.

● Water at ground level with a soaker hose or drip irrigation to avoid wetting leaves.

● Grow fountain grass in a location that provides good sun exposure and air circulation.

● In areas where fountain grass is hardy (zone 6 and warmer), cut the plant to 6 inches above ground in late fall. Rake up and dispose of mulch and debris near the plants.

Leaves have tan spots that turn into long streaks

Problem: Leaves show numerous tan spots, especially near their tips. The spots develop into streaks that run lengthwise down the leaves.

Cause: Leaf spot is a fungal disease.

Solution: Remove and dispose of infected leaves, spray with fungicide, and keep the foliage as dry as possible.

● If only part of a clump shows symptoms, cut out the diseased leaves close to the ground and dispose of them.

● Avoid overhead watering to keep leaves dry.

Plant does not produce new growth in spring

Problem: By late spring, a plant that grew the previous season fails to show signs of life.

Cause: Cold temperatures will kill fountain grass that is not sufficiently hardy for the region or that has not been given adequate winter protection.

Solution: Select a species appropriate to the climate. Grow fountain grass as an annual in cold areas. Provide winter protection.

● Check the winter hardiness of the desired fountain grass species before purchasing. *P. alopecuriodes* is hardy to zone 6, whereas *P. setaceum* and *P. villosum* are hardy only to zones 8 and 9, respectively.

● In areas where the desired species is not hardy, grow fountain grass as an annual. Start seeds indoors in early spring and set out when danger of frost has passed.

● In cold climates, you can also dig up tender plants and overwinter them in a garage or other place not exposed to a hard freeze.

● In regions where a species is marginally hardy, wrap the base of an outdoor clump in burlap in late fall to provide protection from cold; remove burlap in early spring.

Hosta
Hosta spp.

LIGHT: Partial to full shade

SOIL: Rich, well drained; pH 5.0 to 7.5

MOISTURE: Moist to seasonally dry

HARDINESS: Zones 3 to 8

Pale leaves have brown edges

Problem: Leaves appear bleached or washed out. Leaf margins and tips turn brown, dry, and crisp; leaves shrivel.

Cause: Strong sunlight causes sunscald on hostas' shade-loving foliage, and warm air and insufficient soil moisture cause leaf burn.

Solution: Provide adequate soil moisture and proper growing conditions.

- Water when the soil is dry 1 inch beneath the surface.
- Limit the amount of direct sunlight the plants receive. Either transplant the hostas to a shady site or plant taller plants nearby to provide shade.
- Before planting the following season, prepare the planting area properly. In fall or early spring, incorporate a 3- or 4-inch layer of finished garden compost, commercial compost, or well-rotted manure into the soil to provide a rich, moisture-retentive, quick-draining growing medium.

Foliage is ragged and marked with slimy streaks

Problem: Foliage is ragged and chewed; the lower leaves are usually damaged first. Slimy silver trails appear on the plant or ground.

Cause: Slugs and snails are mollusks that feed on tender foliage. Moist soil, cool weather, and humidity encourage their activity.

Solution: Remove the pests, use traps to reduce further infestations, and clean up garden debris.

- Handpick and dispose of slugs and snails. An hour after sundown is the best time to find them feeding on plants.
- Set shallow containers in the ground and fill them with an inch of stale beer. Slugs and snails will crawl in and drown. Refresh beer every other day.
- Keep the garden free of decaying vegetation and other debris to eliminate daytime hiding places.
- If necessary, take other steps to control slugs and snails (p.49).

Foliage has dark specks

Problem: Leaves and stems are covered with small reddish or purplish bumps encased in a thick, whitish pink, waxy coating. Sticky, clear secretions and black, sooty mold may be present.

Cause: Florida wax scale are small sucking insects. The stationary adults cover their eggs with their bodies. Tiny, crawling young collect on leaf undersides.

Solution: Use insecticide and introduce beneficial insects, which prey on scale.

- Spray infested foliage with insecticidal soap every three to five days, as needed, until the pests are gone.

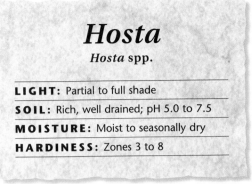

• Or spray plants with the botanical insecticide neem oil or a refined horticultural oil. Follow label directions carefully.

• If problems persist, apply a synthetic insecticide registered for hostas that contains the active ingredient bifenthrin. Follow label directions carefully.

• Grow small-flowered nectar plants nearby, such as sweet alyssum and scabiosa, to attract predatory insects, including lacewings, ladybugs, and parasitic wasps, which parasitize or feed on scale.

Tops of leaves turn yellow; undersides have orange blisters

Problem: Leaves turn yellow, and small, powdery yellow spots form on leaf undersides.

Cause: Rust is a fungal disease caused by several species of fungi. It develops in damp weather and can spread quickly when the spores are blown or splashed onto wet leaves.

Solution: Remove infected leaves, use fungicide, water properly, and practice good garden sanitation. Relocate plants if necessary.

• Pick and destroy diseased leaves.

• If the rust infection is severe, spray with an organic sulfur fungicide. Follow label directions carefully.

• Water at ground level, and water early in the day so that leaves can dry quickly.

• Clean up leaf debris during and at the end of the season, to eliminate overwintering sites for disease spores.

• If rust persists, move plants into an area with full sun, well-drained soil, and good air circulation.

Gray patches appear on leaves; leaf tips die

Problem: Leaves develop gray patches, and the leaf tips die back. Plant may rot at the crown, or base.

Cause: Gray mold is a fungal disease that becomes active in wet weather when temperatures are around 60°F. It spreads quickly among plants in low-lying areas and where nights are cool and damp. Spores are carried by water and air, and new infections can start every few days if moisture is sufficient. The disease overwinters in plant debris.

Solution: Practice good garden sanitation, fertilize, use fungicide, and plant properly.

• Remove and destroy infected plant material.

• Drench the soil with disease-inhibiting compost tea (p.392) when conditions favor the disease.

• Spray with an organic fungicide that contains copper sulfate and hydrated lime. Start treatment when the plant is 6 inches high and continue every 10 to 14 days until flowering. Follow label directions carefully.

• If problems persist, apply a synthetic fungicide registered for hostas that contains the active ingredient mancozeb. Follow label directions carefully.

• Thoroughly remove plant debris in fall. Mulch lightly after cleanup to create a barrier between the foliage and spores.

• In the future, avoid planting in low spots and space plants to allow for air circulation.

Lamb's Ears
Stachys byzantina

LIGHT: Full sun to afternoon shade

SOIL: Moist, well drained; pH 6.0 to 7.0

MOISTURE: Moist to seasonally dry

HARDINESS: Zones 4 to 7

Leaves turn brown and rot

Problem: Leaves turn brown and rot. Patches of plants die in hot, humid weather.

Cause: The woolly leaves trap moisture. Wet foliage, along with high night temperatures and humidity, encourage various fungal diseases.

Solution: Destroy infected foliage, prune plants, keep leaves dry, and site plants well.

- Remove and discard diseased leaves.
- Cut back foliage in late summer. Healthy new growth will look good by fall.
- Water at ground level with a soaker hose or drip irrigation and water early in the day so that leaves dry quickly.
- Place new plants in full sun.

Plant turns yellow, wilts, rots at the base, and dies

Problem: The leaves of lamb's ears plants growing in poorly drained soil turn yellow and wilt. Foliage blackens at the base of the plant, or crown, and dies. The roots also turn black and die.

Cause: Root rot is a soilborne fungal disease. It is persistent and difficult to treat. Plants in poorly drained soil are most susceptible. Warm, wet weather encourages the disease.

Solution: Remove affected plants and soil, apply a soil drench, water and mulch properly, and improve drainage.

- Remove and destroy diseased plants. Also remove the surrounding 6 inches of soil.
- Drench infected soil with disease-fighting compost tea (p.392).
- Avoid overhead watering and allow soil to dry out between waterings.
- Pull mulch a few inches away from crowns.
- Improve drainage by working 2 to 4 inches of compost into a new planting area or grow lamb's ears in raised beds.

Leaves have ragged holes

Problem: Silver trails appear on leaves and soil. Leaves have ragged holes. Damage usually begins on lower leaves first.

Cause: Slugs and snails. These night-feeding mollusks can devastate lamb's ears, especially young plants. Damp, cool weather, moist soil, and humidity encourage their activity. Leaf litter and debris like boards and broken pots left on the ground provide them with daytime hiding places.

Solution: Use handpicking, trapping, and good garden sanitation to reduce damage.

- Hunt these pests after dark by flashlight and dispose of them.
- Set out homemade beer traps (p.49) or commercial traps. Empty and renew the traps every three days.
- Remove mulch and debris to reduce hiding places.

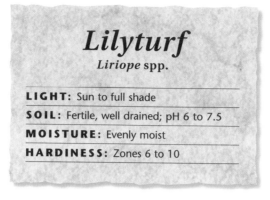

Lilyturf

Liriope spp.

LIGHT: Sun to full shade

SOIL: Fertile, well drained; pH 6 to 7.5

MOISTURE: Evenly moist

HARDINESS: Zones 6 to 10

Leaves turn brown in winter

Problem: Plant appears ragged and brown after exposure to cold temperatures.

Cause: Although lilyturf is evergreen and winter hardy to zone 6, temperatures below 20°F often damage the leaves. Following a very cold winter or exposure to accumulated ice, leaves often turn yellowish brown.

Solution: Prune damaged growth and fertilize to stimulate healthy new growth.

- Leave the damaged foliage on the plant throughout the winter to help insulate the plant's base, or crown, from cold weather. In spring, carefully trim off the affected leaves with pruning shears, a lawn mower, or string trimmer.

- Fertilize plants in spring or early summer with a balanced fertilizer, such as 10-10-10 (p.324). Do not fertilize late in the season; late feeding may stimulate the growth of tender new leaves, which will be more susceptible to frost damage than old growth.

Leaf margins and tips brown

Problem: Leaves develop brown patches that spread along the margins and leaf tips.

Cause: Leaf anthracnose is caused by fungi and can infect lilyturf when the weather is rainy.

Solution: Prune infected plant parts and apply mulch. There is no fungicide registered for use against leaf anthracnose on lilyturf.

- At the first sign of disease, prune and dispose of infected leaves. If necessary, remove the entire plant. Be careful not to cut into the plant base. Sterilize (p.310) pruners with rubbing alcohol between cuts.

- To prevent future problems, mulch around healthy plants to keep soilborne disease spores from splashing onto them.

Leaves have ragged holes

Problem: Leaves have irregular holes chewed along their edges, especially the leaves on the outside of the clump.

Cause: Slugs and snails thrive in the same moist, shady locations lilyturf favors. These mollusk pests feed on foliage at night and hide under mulch and low-lying foliage during the day.

Solution: Trap and remove slugs and snails. Make the area uninviting to these pests.

- Handpick at night by flashlight for three consecutive nights. Dispose of the pests.

- If the pests persist, use traps baited with beer (p.49) or commercial traps baited with the synthetic ingredient metaldehyde or mesurol. Follow label directions carefully. Clean and rebait every three days until the problem is under control.

- Remove nearby mulch and plant debris to deny slugs and snails daytime hiding places.

Maiden Grass
Miscanthus sinensis

LIGHT: Full sun to partial shade

SOIL: Average, well drained; pH 5.5 to 7

MOISTURE: Moist to dry

HARDINESS: Zones 5 to 9

Plant flops over

Problem: Instead of standing straight, a plant bends over and arches in different directions.

Cause: Maiden grass, which can range in height from 4 to 10 feet, will flop over if it is grown in too much shade or in poorly drained or excessively rich soil. Also, an old, overgrown plant may grow so weakly that it has trouble standing erect.

Solution: Transplant maiden grass to a sunny, well-drained site; divide older specimens. Fertilize sparingly.

- In early spring, prepare a planting area with full sun exposure and moist but well-drained soil, and dig up the affected plant. If the plant is young, move the entire clump to the new location. If the plant is older, cut away and discard the interior portion of the clump. Cut 6-inch-wide, healthy clumps from the perimeter and replant these divisions in the new site.

- Do not fertilize maiden grass during the first season after planting unless it is growing in very porous, sandy soil. For plants in infertile soil, feed every six weeks with a balanced fertilizer, such as 10-10-10 (p.324), at half the rate recommended on the label.

No growth emerges in spring

Problem: A month after the last spring frost, there are no signs of life from an established clump of maiden grass.

Cause: Lack of spring growth often results from winter injury due to cold temperatures. In mild-winter areas, the problem may be caused by excessive soil moisture, which rots the plant's roots during the winter.

Solution: Provide winter protection in areas where maiden grass is marginally hardy. In warmer climates, improve soil drainage.

- In late fall in zones 5 and 6, cut back maiden grass to 6 inches above the ground. Wrap the pruned clump with burlap and hold it in place with bricks or wire pins. After a snowfall, pack snow around the wrapped bundle to further insulate the crowns from cold. Remove the burlap about two weeks before the last expected spring frost to allow new growth.

- In mild climates, improve drainage by working finished compost, well-rotted manure, or other organic matter into the soil. Alternatively, grow maiden grass in raised beds (p.328) of well-drained soil.

Leaves have reddish brown spots and streaks

Problem: Reddish brown spots develop on the leaves, and the edges and tips of older leaves turn brown. A young plant may turn entirely brown and die in early summer.

Cause: Miscanthus leaf blight is a fungal disease that often appears in late spring and into early summer.

Solution: Dispose of infected leaves, apply fungicide, and use good garden sanitation.

- Prune off and destroy affected leaves as soon as the spots appear.

- Spray the remaining foliage with an organic copper-based fungicide. Follow label directions carefully.

- In late fall, rake up and dispose of any withered leaves and other plant debris.

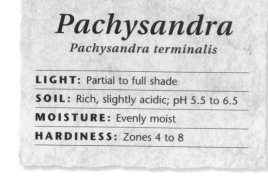

Pachysandra
Pachysandra terminalis

LIGHT: Partial to full shade

SOIL: Rich, slightly acidic; pH 5.5 to 6.5

MOISTURE: Evenly moist

HARDINESS: Zones 4 to 8

Brown blotches mar leaves

Problem: Leaves have chocolate brown blotches, and the stem tips shrivel. The symptoms spread to nearby plants, which also turn brown and die.

Cause: Volutella leaf blight is a fungal disease, most common in plantings that are weakened by the feeding of scale insects or are smothered by a layer of damp leaves.

Solution: Remove diseased and older foliage and debris. Treat with fungicide and, if needed, insecticide. Add compost and fertilizer.

- Pull out old stems and those that show blight symptoms. Also remove dead leaves and plant debris from around the foliage.

- Avoid future problems by applying a synthetic fungicide registered for pachysandra that contains the active ingredient copper chloride. Follow label directions carefully.

- If scale (entry, right) is present on foliage, treat with appropriate insecticide.

- In early spring, add a 1-inch layer of compost to the soil to introduce disease-fighting organisms.

- In early summer, apply a slow-release, balanced fertilizer, such as 10-10-10 (p.324).

Plant has yellowing leaves

Problem: Leaves turn light yellow-green, and the plant grows slowly.

Cause: Full sun will scorch pachysandra, which requires shade. Low soil fertility will stunt its growth.

Solution: Provide pachysandra with shade and moist, fertile, well-drained soil.

- Grow plants in an area that receives less than six hours of direct sun daily.

- Supplement rain as needed to supply 1 inch of water per week in the growing season.

- In spring, incorporate organic matter into beds. In early summer, apply a slow-release, balanced fertilizer, such as 10-10-10 (p.324).

Plant has yellowing foliage with dark specks

Problem: New leaves may be small and pale, and small, dark disks are on leaves and stems.

Cause: Scale is a persistent, sap-sucking pest. Females are dark brown or gray, males are white, and immature scales are orange.

Solution: Spray infested plants. Thin and fertilize to promote growth. Avoid host plants.

- To control light infestations, apply horticultural oil, insecticidal soap, acephate, or pyrethrum. Follow label directions carefully.

- For severe infestations, spray the plants with a synthetic insecticide registered for pachysandra that contains the active ingredient carbaryl or bendiocarb. Follow label directions carefully.

- In early spring, thin plants and fertilize with rotted manure to encourage growth.

- Don't grow pachysandra near plants that can harbor scale, like Japanese euonymus.

Pampas Grass

Cortaderia selloana

LIGHT: Full sun

SOIL: Well drained; pH 5.5 to 7

MOISTURE: Dry to wet

HARDINESS: Zones 8 to 10

New plants appear where they are not wanted

Problem: Seedlings become a weedy nuisance.

Cause: A species that closely resembles true pampas grass is a rampant self-seeder in warm climates. Classified as *C. jubata*, it has shorter leaves and fewer feathery plumes than does the ornamental garden variety *C. selloana*.

Solution: Destroy unwanted plants and replant with true pampas grass (*C. selloana*).

● Dig up and remove the unwanted plants from the garden and replace them with a labeled plant from a reputable nursery.

● You may also spray individual seedlings with a synthetic herbicide registered for pampas grass that contains the active ingredient fluazifop or glyphosate. Follow label directions carefully.

Thick, dead foliage is difficult to prune

Problem: Clumps grow so large as they mature that they are hard to prune.

Cause: The size of this grass, which can reach 12 feet tall, makes it difficult to cut back in late winter, but annual pruning is needed to make way for new growth in spring.

Solution: Use the proper tools and techniques

to prune pampas grass annually. Wear thick gloves and protective clothing when pruning; the leaves have very sharp edges. It's best to prune pampas grass in late winter, before new growth appears. But it can be pruned when it goes dormant in late fall, in very warm climates, and in areas where the dry foliage would pose a fire hazard over the winter.

● If the clump is less than 1 foot across, use long-handled lopping shears to prune it back to about 6 inches above the ground in late winter. In warm climates, check for green growth and avoid cutting into it.

● On larger plants, cut the clump down to 6 inches above ground with a scythe. Alternatively, bind the stems together around the middle of the clump with twine or packing tape. Then cut the plant back, using a weed trimmer fitted with a blade attachment.

Narrow tan spots mar leaves

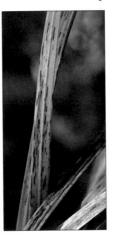

Problem: The leaves are marked with oblong tan spots.

Cause: Leaf spot is a disease caused by fungi that are most active during the growing season in periods of wet weather.

Solution: Remove diseased leaves, keep foliage dry, irrigate properly, and use fungicide. Divide overgrown clumps.

● Cut off and dispose of diseased leaves.

● When spots appear, use a synthetic fungicide registered for pampas grass that contains the active ingredient maneb or thiram. Follow label directions carefully.

● Keep irrigation water off foliage.

● Divide clumps that have grown so broad that the leaves in the center dry slowly (p.29). Remove dead foliage from the center to improve air circulation and help keep the plant's interior dry.

Periwinkle

Vinca minor

LIGHT: Partial to full shade

SOIL: Well drained; pH 6 to 8

MOISTURE: Moist

HARDINESS: Zones 3 to 8

Stems turn brown and die

Problem: Growing tips turn brown; then entire stems turn black and die to the ground.

Cause: Dieback is a wet-weather fungal disease. It spreads rapidly when weather conditions are warm and damp, and can be fatal.

Solution: Prune affected stems and thin the plant to promote better air circulation. Treat foliage with fungicide.

- Clip off and dispose of as many diseased vines as possible to reduce the number of spores present.
- To increase air circulation and discourage the development of spores, thin dense, overlapping growth, where the foliage stays wet after rain or watering.
- To control a serious outbreak, spray the infected plant with an organic copper-based fungicide. Follow label directions carefully.

Plants spread beyond their beds

Problem: Plants invade lawns or flower beds.

Cause: When growing conditions are ideal, periwinkle stems develop roots where they touch the soil and can become invasive.

Solution: Remove unwanted plants. Create barriers, edge plant beds, and spread mulch. Site plants carefully.

- When a plant spreads where it is not wanted, dig up new roots and cut back the stem to the desired length. Remove new plants to prevent them from becoming established.
- When growing periwinkle in partial sun, line the bed with a deep edging that will prevent the vine roots from spreading.
- Use a weed trimmer or shears to trim the edges of plantings often in the summer to keep vines from rooting outside the bed.
- Mulch around nearby plants to discourage wandering periwinkle stems from rooting.
- Locate new plantings in shade to slow their spread; they thrive where few plants grow.

Leaves have brown spots

Problem: Circular or oval brown spots appear on the leaves.

Cause: Leaf spot, a fungal disease, is most likely to appear during periods of cool and damp weather. Spores are spread by splashing water, and they overwinter in plant debris.

Solution: Remove infected leaves. Water carefully. Spray with a fungicide.

- Clip off and dispose of the infected leaves and remove surrounding plant debris.
- Water in the morning so foliage dries rapidly. Water at ground level to keep leaves dry.
- If a case is severe, spray the foliage with an organic sulfur fungicide. Follow label directions carefully.

Sedum
Sedum spp.

LIGHT: Full sun to light shade

SOIL: Well drained; pH 5.5 to 7.0

MOISTURE: Moist to seasonally dry

HARDINESS: Zones 3 to 8

Leaves are yellow and distorted

Problem: Leaves turn yellow or brown and may be puckered.

Cause: Aphids are small, soft-bodied sucking insects.

Solution: Hose off aphids and spray with insecticide soap.

- Dislodge aphids with a strong stream of water from a hose.
- Spray leaves with insecticidal soap every three to five days until aphids are gone.

Leaves have yellow spots

Problem: Small yellow spots form on leaf undersides. The leaf tops develop yellow or dark areas.

Cause: Rust is a fungal disease that thrives in damp weather. Its orange spores blow or splash from plant to plant, developing on wet leaves.

Solution: Remove affected leaves and apply fungicide. Water carefully and practice good garden sanitation. Relocate plant if needed.

- Handpick and destroy infected leaves.
- If the case is severe, apply organic sulfur fungicide. Follow label directions carefully.

- Water in the morning so plants dry quickly.
- Thin foliage to increase air circulation.
- At season's end, clean up leaf debris to prevent spores from overwintering in it.
- If rust is a persistent problem, transplant sedum to a new location that provides full sun exposure and good air circulation.

Stem rots at ground level

Problem: White, threadlike fungal strands form on the stem at soil level. Round tan or yellowish structures the size of a pinhead appear in the soil around stems. Lower leaves rot, and the plant topples over.

Cause: Crown rot, or Southern blight, is a soilborne fungal disease that is active in hot, humid weather.

Solution: Remove infected plants and surrounding soil. Amend the soil.

- Remove and discard the diseased plant and the surrounding 6 inches of soil. Apply ammonium nitrate, a high-nitrogen fertilizer, to the area, according to package directions, to suppress fungal growth.
- In summer, drench plants and soil with disease-inhibiting compost tea (p.392).

TIME-TESTED TECHNIQUES

PRUNING SEDUM

Despite its floppy appearance, sedum 'Autumn Joy' can be a handsome groundcover. Simply cut it back once in early summer to give it a pleasing, ground-hugging shape. As a bonus, the plant will produce more flowers later in the season. When the plant is 8 inches tall, cut the stems down to 4 inches with pruning shears, making each cut about ¼ inch above a leaf joint.

CHAPTER FIVE

SHRUBS AND VINES

ROM THE BRIGHTLY COLORED display of azaleas in spring to the profuse and long-lasting fruits of cotoneasters in fall to the year-round sculptured elegance of boxwoods, shrubs bring form, foliage, flowers, and fragrance to the landscape. Whether you need a low creeping plant to cover a bank or a tall bushy one as a focal point in the garden, there is a shrub to suit your every need.

If you want to create a dramatic vertical element that leads the eye upward or need to camouflage an eyesore, vines can provide a fast solution. The vigorous trumpet vine and hardy clematis are good candidates for the jobs.

As a group, shrubs and vines are remarkably healthy plants. But when insects or diseases do cause trouble, this chapter has solutions. Remember to use environmentally friendly solutions first. For the safe use of commercial treatments, see page 9 and pages 390 to 399.

Quick Troubleshooting Guide

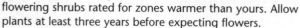

FLOWERS

POOR FLOWERING

Cause: Shade, ill-timed pruning, overfertilizing, lack of dormancy, young plant

Solution: Move plants into sun, or thin trees. Prune early-spring-flowering shrubs as flowers fade. Avoid high-nitrogen fertilizers. Don't plant flowering shrubs rated for zones warmer than yours. Allow plants at least three years before expecting flowers.

SPOTS MAR FLOWERS AND LOWER LEAVES; TWIGS DIE BACK

Cause: Fungal blight

Solution: Prune infected stems and thin plants for better air penetration. Spray infected plants with organic copper-sulfur fungicide. Remove plant debris and space plants widely for more air circulation. Insulate roots with a 4-inch-thick layer of compost.

LEAVES

BROWN SPOTS ARE ON LEAVES

Cause: Fungal leaf spot

Solution: Remove and destroy infected foliage. Treat badly infected plants with an organic copper fungicide. Follow the label. Allow soil to dry between waterings. Remove plant debris.

LEAVES HAVE PALE WINDING TRAILS

Cause: Leafminer

Solution: Destroy infested leaves. Lay a barrier of plastic under plants and cover with mulch to keep larvae from dropping to the soil and maturing. Clear the garden of pest-harboring plant debris.

SMALL WINGED INSECTS INFEST LEAVES

Cause: Whitefly

Solution: Dislodge whiteflies with a jet of water. Follow up with insecticidal soap spray. Target leaf undersides, where all stages of whitefly are present. Postpone pruning to limit susceptible new growth.

STIPPLED AREAS DISFIGURE LEAVES

Cause: Spider mite, lacebug, leafhopper

Solution: Keep plants healthy: fertilize and water regularly. Dislodge pests with a jet of water from a hose. Control large populations with the botanical insecticide neem or pyrethrum. Follow the label directions carefully.

DISTORTED, STICKY LEAVES

Cause: Aphid

Solution: Knock these small, pear-shaped, sap-sucking insects off plants with a forceful spray of water from a hose. Spray heavy infestations with the botanical insecticide neem or pyrethrum. Follow the label. Plant nectar-heavy alyssum and scabiosa to attract insect predators. Repel aphids with commercial garlic oil or capsaicin spray.

LEAVES ARE YELLOW AND GREEN

Cause: Nutritional deficiency

Solution: Test soil and amend as recommended. Spray leaves of iron-deficient plants with a liquid fertilizer containing chelated iron. Increase soil acidity by working garden sulfur into soil; mulch with acidic oak leaves or pine needles. Magnesium-deficient plants can be treated with magnesium sulfate applied at regular intervals during the growing season. Follow package labels.

POWDERY DEPOSITS: ORANGE, WHITE, OR BLACK, SHOW ON LEAVES

Cause: Sooty mold, rust, or powdery mildew

Solution: Destroy infected leaves. Use organic sulfur fungicide. Sooty mold forms on insect droppings; control pests with insecticidal soap. Space plants widely and water at ground level.

LEAVES APPEAR SCORCHED AND CLING TO TREE

Cause: Fireblight

Solution: Control outbreaks by pruning well below infected area and sterilizing tools between cuts. Spray new growth with an organic copper fungicide as a preventive. Plant resistant varieties.

LEAVES HAVE LARGE, RAGGED HOLES

Cause: Snail, slug, beetle, caterpillar, weevil

Solution: Collect and destroy insects. Treat caterpillars with the biological insecticide BT. Spray beetles with the botanical insecticide neem or pyrethrum. Follow labels. Trap slugs and snails in saucers of beer, or commercial traps.

STEMS AND LEAVES YELLOW AND ARE DISTORTED

Cause: Weed-killer damage

Solution: Plants may recover with watering; fertilize in spring with a balanced formulation. Treat weeds with an herbicide containing only the active ingredient dicamba rather than combination products. Follow label directions.

BRANCHES

BRANCHES HAVE DARK, SUNKEN AREAS

Cause: Canker

Solution: Prune and destroy branches that have fungal lesions. Prune again, lower, if dark brown wood appears under bark. Sterilize pruning shears with rubbing alcohol.

SWELLINGS OR GROWTHS MAR TWIGS OR TRUNK

Cause: Gall

Solution: Prune and dispose of fungal galls. Spray antibiotic streptomycin on plants it is labeled for. Discard severely infected plants. Sterilize pruners between cuts; avoid injuring plants when cultivating near roots and stems. Lower soil pH with garden sulfur.

WAXY BUMPS APPEAR ON STEMS OR TRUNK

Cause: Scale

Solution: Prune and destroy infested branches. Spray dormant oil in winter. In late spring, spray neem, an organic insecticide. Follow the label directions carefully.

WHOLE PLANT

LEAVES WILT; BRANCHES DIE

Cause: Fungal root or crown rot

Solution: Remove infected plants and replace soil before replanting, or replant in a raised bed. Prevent by cultivating carefully around shrubs. Do not mulch plants.

LEAF EDGES OR NEEDLES TURN BROWN

Cause: Leaf or needle scorch due to heat, wind, or drought

Solution: Apply a 4-inch-thick mulch (keep it away from trunk) to conserve moisture and insulate roots. Do not fertilize or prune past midsummer. Avoid damage: provide plants with afternoon shade in summer; use a windbreak and shake off snow in winter.

BRANCH TIPS WILT; LEAVES YELLOW

Cause: Borer: larvae of moth or beetle

Solution: Prune and destroy damaged branches. Seal cuts with household white glue and water. Spray the botanical insecticide neem in spring and summer, following label.

Annual Vines
Various species

LIGHT: Full sun

SOIL: Well drained; pH 6.0 to 7.5

MOISTURE: Consistently moist

HARDINESS: Tender annual

Leaves have brown, sunken spots

Problem: The leaves develop circular, sunken, tan to brown spots about the size of a pin-head, most often in spring through summer.

Cause: Fourlined plant bugs are small insects that suck sap from a number of plants, including many annual vines. The bugs are yellow-green with black longitudinal stripes down their backs. If you startle them while they feed, they will often hide under the leaf or in the petals of a nearby flower. The bugs cause mostly cosmetic damage to leaves; rarely do they seriously threaten plant health.

Solution: Control fourlined plant bugs with insecticide and good garden sanitation.

- If the spots or insects are present, spray the plant with the botanical insecticide pyrethrum or neem or a combination of insecticidal soap and neem. Follow label directions carefully.

- Apply garlic oil or capsaicin to foliage as a repellent. Follow label directions carefully.

- In fall, clean up the garden to remove over-wintering insects and their eggs.

Seeds don't germinate

Problem: Seeds sown in the soil don't germinate. This occurs most often with morning glory (*Ipomoea purpurea*), moonflower (*I. alba*), cardinal climber (*I. × multifida*), starglory (*I. lobata,* also known as *Mina lobata*), sweet pea (*Lathyrus odoratus*), and cup-and-saucer vine (*Cobaea scandens*).

Cause: Many types of annual vines have hard seed coats that often inhibit germination. Called seed coat dormancy, this condition means the seeds require special treatment before they will sprout.

Solution: To remedy seed coat dormancy in annual vines, presoak the seed or scratch the seed surface before sowing.

- Before planting most annual vines, soak the seeds overnight in lukewarm water.

- Before planting annual *Ipomoea* vines of the morning glory genus, scratch or nick the seed coat with a nail file, then soak the seeds overnight in lukewarm water.

- After soaking the seeds overnight, sow them in well-drained, moist soil. Most types of annual vines will germinate in about two weeks.

Clusters of small insects appear on leaves

Problem: Small, soft-bodied insects appear on leaves, shoots, and buds. The leaves look yellow, and new leaves and flowers are distorted. These symptoms are most common on plants of the genus *Tropaeolum*, such as canary-bird vine (*T. perigrinum*) and nasturtium (*T. majus*), and plants of the genus *Ipomoea*, such as cardinal climber (*I. × multifida*), moonflower (*I. alba*), morning glory (*I. purpurea*), and starglory (*I. lobata*).

Cause: Aphids are small insects that feed on the sap of plants. Of the many different kinds and colors, all can cause real damage. They are prolific and multiply rapidly, making a control program important.

Solution: Aphids are easy to control by hosing them off, spraying insecticides, using repellents, and attracting predators.

- Knock aphids from the plant with a daily forceful spray of water from a hose.
- Spray foliage with the botanical insecticide neem or pyrethrum, or a combination of insecticidal soap and neem, every 5 to 10 days beginning when the insects first appear. Follow label directions carefully.
- Repel aphids with garlic oil or capsaicin spray. Follow label directions carefully.
- Plant nectar plants such as alyssum to attract aphid predators including ladybugs.

Leaves are eaten or skeletonized

Problem: Leaves and flowers are chewed or skeletonized. Bronze-colored beetles are on leaves, stems, and flowers. The problem is most severe from midsummer to fall. The annual vines that are most often affected include scarlet runner bean (*Phaseolus coccineus*) and hyacinth bean (*Dolichos lablab*).

Cause: Japanese beetles are insects with bronze wing covers and metallic green to black coloring. The white grub larvae feed on the roots of grasses while the adult beetles devour the leaves and flowers of a vast array of plants. In large numbers, the beetles can defoliate entire plants.

Solution: Handpick and spray to control beetles. Treat grass to control the larvae.

- In the early morning, handpick Japanese beetles from the plant and drown them in a container of soapy water.
- If the infestation is severe, spray the plant with the botanical insecticide neem or pyrethrum. Or use a synthetic insecticide registered for the annual vine you are treating that contains the active ingredient carbaryl or methoxychlor. Follow label directions carefully.
- To control grubs and prevent future infestations, treat grassy areas with milky spore disease or beneficial nematodes (p.126). Or use a synthetic insecticide registered for grass that contains the active ingredient diazinon. Follow label directions carefully.

Seedling emerges, then dies

Problem: Seedling emerges and seems healthy but soon dies. The base of stem may be black and soft. The roots are rotted.

Cause: Damping off, root and stem rot in seedlings, is produced by many fungi, most often in seedlings sown in wet, cool soil or in soil where infected plants once grew.

Solution: Control and prevent the disease with fungicides and good garden sanitation.

- Drench the soil with a synthetic fungicide registered for use on the annual vine you are treating that contains the active ingredient captan as soon as symptoms appear. Follow label directions carefully.
- In fall, remove plant debris from garden. Solarize the soil (p.117) before replanting.
- Next season, dust seeds with a synthetic fungicide registered for use on the annual vine you are treating that contains the active ingredient thiram. Follow label directions carefully.

Vine grows well but flowers poorly

Problem: Vine has abundant, dark green leaves but few or no flowers. It has no noticeable problems and gets water and full sun.

Cause: Most annual vines need little or no fertilizer. Too much stimulates excess leaf growth and inhibits flower bud formation.

Solution: Be careful about which vines you fertilize.

- Don't apply fertilizer to canary-bird, cardinal climber, moonflower, morning glory, nasturtium, or starglory annual vines.

Boxwood

Buxus spp.

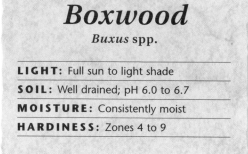

LIGHT: Full sun to light shade

SOIL: Well drained; pH 6.0 to 6.7

MOISTURE: Consistently moist

HARDINESS: Zones 4 to 9

Leaves are yellow; stems and leaves have corky growths

Problem: Leaves are pale green or yellow with sunken spots or corky growths on the undersides. Stems are lumpy and may have small, pitted holes. Overall, the shrub grows poorly.

Cause: At least five species of scale insects commonly attack boxwood. They cover themselves with a waxy coating that protects them from most sprays. They are most vulnerable after hatching, when they are mobile, looking for a feeding place. Once they settle, they grow the protective coat and don't move again.

Solution: Prune infested branches. Spray and use natural enemies for a severe problem.

- Prune and discard infested branches.
- To control the crawling stage, spray in May with the botanical insecticide neem. Or use a synthetic insecticide registered for boxwoods that contains the active ingredient malathion, carbaryl, acephate, or diazinon. Follow directions carefully.
- Encourage insect predators by growing nectar plants such as alyssum and dill.
- Spray dormant oil to kill overwintering scale.

Leaves turn yellow and wilt; plant dies suddenly

Problem: Leaves turn yellow and may be smaller than usual on the entire plant or just on one side. The leaves wilt and fall. The plant dies.

Cause: Root rot, a fungal disease, invades the root system, cutting off the plant's water and nutrient supply. It generally gains entry through damaged roots. Hard, brown, fruiting bodies may form at the diseased plant's base or in the ground.

Solution: Remove the infected plant. Be careful not to damage roots of other boxwoods.

- Remove the infected plant. Replace the soil before planting boxwoods at the same site.
- Cultivate carefully around boxwoods, since they have a shallow root system. Pull weeds by hand rather than hoeing them.

Leaves turn yellow; bark peels

Problem: Leaves look unhealthy and turn pale green to yellow. The bark lifts up and peels away. Pustules on the bark may exude sticky sap.

Cause: Boxwood blight, caused by several fungi, is most common on plants stressed by poor soil, drought, or winter injury.

Solution: Prune infected branches, spray, and improve growing conditions.

- Prune blighted branches and clear dead leaves, which accumulate inside the shrub.
- Spray with organic copper or lime-sulfur fungicide. Follow label directions carefully. Spray just before spring growth starts, again when half grown, and when fully grown.
- Mulch with a 4-inch-thick layer of compost or well-rotted manure to reduce soil evaporation, and water well during droughts.

Branches die in winter

Problem: In winter some branches turn brown and die; sometimes the entire plant dies. Or in the spring, branches may have dead tips and reddish lower leaves.

Cause: Winter injury results when drying winds and frozen soil hamper a plant's water uptake, or when cold kills immature late-fall or winter growth. Growing boxwood at the limits of its hardiness invites winter damage.

Solution: Limit fertilizing, protect plant, and choose hardier varieties.

- Don't fertilize later than midsummer. Late fertilizing promotes injury-prone growth.
- Shelter plant in winter with a burlap wrap.
- Mulch in fall to prevent frost damage to roots and to help roots to take up water.
- Plant hardier varieties (box, below).

WISE CHOICES

The Korean boxwood (*Buxus microphylla* var. *koreana*) is one of the hardiest varieties and has been used to develop semi-evergreen Canadian hybrids, such as 'Green Gem', 'Green Mountain', and 'Green Velvet', which keep their color better in winter. The Japanese boxwood (*B. microphylla* var. *japonica*) tolerates heat and harmful soil nematodes, making it the best choice for the South.

Common boxwood (*B. sempervirens*) varieties are best for hedging. 'Suffruticosa', when regularly trimmed, can be kept under 3 feet tall.

Leaves turn brown

Problem: New growth turns brown, often on one side of the plant. Leaves may have brown margins or brown patches.

Cause: Heat stress is most prevalent at the southern limits of boxwood's hardiness range and in hot-summer areas.

Solution: Prune carefully. Plant new shrubs in a protected area; select a heat-tolerant variety.

- Do not overprune. Severe pruning allows sunlight to penetrate and scorch foliage.
- In the South, plant boxwood in dappled shade and away from light-reflecting walls. Select a heat-tolerant variety (box, left).

Leaves are yellow and blotchy

Problem: Leaves have small blisters and yellow spots or flecks. They may yellow completely and drop. Branches die back. Plant grows poorly, looks sickly, and dies in several years.

Cause: Boxwood leafminers are a serious pest. The larvae overwinter between the surfaces of leaves. Adults are small flies that emerge in spring, swarm in the morning, and lay eggs under the leaf surface, creating new blisters.

Solution: Apply insecticide, remove debris, and plant a resistant variety.

- Just before adults emerge, spray with a synthetic insecticide registered for boxwoods that contains the active ingredient acephate. Follow label directions carefully.
- If adults have laid eggs, spray with a synthetic insecticide registered for boxwoods that contains the active ingredient dimethoate. Follow label directions carefully.
- Rake up and discard fallen leaves.
- Select common boxwood (*B. sempervirens*), which is resistant to the pest.

Plant is stunted and wilts easily

Problem: The plant is stunted, wilts easily, and doesn't respond to watering.

Cause: Harmful nematodes—microscopic wormlike creatures—invade the roots, stunting them and starving the plant.

Solution: Remove a dying plant. For a new planting, cleanse soil; use a resistant variety.

- Remove a severely infested plant.
- Before replanting, solarize the soil (p.117) or have it fumigated by a professional.
- Plant a resistant variety (box, left).

Butterfly Bush
Buddleia spp.

LIGHT: Full sun

SOIL: Fertile, well drained; pH 6.0 to 7.5

MOISTURE: Seasonally moist to dry

HARDINESS: Zones 5 to 9

Leaves wilt; plant is unhealthy

Problem: Plant grows poorly and looks sick. Leaves turn yellow and wilt, and flowers may not open. The plant eventually dies.

Cause: Southern root-knot nematodes are microscopic worms that invade plant roots and destroy the root cells. The plant develops swellings (knots) at the points of attack and eventually is unable to take up water. The pest, a significant problem in the South, is killed by low temperatures.

Solution: There's no cure. Remove the plant, and treat or replace the soil.

- Dig up and remove the infected plant.
- Before replanting, solarize the soil (p.117). Or replace it with uncontaminated soil.

Leaves have holes; caterpillars are present

Problem: Holes appear in leaves and flowers. Dark blue caterpillars with orange markings are on the shrub.

Cause: The larva of the checkerspot butterfly is the only type of caterpillar that feeds on both flowers and leaves of butterfly bush. The adult is mostly pale brown with about a 2-inch wingspan. Unless the attack is severe enough to defoliate the shrub, you may prefer to leave the larvae undisturbed, especially if you are growing the shrub to bring butterflies into your garden.

Solution: If the attack is moderate to severe, handpick and relocate, or spray to reduce the damage.

- Gently handpick the caterpillars and move them to parsley, dill, or other plants on which butterfly caterpillars feed.
- If the infestation is severe, spray with the botanical insecticide neem. Follow label directions carefully.

Flowering is sparse

Problem: Few flowers are produced. Those that do form appear late in the season.

Cause: There are two likely causes: growing plants in the shade and untimely or improper pruning the prior season. Both reduce the number of flowers.

Solution: Careful and timely pruning will encourage flowering; relocate shrub if needed.

- To preserve flower buds, do not prune in late spring or early summer (when most other shrubs are pruned). Avoid giving the shrub a haircut when it gets too large. Proper pruning methods and timing vary according to the species (sidebar, left).
- If shrubs are being shaded by trees or buildings, consider digging them up and replanting them in an area that receives full sun.

Tips of branches fail to develop leaves

Problem: New growth develops on the lower stem, but the branch tips don't produce any.

Cause: Winter injury often happens when a plant is grown at the limit of its hardiness zone. It can result when a midwinter thaw causes premature budding and the buds are killed when cold returns or when a late frost kills spring buds.

Solution: Prune, fertilize, and mulch to encourage new growth.

- Prune in early spring, leaving four or five buds at the base of each shoot.
- Fertilize with a balanced 10-10-10 formulation (p.324) immediately after pruning to promote good growth.
- Mulch with compost or well-rotted manure to control water loss and add nutrients.

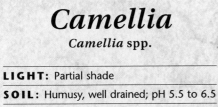

Camellia
Camellia spp.

LIGHT: Partial shade

SOIL: Humusy, well drained; pH 5.5 to 6.5

MOISTURE: Consistently moist

HARDINESS: Zones 7 to 9

Brown spots appear on leaves

Problem: Small brown spots appear on the leaves. They soon run together to form large blemishes. Tiny black dots appear in the infected areas.

Cause: Camellia leaf spot is a serious fungal disease that attacks all species. It causes premature leaf drop and may also infect and kill flower buds.

Solution: Use good garden sanitation and fungicidal spray to combat this disease.

- Pick off and dispose of infected leaves.
- Spray a severely infected plant with organic sulfur fungicide. Follow label directions carefully.

Leaf edges are notched

Problem: Leaves have irregular notches around the edges. In severe cases, only the main vein is left. The bark is missing at ground level. The plant wilts and in time may die.

Cause: Black vine weevils are beetle-like insects that feed on foliage, weakening the plant. But the most serious damage is caused by their larvae, which feed on the roots and eat the bark off the base of the trunk. Control is difficult because the weevils resist many chemicals.

Solution: Dislodge the adults, use natural parasites, spray, and check new plants for pests.

- Spread a white sheet under the plant and shake the plant. Collect and dispose of weevils that fall on the sheet.
- Add beneficial nematodes (p.126) to the soil every three months to control larvae.
- If the problem persists, spray the plant with a synthetic insecticide registered for camellias that contains the active ingredient bendiocarb. Follow label directions carefully.
- Inspect plants for larvae before buying.

Leaves are covered with white spots and tiny black pests

Problem: Leaves are mottled with white or yellow pin-sized spots. Leaf undersides have small black pests and some clear, sticky areas.

Cause: Florida red scale, tea scale, and camellia scale infest camellias. These insects are active right after hatching, but later settle in one spot to feed. Scale produce several generations each year. In zone 9 and above, immature scale are present all year long.

Solution: Spraying and attracting natural predators will help control scale.

- To kill adults and crawlers, spray with horticultural oil or oil emulsion when temperatures are below 85°F.
- To control the crawling stage, spray during warm weather with insecticidal soap or the botanical insecticide neem. Or use a synthetic insecticide registered for camellias that contains the active ingredient carbaryl. Follow label directions carefully.
- Encourage natural predators to move into your garden by growing nectar plants such as alyssum and scabiosa.

Leaves have dark powdery spots

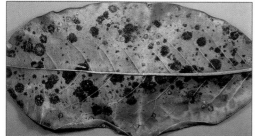

Problem: Leaves and stems become covered with a dark, sooty substance. The infected plant weakens, and the foliage may die.

Cause: Sooty mold is a fungus that feeds on the sticky, clear excretions of aphids, mealybugs, and scale insects. The fungus does not attack a plant directly, but it blocks sunlight, hindering the plant's ability to produce food.

Solution: Remove the infected foliage, and spray to control insects. Fertilize the plant.

- Pick off and dispose of sooty foliage. Remove secretions with soapy water.
- Spray insects with insecticidal soap or with a synthetic insecticide registered for camellias that contains the active ingredient malathion. Follow label directions carefully.
- Fertilize with an organic fertilizer, such as fish emulsion, or with a balanced 10-10-10 formulation (p.324).

Buds brown and drop

Problem: Buds open partly, brown at the edges, and fall. Or buds drop before opening.

Cause: Bud drop is common when a camellia is exposed to sudden cold after an early warm spring. Inadequate watering and a marginal hardiness zone may also be factors.

Solution: Protect the plant from winter cold, and provide a regular supply of water.

- Throw an insulating fabric floating row cover over shrubs when frost is expected.
- Or build burlap-covered cages over small plants to shelter them from spring frost.
- Keep soil consistently moist, but well drained. Excess water also causes bud drop.

Flowers have brown blotches

Problem: Flowers have small brown spots that spread rapidly to form blotches. Infected flowers have darker veins, giving a netted appearance. They become leathery but stay on for weeks before falling. The problem is most common in the South during periods of warm, moist weather.

Cause: Flower blight is a fungal disease in which spores overwinter in soil and infect flowers when it's warm and moist in spring.

Solution: Use good sanitation and spray.

- Handpick and remove infected flowers. If severe, remove all flowers and buds.
- If necessary, drench the soil under shrub before buds open with a synthetic fungicide. Use one registered for camellias that contains the active ingredient captan or PCNB. Follow label directions carefully.
- If diseased flowers have fallen on ground, spread a 3-inch layer of wood chips or pine bark under shrub to block release of spores.
- To help prevent spread, spray healthy blooms with a synthetic fungicide registered for camellias that contains the active ingredient ferbam, maneb, or ziram. Follow label directions carefully.

Clematis

Clematis spp.

LIGHT: Sun to partial shade

SOIL: Humusy and cool; pH 5.5 to 7.5

MOISTURE: Consistently moist

HARDINESS: Zones 3 to 8

Plant is not growing well

Problem: A new plant starts to decline in midsummer. Or an older plant that had been doing well suddenly declines.

Cause: Soil that is too warm commonly causes a newly planted clematis to do poorly. With an older plant, the cause is often some change that lets the soil overheat, such as removing a shrub that once shaded the roots.

Solution: Keep the soil moist and shade the roots from direct sunlight.

- Apply a 4-inch layer of an organic mulch, such as bark chips, around the base of the plant to shade the roots.
- Or shade the roots with a spreading shrub, such as juniper, or a spreading annual, such as verbena or petunia. But provide extra water, because the groundcover will compete with the clematis for moisture.

Leaves have pale spots with dark borders

Problem: A stem or two suddenly wilts, or leaves develop light spots with dark, reddish borders. Damage begins at the bottom of the plant. The rest of the plant seems healthy. Occasionally the entire plant is affected and may die.

Cause: Ascochyta leaf spot and stem rot is a fungal disease that enters a plant through damaged tissue, often where a stem is tied to a support. The fungus prevents water from reaching the foliage. It's most common in very old or newly planted shrubs. The fungus produces spores that may attack other stems. It may travel to the roots, killing the entire plant.

Solution: Use pruning, spraying, and proper planting techniques to combat this disease.

- Prune wilting stems just above soil level.
- To protect healthy plants, spray the leaves with an organic sulfur fungicide. Follow label directions carefully.
- When planting clematis, place it lower in the soil than it grew in the pot, putting some buds below soil level to ensure new growth if the top is killed.

WISE CHOICES

The familiar, large-flowered clematis hybrids are typically summer bloomers. But you can have flowers from spring to fall by growing these and a few species clematis. The alpine clematis (*Clematis alpina*) has small nodding bell-shaped pink, blue, and white flowers in early spring. In summer, the virgin's bower clematis (*C. virginiana*) has flowers ranging from blue and pink to purple. Sweet autumn clematis (*C. paniculata*) has profuse small white flowers in fall.

Plant is stunted; shoots wilt

Problem: The plant doesn't grow well and seems stunted. The leaves are soft and hang down. Individual shoots or the entire plant eventually wilts and dies.

Cause: Clematis borers, the creamy white larvae of clearwing moths, tunnel and feed inside plant roots and crowns. Larvae hatch from eggs laid at soil level from spring to early summer. Once inside the plant, larvae are not easy to control chemically.

Solution: Remove infested plant parts, and spray to control moths.

- Dig around the base of the plant and try to find the entry holes. Cut out and dispose of infested roots.

- Every two weeks, spray the plant base and surrounding soil with a synthetic insecticide registered for clematis that contains the active ingredient chlorpyrifos. Follow label directions carefully.

Leaves are yellow with many tiny spots

Problem: The foliage turns pale and may have a yellow, gray, or bronze tinge. Close examination reveals tiny spots on the leaves. Leaf undersides may have very fine webs and, in severe attacks, the webbing may stretch from leaf to stem or from stem to stem.

Cause: Spider mites are relatives of spiders so tiny that you need a magnifying glass to see the individuals. They build up rapidly in hot weather and feed on the leaf undersides, causing discoloration. In large numbers, they weaken a plant and can kill it. When clematis is grown on a wall trellis, heat reflected from the wall provides ideal conditions for rapid mite increase. Clematis climbing through trees or shrubs are less prone to severe attacks.

Solution: Hose mites off plants and spray plants with an insecticide.

- Spray the plant with a strong jet of water from a hose. Make sure the water hits the undersides of the leaves. Repeat the spray every other day for at least two weeks to dislodge mites as they hatch.

- Spray severely infested foliage with the botanical insecticide neem or pyrethrum. Follow label directions carefully.

Holes appear in flowers and leaves

Problem: In June or July, holes appear in both the leaves and flowers, and you see narrow black beetles about ½ inch long feeding on the plant. The pests can be numerous and do considerable damage in a short time, often completely destroying a plant.

Cause: Black blister beetles get their name from a fluid in their body that blisters human skin when one of the insects is crushed. The beetles are especially drawn to clematis, often attacking it and doing serious damage. They most frequently appear in June and July, but they can show up later in the season. Black blister beetles are most commonly found in southern areas. Surprisingly, the larvae of this pest are beneficial. They live in the soil and feed on grasshopper eggs.

Solution: Handpick or spray the beetles to control the damage.

- If the infestation is slight, handpick the insects, wearing rubber or plastic gloves to protect your skin. Ordinary cloth garden gloves don't offer adequate protection.

- If the pests are numerous, spray with insecticidal soap or with the botanical insecticide neem or pyrethrum. Follow label directions carefully. Because the beetles often appear in swarms, you may need to spray weekly until they are under control.

TIME-TESTED TECHNIQUES

HELPING CLEMATIS TO CLIMB

A self-clinging vine such as English ivy scales a wall with little help. But clematis is a twining vine that needs to wrap its tendrils around a support such as wire or string. A rigid plastic 4- to 6-inch mesh provides good support. Position it 1 inch from a solid wall to let air circulate and prevent disease. Tie young shoots to the mesh with string, plant rings, or twists. After this, new shoots should twine without further help.

If you want to grow clematis on a wooden trellis, give the vine something to start on by stapling netting to the trellis or by running a few strings from the ground to the top of the trellis. Tie young shoots to the mesh or strings.

Cotoneaster
Cotoneaster spp.

LIGHT: Full sun to partial shade
SOIL: Well drained, fertile; pH 5.5 to 7.5
MOISTURE: Seasonally moist to dry
HARDINESS: Zones 3 to 8

Leaves look scorched

Problem: Some leaves wilt and look burned. Flowers may look water soaked, and the bark develops sunken cankers.

Cause: Fireblight is a bacterial disease. A sweet gum oozing from the cankers attracts insects that spread the bacteria.

Solution: Remove infected branches, and spray. Plant a resistant variety.

- Prune branches well below the infected area. Sterilize (p.310) tools between cuts.
- As a preventive, spray organic copper as leaves unfurl. Follow label directions.
- Plant creeping cotoneaster (*C. adpressus*), which is resistant to fireblight.

Leaves have winding lines

Problem: Some leaves have tan, winding lines on them, but the lines do not turn into holes.

Cause: Leafminers are the larvae of small flies that lay clusters of minute white eggs on the leaf undersides. The larvae hatch and tunnel between upper and lower leaf surfaces. Then they drop to the ground where they develop into adult flies. The larvae overwinter under fallen leaves. Leafminers can disfigure a plant, but rarely damage it.

Solution: Practice good garden sanitation and use barriers and biological predators to control leafminers.

- If only a few leaves are attacked, handpick and dispose of them.
- Remove fallen leaves and other plant debris from the garden.
- Place landscape fabric under shrubs and cover it with an attractive mulch, such as bark chips. The fabric will prevent larvae from dropping to the soil where they complete their life cycle.
- Cover plants with insect-excluding fabric floating row cover in the spring to keep flies from laying eggs on the leaves.
- Apply beneficial nematodes (p.126) to the soil in early spring to control developing larvae.

Bark has small bumps; growth is stunted

Problem: Bark has small brown or grayish bumps. The plant's growth may be stunted.

Cause: Scale insects attach themselves and grow a protective waxy covering that sprays run off. Scales are vulnerable after hatching when they are mobile.

Solution: Remove infested branches. Use sprays and natural parasites to control scale.

- Prune and discard infested branches.
- Spray a serious infestation with dormant oil in winter to kill overwintering scale. Follow label directions carefully.
- In May and again in June, spray with the botanical insecticide neem or with a synthetic insecticide registered for cotoneaster that contains the active ingredient carbaryl. Follow label directions carefully.
- Grow nectar plants such as alyssum and scabiosa to attract natural parasites.

Dutchman's Pipe

Aristolochia durior

LIGHT: Full sun to partial shade

SOIL: Well drained; pH 6.0 to 7.5

MOISTURE: Consistently moist

HARDINESS: Zones 4 to 8

Small dark-colored bumps appear on stems

Problem: Hard, dark-colored bumps appear on stems and sometimes on leaves. The bumps can be scraped off with a fingernail. The foliage may be pale or spotted with yellow. The plant's growth may begin to slow down.

Cause: Scales are small, soft-bodied insects that encase themselves in hard, waxy shells. They feed on sap and are most numerous during warm weather. Their waxy coating repels sprays, making them difficult to control. They are most vulnerable soon after they hatch, when they move around looking for a place to feed. Once they settle in a spot, they grow their protective shell and don't move again.

Solution: Selective pruning and timely spraying with insecticides offer effective control of scale insects. Try botanical controls.

- Prune and destroy severely infested stems. Sterilize (p.310) your pruning shears between cuts.
- Spray with the botanical insecticide neem beginning in spring, spraying every 10 days until infestation is under control. Or use a synthetic insecticide registered for Dutchman's pipe that contains the active ingredient carbaryl. Follow label directions carefully.
- Encourage insects that prey on scale by growing nectar plants such as alyssum and dill.

Dark spots form on leaves

Problem: Small, dark-colored spots appear on the leaves. They form most often on older leaves during warm, moist weather and on plants grown in partial shade.

Cause: Fungal leaf spot is caused by several different fungi. On Dutchman's pipe, the damage is most often cosmetic, not a serious threat to the plant.

Solution: Control leaf spot with fungicide and good gardening practices.

- Apply an organic sulfur fungicide to the foliage. Follow label directions carefully.
- Rake up and dispose of all leaves in fall.
- If leaf spot is an annual problem, apply sulfur fungicide in spring before the leaves show symptoms.

Stems have fuzzy white clumps

Problem: Clusters of white cottony fluff appear near the tips of growing points and at the bases of leaf stems. Under the fuzz are small grayish white insects. Plant leaves may be pale green to yellow and fall prematurely. Growth may be stunted.

Cause: Mealybugs are small, soft-bodied insects that feed on plant sap. A waxy, fuzzy white substance covers the adults.

Solution: Limit mealybug damage with insecticidal sprays or botanical controls.

- Spray foliage with the botanical insecticide neem. Or use a synthetic insecticide registered for use on Dutchman's pipe that contains the active ingredient chlorpyrifos or carbaryl. Follow label directions carefully.
- Purchase mealybug destroyers from a catalog or a garden center. These insects attack mealybugs at all stages and work best between 60° and 90°F.
- Encourage predatory insects by growing nectar plants such as alyssum and dill.

Euonymus
Euonymus spp.

LIGHT: Full sun to shade

SOIL: Well drained; pH 5.5 to 7.5

MOISTURE: Seasonally moist to dry

HARDINESS: Zones 4 to 8

Leaves and stems have small, brownish spots

Problem: Small spots appear on leaves and stems. They may be brown, pink, or purple. The spots gradually enlarge, then become water soaked. The leaves fall off after small, fruiting bodies appear. On twigs, the bark becomes rough, corky, and brown, and starts to peel.

Cause: Anthracnose, a widespread fungal disease, is found primarily on the evergreen euonymus species such as Japanese and winter creeper euonymus. The disease is most common in the South but occurs elsewhere in warm, moist springs. The fungus is almost always present in the soil, and it attacks in suitable weather conditions. Plants under stress from drought, winter injury, and poor nutrition are also susceptible to infection.

Solution: Use a combination of pruning, spraying, and good gardening techniques to limit this disease's damage.

- As soon as you notice the disease, pick off infected leaves, prune infected stems, and dispose of them.
- In winter, spray the plant with the organic fungicide lime sulfur; spray again after leaves begin to form in spring. Follow label directions carefully.
- Mulch around plant with a 2- to 4-inch layer of bark chips to prevent spores from splashing on it.
- Fertilize in spring using a balanced 10-10-10 formulation (p.324).

Knobby galls appear on stems

Problem: Rough textured galls, up to several inches in diameter, cluster along stems or near the soil line.

Cause: The bacteria that cause galls enter the plants through wounds in the stems or roots. They overwinter in the soil and are spread among the plants by splashing water and dirty tools.

Solution: Practice good garden sanitation and modify soil acidity for control.

- Prune and dispose of diseased plant parts, or the entire plant if it is severely affected. Sterilize (p.310) tools between cuts, and take care not to injure the plants when cultivating.
- Add garden sulfur to soil or amend it with organic materials to lower the pH to 5.5, since bacteria do not survive in acidic soil.
- Don't plant euonymus in locations where this disease has previously occurred.

Leaves have yellow spots or blotches

Problem: Leaves are speckled with small yellow spots or have pale green to yellow blotches. The plant doesn't grow well and sheds leaves. There is some dieback, and the plant seems stunted. The bark is corky with brown or grayish bumps. Leaf undersides (and occasionally the entire plant) have tiny, dark, cone-shaped pests and many smaller white pests.

Cause: Several different scales attack euonymus. The worst is euonymus scale, common on plants

REGIONAL FOCUS
NORTHEAST

The euonymus caterpillar, a pest from Europe first identified in 1967, is causing problems in the Northeast. The caterpillars are pale with two lines of black dots on their back. They construct web tents in the tips of branches, feeding on foliage, and their woolly cocoons hang in clusters. The adults are small white moths with black dots. To control these pests, destroy their webs and cocoons, and spray with BTK. Follow label directions carefully.

growing close to buildings where air movement is minimal. Scales have a waxy covering that repels sprays, making them difficult to control. They are most vulnerable soon after hatching, when they are mobile and seeking a place to feed. Once they find a spot, they grow their protective coats and don't move again. Scale may produce as many as three generations a year in the South.

Solution: Prune and discard infested branches. Use insecticidal sprays and natural parasites to control infestations.

- If the infestation is localized, prune the infested branches. Sterilize (p.310) your pruning shears with alcohol between cuts.

- Control the crawling stage of scale by spraying the plant in early summer with the botanical insecticide neem, or with a synthetic insecticide registered for euonymus that contains the active ingredient carbaryl. Follow label directions carefully. In the South, spray again in August.

- Limit the spread by encouraging insects that prey on scale. Attract them by growing nectar plants such as alyssum and dill.

- Spray dormant oil during late winter to kill overwintering scale.

TIME-TESTED TECHNIQUES

PLANTING SHRUBS IN CLAY SOIL

Putting shrubs in areas with heavy clay soil requires special care. As you dig in clay soil, the spade glazes the inside of the hole, forming an almost waterproof surface. When you plant and refill the hole, it may fill with water that cannot drain away, thus causing the plant to drown. Here's how to avoid this:

- Before planting, break up the base of the hole with a garden fork and drag the tines up the sides to break the glaze left by your spade.

- On low sites with poor drainage, plant above the grade level. Dig a shallow hole and use additional soil to cover the roots, forming a shallow mound. Stake the plant until the roots are established.

Leaves are covered with a gray powder

Problem: In late summer or early fall, leaves become covered with a white or gray powder. The powder appears first in small spots and rapidly spreads to cover much of the leaf surface.

Cause: Powdery mildew is a very common fungal disease. It usually appears late in the growing season and, while disfiguring, is rarely serious.

Solution: Practice good garden sanitation and spray with fungicide to keep powdery mildew from spreading.

- Collect and dispose of infected leaves, especially those that have fallen to the ground.

- Spray healthy leaves with organic lime-sulfur fungicide. Follow label directions.

- Space new plants for good air circulation.

Leaves have ringed spots

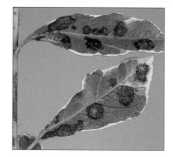

Problem: Leaves have small yellow, pink, purple, or brown spots with distinct pale or dark margins. Later, the spots run together to form large discolored areas, and leaves fall.

Cause: At least 10 different fungi cause leaf spot on euonymus. Leaf spot is most destructive during long periods of warm, wet weather. Excessive early leaf loss makes the plant susceptible to other pests and diseases.

Solution: Remove diseased leaves, spray plants with fungicide, and mulch.

- If the attack is slight, handpick and remove diseased leaves.

- If many leaves are affected, spray the plant with organic copper fungicide. Make several applications, 10 to 15 days apart. Follow label directions carefully.

- Mulch to keep soilborne spores off plant.

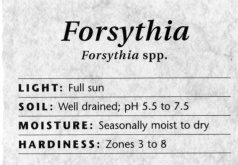

Forsythia
Forsythia spp.

LIGHT: Full sun

SOIL: Well drained; pH 5.5 to 7.5

MOISTURE: Seasonally moist to dry

HARDINESS: Zones 3 to 8

Few flowers form in spring

Problem: The plant is healthy, but in spring, it produces just a few, widely scattered flowers, or only the lower branches flower.

Cause: Untimely pruning is a likely cause. Forsythia forms next year's flower buds soon after flowering. A plant should be pruned immediately after the bloom finishes. Pruning in summer, fall, or winter removes the next year's flower buds. In the North, flowers may not form because the buds were killed by winter cold. If so, only lower buds that were protected by snow may flower.

Solution: Prune in spring. Or replace the plant with a hardier variety.

- Prune in spring immediately after the plant flowers.
- If cold damaged, replace with a hardier variety, such as 'Northern Gold', 'Northern Sun', 'Ottawa', or 'Vermont Sun', or the groundcover 'Happy Centennial'.

Leaves have pin-sized dots

Problem: The leaves are pitted with small dark or transparent dots, often in clusters. The centers may fall out, leaving open holes.

Cause: Fourlined plant bugs feed on foliage, causing this damage. Yellow-to-red nymphs hatch from May to June and, a month later, become yellow-to-green adults. Both have

four telltale black stripes, and both feed on foliage. Control adults before they lay eggs. Eggs overwinter in plant debris.

Solution: Spray and remove plant debris.

- Spray foliage with insecticidal soap. Or use a synthetic insecticide registered for forsythia that contains the active ingredient carbaryl. Follow label directions carefully.
- Remove plant debris from garden in fall.

Stems have swollen lumps

Problem: Swollen growths, called galls, appear on the shoots and roots. The galls are spongy at first but become hard, woody, and very rough. Initially, they are the same color as the plant—green on new shoots, brown on older shoots— but become dark brown as they age. If the galls are numerous, the plant becomes stunted, weakened, and susceptible to drought or winter injury. If the gall occurs at the plant crown (where stems and roots join), the plant usually dies.

Cause: Crown gall is a bacterial infection that enters the plant through wounds caused by pruning, transplanting, or pest feeding. It causes plant cells to divide, forming the swollen gall. It is most active between 70° and 85°F. A dormant plant that was infected in the fall may not show symptoms until spring. Old galls release bacteria into the soil to infect other plants.

Solution: Remove diseased shoots or the entire plant.

- Prune infected shoots as soon as the galls appear. If necessary, cut the plant back to near ground level; the shrub will regrow. Sterilize (p.310) shears between cuts. Be careful not to injure healthy wood.
- If poor growth continues, dig up the plant and destroy it before galls infect the soil. Take care not to injure healthy plants.

The holly bud moth is a particular pest in the Northwest. This small brown insect lays eggs close to holly buds. Its larvae, sometimes called blackheaded fireworms, feed on buds and stem tips, tying leaves together with webbing. To control the moths, spray in summer with insecticidal soap or with a synthetic insecticide registered for hollies with the active ingredient methoxychlor. Follow label carefully.

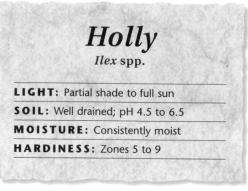

Holly
Ilex spp.

LIGHT: Partial shade to full sun

SOIL: Well drained; pH 4.5 to 6.5

MOISTURE: Consistently moist

HARDINESS: Zones 5 to 9

Irregular translucent lines or spots appear in leaves

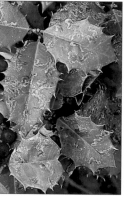

Problem: On Japanese holly, small round scars develop on leaf surfaces. On American and English hollies, there are also small opaque spots or blotches on the leaves.

Cause: Native holly leafminers are the tiny larvae of a small fly. The female fly pierces the leaf surface of the leaf underside and deposits eggs. The hatching larvae tunnel and feed between the upper and lower surfaces. On American and English hollies, eggs are laid inside the leaf, resulting in tunnel-like mines. The larvae do not mature within English holly leaves, but in American holly, they pupate and overwinter within leaves, emerging as adults in spring.

Solution: Practice good sanitation and spray to control both larvae and flies.

● For a mild infestation, handpick and dispose of the infested leaves in winter. Wear heavy gloves; holly leaf points are sharp.

● Spray a serious infestation with a synthetic insecticide registered for hollies that contains the active ingredient carbaryl or diazinon in mid-May and again in early June to control adult flies. Follow label directions carefully.

● Clean up and dispose of plant debris where larvae can also overwinter.

Brown areas appear on leaves

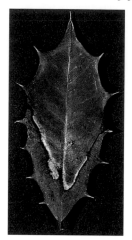

Problem: In late winter or early spring, leaves develop brown areas, beginning along the edges. In severe cases, the leaves wilt and fall.

Cause: Holly leaves turn brown due to drying winds and frozen soil, which hamper the plant's water uptake. This problem especially affects young plants with few roots.

Solution: Water plant in fall. In winter, shade it or protect it with a windbreak and mulch.

● Water holly plant well through fall to keep it supple.

● Shade a bush from early morning sun to prevent scorching.

● Shelter a newly planted holly over the winter with a burlap windbreak.

● Before a freeze, mulch with 6 inches of bark chips to prevent frost damage to roots.

Leaves have colored spots

Problem: Leaves have small brown, yellow, black, purple, or pink spots. In time, they may run together to form large areas of dead tissue. Centers may fall out, leaving holes.

Cause: Fungal leaf spot is caused by many different fungi, and more than one type may appear on a single leaf. The disease is most common in warm areas like the South and on plants stressed by poor growing conditions or winter frost injury.

Solution: Remove infected leaves, spray, and improve growing conditions to limit leaf spot.

● Handpick infected leaves, and rake up any fallen leaves that might harbor infection.

- In late summer and early fall, spray with an organic copper fungicide. Follow label directions carefully.
- Mulch with oak leaves or pine needles to improve soil acidity. Water in dry periods.

Leaves have yellow spots that turn black

Problem: Leaves of an American or English holly have yellow spots in spring that turn rusty brown and then eventually black, with narrow yellow borders.

Cause: Tar spot, a fungal leaf spot, is a common problem in warm climates. If rainfall is heavy, the fruit may also become spotted.

Solution: Remove diseased plant parts, and spray with fungicide.

- Collect and destroy badly infected foliage.
- Spray with the organic fungicide Bordeaux mixture, a mix of copper sulfate and hydrated lime, at two-week intervals. Repeat the following year in late spring. Follow label directions carefully.

Lower leaves have dark spots; twigs die

Problem: In cool, rainy weather, English holly develops small, dark spots on lower leaves. The symptoms move up the plant during fall and early winter. Young twigs die; older stems develop sunken cankers.

Cause: Holly blight, also called twig dieback, is a fungal disease associated with cool, damp weather. It is unlikely to occur where summers are hot.

Solution: Prune and spray to control. Site new shrubs in areas with good air circulation.

- Prune and dispose of infected stems. Thin plant to allow air flow through shrub.
- Spray with an organic copper-sulfate fungicide, starting when the weather turns cool and wet. Follow label directions carefully.
- Plant shrubs in open areas with air movement; avoid planting in sheltered areas.

Berries don't turn red

Problem: In fall, the berries on American holly bushes fail to change color, staying green all winter.

Cause: Maggots of the hollyberry gall midge invade berries and keep them from maturing. The midges emerge in May to lay eggs. Early-blooming hollies are more susceptible.

Solution: Remove infested berries, and spray. For new plantings, choose late-bloomers.

- Handpick berries that stay green in winter.
- Spray a severe infestation with insecticidal soap in early June to kill adult midges. Follow label directions carefully.
- For new hollies, choose a late-flowering variety recommended by a local nursery.

Entire leaves are pale or yellow

Problem: Leaves are pale green or yellow, often with dark veins. More leaves yellow as the summer progresses.

Cause: Chlorosis is caused by a lack of available iron. Most hollies grow best in acidic soil and can't absorb adequate iron from alkaline soil.

Solution: Treat with an iron supplement, and acidify soil. Plant alkaline-tolerant varieties.

- Spray plant and soil with chelated iron.
- Work powdered garden sulfur into the soil surface and mulch with oak leaves, pine litter, or peat moss to increase soil acidity.
- If your soil is neutral or slightly alkaline (pH 7.0 or higher), plant semi-alkaline-tolerant Chinese holly varieties (*I. cornuta*).

WISE CHOICES

The popular hybrid blue hollies, hardy to zone 4, resulted from a desire to develop hardy evergreen hollies, but they are also heat tolerant and do well in the South. Like all hollies, you need both male and female plants to get berries. One male, such as 'Blue Boy', 'Blue Prince', or 'Blue Stallion', will pollinate several female plants. Popular females include 'Blue Girl', 'Blue Maid', and 'Blue Princess'.

Honeysuckle
Lonicera spp.

LIGHT: Full sun to light shade

SOIL: Well drained; pH 5.5 to 7.5

MOISTURE: Consistently moist

HARDINESS: Zones 4 to 9

New growth is tassel-like

Problem: New growth is distorted, with undersized pale green and folded leaves. Many new shoots hang downward, giving a tassel-like, witches'-broom appearance. Later, mature leaves curl upward and contain small green insects. The tassels are killed by frost in winter, making the plant look unsightly.

Cause: Honeysuckle, or Russian, aphids lay eggs in fall on the buds at the stem tips, and the eggs hatch in spring just as buds start to enlarge. The deformity results from toxins that the aphids inject as they feed on the opening buds. Later generations move onto the leaves and feed on the upper surface, causing the leaves to curl.

Solution: Remove the tassels, and spray the plant with an insecticide.

- Watch for tassels in spring, and prune off and destroy them as soon as they appear.

- If cupped leaves occur, spray the plants with insecticidal soap or with a botanical insecticide, such as neem or pyrethrum, making sure to cover the upper leaf surfaces. Repeat 10 days later. Follow label directions carefully.

- In winter, prune off any remaining tassels to improve the plant's appearance.

- In late winter, spray with dormant oil to kill overwintering eggs.

Plant is not growing well or is flowering poorly

Problem: The plant is not putting on much new growth, but it does flower. Alternatively, the plant is growing well but it either does not flower or flowers are sparse.

Cause: Honeysuckle has a height limit. A shrub or vine still flowering well and growing wider, rather than taller, has probably reached its maximum height. An imbalance in soil nutrients, insufficient light, and incorrect pruning all cause poor flowering.

Solution: Provide fertilizer and sunlight as needed; prune properly for good flowering.

- Feed the plant in spring with a fertilizer that contains trace minerals. Also spray leaves with nutrient-rich fish emulsion or liquid seaweed.

- Thin nearby trees to increase light.

- Prune honeysuckle immediately after flowering to shape or rejuvenate an overgrown shrub without sacrificing flowers.

Leaves are disfigured with winding tan lines

Problem: Leaves are disfigured by pale, winding lines or light-colored, rounded blotches.

Cause: Leafminers are the tiny, yellowish or pale green, maggotlike larvae of small flies, which lay eggs on leaf surfaces. The hatching maggots burrow between the leaf surfaces where they feed. Leafminer damage is unsightly, but rarely health threatening.

Solution: Remove infested foliage, create barriers, and practice good garden sanitation. Chemical control is not effective because miners are protected by the leaf surfaces.

- Handpick and dispose of infested leaves.

- Mulch with plastic sheets to keep maggots from dropping to the soil and maturing.

- In fall, remove dead leaves and other plant debris to eliminate overwintering sites.

Hydrangea

Hydrangea spp.

LIGHT: Partial shade

SOIL: Well drained; pH 5.5 to 7.0

MOISTURE: Consistently moist

HARDINESS: Zones 3 to 9

Leaves are yellowing and have many tiny pale spots

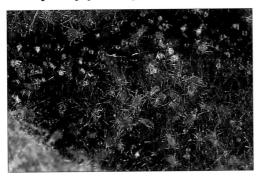

Problem: Foliage turns pale and may be yellowish, grayish, or have a bronze tint. Close examination shows that the leaves are covered with tiny yellow or tan spots. Leaf undersides and stems may have fine webs.

Cause: Spider mites have attacked the plant. These tiny, sap-sucking relatives of spiders build up rapidly in hot weather and feed on the leaf undersides, causing a mottled discoloration. In large numbers, they can severely weaken a plant and can even kill it. Spider mites flourish in hot, dry weather and seek drought-stressed plants. They are so small a magnifying glass is needed to see them.

Solution: Remove the mites from the plant, water well, and spray with a pesticide.

- At the first sign of mites, spray the plant with a strong jet of water, taking care to rinse the leaf undersides. Repeat this every other day for at least two weeks to dislodge immature mites as they hatch.
- Keep soil evenly moist during droughts.
- If problems persist, spray the plant with neem or pyrethrum, both botanical pesticides. Or use a synthetic pesticide registered for hydrangeas that contains the active ingredient malathion. Follow label directions carefully.

Flowers are not the right color

Problem: Flowers, especially the blue or pink blossoms of the bigleaf type hydrangea (*H. macrophylla*), are not the true color.

Cause: The flower color of these plants is affected by the availability of aluminum in the soil. Aluminum availability is governed by the level of soil acidity. Blue flowers of the bigleaf hydrangea are more blue when the plant grows in an acidic soil with a pH of 5.0 to 5.5. The higher the soil's alkalinity, the more pinkish the color becomes. Pink-flowered varieties are more pink when plants grow in soil that is slightly less acidic, with a neutral pH of 6.0 to 7.0.

Solution: Test soil and adjust pH as directed.

- Test soil pH (p.329), and acidify soil by adding aluminum sulfate as directed.
- Or incorporate lime into the soil to increase alkalinity as directed.

White or gray spots mar leaves

Problem: Leaves have small white or gray powdery spots that enlarge to form blotches. They turn yellow and fall prematurely. Flower buds may become deformed and stunted. Tender new leaf growth may die.

Cause: Powdery mildew is a fungal disease. In warm regions, this fungus is present year-round. In areas where summers are hot and dry, or winters are cold, the fungus is dormant during periods of adverse weather and reappears when conditions are mild and humid, although the fungal spores do not need water to develop.

REGIONAL FOCUS
SOUTHWEST

Hydrangeas are easily scorched by sun and dry heat. The growing tips and top leaves turn yellow with brown margins. Plants growing in full sun when temperatures are above 102°F are especially at risk. Tops of badly burned plants can die, resulting in no flowers and stunted growth. Provide relief by shading with lattice or burlap, or by moving plants to a shadier area.

Solution: Handpick or spray infected leaves; avoid growing hydrangeas near host plants.

- Handpick and dispose of infected leaves.
- Spray with wettable sulfur, an organic fungicide. Follow label directions carefully.
- Plant hydrangeas far from serviceberry, acacia, black locust, and gardenia, because these plants can carry the disease.

Leaves are yellow; veins green

Problem: Leaves gradually turn yellow, but the veins remain green. The plant is stunted and grows poorly.

Cause: Neutral or alkaline soil typically causes hydrangeas to suffer. This is most noticeable on the bigleaf hydrangeas (*H. macrophylla*). Iron, which plants use to produce chlorophyll, is not as available to a plant in alkaline soil.

Solution: Increase the amount of iron in the soil, and acidify soil to make iron available.

- For immediate relief, drench the soil around the plant with ammonium sulfate.
- For another fast-acting, short-term cure, spray the plant with a solution of chelated iron, which is then absorbed by the foliage.
- For a long-term cure, increase the soil acidity by working in powdered sulfur according to package directions, and by mulching with acidifying pine needles or oak leaves.

Flowers and leaves are eaten

Problem: Pale brown, slow-moving beetles are consuming flowers and leaves. If many are present, a plant can be weakened, and unsightly. The damage usually begins in early June and lasts for about a month.

Cause: Adult rose chafers feed on hydrangea and other plants, while their larvae infest lawns and eat grass roots. Rose chafers are most common in areas with sandy soil.

Solution: Remove the chafers or spray the plant with insecticides.

- If the infestation is light, handpick chafers. Dispose of them so that birds can't feed on them because they are toxic to birds.
- Spray the infested plant with the botanical insecticide neem or pyrethrum. Or use a synthetic insecticide registered for hydrangeas that contains the active ingredient methoxychlor or carbaryl. Follow label directions carefully.

Plant looks sick; upper branches are corky

Problem: Plant looks unhealthy, with yellowing leaves, stunted growth, and wilting tips. Stems, particularly the upper ones, seem to have a corky growth.

Cause: Scale, especially oyster-shell scale, generally colonize one or two shoots before infesting the rest of the plant. After hatching in spring, the pests crawl to a new location, become attached to the plant, and develop a waxy covering. In the North there is only one generation per year, but there may be two in the South.

Solution: Prune and spray to control scale.

- Prune the first infected shoots to stop the insects from spreading to other branches.
- In late May or early June, spray with the botanical insecticide neem or pyrethrum. Or use a synthetic insecticide registered for hydrangeas that contains the active ingredient malathion or carbaryl. In the South, spray a second time in mid-July to control crawlers. Follow label directions carefully.
- In late winter, spray with dormant oil to kill overwintering adults and eggs.

TIME-TESTED TECHNIQUES

TIMELY PRUNING IS THE KEY TO ABUNDANT FLOWERS

The many varieties of hydrangea differ greatly in their pruning requirements. Pruning in the wrong way, or at the wrong time of year, can result in a loss of flowers. Both smooth hydrangea (*Hydrangea arborescens*) and panicle hydrangea (*H. paniculata*) bloom on new wood and can be cut back almost to the ground in late winter or very early spring. The tree form of panicle hydrangea should only be cut back to the top of the trunklike stem. Bigleaf (*H. macrophylla*) and oakleaf (*H. quercifolia*) hydrangeas bloom on old wood and should be pruned immediately after flowering. Climbing hydrangea rarely needs pruning.

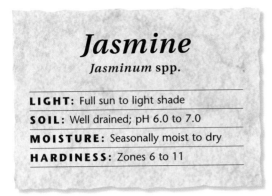

Jasmine
Jasminum spp.

LIGHT: Full sun to light shade

SOIL: Well drained; pH 6.0 to 7.0

MOISTURE: Seasonally moist to dry

HARDINESS: Zones 6 to 11

A young plant wilts suddenly and dies

Problem: A plant on which the bark has not yet fully developed wilts suddenly and dies. A white mat of fungus is visible on the base of the stem and on surrounding soil.

Cause: Southern blight is a fungal disease that can occur in the North as well as the South. Spores enter a plant at soil level, often through a small wound, and spread a mat of tendrils up the plant and out onto the surrounding soil. Droplets of acidic liquid produced by the mat kill plant cells on contact. Plants often die within a month of infection. This fungus can infect a variety of vegetables and flowers as well as shrubs.

Solution: Southern blight is incurable. Destroy infected plants. To prevent the recurrence and spread of the disease, practice good garden sanitation, add soil amendments and fertilizer, and use proper cultivation methods.

- Dig up the infected plant along with the surrounding 6 inches of soil. Take extra care not to drop any contaminated soil back into the hole. Make sure to destroy the infected plant material.
- Reduce the chances of repeated outbreaks by working organic material, such as compost, into the soil to increase drainage and introduce disease-inhibiting organisms.
- Keep the nitrogen level of the soil high, using a complete fertilizer with a 10-10-10 formulation (p.324), because the disease does not thrive in nitrogen-rich soil.
- When planting or hoeing around plants, take care not to damage the lower stem, as this disease enters through small wounds near the soil.

Flowers are spotted

Problem: Flowers have dark spots that rapidly join to form blotches. They turn brown and collapse. This problem is most common during periods of warm, moist weather.

Cause: Flower blight is a fungal disease. Infected flowers gradually turn brown and, after several weeks, fall to the ground. The disease spores overwinter in the soil.

Solution: Good sanitation and proper growing conditions will help control flower blight.

- Pick off infected flowers to keep the fungus from forming spores; remove plant debris.
- Mulch to keep spore-laden soil from splashing onto plants.
- When planting new jasmines, space the shrubs widely for adequate air circulation, and avoid planting in low-lying areas.

Small white flies are on plant

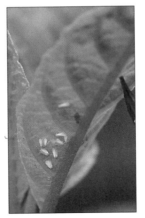

Problem: Tiny triangular white flies flutter up in clouds whenever the plant is disturbed. A black sooty powder may make some of the leaves look dark and dirty. The plant becomes pale and stunted.

Cause: Citrus whiteflies are ½-inch insects that are active year round in warm climates. The flies lay eggs on leaf undersides, where larvae and adults suck sap. The sticky, clear substance called honeydew that the insects excrete often causes a sooty mold fungus to develop on the leaves.

Solution: Spray with insecticide to control current problem. Release beneficial predators for longer term control.

- Spray plant with insecticidal soap or the botanical insecticide pyrethrum. Or use a synthetic insecticide registered for jasmines that contains the active ingredient chlorpyrifos. Follow label directions carefully.
- For long-term control, buy predators such as green lacewings from a catalog.
- Use a wet rag to wipe off mold; it will be less of a problem once flies are controlled.

Juniper

Juniperus spp.

LIGHT: Full sun to light shade

SOIL: Heavy to light; pH 5.5 to 8.0

MOISTURE: Moist to dry

HARDINESS: Zones 3 to 9

Twigs turn brown and die

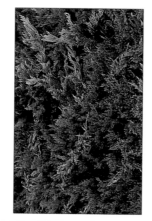

Problem: The tips of the branches remain green, but the lower portions die off. Or the immature needles at the tip of a branch get yellow spots, turn pale, then brown. Young shoots die, but old foliage survives.

Cause: Two unrelated fungi cause twig blights: cercospora needle blight and phomopsis tip blight. Needle blight infects plants mainly in summer, but damage is often not seen until fall. The disease starts on small side shoots near the base of the branch, causing infected limbs to turn brown and fall off after a couple of months. Tip blight invades the stems, causing lesions, or cankers. On a young plant, if the canker occurs on the main stem, the plant will die. On older plants, new growth is affected, and the shrubs seldom die.

Solution: Combine pruning and spraying.

- Prune out infected wood; use gloves for protection against the prickly needles.
- For needle blight, spray in June and July with Bordeaux mixture. Follow label directions carefully. Or remove the plant.
- For tip blight, spray with a synthetic fungicide registered for junipers that contains thiophanate-methyl. Follow label directions carefully.

Pointed nests hang on branches

Problem: Small nests of brown shoots hang from branches. Insect larvae feed on needles, leaving bare twigs.

Cause: Bagworms make nests using small pieces of juniper woven together with silk. The larvae live inside the nests for protection from predators. They overwinter as eggs, and larvae emerge in spring to feed and build nests.

Solution: If you notice nests early, handpicking is sufficient. Later, spraying is needed.

- Handpick in winter or early spring, and burn the nests to prevent egg laying.
- If there are numerous nests, spray the plant in summer with the biological insecticide BTK. Follow label directions carefully. Spray a second time if the bagworms are still alive after two weeks.
- If problems persist, spray with the botanical insecticide neem or pyrethrum. Or use a synthetic insecticide registered for junipers that contains carbaryl or malathion. Follow label directions carefully.

Needles turn yellow

Problem: Individual branches of needles yellow; then entire branches turn brown. Branches also become stunted, and the entire shrub looks sickly.

Cause: Juniper scales are tiny insects that are frequently overlooked because of their small size. These circular pests are white when young, turning black as they mature. Their waxy covering makes them hard to control.

Solution: Control scale insects by spraying with insecticides.

- To control scale, spray in May and June when newly hatched insects are active with insecticidal soap or the botanical insecticide neem. Or use a synthetic insecticide registered for junipers that contains the active ingredient malathion or methoxychlor. Follow label directions carefully.

- Kill overwintering eggs in late winter by spraying with dormant oil. Follow label directions carefully.

Tips of branches turn brown or are broken

Problem: Small branches are brown at the tips or are broken. In extreme cases, the entire center of the shrub may be broken and crushed.

Cause: Even though junipers are cold-hardy plants, they still may suffer from injury during winter storms. Tips of branches can be killed when prolonged windy weather dries the branches out and the roots cannot take up water to replace the loss because the soil is frozen. Junipers are particularly susceptible to damage from freezing rain. When branches are coated in ice, the weight of the ice can break them; branches that are coated and do not break often suffocate and die. Junipers used as foundation plantings can also be badly damaged by ice or snow sliding off the roof and crashing onto them, weighing them down and breaking branches.

Solution: Protect the plant from the damaging effects of winter weather.

- If the temperature is just below freezing following a rainstorm, spray plants with cold water to melt the ice.

- Erect open-sided A-frame structures over plants growing under overhangs, to break the force of falling snow.

- To keep foliage from drying out, put up a windbreak, such as burlap on stakes.

Branches have orange growths

Problem: In early spring, small green growths, called galls, appear on branches. As summer progresses, galls turn greenish brown. The following spring, they put out bright orange tentacles. The stem beyond galls often dies.

Cause: Cedar-apple rust is a fungal disease that spends its life cycle alternating between apple trees and junipers. Spores released from apple trees in summer infect junipers in late summer, and galls develop the following summer. The orange, jellylike tentacles release spores in spring that then reinfect apple trees, sometimes causing them to defoliate. The disease mainly infects eastern and southern red cedar and Rocky Mountain juniper.

Solution: Cut off and destroy all galls, spray fungicide, and avoid growing host plants.

- In winter, cut off and destroy all galls.

- Spray junipers with the organic fungicide sulfur in August to discourage spores released by apple trees from infecting them.

- If cedar-apple rust has been a problem in the past, avoid growing junipers and apple trees within a half mile of each other.

WISE CHOICES

Be careful when buying junipers. The cute little plant in a gallon pot may quickly grow into a monster with a 10-foot spread. Some spreading varieties with more refined growth include these.

- 'Blue Rug' (*Juniperus horizontalis*), or 'Wiltonii', is a ground-hugging 6 inches in height and blue green.

- 'Yukon Belle' (*J. horizontalis*) is under 6 inches tall and silver blue.

- 'Arcadia' (*J. sabina*) is 1 foot tall and bright green.

- 'Blue Carpet' (*J. squamata*) grows 5 feet tall and is blue green.

- 'Blue Star' (*J. squamata*) reaches 3 feet tall and is blue green.

Lilac

Syringa spp.

LIGHT: Full sun

SOIL: Well drained; pH 6.5 to 7.5

MOISTURE: Consistently moist

HARDINESS: Zones 3 to 7

Branches wilt and have cracked bark

Problem: Piles of pale sawdust are on the bark or on the soil beneath the plant. Leaves wilt, and branches also wilt, breaking easily in the wind. Bark near the sawdust cracks and lifts away from the swollen stems underneath.

Cause: The female clearwing moth lays about 400 eggs in crevices in the bark during her week-long life. The eggs hatch, and the larvae, called lilac borers, tunnel into branches, causing wilting. Later, the pests bore deeper into the branch, pushing their sawdustlike excrement, called frass, out the entry hole. Borers overwinter in the tunnels and, after pupating, exit the following spring through a second hole, about 3 inches above the first.

Solution: Careful pruning and insecticidal spray offer effective control.

- Look for signs of borers, such as holes in the stems, especially after leaf-drop in fall. Cut off and destroy damaged tissue.

- In April, spray the stems with a synthetic insecticide registered for lilacs that contains the active ingredient endosulfan. Follow label directions carefully.

Plant is stunted and sickly

Problem: The plant becomes stunted. Leaves are small, yellowing, and twisted. If left untreated, sprays of tiny side branches, called witches'-brooms, develop on stems. Leaves may look scorched, and stems may die.

Cause: Mycoplasma-like organism (MLO) is an increasingly common problem in lilacs. The action of these single-celled organisms, which are not fungus, bacterium, or virus, is still not fully understood. MLO is most common on Hungarian, late, and nodding lilacs, and their hybrids, such as the Preston lilacs. It also occurs on Japanese tree lilac. Common lilac seems to be immune.

Solution: There is no cure. Remove infected plants, practice good garden sanitation, and grow resistant species to prevent spread.

- At the first sign of infection, remove plants.

- Dispose of potentially infected leaf litter.

- Plant resistant common lilac (*S. vulgaris*) and its varieties.

Leaves have a whitish powder

Problem: Lower leaves become covered with a white dust that slowly spreads upward. The problem is most common late in the season.

Cause: Powdery mildew is a common lilac disease. The fungus that causes it feeds on the upper leaf surfaces and doesn't penetrate into the leaf itself. If the disease doesn't show up until late in the growing season, it does little damage. But a plant infected in midsummer or before can be weakened and stressed.

Solution: Spray if mildew appears early. Practice good garden sanitation to control.

- If the disease strikes early in the growing season, spray the plant with an organic fungicide, such as lime sulfur or sulfur. Follow label directions carefully.

- In fall, dispose of infected or fallen foliage.

- Don't remove snails. This is one case where they are beneficial. They feed on the powdery mildew without eating the leaf underneath. Zigzag tracks in the mildew are a sign that snails are eating powdery mildew.

Stems blacken; leaves shrivel

Problem: In spring, when the weather is warm and moist, young shoots turn black or brown. Leaves at the tip of these shoots wither and darken. Older leaves have small spots that run together to form blotches. Flower stems wilt and turn brown; buds blacken.

Cause: Two diseases produce these symptoms. Bacterial blight causes shoot blackening, while those turning brown have phytophthora fungal blight. The fungal blight is the more severe and may eventually kill the plant. White-flowered varieties of the common lilac (*S. vulgaris*) are most susceptible.

Solution: Control these blights with pruning, fungicidal sprays, and proper plant care.

- Cut out infected shoots well below the infected area. Sterilize (p.310) pruners between each cut.

- For more control, spray with an organic copper fungicide, such as copper sulfate, or wettable sulfur. Follow label directions.

- Don't fertilize plants more than once in spring, because new growth is more prone to infection.

- Fungal blight also attacks rhododendrons; don't plant lilacs near rhododendrons.

Leaves are folded and tied

Problem: At any time during the growing season, the leaves develop brown blotches of dried tissue. Later, the leaf folds in half, and the edges are joined together with silk.

TIME-TESTED TECHNIQUES

INTEGRATED PEST MANAGEMENT

If you can tolerate a few pests in your garden, try integrated pest management (IPM) to maintain plant health. Knowing that pests and diseases attack weakened plants, IPM practitioners avoid trouble by growing plants in a stress-free manner. To do this, select plants that grow well in your climate and soil. Encourage beneficial insects and animals by providing habitats they enjoy. Put up birdhouses to encourage insect-eating birds. Provide suitable homes, such as overturned pots, for toads and lizards. You'll seldom see these creatures, but they'll eat many garden pests. Grow small-flowered nectar plants such as dill, alyssum, and scabiosa to attract beneficial insects.

Cause: Lilac leafminers are the larvae of a small moth. The moth lays its eggs on leaf undersides, and the hatching larvae tunnel into the leaf tissue, where they feed. Where several trails occur in one leaf, they may run together, forming a large brown area. After feeding, larvae leave the mines and form cocoons, overwintering in fallen foliage or in soil under the shrub.

Solution: Handpick, spray, practice good garden sanitation, and use barriers.

- If there are only a few blotched leaves, and the plant is a manageable size, handpick the damaged foliage.

- For severe infestations, spray the plant with a synthetic insecticide registered for lilacs that contains the active ingredient acephate. Follow label directions carefully.

- Rake up and dispose of infected foliage as it falls, to prevent pupae development.

- Place plastic sheeting under the shrub to prevent the dropping pupae from reaching the soil, where they mature.

- If leafminers have been a problem previously, drench the soil under the shrub with a synthetic insecticide registered for lilacs that contains the active ingredient diazinon. Apply it in spring, to control emerging moths. Follow label directions carefully.

Mock Orange

Philadelphus spp.

LIGHT: Full sun to partial shade

SOIL: Well drained; pH 5.5 to 7.5

MOISTURE: Consistently moist

HARDINESS: Zones 4 to 8

Buds are distorted and covered with tiny insects

Problem: Leaves become twisted, with curled edges, particularly at the top of the plant. Buds and tender new growth are covered with small, dark or pale green insects. Curled leaves and older leaves lower down on the plant have sticky and shiny patches. Later, a powdery black mold covers the leaves.

Cause: Two species of sap-sucking aphids feed on leaf undersides. The bean aphid is dark green to black. The green peach aphid is pale green with dark lines on its back. Populations of these pests build up rapidly in warm weather, and if left unchecked, may severely stunt growth. The clear sticky substance, called honeydew, is excreted by the aphids. Eventually, black sooty mold grows on the honeydew, blocking light to the leaves.

Solution: Hose off aphids or spray with insecticides. Use repellents.

- Dislodge aphids with a strong stream of water from a hose.
- Or spray the plant with insecticidal soap or with the botanical insecticide neem. Follow label directions carefully.
- Once aphids are under control, spray the plant with garlic oil or with capsaicin to repel further infestations. Follow label directions carefully.

Shrub does not flower well

Problem: Few flowers are produced, and the entire shrub seems to lack vigor. But abundant soft growth is produced.

Cause: Too much shade prevents a mock orange from flowering fully. As surrounding plants grow, they may start to shade a plant that was originally planted in sun. Lack of pruning will also affect the amount of flowers that a mock orange produces. A plant with a mass of congested stems will not grow well or bloom freely. Mock orange blooms on the previous year's wood, so pruning at the wrong time of year, or shortening the top of the plant, will result in few flowers.

Solution: Prune mock orange properly. Thin nearby plants for more light or move plant.

- Soon after flowering, prune by removing the oldest shoots, not by trimming back all of them. Also remove a few of the branches that grow close to the ground.
- Thin surrounding plants to allow more direct sunlight to reach the mock orange.
- If you can't provide more light, dig up the plant and relocate it to a sunnier area.

Stems have rough, cracked areas; tips die

Problem: Individual stems die, starting at the tips. Below the dead region, there is an area of roughened bark that is cracked and may be slightly swollen. If left untreated, small, black fungal growths will develop. Later, pink to red pustules also may appear.

Cause: Canker from a fungal infection causes dead shoots and rough bark. The pink pustules are a secondary fungus, known as coral spot, that invades the weakened wood. The lesions infect the soft wood just under the bark, staining it brown and causing the stems to die.

Solution: Remove the infected branches.

- Prune and destroy infected branches. Cut well below the rough area of bark and examine the cut surface. If there is still a ring of brown wood just inside the bark, prune again lower down. Sterilize (p.310) your shears between cuts.

Mountain Laurel

Kalmia latifolia

LIGHT: Sun to shade

SOIL: Well drained; pH 5.0 to 6.5

MOISTURE: Consistently moist

HARDINESS: Zones 4 to 9

Stems have hard waxy bumps; plant declines

Problem: At any time during the growing season, stems develop small, hard, waxy bumps that look like tiny flat discs. A heavily infested plant declines, and may die within the year.

Cause: Scale insects attach themselves to tender stems and suck out plant juices. They are a significant problem affecting mountain laurel and other shrubs. Adults are stationary and protected by hard, waxy shells. They are most common in warm climates, where they have several overlapping generations, which makes treatment difficult. Larvae, or crawlers, hatch from eggs protected under the shells of female adults, and migrate to other leaves and branches.

Solution: Spray a serious infestation and release natural predators.

- To kill newly hatched crawlers, spray in spring with insecticidal soap. Repeat applications regularly to catch new generations.

- Or spray with an insecticide registered for mountain laurels that contains the active ingredient imidacloprid. Follow label directions carefully.

- For long-term control of minor outbreaks, release predatory lacewings (p.103), available from mail-order catalogs.

Brown spots appear on leaves

Problem: Leaves have brown spots that become light gray in the center with a purplish margin. The blemishes first appear in spring on the new foliage, at flowering time. Small, black, fruiting bodies appear in summer. Severely infected plants, especially when growing in shade, may be slightly stunted and have few flowers.

Cause: Kalmia leaf spot is a fungal disease that occurs wherever mountain laurel grows. The fruiting bodies release spores in spring to infect the newly opened leaves.

Solution: Use good garden sanitation and spraying to prevent serious problems.

- Handpick infected leaves, and dispose of foliage that falls to the ground.

- Spray healthy foliage with a synthetic fungicide registered for mountain laurels that contains the active ingredient triadimefon, mancozeb, myclobutanil, maneb, or ferbam. In winter, spray with an organic sulfur fungicide. Follow label directions carefully.

WISE CHOICES

The range of mountain laurel flower colors has been greatly extended in recent decades. There are now more than 50 named varieties with flowers in white and in solid or bicolored shades of pink, red, and burgundy. Here are some of the best choices.

- 'Bravo': Dark pink buds and flowers
- 'Carol': Red buds open to pink flowers
- 'Heart's Desire': Red flowers with a white band at the edge
- 'Hoffman's Pink': Dark pink buds open to pale pink flowers
- 'Raspberry Glow': Burgundy buds open to pink flowers
- 'Shooting Star': White, star-shaped flowers
- 'Sunset': Dark red buds and nearly red flowers
- 'White Mountain': White buds and flowers
- 'Yankee Doodle': Pink buds open to white flowers with a narrow red border

Mountain laurel is the finest native shrub for the Northeast. Plants flower best in full sun, but the foliage looks better when plants grow in shade.

The shrub's bell-shaped flowers have curious pockets in the petals that house stamens. When an insect enters the flower, the stamens spring forward to deposit pollen.

Mountain laurel makes a good companion plant for ground-hugging heaths and heathers.

Flowers have small spots and turn brown

Problem: Flowers have small spots that rapidly grow and join to form blotches. Eventually, the entire flower turns brown and droops. A plant in full bloom can be reduced to a mass of withered flowers almost overnight. This problem is most common during periods of warm, moist weather, especially in the South and where mountain laurels are planted close to azaleas.

Cause: Flower blight, also called petal blight, is a fungal disease. The infected flowers turn brown and hang on the plant for several weeks, later falling to the ground. During this time, spores form that eventually get washed into the soil where they overwinter. In warm, moist weather the following spring, spores germinate and infect opening flowers.

Solution: Good garden sanitation and fungicidal sprays are the best control.

- Pick infected flowers, and remove them from the garden. Spores from nearby plants can still cause infection; continue to check the mountain laurel for spotted flowers every few days.
- Spray healthy flowers with a synthetic fungicide registered for mountain laurels that contains the active ingredient triadimefon, mancozeb, myclobutanil, or maneb. Follow label directions carefully.

Leaf edges are chewed; bark is missing at ground level

Problem: Leaves have jagged edges. In severe cases, only the main leaf vein remains. Roots are eaten and bark is missing at ground level. The plant wilts and may gradually die.

Cause: Black vine weevils produce these symptoms. The beetlelike adult insects feed on the foliage and can weaken the plant. The larvae are also a problem, eating the roots and removing the bark from around the base of the main stem.

Solution: Remove beetles or spray infested plants with insecticide. For long-term prevention, use biological control and select new plants carefully.

- Spread a white sheet beneath each plant, then shake the plant. Collect and destroy beetles that drop onto the sheet.
- If the problem persists, spray the infested plants with a synthetic insecticide registered for mountain laurels that contains the active ingredient chlorpyrifos. Follow label directions carefully.
- To control weevil larvae, apply beneficial parasitic nematodes (p.126) to the soil around the plants four times a year.
- When buying new plants, check for larvae in top few inches of soil.

Leaves have spots and tips die

Problem: Large circular or oval spots appear on the leaves. The spots are numerous, and brown or purplish with a dark margin. In heavy attacks, shoot tips may die. The damage is easy to confuse with winter injury in a plant grown at the limits of its hardiness.

Cause: Phomopsis blight is a fungal disease that causes dieback and lesions on leaves. Severely infected leaves with many spots tend to drop during the summer, rather than remaining evergreen.

Solution: Use good garden sanitation and spray with fungicide to control this disease.

- Handpick infected leaves, and rake up and dispose of foliage that falls to the ground.
- Spray leaves with a synthetic fungicide registered for mountain laurels that contains the active ingredient mancozeb or thiophanate-methyl. Follow label directions carefully.
- In late winter, apply organic sulfur fungicide to the plant to kill overwintering spores. Follow label directions carefully.

Privet
Ligustrum spp.

LIGHT: Sun to shade

SOIL: Sandy to clay; pH 5.5 to 7.5

MOISTURE: Moist to dry

HARDINESS: Zones 3 to 11

Leaves turn brown and twigs die unexpectedly

Problem: Leaves turn brown and die but remain on the branches. Small twigs are killed, and lesions develop at the base of main stems. The lesions grow pink blemishes, and if affected stems are cut through, there is brown wood inside. Cracks develop in the bark, which then peels away.

Cause: Anthracnose, or twig blight, is a common fungal disease, especially on plants weakened by stress, drought, poor nutrition, or attacks from other pests and diseases.

Solution: Prune infected branches and spray with fungicide. Prevent future problems by growing resistant varieties.

- Cut off infected shoots and branches, using a sharp pruning saw to make a clean cut. Saws styled like Japanese bonsai saws are ideal, because they make an exceptionally smooth cut. Sterilize (p.310) pruning tools between cuts to prevent reinfection.

- Each week, starting in early spring when the weather is warm and damp, spray the organic fungicide Bordeaux mixture, a blend of copper sulfate and hydrated lime. Follow label directions carefully. Continue treating the plant until no further disease outbreaks occur.

- Grow resistant species, such as amur privet (*L. amurense*), regal privet (*L. obtusifolium*), Californian privet (*L. ovalifolium*), or glossy privet (*L. lucidum*).

Leaves are spotted or streaked with yellow

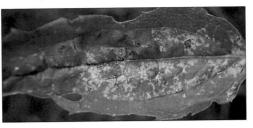

Problem: Leaves develop random yellow spots, blotches, streaks, or rings.

Cause: Viral diseases can be transmitted during grafting and are also spread from plant to plant by sap-sucking insects, such as aphids and leafhoppers, as they feed in the garden.

Solution: There is no cure for viral diseases. To prevent disease spread, destroy infected plants and control insects.

- Dig up and destroy infected plants.

- Spray plants during growing season with insecticidal soap to control sap-sucking insects. Follow label directions carefully.

- Remove nearby weeds that shelter insects.

Leaves have small pale spots that turn brown

Problem: Leaves are covered with small, pale spots that later turn brown. The spots have a yellow edge, and affected leaves may fall prematurely. This problem is most common in the South in wet weather.

Cause: Leaf spot is a fungal disease occurring most frequently on overgrown or crowded shrubs, or wherever air circulation is poor.

Solution: Prune the plant and use proper watering techniques to control leaf spot.

- Remove and dispose of diseased leaves.
- Prune a few old branches to increase air circulation in the shrub's interior and discourage germination of disease spores.
- Water early in the day, and water at ground level to keep the foliage as dry as possible.

☙ TIME-TESTED TECHNIQUES ☙

KEEPING HEDGES SHAPELY

Privet makes an ideal hedge. The plants respond well to trimming and can be kept any shape. They can be trimmed as low as 2 feet or allowed to grow to a height of 10 feet. Trimming twice, once in late spring and again in midsummer, is the minimum requirement, but three or even four trimmings per year will result in a denser, neater hedge. To prevent privet hedges from going bare at the base, prune them to a tapering shape that's narrower at the top. Cut neglected hedges back almost to the ground; then let them regrow.

Leaves have tiny pale dots

Problem: Leaves have tiny puncture marks that are bleached out. Where spots are numerous, the leaves have a grayish appearance. The symptoms are most pronounced when the plant is used as a hedge.

Cause: Privet thrips are minute flying insects that feed on leaf undersides. They are most active during dry weather.

Solution: Hose off pests, water plant, and spray with insecticide.

- Hose off plant frequently to dispel insects. Water plant frequently during droughts.
- To control thrips, spray the plant with insecticidal soap or the botanical insecticide neem, rotenone, or pyrethrum. Or use a synthetic insecticide registered for privet that contains the active ingredient carbaryl. Follow label directions carefully. Respray in two weeks.

Leaves are curled or dotted

Problem: Leaves curl lengthwise, or they become yellowish, with small dots. Leaves have a sticky, shiny film. In time, the leaves may turn black.

Cause: The folded leaves are infested by privet aphids, and the yellowish leaves have been attacked by citrus white fly. Both of these common pests feed on sap and secrete a sticky substance called honeydew. Their feeding can weaken the plant and make it susceptible to diseases. Honeydew can be a host for black, sooty mold, which covers the leaf surface and blocks light, causing leaves to die.

Solution: Spray to control both pests.

- Spray with insecticidal soap or with the botanical insecticide neem. Follow label directions carefully.
- If the problem persists, spray with a synthetic insecticide registered for privet that contains the active ingredient malathion or carbaryl. Follow label directions carefully.

Leaves have powdery spots

Problem: Upper surfaces of privet leaves are covered with a powdery white dust, usually starting on lower leaves. The problem is most common late in the season.

Cause: Powdery mildew is a fungal disease that attacks the upper leaf surface, but it doesn't penetrate the leaf itself. When it shows up late in the season, it does little damage. But plants that are infected in midsummer or earlier can be weakened.

Solution: Spray and practice good sanitation.

- Spray the infected plant with organic wettable sulfur fungicide. Follow label directions carefully.
- In fall, rake up and dispose of infected foliage that has dropped to the ground.

Rhododendron and Azalea

Rhododendron spp.

LIGHT: Partial shade

SOIL: High in humus; pH 5.0 to 6.5

MOISTURE: Consistently moist

HARDINESS: Zones 4 to 9

Leaf edges are notched; plant is wilted

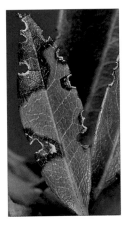

Problem: Leaves have irregular notches around the edges. In severe cases, only the main leaf vein is left. Roots are eaten and the bark is missing at ground level. The plant wilts and may eventually die.

Cause: Strawberry and black vine weevils both cause these symptoms. The adults are beetlelike insects that feed on the foliage, weakening the plant. Their root-feeding larvae do even worse damage, eating the bark off roots at the base of the stems, which eventually kills the plant. Control is very difficult because these pests resist many chemicals.

Solution: Remove the insects or spray with insecticide. Use parasitic nematodes to control larvae. Inspect new plants for problems.

● Spread a white sheet under the plant, shake the plant and destroy insects that fall on it.

● If the problem persists, spray the foliage with a synthetic insecticide registered for rhododendrons that contains the active ingredient acephate. Follow label directions carefully.

● To control weevil larvae, apply parasitic nematodes (p.126), a biological control, to the soil. Repeat as needed.

● Before purchasing a new plant, carefully inspect the soil in the container for larvae. Reject plants with symptoms.

Leaf surfaces are speckled with pale dots

Problem: Small pale green to yellow dots appear on upper leaf surfaces. The leaf undersides have small brown or black tarlike spots.

Cause: Lace bugs are destructive insects that overwinter as eggs laid along the main leaf veins. They hatch in spring and begin to feed. There are two generations per year in the North and three or more in the South.

Solution: Insecticidal sprays will help control lace bugs. Try to control the pests in the juvenile (nymph) stage before they develop wings and spread to other plants. Because there are several generations per year, repeated spraying is needed. Be careful to concentrate on the leaf undersides.

● Spray the plant with insecticidal soap. Repeat the application as needed. Follow label directions carefully.

● Or spray with a synthetic insecticide registered for rhododendrons that contains the active ingredient carbaryl, acephate, or malathion. Follow label directions carefully.

WISE CHOICES

Many rhododendron varieties can lend spring and early summer color even to cold, Northern gardens. Here are some of the toughest varieties, hardy to about −25°F.

● *Rhododendron catawbiense* 'Album', 'English Roseum', 'President Lincoln', 'Purpureum Elegans', 'Roseum Pink', and 'Roseum Superbum'

● *R. mucronulatum* 'Alba', 'Cornell Pink', 'Mahogany Red', and 'Shrimp Pink'

● *R.* PJM hybrids 'Black Satin' and 'Elite'

● *R.* hybrids 'Nova Zembla', 'Shamrock', 'Sham's Candy', and 'The General'

REGIONAL FOCUS
SOUTHEAST

While severe winters limit the range of azaleas in the North, it is the hot, humid summers that act as the limiting factor in the Southeast. Heat tolerance varies depending on the type of azalea grown, with the Indica type being the best choice in the South (box, right).

Where heat stress is a factor, plant azaleas in dappled shade and avoid planting where light is reflected from nearby buildings. Sunscald, the sudden browning of one side of the plant, is a problem that can occur when light intensity suddenly changes, as when a shade tree is removed.

WISE CHOICES

Indica azaleas are excellent choices for growing in areas with warm sunny climates. Here are some of the best southern Indica azalea varieties.

'Brilliant', 'Daphne Salmon', 'Elegans', 'Fielder's White', 'Fisher Pink', 'Formosa', and 'George L. Taber'

Leaves turn yellow, but veins remain green

Problem: The plant grows slowly. Its leaves turn pale at first, eventually turning yellow. The leaf veins, however, remain dark green.

Cause: These symptoms result when the plant does not receive enough iron, an essential nutrient. Frequently, the soil contains enough iron for healthy growth, but because it's alkaline, the plant is unable to absorb the iron. Even in an area with acidic soil, planting close to a cement foundation, walk, or driveway may lead to iron-deficiency as a result of alkaline lime being leached from the concrete.

Solution: Give the plant supplemental iron as a quick fix. Make the soil more acidic using sulfur, mulch, and fertilizer.

- As a short-term solution, spray the plant with a form of chelated iron absorbable through the leaves. Drench the soil under the plant with the same solution. In a few days, the leaves will turn green.

- For a longer term solution, test the soil pH (p.329) and adjust it to make it more acidic. Follow test recommendations and incorporate sulfur in soil to raise it to a pH level of 5 to 6.5.

- Mulch around the plant with naturally acidic oak leaves or pine needles.

- Apply an acidifying fertilizer, such as cottonseed meal or ammonium sulfate. Follow label directions.

Leaves or buds have spots and pale, fleshy growths

Problem: Some leaves have red or yellow spots. Other leaves, and occasionally flower buds, become deformed, developing pink or white, soft fleshy growths. The growths eventually become brown and hard.

Cause: Azalea leaf gall is a fungal disease that's more unsightly than serious. The leaf swellings are called pinkster apples. The disease can also attack growing tips, producing fleshy leaves and flower buds that harden and fail to open.

Solution: Handpick and remove infected plant parts. Spray if necessary.

- On a small bush, handpick the infected growth and dispose of it.

- If the plant is large or the damage is extensive, spray in early spring with a synthetic fungicide registered for azaleas that contains the active ingredient triadimefon. Follow label directions carefully.

- In late winter, spray the plant with organic copper-sulfate fungicide. Follow label directions carefully.

Leaves wilt; stems break easily

Problem: Leaves of individual shoots curl and wilt from the top of the shoot down. Small holes filled with insect waste (frass) are on the stems. Brittle, weakened stems may break in strong winds.

Cause: Larvae of the azalea stem borer are tunneling inside the shoots. The adult beetle feeds on leaf undersides, causing them to curl.

In June or July, the beetles lay eggs on stems. After hatching, the grubs tunnel into the stem and move down, overwintering the first year inside the stem. The second year, they continue downward into the root, where they feed, and then pupate. Because they are protected in stems, borers are difficult to control.

Solution: Deter infestations with pruning and insecticidal spray.

- Cut and destroy wilting stems, inspecting the cut ends to make sure borers are inside.

- To discourage infestations, spray the plant in spring and early summer with the botanical insecticide neem. Follow label directions carefully.

Flowers have spots or blotches

Problem: Small spots appear on the flowers. The spots rapidly enlarge and join to form blotches. Soon the entire flower collapses—sometimes almost overnight. This problem is most common during periods of warm, moist weather.

Cause: Ovulinia petal blight, a fungal disease, causes blossoms to turn brown and hang from the plant. After several weeks, they fall to the ground. During this time, spores wash into the soil where they overwinter. In the warm, humid weather of spring, spores produce fruiting bodies that shoot new spores into the air to infect opening flowers.

Solution: Good sanitation is the best control but large plants may require a fungicide.

- Handpick infected flowers to prevent overwintering spores. Remove any spotted flower immediately.

- In severe attacks, remove all flowers and buds for one season.

- If picking is not possible, treat the soil under the shrub with a synthetic fungicide that contains the active ingredient captan or PCNB to kill the fruiting bodies. Apply it before buds show color. Spray the flowers with a synthetic pesticide that contains the active ingredient mancozeb, propiconazole, or ziram. Use formulations registered for azalea. Follow label directions carefully.

Flower buds look dried out and have tiny dark spots

Problem: Flower buds are small and dried out, and have many tiny black dots. Leaf buds may have similar symptoms, and their twigs may die.

Cause: Bud and twig blight is a fungal disease that affects rhododendrons and azaleas. The disease overwinters on dead twigs, and may live to reinfect the shrubs for up to three years.

Solution: Careful and timely pruning together with good garden sanitation can control bud and twig blight.

- Prune and destroy infected twigs, leaves, and flower buds.

- In fall and again in spring, prune and destroy all dead twigs. Remove and dispose of all garden plant debris.

- If bud and twig blight has been a problem in the past, spray plants with Bordeaux mixture, an organic fungicide containing sulfur and hydrated lime. Begin spraying before flower buds open and continue at monthly intervals through the growing season. Follow label directions carefully.

TIME-TESTED TECHNIQUES

YES, YOU CAN GROW AZALEAS!

You can grow acid-loving azaleas even if your soil is alkaline. But don't try to acidify a flower bed. Minerals leaching from surrounding soil will bring the bed back to its original state. Instead, construct a raised bed (p.328). Azaleas have a shallow root system, so the bed needs to be only about 12 inches deep. Add peat moss, pine needles, or decomposed oak leaves to the soil. Mix in iron sulfate for immediate acidity and powdered sulfur for long-term acidity. Test the soil yearly and amend it as needed to maintain its acidity (p.329).

REGIONAL FOCUS
NORTHWEST

Rhododendrons on the West Coast, especially in Washington and California, may be attacked by the rhododendron whitefly. This pest causes leaves to yellow and their edges to curl. The nymphs feed on the undersides of the leaves and drop a sweet substance called honeydew onto lower leaves. A sooty mold grows on the honeydew, blocking sunlight from the leaves. The whitefly prefers varieties that have smooth underleaves; those with a felty undersurface are less likely to be attacked.

Rose
Rosa spp.

LIGHT: Full sun
SOIL: Fertile, well drained; pH 6.0 to 6.8
MOISTURE: Consistently moist
HARDINESS: Zones 3 to 11

Buds open unevenly; petals have brown edges

Problem: On a white or pale pastel rose, the buds droop and may only partially open. Petals on open blossoms have brown scratches and bumps and often brown, curled edges.

Cause: Thrips are tiny insects that feed inside the flowers. You can only see them if you tap a blossom over a sheet of colored paper and examine the paper for tiny, squirming, shardlike insects.

Solution: Remove diseased plant parts, spray, and deadhead flowers. Grow a different variety of rose less likely to attract thrips.

- Handpick the affected blossoms, and remove them from the garden.
- Spray the plant with insecticidal soap or with the botanical insecticide neem, pyrethrum, or rotenone.
- If problems persist, use a synthetic insecticide registered for roses that contains the active ingredient malathion, carbaryl, or diazinon. Follow label directions carefully.
- Spray the plant with garlic oil to repel future infestations.
- Deadhead roses as soon as blossoms fade. Even healthy faded flowers can host thrips.
- If thrips are a recurrent problem, grow mostly dark-colored red roses; they're less attractive to thrips than pale ones.

Buds blacken in spring

Problem: When spring is cool and damp, a black mold develops on rose buds, usually accompanied by fuzzy gray mold on nearby leaves and stems. Any blossoms that do open reveal brown specks and spots of soft gray mold; they fall apart when touched.

Cause: Botrytis blight, also called gray mold, is caused by a fungus that thrives in cool, damp conditions.

Solution: Prune, spray, and keep the plant as dry as possible to control the blight.

- Clip off affected buds, blossoms, and stems. Prune the plant to improve air circulation, so that buds and leaves will dry quickly when dampened by rain.
- If damp weather persists, spray the affected rose and its neighbors with organic copper-sulfate fungicide or the botanical fungicide neem. Or spray them with a synthetic fungicide registered for roses that contains the active ingredient captan. Follow label directions carefully.
- To discourage future outbreaks, water the plant in the morning so that it has time to dry before nightfall.

Leaf undersides have powdery orange deposits

Problem: In late spring and summer, small deposits of orange powder appear on the leaves. The affected leaves become mottled with yellow, and new stems may be twisted.

Cause: Rust is a fungal disease that can spread rapidly in droplets of windblown rain.

Solution: To control rust, spray, practice good garden sanitation, and keep foliage dry.

- Spray an outbreak with the botanical pesticide neem. Or use a synthetic fungicide registered for roses that contains the active ingredient ferbam, mancozeb, or maneb. Follow label directions carefully.
- Remove all fallen leaves and stems, whether or not they show signs of rust.
- In late winter, spray the dormant plant with organic lime-sulfur fungicide. Follow label directions carefully.
- Water the plant in the morning so that it has time to dry before nightfall.

Tiny insects appear on stem tips

Problem: From spring to early summer, hundreds of tiny, wedge-shaped insects cling to young green stems and flower buds. New leaves may be curled and yellow.

Cause: Aphids are tiny insects that damage roses by sucking plant juices. Large groups of these soft-bodied pests feed on tender young stems, buds, and leaves. They excrete a sticky substance called honeydew that often causes a sooty black mold to develop. A light aphid infestation that is not seriously injuring a plant may actually be helpful, because aphids attract beneficial insects, such as ladybugs and lacewing larvae.

Solution: Dislodge the pests with water, and spray with insecticides to control them.

- Hose the aphids off the plant on a dry, breezy day when leaves will dry quickly.
- Spray the infested plant with insecticidal soap or the botanical insecticide neem, pyrethrum, or rotenone. Follow label directions carefully.
- Or spray with a synthetic insecticide registered for roses that contains the active ingredient malathion, diazinon, or dimethoate. Follow label directions carefully.
- For a chronic problem, spray with light horticultural oil in early spring to smother eggs. Also spray with capsaicin or garlic oil to repel aphids.

Rounded holes appear in leaf edges

Problem: Healthy green rose leaves suddenly develop cleanly cut circles or semicircles along the edges. The damage is often limited to a single plant.

Cause: Leaf-cutter bees harvest bits of rose leaves to use in building their nests. These insects are widespread, but there are so few of them that damage to roses is more interesting than alarming. These bees help pollinate other plants, so it is best to accept them as part of your garden's insect community and tolerate the light damage they cause to roses. The bees themselves are blue-black and shiny. They are most active during the late morning.

Solution: Prune unattractive stems to improve the plant's appearance.

- If leaf-cutter bees scallop the edges of leaves on single branches, simply prune the unsightly stems.

Corky, rounded knobs protrude from lower stems and roots

Problem: Woody knobs form on the lower stems and on the highest roots of the plant. Over time, the growths kill the plant as they encircle the main stem and strangle it.

Cause: Crown gall is a bacterial disease that causes the knobby growths, called galls. It is usually brought into the garden on infected plants and can spread to healthy plants on pruning shears or on other garden tools.

Solution: Depending on the disease's severity, prune the affected area, spray with an antibiotic, or remove the plant.

- Prune small growths that appear above the graft if the plant is otherwise healthy. Disinfect (p.310) your shears between cuts.

- Spray the foliage with the antibiotic streptomycin. Follow label directions carefully.
- In winter, spray with organic lime-sulfur, which helps control this bacterial infection. Follow label directions carefully.
- Remove a badly infected plant. Don't grow roses in the same area again; the bacteria can persist in the soil for years.

Black spots appear on leaves

Problem: Round black spots with fringed edges develop on the upper sides of leaves, and the leaf tissue around the spots slowly turns yellow. At first, affected leaves appear in clusters. Within a few weeks, many more spots appear on the rest of the plant.

Cause: Rose blackspot is a fungal disease that can infect almost any type of rose. It is a widespread problem in all but the most arid climates. Blackspot flourishes when temperatures range between 50° and 80°F. As the fungi mature, they release thousands of microscopic spores. The spores germinate on new leaves that remain continuously damp for more than six hours.

Solution: Prune, spray, and practice good garden sanitation. Grow resistant varieties.

- Clip off and dispose of affected leaves. Prune an infected branch back to a healthy, outward-facing bud. Pick up and destroy any leaves that fall to the ground.
- Spray with organic copper-sulfate fungicide or the botanical pesticide neem. Or use a synthetic fungicide registered for roses that contains the active ingredient captan or mancozeb. Follow label directions carefully.
- Water the plant in the morning so that leaves can dry completely by nightfall.
- Mulch with an organic material such as shredded bark, pine needles, or straw to prevent water splashing onto leaves.
- In humid climates, grow blackspot-resistant English, shrub, and rugosa roses.

Dusty powder forms on leaves

Problem: In spring or fall, grayish white powdery deposits appear on young leaves, stems, and buds. Leaves curl up.

Cause: Powdery mildew is a widespread fungal disease that flourishes when temperatures range between 50° and 80°F. Older leaves and glossy-leaved varieties resist invasion, but young tissues are at high risk.

Solution: Spray and practice good garden sanitation. Grow resistant varieties.

- Spray the plant with an organic sulfur, lime-sulfur, or copper-sulfate fungicide or the botanical pesticide neem. Or use a synthetic fungicide registered for roses that contains the active ingredient ziram. Follow label directions carefully.
- Remove old leaves in fall, replace mulches in spring, and prune to promote air flow.
- As soon as they leaf out in spring, spray susceptible plants weekly with a mixture of baking soda and light horticultural oil (p.392). Between applications, hose the plants on dry, breezy mornings to dislodge spores on infected leaves.
- Plant resistant roses, including many shrub, English, and glossy-leaved varieties.

Buds and petals have small holes in them

Problem: Buds are riddled with clean, round holes that cause the petals to look ragged when the blossoms open. A small beetlelike insect may be present.

Cause: Rose curculio is a small insect with a red back and black belly. Curculio larvae feed in rose fruits, called hips, in late summer and fall, so they are most likely to be found in

PRUNING ROSES

Pruning is one of the best ways to keep rose plants vigorous and beautiful while avoiding many pest and disease problems. Much has been written about the subtleties of pruning, but keeping these flowering shrubs in shape is no more complicated than a few basic cuts made annually in early spring. Here are directions:

1. In early spring, just as the buds on the canes begin to swell, pull back any mulch from the plant's base. Prune winter-damaged canes, cutting at least 2 inches below the damaged section and ¼ inch above a plump, healthy bud that points toward the outside of the plant.

2. Remove canes more than three or four years old, and those that died back, to the base of the plant. Make a straight cut flush with the base (crown), using loping shears or a pruning saw. Removing deadwood removes overwintering sites for pests and diseases.

3. Examine the remaining canes and remove those less than ¼ inch in diameter. To encourage climbers to grow and bloom vigorously, trim the side (lateral) branches back to three or four buds from the main branch.

4. In summer, roses need only light pruning. Clip off dead or diseased branches, leaves, and faded flowers. When clipping flowers, cut above a cluster of five leaflets (not clusters of three) to promote more bloom.

areas where roses that bear fruit, such as rugosas, are grown.

Solution: Remove curculios, spray, and cut off larvae-infested rose hips.

- Shake rose curculios, which are not strong fliers, to the ground when they are feeding on blossoms. Collect them in a jar of soapy water or simply crush them.

- Spray severe infestations with the biological insecticide *Beauveria bassiana* GHA. Follow label directions carefully.

- Or spray with a synthetic insecticide registered for roses that contains a mixture of the active ingredients methoxychlor and malathion. Follow label directions carefully.

- Spray healthy plants with capsaicin or garlic oil to repel the insects. Follow label directions carefully.

- In late summer, clip off and destroy rose hips infested with curculio larvae, which look like little maggots.

WISE CHOICES

Although many roses are sensitive to harsh climates, some have been bred to flourish where no rose has grown before.

Canadian Explorer Roses

- 'William Baffin' is tough and beautiful. Hardy to –50°F, this shrubby climber has strawberry red blossoms with white in the center. It's highly disease resistant and tolerates windy, exposed sites and partial shade. Zones 2 to 7

- 'Champlain' is a shrub rose with velvety red blossoms and excellent disease resistance. Zones 3 to 7

Morden Roses

- 'Prairie Dawn', a climber bred at the Morden Research Station in Manitoba, is noted for hardiness. The semidouble flowers are a soft pastel pink and bloom in flushes from summer to first frost. It's good for windy, exposed sites. Zones 3 to 7

- 'Morden Blush' is a shrub that bears abundant pale pink flowers for months. Zones 3 to 7

- 'Assiniboine' has stunning wine red blossoms marked with a cluster of yellow stamens. Zones 3 to 7

Griffith Buck Roses

- 'Golden Unicorn', a shrub rose from the noted breeder Griffith Buck, bears butter yellow, double flowers edged in orange—unlike most extra hardy rose blossoms, which are red or pink. They contrast nicely with the dark, glossy foliage. Zones 3 to 7

- 'Country Dancer' has bountiful pink blossoms and excellent disease resistance. Zones 3 to 8

- 'Carefree Beauty' also boasts plentiful pink flowers and good disease resistance. Zones 4 to 8

Holes are chewed in leaves

Problem: In early summer, ragged holes appear between leaf veins. By the time flowers open, many long-legged, brown or gray beetles are feeding on leaves and flowers.

Cause: Rose chafers are beetles that feed intensively for about a month in summer. Their populations are much higher in some years than in others. In bad years, they feed on many other plants besides roses. Chafers overwinter underground as white grubs, feeding on grass roots until early summer when they emerge as adults. Lawn areas with sandy soil are ideal nurseries for rose chafers.

Solution: Handpick or spray to kill adult beetles. Treat the soil to control larvae.

- Handpick the beetles if there are only a few.

- Spray an outbreak with the botanical insecticide neem or rotenone. Or use a synthetic insecticide registered for roses that contains the active ingredient carbaryl or methoxychlor. Follow label directions carefully.

- Next spring, treat your lawn with beneficial nematodes (p.126) four weeks before you normally see chafers on roses.

- Also in spring, spray the plant with garlic oil or capsaicin to repel beetles. Follow label directions carefully.

Leaves turn pale; have specks

Problem: Leaves turn pale, with tiny yellow specks. They feel gritty and have a faint webbing on their undersides.

Cause: Spider mites feed in colonies on leaf undersides, from midsummer to fall. To check for them, tap a leaf over white paper and look for tiny moving red specks.

Solution: Spray foliage. Take preventive measures to deter the return of spider mites.

- Spray leaf undersides with light horticultural oil. Repeat after three days. If mites survive, spray with insecticidal soap.

- If the problem persists, spray with the botanical insecticide neem. Or use a synthetic insecticide registered for roses that contains the active ingredient dimethoate. Follow label directions carefully.

- As a deterrent, water the plant often and spray with capsaicin or garlic oil. In early winter, prune the plant, and apply horticultural oil. Remove nearby weeds.

Beetles eat buds and blossoms

Problem: As soon as buds form, they are eaten by groups of copper-colored beetles with green and white markings; they also skeletonize leaves.

Cause: Japanese beetles eat roses and many other plants. The eggs overwinter in the soil and hatch into white grubs that feed on grass roots. Adult beetles emerge in early summer and feed voraciously for about six weeks before laying eggs in the soil.

Solution: Handpick or spray to kill adults. Treat lawn soil to control grubs.

- Handpick the beetles and destroy them.

- Spray a heavy infestation with the botanical insecticide neem, pyrethrum, or rotenone, or with the biological control *Beauveria bassiana* GHA. Follow label directions carefully.

- If necessary, spray with a synthetic insecticide registered for roses that contains the active ingredient carbaryl or methoxychlor. Follow label directions carefully.

- To kill grubs, inoculate your lawn with milky spore disease in spring or fall.

- In late spring and early fall, treat your lawn with beneficial nematodes (p.126).

- Or drench your lawn with a synthetic grub-control product registered for lawns that contains the active ingredient imidacloprid. Follow label directions carefully.

New growth yellows and wilts

Problem: Leaf tips suddenly stop growing, turn yellow, and wilt. The stem appears swollen 6 inches or so below the tip.

Cause: Cane borers of several different species enter stems through breaks or pruning cuts and feed on the stems from the inside. They look like slender caterpillars. Certain wasps also occasionally invade rose stems and cause small growths, called galls, to form.

Solution: Remove infested plant parts, seal wounds, and spray preventively.

- Prune and dispose of affected stems, cutting below the borer swelling or gall.

- If cane borers are a recurrent problem, paint over pruning cuts with tree wound paint or apply a thin mixture of white glue and water.

- To repel borers, spray the plant with the botanical insecticide capsaicin or with garlic oil. Follow label directions carefully.

Leaves suddenly become discolored or distorted

Problem: Leaves suddenly become discolored, blotchy, or twisted and distorted. Or they die. Nearby unrelated plants may display similar damage.

Cause: Weed killers affect many plants, including roses, as a result of misdirected spray, drift, or vaporization caused by rain or heat. Excessive herbicide applied to soil can be absorbed by roots.

Solution: Use weed killers cautiously and only when necessary.

- Control weeds in rose beds by shallow cultivation, hand pulling, and mulch.

- Use only postemergence herbicides. Apply it evenly and only where needed. Use only the recommended amount.

- To prevent drift, spray with low pressure and when it's not windy. Also, avoid hot or wet days if label so directs.

New growing tips turn yellow and die back

Problem: At any time during the growing season, small insects that look like tiny, flat disks attach themselves to tender stems and suck out plant juices. As a result, new growth turns yellow and may die.

Cause: Rose scale insects often appear suddenly in early summer on large shrub roses not routinely pruned in winter, but they can infest any type of rose. While they are feeding, scale insects hardly move and look like oval or circular flat growths attached to the stems.

Solution: Prune to control scale. Use timely sprayings to prevent future problems.

- Prune and dispose of infested plant parts frequently.

- To kill newly hatched crawlers, spray in spring with insecticidal soap or the botanical insecticide neem.

- Or spray with a synthetic insecticide registered for roses that contains the active ingredient diazinon, carbaryl, or acephate. Follow label directions carefully.

- In summer, prune infested canes; then spray plant with a mixture of insecticidal soap and light horticultural oil (p.392). Spray with garlic oil to repel the insects.

- In winter, apply dormant oil to smother overwintering adults and eggs.

Leaves have holes or tan patches

Problem: Leaves are dotted with skeletonized patches or holes that most often appear between large veins. Severely infested leaves turn brown and curl.

Cause: European and bristly rose slugs frequently infest roses. Both are green, wormy larvae of sawflies. European rose slugs appear in spring and skeletonize the upper surface of young leaves. Bristly rose slugs feed on leaf undersides in summer, leaving holes between the leaf veins. Extensive damage can occur in only a few days.

Solution: Remove the slugs or spray them.

- If there are only a few slugs, handpick them and drown them in a jar of soapy water.

- To control numerous slugs, spray the plant with the botanical insecticide neem or with a combination of the organic insecticides rotenone and pyrethrum.

- Or apply a synthetic insecticide registered for roses that contains the active ingredient carbaryl. Follow label directions carefully.

Silver-Lace Vine

Polygonum aubertii

LIGHT: Full sun to partial shade

SOIL: Sandy to clay; pH 6.0 to 7.5

MOISTURE: Consistently moist to dry

HARDINESS: Zones 4 to 8

Leaves are skeletonized by metallic brown beetles

Problem: In mid-summer, beetles with metallic brown wing covers begin to eat the foliage. The damage often continues for about six weeks, tapering off in late summer.

Cause: Japanese beetles are large insects with emerald green heads and coppery brown wing covers. They feed on hundreds of plants and are most often seen in eastern North America. Japanese beetles are voracious feeders and can strip a plant of leaves in just a few days. The immature forms, called grubs, feed on grass roots and can do considerable damage to lawns.

Solution: Handpick and spray to control adult beetles. Use predators to kill grubs.

- Handpick and destroy beetles in the morning while they are still sluggish.
- Spray a serious infestation with the botanical insecticide neem or pyrethrum. Or use a synthetic insecticide registered for silver-lace vine that contains the active ingredient malathion or carbaryl. Follow label directions carefully.
- To control grubs, inoculate your lawn with milky spore disease in spring or fall.
- In late spring and early fall, treat your lawn with beneficial nematodes (p.126).
- Or drench your lawn with a synthetic grub-control product registered for lawns that contains the active ingredient imidacloprid. Follow label directions carefully.

Vines grow aggressively on nearby plants

Problem: The vines grow onto nearby plants, strangling them, or new vines appear in the garden near the parent plant.

Cause: Silver-lace vine is a vigorous plant that can grow from 10 to nearly 20 feet in a single season. In addition to its fast growth rate, the plant spreads easily from underground stems called rhizomes, allowing a single plant to quickly become a colony if not controlled.

Solution: Prune aggressively, install root barriers, and spray to restrain a vine's growth.

- After the plant goes dormant in late fall, prune back the vine and remove stems that have wrapped around trees and shrubs.
- When planting silver-lace vine near other beds, install metal or plastic edging that extends 1 to 2 feet below the soil surface to stop the spread of rhizomes.
- If a vine is totally out of control, spray it when it's actively growing with a synthetic herbicide registered for silver-lace vine that contains the active ingredient glyphosate. Follow label directions carefully.

Foliage is pale and dingy

Problem: Leaves look dingy, feel gritty, and are dull green or spotted with small yellow dots. The leaf undersides may have strands of fine webbing.

Cause: Spider mites are tiny relatives of spiders that feed on sap. They can multiply rapidly, especially in warm, dry weather, and can stunt the growth of an affected plant.

Solution: Spray to control spider mites.

- Starting when you first notice mites, spray with the botanical pesticide neem or pyrethrum every 10 days for a month.
- Or spray with a synthetic pesticide registered for silver-lace vine that contains the active ingredient malathion. Follow label directions carefully.

Trumpet Vine
Campsis spp.

LIGHT: Full sun

SOIL: Sandy to clay; pH 5.5 to 7.5

MOISTURE: Moist to dry

HARDINESS: Zones 4 to 9

Leaves are covered with a white powder

Problem: Late in the growing season, leaves become covered with a powdery white dust, usually starting on the lower leaves and moving upward. This occurs most often after a period of humid weather.

Cause: Powdery mildew is a fungal disease that feeds on the upper leaf surface but doesn't penetrate into the leaf itself. When the disease doesn't show up until late in the growing season, it does little damage. But a plant that is infected in midsummer or earlier can be weakened and stressed.

Solution: Spray and practice good garden sanitation to control powdery mildew. Provide proper growing conditions for new plants.

- If the disease strikes early in the growing season, spray the plant with baking soda solution (p.392).
- In fall, rake up and dispose of infected foliage that drops to the ground.
- Plant new vines in a sunny site.

Stems are studded with colonies of white insects

Problem: In summer, scattered clusters of white, cotton-covered insects can be found on stems. They look like mealybugs but jump when disturbed. If the infestation is severe, leaves become yellow and are coated with a sticky substance.

Cause: Plant hoppers are gray to brown bugs that lay eggs in bark slits in late summer. The egg laying may cause some stem tips to die. The larvae hatch in spring and feed on the stems, covering themselves with a waxy substance. A sticky material, called honeydew, is excreted by the larvae. There is usually only one generation per year.

Solution: Depending on the severity, either ignore plant hoppers or spray them.

- With a light infestation, damage will be negligible and the insects can be ignored.
- If there are enough pests to cause leaf yellowing, spray the plant with the botanical insecticide neem or pyrethrum. Follow label directions carefully.

WISE CHOICES

The most commonly grown trumpet vine is the wild plant *Campsis radicans*, native from Pennsylvania to Texas, noted for its orange flowers. Some varieties have different colored flowers worth finding. 'Crimson Trumpet' has bright red flowers without the orange tinge, while the flowers on 'Flava' are yellow.

C. × *tagliabuana* 'Mme Galen', a hybrid between *C. radicans* and the Chinese trumpet vine (*C. grandiflora*), is even more free flowering than either parent. It thrives in heat and is hardy to zone 6.

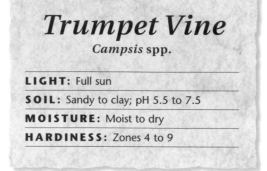

Viburnum

Viburnum spp.

LIGHT: Sun to shade

SOIL: Well drained; pH 6.0 to 6.7

MOISTURE: Consistently moist

HARDINESS: Zones 3 to 9

Buds are chewed; foliage is distorted

Problem: In spring, small insects feed on the opening buds of flowers and stems. If their feeding kills the buds entirely, secondary buds will grow, making the shrub very bushy and misshapen. The shoots that survive may have distorted leaves. Where flower buds are eaten, the resulting blooms may be distorted or have brown spots.

Cause: Tarnished plant bugs, while not a major pest, can cause considerable damage in some regions. Overwintering insects do the most damage. There are three to five generations each year, and by fall there can be a large adult population. The bugs have mottled white, yellow, and black bodies, making them look tarnished. Adults hibernate in weeds and under leaves and debris.

Solution: Spray with insecticide and use good garden sanitation to control the bugs.

- If you see adults feeding, spray the plant with insecticidal soap. Or use a synthetic insecticide registered for viburnums that contains the active ingredient carbaryl or malathion. Follow label directions carefully.
- In fall, clean up the garden and dispose of weeds, leaves, and other plant debris. Pick up pieces of wood or other objects that might provide shelter for the pests.

Leaves are badly distorted

Problem: In early spring, soon after unfurling, leaves become distorted. They are curled, yellow, and puckered. In a severe attack, even the leaf stalk may be twisted. The plant is severely weakened if the majority of shoots are affected.

Cause: Aphids overwinter as eggs laid on the twigs and buds in fall. They hatch just as the viburnum buds start to open, and the young aphids feed for about eight weeks on developing leaves. The aphids are gray to bluish white and are dusted with a white powder.

Solution: Spray to control aphids.

- As soon as the buds start to break, spray the plant with insecticidal soap or the botanical insecticide neem, pyrethrum, or rotenone.
- Or spray with a synthetic insecticide registered for viburnums that contains the active ingredient malathion or carbaryl. Follow label directions carefully.
- In late winter, spray the bark on the main stem and branches with dormant oil to kill the overwintering eggs.

Leaf undersides have bright yellow spots

Problem: In summer and early fall, bright yellow spots appear on leaf undersides. The leaves gradually fade to a dull yellow and then to a pale brown, at which time they release spores.

Cause: Rust disease of this type can be found on viburnum in any area where jack pine is native. Two stages of this fungal disease live on the jack pine and the other two on several species of viburnums. At least two other rusts use viburnums for a

In 1978, the European viburnum beetle was discovered in eastern Canada. Since then, it has spread and is now a major pest in the Northeast. Both the dark beetle and its green larvae feed exclusively on viburnum foliage. Eggs overwinter in the bark, and the larvae emerge in spring to feed on young leaves. They chew holes and can skeletonize a leaf in a short time. After pupating, they continue the destruction. Insecticidal soap and the botanical insecticide neem are effective on these pests. Follow label directions carefully.

part of their life cycle; one of these occurs in Florida, the other in the northern United States from New Hampshire to Idaho. Rust is seldom serious enough to require control measures.

Solution: Spray a serious outbreak. Don't grow viburnums if jack pines are nearby.

- If the outbreak is severe, spray the infected plant with the botanical pesticide neem. Follow label directions carefully.
- If you live near a stand of jack pines, you are better off not growing viburnums.

Swollen lumps form on stems and stem bases

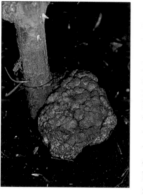

Problem: Swollen growths, called galls, appear on stems and near the plant base. The galls are spongy at first but, in time, become hard and woody. They are the same color as the plant—green on new shoots, brown on older shoots. The plant becomes stunted, weakened, and susceptible to drought and winter injury. Branches above the galls eventually die.

Cause: Crown gall, a bacterial infection, enters the plant through wounds caused by pruning, transplanting, or pest feeding. It is most active when temperatures are between 70° and 85°F. A plant that is infected while dormant may not show symptoms until the following spring.

Solution: Pruning and spraying help control crown gall. Take care when working around the plant. Select new plants carefully.

- Prune infected shoots as soon as you see galls. Sterilize (p.310) shears between cuts to prevent reinfecting healthy tissue.
- When the plant is dormant, spray it with organic lime-sulfur pesticide, which helps control this bacterial infection. Follow label directions carefully. This is not recommended for evergreen varieties (sidebar, p.225).
- Take care not to wound stems while hoeing weeds or cultivating around plants.
- Inspect new plants carefully for suspicious swellings, especially at the base of stems.

Leaves develop brown patches between veins

Problem: Pale spots appear on the upper leaf surface. These darken and spread between the veins to form angular blotches. The leaves become puckered and fall prematurely if the infection is severe. The symptoms usually start on the lower part of the plant and move upward. The infected leaves have small gray tufts on their lower surface, corresponding with the blotches above.

Cause: Downy mildew, so called for the downy spores it produces, is a fungal disease that strikes during moist weather. In warm climates, it may be a year-round problem.

Solution: Spray, thin foliage, and use good garden sanitation to control the mildew.

- Spray with an organic copper-based fungicide. Follow label directions carefully.
- Prune to allow good air flow. This will dry leaves quickly following rain.
- Rake up and dispose of fallen infected foliage regularly.

TIME-TESTED TECHNIQUES

BUYING SHRUBS

In a garden center, you have a choice of bare-root, container-grown, or balled-and-burlapped shrubs. Each type has its advantages, but not all shrubs are available in all forms.

Bare-root shrubs are usually the least expensive, but you have to plant them while they are dormant. If stored properly, they can be a good buy, but don't purchase them after leaves appear.

You can plant container-grown and balled-and-burlapped plants any time the weather is moderate, but not when it's below freezing or above 90°F. Store in a cool place until conditions improve.

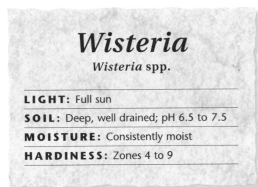

Wisteria

Wisteria spp.

LIGHT: Full sun

SOIL: Deep, well drained; pH 6.5 to 7.5

MOISTURE: Consistently moist

HARDINESS: Zones 4 to 9

Leaves become yellow and wilt

Problem: Leaves turn yellow or bronze and wilt. They rapidly dry, and the plant dies.

Cause: Cotton root rot is a fungal disease that invades the upper roots of a plant. Because the cells that move food and water from the soil into the plant are plugged, the upper part of the plant dies. The disease is common in alkaline soil in southern areas of the Southwest. The fungus can't survive in acidic soil or where temperatures dip below freezing.

Solution: There is no cure. Dispose of infected plants, treat the soil, and site plants carefully.

- Remove infected plants. Soil pasteurization, a task for professionals, kills most disease spores in the soil. Solarizing the soil (p.117) yourself may help.

- Don't plant wisteria in a location where this disease has occurred.

Leaves have small yellow spots

Problem: During summer, usually after a spell of wet weather, leaves develop small yellow spots that enlarge and turn brown. They may look water-soaked and may cause the leaves to twist and become distorted. Eventually, the spots become dark brown or black and often fall out. Growth may be weakened, but if the number of leaves affected is not large, the plant recovers.

Cause: Fungal leaf spots are caused by at least three different fungi, so symptoms may differ slightly. In severe attacks, the entire area around a spot may become bright yellow. Leaf spots are most common on plants under stress from other pests, poor growing conditions, or injury.

Solution: Keep leaf spots in check with good garden sanitation. If the plant is severely weakened from other problems, use a fungicidal spray.

- Pick off spotted leaves and destroy them. Rake up any fallen leaves and dispose of them.

- If problems persist, spray the foliage with an organic copper-based fungicide. Follow label directions carefully.

Stems and leaves are distorted

Problem: Shoots are twisted, with gaps between leaves. Leaves are twisted and distorted and may have pale or white areas. Shoots may fail to elongate, and leaves fail to unfurl. By late spring the vine appears dead.

Cause: Lawn weed killers frequently produce these symptoms. Wisteria is very sensitive to 2,4-D and mecoprop, two synthetic herbicides. Distorted growth is common when spray drift is absorbed by leaves and shoots. Abnormal growth or growth failure is common when the area over the roots has been sprayed and the roots absorbed the chemicals. Other chemicals, such as pesticides applied at higher than recommended concentrations, may cause similar symptoms.

Solution: With consistent care, a plant that has absorbed spray drift will usually recover.

- Keep the soil around the plant consistently moist, and fertilize in spring, using a balanced fertilizer such as a 10-10-10 formulation (p.324).

- If you have a serious weed problem, use a synthetic herbicide that contains only the active ingredient dicamba, rather than the more common combination weed sprays, because wisteria is not as sensitive to this chemical. Follow label directions carefully.

DID YOU KNOW?

Japanese and Chinese wisteria look very much alike, but you can tell the difference between the two by examining the way they climb. The stems of Japanese wisteria (*Wisteria floribunda*) twine around their support in a clockwise direction, while the stems of Chinese wisteria (*W. sinensis*) twine in a counterclockwise direction.

Plant lacks flowers

Problem: The plant is growing well, but blooms poorly or not at all.

Cause: Grafted plants must be three to five years old to bloom, so it's best to buy sizable plants. Seedlings may take even longer. Also, using a high-nitrogen fertilizer promotes rapid growth but suppresses flowering. Older plants, especially in the South, may bloom poorly if grown in rich soil.

Solution: Proper pruning and fertilizing and careful plant selection will ensure blooms.

- In summer, prune straggly growth. Leave a few strong stems, but prune these in half.
- Fertilize in spring with high-phosphorus formula, such as a 10-30-20 (p.324).
- Plant recommended varieties (box, right).

Small white pests are on leaves and stems

Problem: During spring and summer, small white pests are found in colonies on leaf undersides and clustered at the base of shoots. They excrete a sticky substance called honeydew that collects dust and promotes the growth of black mold. In summer, woolly patches develop on the main stems and branches.

Cause: Comstock mealybugs are the problem. The woolly patches on the main stems are the egg sacks and dead females. Overwintering eggs hatch in spring and feed on the new foliage and shoots. Severe feeding on the shoot bases causes the formation of growths, called galls, on which the next generation feeds. Comstock mealybugs thrive best on plants that have been heavily fertilized and have a lot of succulent growth. The honeydew they secrete may be host to a sooty mold that can block light from reaching the leaves and cause premature leaf drop.

Solution: Spray with insecticide for immediate control. For a long-term cure, release beneficial insect predators, and attract beneficial birds into your yard.

- In late spring and midsummer, spray the plant with summer oil or the botanical insecticide pyrethrum. Or spray with a synthetic insecticide registered for wisteria that contains the active ingredient methoxychlor. Follow label directions carefully.
- Consider releasing commercially available predators, such as green lacewings and mealybug destroyers, to keep the mealybug population under control.
- Install a bird feeder to attract birds, such as woodpeckers and chickadees, that will feed on the egg masses during winter.

Leaves are tied together

Problem: Leaves are tied together and appear to be eaten in places. The damage occurs at night, and severe defoliation can result. Inside each tied-up leaf is a small yellow to green caterpillar with a reddish brown head.

Cause: Larvae of the silverspot skipper butterfly tie the leaves. The small brown butterfly lays eggs on the leaves, and the caterpillars that emerge have yellow-spotted heads. The pests overwinter as pupae in the soil.

Solution: Either disregard the insects, or spray with an insecticide.

- If symptoms are mild, ignore the pest. The butterfly is attractive, and wisteria can tolerate some damage.
- If damage is severe, spray the plant with a synthetic insecticide registered for wisteria that contains the active ingredient malathion. Follow label directions carefully. For best results, spray late in the evening, just before the larvae start to feed.

Yew

Taxus spp.

LIGHT:	Sun or shade
SOIL:	Well drained; pH 6.0 to 7.5
MOISTURE:	Consistently moist
HARDINESS:	Zones 4 to 7

Needles turn yellow, then brown

Problem: In summer, needles on one side or the top of the plant turn yellow, then die and fall. In winter, one side of the plant, or the entire plant, turns brown, but the needles hang on for a long time before falling. The upper part of the plant is usually dead. In spring, especially after unusually mild spells, the plant turns yellow, then brown, and the tops of shoots are killed.

Cause: High temperatures and drying winds can evaporate moisture from the needles faster than the roots can take in water. In the southern part of zone 7, high temperatures alone can kill stem tips and cause needle browning. Where winters are harsh and the soil freezes, wind can dry out branches when roots can't absorb water from the frozen soil. Sometimes unusually warm spring temperatures can prompt growth, which is killed when cooler seasonal temperatures return.

Solution: Provide protection, depending on the season. Consider more tolerant plants.

- In summer, especially in the South, provide shade for the plant during the heat of the day, or plant more heat-tolerant evergreens.

- In winter, especially in the North, protect the plant from drying winter winds with a fence or screen to act as a wind break. If deep snowfalls are common, make sure you protect branch tops above snow level.

- In spring, when frosts are forecast after a early warm spell, protect the plant with old drop cloths.

Needles and stems are distorted

Problem: Young growth in spring is distorted with twisted needles, or buds fail to open and develop. Flower buds may become enlarged, fail to open, and be mottled yellow or brown.

Cause: Taxus bud mites are tiny pests that live under the scales covering a developing bud, feeding on the tissue. In a severe infestation, up to 1,000 mites may live on a single bud, causing the buds to enlarge and turn into swellings called galls. Lightly infected buds will still grow, but the shoots and foliage will be malformed.

Solution: Timely spraying is the best control.

- As soon as new buds form and mites start to colonize them, spray with the botanical pesticide neem. Or use a synthetic pesticide registered for yews that contains the active ingredient endosulfan or malathion. Follow label directions carefully.

Leaves are yellow and notched

Problem: Leaves are yellow and have irregularly notched edges. Bark is missing at ground level. Individual branches, or the entire plant, wilt and eventually die.

Cause: Black vine weevils, also called taxus weevils, are beetle-like insects that feed on foliage and can weaken the plant. But their larvae produce the worst damage; they attack the roots and can kill the plant. Control is difficult; the weevils resist many chemicals.

Solution: Remove the pests, or spray with insecticide. Use parasites and take care buying new plants.

- Spread a white plastic sheet over the soil and shake the plant. Dispose of any pests that fall onto the sheet.

- If the problem persists, spray with a synthetic insecticide registered for yews that contains the active ingredient bendiocarb. Follow label directions carefully.

- Apply beneficial nematodes (p.126) to control larvae.

- Inspect new plants carefully before purchasing them.

CHAPTER SIX

TREES

Trees are the mainstay of any home landscape. Deciduous trees shade a house or a yard in summer and admit the sun's warming rays in winter. Evergreens shelter a yard or a terrace from wind, hide undesirable views, and offer year-round privacy. The diversity of trees is astounding. The foliage can be red, purple, or yellow, as well as green. It is possible to create a colorful garden using only trees. Trees also come in a wide variety of sizes and shapes, from ground-hugging junipers and small Japanese maples to soaring pines and spreading oaks.

A healthy tree, well-fed and watered during dry spells, can fight off many infections and pests. But problems can arise. If you have large trees, you may not be able to see into the crowns to identify pests, even with binoculars; check fallen foliage for the culprit. To reach pests at such heights, use a high-pressure sprayer. For safe use of commercial treatments, see page 9 and pages 390 to 399.

Quick Troubleshooting Guide

FLOWERS

FLOWER BUDS DIE OR FALL

Cause: Frost, lack of water or nutrients, transplant shock

Solution: Wait for next spring's flowers. Water deeply if there is no rain for a week. Fertilize in spring with a balanced fertilizer. To transplant, wait until tree is dormant. Plant in an area where cold air doesn't collect.

LEAVES

HOLES ARE EATEN IN LEAVES

Cause: Beetle, caterpillar, slug, and snail

Solution: Handpick. Spray insects with insecticidal soap and spray caterpillars with BT. Trap slugs and snails in saucers of beer or commercial traps placed on the soil.

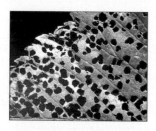

YELLOWING LEAVES ARE CURLED AND STICKY

Cause: Aphid

Solution: Knock pests off the tree with a strong spray of water from a garden hose. Spray insecticidal soap or the botanical insecticide neem. Irrigate deeply when a week passes without rain. Mulch to conserve soil moisture.

LEAVES AND TWIGS LOOK SCORCHED

Cause: Fireblight

Solution: Prune fungal-infected branches 1 foot below the discoloration and destroy them; sterilize pruners after each cut. Spray the tree with organic fungicides—lime-sulfur in winter and copper-hydroxide in spring.

LEAVES HAVE SOOTY, DUSTY, OR RUSTY SPOTS

Cause: Sooty mold, powdery mildew, rust

Solution: Sooty mold is a fungal disease that grows on the secretion of insects. Wash it off with a strong spray of water. Control insects with insecticidal soap. Powdery mildew and rust require synthetic fungicides that are labeled for use on your specific tree species. Follow label directions carefully.

LEAVES TURN YELLOW BETWEEN VEINS

Cause: Nutrient deficiency

Solution: Spray foliage with a solution of chelated iron. Correct soil pH. Apply a balanced fertilizer in early spring. Identify and treat for the lack of a specific nutrient.

LEAVES ARE DISTORTED, EATEN, OR ROLLED

Cause: Leaf roller, leaf miner

Solution: Use synthetic insecticides labeled for the pests and tree species. Spray for rollers in early spring. Spray for adult miners in spring, May 1, and July 1. Follow labels.

LEAVES HAVE SPOTS OR BLOTCHES

Cause: Fungal leaf spot, insect or sun damage

Solution: Identify the fungal disease; use a fungicide labeled for the species and follow label directions carefully. Identify and control pests with insecticidal soap. Select a tree species that tolerates strong sun or plant in partial shade. Water deeply when a week passes without rain.

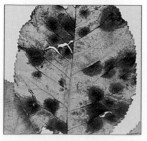

TRUNK AND BRANCHES

BARK HAD WHITE COTTONY COATING

Cause: Cottony cushion scale, wooly aphid

Solution: Spray foliage with synthetic insecticides labeled for your specific tree species, following label directions carefully. Spray horticultural oil in early spring.

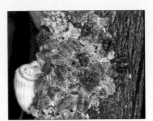

SHOOTS OR TWIGS HAVE CRUSTY OR SCALY BUMPS

Cause: Scale

Solution: Prune infested foliage. Spray with botanical insecticide pyrethrum when 'crawlers' are active. Spray in early spring with horticultural oil. Grow small-flowered nectar plants to attract lacewings and other scale-eating insects.

BARK HAS SWOLLEN GROWTHS

Cause: Fungal or insect gall

Solution: Prune and destroy branches and growth, or gall. Avoid injuring bark. Identify the disease or insect causing the growth and treat with a pesticide labeled for it.

TRUNK OR BRANCHES OOZE SAP

Cause: Mechanical injury, disease, borer

Solution: Avoid injuring trees. Prune affected branches or cut out diseased cankers. Prune when tree is dormant. Water and fertilize to keep the tree healthy. Control borers with synthetic insecticide registered for the tree species.

TWIGS DIE, BREAK OFF

Cause: Twig girdler, twig pruner

Solution: Wood-boring beetles make twigs break. Spray after tree leafs out with synthetic insecticide labeled for the species; repeat in a month. Destroy dropped twigs.

BARK HAS HOLES OR CRACKS

Cause: Animal, bird, borer, sun or frost damage

Solution: Wrap trunk with wire mesh to ward off animals and birds. Control borers with a synthetic insecticide labeled for the tree species. Protect trunk from elements by applying tree wrap or a coat of white latex paint in winter.

BRANCHES HAVE TUFTS OF SMALL TWIGS

Cause: Fungus, insect

Solution: The twig clusters, called witches' broom, can be caused by a fungus or an insect. Prune the affected growth and identify the problem. Use a pesticide labeled for the problem and species.

WHOLE PLANT

LEAVES ARE CHEWED; SILKEN NESTS ARE PRESENT

Cause: Tent caterpillar, fall webworm, bagworm

Solution: Remove nest or prune affected branch and destroy. Spray nests with the biological insecticide BT when larvae are small.

TREE WILTS; LEAVES MAY YELLOW

Cause: Heat or wind, lack of water, salt damage

Solution: Water deeply when rain is absent for a week. Flush damaging salt from the soil by watering heavily once a month. Spray foliage with water in early morning during extreme hot spells.

NEW TREE WILTS, MAY LOSE LEAVES AND BUDS

Cause: Transplant shock

Solution: Protect the tree from strong sun. Keep the tree well watered. Next time, install a tree when it is dormant. Transplant on a cool, overcast day. Avoid injuring tree roots when planting.

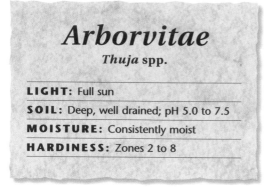

Arborvitae
Thuja spp.

LIGHT: Full sun

SOIL: Deep, well drained; pH 5.0 to 7.5

MOISTURE: Consistently moist

HARDINESS: Zones 2 to 8

Tips of needles turn brown

Problem: The tips of needles turn brown in summer. A few needles or most of the tree may be affected. Browned needles eventually fall off, which may leave a mass of bare stems.

Cause: Arborvitae leaf miners, the larvae of a small gray moth that lays eggs on foliage in spring and early summer, hatch and tunnel into needles to feed. Damage is minor at first, but by the following spring, trees start to turn yellow, then brown. Larvae eventually come out of the needles and spin whitish cocoons on the foliage. Because the living wood is not attacked, trees usually turn green again after treatment.

Solution: Use pruning and insecticidal sprays to control problem cases.

- Inspect trees in midsummer: Hold small shoots up to the light. If you see semitransparent areas in the needles, indicating miners, trim the new growth and dispose of it.

- If you see small gray moths in late spring, spray with insecticidal soap or a synthetic insecticide registered for arborvitae that contains the active ingredient diazinon. Apply two or three times, at seven-day intervals. Follow label directions carefully.

- Spray with the botanical insecticide neem to discourage future leafminer infestations. Follow label directions carefully.

Foliage looks scorched and falls

Problem: On western red cedar, and sometimes on eastern white cedar, the foliage on lower branches looks scorched. New growth forms pale patches that later turn brown. By autumn, the affected needles drop, leaving bare branches.

Cause: Arborvitae leaf blight, a fungal disease, attacks and sometimes kills small trees, especially ones growing in shaded areas that remain wet late into spring. The fungus releases its spores during the summer.

Solution: Spray with a fungicide to control the disease. Plant new trees in suitable sites.

- Spray young trees with an organic copper fungicide several times in summer and early autumn. Follow label directions.

- Plant new arborvitae in sunny places with good soil drainage and air circulation.

Tips of needles turn yellow

Problem: In late spring and early summer, tips of needles turn yellow, then brown. When you hold a needle to the light, there are no semitransparent areas indicating leaf miners (entry, left).

Cause: Tip blight is a disease caused by a fungus that attacks new growth, especially on plants stressed by poor growing conditions, by being grown near the limit of their hardiness zone, or by drying winter winds.

Solution: Spray to kill fungus. Protect tree from winter cold and wind, and nurture it.

- Spray tree with an organic copper fungicide, such as copper sulfate, in late summer and fall. Follow label directions carefully.

- In a cold or windy area, protect the tree with a burlap screen in winter (p.252).

- Keep plants healthy by fertilizing (p.324) in spring and watering (p.273) as needed.

Ash

Fraxinus spp.

LIGHT: Full sun

SOIL: Well drained; pH 6.0 to 8.0

MOISTURE: Moist to dry

HARDINESS: Zones 3 to 9

Small, dark, sunken areas appear on stems

Problem: The stems have small sunken areas, often darker in color than the surrounding bark. If more than one year old, these areas may look target-like, with several rings of bark showing. The foliage on infected branches may be small and yellow.

Cause: Canker in ash is caused by at least six different fungi. The disease typically enters tree tissue through wounds, such as borer tunnels, cracks in bark opened by winter damage, or twigs chewed by animals. The fungus needs to establish itself before it can cause problems, and a healthy tree usually develops natural barriers that isolate the infected site before the fungus can spread.

Solution: Prune, spray, and nourish the tree to discourage the spread of canker disease.

- Prune and dispose of any branches that show signs of the disease.
- If a tree is dormant, apply an organic sulfur fungicide. Follow label directions carefully.
- If a tree is actively growing, spray with a synthetic fungicide registered for ashes that contains the active ingredient myclobutanil. Follow label directions carefully.
- Fertilize with a granular balanced 10-10-10 formulation (p.324). Fertilize in spring to avoid producing lush late-season growth that is susceptible to winter damage.
- Water (p.273) your tree in summer as needed in dry periods to equal 1 inch a week.

Leaves have yellow spots

Problem: Yellow powdery spots develop on the leaves, which curl and die. Stems are spotted and corky.

Cause: Ash rust is a fungal disease that attacks in early spring. Most prevalent in coastal regions, it is often hosted by cordgrass, a tall marsh grass.

Solution: Control with fungicide. Grow ash in problem-free areas.

- Spray in early spring with an organic sulfur fungicide. Or use a synthetic fungicide registered for ashes that contains the active ingredient myclobutanil. Follow label directions carefully.
- If you live near a coastal marsh, avoid planting ash trees.

Leaves have dead patches

Problem: Soon after leaves open, they develop water-soaked spots that turn into dead orange-brown patches. Damaged leaves fall, and the plant may wilt.

Cause: Anthracnose is a fungal disease most active during a prolonged cool, wet spring. Disease spores overwinter on twigs and old foliage.

Solution: Use good sanitation and spray.

- Clean up and dispose of infected leaves.
- Spray with an organic lime-sulfur fungicide in late winter to kill overwintering spores. Follow label directions carefully.
- If spring is cool and wet, spray with an organic copper-hydroxide fungicide. Spray when leaves unfurl, are half open, and fully open. Follow label directions carefully.

Beech

Fagus spp.

LIGHT: Full sun

SOIL: Well drained; pH 5.0 to 6.5

MOISTURE: Consistently moist

HARDINESS: Zones 3 to 9

Bark has woolly patches; tree has dead twigs

Problem: Crevices in the bark on the main branches and on the trunk have thin white lines, which are patches of a woolly material. There may be dead branches in the canopy, and in an advanced case, there may be circular marks or pustules on the trunk.

Cause: Beech bark disease is transmitted by a scale insect that shelters in bark ridges. The insect, which is no larger than the head of a pin, quickly puts out a protective woolly covering. Where colonies of scales feed, a canker-causing fungus gains entry, weakening and occasionally killing the tree.

This disease most often spreads to garden beech trees from native beeches in nearby wooded areas.

Solution: Spray insecticide, and consider growing a different species of tree.

- If you see white woolly patches during the growing season, apply a synthetic insecticide registered for beeches that contains the active ingredient carbaryl or acephate. Follow label directions carefully.

- If an infestation occurs after the leaves have fallen, spray the bark with organic lime-sulfur pesticide. Follow label directions carefully.

- If you are near a wooded area that contains native beeches, plant a different species of tree.

Bark develops vertical cracks

Problem: The trunk and some major branches have vertical cracks. The bark appears dead and lifts, exposing wood. The injuries are on the tree's southwestern side.

Cause: Winter bark damage occurs mainly on smooth-barked trees like beech that have a southwestern exposure. After the sun warms the tree, the rapid temperature drop in the evening causes the bark to split and separate. This seldom occurs where trunks are shaded.

Solution: Protect bark with artificial shade.

- In winter, wrap the trunk with burlap, or tie a board against the southwestern side.

- Or paint affected areas with a coat of white interior latex paint to reflect sunlight. It will gradually wash away over the winter.

Bare trunk area oozes sap

Problem: A region near the base of the trunk is missing its bark, and a thick sap is weeping from the damaged area.

Cause: Bleeding canker is a soil-borne fungal disease that often enters through wounds made by mowers or power trimmers. Although it can attack mature trees, it is chiefly a problem of young trees. Newly planted ones are especially susceptible due to transplant injuries. By the time the disease becomes visible, it is usually too entrenched to be treatable, but many trees recover on their own.

Solution: Use good garden techniques and take care in selecting new trees.

- When working around a tree, be careful not to damage the bark.

- Don't fertilize a healthy looking tree. New growth is susceptible to canker.

- Inspect nursery plants carefully. Don't purchase any that have injuries.

Birch
Betula spp.

LIGHT:	Full sun to light shade
SOIL:	Deep, well drained; pH 5.0 to 6.5
MOISTURE:	Consistently moist
HARDINESS:	Zones 2 to 6

Leaves turn yellow, and the canopy is thin

Problem: Tree does not fully leaf out, and foliage turns yellow soon afterward, starting at the top of the tree and spreading downward. The bark has a lumpy, swollen texture.

Cause: Birch borers are beetles that feed on birches. The larvae take about two years to mature. During this time they tunnel and also feed beneath the bark, destroying the tissue that transports nutrients and water. Trees that are unhealthy and under stress are much more susceptible to attack.

Solution: Prune branches or remove tree. Spray with insecticide. Keep trees healthy. Plant a less susceptible species.

- Prune and dispose of dying branches.
- Remove a severely infested young tree.
- Spray leaves and bark with a synthetic insecticide registered for birches that contains the active ingredient chlorpyrifos. Follow label directions carefully.
- Fertilize the tree with a balanced fertilizer, such as a 10-10-10 formulation (p.324).
- Water the tree so that it receives the equivalent of 1 inch of water a week (p.273) from spring through fall. Birches can't thrive in dry soil and high summer temperatures.
- When planting, choose a species that is less susceptible to borer attacks (box, p.238).

Sap oozes from cuts or wounds on trunk

Problem: Sap flows excessively from wounds or pruning cuts in late winter or spring.

Cause: Birches have a strong sap flow in late winter and weep sap if wounded at this time.

Solution: Repel woodpeckers and time pruning carefully.

- Linear puncture wounds in bark are usually caused by sapsuckers, a woodpecker fond of thin-barked birches. If damage is severe or repetitive, tie reflective tape or shiny disposable pie pans in the tree to scare birds away in spring.
- Prune birches in the fall, so that the cuts will quickly dry and heal.

Trunk has small, sunken areas or hard lumps

Problem: The trunk has sunken areas that may show several layers of bark. Later on, small bumps form on the bark.

Cause: Cankers are depressed areas caused by a fungal infection. Pruning cuts and other bark damage invite infection. If left untreated, a secondary fungus will attack the cankers, forming a scaly lump. The tree will die slowly as the fungi invade the sapwood.

Solution: Spray with fungicide, keep tree healthy, and minimize damage to bark.

- When the tree is dormant, apply organic lime-sulfur fungicide to the trunk and limbs. Follow label directions carefully.
- Water the tree so that it receives the equivalent of 1 inch of water a week (p.273). Feed the tree regularly with a balanced fertilizer having a 10-10-10 formulation (p.324).

- Prune only in late fall or early winter when the spore levels are low.
- When working around trees, take care not to damage the bark. If wood-boring sapsuckers are common in your garden, hang bird scarers in the tree to frighten them off.

WISE CHOICES

The most common birches are all susceptible to birch borer. Paper birch (*Betula papyrifera*) and European white birch (*B. pendula*) are very susceptible; yellow birch (*B. alleghaniensis*) and sweet (or black) birch (*B. lenta*) are somewhat less susceptible. When shopping for new trees, select resistant birches, such as the following.

- River birch (*B. nigra*) is almost immune to birch borer.
- Asian whitebark birch (*B. platyphylla* var. *japonica*) 'Whitespire' is somewhat resistant.

Leaves have large, dead areas

Problem: Leaves open normally but develop small opaque areas that rapidly enlarge. The tree loses some leaves and grows a second crop. The new leaves may be attacked in turn.

Cause: Birch leafminers are a serious pest and often lead to an attack of borers (p.237). Leafminers tunnel inside the leaf, eating tissue. Mature larvae cut holes in the leaves and drop to the ground, where they pupate. If left untreated, a birch may rapidly decline and die within a few years.

Solution: Spray and keep larvae out of the soil. Don't plant susceptible birch species.

- Spray leaves with the botanical insecticide neem. Or use a synthetic insecticide registered for birches that contains the active ingredient carbaryl, diazinon, or acephate. Follow label directions carefully.
- Spread plastic sheeting under the tree to keep larvae from pupating in the soil.
- Avoid planting susceptible gray birch (*B. populifolia*) or paper birch (*B. papyrifera*).

Small, irregular holes appear on leaves

Problem: Numerous, small chewed areas with jagged edges appear in the leaves. The leaf surfaces are still intact, and the small veins that are left give a lattice effect.

Cause: Birch leaf skeletonizer, a moth caterpillar, eats the lower surface and green tissue of leaves. If disturbed, the small caterpillar drops from the leaves and hangs suspended on a silken thread, which can be a nuisance if the tree is near a walkway.

Solution: Spray to control the caterpillars.

- At first sign of an attack, spray the leaves with insecticidal soap or with the biological insecticide BT or BTK. Follow label directions carefully. Make sure to cover the leaf undersides completely.

Leaves turn yellow between the leaf veins

Problem: Leaves of a river birch (*B. nigra*) slowly turn yellow between the veins, which will remain a bright green color.

Cause: Iron chlorosis is a problem that results from iron deprivation. River birch needs acidic soil to grow well, and if grown in alkaline soil it will suffer from iron chlorosis. There may be plenty of iron in the soil, but the high pH makes it unavailable to the plant.

Solution: Give the plant supplemental iron and acidify the soil.

- For a quick fix, spray the tree leaves with a solution of chelated iron. Also apply the solution to the soil every spring, spreading it over the entire root zone. Follow label directions carefully.
- To achieve optimum soil acidity, apply garden sulfur to the soil according to package directions to reach a pH level of 5.0 to 6.5.

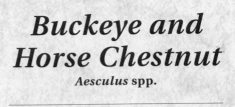

Buckeye and Horse Chestnut
Aesculus spp.

LIGHT: Full sun

SOIL: Deep, well drained; pH 6.0 to 7.5

MOISTURE: Consistently moist

HARDINESS: Zones 3 to 7

Leaves develop brown blotches, dry out, and drop

Problem: In summer, small water-soaked spots on leaves enlarge rapidly, turning into ginger-brown blotches with yellow margins. The leaves often curl, dry up, and fall.

Cause: Leaf blotch, a fungal disease, can defoliate young plants. Repeated attacks may kill them. The damage is similar to blotching caused by drought, but leaf blotch can be identified by the presence of small, black, fruiting bodies on the diseased leaf parts.

Solution: Remove infected leaves and spray fungicide to control the disease.

- Collect and destroy infected foliage.
- Spray with a synthetic fungicide registered for horse chestnuts that contains the active ingredient mancozeb. Follow label directions carefully.
- In spring, spray unfurling leaves several times at 10-day intervals with a synthetic fungicide registered for horse chestnuts that contains the active ingredient maneb. Follow label directions carefully.

Leaves look burned or stripped

Problem: In summer, the tree top suddenly looks scorched on the south side. Leaves are stripped off.

Cause: Japanese beetles attack in this pattern. They are metallic green beetles with coppery wing covers. They move on quickly, making control hard. Their larvae, called grubs, eat grass roots in the spring.

Solution: Apply insecticides to control beetles and their larvae.

- Spray infestations with the organic insecticide pyrethrum or rotenone. Follow label directions carefully.
- If the problem persists, spray with the botanical insecticide neem. Or use a synthetic insecticide registered for horse chestnuts that contains the active ingredient carbaryl. Follow label directions carefully.
- To kill larvae in spring, spray lawns with the biological insecticide milky spore disease, or apply beneficial nematodes (p.126) in spring or fall when soil is above 50°F.

Canker oozes a dark fluid

Problem: Lesions several feet long form on the trunk and major limbs of a tree. The cankers secrete a fluid that looks like a blood stain when dry. Affected branches wilt and die back, weakening the tree.

Cause: Bleeding canker is a fungal disease that enters through damaged tree roots.

Solution: Prune branches and limit watering and fertilizing. If serious, call a professional.

- Prune and destroy infected branches, cutting well below canker. Sterilize cutting tools (p.310) afterward.
- Allow soil to dry between waterings; avoid fertilizing until the tree recovers.
- In extreme cases, have a professional apply systemic fungicide.

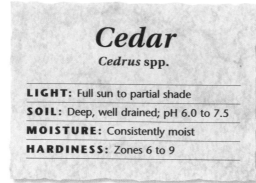

Cedar

Cedrus spp.

LIGHT: Full sun to partial shade

SOIL: Deep, well drained; pH 6.0 to 7.5

MOISTURE: Consistently moist

HARDINESS: Zones 6 to 9

Small sacks of plant debris hang from branches

Problem: Small silk sacks, made with bits of cedar needles, hang on small branches. Needles are eaten, reducing branches to bare twigs. The problem occurs mostly on deodar cedar (*C. deodara*), but other species may also be affected.

Cause: Bagworms make their homes of silk and pieces of the host plant. They live inside the sacks and partly emerge to feed on nearby foliage. The females are wingless and cannot fly to a new host plant, so an infested plant may have a large population of the pests. Bagworms attack a wide range of plants in the East and Midwest and also along the West Coast.

Solution: Handpick, prune, spray, and use sticky traps to eliminate bagworms.

- Handpick bags, or prune affected branches and burn them or put them in the trash.
- Spray infested plants with the biological insecticide BTK as soon as you discover bagworms. Follow label directions carefully.
- Spray a severe infestation with a synthetic insecticide registered for cedars that contains the active ingredient carbaryl. Follow label directions carefully.
- Place sticky bands (available at garden centers) around the trunk and main branches to trap females as they climb to lay eggs.

Needles turn yellow and fall, and the tree dies rapidly

Problem: Needles on an atlas (*C. atlantica*) or deodar cedar (*C. deodara*) turn yellow, and the tree dies quickly. Symptoms are often seen first on a single branch, which may die before others show any signs of infection. Death may be so rapid that the needles don't have time to fall, or it may be slower, with foliage falling first.

Cause: Pine wilt nematodes are microscopic worms that attack many conifers. These pests make their homes in branches and stems, which they cause to wilt and die. Their eggs can be spread by sap-sucking and borer insects. The nematodes can also survive in cut timber to infect other trees. There is no cure.

Solution: Destroy an infected tree. Control sap-sucking and borer insects.

- Remove an infected tree as soon as possible, and dispose of it.
- Identify and control sap-sucking insects.

New shoots curl and die, older needles fall

Problem: On any species of cedar commonly grown, new growth may be stunted and even curl over. Eventually, it turns brown and dies. Needles on older branches have brown patches and fall early, leaving bare twigs. Young trees may turn brown and die.

Cause: Deodar weevils, also called eastern pine or southern pine weevils, are small, dark brown beetles with a long snout. Adults feed on the inner bark of shoots on mature trees as well as on the trunk of young trees. They excavate pits as they feed, weakening small branches and making them liable to break in a wind. Eggs are laid in some of these pits, especially ones near the base of the tree, and the pits are then plugged with insect waste. When the larvae hatch, they tunnel beneath the bark. The damage can make a tree susceptible to other diseases, and a severe attack can kill a tree. But a healthy, well-nourished tree is better able to survive the weevils.

Solution: Spray insecticide and keep the tree in good health to control this pest.

- To control adults, spray in spring with insecticidal soap or the botanical insecticide pyrethrum. Or use a synthetic insecticide registered for cedars that contains the active ingredient chlorpyrifos. Follow label directions carefully.

- Apply fertilizer with a 10-5-5 formulation (p.324) in spring and summer to keep the tree growing strongly.

- Water the tree during dry spells to ensure that it gets the equivalent of 1 inch of water per week (p.273).

New growth is distorted

Problem: New growth opens normally but quickly becomes distorted. Individual needles may be twisted and curled, new shoots may be crooked or flattened, and needles may be pale yellow or whitish. Only part of the tree may be affected.

Cause: Weed-killer injury to trees is caused by synthetic herbicides commonly used to control weeds in lawns. These herbicides contain growth hormones that kill weeds by upsetting their hormonal balance and growth. Minute doses can cause strange growths on other plants that are exposed to the herbicides. Trees can be affected by spray droplets that drift in the wind, by vapors given off as the herbicide dries on the grass, or by absorption through the roots, especially of the herbicidal active ingredient dicamba. Deodar cedar (*C. deodara*) is particularly sensitive to this chemical. Spray drift is the most common cause of problems, and it will generally affect only the lower branches on the downwind side of the tree. If the damage is not too severe, the tree will recover.

Solution: Prune and dispose of any distorted growth that does not recover within a few months. Keep the tree in good health. Avoid using weed killers near trees.

- Trim twisted and flattened shoots.

- Fertilize the tree in spring and summer, using a 10-5-5 formulation (p.324).

- Water the tree during dry spells to ensure

that it gets the equivalent of 1 inch of water per week (p.273).

- Avoid using weed killer on your lawn near a cedar, especially upwind from the tree. Don't use a lawn weed killer that contains the synthetic active ingredient dicamba, to which cedars are especially sensitive.

Tree grows poorly

Problem: The tree exhibits sudden dieback, or is slowly failing to thrive. There is no visible sign of insect damage or disease.

Cause: Cedar trees are subject to winter damage or root disease if they are poorly sited or carelessly planted. Dieback caused by drying winter winds can result from extreme cold snaps of even a short duration. Moderately cold winters that keep the soil frozen for long periods keep the roots from absorbing moisture. In milder climates, poorly drained soil makes the roots susceptible to root rot over winter, which gradually kills the tree. Branches that are damaged by winter wind or ice breakage can be also invaded by disease.

Solution: Give special attention to the habitat requirements of cedars. Relocate trees if possible and choose hardy varieties for new plantings. Site them carefully.

- If the tree is small, and damage is not severe, dig the tree up, making the soil ball as large as possible. Transplant it into fertile, well-drained soil in a location that receives full sun.

- For a new planting, choose a cold-hardy variety of cedar, such as 'Kashmir' or 'Kingsville'. Or consider planting cedar of Lebanon (*C. libani*), a species hardy to zone 6.

- Avoid using sites for new trees and transplants that are exposed to cold winter wind.

Crab Apple
Malus spp.

LIGHT: Full sun

SOIL: Well drained; pH 5.0 to 6.5

MOISTURE: Consistently moist

HARDINESS: Zones 4 to 8

Leaves and fruits have small, olive-green spots

Problem: Small, olive-green spots appear on leaves soon after they unfurl. The spots grow, and the leaves turn yellow and fall from the tree. On fruits, the spots form slightly raised areas that develop a rough, scablike surface.

Cause: Apple scab is one of three serious diseases that can attack both crab and culinary apples. The others are cedar-apple rust (p.245) and fireblight (p.244). Apple scab is a fungal disease that is at its worst in spring when humidity is high and temperatures are cool. The scabs affect foliage, fruits, and shoots. The raised areas on fruits eventually look sunken as the unaffected parts of the apples enlarge around them. On shoots, the infection causes corky patches that release spores that infect new leaves the following year.

Solution: Spray fungicide to control scab.

- At the first sign of disease, spray with a synthetic fungicide registered for crab apples that contains the active ingredient propiconazole. Follow label directions carefully.

- When the tree is dormant, spray with an organic lime-sulfur fungicide. Follow label directions carefully.

- Next spring, as a preventive, starting when the leaves are half open, spray at 10-day intervals with a dilute organic lime-sulfur fungicide. Or apply a synthetic fungicide registered for crab apples that contains the active ingredient captan. Follow label directions carefully.

Tree flowers and fruits poorly

Problem: The tree seems to be growing well, but it often fails to flower, it flowers poorly, or it flowers only on one side. The tree goes on to produce only a few fruits.

Cause: The tree's variety, improper pruning, or insufficient sunlight may be the cause of the problem. Many older varieties of crab apple are alternate bloomers, meaning that they flower well one year and sparsely the next. Incorrect or excess pruning can also reduce flowering and fruiting for a

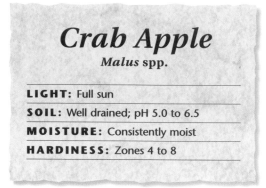

year or two. Another possible cause is that the crab apple may not be getting enough sunlight to form flower buds because surrounding trees have grown much larger than it has and are shading it.

Solution: Use a wait-and-see approach. Thin any trees shading the crab apple.

- Observe the tree for a few seasons to see if alternate blooming is the case. If it is, there's no remedy; it's a natural condition.
- Let time correct a poor pruning job. Prune (p.293) more carefully in the future.
- If shade is cast by surrounding trees, consider thinning their canopies to let enough light reach the crab apple to promote flower bud formation.

Leaves have brown spots; branches have cankers

Problem: Soon after opening, the leaves develop small brown spots with purple margins. Small purple pimples and black spots form on the fruits. But the main damage is on the branches, which develop elongated cankers.

Cause: Black rot canker is a serious disease of edible apple and crab apple trees. It is caused by a fungus that normally enters through pruning wounds and other injuries. It appears mostly on trees under stress from environmental causes or another disease, such as fireblight (p.244).

Solution: Use good gardening practices to keep the tree healthy and avoid canker.

- Fertilize in spring with a 12-6-6 or 10-5-5 formulation (p.324). Water during dry periods to equal 1 inch of water a week (p.273).
- Mulch under the tree to avoid injuring surface roots while mowing. Don't pile mulch against the trunk where retained moisture could increase disease susceptibility.
- In fall, remove any branches that have elongated patches of darker bark, which might be a source of infection next spring.

Webs appear at branch tips late in the growing season

Problem: In late summer and fall, web-like silky masses cover the branch tips. Pale green or yellow, hairy caterpillars eat the leaves.

Cause: Fall webworms are the larvae of a small moth. After hatching, the young spin a nest at the end of a branch and begin feeding on the leaves inside. Webworms are not as damaging as tent caterpillars (p.245) and seldom require spraying. They tend to come and go in cycles, producing up to four generations in mild-winter climates like the South. Nests become more and more abundant until natural predators start to control them.

Solution: Remove the webbed nests. Spray only severe infestations. Kill eggs in winter.

- If you can reach them, cut off the branch tips with nests and destroy them.

WISE CHOICES

Many common crab apple varieties are susceptible to fungal diseases, such as apple scab and cedar-apple rust, and to the bacterial disease fireblight.

Crab apple varieties that resist apple scab, cedar-apple rust, and other fungal diseases include 'Ames White', 'Baskatong', 'Beauty', 'Centennial', 'Centurion', 'Color Parade', 'Evelyn', 'Excalibur', 'Harvest Gold', 'King Arthur', 'Lancelot', 'Prairiefire', 'Professor Springer', 'Sea Foam', 'Strawberry Parfait', 'Sugar Tyme', and 'Thunderchild'. For Southern gardens, the variety 'Callaway' is the best choice.

Varieties that resist fireblight include 'Adams', 'Adirondack', 'David', 'Dolgo', 'Harvest Gold', 'Indian Summer', 'Jewelberry', 'Liset', 'Profusion', 'Red Baron', 'Selkirk', and 'Sentinel'.

- Spray a severe infestation during the day when the caterpillars feed openly, using the biological insecticide BT.
- If you need to spray in the evening or on a damp day, break open the silky nests with a stick and spray each with the botanical insecticide pyrethrum.
- In winter, spray susceptible trees with dormant oil to kill overwintering egg masses.

Leaves appear burned

Problem: On one or more shoots, leaves wilt and rapidly turn brown. They look scorched but hang onto the branch. Flowers may look water soaked, and twigs and branches may have cankers.

Cause: Fireblight is a bacterial disease that attacks rose-family members, including crab apples, throughout North America. The name comes from the scorched appearance of infected leaves. The wilted leaves that stay on the branch and a red-brown discoloration of the sapwood help to identify the disease. Crab apples are most susceptible to serious injury or death from fireblight in the first three to five years after planting. The disease overwinters in infected wood and is carried from tree to tree in spring by bees as they pollinate the flowers.

Solution: Remove infected branches, spray with an antibiotic, and fertilize with caution. Plant resistant varieties.

- Prune and destroy infected branches. Cut well below any wood that is stained with reddish discoloration. Disinfect tools (p.310) between cuts to prevent reinfection.
- Spray the leaves and branches with the antibiotic streptomycin. Follow label directions carefully.
- Avoid fertilizing infected trees in early spring, because the resulting lush growth is especially prone to fireblight.
- When planting, select varieties that resist fireblight (box, p.243).

TIME-TESTED TECHNIQUES

TREES EXPERIENCE STRESS, TOO

If you think life is stressful, take a look at trees. You can get a drink if you're thirsty, or turn on a fan if you're hot, but trees must stay put and take whatever comes their way. Here is how to reduce environmental stress on trees.

Heat and water stress are usually most damaging in late spring when a tree is actively growing and new growth is still soft and succulent. Hot, dry weather at this time can wilt or brown tender leaves and sometimes kill entire shoots.

To lessen the impact of heat, make sure that a tree, especially a small or newly planted one, has a 3-inch layer of organic mulch over the root area, but keep it several inches from the trunk. Water the tree during dry periods to provide the equivalent of 1 inch of water per week (p.273).

Tree flowers well but doesn't produce fruit

Problem: The tree flowers freely each spring, but produces few fruits or none at all.

Cause: A lack of bees to pollinate the flowers is the usual cause, especially in polluted downtown locations, in areas where pesticides are used heavily, or when freezing weather coincides with blossoming. Disease has also decreased the number of honeybees. Another cause may simply be the kind of crab apple. Varieties with double flowers often produce extra petals at the expense of reproductive parts, and so produce few fruits.

Solution: Hand-pollinate a small tree. Select new varieties with care.

- Try hand-pollinating if the tree is small, dabbing a small artist's brush into one flower and then another until many are pollinated.
- Be aware that some ornamental, double-flowered varieties, such as 'Klems' and 'Madonna', are bred to be nearly fruitless to reduce yard litter.

Many small branches die, and twigs break off in the wind

Problem: The upper part of the tree develops a great many small, dead branches, and these twigs snap off in the wind.

Cause: Periodical cicadas can cause this problem as they lay their eggs. The female makes deep cuts through the bark and into the heart of a twig and lays eggs there, weakening it. After hatching, the nymphs drop to the ground where they feed on the tree roots, causing little damage. Adults suck sap from leaves and tender stems, making the tree susceptible to fungal attacks. You can tell adult cicadas are present by their loud mating calls.

Solution: Use a combination of pruning, spraying, protective coverings, and timely planting to control cidadas.

- Prune and destroy infested twigs.
- At the first sign of adults, spray with a synthetic insecticide registered for crab apples that contains the active ingredient chlorpyrifos. Follow label directions carefully.
- During an outbreak of cicadas, cover a small tree with an insect-excluding fabric floating row cover to prevent egg laying.
- Don't plant new trees at a time when cicadas are active.

Silky webs appear in branch forks in spring

Problem: A mass of silk threads develops in the forks of branches, and many small, black-and-white-striped caterpillars eat leaves.

Cause: Tent caterpillars overwinter as dark, shiny egg masses encircling small twigs. After hatching, larvae spin a silken nest at a branch fork and feed on the leaves inside. They enlarge the nest as they seek new leaves. If an infestation is severe, they can defoliate a tree. The eastern tent caterpillar, which is found as far west as the Rockies, is dark with a white-striped back and blue-spotted sides. The western tent caterpillar, which lives west of the Rockies, has blue and orange spots.

Solution: Remove nests and egg masses, and spray with insecticide to control tent caterpillars.

- Destroy nests you can safely reach.
- If caterpillars are small, spray with the biological insecticide BT. Use a high-pressure sprayer to penetrate the nests. Follow label directions carefully.
- Or spray with a synthetic insecticide registered for crab apples that contains the active ingredient acephate. Follow label directions carefully. Use a high-pressure sprayer.
- In winter, prune twigs with egg masses.

Brown or orange spots appear on the leaves

Problem: Spots, yellow at first but turning orange or brown, appear on the leaves in early summer. They may be edged with a red band and have tiny yellow dots in their centers. Fruits may have brown spots.

Cause: Cedar-apple rust is a fungal disease that alternates between two unrelated host plants; in this case, junipers and apples.

Solution: Spray with fungicide, and remove fungal growths from nearby junipers.

- Spray with a synthetic fungicide registered for crab apples that contains the active ingredient mancozeb. Apply it four or five times at seven- to ten-day intervals. If possible, spray when rain is not expected for 24 hours. Follow label directions carefully.
- In winter, look for dark, reddish brown, 1-inch growths, or galls, on junipers, especially eastern red cedar (*Juniperus virginiana*), and remove them before the disease spreads to crab apples.

REGIONAL FOCUS
NORTHEAST

A late-spring frost can cause flower buds on a dogwood to shrivel and die. If you expect frost, spray the tree with cold water early in the morning before the sun warms it. The water lets the ice melt slowly, preventing serious damage.

Also, don't plant an early-blooming tree in a low area, such as the base of a slope where cold air pools, forming a frost pocket.

In general, pink-flowering varieties are more tender than the white-flowering ones.

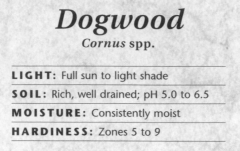

Dogwood

Cornus spp.

LIGHT: Full sun to light shade

SOIL: Rich, well drained; pH 5.0 to 6.5

MOISTURE: Consistently moist

HARDINESS: Zones 5 to 9

Leaves are spotted or blotched

Problem: Leaves develop purple-margined brown spots, which may run together to form large blotches. Affected leaves die, but many remain attached. Flowers may also be damaged and the twigs may be killed back to their base.

Cause: Dogwood anthracnose is a serious fungal disease of flowering dogwoods in the mid-Atlantic and southern New England states. It is slowly spreading south and west, but the less-humid weather conditions of some regions seem to limit its activity. A diseased tree generally dies in two to three years.

Solution: Prune, spray, and keep the tree healthy. Plant resistant hybrids.

- Prune and destroy infected shoots.

- Spray foliage in early spring with organic copper-sulfate fungicide. Then spray with synthetic fungicide registered for dogwoods that contains the active ingredient mancozeb, myclobutanil, or maneb. Follow label directions carefully.

- Keep a dogwood strong by applying a 5-10-10 fertilizer (p.324) and watering it well (p.273), especially during dry spells.

- Plant resistant cultivars, such as these hybrids created by crossing flowering dogwood and the naturally resistant species kousa dogwood (*C. florida* × *C. kousa*): 'Aurora', 'Celestial', 'Constellation', 'Galaxy', 'Ruth Ellen', and 'Stellar Pink'.

Leaves are yellow and small

Problem: A tree produces leaves in spring, but they are small and quickly turn pale yellow, or may be misshapen and have pale spots or rings. Flower petals are narrow and twisted, often with distorted tips.

Cause: Cherry leaf roll virus is spread by sap-sucking insects, such as aphids and leafhoppers. The yellowing or spots may disappear during the summer, but the tree still looks thin and undernourished. There is no cure for this disease, although the tree may live for several more years with regular fertilizing and watering.

Solution: Destroy infected plants and control insects. Keep a plant well fed and watered.

- If healthy dogwoods are nearby, remove and destroy an infected tree to prevent the disease from spreading.

- To control insects that carry the disease, spray with the organic pesticide neem or pyrethrum. Or use a synthetic pesticide registered for dogwoods that contains the active ingredient diazinon or malathion. Follow label directions carefully.

- Keep a dogwood strong by applying a 5-10-10 fertilizer (p. 324) in spring, and watering it well (p.273) during dry periods.

Patches of bark fall off, or leaves may curl

Problem: Bark lifts in patches and falls off; sawdust and insect waste may be visible in bark crevices. Or the leaves curl downward. The tree looks unhealthy and grows poorly.

Cause: Several borers feed on flowering dogwoods. Dogwood borers, the most serious, are the larvae of a clearwing moth. They can't chew through mature bark but gain entry through wounds, such as woodpecker and squirrel damage. They feed just under the bark, causing it to lift and small branches to die. The dogwood twig borer is a beetle that feeds on leaf undersides, causing them to curl downward. It lays eggs in twigs. Its larvae tunnel inside the twig for two years, making many holes to push out waste. Borers are not easy to control, especially the dogwood twig borer.

Solution: Well-timed spraying is the best control for borers.

- To control dogwood borers, spray the bark with a synthetic insecticide registered for dogwoods that contains the active ingredient chlorpyrifos in mid-May and in mid-June. Follow label directions carefully.

- To control dogwood twig borers, watch for the characteristic downward curl of the leaves, then spray the foliage with the botanical insecticide neem. This kills the beetles before they lay their eggs. Follow label directions carefully.

Leaves have brown areas

Problem: Flower petals develop light to medium brown patches and drop early. Leaves may also become infected, turning brown, starting at the tips. The condition is most severe when spring is wet and cool.

Cause: Flower and twig blight, also called botrytis blight, flourishes as long as the temperature is above freezing and the humidity is high. The disease is also known as flower and leaf blight on flowering dogwoods and Pacific dogwoods.

Solution: Prune and spray to control.

- Thin inner branches for air circulation.
- Spray a previously infected tree with synthetic fungicide registered for dogwoods that contains the active ingredient benomyl or captan as soon as flowers start to open when wet conditions are predicted. Repeat weekly during the flowering period. Follow label directions carefully.

Leaves are skeletonized by orange beetles

Problem: Leaf undersides are eaten and reduced to skeletons by small orange-and-black beetles. Occasionally, irregularly shaped tunnels are visible under the leaf surfaces.

Cause: Locust leaf miners are bright orange beetles with a black head and legs and a black stripe down the center of their back. Their leaf-mining larvae live mainly on black locust and sometimes on other plants, such as dogwoods. Adults feed on many different plants and, if numerous, can defoliate a plant.

Solution: Handpick beetles or spray with insecticide, depending on the size of the tree.

- With a small tree, handpick the beetles and destroy them.

- With a large tree, spray with a synthetic insecticide registered for dogwoods that contains the active ingredient chlorpyrifos when you first see the beetles. Follow label directions carefully.

White frothy bubbles appear on dogwood twigs

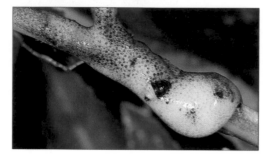

Problem: White, bubbly foam is found on the twigs. On close examination, these frothy masses contain one or more small larvae.

Cause: Dogwood spittlebugs are the larvae of a small yellow-and-black beetle that flies away quickly if disturbed. While seldom numerous enough to kill the tree, sap-sucking spittlebugs are unsightly, and several on one shoot can stunt its growth. Although control is seldom needed to save the tree, the foam is unattractive, and most gardeners prefer to remove them for aesthetic reasons.

Solution: Hose off or spray spittlebugs.

- Spray foliage with a strong stream of water from a hose to dislodge the insects.
- Or spray the foamy masses with insecticidal soap, repeating as needed for control. The soap formulation penetrates the bubbles to reach and kill the pests inside. Follow label directions carefully.

Trunk oozes red sap; leaves turn pale, then red

Problem: Leaves on the topmost branches are small and light green and turn prematurely red in late summer. Twigs and branches may die. Reddish sap oozes from the trunk base. The damaged area shrinks and its bark crumbles.

Cause: Crown canker is caused by a soilborne fungus that enters through bark wounds. Often the only early sign of infection is the weeping of a reddish sap from the base of the trunk. If the roots become infected, the canker can develop unseen; only its effects are visible. Eventu-

ally the disease spreads, affecting the movement of sap, and the leaf symptoms occur. Unfortunately, when the disease has progressed enough to cause leaf symptoms, control is not possible. If cankers encircle the trunk, the tree will die.

Solution: Remove small cankers, and protect the tree trunk from damage.

- If a canker is small, cut it out. Paint the wound with shellac to prevent reinfection.
- Mulch around the base of the trunk to prevent mower or trimmer injury. Don't let mulch touch the tree trunk to avoid introducing additional diseases.

Leaves are chewed or eaten; tree may be defoliated

Problem: Larvae that look like caterpillars rapidly consume leaves, sometimes defoliating an entire tree.

Cause: Dogwood sawflies lay eggs in large clusters on the underside of dogwood leaves. When the eggs hatch, their translucent yellow larvae feed in groups. As they grow, the larvae develop a powdery gray coating that mimics bird droppings. The pests burrow into soft wood to overwinter, emerging as adults from spring through early summer.

Solution: Spray and release beneficial predators. Watch for a repeat infestation.

- As soon as you see caterpillars, spray the trees with a synthetic insecticide registered for dogwoods that contains the active ingredient carbaryl or malathion. Follow label directions carefully.
- Purchase and release beneficial wasps of the *Trigonaloidea* group (available from garden supply catalogs) to prey on sawflies.
- In future years, monitor plants closely if they have a history of infestation, because sawflies tend to reinfest plants.

Eucalyptus
Eucalyptus spp.

LIGHT: Full sun

SOIL: Tolerates most soils; pH 6.0 to 8.0

MOISTURE: Wet to dry; species vary

HARDINESS: Zones 9 and 10

Branches die; leaves wilt

Problem: Branches are dead or dying. Foliage becomes pale and wilts, and dead leaves stay on branches. Small holes that ooze liquid are in the bark.

Cause: Eucalyptus longhorned borers are glossy brown insects with long antennae with a cream-colored band running across their back. Their cream-colored larvae burrow in the wood. The insects are most common on trees stressed by drought or disease. Healthy trees are less prone to attack and are more likely to survive an infestation.

Solution: Destroy infested branches. Water regularly. Plant resistant species.

- Prune and burn infested branches in winter.
- Water the tree throughout the year to ensure it receives the equivalent of 1 inch of water per week (p.273).
- Replace infested trees with red gum (*E. camaldulensis*), sugar gum (*E. cladocalyx*), swamp mahogany (*E. robusta*), or red ironbark (*E. sideroxylon*), which are species that resist infestation.

Leaves are yellow between veins

Problem: Leaves open normally but soon turn yellow between the veins. Growth slows and the tree declines.

Cause: Iron chlorosis is an iron deficiency caused primarily by alkaline soil, especially if it is shallow. If a tree is left untreated, it will die in a few years.

Solution: Supply iron. Acidify and fertilize soil.

- For a quick fix, spray foliage and drench soil with iron chelate solution each spring.
- For a longer term solution, work powdered sulfur into the soil above roots to reach the ideal pH (p.329).
- Use an acidic mulch, such as pine needles.
- Treat soil with an acidifying additive, such as ammonium nitrate or ammonium sulfate.
- Apply a balanced fertilizer, such as a 10-10-10 formulation (p.324), in spring and late summer for tree health.

Leaves are pale and small

Problem: Leaves become small and pale, small branches die, and the entire tree looks sick and undernourished. Fertilizing doesn't help.

Cause: California prionus, a root borer, lays eggs in the soil close to the tree roots. The larvae dig into the roots and feed just below the bark, creating tunnels that often form a spiral. A tree may have many tunnels. If the holes girdle a root, it dies. Because the larvae are inside the roots, they cannot be reached with chemicals.

Solution: In a severe case, remove the tree. Water and feed a tree to keep it healthy.

- Dig around the tree to expose roots and find entry holes and insect waste. If a tree is badly infested, remove it and grind the stump to kill all larvae before they mature and infect other trees.
- Water as needed to supply the equivalent of 1 inch of water each week (p.273).
- Apply a balanced 10-10-10 fertilizer (p.324) regularly, following the advice of a local garden center.

**REGIONAL FOCUS
NORTHEAST**

Eucalyptus is surprisingly hardy. Some species survive in zone 8, where they die back to the ground during cold winters and resprout in spring. But a eucalyptus tree will eventually decline from stress if it is routinely subjected to freezing temperatures. Select a species that's rated hardy in your hardiness zone. Avoid planting in a windy, exposed site.

False Cypress

Chamaecyparis spp.

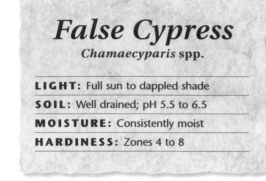

LIGHT: Full sun to dappled shade

SOIL: Well drained; pH 5.5 to 6.5

MOISTURE: Consistently moist

HARDINESS: Zones 4 to 8

Foliage turns brown on a variegated variety

Problem: Needles turn brown and look burned, while those of nearby evergreens are not damaged. The problem is more common on varieties with golden or silver-tipped foliage.

Cause: Needle burn of this type is a weather-related problem. The foliage on many ornamental forms of false cypress with colorful needles is sensitive to weather extremes. Late frost in spring, an extra-early frost in fall when the trees are not properly hardened, unduly hot weather in summer, or prolonged periods of drought, especially when coupled with high temperatures, can cause needle burning. There is no quick remedy, but a damaged tree should recover in time. If the problem occurs frequently, however, the shape of the tree may change.

Solution: Water the tree during dry spells. Select new varieties that suit your climate.

- Water the tree frequently during dry periods in summer so that it gets the equivalent of 1 inch of water each week (p.273).

- Before planting an ornamental false cypress, ask local garden-club members which varieties they recommend.

Small sacks hang on branches

Problem: Small sacks, made with pieces of twigs and needles, hang from small branches. New growth is eaten, and nearby branches are reduced to twigs.

Cause: Bagworms make nests of silk mixed with bits of plant. They live in the sacks and partly emerge to feed on nearby foliage. The wingless females can't fly to a new tree, so a tree may be home to a large population.

Solution: Use sprays and sticky traps.

- Spray the plant with the biological insecticide BTK as soon as you see bagworms.

- Spray the foliage with the botanical insecticide pyrethrum. Or use a synthetic insecticide registered for false cypresses that contains the active ingredient carbaryl or malathion. Follow label directions carefully.

- Place sticky bands (available from garden centers and catalogs) around the trunk and main branches to trap females as they climb to lay eggs.

Needle tips turn yellow

Problem: In late spring or early summer, needle tips turn yellow, then brown. Small, black, fruiting bodies appear in late summer.

Cause: Tip or needle blight is caused by a fungus that lives mainly on dead or dying foliage. It can also attack new growth and is then called shoot blight. It is most prevalent on trees under stress from poor growing conditions or winter cold. Trees grown near the limits of their hardiness zone or dried out by winter winds are more susceptible to attack.

Solution: Spray to control the fungus. Protect the plant in winter, and keep it healthy.

- Spray with an organic copper fungicide in late summer and fall. Follow label directions carefully.

- Give winter protection by wrapping the tree or erecting a screen (p.252).

- Feed the plant in spring with a high-nitrogen 14-7-7 fertilizer (p.324).

- Water the tree during dry spells to provide 1 inch of water each week (p.273).

Fir
Abies spp.

LIGHT: Sun to light shade

SOIL: Well drained; pH 5.0 to 6.0

MOISTURE: Consistently moist

HARDINESS: Zones 3 to 7

Needles are twisted, curled, and shiny

Problem: Needles are curled, and they have a glossy shine. The bark of twigs is sometimes rougher than normal and marked by white, waxy deposits. On close examination, you see small, soft-bodied insects at the ends of twigs and near the base of needles.

Cause: Balsam twig aphids are small gray insects that most frequently attack fir trees in early summer, clustering at the tips of young, succulent growth. Although a severe infestation can weaken the tree, the pests usually produce only cosmetic damage to the needles. The glossy sheen sometimes seen on the needles results from the accumulation of honeydew, a sticky substance exuded by the aphids as they feed.

Solution: Ignore a minor infestation. Spray to control cosmetic damage. Use repellents.

- If the infestation is not extensive or unsightly, no action is necessary.
- Spray with insecticidal soap or the botanical insecticide neem or pyrethrum. Or use synthetic insecticide registered for firs that contains the active ingredient carbaryl. Follow label directions carefully.
- To repel future infestations of aphids, spray the tree with garlic oil or capsaicin. Follow label directions carefully.

Needles have brown spots

Problem: In spring, needles develop yellow spots, which turn a mottled reddish brown, brown or sooty black. The needles die within a year instead of living to the usual eight. The tree looks thin.

Cause: Needle cast is a fungal disease that causes needles to drop prematurely. Needle loss may occur over the entire tree and may kill very small trees.

Solution: Use pruning, spraying, and fertilizing to control the disease.

- Prune and destroy infected shoots. Do this on a dry day to lessen the chance of spreading the disease. Be sure to sterilize your shears (p.310) afterward.
- In spring, spray with the organic fungicide Bordeaux mixture. Spray as new needles develop. Spray again twice at 10-day intervals.
- In early summer, spray with an organic lime-sulfur fungicide to limit spore activity.
- To keep the tree strong, fertilize it in early spring, using a balanced 10-10-10 formulation (p.324).

PROTECTING TREES IN WINTER

Winter weather can damage trees in many ways. Snow and ice can break branches, alternating warm and cold temperatures can heave roots out of the soil, wind and sun can burn foliage, and bark can split after sunny days. In winter, hungry rodents can also gnaw off pieces of bark.

• To prevent snow and ice damage, protect trees, such as arborvitae, by wrapping a roll of burlap around the entire tree, beginning at the base and spiraling upward. Leave a foot or so of space between each strip.

• A 3-inch layer of loose mulch, such as pine bark or dried leaves, spread beneath small trees after the ground freezes will inhibit heaving of the soil, which can damage the root system.

• Protect small evergreens with a screen of burlap a few feet from the trees. For sun protection, place the screen on the south and west sides. For wind protection, place it in the direction of the prevailing wind.

• To deter small rodents, wrap the base of the tree with small-meshed fencing.

Small sacks hang on branches; foliage is eaten

Problem: Small silken sacks, made with pieces of needle and bark, hang from small branches. The needles near the sacks are eaten, and the branchlets are often reduced to twigs.

Cause: Bagworms make nests of silk strengthened with bits and pieces of the tree. They live inside the sacks and partly emerge to feed on nearby foliage. Females have no wings and can't fly to a new tree, so an infected tree may become home to a large population of the pests.

Solution: Spray with insecticide, use traps, and handpick bags to prevent spread.

• Spray with the biological insecticide BTK as soon as you see bagworms. Follow label directions carefully.

• Place sticky bands (available from garden centers and catalogs) on the trunk and main branches to trap females as they climb to lay eggs.

• Handpick and dispose of bags in winter to reduce infestation the following season.

Needles are eaten

Problem: Small loopers or inchworms feed on the needles, often eating only part before moving to another needle. The loopers are yellow with white spots and a dark line on each side of their body. Damaged needles turn brown and fall. Severe defoliation can occur, weakening the tree.

Cause: Balsam fir sawfly larvae, also known as hemlock loopers, hatch in late spring from eggs laid on the bark. The larvae feed on the new foliage at first but later move to older needles. They mature by late summer. The adult sawflies lay eggs in fall.

Solution: Use insecticidal sprays to control hemlock loopers.

• With hemlock loopers, spray the larvae with the biological insecticide BTK when you first see them.

• Or spray the foliage with a synthetic insecticide registered for firs that contains the active ingredient methoxychlor or carbaryl. Follow label directions carefully.

• During the winter, spray a tree that is infested with hemlock loopers with dormant oil to kill eggs in bark crevices. Follow label directions carefully.

Ginkgo or Maidenhair Tree

Ginkgo biloba

LIGHT: Full sun

SOIL: Deep, well drained; pH 5.5 to 7.5

MOISTURE: Consistently moist

HARDINESS: Zones 3 to 8

Pale green or brown spots appear on leaves

Problem: Pale green or yellow-green spots appear on the leaves of the ginkgo. The spots sometimes turn brown or pale tan with dead tissue in the center.

Cause: Anthracnose leaf spot is a common fungal disease that infects many different plants, from perennials to shade trees. It is one of the few diseases to attack ginkgo. It is most often seen on trees suffering from water stress, poor nutrition, or weather damage.

Solution: Spray with fungicide. Feed and water the tree to keep it healthy.

- At the first sign of the disease, spray the foliage with an organic copper-hydroxide fungicide or with a synthetic fungicide registered for ginkgos that contains the active ingredient benomyl or thiophanate-methyl. Follow label directions carefully.

- Feed the tree in spring with a granular fertilizer with a balanced 10-10-10 formulation (p.324) to help keep it healthy.

- Provide the tree with supplemental water during extended dry periods so that it receives the equivalent of 1 inch of water each week (p.273).

Tree grows slow and turns green late in spring

Problem: Even years after planting, the tree grows little each year. Leaves don't appear until most other trees are fully green.

Cause: Slow development and late greening are natural. Ginkgos are notoriously slow to establish, especially in cool climates. Once established, the growth rate is sometimes only 3 to 4 inches each year. They are also slow to turn green in spring. These are small prices to pay for a tree with few problems, outstanding fall color, and salt and pollution tolerance.

Solution: No action is needed.

- Be patient and let a ginkgo develop at its own natural speed.

Fruits are messy and have a bad odor

Problem: Fruits falling off the tree have an offensive odor. They are messy, and if they fall on a sidewalk they leave a stain that is difficult to wash away.

Cause: As part of this ancient tree's primitive reproductive cycle, the rotting odor is necessary to attract animals that disperse the fallen seeds. Ginkgo trees can be male or female; only the female trees produce fruits. On a hard surface, the fruits can not only produce a stain but can also become slippery as they decay, making walking dangerous.

Solution: Clean up fallen fruits and debris. Consider growing male ginkgos.

- Scrape up fallen fruits daily, especially to keep a walkway safe to use. Wear rubber gloves; the fruit flesh can cause a rash.

- Plant male ginkgos, which don't produce fruit, such as the variety 'Princeton Sentry'. Most named varieties of ginkgo trees are male.

Hawthorn

Crataegus spp.

LIGHT: Full sun

SOIL: Well drained; pH 5.5 to 7.5

MOISTURE: Moist to seasonally dry

HARDINESS: Zones 3 to 8

Leaves appear scorched

Problem: On one or several shoots, leaves wilt and rapidly turn brown but remain attached to the branch. Flowers may look water soaked, and twigs and branches have cankers.

Cause: Fireblight is a bacterial disease that gets its name from the leaves' scorched appearance. A widespread problem in North America, fireblight is identifiable by the retention of wilted leaves and a reddish brown discoloration of the sapwood. The bacteria overwinter on stems and branches in dark-colored cankers. In spring, the disease is spread by insects, wind, rain, and animals.

Solution: Prune and spray, but don't fertilize the tree. Plant resistant varieties.

- Prune branches, cutting well below the infected discolored area. Sterilize (p.310) your pruning tool between cuts.

- In winter, spray with organic lime-sulfur, which has antibiotic properties. Follow label directions carefully.

- In spring, as leaves unfurl, spray with organic copper-hydroxide, which has antibiotic properties. Or spray with the antibiotic streptomycin. Follow label directions carefully.

- Avoid fertilizing an infected tree in early spring, because the resulting lush growth is especially prone to fireblight.

- Plant fireblight-resistant cultivars, including *C. punctata* 'Ohio Pioneer' and *C. viridis* 'Winter King'.

Leaves have orange spots

Problem: Yellow or orange spots appear on leaves in early summer. Entire leaves may yellow and fall. If infected, fruits develop small, pinkish fruiting bodies in fall.

Cause: Cedar-hawthorn rust is a fungal disease that alternates between junipers and hawthorns and may infect hosts other than hawthorn. Similar diseases, such as cedar-apple rust, attack other members of the rose family, notably apples, quinces, and serviceberries.

Solution: Eliminate growths from host trees, spray, and plant resistant species.

- In winter, prune dark orange ball-like growths on nearby junipers. They turn bright orange and slimy in spring when they release spores.

- Spray the infected hawthorn in spring with an organic wettable sulfur fungicide. Follow label directions carefully.

- Plant Washington or cockspur hawthorns—such as 'Presidential', a rust-resistant Washington hawthorn, or 'Cruzam', a thornless cockspur hawthorn—which are almost immune to rust diseases.

Dark sluglike insects feed on leaves

Problem: In late spring, leaves have areas where they have been reduced to veins. Small, dark, sluglike pests are present, but don't leave a slime trail as true slugs do.

Cause: Sawfly larvae, called pear slugs, cause early leaf drop, and in a severe attack can defoliate the tree. Larvae drop to the ground and pupate, emerging as a second generation in late summer. The larvae from this next

generation overwinter in the soil. There may be as many as three generations in areas with a long growing season.

Solution: Use sprays and drenches and good garden techniques to control sawflies.

- Spray with insecticidal soap or the botanical insecticide pyrethrum. Follow label directions carefully.

- Or spray with synthetic insecticide registered for hawthorns that contains the active ingredient rotenone. Follow label directions carefully.

- Cultivate the soil under an infested tree after the leaves have fallen to help kill overwintering larvae. But be aware that larvae can burrow back into the soil because they don't pupate until early spring.

- Treat the soil under the tree with synthetic insecticide registered for hawthorns that contains the active ingredient diazinon in early spring to kill sawflies as they emerge. Follow label directions carefully.

Brown spots are on leaves

Problem: Small brown or red spots appear on leaves in spring or summer. They run together to form blotches, often surrounded by a yellow zone. Leaves fall prematurely, and the entire tree may be defoliated. If a second crop of leaves is produced, it is also affected.

Cause: Hawthorn leaf blight, a fungal disease, is the most common cause of severe leaf drop on ornamental hawthorns. The disease overwinters on bark and fallen foliage.

Solution: Use good garden sanitation and spray a fungicide to control leaf blight.

- Rake up and dispose of infected leaves.

- Spray foliage as the flower buds open, using a synthetic fungicide registered for hawthorns that contains the active ingredient benomyl or propiconazole. Repeat treatment if leaf spots reappear. Follow label directions carefully.

- In late winter, spray with an organic lime-sulfur fungicide to kill spores on the bark.

Silky webs appear in branch fork in spring

Problem: A mass of silken threads forms in the fork of one or more branches. Small caterpillars are feeding on the foliage.

Cause: Tent caterpillars overwinter as shiny black egg masses encircling a small twig. After hatching, the young gather at a branch fork and spin a silken nest. They feed during the day and return to the nest at night. A severe attack can result in complete defoliation. The green eastern tent caterpillar is found as far west as the Rocky Mountains. The yellow and black western tent caterpillar is only a problem west of the Rockies.

Solution: Hose off nests and spray with insecticide to control tent caterpillars.

- Spray nests with a strong stream of water from a hose to dislodge caterpillars.

- Spray larger caterpillar colonies with the biological insecticide BTK on sunny days when the pests are visible and out of their nest. Follow label directions carefully.

- Or break open the nest with a pole in the evening (or on a damp day) and spray with the botanical insecticide pyrethrum. Follow label directions carefully.

- Protect hawthorns and other susceptible trees, such as cherries and crab apples, by spraying them with dormant oil in winter to kill the egg masses. Follow label directions carefully.

Hemlock
Tsuga spp.

LIGHT: Full sun to medium shade

SOIL: Rich in humus; pH 5.0 to 6.0

MOISTURE: Moist

HARDINESS: Zones 3 to 7

New foliage yellows and droops

Problem: New foliage on a Canada hemlock (*T. canadensis*) or Carolina hemlock (*T. caroliniana*) turns yellow and droops. It is often covered with yellow powder. Needles fall, leaving a crooked twig. Cones are also attacked. On a badly infected tree, most shoot tips turn brown and die, making the tree look scorched.

Cause: Hemlock needle rust can be caused by two closely related fungi. The yellow, dusty spores either overwinter on the dead shoots or drift to an alternate host in the poplar family, which includes aspen and cottonwoods as well as poplar trees.

Solution: Spray fungicide and practice good garden sanitation to limit the spread of rust.

- If a tree is small, spray organic lime-sulfur fungicide weekly for a month, starting when new growth first emerges. Follow label directions carefully.
- To minimize future problems, rake and dispose of fallen leaves of host trees in the poplar family, through summer and fall.
- In late winter, spray infected trees with an organic lime-sulfur fungicide to kill overwintering spores. Follow label directions carefully.

New shoots have gray fuzz

Problem: New shoots become covered with a gray, feltlike fuzz. Needles are dark brown or black at base. Shoots wilt and eventually die.

Cause: Gray mold, also called bud blight, is a fungus prevalent in warm, humid areas. It is particularly active on plants growing in shade or close together. If humidity is high, it will grow at most temperatures above freezing.

Solution: Spray with fungicide. Choose new planting locations with care.

- Spray the tree with an organic sulfur fungicide. Follow label directions carefully.
- In future plantings, avoid damp, windless sites, and space trees widely for air flow.

Needles on some branches turn brown and drop

Problem: In spring, scattered branches (or occasionally the entire tree) take on a bluish tinge. Needles gradually turn yellow, then brown, and fall by midsummer.

Cause: Hemlock rust mites are tiny, slow-moving insects that can be seen only with a magnifying glass. Related to spider mites, rust mites feed on needles in spring and can rapidly become a major problem. The infested plant looks rusty, but don't confuse this problem with needle rust (entry, left).

Solution: Hose off the mites. Spray to avoid further infestations.

- If the tree is small, spray the underside of the needles frequently with strong jets of water to dislodge the mites. Spray early in the day, so that the tree dries before night, to discourage potential fungal infections.
- Spray a larger tree with commercial garlic oil or capsaicin to repel mites. Follow label directions carefully.
- To discourage further infestations, spray in early spring with insecticidal soap or the botanical pesticide neem. Follow label directions carefully.

Cottony masses grow at base of needles and on bark

Problem: Small, cottonlike masses develop at the base of needles and on the bark. Infected needles gradually turn yellow, then brown, and fall off. Trees appear somewhat stunted and in poor health. In a severe attack, so much foliage may be lost that the tree dies.

Cause: Hemlock woolly adelgids are insects related to aphids that damage trees by sucking sap. Eggs are laid in early spring by overwintering adults. After hatching, the larvae crawl to a fresh spot and settle down to feed, covering themselves with white cottonlike fibers. The young pass through several stages before becoming adults in fall, but after the crawling stage, they don't move again.

Solution: Use forceful or well-timed spraying with insecticide to control adelgids.

● Spray with insecticidal soap, using a powerful sprayer to break the pests' covering. Follow label directions carefully.

● Or spray several times, at one-week intervals, with a contact insecticide in mid- to late spring to kill crawlers. Use the botanical insecticide pyrethrum or a synthetic insecticide registered for hemlocks that contains the active ingredient malathion or diazinon. Follow label directions carefully.

Needles gradually turn yellow

Problem: In late spring, a few needles on some of the tree's new shoots turn pale, swell slightly, and then gradually begin to turn yellow. By midsummer, white growths appear on the underside of the needles. New growth on young trees is most severely affected, but low branches on older trees may also have the same symptoms.

Cause: Blister rust is a fungal disease that comes in two species. One attacks Canada hemlock (*T. canadensis*) and Carolina hemlock (*T. caroliniana*), and this variety has hydrangeas as its alternate host. The other form of the disease is found on all hemlocks and has members of the heather family, including rhododendrons, azaleas, mountain laurel, and blueberries, as its alternate host.

Solution: Prune infected branches and spray with fungicide. Avoid planting host plants.

● Prune and dispose of infected needles and branches.

● Spray the tree with an organic sulfur fungicide. Follow label directions carefully.

● Don't grow hydrangeas or heather-family plants within a half mile of hemlocks.

Large patches of brown needles suddenly appear

Problem: Brown needles develop in patches. The patches spread, affecting entire branches, which then begin to die. The tree shows no signs of insect damage or disease.

Cause: Hemlocks are sensitive to weed killers. They can be accidentally exposed when herbicide spray drifts to them on the wind, or when herbicide applied to the soil migrates into their root zone.

Solution: Use weed killers cautiously, as directed, and only when necessary.

● Spray only on a windless, cool, dry day.

● Never exceed label concentrations, and never apply a weed killer where weeds can be controlled without using herbicides.

● Use low pressure when spraying weed killers to prevent forming a mist of fine herbicide droplets that can drift off target with air currents.

● Avoid soil-active herbicides, such as tebuthiuron, which damage or kill large hemlocks and other species growing over 100 yards away, through root absorption.

**REGIONAL FOCUS
CENTRAL**

During prolonged hot weather, hemlocks are prone to sun scorch. The tips of branches die back for several inches, and the tree looks scorched. The cause is high temperatures (above 95°F for several days) rather than sunlight, and the problem occurs all over the plant, not just on the sunny side. There is no cure. In time the tree will put out new growth. On small trees, shear lightly to remove damaged tips. It's best to avoid planting hemlocks in areas with very hot summers, such as the lower Midwest and the Southeast.

Hickory
Carya spp.

LIGHT: Full sun

SOIL: Rich, well drained; pH 5.5 to 6.5

MOISTURE: Seasonally dry

HARDINESS: Zones 4 to 9

REGIONAL FOCUS

SOUTHEAST

In Southern regions where pecans are commonly grown, especially Florida, the pecan casebearer can be a serious pest for the hickory, causing defoliation, weakened trees, and crop reduction. Tiny larvae mine into leaves while feeding. To kill overwintering larvae that attach their cases to twigs and branches, spray the tree with dormant oil in winter.

Leaves are yellowish with brown spots

Problem: In late summer, the leaves turn yellow-green with small brown spots. The spots have indistinct margins and often run together to form brown patches. The leaves curl and tend to fall slightly earlier than normal.

Cause: Anthracnose leaf spot is caused by a fungus that overwinters on fallen foliage. It infects newly opened leaves in spring, but symptoms do not appear until later.

Solution: Practice good garden sanitation and spray in spring to help limit the disease.

● Collect and dispose of all infected foliage in fall to prevent reinfection next spring.

● If the tree is small, spray the spring after an infection with an organic copper-hydroxide fungicide. Follow label directions carefully. Spray as leaves start to open, are half open, and are fully open.

Branches in tree crown have sunken areas and die

Problem: Dead branches with brown leaves appear in the crown. There are small, sunken areas on the bark of affected branches.

Cause: Canker is caused by a fungus that usually enters through a wound. Old cankers are circular and targetlike, with several layers of bark visible. This disease is seldom fatal to a tree unless cankers occur near one another in a cluster on the trunk.

Solution: Remove diseased branches and spray. Keep the tree healthy and injury free.

● Prune and dispose of infected branches.

● If a case is severe, spray the tree with an organic lime-sulfur fungicide. Follow label directions carefully.

● To keep the tree healthy, water it when rains are lacking. It should get the equivalent of 1 inch of water a week (p.273).

● To avoid injury, keep mowers and trimmers away from trunk and limit pruning.

Branches have knobby swellings

Problem: In the growing season, knotty swellings appear on twigs and branches. The swellings, called galls, remain throughout the year.

Cause: A variety of mites, midges, and wasps lay eggs under the bark, injecting substances that cause galls to form as chambers for their larvae. The hickory onion gall midge is a common culprit. Although the galls are unsightly, they don't threaten the health of the tree.

Solution: Prune, attract birds, or spray.

● Prune and destroy infested plant parts.

● Allow insect-eating birds to eat larvae from galls that cannot be reached with pruners.

● Or in spring, hire a professional to identify the pest and spray appropriately.

Dead twigs litter ground

Problem: Small branchlets turn brown in summer and fall, littering the ground.

Cause: Twig girdlers lay eggs on twigs in spring. Their larvae spend the summer inside the twigs, weakening them, then overwinter in fallen debris, emerging in spring as adults.

Solution: Use insecticides and garden cleanup to control girdlers.

● Spray the tree with a synthetic insecticide registered for hickories that contains the active ingredient carbaryl. Follow label directions carefully.

● Before spring, dispose of fallen twigs.

Honey Locust
Gleditsia triacanthos

LIGHT: Full sun

SOIL: Well drained; pH 6.5 to 8.0

MOISTURE: Consistently moist

HARDINESS: Zones 3 to 9

Trunk bark is cracked and lifted

Problem: The bark develops large sunken patches, then cracks and lifts away from the wood, which has brown streaks. The foliage gets sparser each year.

Cause: Canker is produced by any of five fungi that can infect the trunk and main branches and eventually kill the tree. They often gain entry through pruning cuts or damaged bark, and are difficult to treat successfully.

Solution: Try pruning and spraying to improve the health of the tree.

- Prune infected branches if possible. Leave major pruning until fall so that the cuts can harden over the winter.
- Spray dormant tree with organic lime-sulfur fungicide. Follow label directions carefully.

Leaves yellow; growth is stunted

Problem: Leaves become distorted, turning yellow with brown spots. The tree's growth is stunted.

Cause: The honey locust plant bug, along with some lesser plant bugs and leafhoppers, has become a major problem as the popularity of honey locust has increased. Both adults and young pests feed on the foliage, causing extensive damage. They are particularly difficult to detect, because they are the same color as the leaves.

Solution: Use an insecticidal spray to control the honey locust plant bug.

- Give the foliage three sprays of insecticidal soap at one-week intervals. Follow label directions carefully.
- If the problem persists, spray with a synthetic insecticide registered for honey locust that contains the active ingredient carbaryl. Follow label directions carefully. Apply when the leaves are fully open; repeat at 10-day intervals until the infestation is controlled.

Leaves yellow, and branches begin to die back

Problem: Foliage gradually turns yellow, and the branches begin to die back. Root damage and winter injury are not suspected causes, and close inspection reveals small, elongated, sunken cankers girdling affected branches. In a severe case, the tree dies.

Cause: Branch dieback is a fungal disease that blocks the flow of nutrients and water throughout the tree. Trees weakened by it are susceptible to other fungal infections.

Solution: Remove cankers or have a professional apply fungicide to control the disease.

- Prune and destroy infected branches. Cut well below the cankers and sterilize (p.310) tools between cuts. If the tree shows few symptoms after pruning, it will recover without further treatment.
- In a severe case, hire a professional arborist to treat the tree with a commercial-strength fungicide.

Linden

Tilia spp.

LIGHT: Full sun

SOIL: Fertile, well drained; pH 5.5 to 7.5

MOISTURE: Seasonally dry to moist

HARDINESS: Zones 3 to 7

Leaves are chewed at the edges

Problem: A yellow inchworm, or looper, with dark lines on its back, eats the leaf from the edge inward. Populations of this pest can rapidly defoliate a tree and weaken it.

Cause: Linden loopers, the larvae of small moths, hatch as leaves unfurl in spring. They feed for about a month, then crawl to the ground, bury themselves, and pupate. In late fall, the adults emerge to mate; the wingless females crawl up the tree to lay eggs under pieces of loose bark.

Solution: Spray with insecticides and use barriers to control loopers and their larvae.

- To control loopers at the larval stage, spray the tree with the biological insecticide BTK. Follow label directions carefully. Use a high-pressure sprayer to reach far into the tree's canopy.

- Place a sticky band (available from garden centers and gardening catalogs) around the trunk of each linden tree to trap the wingless females as they climb the trunk to lay their eggs.

- In winter, when the tree is dormant, spray the trunk and all of the limbs with dormant oil to kill the overwintering eggs of the loopers.

Leaves have ragged holes

Problem: Leaves have ragged holes produced by small, yellow-headed larvae. The adult looks like a small yellow ladybug with stripes instead of spots. Both adults and larvae eat leaves.

Cause: Linden leaf beetles, also called calligrapha beetles, lay eggs on new foliage in spring. There is a second generation in midsummer that feeds until fall before hibernating.

Solution: Spray the tree with insecticide and remove debris at the base to control beetles.

- As soon as you notice beetles, spray them with insecticidal soap. Follow label directions carefully.

- For severe infestations, spray with a synthetic insecticide registered for lindens that contains the active ingredient carbaryl. Follow label directions carefully.

- Keep the area around the tree free of leaves and other litter to reduce the number of places where the beetles can hibernate.

Brown spots appear on leaves

Problem: Leaves develop light brown patches, mostly along the veins and toward the tips. A severe attack may defoliate the tree.

Cause: Linden anthracnose, a fungal disease, can be distinguished by the thin black line that separates the infected area from the rest of the leaf.

Solution: Practice good garden sanitation to limit damage. Spray a fungicide if necessary.

- Rake up and dispose of potentially spore-infected foliage as it falls.

- If the problem is severe, spray with an organic lime-sulfur fungicide when the tree is dormant in winter. Then spray three times in spring with organic copper-sulfate fungicide. Follow label directions carefully.

Locust
Robinia spp.

LIGHT: Full sun to light shade

SOIL: Any soil

MOISTURE: Moist to dry

HARDINESS: Zones 3 to 8

A web containing sawdust hangs from branches

Problem: A cobweb bag filled with sawdust and small wood chips hangs from branches or from bark on the trunk. The branches are weakened and may break off in a storm. In a serious attack, the entire tree may blow down.

Cause: Carpenterworms are wood-boring caterpillars, the larvae of a small moth. They mature in one year in the South but may take up to four years in the North. They tunnel mostly in the sapwood, just below the bark. A beetle larva, locust borer, also attacks locusts by tunneling into the wood. The mottled brown female moths are difficult to distinguish from the bark. And either pest can pose serious problems for black locusts.

Solution: Prune and spray an insecticide to control these wood borers.

- If the attack is localized, prune off and destroy the injured branches.
- Spray the tree with a synthetic insecticide registered for locusts that contains the active ingredient carbaryl. Follow label directions carefully.
- In the South, where adults can be present every spring, spray the trunk and branches with insecticidal soap as the leaves unfurl. Follow label directions carefully.
- Repel future infestations of carpenterworms by spraying the tree with the botanical repellent capsaicin or garlic oil. Follow label directions carefully.

Sap runs after pruning

Problem: After pruning the tree in spring, the sap flows freely from the pruning cuts.

Cause: Sap flow is high in black locusts in late winter and early spring. Trees may bleed excessively when pruned or injured then.

Solution: Time pruning to avoid the period in late winter to early spring when sap flow is high. Avoid injuring the tree.

- Prune in late fall, when sap is low, to give cuts time to dry and seal before spring.
- Avoid injuring the tree with a mower or trimmer to reduce loss of sap and eliminate entry points for disease.

Small branches with sunken areas suddenly wilt

Problem: The tree produces leaves normally, but during the summer, scattered small branches develop sunken areas of bark, then suddenly wilt with leaves turning brown. The branches eventually die.

Cause: Cankers on locust twigs result from infection by one of three different fungi. The fungus gains entry through wounds caused by branches rubbing together, squirrels feeding, or birds breaking off side shoots for nesting material. If the damage is limited to small branches, the cankers are unlikely to spread into the main branches of the tree.

Solution: Remove infected branches and spray to reduce canker outbreaks.

- Prune infected branches just below the dead portion and destroy the cuttings. Sterilize (p.310) tools between cuts.
- Spray with an organic lime-sulfur fungicide. Follow label directions carefully.

Magnolia

Magnolia spp.

LIGHT: Full sun to light shade

SOIL: Well drained; pH 5.0 to 6.5

MOISTURE: Moist

HARDINESS: Zones 3 to 9

Leaves develop small tunnels or irregular holes

Problem: Leaves either have holes eaten into them or, in the case of thick-leaved evergreen magnolias, have much of the tissue on the surface removed. The tips of the leaves may have large tunnels where the tissue inside the leaf has been eaten away.

Cause: The sassafras weevil, also known as the yellow poplar weevil, the magnolia leaf miner, and the tulip tree leafminer, is a small, dark-colored beetle with a long snout. Adults emerge in spring, lay eggs, and feed on the leaf undersides. Larvae tunnel into the leaf tips, pupate, and emerge in summer to feed, before hibernating in litter under the trees. This pest is more of a nuisance that causes cosmetic damage than a serious problem.

Solution: Remove overwintering sites and spray the tree with an insecticide.

- If many leaves are chewed, remove mulch from under the tree to eliminate overwintering sites for the weevil.

- At the first sign of injury, spray the tree with insecticidal soap or with a synthetic insecticide registered for magnolias that contains the active ingredient carbaryl. Follow label directions carefully.

Small branches in crown die

Problem: Small dead branches are scattered throughout the crown of the tree. Small sunken areas are on the branches.

Cause: Nectria canker is caused by a fungus that gains entry through wounds. The small, dark, sunken areas of bark are hard to detect initially. After the first year, the cankers become more visible as they form targetlike wounds with rings of overlapping bark. On main branches, the cankers can become large without any other symptoms and may escape detection, especially when they attack evergreen magnolias. Smaller branches may die. Healthy trees are unlikely to be attacked.

Solution: Prune, spray, and keep the tree healthy and unstressed.

- Prune infected branches. On the trunk, infections are more difficult to eliminate.

- Spray the tree when dormant with an organic lime-sulfur fungicide. Follow label directions carefully.

- Inspect the tree annually for signs of infection, and prune affected branches.

- In spring, feed the tree with an acidifying fertilizer with a 21-7-7 formulation (p.324).

- Keep the tree well watered (p.273) during dry periods of more than a week.

- Don't plant a magnolia in poorly drained or alkaline soil, or in an area subject to lingering frost; these are stressful conditions.

Ragged holes appear in leaves overnight

Problem: Leaves have holes eaten in them. Some are so badly chewed that they are reduced to skeletons. No pest can be found feeding during the daytime. The problem is most prevalent on a young tree.

Cause: Slugs and snails climb into the tree at dusk and feed all night, returning to the ground at daybreak to hide in debris.

Solution: Handpick the mollusk pests. Use barriers and traps to foil them.

- Using a flashlight at night, handpick and dispose of as many slugs or snails as you can reach.
- Repel them by putting copper edging (available at garden centers) in the soil around the tree trunk. The pests will receive a mild electrical shock upon contact.
- Put beer traps (p.49) in the soil under the tree. The pests are attracted to beer and will crawl in and drown.

Leaves are coated with a powdery black mold

Problem: Leaves of a deciduous or evergreen magnolia become coated with a black mold that resembles a dark powdery mildew. If the attack is heavy, the leaves fall prematurely.

Cause: Mealybugs feed on magnolias and excrete a sticky substance called honeydew, which encourages the growth of sooty mold. If the mealybug attack is severe, the mold can be dense enough to block light to the leaves, which can cause them to turn brown and drop. In the South, another possible cause of the problem may be a different fungal disease called black mildew, which also causes early defoliation. A clue that your magnolia has a mealybug problem instead of a mildew problem is that the green parts of leaves—the parts not covered with mold—will be sticky with clear, shiny honeydew.

Solution: Spray the tree with insecticide to control mealybugs. Hose off mold.

- To control mealybugs, spray with insecticidal soap. This also helps to wash some of the honeydew off the leaves, discouraging the growth of black sooty mold. Follow label directions carefully.
- Spray the foliage often with a strong stream of water from a hose to wash off the honeydew and black mold.

Leaves turn yellowish green

Problem: Leaves open normally but fade to a pale yellow-green as summer passes. In severe cases, they are bright yellow with green veins.

Cause: Chlorosis is a condition caused by alkaline soil, which inhibits the uptake of several essential nutrients, often iron.

Solution: Give your tree easily absorbed iron and acidify the soil.

- For a quick fix, spray the leaves and drench the ground with chelated iron solution.
- For a long-term solution, lower the pH (p.329) of the soil to between 5.0 and 6.5. Add powdered sulfur to the top few inches, or mulch with pine needles or oak leaves.

Buds and flowers darken

Problem: In the spring, flower buds fail to open and become dark. Or the flowers open, but then turn partly dark.

Cause: Cold winters can kill flower buds. This is common at the northern limits of a tree's hardiness zone. A late spring frost can also kill them. This kind of damage can happen even in warm regions where magnolias normally grow well.

Solution: You can't save dead buds. Spray with water to prevent frost damage next time.

- If buds have been killed by low temperatures, do nothing. You'll lose a season of flowers, but the tree will leaf out normally and form buds again next season.
- Next time there's a late frost, spray the buds with cold water before the morning sun heats them. The film of water lets buds thaw gradually, saving them.

Maple

Acer spp.

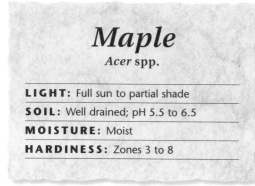

LIGHT: Full sun to partial shade

SOIL: Well drained; pH 5.5 to 6.5

MOISTURE: Moist

HARDINESS: Zones 3 to 8

Tree dies slowly from the top downward

Problem: The tree has dead twigs high up among the foliage. The problem gradually spreads downward (sometimes down just one or two branches), taking three or four years for dying foliage to reach the trunk.

Cause: Maple decline is caused by environmental stress. It is most common on trees growing in cities and those planted close to roadways. Salt damage, especially in the North, and vehicle pollution are thought to be the major causes. Sugar maple (*A. saccharum*) is especially susceptible.

Solution: Minimize stress and keep trees healthy with fertilizer and proper care. Avoid planting pollution-sensitive species.

- Fertilize in spring with a high-nitrogen fertilizer, such as a 15-10-10 (p.324) formulation, and neutralize soil as needed with crushed limestone.
- Water well during dry spells, making sure the tree gets the equivalent of at least 1 inch of water each week (p.273).
- Mulch with a 3-inch-thick layer of wood chips, to reduce evaporation from the soil. Don't let mulch touch the trunk.
- Avoid compacting the soil under the tree. Don't walk on the soil when it is wet.
- In urban areas, don't plant sugar maples. If road salt is the problem, try ginkgo, honey locust, or Norway maple, which are more salt tolerant.

Leaves turn yellow and drop in summer

Problem: Leaves yellow and fall early, mostly from the lower branches. They have almost no stalk, or the stalk is slightly swollen and black at the end.

Cause: Insect borers from one of two unrelated species, a moth and a sawfly, tunnel into the leaf stalks of maples. After the leaves fall, the larvae live in the remains of the stem until they mature. The larvae then drop to the ground and pupate. They emerge as adults the following spring.

Solution: Spray the infested tree with an insecticide to control the borers.

- Spray with insecticidal soap. Follow label directions carefully.
- If problem persists, spray with a synthetic insecticide registered for maples that contains the active ingredient malathion or carbaryl. Spray every 10 days; start when leaves open fully and continue until larvae are gone. Follow label directions carefully.

Maple seedlings spring up everywhere

Problem: Seedlings sprout in flower beds, driveway cracks, and other untended spots.

Cause: Copious seed production is natural for maples, whose seedlings must compete for light in the forest, where most die from lack of light. But in yards and gardens, they flourish. Some are more prolific than others.

Solution: Remove the seedlings. Choose species wisely when planting maples.

- Pull the seedlings by the roots as soon as you notice them, before the roots can spread and become established.
- Select new maples with care. Box elder (*A. negundo*) has an almost weedlike ability to colonize any vacant spot. Norway maple (*A. platanoides*), an introduced species, is best avoided in rural areas where it can spread into nearby woods. Look for male varieties, which are seedless.

A street tree dies on one side

Problem: In spring, a curbside tree has many dead leaves on the side next to a street light.

Cause: Street lights and other outdoor lights can upset a nearby tree's natural dormancy. When lights are on all night, the side of a tree that's closest to the lights keeps growing late into fall and is not fully dormant by winter, causing it to die of exposure.

Solution: Use proper maintenance and take care in locating a new tree.

- Don't fertilize the tree in late summer or fall. The resulting new growth will be prone to frost damage.
- Don't plant a tree close to a street or porch light, especially if the light is on all night.

Leaves have brown blotches and soon fall

Problem: Leaves open normally but soon develop large brown patches between the veins and appear scorched. The blotches run together and the leaves fall from the tree.

Cause: Maple anthracnose, a fungal disease, thrives in cool, wet springs and on stressed trees, such as those in urban gardens.

Solution: Practice good garden sanitation, keep the tree healthy and stress-free, and spray infected trees with a fungicide.

- Collect and dispose of all infected foliage, as it drops in summer and in fall.
- Keep the tree healthy by watering (p.273) to supply the equivalent of 1 inch of water per week and by fertilizing (p.324) in spring.
- Minimize stress by avoiding lawn weed killers over the root area.
- The season after an infection, spray the tree with an organic copper-sulfate or lime-sulfur fungicide. Spray when leaves start to unfurl, are half open, and again when they're fully open. Follow label directions carefully.

Leaves have circular holes

Problem: Leaves have oval or circular holes. Over time, the leaves in the canopy may be almost completely consumed.

Cause: Maple leaf cutters are ¼-inch-long caterpillars that are the larvae of a small blue moth. A leaf cutter tunnels inside a leaf in the spring. When it emerges, it cuts two circles from the leaf, fastens them together, and lives inside, partly emerging to eat more of the leaf. Damage is not often serious but can be epidemic in an area. Repeated defoliations can weaken and kill a tree. Nearby trees of other species may also be attacked.

Solution: Spray insecticide and practice good garden sanitation to control maple leaf cutter.

- Spray the foliage with a synthetic insecticide registered for maples that contains the active ingredient acephate. Follow label directions carefully.
- Rake up and destroy infested foliage in fall to remove the overwintering pupae. During this period, the larvae are protected by their leafy homes, so spraying is not effective.

Leaves open normally, then turn dark and shrivel

Problem: In the spring, leaves of a Japanese maple (*A. palmatum*) or fullmoon maple (*A. japonicum*) open normally, then turn brown or black, become distorted, and die. Eventually, the tree puts out a second set of leaves that mature normally.

Cause: Late frost has frozen the newly opened foliage. When this is followed by the sun's sudden heat in the morning, crystals form in the frozen leaves that rupture the cell walls and kill the leaves. The second set of replacement leaves opens after the danger of frost is past, but if this happens frequently, the tree will be severely weakened. Trees in valleys and other low areas where cold air settles are more likely to be affected.

Solution: Give the tree a protective water spray. Plan for late frosts when selecting trees.

- When a late frost occurs, spray the tree with cold water early in the morning after frost has formed. The water helps the leaves thaw slowly so that they are not damaged.

- Don't plant Japanese or fullmoon maples in frost-prone low-lying areas.

- If late frost is common, ask a local garden center to recommend a hardier species.

Leaves fail to show fall color

Problem: A maple planted for its good fall color fails to perform. Instead, the leaves turn brown and fall off.

Cause: Droughts in summer, or cold or warm periods in early fall, can cause poor fall color. Also, not all maples have good fall color. Norway maples (*A. platanoides*) are not reliable, sycamore maples (*A. pseudoplatanus*) turn brown, and silver maples (*A. saccharinum*) turn yellow but are unpredictable.

Solution: Water well. Plant colorful varieties.

- Supplement rain with watering (p.273) as needed to supply 1 inch of water each week during dry periods in summer.

- Grow varieties that turn color (box, p.267).

Small black spots appear on leaves

Problem: In summer, shiny black spots develop on the upper surface of leaves. The spots may be up to ½ inch in diameter, and they are usually surrounded by a brownish yellow halo. The tree may shed its leaves early.

Cause: Tar spot is a fungal disease that attacks maples. It disfigures foliage but rarely inflicts significant damage. In late spring, yellow areas develop on leaves. The black spots erupt later. A related disease causes tiny black speckles on the leaf in nearly circular patches.

Solution: Practice good garden sanitation and spray with fungicide next spring.

- Rake up and remove leaves in fall to get rid of overwintering spores.

- Next spring, as leaves unfurl, spray with an organic copper-based fungicide, such as copper sulfate or copper oxychloride sulfate. Follow label directions carefully.

TIME-TESTED TECHNIQUES

MAPLE SUGARING

If you live in the upper Midwest or from the mid-Atlantic states northward, you can grow one of the most brilliantly colored maples of fall, the sugar maple (*Acer saccharum*). And you can indulge in the time-honored tradition of making your own delicious maple syrup.

When the sap starts to run in very early spring, often when snow still lingers, drill a ½-inch-diameter hole into a mature tree at waist height, going about one-third of the way into the trunk. Insert a tight-fitting piece of pipe into the hole and hang a lightweight bucket on the pipe to collect the dripping sap. Collect the sap daily, keeping it in a cool place, until you have enough for a batch of syrup. Have patience—it takes 33 quarts of sap to boil down into 1 quart of syrup!

Leaves quickly wilt and die on one side of tree

Problem: Leaves suddenly wilt and die on scattered branches, usually on one side of a tree. Other leaves may be small, pale green or yellow, have brown patches, or show early fall color.

Cause: Verticillium wilt is a fungal disease that attacks a wide range of woody and nonwoody plants. Among maples, it occurs most often on silver (*A. saccharinum*), sugar (*A. saccharum*), red (*A. rubrum*), and Norway (*A. platanoides*). Once the fungus becomes entrenched, a tree stands little chance of surviving. The disease can kill a tree in one season, but it may survive for years, not showing symptoms every year. Cut wood reveals an olive-green discoloration under the bark of diseased branches.

Solution: Depending on the stage of infection, fertilizer or a fungicide may help the tree survive. Replace a badly infected tree.

- If the disease is in the early stages, feed the tree in spring with a high-nitrogen fertilizer, such as a 15-10-10 (p.324) formulation. This may make the tree grow fast enough to seal off the fungus under new wood.

- If the fungus is well established, try injecting (or having a professional inject) the tree with a synthetic fungicide registered for maples that contains the active ingredient benomyl. Follow label directions carefully.

- If a tree is badly infected, cut it down and dig up the roots. Replace it with a wilt-resistant tree species, such as a narrow- or broad-leaf evergreen tree, or a beech, chestnut, ginkgo, hickory, sycamore, willow, or zelkova tree.

Twigs have white pests

Problem: In midsummer to late summer, leaf undersides have cottony masses, mostly along veins. Later, branches and twigs are covered with white, popcornlike pests.

Cause: Cottony maple scale is a soft-scale insect. Females overwinter on small branches and lay up to a thousand eggs each in late spring. When the eggs hatch in summer, the insects emerge and move onto the leaf undersides to feed. During this time, they look like aphids and produce a sticky secretion called honeydew, which often is the host for sooty mold. In fall, the females move to the woody parts to overwinter, protecting themselves with a cottony covering.

Solution: Treat with well-timed sprays of insecticide. Encourage natural predators.

- Use insecticidal soap in late June and July to kill crawling-stage females. Follow label directions carefully.

- If the problem persists, spray with a synthetic insecticide registered for maples that contains the active ingredient carbaryl. Follow label directions carefully.

- To kill overwintering insects, spray trunk and branches in late winter with dormant oil, covering undersides of the branches.

- Encourage natural predators, such as lacewings (p.103).

WISE CHOICES

Here are some varieties of maple that will usually provide good fall color even with unfavorable weather conditions.

- Amure maple (*Acer ginnala*) 'Flame'

- Japanese maple (*A. palmatum*) 'Bloodgood', 'Crimson Queen', 'Filigree', 'Moonfire', 'Osakazuki', 'Red Filigree Lace', and 'Waterfall'

- Red maple (*A. rubrum*) 'Autumn Flame', 'Morgan', 'Northwood', 'October Glory', and 'Red Sunset'

- Sugar maple (*A. saccharum*) 'Commemoration', 'Flax Mill Majesty', 'Green Mountain', and 'Legacy'

Mountain Ash
Sorbus spp.

LIGHT: Full sun to light shade

SOIL: Well drained; pH 5.5 to 6.5

MOISTURE: Average

HARDINESS: Zones 3 to 7

Leaves have yellow blotches

Problem: Leaves develop bright yellow streaks, stipples, and blotches. From a single branch, the condition can spread to infect the entire tree, stunting or even killing it.

Cause: Apple mosaic virus is thought to be spread by sap-sucking insects such as aphids, lacebugs, or leafhoppers. If caught in the early stages, it can be eliminated, but once the entire tree is infected, there is no cure.

Solution: Remove the affected parts.

● Prune and destroy the infected shoots as early as possible to control disease spread.

Leaves have small brown spots with yellow edges

Problem: Leaves have small brown spots and blotches, edged in yellow. Later, triangular parts turn brown and fall out.

Cause: Japanese leafhoppers feed on the leaf undersides as small, white-spotted, brown nymphs. Adults are gray and active, moving quickly if disturbed. Damage can be severe and weaken the tree.

Solution: Spray to control leafhoppers.

● Spray with the botanical insecticide neem in late May or when you first spot damage. Make sure the spray hits the leaf undersides. Follow label directions carefully.

Leaves are tied together

Problem: Leaves are pulled together and tied with fine silk threads. An insect feeding inside distorts the leaves.

Cause: Obliquebanded leafrollers attack a wide range of trees and shrubs. Larvae roll the leaves into a tight cylinder and also feed on the terminal bud at the tips of shoots. In the North, eggs hatch in late June or July and spread from tree to tree on silken parachutes. They overwinter under the scales covering winter buds. There may be several generations a year in the South.

Solution: Spray to control leafrollers.

● Spray with the botanical insecticide neem as soon as you see damage. The protective rolled leaves make them hard to kill.

● Spray with dormant oil in late winter to kill overwintering pests.

Leaves have red-yellow spots

Problem: Pale yellow spots appear on leaves. They are round at first but may become irregularly shaped later. The leaf surface becomes thickened. Eventually orange cups appear on the leaf undersides, below the spots.

Cause: Cedar-apple rust is caused by a fungus that spends part of its life cycle on eastern red cedar or other junipers and part on mountain ash or other rose-family members.

Solution: Spray the mountain ash. Eliminate or prune alternate-host junipers.

● Spray with an organic sulfur fungicide or with a synthetic fungicide registered for mountain ashes that contains the active ingredient ferbam. Or use a mix of the two. Spray several times at seven- to ten-day intervals, starting as soon as leaves open fully. Follow label directions carefully. Do not spray when rain is likely.

● If possible, remove junipers, the alternate host plants, from your yard.

● Or in winter, prune juniper twigs that have dark red-brown round growths, or galls.

Leaves appear burned

Problem: On one or several shoots, leaves wilt and rapidly turn brown but remain hanging. Flowers may look water soaked, and branches may have cankers.

Cause: Fireblight, named for the scorched appearance of the leaves, is a bacterial disease widespread in North America, especially on mountain ash and other rose-family members. But the risk is reduced if a tree is kept growing strongly and free from other pests and diseases. The retention of leaves and a reddish brown discoloration of sapwood help to identify fireblight.

Solution: Prune and spray, but don't fertilize.

- Prune branches, cutting well below the infected area. Look for unstained wood. Disinfect (p.310) tools between cuts.
- Spray organic fungicides with antibiotic properties—lime sulfur in winter and copper hydroxide in spring as leaves unfurl. Follow label directions carefully.
- Avoid fertilizing in early spring (or use a slow-release fertilizer); the resulting lush growth is especially prone to fireblight.

Small larvae eat leaves

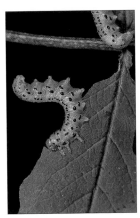

Problem: In early to midsummer, leaves are devoured by colonies of small green caterpillars that eat all the leaf except the midvein, starting from the edge.

Cause: Mountain ash sawfly larvae emerge from May to July and lay eggs near the leaf edges. The larvae feed in groups; there may be several sizes present, depending on when they hatched. After stripping one branch, they all move onto a fresh one. A severe attack can quickly defoliate a tree, making it vulnerable to other diseases. A second generation may appear in late August or September.

Solution: Spray the tree with insecticide to control the larvae.

- Spray with insecticidal soap until the larvae are no longer present. Follow label directions carefully.
- Or spray with synthetic insecticide registered for mountain ashes that contains the active ingredient methoxychlor or carbaryl. Follow label directions carefully.

Knobby swellings form on trunk or branches

Problem: Swollen, knobby growths develop on the trunk or branches. They grow larger each year but don't seem to affect the tree's growth.

Cause: Crown gall is a bacterial disease that attacks many trees, especially ones in the rose family. The growths, called galls, are spongy at first, but with age, they become hard, rough, and fissured—and grow larger. In mountain ash, crown gall is seldom a serious problem. But it weakens the tree, making it susceptible to other diseases.

Solution: Prune the galls and spray the tree.

- Cut out the galls if you can do so without creating large wounds.
- Spray the tree when dormant with organic lime-sulfur, which has antibiotic properties. Follow label directions carefully.

Oak

Quercus spp.

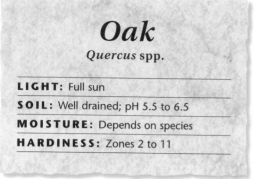

LIGHT: Full sun

SOIL: Well drained; pH 5.5 to 6.5

MOISTURE: Depends on species

HARDINESS: Zones 2 to 11

Foliage is distorted or has brown blotches

Problem: Newly opened leaves become twisted and shriveled. Fully opened leaves develop brown spots and blotches that spread along leaf veins. In cool, wet springs, lower branches are affected first and the disease then spreads upward. Leaves may fall early, causing more stress.

Cause: Oak anthracnose is a fungal disease most prevalent on species of white oak, particularly eastern white oak (*Q. alba*). But this and similar diseases will attack many others, including some live oaks (*Q. virginiana*). While it is a problem in spring, infection can occur in summer on new growth, especially if the tree suffered early defoliation.

Solution: Spray fungicide and practice good garden sanitation to discourage infections.

- In spring, spray with an organic copper-sulfate fungicide. Follow label directions carefully. Spray first when leaves unfurl, when they are half open, and again when they reach full size.
- Rake up and dispose of all fallen foliage.

Small branches clutter ground under a tree

Problem: In late summer, the ground under the tree becomes littered with small branches that have cleanly cut ends.

Cause: Twig pruners are the small wood-boring larvae of one or more species of beetle. After the beetle lays eggs near the twig tip in spring, the larvae burrow into the twig and eat their way down the center. Because the sap flow is not affected at this stage, leaves do not wilt or turn brown. In late summer, the larvae chew through the wood at the base of the twig, which breaks off in the wind with the larvae inside and drops to the ground.

Solution: Practice good garden sanitation.

- Collect and burn fallen twigs to destroy the larvae that overwinter in them.

Sunken areas develop on bark

Problem: Areas of bark are recessed and yellow in color. On a young oak, the depressions start small but grow rapidly, often girdling the trunk and killing the tree. On a larger tree, the areas spread slowly while the tree is dormant and are walled off by the new growth in spring, only to spread again the following winter. This results in a sunken depression with layers of bark around the edges. The depressions are often on old branch stubs.

Cause: Strumella canker is a serious fungal disease in young oaks. On older trees, the cankers appear as areas of missing bark with rotten wood in the center.

Solution: Remove infected areas and keep the tree healthy to discourage the fungus.

- Prune infected branches where possible. Cut out small cankers on the trunk if you catch them at an early stage.
- Fertilize the tree in spring with a granular, balanced fertilizer, such as a 10-10-10 formulation (p.324). Water deeply (p.273) once a week during dry periods.

Raised blisters develop on leaf surfaces

Problem: Upper surfaces of leaves have many raised, yellowish blisters. On the underside of each leaf is a corresponding round, brownish depression.

Cause: Oak leaf blister is a fungal disease that most often attacks in cool, wet springs and can affect nearly all species of red oak (*Q. rubra*). The leaves rarely fall early and seem able to carry out their normal function, so the tree is not weakened to any great extent.

Solution: Remove fallen leaves and, if necessary, spray a fungicide to limit damage.

● Rake up and destroy infected foliage that falls to the ground.

● If the attack is serious, spray with an organic copper-sulfate fungicide once in early spring. Or apply a synthetic fungicide registered for oaks that contains the active ingredient maneb or ziram as buds open. Follow label directions carefully.

Leaves are eaten by dark caterpillars

Problem: Masses of dark, hairy caterpillars rapidly consume oak leaves.

Cause: Gypsy moth caterpillars are extremely destructive. The pests originated on the East Coast and are quickly spreading across the United States. Although oaks and apples are their preferred food, the caterpillars will feed on just about anything, including grass if no other food source is available. They feed for about seven weeks, moving from plant to plant, and then pupate, often on the host tree. After emerging in midsummer, the flightless females mate and then crawl up the tree to lay eggs in crevices or on the undersides of branches.

Solution: Spray caterpillars. In winter, remove eggs and attract bird predators.

● Spray caterpillars with the biological insecticide BTK when you see them. Or use a botanical insecticide, such as neem or pyrethrum. Follow label directions carefully.

● If the problem persists, spray with a synthetic insecticide registered for oaks that contains the active ingredient cyfluthrin, acephate, methoxychlor, or carbaryl. Follow label directions carefully.

● In winter, look for tan, fuzzy egg masses on tree limbs and scrape them off.

● Set up bird feeders to attract winter birds, such as chickadees, so that they can feed on eggs you may have missed.

WISE CHOICES

As a tree matures, its far-reaching roots can actually buckle pavement. To avoid this, don't plant shallow-rooted or fast-growing trees near streets, driveways, or sidewalks. As a rule, keep a small tree 5 feet away from a paved surface. Keep a medium to large tree 10 feet away. Here are some trees that make good neighbors for sidewalks and driveways.

Small to Medium Trees (under 30 feet tall)
- Apple serviceberry, *Amelanchier × grandiflora* 'Princess Diana' or 'Autumn Brilliance'
- Eastern redbud, *Cercis canadensis*
- European mountain ash, *Sorbus aucuparia* 'Cardinal Royal'
- Flowering crab apple, *Malus* 'Adirondack' or 'Red Baron'
- Flowering plum, *Prunus cerasifera* 'Newport'
- Goldenrain, *Koelreuteria paniculata*
- Japanese snowbell, *Styrax japonica*
- Kousa dogwood, *Comus kousa* 'Ballerina' or 'Par Four'

Medium to Large Trees
- European hornbeam, *Carpinus betulus* 'Fatigiata'
- Ginkgo (or maidenhair), *Ginkgo biloba* 'Autumn Gold' or 'Princeton Sentry'
- Katsura, *Cerdidiphyllum japonicum*
- Red oak, *Quercus rubra*
- Scarlet oak, *Q. coccinea*
- Swamp white oak, *Q. bicolor*

REGIONAL FOCUS
SOUTHEAST

In the Southeast, a fungal disease similar to oak anthracnose (facing page) has varying symptoms. On some species (laurel, pin, Shumard, water, and willow oak), the leaf disease may show up as small dark spots on leaves varying from a pinpoint to ⅛ inch in diameter. The spots may have a yellowish halo. Infected spots may fall from the leaves in some species, giving a shot-hole effect. Although the symptoms vary, the treatment is the same as for anthracnose.

A twig-girdling beetle in southern California attacks live oaks. The larvae tunnel just below the bark, spiraling down the twig to the base. Because the sapwood is destroyed, the leaves wilt and die. The crown may contain many small dead branches. The larvae feed for two years and pupate inside the attached twigs.

A healthy tree is more resistant to beetle attacks. Keep a tree watered (facing page), especially during extreme droughts. Feed it at the beginning of the growing season with a granular, balanced fertilizer, such as a 10-10-10 formulation (p.324).

Leaves wilt and quickly fall

Problem: Leaves at the top of the tree suddenly wilt and fall. They may turn brown or curl first, or just turn brown at the tips or along the veins. Cut branches reveal brown streaks.

Cause: Oak wilt is a fungal disease most virulent in red oaks (*Q. rubra*), often killing trees within a year. It will also attack other oaks, though the white oak (*Q. alba*) is fairly resistant. This disease is most common in the Midwest, but sap-sucking insects can carry it to other regions.

Solution: Have the tree professionally treated or remove an infected tree.

- Have a tree-care professional inject the tree with the synthetic fungicide propiconazole, the only effective chemical control.
- Or cut down and dispose of the infected tree. This disease is most virulent early in the season; remove the tree as soon as possible to control its spread, and dig a trench between the stump and surrounding oaks.

Leaves or twigs have unusual, swollen growths

Problem: Unusual swellings or growths develop on leaves or twigs. The growths can vary in size from small bumps to apple-size swellings on leaves or the branches. The growths are often brown and may be round or conical.

Cause: Galls, as the growths are known, are the home of insect larvae. Oaks are one of the favorite host plants for many species of wasps and midges. The insects lay their eggs on the tree; the larvae that emerge produce a chemical that causes plant cells to multiply rapidly, forming the growths that house them. Unless galls are formed around a shoot, most are more unsightly than harmful.

Solution: Remove infested branches and, in a severe case, spray with insecticide.

- Prune off and dispose of heavily infested branches during the summer, especially where the galls are on the branch itself.
- If necessary, spray the tree with a synthetic insecticide registered for oaks that contains the active ingredient carbaryl. Follow label directions carefully.

Leaves are yellow between veins

Problem: Leaves open normally but quickly turn a yellowish green. The veins remain green, but the entire tree resembles a golden variety.

Cause: Chlorosis is an iron deficiency caused by alkaline soil. Iron is a major part of the green chlorophyll in leaves. Without iron, the leaves cannot function properly, and they turn yellow. Iron becomes unavailable to the tree as the pH (p.329) increases and the soil becomes more alkaline. Even though iron may be present, the tree's roots cannot absorb it. Pin (*Q. palustris*), scarlet (*Q. coccinea*), and red oak (*Q. rubra*) in particular are subject to chlorosis when grown on soils with a pH above 6.5. Members of the red oak group need more iron than do white oaks (*Q. alba*), and they grow best in acidic soils.

Solution: Treat with an iron supplement for a quick improvement. For the longer term, take measures to make the soil more acidic.

- Spray the foliage with iron chelate, a soluble form of iron that can be absorbed through the leaves, or have an arborist install iron implants into the tree to restore green to the leaves.
- Every spring, drench the soil with iron chelate around the root zone of the tree.
- Mulch under the tree with pine needles or partly rotted oak leaves to increase the soil acidity. Don't let the mulch, which can harbor some diseases, touch the tree trunk.
- Test the soil pH (p.329) and add sulfur as needed to lower the pH to 5.5 to 6.5.

CARING FOR TREES

Basic tree care involves proper selection, planting, watering, fertilizing, and pruning. When planting a new tree, try to do it when the roots are actively growing, but while the top is dormant, in early spring. Or plant the tree when the top has matured after its summer growth flush, in the fall. Roots grow when soil is above 40°F.

PLANTING NEW TREES

Dig a planting hole at least as wide as the tree's canopy and as deep as the height of the root ball. Set the tree no deeper than it grew in the nursery, or slightly higher in poorly drained soil. Crumble the soil removed from the hole and fill around the tree, compacting the soil only enough to remove air pockets. Mound some of the soil a foot or so from the trunk of the tree, forming a levee. Fill the basin inside the levee with water to settle the soil.

WATERING TREES

Water new trees during the growing season, whenever there is less than an inch of rain in a week, by filling the basin. Increase the irrigation by 1 inch for each inch of the trunk diameter until a sudden spurt of growth indicates that the tree is established. An established tree adapted to your region should only need supplemental watering during severe droughts. An occasional deep soaking of 1 inch of water during hot weather will help the tree resist pests and diseases.

Apply a 3-inch layer of organic mulch, such as wood chips, to smother weeds and reduce evaporation. Keep the mulch from touching the trunk to keep trapped moisture from fostering diseases.

FERTILIZING TREES

A tree growing in average soil with good drainage and a pH (acidity) suited to the species does not need supplemental fertilizer. If soil tests (p.329) reveal nutrient deficiencies, periodic fertilization will increase a tree's health and vigor. Scatter nitrogen fertilizer on the ground under and beyond the tree crown annually, at a rate of 3 pounds of nitrogen per 1,000 square feet of ground. The first number in a fertilizer analysis is the percentage of nitrogen, so if an analysis of 10-10-10 contains 10 percent nitrogen, applying 100 pounds of fertilizer will yield 10 pounds of nitrogen. Add other amendments as indicated by a soil test.

PRUNING TREES

Pruning usually is better for the tree if done with restraint. Remove dead or diseased branches and thin those that rub against each other or restrict air and light inside the crown. Gradually raise the crown by removing lower branches over several years, always leaving at least 60 percent of the crown intact. Then enjoy the shade.

Ornamental Cherry and Plum

Prunus spp.

LIGHT: Full sun

SOIL: Well drained; pH 6.0 to 7.5

MOISTURE: Consistently moist

HARDINESS: Zones 2 to 10

Trunk exudes amber, sticky gum

Problem: Trunk or branches exude a sticky, yellow gum. Tree grows poorly; leaves turn yellow.

Cause: Gummosis is caused by two borers. The greater peach tree borer burrows into the base of the trunk and upper roots; the lesser peach tree borer burrows along the trunk.

Solution: Remove or treat larvae.

- Push wire into holes to spear larvae.

- Inject beneficial nematodes (p.126), a biological control, into borer tunnels. Or spray with a synthetic insecticide registered for cherry and plum trees that contains chlorpyrifos in May and June for lesser peach tree borer or in August for greater peach tree borer. Follow label directions carefully.

Leaves are curled and distorted

Problem: New leaves are twisted, curled, or deformed and have clear, sticky spots. Leaves may also have black, sooty areas.

Cause: Black cherry aphids are tiny, pear-shaped insects that feed in masses, sucking sap from tender new growth, causing buds and leaves to curl. The sticky, clear waste, called honeydew, secreted by aphids, is an ideal growing medium for sooty mold, which blocks off light, causing leaves to yellow and drop prematurely. Feeding aphids weaken mature trees and can kill young ones.

Solution: Hose off aphids. Spray and use beneficial predators.

- Knock off aphids with a stream of water.

- Spray leaves with insecticidal soap. Follow label directions carefully.

- In winter, spray bark with dormant oil to kill overwintering aphid eggs.

- In spring, release insect predator lacewings (p.103), available from garden catalogs.

Web appears in branch fork

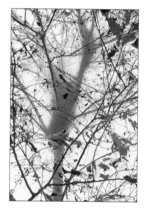

Problem: A mass of silken threads appears in the forks of branches. Feeding on nearby leaves are hairy, black caterpillars, each with a white stripe bordered by brown on their back, and blue-dotted sides.

Cause: Tent caterpillars overwinter as shiny egg masses on a small twig. After hatching, the young spin a silken nest at a branch fork. The caterpillars go out to feed during the day and return to the nest at night. A severe attack can defoliate a tree. There are similar-looking tent caterpillars both east and west of the Mississippi River.

Solution: Spray caterpillars, nests, and eggs.

- During the day, spray feeding caterpillars with the biological insecticide BT or BTK. Follow label directions carefully.

- If you spray in the evening or on a damp day, break open the nest with a stick and spray it with the botanical insecticide pyrethrum or with a synthetic insecticide registered for cherry or plum trees that contains the active ingredient bendiocarb, carbaryl, malathion, or methoxychlor. Follow label directions carefully.

- Spray susceptible trees with dormant oil in winter to kill the overwintering egg masses.

Leaves are covered with small, blister-shaped swellings

Problem: Leaves are liberally sprinkled with small, raised swellings.

Cause: Gall mites, also called blister mites, feed in mass, sucking sap from the leaves of trees, weakening them and causing the small, blister-like swellings on leaves. The minute spider relatives are most active in dry weather.

Solution: Hose off mites and, if needed, spray.

- Hose foliage with a strong stream of water frequently to dislodge mites.
- If symptoms are severe, spray with insecticidal soap. Or apply a synthetic insecticide registered for cherry or plum trees that contains the active ingredient diazinon. Follow label directions carefully.
- In early spring, spray the bark with dormant oil or an organic lime-sulfur fungicide, which has insecticidal properties, to kill eggs. Follow label directions carefully.

Black growths form on branches

Problem: Branches have irregular black growths that start small but spread downward. Cankers with small black eruptions may also appear on trunk and limbs.

Cause: Black knot is a serious fungal disease. Infected trees that are untreated will die, and fungus on dead wood can infect others.

Solution: Prune and spray with fungicide.

- Prune and dispose of infected branches in winter, cutting 6 inches below the knots.
- Spray a synthetic fungicide registered for cherry or plum trees that contains the active ingredient benomyl. Spray in spring before buds open. Then spray twice again at 7- to 10-day intervals. Follow label directions carefully.

Leaves are sprinkled with holes of varying sizes

Problem: The leaves are riddled with holes of various shapes, and the leaf edges may be ragged.

Cause: Caterpillars of various species eat the leaves of cherry and plum trees as well as other trees in the *Prunus* genus.

Solution: Handpicking and spraying are the best controls for caterpillars.

- If the infestation is light and the tree is small, handpick and dispose of caterpillars.
- Spray larger populations with the biological control BT or BTK while the pests are small.
- In winter, spray bark with dormant oil or an organic lime-sulfur fungicide, which has insecticidal qualities, to kill eggs. Follow label directions carefully.

Leaves yellow and curl; twigs form witches' brooms

Problem: Leaves of a Japanese, yedo, or pin cherry thicken, turn yellow or pink, and pucker. Later, twigs swell and may grow many side shoots to form small witches' brooms.

Cause: Leaf blister is a fungal disease related to peach leaf curl (p.307). Brooms don't always develop, but typically they are small and numerous. They tend to grow leaves early, making them susceptible to late frosts.

Solution: Remove brooms and spray.

- Prune and destroy the brooms. Cut well below the swollen part of the stem.
- Spray with a synthetic fungicide registered for cherry or plum trees that contains the active ingredient ziram. Follow label directions carefully.

Ornamental Pear

Pyrus calleryana

LIGHT: Full sun

SOIL: Well drained; pH 6.0 to 7.5

MOISTURE: Seasonally moist

HARDINESS: Zones 5 to 8

Wind damages tree badly

Problem: A mature tree is badly damaged by a storm that doesn't harm other trees.

Cause: Narrow branch forks of pears are prone to splitting after about 20 years. This is especially a problem with the variety 'Bradford', on which many branches emerge in a short trunk area.

Solution: Replace damaged tree; prune well.

- Cut down and remove the damaged tree.
- Replace it with a variety that has a wider wind-resistant branch angle (box, below).
- Prune young trees to reduce the number of crowded branches.

WISE CHOICES

The chances of disease or other problems on an ornamental pear are often determined by the variety that you select. Here are some to consider.

- 'Aristocrat'—resists storm damage but is susceptible to fireblight
- 'Autumn Blaze'—good fall color but susceptible to fireblight
- 'Chanticleer'—resists storm damage and also fireblight
- 'Fauriei'—susceptible to storm damage and has slow growth rate
- 'Paradise'—resists storm damage

Leaves curl downward and have a purplish color

Problem: The tree lacks vigor. Leaves curl downward, have a purplish tinge, and may fall prematurely.

Cause: Pear decline is an incurable disease caused by a microscopic organism known as a mycoplasma-like organism, or MLO. It can rapidly kill a fruiting pear, but an ornamental pear in otherwise good health is generally able to survive for many years. The disease is probably spread by sap-sucking insects and dirty pruning tools.

Solution: Keep an infected tree healthy to extend its life. Protect other trees.

- Feed the tree each spring with a nitrogen-rich fertilizer (p.324), such as 10-5-5.
- Provide the equivalent of 1 inch of water a week (p.273) during dry spells.
- Deal with other diseases promptly.
- Sterilize (p.310) pruners after using them to avoid infecting other trees.

Leaves at branch tips are brown

Problem: In summer, branch-end leaves and sometimes the tip of a branch turn brown and hang down but do not fall.

Cause: Fireblight, a bacterial disease to which pears are prone, takes its name from the scorched appearance of the leaves. It is identifiable by the retention of wilted leaves and a reddish brown discoloration of wood beneath the bark.

Solution: Prune and spray to control fireblight. Plant resistant varieties.

- Prune infected branch tips, cutting back into wood that does not have a brown stain. Sterilize (p.310) pruners between cuts.
- Spray organic lime-sulfur, a fungicide with antibiotic properties, in spring before leaves unfurl. Follow label directions carefully.
- Plant resistant varieties (box, left).

Palm
Various genera

LIGHT: Full sun

SOIL: Well drained; pH 6.0 to 7.5

MOISTURE: Seasonally dry

HARDINESS: Zones 8 to 11

Plant wilts; fronds droop

Problem: The plant seems wilted. Fronds droop on the entire plant. Large fruiting bodies are at the trunk's base.

Cause: Butt rot, an incurable fungal disease, is especially prevalent on queen palms and is related to fungi that cause heart rot in hardwoods. The disease is soilborne and typically enters through wounds at the tree base, often caused by lawn mowers.

Solution: Destroy the infected tree and protect healthy trees.

- Remove and destroy an infected palm.
- Don't plant another palm in the same spot for several years, or remove the soil and replace with fresh.
- Remove grass from around healthy palms to avoid mower damage.

Fronds have brown patches

Problem: The mature fronds have small to large brown patches, and their undersides have a loose, wrinkled look. Fronds seldom die, but they become unsightly.

Cause: Palm leaf skeletonizers are small moths whose larvae are one of palms' most destructive pests. With no season-related life cycle, they are active year-round; successive generations feed on frond undersides. Eggs are laid on the underside. On hatching, the young feed in the protection of the egg case, then congregate and spin a fine, protective web with a wrinkled appearance. Larvae feed on the leaf, expanding their web as they grow, and pupate while attached to the leaf.

Solution: Prune infested fronds and spray.

- Prune and destroy badly infested fronds.
- Spray fronds with insecticidal soap or the biological insecticide BT. Or use a synthetic insecticide registered for palms that contains the active ingredient carbaryl. Follow label directions carefully. Spray several times to kill all stages of the pest.

Fronds have yellow spots with black scabs

Problem: Fronds develop yellow spots that may run together. Each spot has a small black scabby area with a hard outer coating.

Cause: False smut, a fungal disease, attacks many palms and is most serious in regions with high summer humidity. Badly infected fronds may die and fall, but not before releasing spores to infect other leaves.

Solution: Prune infected fronds and spray to control false smut.

- Remove or trim back infected fronds.
- Spray fronds with an organic copper-sulfate fungicide. Follow label directions carefully.

REGIONAL FOCUS
SOUTHWEST

One fungus (*Penicillium vermoeseni*) attacks several species of palm with different results. On queen palm, it causes an unseen trunk canker that weakens the plant until it blows down. On Canary Island date palm, it rots the bases of the leaves. On Washington palm, it causes a bud rot on new growth. To control the disease, have a professional inject the tree with a synthetic fungicide registered for palms that contains the active ingredient carbendazim.

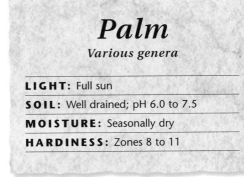

Pine

Pinus spp.

LIGHT: Full sun

SOIL: Well drained; pH 5.5 to 6.5

MOISTURE: Seasonally moist

HARDINESS: Zones 2 to 9

Branches die, and damaged bark oozes resin

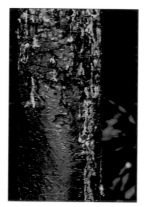

Problem: A mature tree has some dead branches. The bark becomes blistered and turns brown. Bark may exude a clear liquid or a resin and have streaks of white, crystallized resin.

Cause: White pine blister rust is a destructive fungal disease that attacks all five-needle pines, including eastern white (*P. strobus*), western white (*P. monticola*), Japanese white (*P. parviflora*), bristlecone (*P. aristata*), limber (*P. flexilis*), sugar (*P. lambertiana*), and Swiss stone (*P. cembra*). In larger trees, infection is usually limited to branches or upper limbs, but white pine blister rust often kills small trees. The fungus is most active in cool, moist weather. Currants and gooseberries are its alternate host. It takes four to six years to complete its life cycle, spending half the time on each host.

Solution: Prune infected parts and remove host plants.

- Prune and destroy badly infected branches.
- Remove small areas of infected bark, cutting into healthy bark 2 inches on each side and 4 inches above and below damage.
- If a branch is infected within 6 inches of the trunk, remove a circle of bark around the branch stub, cutting into the trunk.
- Remove all currant and gooseberry bushes growing within several hundred feet.

Tree has dead branch tips in spring

Problem: In late fall, the shoot tips start to yellow. By spring, they turn reddish brown and die, but needles stay on branches until late summer when they fall.

Cause: Pine twig blight is a fungal disease that is also called pruning disease because it kills the lower branches and thus prunes the tree. Once the needles have fallen, small black fruiting bodies appear on the shoots and release spores to infect healthy shoots.

Solution: Prune, spray, and fertilize the tree to control pine twig blight.

- Prune and destroy infected shoots. Work on a dry day to avoid spreading the disease.
- Immediately after the infected needles fall, spray with an organic copper fungicide or with a synthetic fungicide registered for pines that contains the active ingredient benomyl. Spray three times at weekly intervals. Follow label directions carefully.
- Fertilize the tree in early spring with a balanced fertilizer, such as a 10-10-10 formulation (p.324) to encourage strong growth.

Tips of new growth turn brown in summer

Problem: New growth turns brown at the tip. On close examination, you find a mass of pitch-covered silk at the tip. New growing tips, called candles, may be deformed, or new growth may be curled. Bushy, stunted growth may result from the dying growth tips. If the attack is severe, the entire tree may have a reddish cast due to the dying needles.

Cause: European pine shoot moth larvae tunnel into growing tips and kill them. The small brown adult moth lays eggs at the bases of new needles in spring. The tree weeps pitch through the wounds. Larvae overwinter and pupate inside the shoot. Loss of the growing tips causes secondary buds to grow, giving the branch a bushier look. Mugo (*P. mugo*), red (*P. resinosa*), Austrian (*P. nigra*), Scotch (*P. sylvestris*), and Japanese black (*P. thunbergi*) are the pines most susceptible to attack.

Solution: Prune and spray insecticide.

● Prune infested shoots in May and June.

● In April or early May, spray with insecticidal soap or with a synthetic insecticide registered for pines that contains the active ingredient diazinon or carbaryl. Follow label directions carefully.

Stems have swollen regions, and shoots are deformed

Problem: Globular swellings, or galls, emerge on shoots, branches, or the main stem. Tips of shoots look inflated. The needles may die or the growth may proliferate, forming twiggy branch clusters called witches' brooms.

Cause: Western gall rust is a fungal disease found all across North America, not just in the West. Severe attacks can kill the tree. There is no known alternate host for this fungus as there is for most rusts; the entire reproductive cycle takes place on one plant.

Solution: Remove infected plant parts and spray to help control this disease.

● Prune and destroy all infected shoots and galls on the plant.

● Spray the foliage with a synthetic fungicide registered for pines that contains the active ingredient mancozeb. Follow label directions carefully.

● As new growth emerges next spring, spray the tree with organic wettable sulfur fungicide to control the spread of spores. Spray three times, at 10-day intervals. Follow label directions carefully.

Tips of branches turn yellow, and lower branches die

Problem: In spring, new growth yellows and dies. Branch tips are stunted and resin soaked. Small black growths mar the needles. Lower branches may die. The affliction is most common on Austrian (*P. nigra*), ponderosa (*P. ponderosa*), and Scotch (*P. sylvestris*) pines, but others are susceptible.

Cause: Tip blight is a serious fungal disease. In young trees, the disease enters the main shoot, killing the

---

WISE CHOICES

Pine trees offer far more to a landscape than rugged good looks. Different species and varieties provide form and style to settings ranging from small rock gardens and Oriental gardens to low-growing foundation plantings and salt- and wind-tolerant seaside plantings. The following pines combine attractiveness with a minimum of problems.

• Japanese black pine (*Pinus thunbergii*) is hardy from zones 5 to 8. It grows 12 to 18 inches a year, reaching a mature height of 30 feet with a spread of 20 feet. The cultivar 'Majestic Beauty' tolerates smog and salt spray, making it an excellent choice for urban plantings or coastal gardens.

• Japanese red pine (*P. densiflora*) is hardy from zones 3 to 7. With an annual growth of less than 12 inches, it reaches a mature height of 50 feet with a spread of 50 feet. The cultivar 'Umbraculifera' (Tanyosho pine) has scaly, orange bark and multiple stems reaching 15 feet tall and topped with a dense, flat canopy of deep green needles.

• Swiss stone pine (*P. cembra*) is hardy from zones 4 to 7. It grows less than 12 inches a year, reaching a mature height of 35 feet with a spread of 15 feet. The cultivar 'Pygmaea' has a compact, pyramidal shape and is very slow growing, adding only about 3 inches each year.

If your Monterey pine (*Pinus radiata*) or bishop pine (*P. muricata*) has a brownish cast, it may be due to the pine needle weevil. This small beetle eats the base of year-old needles in late winter, causing browning. The damage usually ceases by early summer, and young foliage is not affected. At the first sign of attack, spray the botanical insecticide pyrethrum or a synthetic insecticide registered for pines that contains the active ingredient carbaryl or malathion. Follow label directions carefully.

plant. In mature trees, the disease attacks two-year-old cones, which become brown and covered with black fruiting bodies. Cones are often infected before symptoms appear on needles. On healthy trees, the dieback from tip blight is limited to shoot tips. But weak trees sustain much more damage.

Solution: Control tip blight with pruning, sprays, and good gardening practices.

- Prune infected growth and destroy the clippings. Prune when the needles are dry to avoid spreading spores.
- Spray the tree with a synthetic fungicide registered for pines that contains the active ingredient thiophanate-methyl. Follow label directions carefully.
- As new growth appears in spring, spray with an organic copper fungicide, such as copper sulfate. Repeat twice, at weekly intervals. Follow label directions carefully.
- In spring, fertilize with a 10-5-5 formulation (p.324), and water during dry periods to equal 1 inch per week (p.273).

Branches have white patches

Problem: Undersides of branches develop white fuzzy patches. The bark on the main trunk of a mature pine turns white in larger patches.

Cause: Pine bark adelgids, which are sap-sucking insects related to aphids, overwinter as eggs under a protective woolly cover. In spring, eggs hatch, and the young crawl to a new feeding spot and cover themselves with a cottony coat. There may be several generations each summer, and an infestation can spread rapidly.

Solution: Spray to control pine bark adelgids.

- Spray the tree with synthetic insecticide registered for pines that contains the active ingredient chlorpyrifos. Follow label directions carefully.
- In early spring, spray with dormant oil to smother overwintering eggs.

Needles have yellow spots

Problem: In spring, older needles on the lower branches develop yellow patches. In a severe case, the entire needle may be yellow. Small white pustules appear on the yellow portion, eventually opening to release spores.

Cause: Needle rust is a fungal disease. Spores released from the needles of two-needle pine (*P. edulis*) infect the alternate host, members of the daisy family, especially asters and goldenrod. On these plants, the fungus releases spores in late summer to reinfect pines, but symptoms aren't obvious until spring. The disease is found coast to coast. In California and Oregon, a related fungus attacks Coulter (*P. coulteri*), Jeffrey (*P. jeffreyi*), and Monterey (*P. radiata*) pines.

Solution: Spray fungicide and remove hosts.

- In early spring, spray with an organic sulfur fungicide. Follow label directions carefully.
- Remove and destroy any asters or goldenrods growing near two-needle pines.
- Don't grow any ornamental plants in the daisy family, including China aster, golden aster, and fleabanes, for several years.

Numerous small holes weep resin on the trunk

Problem: Small holes on the trunk weep resin, and there may be wood dust present.

Cause: Pine bark beetles feed by tunneling just under the bark. Several species populate different parts of the country and attack pines at different heights above the ground, but the damage is similar. All tunnel under the bark and lay eggs; the larvae then feed on the sapwood. A single tree may be host to different species, and there may be up to nine generations a year in warm-winter climates. Bark beetles tend to attack pine trees that are in poor health.

Solution: Destroy a small tree. Debark spots and spray large trees. Keep pines healthy.

- Destroy a small tree if it is badly infected.

- If the tree is large, strip off bark in the infected areas and destroy exposed pests.

- Then spray a large infected tree with a synthetic pesticide registered for pines that contains the active ingredient chlorpyrifos. Follow label directions carefully.

- In spring, fertilize with a 10-5-5 formulation (p.324) to help keep the tree strong.

- During dry spells, water the tree to equal 1 inch of water each week (p.273).

- Thin groves for light and air circulation.

Needles are eaten; silk nests appear on branches

Problem: Masses of silk filled with bits of plant and also insect debris appear near the ends of the tree branches. Nearby needles have been completely eaten.

Cause: Webworms feed on pines across North America. Eggs are laid on the underside of needles, and the young insects tunnel into the needles. Eventually, they congregate and build nests. They pupate in the soil and emerge as small moths. There is one generation per year in the North, two in the South. This pest generally goes unnoticed until it forms nests, by which time spraying an insecticide is often necessary. To a limited extent, small populations of webworms can be ignored, but they may kill the growing tips of the tree.

Solution: Monitor a small infestation. Spray the tree and treat the soil with insecticide if the infestation becomes serious.

- If the infestation is small, wait and watch it closely to make sure that it doesn't spread.

- If the pests cause serious problems, break

open the nests with a stick and spray them during the day with insecticidal soap or the botanical insecticide pyrethrum. Or use a synthetic insecticide registered for pines that contains the active ingredient carbaryl. Follow label directions carefully.

- If the attack is severe, drench the soil under the tree in early spring with a synthetic insecticide registered for pines that contains the active ingredient diazinon to kill emerging moths. Follow label directions carefully.

Small larvae eat needles

Problem: In late spring and early summer, small white grubs with black spots and a red head defoliate the shoots.

Cause: Redheaded pine sawfly larvae are a major pest of many pines, but three other sawflies also attack pines, so you may find larvae of other colors. There is one generation per year in the North but up to three in the South. Larvae feed for about a month before dropping to the ground to pupate. But pupae of the redheaded pine sawfly may stay in a pupal stage for two years or more, so one treatment is no guarantee of future immunity.

Solution: Spray and treat soil with insecticide.

- Spray an infestation with insecticidal soap. Follow label directions carefully.

- Or spray with a synthetic insecticide registered for pines that contains the active ingredient chlorpyrifos. Follow label directions carefully.

- In spring, kill emerging adults by treating soil under the tree with a synthetic insecticide registered for pines that contains the active ingredient diazinon. Follow label directions carefully.

Spruce

Picea spp.

LIGHT: Full sun to light shade

SOIL: Well drained; pH 5.5 to 6.5

MOISTURE: Seasonally moist

HARDINESS: Zones 2 to 7

Green larvae eat needles

Problem: Needles are eaten by small caterpillar-like larvae. In severe cases, the tree may be completely defoliated. At best, its canopy has many patchy holes.

Cause: Sawfly larvae of two types feed on spruce trees. The yellow-headed sawfly larvae eat both new and old needles. A severe infestation can quickly defoliate a tree and may kill it. The larvae have a green-and-white striped body and a yellow head. The European spruce sawfly feeds only on old needles. Although it may make a tree look bare, it doesn't do serious damage. Its larvae have gray stripes and a black head. When they mature, the larvae of both species drop to the ground and pupate underground, emerging the following spring as small flies.

Solution: Use insecticide to control sawflies and their larvae.

- Spray with insecticidal soap or the botanical insecticide neem. Or use a synthetic insecticide registered for spruces that contains the active ingredient carbaryl. Follow label directions carefully.
- To kill the sawflies before they emerge in spring, treat the soil with a drench or crystals of a synthetic insecticide registered for spruces that contains the active ingredient diazinon. Follow label directions carefully.

Lower branches turn yellow and ooze white resin

Problem: Needles on lower branches turn yellow then brown. White resin oozes from the branches and often from the trunk. The disease spreads slowly up the tree. Dead branches retain their twigs and stand out against green ones.

Cause: Cytospora canker is a destructive fungal disease on Engelmann (*P. engelmannii*), Norway (*P. abies*), red (*P. rubens*), white (*P. glauca*), and Colorado (*P. pungens*) spruces. It spreads each year, moving up one tier of branches.

Solution: Remove damaged branches and spray fungicide to eliminate the disease.

- Prune branches below the diseased region, sterilizing the tool between cuts (p.310). Prune only in dry weather.
- Cut out cankers on trunk, removing bark well beyond the infected area.
- Spray with an organic copper fungicide three or four times in spring. Follow label directions carefully.

New growth is eaten, leaving bare twigs

Problem: Early in the season, small caterpillars feed on the shoots inside silken cocoons. Later, they feed openly, defoliating the twigs.

Cause: Spruce budworm is a destructive pest of conifers in the East. Related budworms are found throughout North America. Females can fly long distances to lay eggs in summer. The larvae overwinter in a silken nest. In spring, they feed on old, then new foliage, killing growing tips and sometimes the tree.

Solution: Control infestations of spruce or other budworms by spraying the infested tree with insecticides.

- Apply insecticidal soap when insects are first noticed. It will help other sprays to soak through the cocoons.

- Spray with the biological insecticide BTK or the botanical insecticide neem. Or use a synthetic insecticide registered for spruces that contains the active ingredient carbaryl. Follow label directions carefully.

Needles are mottled with tiny yellow spots

Problem: In both early summer and fall, the tree's older needles have a mottled appearance and are covered with tiny yellow spots. There may be fine webbing spread between the needles.

Cause: Spruce spider mites are tiny pests related to spiders—you may need a magnifying glass to see them. They mature quickly, and a few soon become many. They overwinter as eggs on twigs and needles.

Solution: Hose mites off tree and spray to control them.

- To dislodge spider mites, spray with a strong jet of water, especially on the underside of the branches. Repeat every few days to control newly hatched nymphs.

- Spray infested foliage with the botanical insecticide neem. Follow label directions carefully.

- In late winter, spray with dormant oil or organic lime-sulfur, a fungicide with insecticidal properties, to kill overwintering eggs. Follow label directions carefully. Don't use dormant oil on blue spruce; it removes the blue color.

- To control surviving mites, spray in spring with insecticidal soap. Follow label directions carefully.

Branches have small growths

Problem: Small growths, or galls, form on tips of Engelmann (*P. engelmannii*), Sitka (*P. sitchensis*), and Colorado (*P. pungens*) spruces. On Norway (*P. abies*), white (*P. glauca*), and red (*P. rubens*) spruces, they appear at the base of shoots.

Cause: Spruce gall adelgid, a tiny insect, causes unattractive, but not life-threatening, galls. It produces a second generation in summer and overwinters under bud scales. The Cooley spruce gall adelgid also lives on Douglas fir.

Solution: Spray and keep host trees apart.

- Spray with the botanical insecticide neem. Follow label directions carefully.

- In late summer, spray with insecticidal soap or with a synthetic insecticide registered for spruces that contains the active ingredient carbaryl to kill the second generation. Follow label directions carefully.

- In late winter, spray with an organic lime-sulfur pesticide to kill overwintering pests. Follow label directions carefully.

- Don't plant spruce near Douglas fir.

Small sacks hang on branches

Problem: Sacks, made with needles and silk, hang from branches. Needles are eaten.

Cause: Bagworms live in the sacks and partly emerge to feed. The wingless females can't fly, so an infected plant may host a large population.

Solution: Spray insecticide, trap, and handpick pests.

- Spray with the biological insecticide BTK.

- Place sticky bands (sold by garden suppliers) on the trunk and main branches to trap migrating females before they lay eggs.

- Handpick and destroy sacks in winter.

Willow

Salix spp.

LIGHT: Full sun

SOIL: Any; pH 5.5 to 7.0

MOISTURE: Wet to consistently moist

HARDINESS: Zones 2 to 8

Leaves are devoured by small black larvae

Problem: Sluglike larvae feed at first on the lower leaf surface but ultimately consume both sides of the leaf. They eat the green tissue, leaving a network of veins. Also, shiny black or metallic blue beetles may be eating irregular notches in leaves.

Cause: Willow leaf beetles overwinter as adults under loose tree bark or in leaf litter on the ground. In spring, they lay eggs that hatch into leaf-eating larvae. In warm climates, there can be up to four generations hatching each year.

Solution: Use good garden sanitation and spray insecticide to control larvae and beetles.

- Keep the area around the tree clear of fallen leaves.
- Spray with the botanical insecticide pyrethrum. Or use a synthetic insecticide registered for willows that contains the active ingredient rotenone, carbaryl, methoxychlor, chlorpyrifos, or acephate. Follow label directions carefully.
- In late winter, spray the tree's bark with dormant oil to kill overwintering beetles.

Undersides of leaves are spotted

Problem: Bright yellow spots develop mostly on lower leaf surfaces in late spring. Later, they turn brown and release dustlike spores. The infected leaves may fall early.

Cause: Rust is a fungal disease that alternates between willow and other hosts: currant, gooseberry, hemlock, or larch.

Solution: Use good garden sanitation and preventive spraying. Choose plants wisely.

- Destroy diseased foliage as it falls.
- In spring, spray with an organic copper or lime-sulfur fungicide as leaves unfurl. Follow label directions carefully.
- Don't plant rust-host plants near willows.

Knobby swellings appear on roots, trunk, or branches

Problem: Swollen, knobby growths form on the tree's roots, trunk, or branches. They grow larger year by year but don't seem to affect the tree's overall health or growth.

Cause: Crown gall is a widespread bacterial disease. In many plants, it attacks the roots or base of stems, but in willows it is also common above ground. The growths, or galls, are spongy when small, but enlarge each year becoming hard and fissured. In a willow, the disease is seldom serious, but it weakens the tree, making it susceptible to other diseases.

Solution: Remove galls and spray.

- Prune and dispose of branches with galls.
- In winter, spray the tree with organic lime-sulfur, a fungicide with antibiotic properties. Follow label directions carefully.

Zelkova, Japanese

Zelkova serrata

LIGHT: Full sun

SOIL: Deep, well drained; pH 6.0 to 7.5

MOISTURE: Consistently moist

HARDINESS: Zones 5 to 8

Young foliage turns black

Problem: Buds open normally but new foliage turns black and becomes distorted.

Cause: Frost damages unfurling zelkova leaves mostly during the first few years after planting. Established trees are less susceptible.

Solution: Protect vulnerable plants from cold, and choose new planting locations carefully.

- If a spring frost is forecast, protect tree with a tightly woven fabric floating row cover.
- If necessary, spray frozen leaves with cold water in the early morning to let them thaw gradually as the sun warms them.
- Don't plant a new zelkova in a low-lying frost pocket, such as at the base of a slope.

Branches fail to leaf out or leaves suddenly wilt

Problem: Most often on newly planted trees, some branches fail to grow leaves in spring or new leaves suddenly wilt and fall. Dark, sunken areas form on the bark. If left untreated, the dead branches develop coral pink spots. The tree may ultimately die.

Cause: Nectria canker is a fungal disease, called coral spot fungus in its later stages. It attacks trees weakened by transplant shock, other diseases, ice damage, or by sapsuckers, members of the woodpecker family.

Solution: Use good garden practices and spray with fungicide to control this disease.

- Check a tree for cankers during its first year after planting. Cut out any sunken areas of bark and dispose of them.
- If canker symptoms appear, spray the dormant tree with an organic lime-sulfur fungicide. Follow label directions carefully.

- Irrigate a newly planted tree as needed to equal 1 inch of water a week (p.273). Check it regularly for pests and diseases. Don't fertilize it for the first two years.

Leaves are skeletonized; upper surface remains

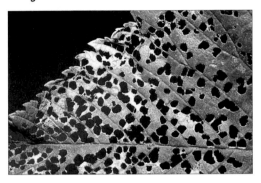

Problem: Starting in spring, the tree's leaves are skeletonized from the underside, leaving only the veins and upper surface. In a serious attack, the leaves curl and may fall early. New leaves, produced after a leaf fall, are eaten as they grow. Branches or the entire tree may die.

Cause: Elm leaf beetles emerge in spring and feed on the leaf undersides of Japanese zelkova trees. The female beetle lays up to 800 yellow eggs in small clusters. Larvae are black at first, becoming yellow with black stripes. They feed on lower leaves and pupate on the ground beneath the tree or on the bark. A second generation feeds in late summer and also pupates. The dark green, black-striped adults overwinter under bark or roof shingles or in garages or homes. In the South, there may be as many as three generations a year.

Solution: Spray with insecticide to control infestations of elm leaf beetles on zelkovas.

- Spray an infested tree with insecticidal soap. Follow label directions carefully.
- Spray a severe infestation with a synthetic insecticide registered for Japanese zelkova that contains the active ingredient carbaryl, bendiocarb, acephate, or methoxychlor. If needed, spray two or three times at one-week intervals to kill all larvae. Follow label directions carefully.

CHAPTER SEVEN

FRUITS AND NUTS

RUIT YOU PICK AT THE PEAK OF
ripeness and eat on the spot can be the
treat of a lifetime, whether they be juicy
strawberries, crisp delicious apples, or tree-ripened
peaches. Fruit and nut trees, grape vines, and berry
bushes need more care than most plants. And their
fruits are just as tasty to insects, birds, and four-
footed pests as they are to gardeners. These plants
often require special tactics to thwart pests and
diseases, ranging from bird netting to red, sticky
balls and pheromone traps that lure pests.

Always consult a local nursery for varieties
that resist the problems common to your area.
Practice careful garden sanitation, picking up
dropped fruit throughout the season and raking
away fallen leaves in autumn to keep pests from
overwintering near your trees, vines, or bushes.
Always use environmentally friendly solutions first.
For the safe use of commercial treatments on fruits
and nuts, see page 9 and pages 390 to 399.

Quick Troubleshooting Guide

FRUITS

FRUIT HAS HOLES OR IS EATEN

Cause: Bird, squirrel, or other animals

Solution: Protect plants by covering them with bird netting or wire mesh. Hang bars of soap to repel deer. Just before fruit ripens, hang disposable aluminum pie pans or reflective tape around plants to scare animals.

FRUIT HAS SMALL HOLES AND BLEMISHES

Cause: Grub, maggot, or other boring insects

Solution: Hang red balls coated with commercial tacky product, two to a plant, as fruit ripens. Destroy infested fruits. Cultivate soil under plants to destroy larvae.

FRUIT HAS VELVETY SPOTS OR CORKY LESIONS

Cause: Scab

Solution: Remove fruits infected with this fungal disease. Remove plant debris. Spray in spring with organic fungicide lime sulfur. Mulch and thin plants for air circulation.

FRUIT HAS SOFT SPOTS THAT MAY BE FUZZY

Cause: Fruit rot, gray mold

Solution: Remove fungal infected fruits. Drench the soil with anti-fungal compost tea. Spray organic fungicide Bordeaux mixture. Remove plant debris, spread mulch, and water at ground level to keep foliage dry.

FRUIT IS OF POOR QUALITY

Cause: Temperature or moisture extremes, nutrient deficiency

Solution: Test the soil and correct soil pH if needed. Water deeply when a week passes without rain. Apply a 3-inch-thick layer of mulch to conserve soil moisture. In spring, apply a balanced fertilizer.

FRUITS ARE SMALLER THAN NORMAL

Cause: Improper pruning or thinning

Solution: When the plant is dormant, prune it to a style appropriate for the species (p.293). Thin immature fruits one to two months after fruit set to encourage larger, but fewer, fruits.

LEAVES

LEAVES HAVE POWDERY SPOTS

Cause: Powdery mildew

Solution: Spray plant with the organic fungicide sulfur. Rinse spores off leaves daily. Thin dense clusters of stems to increase air circulation. Clean up plant debris in fall. In the future, select a disease-resistant variety.

SMALL REDDISH BROWN SPOTS APPEAR ON LEAVES

Cause: Anthracnose

Solution: Prune fungal infected leaves and stems. Spray an organic copper sulfate fungicide after harvest. Water at ground level with a soaker hose or drip irrigation to keep leaves dry. In the future, select disease-resistant plants.

LEAVES TURN YELLOW AND MAY DROP

Cause: Iron deficiency

Solution: Spray leaves and soil with chelated iron, following package directions. Test the soil; if it is alkaline, amend with sulfur to achieve the proper pH level for the plant and spread an acidic mulch.

LEAVES ARE MISSHAPEN AND STUNTED

Cause: Aphids

Solution: Prune and dispose of infested leaves and stems. Spray plant with insecticidal soap or the botanical insecticide neem. Spray plant with dormant oil in early spring, when leaf buds begin swelling but before they turn green.

LEAVES HAVE COTTONY GROWTHS

Cause: Downy mildew

Solution: Remove fungal infected leaves and stems. Spray organic fungicides copper sulfate or Bordeaux mixture just before bloom, just after bloom, and one week later. Clean up debris in fall.

LEAVES TURN BROWN AND LOOK SCORCHED

Cause: Fireblight

Solution: Prune stems 6 inches below the bacterial infection. Spray with antiseptic copper sulfate or Bordeaux mixture before blossoms open and repeat once a week until blossoms drop. Select disease-resistant varieties.

LEAVES ARE DISCOLORED; PLANT IS STUNTED OR WILTED

Cause: Root or crown rot, nematode, crown gall

Solution: Remove a dying plant. Before replanting, solarize the soil to kill nematodes and disease spores. In the future, select a variety resistant to root and crown rot.

TRUNK AND BRANCHES

LEAVES OR BARK HAVE PATCHES OF A WHITE, COTTONY COATING

Cause: Cottony cushion scale, wooly aphid, mealybug

Solution: Spray foliage and bark with insecticidal soap or synthetic insecticide labeled for the species. Spray horticultural oil in early spring.

GUMMY SAP OOZES FROM HEALTHY BRANCHES

Cause: Gummosis

Solution: Fruit trees, including cherry and peach, naturally ooze sap. Avoid injuring bark, allow soil to dry between waterings, and prune when tree is dormant to reduce the incidence of gummosis.

BARK HAS SUNKEN LESIONS; BRANCHES DIE

Cause: Bacterial or fungal canker

Solution: Prune and destroy the affected branch or stem, or scrape off diseased bark to expose healthy tissue. Spray the tree with organic copper sulfate. Remove plant debris and mulch, keeping mulch away from the trunk. Select a disease-resistant variety.

PLANT HAS PATCHES OF CRACKED OR DEAD BARK

Cause: Sunscald

Solution: Water and fertilize the plant to stimulate new growth. In the fall, wrap the trunk with paper tree wrap or paint trunk with white latex paint or whitewash to protect bark from winter sun.

BUMPS FORM ON TWIGS, LEAVES, AND FRUITS

Cause: Scale

Solution: Spray the botanical insecticide neem when young scale are active. Spray summer oil in early fall. Introduce lacewings, parasitic wasps, and other beneficial insects that prey on scale.

Apple
Malus spp.

LIGHT: Full sun

SOIL: Average, drained; pH 5.5 to 6.5

MOISTURE: Consistently moist

HARDINESS: Zones 3 to 11

Rotting spots develop on fruits

Problem: Fruits rot on the tree. The rotted areas are discolored and may be sunken. The fruits may dry, or mummify, and hang on the tree over winter.

Cause: Various fungi cause similar symptoms, known collectively as summer disease, but the decay varies in appearance. Black rot decay shows alternating rings of brown and black. Bitter rot causes tan and slightly sunken spots. White rot leads to watery decay. All can overwinter in mummified fruit and in small lesions, called cankers, in the wood.

Solution: Practice good garden sanitation. Apply fungicide. Plant resistant varieties.

- In winter, collect and dispose of all fallen or mummified fruits. Prune infected branches, making cuts 6 inches below the cankers.

- To combat black rot, spray the tree with sulfur or copper sulfate, which are organic fungicides, or with a synthetic fungicide containing the active ingredient captan. Apply when the disease appears after petal fall. Use a formulation registered for apples and follow label directions carefully.

- The following season, grow resistant apple varieties (p.291).

Spots on leaves and fruits turn yellow, then orange

Problem: In spring, leaves and fruits develop small yellow spots that turn orange and then become dark and sunken. Leaves may fall, and fruits may be small and misshapen.

Cause: Cedar-apple rust is a fungal disease that infects both eastern red cedar (*Juniperus virginiana*) (p.205) and apple species. It causes growths, called galls, to form on junipers, then its spores infect apple or crab apple trees for a year to complete the life cycle.

Solution: Control galls, use fungicide, plant apple trees away from host junipers, and grow resistant varieties.

- Pick the galls from junipers in late winter, before orange, spore-laden "horns" emerge from them. Rake up fallen apple leaves and fruits and remove them from the garden.

- The following spring, spray apple trees with a synthetic fungicide containing the active ingredient mancozeb, maneb, or triflumizole. Apply when the flower buds show pink, again when 75 percent of petals have fallen, and again 10 days later. Use a formulation registered for apples and carefully follow label directions.

- Site ornamental junipers at least a few hundred yards from apple or crab apple trees.

- Select resistant apple varieties (p.291).

Fruits have dimples and narrow brown tunnels

Problem: Small dark spots, often indented, appear on apples. The fruits have thin, winding tunnels that may contain legless white maggots. Infested fruits may rot throughout and often drop from the tree prematurely.

Cause: Apple maggots, or railroad worms, are the larvae of a small fly. The maggots mature in the soil during winter. The adults look like small houseflies with white bands on the abdomen and conspicuous black zigzag bands on the wings. They emerge in early summer through fall, and the females lay single eggs under apple skin.

Solution: Control adults and remove fallen fruit. Once in the apple, the pest is immune to pesticides.

- By mid-June, hang red sticky traps (p.392) at eye level, 2 to 3 feet into the tree canopy. Use one for a dwarf tree and four to eight for a standard tree. Clean and replace the sticky coating every two to three days.

- Pick up fallen apples, which may contain maggots, once or twice per week.

- Spray the tree with a synthetic insecticide containing the active ingredient carbaryl, methoxychlor, or a mixture of carbaryl and malathion every 7 to 10 days from the end of June to the beginning of September. Use a formulation registered for apples and carefully follow label directions.

Fruit has holes plugged with brown sawdust

Problem: The apple core and tunnels are filled with brown insect waste. Fat, pinkish white caterpillars with brown heads may be visible in the fruits.

Cause: Codling moth larvae, one of the most common apple pests, over-winter as full-grown caterpillars, hiding under loose bark, then mature there in spring. The adult moths emerge and lay eggs just before bloom time. Adults have gray-brown wings with irregular golden brown lines. There are generally two or more generations per season.

Solution: Control pests with traps, barriers, and biological control. Thin fruits on trees, and remove fallen fruits. Once in the apple, the pest is immune to pesticide.

- In late winter, hang one or two pheromone traps (available at garden centers and mail-

order suppliers) per tree. Pheromones are the chemicals that moths produce to attract the opposite sex.

- In early spring, scrape loose bark from the tree and spray the tree with dormant oil to smother eggs. Wrap the trunk with a band of corrugated cardboard or burlap and regularly remove pupae you find behind it.

- Thin the fruits so that they do not touch. If the tree is small, tie paper bags over each fruit in May or June, after thinning. The bags create a barrier between the apples and the moths.

- On a daily basis, remove fallen fruits, which may harbor larvae.

- If problems have been severe in the past, spray the tree with BT, a biological insecticide, two to six weeks after the tree blooms. Follow label directions carefully.

WISE CHOICES

The following varieties resist one or more diseases. Check with nurseries and garden centers to learn the latest resistant varieties and be sure to select a variety that is adapted to your climate. In the list below, the variety is followed by those it resists.

'Akane': scab

'Bramley': scab

'Dayton': cedar-apple rust, scab

'Freedom': scab, summer disease

'Golden Delicious': scab

'Grimes Golden': scab

'Liberty': cedar-apple rust, scab

'Macfree': cedar-apple rust

'Nova Easygro': cedar-apple rust

'Priscilla': cedar-apple rust

'Redfree': cedar-apple rust, scab

'Shay': scab

'Sir Prize': scab

'Williams Pride': cedar-apple rust, scab

Fruit has olive to brown spots

Problem: The fruit develops irregular brown blotches and may be misshapen. The leaves may also have spots and may fall.

Cause: Apple scab is a fungal disease widespread among apples. Spores are carried by wind and also overwinter in fallen leaves and fruit. The disease is most serious where spring weather is damp and mild, with temperatures between 60° to 70°F.

Solution: Practice good garden sanitation, treat with fungicide, prune, and mulch.

- Spray an infected tree with lime sulfur, an organic fungicide, when the buds first show green. On humid days when the temperature is warmer than 59°F, spray expanded leaves with sulfur. Repeat weekly or after each rain until midsummer or until scab diminishes. Follow label directions carefully.

- Pick up all fallen fruits by season's end. Also remove fallen leaves and compost them to eliminate overwintering sites.

- In late fall, spread a 4-inch-thick organic mulch, such as compost, beneath the tree to keep spore-laden soil from splashing it. Keep mulch 6 inches away from the trunk so that air can circulate around the trunk.

- Prune the trees in late winter to promote good air circulation within the canopy.

Fruits do not develop good color

Problem: Some or all of the fruits remain green rather than developing the ripe color appropriate for the variety.

Cause: While some fruits will form where little light can reach them, all fruits need suffi-cient sunlight to turn from unripened green to a good ripe color.

Solution: Prune tree to increase the amount of sunlight that can reach the interior. Site trees carefully.

- Thin interior branches (box, facing page).

- Plant trees where they will receive full sun for most of the day.

Leaves are rolled; tiny insects are present

Problem: Teardrop-shaped insects, usually greenish or pink, appear on buds, leaves, and stem tips. Leaves are often rolled and twisted, and stem tips may be curved. Leaves may be sticky or blackened.

Cause: The most damaging aphids on apple are the apple aphid, which is green in color, and a different species called the rosy apple aphid, which is rose colored. Both cause leaf curl, but the rosy apple aphid causes more severe curling. Both overwinter on apple bark; rosy apple aphid departs in midsummer, but apple aphid continues to feed through summer. Aphids secrete partly digested sap, called honeydew, which attracts a dark gray fungus known as sooty mold.

Solution: Prune tree to remove affected and crowded stems. Spray with insecticide.

- Prune out and dispose of infested stems. Thin dense inner growth in large trees to increase air circulation.

- For serious outbreaks, spray the infested plant with insecticidal soap or neem, a botanical insecticide. Alternatively, use a synthetic insecticide containing the active ingredient malathion, carbaryl, or endosulfan, being careful to get the spray into curled leaves. Be sure to use a formulation registered for apples and follow the label directions carefully.

- Discourage future problems by spraying the tree in spring with dormant oil as leaf buds swell, but before they show green.

PRUNING FRUIT AND NUT TREES

Most fruit- and nut-bearing trees can be pruned to one of three styles designed to strengthen the tree and maximize yields: central leader, modified leader, and open center.

CENTRAL LEADER is the best shape for trees bearing lightweight nuts. The leader is the main stem of the tree, and in the central leader method, this stem is allowed to grow. On a young tree, select six or seven strong side branches, making sure they are well spaced around the tree. Remove the thinnest branches in between so that the spacing between the remaining branches is more or less symmetrical, allowing plenty of sunlight and air to penetrate to the interior branches.

MODIFIED LEADER is used for fruit trees that bear heavy fruits, such as apples and pears. When a tree is 10 feet tall, cut the leader back to about 8 feet. The selection and pruning of the side, or scaffold, branches is the same as with the central leader method above. The first couple of years the tree bears, pick a few fruits, but leave some on the tree. The weight of these fruits will strengthen side branches and help them grow perpendicular to the trunk.

OPEN CENTER is used for trees that bear lighter-weight fruits, such as cherries and plums. The central leader is cut off when it reaches 4 to 6 feet tall, and the strongest side branches are allowed to grow. This produces a tree with no dominant trunk but many large branches. Spacing large branches evenly around the tree produces strong branch unions.

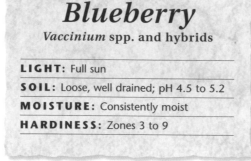

Blueberry

Vaccinium spp. and hybrids

LIGHT: Full sun

SOIL: Loose, well drained; pH 4.5 to 5.2

MOISTURE: Consistently moist

HARDINESS: Zones 3 to 9

Fruit is webbed together

Problem: Groups of berries are connected by webbing. The fruits may be covered with sawdustlike insect waste or may be shriveled.

Cause: Two kinds of moth larvae, the cranberry fruitworm and the cherry fruitworm, web blueberries together while feeding on them. The fruitworms are distinguished by their colors: the cranberry fruitworm is light green, while the cherry fruitworm is pinkish. Each fruitworm can damage as many as six berries before overwintering in a cocoon on the ground. The cherry fruitworm may also overwinter in crevices on the plant.

Solution: Remove affected fruits. Apply insecticide. Cultivate soil.

- Pick damaged berry clusters and fallen fruits and remove them from the garden.
- Spray the plant with a synthetic insecticide containing the active ingredient carbaryl, methoxychlor, or malathion. Use a formulation registered for blueberries and follow label directions carefully.
- When the plant is dormant, spray it with dormant oil to kill overwintering cherry fruitworms in their cocoons.
- Cultivate the soil lightly and frequently to destroy cocoons on the ground.

Branches have lesions and die

Problem: Some branches weaken and die. Examination reveals black or red lesions at the base of the dying portion.

Cause: Several types of stem canker infect blueberries. One type, blueberry cane canker, is most common in the Southeast. It begins as reddish, conical swellings on stems. The following year the swellings become gray, then black, cracked cankers. Another type, fusicoccum canker, is more common in regions with cold winters. The canker begins as red spots on the stem that emerge in wet weather. The spots enlarge and are encircled by concentric rings that kill branches and spread through the plant.

Solution: Remove and destroy infected plant material. Grow resistant varieties.

- Inspect blueberry stems several times per year and prune out and dispose of cankered stems. Cut several inches below the canker, sterilizing (p.310) tools between cuts.
- Rake the ground under bushes, and remove fallen cankered stems.
- In the South, grow highbush varieties that resist blueberry cane canker. Ask suppliers which varieties resist local strains of the disease. In the Southeast, grow rabbit-eye blueberries, which are immune.
- In colder areas, grow blueberry varieties that resist fusicoccum canker, such as 'Burlington', 'Coville', or 'Rubel'.

Leaves are yellowed between the veins

Problem: The leaf veins remain green, but the rest of the leaf turns yellow. The problem starts on the youngest leaves.

Cause: Iron deficiency in blueberries is most often caused not by a true shortage of iron but by a soil pH that is not sufficiently acidic. In the early stages, the young leaves turn green. If the problem continues, new leaves do not green up properly and fewer shoots grow.

Solution: Treat foliage with an iron supplement. Test the soil pH and amend as needed.

- For a quick fix, spray leaves with chelated iron solution, following package directions.

- If the problem persists, test the soil pH (p.329). If it is above 5.2, amend the soil with garden sulfur, as directed on the package label, to lower the soil pH to between 4.5 and 5.2.

- Spread an acidifying mulch, such as uncomposted pine needles or oak leaves, under plants. Replace it with fresh mulch when the foliage begins to decompose.

Soft, shriveled berries fall early

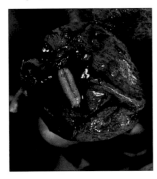

Problem: Some ripening berries are mushy and leak juice, falling from the plant before they are fully ripe. Inspection reveals dark tunnels that may contain small white maggots.

Cause: The maggots are the larvae of blueberry maggot flies, which lay eggs under the skin of green and ripe berries. The maggots feed on fruits for about 20 days, then drop to the ground. They mature in the soil, overwinter, and emerge as adults the next summer.

Solution: Remove infested fruits and treat with insecticide. Erect barriers and traps.

- Remove and destroy all soft, infested berries found on the plant and ground.

- Spray the plant with rotenone, a botanical insecticide, or rotenone premixed with the botanical insecticide pyrethrum. Alternatively, spray with a synthetic insecticide containing the active ingredient carbaryl, diazinon, or malathion. Use a formulation registered for blueberries and follow the label directions carefully. Begin spraying when berries are nearly full size but still green and repeat every 10 days through harvest. Spray again the following year to disrupt the insect's two-year life cycle.

- In spring, as the first blossoms fade, cover the bushes with an insect-excluding fabric floating row cover.

- Before the fruits develop, hang red globe sticky traps (p.392) to attract the flies. Hang one per highbush blueberry or one for several lowbush plants. Place the globes a few feet from the plant and at the same height as the fruits. Clean and recoat globes often.

Blossoms wither and berries drop prematurely

Problem: Blossoms become withered and brown. Ripening berries turn tan, then become shriveled, hard, and gray. Many fall before ripening. Young leaves have black spots. Leaves or whole stem tips wilt and die.

Cause: Mummyberry of highbush blueberry is a potentially serious fungal disease in years with cool, wet springs. Hard, dried berries, called fruit mummies, that are left on the ground from the previous year's infection release spores in spring. In moist conditions, the spores are carried by splashing water onto plants. To develop, the spores must land on growing parts of a plant that have not yet developed a waxy covering.

Solution: Remove infected leaves, stems, and roots, and use a fungicide. Mulch and grow resistant varieties.

- Prune out infected stem tips and remove damaged berries from the plant or ground.

- Spray the plant with a synthetic fungicide containing the active ingredient captan or benomyl. Use a formulation registered for blueberries and follow label directions carefully.

- In spring, as the buds begin to open, cultivate around the plant and add a 2-inch-thick layer of organic mulch to prevent spores from splashing onto the shrub.

- Select resistant varieties, such as 'Bluetta', 'Burlington', 'Collins', 'Dixi', or 'Jersey'.

Bramble Fruits
Rubus spp.

LIGHT: Full sun (part shade in the South)

SOIL: Well drained; pH 6.0 to 6.7

MOISTURE: Consistently moist

HARDINESS: Zones 3 to 11

Powdery orange or yellow spots appear on plant

Problem: The leaves or canes develop raised, powdery, orange or yellow pustules that may turn black later in the season.

Cause: The most common rust fungus infecting blackberries and black (but not red) raspberries is orange rust. Early symptoms are an unusually upright plant that is yellowish with glistening yellow spots on leaf undersides. Masses of orange spores soon appear on the leaf spots. Leaves may become bunched up. This disease is carried in the plant from year to year and spreads among plants during the year. Infected plants never recover.

Solution: Remove infected plants, purchase healthy plants, and resistant varieties. There are no chemical controls.

- Remove the infected plant as soon as symptoms appear.
- In future seasons, purchase certified disease-free plants.
- For future plantings, grow resistant varieties, such as the blackberries 'Ebony King', 'Eldorado', 'Oregon Evergreen Thornless', or 'Snyder'; the dewberry 'Lucretia'; or any variety of boysenberry or red raspberry.

Fruits are small and hard

Problem: Berries and plant are the normal color, but the fruits are small and not tender.

Cause: Underwatered bramble plants will produce small and tough-textured berries.

Solution: Provide the proper growing conditions.

- Water the plant when the soil is dry 1 to 2 inches beneath the surface.
- Incorporate plenty of organic matter, such as compost, into the soil at planting time, and mulch with it, to provide a well-drained soil that also retains moisture.

Spots with reddish borders develop on canes and leaves

Problem: Red-bordered spots appear on the plant. Spots on stems have pale gray centers; those on leaves have yellow centers. Stem tips die, leaves may fall, and fruits may dry out.

Cause: Anthracnose is a fungal disease that damages mostly blackberries and black raspberries, and sometimes red raspberries. The spores spread from last year's infected canes, and the disease can also spread among canes during the season.

Solution: Remove infected canes, apply fungicide, and grow resistant varieties.

- Prune out all infected canes after harvest.
- After harvest, spray the plant with copper sulfate, an organic fungicide. Follow label directions carefully.
- Or, spray the plant after harvest with a synthetic fungicide containing the active ingredient captan. Use a formulation registered for brambles. Follow label directions.
- Grow resistant varieties, such as 'Black Satin' and 'Gem' blackberries; and 'Black Hawk' and 'Jewel' black raspberries.

Entire canes or cane tips die

Problem: Entire canes or cane tips wilt and die. Whole canes are brittle at the base and break off readily. Insect entry holes are visible below the wilted area, and there are white insect larvae inside.

Cause: Two insects cause this damage, primarily to blackberries and raspberries. The raspberry crown borer attacks the cane base. The raspberry cane borer attacks the tip, leaving a ring of tiny black holes on the stem below a wilted tip. The larvae of both insects require two years to complete their life cycles.

Solution: Provide good growing conditions. Remove damaged plant parts. Apply pesticide.

- Water when the soil is dry 1 to 2 inches beneath the surface.
- If the cane base is damaged, dig out and destroy the affected cane.
- If the stem tip is damaged, prune the cane 6 inches below the entry hole, as the insect burrows downward as it feeds.
- When the plant is dormant, apply a synthetic insecticide containing the active ingredient diazinon. Use a formulation registered for brambles and carefully follow label directions.

Canes die and galls appear

Problem: Canes fall over and break, the plant is often stunted, and the berries are dry and seedy. Galls, or warty growths, appear on the canes or at the plant base.

Cause: Cane gall and crown gall are caused by two similar bacteria. While both infect all brambles, cane gall is rare on red raspberries. The diseases survive in the soil, and travel on splashing water and tools, entering the plant through injuries.

Solution: Remove affected canes or the plant. Handle plants carefully. Buy healthy plants.

- Cut out infected canes at ground level.
- Prune and carefully cultivate around plants to avoid injuring them.
- If problems persist, remove infected plants from the garden along with the surrounding 6 inches of soil. Do not replant bramble fruits in that location for three years.
- Before planting new brambles, be sure to obtain certified disease-free plants.

Fuzzy gray mold forms on blackberry and raspberry fruits

Problem: Flowers may turn brown and dry. Berries turn soft and mushy. If infected fruit stays on the plant, berries dry up and "mummify," becoming covered with a gray powder.

Cause: Gray mold is a fungal disease active in wet weather when temperatures are around 60°F. It spreads among plants in low areas and where nights are cool and damp. Gray mold is carried by water and wind, and new infections can start every few days. The fungus overwinters in plant debris.

Solution: Remove affected fruits. Fertilize and water carefully. Apply fungicide and mulch. Site plants properly.

- Remove and destroy infected fruits.
- Drench soil with compost tea (p.392) when conditions favor the disease.
- Water at ground level only, since spores need water on foliage to germinate.
- If problems persist, spray Bordeaux mix, an organic fungicide of copper sulfate and hydrated lime. Start when plants are 6 inches tall and spray every 10 to 14 days until flowering. Follow label directions.
- During the growing season, mulch around the plant to prevent berries from touching spore-laden soil. Remove mulch and plant debris in fall. Lightly mulch plants after fall cleanup to create a barrier between plants and spores left on the soil.
- Space plants widely for maximum air circulation. Avoid planting in low spots and in areas with poor air circulation.

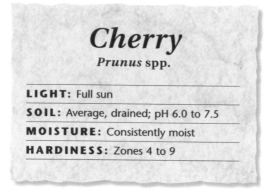

Cherry
Prunus spp.

LIGHT: Full sun

SOIL: Average, drained; pH 6.0 to 7.5

MOISTURE: Consistently moist

HARDINESS: Zones 4 to 9

Smelly sap oozes from the tree

Problem: In fall through spring, dark, wet lesions appear on the trunk and branches. Smelly, amber sap often oozes from them. Leaf buds may be damaged and may not open in spring. In midsummer, the leaves on infected branches may wilt, and the branches may die. Black spots appear on cherries.

Cause: Bacterial canker seriously damages cherry trees. Bacteria are splashed onto dormant buds and branches by water. The disease is most active in cool to cold weather, but infected branches may not die until summer.

Solution: Prune infected branches and spray. Provide good growing conditions, test the soil, and grow resistant varieties.

- Cut branches 6 inches below cankers. Sterilize tools between cuts (p.310).
- Spray copper sulfate, an organic pesticide, when the tree is dormant. Follow label directions carefully.
- Plant in soil deeply amended with compost.
- Have the soil tested for nematodes, which may increase chances of canker.
- If problems persist, select plants that have been grafted onto resistant rootstock or plant resistant varieties, such as 'Bada', 'Burlat', 'Sam', or 'Sue'.

Ripening fruits crack open

Problem: Just before they ripen, cherries split open. While they are still edible, damaged fruits are susceptible to decay.

Cause: Heavy rainfall during ripening causes some varieties to split.

Solution: Protect trees from heavy rain with tarps. Grow resistant varieties.

- Cover small trees during rainfall while the fruit is ripening. Shake the branches of wet trees after rain to remove excess water.
- Grow crack-resistant varieties, such as 'Early Burlat', 'Montmorency', or 'North Star'.

Deformed fruits drop early

Problem: Cherries fall before they are fully ripe. The affected fruits are shriveled, soft, and often underdeveloped on one side. Small white larvae are visible inside the fruits.

Cause: The creamy white maggots are the larvae of the cherry fruit fly. The larvae feed in fruit, then mature in the soil over winter. Adult flies emerge in late spring to lay eggs in the new season's fruit. The flies are smaller than houseflies and marked black, yellow, and white, with a dark band across the wings.

Solution: Remove infested fruits. Use traps and apply insecticide.

- Gather fallen cherries daily and remove them from the garden.
- Next spring, set out red or yellow sticky traps (p.52). At the first sign of flies on the traps, spray with rotenone, a botanical insecticide, or a synthetic insecticide containing the active ingredient malathion, methoxychlor, or carbaryl. Use a formulation registered for cherries and follow label directions carefully.

Citrus

Citrus spp.

LIGHT: Full sun

SOIL: Average, drained; pH 6.0 to 6.5

MOISTURE: Consistently moist

HARDINESS: Zones 9 to 11

Twigs, leaves, or fruits develop oval bumps

Problem: There are small, oval, brown, gray, black, or golden bumps on the twigs, leaves, or fruits. The leaves may turn yellow and drop, or the plant may be covered with a sticky substance and a dark gray powder.

Cause: Various types of scale insects can infest citrus trees. The males can fly, but the females attach themselves to plants and feed without moving. Serious infestations weaken trees and can kill them. If scale are on the fruits, they are California red scale. If they are only on leaves and twigs, they may be brown, citricola, or black scale.

Solution: Apply insecticide. Erect barriers. Introduce natural predators.

- Spray infested plants with neem, a botanical insecticide; follow label directions carefully. Note that, unlike neem, most pesticides will kill beneficial insects, the natural enemies of scale.

- Apply summer oil to smother scale, in late summer to early fall, making sure the spray reaches all parts of the plant. Follow label directions carefully.

- If the infestation continues, seek advice from a local garden center to identify the species of scale, and whether natural predators can be purchased to help control it. Planting nectar plants like alyssum, dill, and scabiosa will attract populations of local beneficial insects.

Fruits fall before they are ripe

Problem: Young fruits or older, nearly ripe fruits fall from the tree.

Cause: It is normal for some young fruits to drop. Excessive drop, however, can occur if the tree is under- or overwatered or the soil is not sufficiently fertile. Older fruits may drop if the plant is underwatered or inadequately fertilized or if the temperature suddenly changes.

Solution: Provide proper growing conditions.

- Water the plant about once a week for the first year, and as needed after that. Don't let the tree wilt; if the weather is particularly warm, dry, or windy, water more often and more deeply. This is especially important when flowers or fruits are developing.

- Plant in well-drained soil. In soggy soil, plant the tree on a 1½-foot-tall mound.

- Fertilize in late winter, early summer, and late summer with a high-nitrogen fertilizer, such as 10-5-5 (p.324).

Leaves are yellowed between the leaf veins

Problem: Leaves, especially young leaves, have green veins, but the area between the veins is yellow.

Cause: Deficiencies of trace nutrients, including iron and zinc, cause these symptoms. Symptoms develop when the soil is too alkaline, limiting the absorption of nutrients needed by citrus.

Solution: Provide adequate nutrients. Test soil and amend the soil pH as needed.

- Spray the leaves with chelated iron. In areas with very alkaline soils, spray the leaves with a solution of iron and zinc.

- Test the soil pH (p.329). If needed, apply sulfur to lower level to between pH 6.0 and 6.5. Follow the package directions.

REGIONAL FOCUS
NORTHEAST

Citrus trees are tender, but where they are not hardy, dwarf specimens can be grown in containers and wintered indoors. A container-grown plant should be watered when the soil is dry 2 inches below the surface. Additional watering rinses out fertilizer, so apply a high-nitrogen fertilizer, such as a 10-5-5 (p.324) formula in late winter, summer, and fall.

Leaves turn yellow and fall from the tree

Problem: Some or all of the leaves fall from the tree.

Cause: While citrus is evergreen, it will shed some leaves. Large numbers of falling leaves may be caused by over- or underwatering or by insufficient nitrogen fertilizer.

Solution: Provide proper growing conditions.

- Water the plant about once a week for the first year, and as needed after that to keep the tree from wilting. If the weather is particularly warm, dry, or windy, water more often and more deeply. This is especially important when flowers or fruits are developing on the tree.
- Fertilize in late winter, early summer, and late summer with a high-nitrogen fertilizer, such as 10-5-5 (p.324).
- Plant trees in well-drained soil. In soggy soil, plant a tree on a 1½-foot mound.

Tiny white insects are on leaves

Problem: Small, ⅛-inch-long, white-winged insects rise in clouds when leaves are disturbed. The leaf undersides are covered with winged adults, stationary pupae that look like translucent scale insects, and crawling nymphs. A clear, sticky substance or sooty, black areas may also be on leaves.

Cause: Citrus whitefly is a sap-sucking pest that can cause serious damage. A secretion, called honeydew, sometimes develops sooty mold, a fungus that reduces the leaves' ability to produce food. Repeated infestations can result in poor plant growth.

Solution: Use sticky traps and insecticide. Limit pruning.

- Place sticky traps (p.52) at plant level to attract and catch whiteflies.
- Spray with insecticidal soap. Monitor the plant for outbreaks and respray as needed.
- Limit pruning to regular hedging or topping, because whiteflies often infest the succulent new growth that follows pruning.

Trunk bleeds sap and fruits rot

Problem: The bark oozes thick, amber sap. Eventually, dark, sunken cankers form. The branches above the canker may die. The fruits, especially on lower branches, may develop brown spots and internal decay. The roots may also rot.

Cause: Brown rot gummosis is caused by a fungus that infects only citrus. Its spores are carried in soil and water. The bark is frequently infected when water from a sprinkler carries spores to the trunk. Root rot develops when the tree stands in irrigation water. The fruits become infected when spores splash up onto lower limbs.

Solution: Remove cankers and apply fungicide. Water carefully, prune tree, and mulch.

- Scrape cankers off the bark until you reach healthy tissue. Let the area dry and spray the area with an organic copper fungicide.
- Spray the leaves with an aluminum-based fungicide or with copper sulfate, both organic fungicides. Follow label directions carefully.
- Water trees at ground level and allow the surface soil to dry out between waterings.
- For a newly planted tree, make an earthen berm 1 foot tall, and a few inches out from the trunk to keep moisture away from the base of the tree when watering.
- Prune limbs that are very near the ground.
- Spread mulch under the tree to keep spore-laden earth from splashing onto it.

Gooseberry and Currant

Ribes spp.

LIGHT: Full sun

SOIL: Average, drained; pH 5.5 to 7.0

MOISTURE: Seasonally moist

HARDINESS: Zones 3 to 8

Leaves are eaten from the edges to the centers

Problem: As the plant comes into full leaf, it defoliates, beginning in the middle and spreading outward. Green larvae with black heads and body spots feed in groups, starting at the edges of the leaves and nibbling toward the centers.

Cause: Imported currant worms are the larvae of a black sawfly with yellow markings. The adults emerge in spring and lay white, flattened, shiny eggs on leaf undersides near the veins. Larvae feed for two to three weeks, then mature, or pupate, on the ground. A second, less destructive generation feeds in midsummer, then pupates on the ground over winter.

Solution: Remove pests from the garden. Apply insecticide.

- Handpick the larvae and dispose of them.
- Spray the plant with pyrethrum, or rotenone, both botanical insecticides. Alternatively, use a mixture of the two. Follow label directions carefully .
- Or use a synthetic insecticide containing the active ingredient malathion. Make sure to spray leaves in the center of the shrub. Use a formulation registered for gooseberries or currants and follow label directions carefully.

Leaves turn yellow; canes die

Problem: In the spring, leaves on some canes turn yellow; canes die.

Cause: Currant borer larvae feed in canes in winter. The adult moths emerge in June and July to lay eggs and infest new canes. The wasplike adult is actually a black-and-yellow moth with transparent wings. Black currants are less prone to infestation than red currants or gooseberries.

Solution: Prune infested canes; destroy larvae.

- Cut out the affected canes, pruning 6 inches below the entry holes.
- Either open pruned canes and destroy the larvae inside or remove damaged canes from the garden and dispose of them.

Leaves turn brown and brittle; foliage growth is reduced

Problem: Leaf size and number are reduced in regions with warm summer temperatures and strong sunlight. Plants may collapse when the soil or air temperature stays continuously above 85°F for several days. Leaf margins may scorch.

Cause: Gooseberries and currants grow best when the soil and air temperatures are cool. Drought stress, high temperatures, and intense sunlight can burn leaves. Both plants have shallow, fibrous roots and are easily susceptible to drought. Leaf margin scorch is caused by potassium deficiency.

Solution: Provide proper growing conditions.

- Keep the soil around the plant cool and moist. Water at ground level regularly until the fruit is harvested; reduce watering after harvest. Apply a 3- to 4-inch-thick layer of moisture-retaining organic mulch, such as compost. Avoid planting in sandy soil.
- If sunscald is a problem, locate new plants where they receive morning sun and afternoon shade.
- Test the soil (p.329). If there is potassium deficiency, apply 1 ounce of potassium per square yard. Don't use potassium chloride; bramble plants are sensitive to chloride.

- Lightly mulch the soil beneath the plant after fall cleanup to keep spores from splashing up from small pieces of debris left on the soil.
- Prune and thin dormant plants to increase air circulation the next season.
- Keep leaves dry by watering at ground level using a soaker hose or drip irrigation. Water early in the day so that leaves dry quickly.
- If the disease cannot be controlled, remove infected plants and plant new, anthracnose-resistant varieties in another location. Space plants 5 feet apart for good air circulation.

Leaves have a powdery white coating; fruits shrivel

Problem: The leaves, stems, and flowers are covered with a white, powdery substance that does not rub off. The fruits may shrivel and develop a brown, velvety coating.

Cause: Various powdery mildew fungi infect gooseberries and currants. The spores overwinter on infected plants and are spread by wind. The disease thrives in humid weather, when temperatures are between 60° and 80°F.

Solution: Prune plants and apply fungicide. Select resistant varieties.

- Prune the shrubs to increase air circulation within each one and between plants.
- If symptoms appear, apply lime-sulfur, an organic fungicide, when the buds first show green. Then spray with an organic sulfur fungicide, three times: as the blooms open, during full bloom, and two weeks later.
- If problems persist, spray with a synthetic fungicide containing the active ingredient benomyl. Use a formulation registered for gooseberries or currants and follow label directions carefully.
- Next season, grow resistant gooseberry varieties, such as 'Hinnomaki Yellow', 'Leepared', or 'Poorman'.

Small, dark brown spots appear on leaves

Problem: Irregular or round leaf spots develop first on lower, older leaves. Sunken, wet spots may also form, with their centers turning into holes. Leaves yellow, and lower leaves may drop. A plant's vigor may be reduced.

Cause: Anthracnose is a fungal disease that occurs most often in humid regions with wet summers. The spores spread by splashing water and overwinter on leaf litter.

Solution: Remove infected plant material and apply fungicide. Spread mulch, prune plants, and water properly. Grow resistant varieties.

- Remove and destroy diseased leaves as they appear. Also remove other plant debris during and at the end of the growing season.
- If the infection is severe, apply sulfur, an organic fungicide, as directed. Also apply sulfur as a preventive measure if anthracnose has been a problem, or if a long period of warm, wet weather is expected.

Grape

Vitus spp.

LIGHT: Full sun

SOIL: Well drained; pH 5.0 to 6.0

MOISTURE: Moderately moist

HARDINESS: Zones 4 to 11

Brown spots appear on fruits

Problem: Brown spots emerge on immature grapes. The spots darken and enlarge until the fruits are black, hard, and shriveled. Red-brown leaf spots also enlarge and darken. Stems develop elongated sunken areas that are dark purple to black.

Cause: Black rot is a serious fungal disease of grapes growing east of the Rocky Mountains. The spores overwinter in infected plant parts, then germinate in warm, moist weather. All parts of the plant are affected. Loss of harvest is often severe.

Solution: Remove infected plant material. Apply fungicide. Select resistant varieties.

- Pick all infected fruits and remove fallen ones from the ground. Also prune out infected canes and tendrils, disinfecting tools between cuts (p.310). Wash your hands before you touch healthy grapes.

- In severe cases, spray with copper sulfate, an organic fungicide, or with Bordeaux mixture, a blend of copper sulfate and hydrated lime. Spray twice: just before plants bloom and again after blooms fade. Follow label directions carefully.

- If problems persist, use a synthetic fungicide containing the active ingredient maneb. Use a formulation registered for grapes and follow label directions carefully.

- Grow resistant varieties, such as 'Beta', 'Campbell's Early', 'Cascade', 'Chancellor', 'De Chaunac', 'Delaware', 'Elvira', 'Fredonia', 'Ives', 'Scuppernong', or 'Worden'.

Leaves are skeletonized

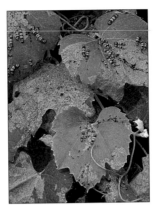

Problem: Rows of caterpillars eat the tissue between leaf veins. Destruction is rapid.

Cause: Two pests cause this damage: grapeleaf skeletonizers in the East and western grapeleaf skeletonizers in California and the Southwest. The larvae of both are yellow caterpillars with black and purplish stripes; western grapeleaf skeletonizers have black hairs that can irritate skin on contact. The insects overwinter in cocoons on leaves and on plant debris under the vines.

Solution: Remove pests and apply insecticide. Practice good garden sanitation.

- If the infestation is light, remove and destroy the leaves and handpick pests.

- In serious cases, spray plants with BTK, a biological insecticide, or with neem, a botanical insecticide. Be sure to coat the leaf undersides as well as surfaces, and follow label directions carefully.

- Rake debris from under the plants in fall to remove any overwintering cocoons.

Few or no grapes form

Problem: The plant looks healthy, and flowers appear, but no fruit forms on the vines.

Cause: Too much nitrogen fertilizer late in the season can result in excessive leafy growth, but no fruits.

Solution: Apply fertilizer at the beginning of the growing season in spring.

- Fertilize the plant with compost or well-rotted manure in spring.

- If the plant is growing slowly early in the season and has yellowish leaves, feed with ¼ pound of nitrogen fertilizer per plant (p.324).

Powdery white coating covers leaves and fruits

Problem: The leaf surfaces, fruits, and fruit stems are covered with a white substance that does not rub off. In severe cases, the leaves turn brown and fall, and the fruits are scarred and crack open.

Cause: Grape powdery mildew is a fungal disease that occurs nationwide but is most damaging in the West, where it is more likely to begin early in the season. Disease spores spread from plant to plant by wind. The disease can seriously weaken plants and prevent them from bearing edible fruits.

Solution: Apply fungicide. Practice good garden sanitation. Select resistant varieties.

- For late-season or light infections, apply an organic, wettable sulfur fungicide as symptoms appear. Do not spray when temperatures are above 85°F. Spray a few leaves as a test before spraying the entire plant, as some varieties may be damaged by sulfur.

- In the West, or when infection has been severe, apply a light coating of sulfur dust five times: when new shoots are 6 to 8 inches long; 14 days later, when they are 12 to 16 inches long; when they are 2 to 3 feet long; when grapes are half-grown; and when grapes begin to ripen.

- Clean up plant debris in the fall, and dispose of it, if infection has been a problem.

- Next season, grow resistant grape varieties, such as 'Canadice', 'Cayuga White', 'Ives', or 'Steuben'.

Leaves have yellow spots and cottony growth

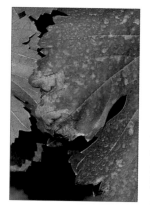

Problem: Yellowish leaf spots turn brown, and the leaves often fall. The shoots, tendrils, flowers, and fruits may be infected. Young fruits darken, then become covered with gray growth; mature fruits show brown rot.

Cause: Grape downy mildew is caused by a fungus that is most severe in the Northeast, where it is common on wild grapes. Spores are released from rotting, infected plant debris in spring and are spread by splashing water. The disease develops most rapidly in cool, moist weather.

Solution: Remove infected plant parts and apply fungicide. Practice good garden sanitation and grow resistant varieties.

- Remove infected plant parts as soon as symptoms appear.

- Apply copper sulfate or Bordeaux mixture, a blend of copper sulfate and hydrated lime. Spray the foliage three times: just before bloom, just after bloom, and again a week later. Follow label directions carefully; these organic fungicides can damage some grape plants.

- At season's end, rake up plant debris and remove it from the garden.

- Plant resistant varieties, such as 'Aurora', 'Baco Noir', 'Canadice', 'Cascade', 'Concord', 'Foch', 'Himrod', and 'Steuben'.

TIME-TESTED TECHNIQUES

INCREASING YOUR YIELD

With a little extra attention, you can encourage grapevines to produce a high yield. Here are three techniques.

- Thinning blossoms. Remove some of the flowers as soon as they appear. The remaining flowers will develop into larger fruit clusters.

- Thinning fruits. After the fruit has set, remove some of the smaller bunches, leaving 12 inches between clusters. As fruits swell, clip off the lower tip of each bunch and a few of the stems with smaller fruits within the bunch.

- Thinning foliage. In late summer, remove some of the leaves to permit the maximum amount of sunlight to reach ripening fruits. Pinch side shoots back to one leaf from the vine.

Vines are stunted and leaves may have green growths

Problem: The vines are smaller than they should be. They have yellowing leaves and poor grape production. In the eastern part of the country, pea-shaped green growths, called galls, form on the leaf undersides.

Cause: Grape phylloxera, or gall aphid, is an aphid that infests only grapes. In the East, some young aphids produce leaf galls, while others form root galls. The leaf galls are relatively harmless, but indicate that root galls may be killing the plant. In California, grape phylloxera infests roots only.

Solution: Treat with insecticide. Select resistant varieties.

- Spray with a synthetic insecticide containing the active ingredient endosulfan or malathion. Use a formulation registered for grapes and follow label directions carefully.
- Select a phylloxera-resistant variety or rootstock (get the advice of a local nursery).

Grapes have holes; larvae may be on fruits

Problem: The grapes and sometimes the leaves are connected by webbing. The fruits turn dark purple and often drop before maturity. Some fruits have larvae or holes.

Cause: Grape berry moth larvae are common in the Northeast and wherever grapes are grown, except on the West Coast. The larvae have greenish bodies and brown heads. Each destroys several berries, then pupates in webbing on leaves or on the ground. A second generation emerges in midsummer.

Solution: Remove affected plant material and apply insecticide.

- Pick and destroy damaged fruits. Remove leaves containing cocoons. Clean up debris under vines as grapes ripen, and in fall.
- If the infestation is heavy, spray with BTK, a biological insecticide. Start just after flowers have faded and follow label directions carefully for repeat applications.
- If problems persist, spray the plant with a synthetic insecticide containing the active ingredient methoxychlor or carbaryl. Use a formulation registered for grapes and follow label directions carefully.

Gray fungus forms on fruit

Problem: Fruits turn soft and watery. White grapes become brown and shriveled; purple grapes turn reddish. Patches of gray fungus grow on infected fruit. Berries shrivel, harden, and drop.

Cause: Gray mold, or botrytis bunch rot, is a fungus affecting all grapes, but it is more serious on tightly bunched species such as *V. vinifera*. The disease overwinters in plant debris and enters plants through injuries on fruits. Humidity, warm temperatures, and moisture cause the disease to develop rapidly.

Solution: Remove diseased fruits. Use good gardening practices and apply fungicide.

- Remove and destroy infected fruits.
- Drench the soil with compost tea (p.392) whenever conditions favor the disease.
- To keep leaves dry, water at ground level.
- If problems persist, spray with Bordeaux mixture, an organic fungicide containing copper sulfate and hydrated lime. Or apply a synthetic fungicide containing the active ingredient mancozeb. Use a formulation registered for grapes and follow label directions carefully.
- Mulch the soil under plants during the growing season to keep berries from touching potentially spore-laden soil. Clean debris from around plants in fall, and mulch to create a barrier between plants and spores left on debris on the soil.

Peach

Prunus persica

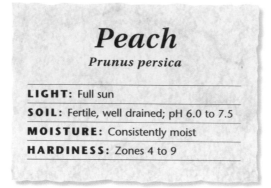

LIGHT: Full sun

SOIL: Fertile, well drained; pH 6.0 to 7.5

MOISTURE: Consistently moist

HARDINESS: Zones 4 to 9

Brown decay appears on fruits; flowers and twigs die

Problem: The blossoms and nearby twigs decay and die. In wet weather, brownish fuzz appears on the blossoms. Small, dark brown, circular spots then appear on young fruits. As fruits ripen, the spots enlarge and the fruits decay. In moist weather, brown fuzz forms on the decaying fruits.

Cause: Brown rot of peaches is caused by two similar fungi. Spores overwinter on infected twigs or on fruits that have hung on the tree all winter or have fallen to the ground. In spring, spores are carried by wind and splashing water to blossoms. Dead blossoms and leaves cling to the tree all season. Fruits may decay on the tree or after harvest. Cherries, plums, and quinces can also carry the disease.

Solution: Remove infected plant parts, use a fungicide, and increase air circulation.

- Prune off infected twigs and sterilize tools afterward (p.310). Remove and discard infected fruits from the tree and ground.

- When buds swell, spray organic lime-sulfur fungicide. As soon as flowers open, spray with organic sulfur fungicide, and spray with sulfur again 10 days later. Follow label directions carefully.

- Each year, thin trees while dormant to promote air circulation among the branches.

Fruit has green or brown spots

Problem: Spots appear on immature fruits, usually near the stem. They start out olive green and later become brown and velvety. The fruits are often small, cracked, and deformed. Spots may also appear on leaves and twigs.

Cause: Peach scab is caused by a fungus that infects peaches and other stone fruits. The spores overwinter on infected plants and are spread in spring by wind and splashing water. Spores are produced throughout summer and continue to infect new parts of the plant.

Solution: Practice good garden sanitation and apply a fungicide to control peach scab.

- Remove infected fruits and clean up all fallen leaves and fruits. Prune off infected twigs and sterilize tools afterward (p.310).

- Spray the foliage with sulfur or lime sulfur, both organic fungicides, or use a synthetic fungicide containing the active ingredient captan. Use a formulation registered for peach and follow label directions carefully.

Larvae appear in fruits; stem tips and young leaves wilt

Problem: New growth wilts 1 inch to several inches from the stem tip. The tree often looks unusually bushy because the side shoots develop after the stem tips die. Later, insect larvae emerge from the fruits.

Cause: Oriental fruit moths damage peaches and other fruits. The gray-and-brown moths lay eggs on leaves and twigs soon after the tree blooms. The larvae, which are pinkish white with brown heads, mature on the bark. A second generation damages stem tips and may enter fruits through stems, tunneling through the flesh and feeding near the pit.

Solution: Destroy infested plant material, use traps, and spray an insecticide.

- Prune off damaged stem tips. Slit some open to confirm the pest's presence. Also remove and destroy infested fruits.

- In spring, set up one or two commercial pheromone traps (available at garden centers) per tree.

- If an outbreak was serious last year, set out pheromone traps in spring and spray with insecticide 10 to 14 days after moths appear on the traps; contact a local garden center to determine the best time to spray. Use neem or pyrethrum, both botanical insecticides, or a synthetic insecticide containing the active ingredient carbaryl, malathion, or methoxychlor. Use a formulation that is registered for peach and follow the label directions carefully.

Young leaves redden and curl

Problem: As the leaves emerge, they develop red areas. They also twist, curl, and thicken. Later the leaves turn pale green, and a gray powder covers them. The affected leaves die and fall. The tree produces more leaves but is weakened. Infected fruits develop raised, rough areas, and may fall.

Cause: Peach leaf curl can weaken and kill peach or nectarine trees. This fungal disease is common in areas with high rainfall or cool, humid weather. The spores overwinter in leaf bud scales, and infect leaves, twigs, and fruits.

Solution: Remove infected plant material, increase air circulation, and use a fungicide.

- Remove infected leaves and fruits. Prune infected twigs and sterilize the tools between cuts (p.310). Rake up and dispose of plant debris.

- Thin tree branches to open the canopy and promote good air circulation.

- When flower buds swell but are not yet showing color, spray lime sulfur or copper sulfate, both organic fungicides. Follow label directions carefully.

- In areas with high rainfall, also spray with copper, an organic fungicide. Spray in fall after the leaves have dropped and follow label directions carefully.

Jagged holes are pecked into the fruits

Problem: Large holes or gashes are pecked in ripe fruits.

Cause: Blackbirds, crows, starlings, and several other kinds of birds feed on fruits.

Solution: Cover the tree with netting and use devices to scare birds away.

- Cover the tree with commercial bird netting mesh. If the tree is small, set up a wooden or pipe frame around the tree and drape the netting over it. This will ensure that birds can't reach through the net and peck the fruits. Secure the base of the netting to the ground or the base of the tree so that birds can't fly into it from the bottom.
- Just before harvest, hang aluminum-foil pie plates from the netting, or cut shapes from cardboard and cover them securely with aluminum foil. Hang these devices from the netting to reflect light and startle birds.

Gummy sap covers stem tips

Problem: Spring growth wilts, 1 inch to a few inches from the tips, and there is often a mass of gummy sap on the stems. Later, fruits develop narrow tunnels near the stem end, usually within ⅜ inch of the surface of the fruits.

Cause: The damage peach twig borers cause is similar to that of the Oriental fruit moth (p.306). But twig borer larvae look different, having pinkish brown bodies with lighter bands. The grayish adult moths are too small to notice. They lay eggs on twigs, fruits, and leaf undersides. The larvae mature on the bark, then a second generation damages the fruits. The pupae stage of the second generation overwinters on the bark, protruding from it like little chimneys.

Solution: Remove infested leaves, stems, and fruits and apply insecticide.

- Prune off and dispose of damaged stem tips and infested fruits. Remove plant debris.
- Spray a synthetic insecticide containing the active ingredient carbaryl or a mix of carbaryl and malathion. Use a formulation registered for peach and follow the label.
- In late winter, spray the tree with dormant oil to kill overwintering pupae.
- At bloom time and several times during the summer, spray with BTK, a biological caterpillar insecticide.

Fruits are small and crowded on the branch

Problem: Fruit is small in size and not of good quality. Limbs break under the weight of crowded fruit.

Cause: Nature ensures the survival of peach trees by encouraging them to develop as much fruit as possible. This in turn ensures enough seeds to propagate the species. However, maximum fruit production diminishes quality, depletes the tree's energy, and may cause branches to break under the weight.

Solution: Thin peaches so that they develop good size, shape, and color.

- Three to four weeks after the flowers bloom, the tree will naturally drop some fruits, usually when the largest ones are about the size of a quarter. After this occurs, remove any diseased, pest-infested, or deformed fruits by hand. Then remove excess fruits, leaving one fruit per cluster and 8 inches of space between fruits.
- Be sure to thin when fruits are no larger than 1 inch in diameter.
- Clean up any fallen fruits, and dispose of those that are diseased or have pests.

Pear

Pyrus communis vars.

LIGHT: Full sun

SOIL: Fertile, well drained; pH 6.0 to 7.5

MOISTURE: Consistently moist

HARDINESS: Zones 4 to 9

Black powder and tiny insects cover twigs and leaves

Problem: Leaves become sticky and may fall from the tree. Often, a nearly black powder forms on twigs or leaves. Tiny insects may be visible, especially where the leaves join the twigs and on leaf undersides.

Cause: Pear psylla are aphid relatives that suck sap from pear leaves. They excrete a substance called honeydew on foliage and fruit that encourages the growth of black, sooty mold. Adult psylla, which look like miniature cicadas, overwinter in bark crevices or under fallen leaves. In spring, they lay eggs near leaf buds. This insect can spread a viral disease called pear decline.

Solution: Treat with insecticide.

● At the first sign of damage, spray the tree with summer oil or insecticidal soap. Spray two more times at weekly intervals, following label directions.

● If problems persist, spray leaves with neem or rotenone, both botanical insecticides, or a synthetic insecticide containing the active ingredient carbaryl or malathion. Use a formulation registered for pear and follow label directions carefully.

● Spray a tree with dormant oil in late winter, and again just before buds swell in spring.

● If fruits mature, wash off the sooty mold and honeydew before eating them.

Fruits are mushy and have poor flavor

Problem: The texture and flavor of the fruits are not of the quality expected for the variety, but there are no signs of disease.

Cause: Except for the 'Seckel' variety, pears should be harvested before they are fully ripe.

Solution: Harvest and store pears properly.

● Harvest pears when the green color of the skin lightens slightly. For early varieties, cut the stem when the pear is still hard but mature. For later varieties, harvest as soon as the stem parts from the branch when lifted with a slight twist.

● After harvest, store pears in a single layer in a dry, cool location, with temperatures between 32° and 40°F.

● Pears ripen best when the temperature is between 65° and 70°F. Bring them to a warmer location, at about 65°F, to ripen for two to three days before eating them.

Leaves, stems, and fruits have black and purple spots

Problem: Spots on leaves start out tiny and gradually enlarge. Infected leaves may turn yellow and drop. Spots on young stems may join to create cankers. Spots on fruits start out red, then become dark and sunken. The fruits may become cracked or misshapen with roughened skin.

Cause: Fabraea leaf spot is caused by a fungus that commonly infects pears east of the Mississippi River. Its spores overwinter on infected twigs and fallen leaves, then spread to leaves and fruits in spring. In severe cases, the disease can defoliate infected trees.

Solution: Remove infected plant parts and treat with fungicide. Grow resistant varieties.

● Prune out diseased twigs and sterilize tools afterward (p.310). Rake up fallen leaves.

● Just before trees bloom, spray with a synthetic fungicide containing the active ingredient mancozeb or ziram. Use a formulation registered for pear and follow label directions carefully. Additional spraying may be needed, depending on your location and the amount of rainfall during the growing season. Check with a local garden center for regional advice.

- If planting new trees, choose resistant varieties, such as 'Maxine' or 'Moonglow'.

Leaves turn brown, and then turn black and die

Problem: Leaves on one or more branches wilt, turn brown, blacken, and curl upward, as if burned. Stem tips bend over, and young fruits on the affected branches are abnormally dark. Cankered areas, often oozing gum, develop on the tree's bark.

Cause: Fireblight is caused by a bacterium that infects edible and ornamental pears, as well as apples, loquats, raspberries, roses, pyracanthas, and hawthorns. It is carried by wind, splashing water, bees, and sucking insects, and it enters the plant through stem tips. If allowed to develop, the disease will spread throughout the plant, eventually killing it.

Solution: Monitor plants carefully and prune infected branches. Spray with fungicide. Grow resistant varieties.

- Check pears and other nearby plants that are susceptible to fireblight, for cankers in early spring and for blackened leaves later. Prune out infected branches, cutting 6 to 12 inches below visible infections. Sterilize tools after each cut (box, left).

- Just before blossoms open, spray with copper sulfate, or streptomycin sulfate, or Bordeaux mixture, a blend of copper sulfate and hydrated lime, all organic fungicides with antibiotic properties. Repeat at five- to seven-day intervals until flowers drop. Follow label directions carefully.

- In the future, grow resistant varieties, such as 'Harrow Delight', 'Luscious', 'Magness', 'Rescue', or 'Seckel'.

Fruits are spotted and cracked

Problem: As the fruits form, they develop olive-brown spots that turn corky and dark brown. Affected fruits may also crack and fall before they mature. There may be blisters on some of the twigs.

Cause: Pear scab is a fungal disease that overwinters in fallen leaves and twig blisters, releasing spores in the spring. The disease is most active in cool spring weather.

Solution: Practice good garden sanitation. Treat with fungicide. Grow resistant varieties.

- Rake up fallen leaves and fruits in the growing season and fall; compost or bury them.

- Prune off and destroy any twigs that have blisters or cankers on them.

- Spray once with lime sulfur, an organic fungicide, before buds begin to open in spring. Follow label directions carefully.

- If pear scab is common in your area, plant resistant varieties such as 'Bartlett', 'Bennett', 'Harrow Delight', or 'Summer Blood Byrne'.

≈ TIME-TESTED TECHNIQUES ≈

STERILIZING PRUNING TOOLS

Sterilizing pruning tools is an effective method of controlling the spread of plant diseases while working in the garden. Traditionally, a mixture of household bleach and water has been a popular solution for sterilizing tools. To sterilize tools, dilute one part bleach with nine parts water. Soak tools for about 20 minutes in the solution. Be sure to dry the tools thoroughly after soaking to prevent rust.

Another way to sterilize tools is to use 70 percent isopropyl alcohol directly from the bottle. Soak a cotton ball or clean rag in alcohol and carefully wipe the blades and handles of the tool after each cut. Let the alcohol evaporate before using the tool. Alcohol is more convenient than bleach for sterilizing a tool, and it does not promote rust or damage clothing if spilled.

Pecan
Carya illinoensis

LIGHT: Full sun

SOIL: Fertile; pH 6.0 to 7.0

MOISTURE: Consistently moist

HARDINESS: Zones 6 to 9

Leaves at branch tips are yellow and mottled

Problem: At first, leaves at the branch tips near the top of the tree turn a mottled yellow. Later, the lower leaves bunch up, crinkle, and turn yellow or reddish brown.

Cause: Pecan rosette, named for the way the leaves bunch together at the branch tips, is a nutrient deficiency problem due to insufficient zinc. Low levels of zinc in the soil or improper soil pH keeps plants from absorbing existing zinc.

Solution: Test the soil pH and adjust as needed. Apply zinc. Grow resistant varieties.

- Test the soil pH (p.329). Where the soil is acidic (below pH 7.0), add garden lime. Follow label directions carefully.
- Where the soil is alkaline (pH 7.0 or higher), use a foliar zinc spray. Mix a tablespoon of zinc sulfate in a gallon of water and spray trees as new leaves form. Repeat once a week as long as new leaves appear.
- In the West, or where alkaline soil is common, grow 'Western Schley', a variety that tolerates zinc deficiency better than others.

Leaves have clusters of small, green galls

Problem: Pecan leaves, and sometimes twigs, develop dozens of small, pale green, knotlike galls. Aside from the galls, the tree appears healthy and bears nuts.

Cause: There are several species of small wasps that produce galls on the leaves of many trees, including oaks and pecans. Adult wasps penetrate the leaf surface, creating galls, where they lay their eggs. Most wasps are considered beneficial insects because they prey on insects that are plant pests. Their galls are numerous and create unsightly leaves, but the tree is not harmed by the wasps or emerging larvae.

Solution: Observe the infested tree, and wait.

- Examine the infested leaves often for signs of other injury or diseases that may enter through gall wounds.
- If the tree seems healthy, wait for wasps to emerge from the galls, and it will recover.

Fallen nuts contain white insect larvae

Problem: Fallen nuts or those clinging to the tree later than usual contain pale, grublike larvae. Creamy caterpillars may also be present on the nuts or leaves.

Cause: Pecan weevils are dark gray or brown beetles with long snouts. Adults emerge from the soil in midsummer to lay eggs on developing nuts, some of which drop. The larvae develop in the nuts and bore out of them, leaving a small hole. They drop to the

FERTILIZING PECANS

Pecan trees thrive—growing between 8 and 15 inches per year—when fertilized generously, particularly with nitrogen. Each spring, top-dress the soil under the canopy with a high-nitrogen fertilizer at a rate of 2 to 4 ounces per square yard. If the tree is growing less than 6 inches per year, apply more fertilizer; if more than 20 inches, apply less. Mulch the soil with compost or rotted manure and keep the area free of weeds, which compete for nutrients and moisture.

ground, where they develop for two to three years. Hickory shuckworms, the caterpillars of a small gray moth, feed in immature nuts, causing them to drop. The last generation of the season can't penetrate mature nut shells, so it feeds in the outer coverings, or shucks.

Solution: Destroy larvae. Apply insecticide. Remove fallen nuts.

- Spread a cloth under the tree. Shake the tree every week in summer. Collect and destroy weevils that fall onto the cloth.

- Spray young trees weekly with neem, a botanical insecticide, or with a synthetic insecticide registered for pecan that contains the active ingredient carbaryl or phosmet. Follow label directions carefully. Spray from the time weevils appear until shucks split from shells. For large trees, spray the trunk, lower limbs, and soil to the drip line, or hire a professional.

- Clean up fallen nuts twice a week.

Leaves die early and nuts fall

Problem: Soon after leaves emerge, leaves and branch tips wilt and die. Immature nuts fall. Olive green or reddish gray caterpillars are in the fallen nuts. Nuts are wrapped in webbing.

Cause: Pecan nut casebearers are the larvae of small gray moths that overwinter at the base of buds. They feed on buds and leaves, and tunnel into young shoots to pupate. Adult moths emerge in May to lay eggs on the nuts. The larvae of this generation spin webs around nuts and enter the nuts to feed.

Solution: Clean up fallen nuts, encourage natural predators, and apply pesticide.

- Remove and destroy fallen nuts weekly.

- Grow morning glory, oleander, or evergreen euonymus nearby. These plants attract ladybugs and parasitic wasps, which are benefi-

cial insects that prey on the casebearers.

- Buy eggs of the parasitic wasp *Trichogramma minutum*. The eggs come on cards, which should be attached to the tree as soon as moths appear. Set out new cards weekly for two to six weeks until infestation subsides.

- Spray trees with the botanical repellent garlic oil or capsaicin. Follow label directions carefully.

- Ask a local garden center when the moths lay eggs in your area. Just after that time, spray BT, a biological insecticide, or a synthetic insecticide registered for pecan that contains the active ingredient malathion or carbaryl. Follow label directions carefully.

Leaves and nuts develop olive-brown spots

Problem: Early in the season, spots appear on leaf undersides and the outer coverings of the nuts. The spots may spread and turn black, the leaves may turn yellow, and the nuts may drop prematurely.

Cause: Pecan scab is a fungal disease that affects growing tissue. Once leaves and nuts mature, they are immune. Spores overwinter in plant tissue, infecting new leaves when the temperature reaches 65°F and the tree is wet for six to eight hours at a time.

Solution: Practice good garden sanitation and use a fungicide. Grow resistant varieties.

- Clean up plant debris in autumn. Shake the tree to knock off dead twigs or shucks.

- Spray young trees with Bordeaux mixture, an organic fungicide, four times: when they leaf out, after flowers fade, three weeks later, and in late July.

- For severe outbreaks, spray copper sulfate, an organic fungicide, or a synthetic fungicide registered for pecan that contains the active ingredient benomyl, dodine, thiophanate-methyl, or ziram. Follow the label. Spray once as buds open and three more times at two-week intervals.

- In humid areas, select resistant varieties such as 'Cheyenne', 'Curtis', 'Gloria Grande', 'Kiowa', 'Moreland', or 'Stuart'.

Plum
Prunus spp.

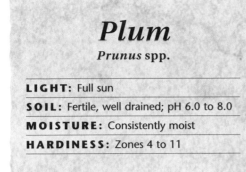

LIGHT: Full sun

SOIL: Fertile, well drained; pH 6.0 to 8.0

MOISTURE: Consistently moist

HARDINESS: Zones 4 to 11

Sunken cankers form in bark and often ooze sap

Problem: Elongated lesions form in the bark and ooze sticky gum. In spring, curled orange threads and black dots form in the cankers. The leaves above the canker may die.

Cause: Cytospora canker is caused by a fungus. Spores released from the cankers in spring can spread the disease. Trees are more susceptible when they have injuries or suffer from sunscald (p.288) in winter. If the oozing sap emits a sour odor, the plum tree may be infected with a bacterial canker.

Solution: Remove infected plant material. Protect the tree from sunscald.

- If the canker is on the trunk or a large limb, carefully chisel out the damaged bark and wood and destroy them.

- In fall and winter, inspect trees carefully. Remove smaller infected limbs, cutting at least 6 inches below the canker. Sterilize tools between cuts (p.310).

- To avoid sunscald the following season, paint the trunk and main limbs exposed to sunlight with white interior latex paint, which protects the bark from strong winter sun, and gradually wears off. Alternatively, wrap the trunk and main limbs with burlap or a commercial paper tree wrap.

Fruits are misshapen and dark; snouted beetles are present

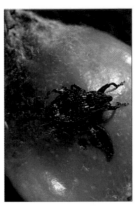

Problem: Fruits are poorly formed, rot, and drop before they are ripe. The skin is marred by deep, half-moon-shaped scars. When you cut open the fruits, you find curved, yellow-gray larvae. Dark brown beetles may be present.

Cause: Plum curculios are a common pest east of the Rocky Mountains. The beetles have a grayish patch on their back and a long, downward-curved snout. The adults come out of hibernation in spring to feed on blossoms, young leaves, and fruits for five to six weeks. Then they slit young fruits and deposit eggs in the cuts. The fruits often drop, and when the larvae finish feeding, they pupate in the soil. The adults emerge, feed on fallen fruits, and then hibernate in debris. In the South, there may be a second generation of larvae in one season.

Solution: Trap and handpick beetles, spray with insecticide, and clean up debris.

- Hang commercial green sticky traps in trees in spring to monitor for plum curculios. When the insects appear,

---

WISE CHOICES

Some plum varieties are self-fertile and don't require pollination, although all will bear better with cross-pollination. The following list includes popular self-pollinating plums.

Damson plums: 'French Damson' and 'Shropshire'

European plums: 'Bluefire', 'Mirabelle', 'Opal', 'Stanley', and 'Victoria'

Gage plums: 'Golden Transparent Gage' and 'Reine Claude' (also called 'Green Gage')

Japanese plums: 'Methley' and 'Santa Rosa'

REGIONAL FOCUS
SOUTHWEST

In regions of the Southwest with mild winters and alkaline soil, plum trees are susceptible to Texas root rot, which is caused by a fungus. If the leaves wilt suddenly and then turn brown, the plant may be infected and could die within two weeks.

Take root samples to a nursery to verify the presence of the disease. In the meantime, try to save the affected tree by pruning off the ailing branches. Work a 2-inch layer of rotted cow manure into the soil around the tree. Also work in sulfur at the rate of one pound per 10 square feet. Water the soil deeply and water again 10 days later.

spread a drop cloth under the tree and shake branches twice daily. Collect and destroy the beetles that fall onto the cloth.

- If problems persist, spray with rotenone, a botanical insecticide, or a synthetic insecticide containing the active ingredient carbaryl or methoxychlor. Use a formulation registered for plum, and follow label directions carefully. Don't spray while the tree is in bloom to protect bees that are pollinating the flowers.

- Pick up all fallen fruits and remove damaged fruits from the tree. Rake up and dispose of debris under the trees to eliminate overwintering sites for these pests.

Black, warty growths appear on the branches

Problem: Soft greenish growths, called galls, form on the branches. They later turn black and warty. Infected branches are stunted and eventually die.

Cause: Black knot disease is caused by a fungus that frequently infects plums. During wet, mild spring weather, with temperatures between 55° and 75°F, the spores germinate on the tree; symptoms appear six months to one year later. The galls enlarge gradually, killing the branch by restricting its ability to transport water and nutrients.

Solution: Treat with fungicide, remove affected branches, and grow resistant varieties.

- Spray a synthetic fungicide with the active ingredient thiophanate-methyl, a formulation registered for plum. Follow the label.

- In winter, prune diseased branches 4 to 6 inches below the infection and destroy them. Sterilize shears between cuts (p.310).

- Just before buds open in spring, spray copper sulfate or lime sulfur, both organic fungicides. When the buds swell, spray with a synthetic fungicide containing the active ingredient benomyl. Use a formulation registered for plum. Follow its label.

- In the future, grow resistant varieties, such as 'AU-Producer', 'Milton', or 'President'.

Fruits are small and crowded

Problem: Fruits are small and poor quality. Limbs break under their heavy weight.

Cause: Plums often set more fruit than they can support. Heavy fruiting ensures plentiful seed production but also prevents individual plums from reaching full size. Too many fruits may cause a tree to deplete its energy or break apart because of excess weight.

Solution: Thin fruits so that they develop good size, shape, and color.

- If the crop is particularly heavy, remove some fruits in late spring. Snap the fruit off the stalk, but leave the stalk on the tree.

- Several weeks after bloom, the tree will naturally drop some fruits. Thin remaining fruits five to eight weeks after bloom, leaving one fruit per cluster and about 4 inches of space between them.

Leaves have reddish or black spots and holes

Problem: Angular reddish or black spots appear on the leaves. The spots may enlarge, join, and make the foliage appear burned or ragged. Twigs have dark blisters that dry, turning into sunken cankers. The fruits have brown or black spots that often exude gum.

Cause: Bacterial leaf spot is common east of the Rocky Mountains. The disease spreads from twig blisters in spring and is carried by splashing water to new leaves and fruits. Infected trees may lose all of their leaves and produce few plums of poor quality.

Solution: Apply fungicides with antiobiotic properties and grow disease-resistant varieties.

- As the buds swell in spring, spray the tree with an organic fungicide, such as copper sulfate or lime sulfur. Follow label directions carefully.

- In the future, plant disease-resistant varieties, such as 'AU-Amber', 'Crimson', 'Green Gage', or 'Simon'.

Strawberry
Frageria spp.

LIGHT: Full sun

SOIL: Fertile, well drained; pH 5.0 to 6.5

MOISTURE: Consistently moist

HARDINESS: Zones 3 to 11

Leaf edges turn dark brown

Problem: Leaves darken at the edges and between veins. Affected leaves may die.

Cause: Strawberries are very sensitive to salts in the soil. Excess sodium may come from the soil, water, or fertilizer. The problem worsens when plants are underwatered or growing in poorly drained soil.

Solution: Test the soil, water carefully, and improve soil drainage.

- Test the soil for salt and fertility (p.324), and amend soil as the test recommends. Work compost into the soil to help plants tolerate salinity. Fertilize less frequently.

- Water when the soil is dry 1 inch below the surface. If your water is high in salts, install a rain barrel under a downspout and water with the salt-free water it collects.

- Before planting, amend soil with organic compost or leaf mold to improve drainage.

Young leaves are deformed

Problem: Emerging leaves are curled, crinkled, and short stemmed. The plant's center becomes a compact mass. Affected leaves appear brownish. Flowers wither and die.

Cause: Cyclamen mites suck plant sap and cause stunting. They also feed on blossoms, causing formation of distorted fruits. The tiny pinkish orange adults crawl on leaf undersides. Mites reproduce rapidly all season, then overwinter in the plant base, or crown.

Solution: Apply insecticide, remove affected plants, and grow disease-free plants.

- Spray the plant with neem, a botanical insecticide. Follow label directions carefully.

- Remove and destroy any plant that shows severe symptoms. Do not handle other plants until you wash your hands.

- In the future, purchase certified disease-free plants, which will also harbor no mites. Do not grow the new strawberry plants near plants with cyclamen-mite symptoms.

Leaves are discolored and wilt

Problem: Early spring growth is gray, bluish, reddish, or otherwise discolored. The plant wilts frequently and produces few berries. The interior of the root is reddish brown, instead of the usual pale yellow.

Cause: Strawberry red stele disease is caused by a root-rot fungus. It is most severe in cool spring weather and may clear up in summer, although infected plants are likely to die prematurely. This disease thrives in heavy or poorly drained soil.

Solution: Apply fungicide, improve soil drainage, and grow disease-tolerant varieties.

- Spray the foliage with an aluminum-based, organic fungicide, or a synthetic fungicide containing the active ingredient metalaxyl. Use a formulation registered for strawberry and follow label directions carefully.

- Amend heavy soil with organic matter, such as compost. Alternatively, plant in a raised bed (p.328).

- If problems persist, replace the infected plant with a disease-tolerant variety recommended by a local nursery or garden center.

Slugs eat leaves and berries

Problem: Holes of varying sizes are chewed in the foliage. Parts of fruits are also missing. Slugs or snails may be present.

Cause: Slugs and snails, nocturnal land-dwelling mollusks, eat the foliage and fruits.

Solution: Harvest fruits quickly, remove the pests, use traps, and clean up garden debris.

- Pick fruits as soon as they are ripe to eliminate a food source for the pests.
- Handpick slugs and snails at night, using a flashlight, and dispose of them.
- Set homemade beer traps (p.49). Slugs and snails will crawl in and drown.
- Keep the garden free of decaying vegetation and other debris to eliminate daytime hiding places for the pests.
- Try other methods of controlling slugs and snails (p.49).

Spots of varying colors mar the leaves

Problem: Leaves are covered with spots that may be tinged red, tan, blue, brown, or black. The affected leaves may die.

Cause: Several different fungi cause strawberry leaf diseases. The fungal spores overwinter on dead leaves and infect green leaves in spring. Infections may worsen year after year and are particularly severe in wet weather.

Solution: Provide proper growing conditions, use fungicide, and remove debris. Rotate crops and choose disease-resistant varieties.

- Water at ground level, using a soaker hose or drip irrigation to keep leaves dry.
- Keep the patch weeded. Don't allow plantings to become thick and matted.
- If damage is severe, spray with copper, an organic fungicide, or with a synthetic fungicide registered for strawberry that contains the active ingredient benomyl every 7 to 10 days during wet weather. Follow label directions carefully.
- Clean up dead leaves and debris. Mulch with compost to keep spores from splashing onto plants from the soil.
- Every few years, start a new strawberry patch in a different location. Select a sunny site with quick-draining soil.
- If these diseases have been a problem, ask at a nursery or garden center for disease-resistant varieties adapted to your area.

Berries are partially eaten

Problem: Berries have holes pecked in them or are partially eaten. When mature, whole fruits may disappear.

Cause: Birds are very fond of strawberries and will peck at maturing fruits to check for ripeness. Once the berries are fully ripe, the birds will eat them, leaving partially eaten fruits, or the birds will remove whole fruits and carry them away.

Solution: Erect barriers and use scare tactics.

- Create a barrier between birds and fruits by covering plants with plastic bird netting.
- When fruits begin to ripen, use reflective Mylar tape or inflatable snakes or hang aluminum pie tins from stakes to scare birds away. Don't use the devices until the berries ripen, to keep birds from becoming accustomed to them.

Leaves are yellow and deformed

Problem: Leaves may be yellow, deformed, or bunched up. The plant may also be stunted. Fruit production is light; fruits are dull and small.

Cause: Viral diseases spread by feeding aphids and mites infect strawberries.

Solution: Control pests, remove affected plants, and rotate crops.

- Spray infested plants with a strong stream of water from a hose or with soapy water from a squirt bottle to dislodge pests.
- Remove and dispose of any plant that shows disease symptoms.
- Move the strawberry patch every few years to a new location, a form of crop rotation (p.115). Avoid sites where plants with viral symptoms had previously grown for at least three years.

Buds have holes; berries are small and brown

Problem: Small brown holes are found at the base of nearly mature flower buds. Buds droop or fall and turn brown. Berry production is reduced. Berries that do develop turn brown. Dark beetles may be on plants.

Cause: The strawberry clipper, or strawberry bud weevil, is a small weevil with a curved, red-brown snout. In spring, females puncture unopened flower buds to lay eggs. Adults clip the flower stems, causing buds to droop or fall to the ground. The pests overwinter in hedgerows, woodlots, and debris.

Solution: Use a trap crop. Treat with insecticide. Select planting sites carefully.

- Because early-flowering varieties are more severely damaged than later ones, plant a few rows of an early variety to act as a trap crop. This reduces damage to later-bearing strawberry varieties.
- When temperatures reach 60°F and flower buds are visible, watch for adult weevils. Treat them with a synthetic insecticide containing the active ingredient carbaryl. Use a formulation registered for strawberry and follow the label directions carefully.
- Locate plantings away from areas where adult weevils overwinter, and clean up and dispose of garden debris.

Fuzzy gray mold forms on fruits

Problem: Flowers may brown and dry. Ripe or ripening fruits develop light brown patches and turn soft and mushy. Berries may dry up and become covered with gray powder.

Cause: Gray mold is a fungal disease that is active in wet weather when temperatures are around 60°F. It spreads quickly in low areas, and during bloom or harvest times in damp weather. Spores spread in splashing water and wind. The disease overwinters on debris.

Solution: Use proper cultural practices and apply fungicide.

- Remove and destroy infected fruits.
- Drench soil with disease-fighting compost tea (p.392) when weather is damp.
- Avoid overhead watering to keep plants dry, and mulch with straw to keep fruits off soil.
- If problems persist, spray with the organic fungicide Bordeaux mixture, starting when plants are 6 inches high and continuing every 10 to 14 days until flowering occurs. Follow label directions carefully.
- Alternatively, spray with a synthetic fungicide registered for strawberries that contains the active ingredient vinclozolin when blossoms open and again 10 days later. Follow label directions carefully.

REGIONAL FOCUS
SOUTHWEST

English walnuts (*J. regia*) growing on black walnut (*J. nigra*) rootstock in the Southwest sometimes develop a condition known as black line. The tree grows poorly, the leaves droop and turn yellow, and shoots die. Eventually, the entire English walnut graft dies, and many shoots sprout from the rootstock. Removal of bark at the graft line reveals a dark brown to black corky ring about ¼ inch wide all around the tree. This is a symptom of a viral disease, transmitted either by contaminated grafting tools or by pollinating insects. There is no cure; remove infected trees.

Walnut
Juglans spp.

LIGHT: Full sun

SOIL: Fertile, well drained; pH 6.0 to 8.0

MOISTURE: Seasonally moist

HARDINESS: Zones 5 to 9

Walnut husks have black spots

Problem: At harvest, soft black spots develop on the nut husks. The blemished husks are difficult to remove. Cream-colored maggots are feeding in the husks. Nuts are not usually damaged, but shells are stained.

Cause: Walnut husk flies are dark and slightly smaller than a housefly. They lay eggs just under the surface of the husk. The maggots feed for several weeks and then fall to the ground, where they pupate over one or two winters. While larvae do not damage the nut kernels, they make the husk black and slimy and leave indelible stains on the shell.

Solution: Tolerate damage, remove infested husks, apply insecticide, use traps, and grow resistant varieties.

- If you do not object to discolored shells, tolerate husk damage.
- Dispose of the infested husks.
- Spray the affected tree with a synthetic insecticide containing the active ingredient malathion or phosmet. Use a formulation registered for walnut and follow the label.
- If husk flies have been a problem in the past, hang four commercial apple maggot traps per walnut tree in early July to trap flies before they lay eggs.
- Grow resistant varieties, such as 'Ashley', 'Payne', or 'Placentia'.

Tree grows slowly, but has no specific symptoms

Problem: The tree grows more slowly than it should, but there are no apparent causes.

Cause: Walnut trees require regular and deep watering, but should not grow in constantly wet soil. Waterlogged soil makes a tree grow poorly and become susceptible to potentially fatal root rot disease.

Solution: Select the planting location carefully and provide proper growing conditions.

- Plant the tree in well-drained soil.
- Water the tree deeply only when the soil is dry 3 to 4 inches below the surface.

Sticky white webs cover leaves at the ends of branches

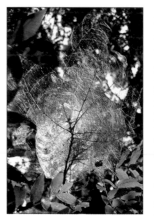

Problem: White webbing encloses the ends of the branches. The nests house caterpillar colonies. Mature caterpillars are 1 inch long and are covered with long, silky gray hairs.

Cause: Fall webworms are found on walnuts and other deciduous trees in summer. Large populations can defoliate branches but the insects do not kill trees. The adult is a white moth that lays masses of green eggs on the leaf undersides. The larvae hatch, spin a web, and feed on the tree leaves enclosed in the web. Caterpillars feed for four to six weeks, then crawl to the ground to pupate in leaf litter. There are usually two broods per season, with the second generation being more noticeable than the first.

Solution: Destroy nests and caterpillars. Apply biological controls.

- Remove nests by pruning off infested branches. Alternatively, snag webs and lift them out of trees using a long wooden pole with nails inserted in the end. Burn the pruned branches or drown the insects in hot, soapy water.
- If webs are still small, apply BT, a biological caterpillar control. To penetrate webs of mature colonies or webs high in trees, use a high-pressure sprayer.

Nuts have sawdust-plugged holes and larvae

Problem: Green nuts fall to the ground. Caterpillars may be inside nuts, or the nuts have holes plugged with sawdust and insect waste.

Cause: The codling moth damages walnuts by laying eggs on nuts or on leaves in spring. The larvae feed inside the nuts, then crawl out to mature, or pupate, on bark. There are generally two or more generations per year, the last one over-wintering as larvae and pupating in spring.

Solution: Control all stages of the life cycle. Grow late-blooming varieties.

- Rake up and remove fallen nuts.

- Wrap the tree trunk with an 8-inch-wide strip of corrugated cardboard or burlap. Regularly remove pupae found behind it.

- In late winter, hang one or two pheromone traps in the tree. Two to six weeks after a moth is caught on a trap, spray the foliage with BTK, a biological caterpillar insecticide, or a synthetic insecticide containing the active ingredient carbaryl. Use a formulation registered for walnut and follow the label directions carefully.

- In early spring, spray the tree with dormant oil to smother coddling moth eggs.

- Grow late-blooming varieties, such as 'Hartley' or 'Vina', which are less susceptible.

Leaves have brown spots

Problem: The leaf buds turn black and die. The stems may have dead, sunken areas, and the leaves have reddish brown spots. When nuts form, they develop hard, dark, sunken lesions that may exude a shiny black fluid. Nuts may drop prematurely. Some nuts are normal, but others are shriveled and inedible.

Cause: Walnut blight is a bacterial disease that overwinters in dormant buds and nuts left on the tree. The disease becomes worse when the weather is warm and wet.

Solution: Use fungicide, increase circulation, keep foliage dry, and grow resistant varieties.

- Spray leaves with the organic copper fungicides copper sulfate or copper hydroxide, which have antiobiotic properties. Follow the label. On the West Coast, some strains resist copper fungicide. If so, ask a local nursery how to control these strains.

- Prune the tree to promote air circulation (p.293).

- Water at ground level to prevent spreading disease by splashing water.

- Select late-blooming varieties, such as 'Hartley' or 'Vina', which show some resistance.

✧ TIME-TESTED TECHNIQUES ✧

FERTILIZING AND WATERING TREES WITH A ROOT FEEDER

Root feeders are tools designed to deliver a fertilizer solution or water directly to the root zone of trees and shrubs, right where they need it. They range from motorized devices used by professionals to inexpensive hand tools for home gardeners.

The most common types have a 2- to 3-foot-long probe attached to a hollow, T-shaped handle that holds a water-soluble fertilizer tablet. The handle has a trigger and a place to attach a garden hose. Once a fertilizer tablet is placed in the handle and the hose is hooked up, the feeder is inserted into the ground and the water turned on. The water travels through the hose and into the handle where it passes over the fertilizer tablet, carrying dissolved nutrients into the soil where the roots are growing. If you only want to water a tree, simply use the root feeder without adding fertilizer.

CHAPTER EIGHT

SOIL AND COMPOST

GOOD SOIL—RICH IN ORGANIC matter and crumbly in consistency —is the foundation of a successful garden. Such soil keeps plants vigorous enough to shrug off most pests and diseases. It holds just enough water so that a plant can take a deep drink without its roots rotting. It affords the correct amount of acidity or alkalinity for the plants it nurtures.

Few gardeners are blessed with perfect soil. That is what this chapter is about. You will learn how to identify and pick plants that are naturally suited to the type of soil that you have. You will also find out how to amend less-than-ideal soil with the correct combination of organic materials to make it suit the plants you want to grow.

And you will discover how easy it is to turn garden and kitchen wastes into clean, organic compost in your own back yard—no fuss, no mess, no odor. Homemade compost is a renewable, free source of organic nourishment for your garden.

THE IDEAL SOIL

Mineral particles weathered from rock, organic matter in various stages of decomposition, beneficial bacteria and fungi, plus billions of other organisms—from the familiar wiggling earthworms and bustling beetles to creatures too small to be seen without a microscope—all can be found in soil. All organisms in the soil, from the smallest bacterium to the largest night crawler, work together to create a healthy home for the roots of plants. Each living member of this complex and intricately functioning ecosystem has an important role to play, consuming and breaking down the organic material and unlocking all the nutrients plants need to thrive.

Some kinds of soil, however, are better for growing plants than others. The nutrient-rich, crumbly soil called loam is the medium that most plants thrive in. When you scoop up a handful, you'll discover that it is dark in color with a sweet, earthy fragrance. It has the consistency of a crumb topping for a pie, clumping together when squeezed, then crumbling easily when you sift it between your fingers.

The advantages of loam come from the diversity and balance of its ingredients. Loam is a mix of roughly equal amounts of decomposed organic matter (humus), sand, silt (soil particles smaller than grains of sand and larger than those of clay), and clay (comprised of the smallest rock particles). The clay and silt particles in loam supply fertility and stability for plant roots by absorbing and

holding moisture. Additionally, clay and silt help all the soil particles stick together, while holding soluble plant nutrients where plant roots can absorb them. The particles of sand in loam loosen its texture and add vital spaces, or pores, for the passage of air and water into the root zone. The organic content lightens soil texture, and boosts the moisture-holding capacity and fertility of loam. Together all these ingredients form a crumbly soil that drains well and is moist and fertile—a condition called tilth, which is everything a garden, and gardener, could want.

Loam solves many problems

Loam not only helps your plants thrive, it makes gardening easier for you as well. Irrigating loam is more efficient than irrigating other kinds of soil because water soaks in quickly instead of running off, as it does with clay. The abundant organic matter soaks up moisture like a sponge, preventing loam from drying out too quickly, as it does with sand. You'll use less muscle to prepare beds of loam, and to transplant or divide plants growing in it, because loam has good tilth—it's light, easy to dig, and easy to lift. Weeding is also less of a chore in loam than in clay because tenacious weed roots give up their grip more easily in friable, or crumbly, loam.

Silt, clay, and organic matter, in loam retain the nutrients that rain would wash away in sandier soil, decreasing the need for repeated applications of fertilizer. The sand contributes spaces that keep the soil drained but moist, supplying air and soluble nutrients to roots. Optimum air spaces in loam filter oxygen and other gases, enabling plant roots and soil organisms to thrive and resist soil diseases that proliferate in wet soil. And as a bonus, some of the microscopic organisms in the organic content of loam produce natural

A community of beneficial soil organisms, from familiar earthworms to minute bacteria, transport bits of organic material from the soil's surface down into the soil where they convert it into nutrients that plant roots can absorb.

SOIL TEXTURE AND STRUCTURE: WHAT'S THE DIFFERENCE?

Soil texture and soil structure may seem like interchangeable concepts, but they are not. Understanding how they are interconnected but distinct will help you determine the type of soil you have, and when and how to build that soil into loam.

Texture describes the size of the particles that make up the three types of soil: clay, silt, or sand. The texture of soil is something you can feel with your fingers. Soil with a sandy

texture feels gritty. Soil with a silty texture feels like flour; and soil with a clay texture feels slippery.

Structure describes how those particles hold together, from crumbs to clods. Structure is something you can see, whether it is a sticky lump of clay or the ideal small crumbs of friable loam. Keep in mind that friable soil is fragile. It's structure be compacted and ruined by foot traffic or vehicles driving on it.

antibiotics that create a condition that makes it difficult for diseases to flourish, helping keep plants healthy.

Because of its balance of air, organic mineral particles, and water, loam is the best soil for most plants' growth. This is because it has a nearly neutral pH level, the measure of soil acidity, which is the optimum level for releasing nutrients. Seeds sown in loam sprout and grow quickly. Most perennials and annuals, shrubs and trees, and all vegetables, establish themselves rapidly when planted in loam.

WONDER-WORKING ORGANIC MATTER

Few gardeners are lucky enough to have a deep layer of natural loam, but it's possible to improve soil by amending and conditioning it with organic matter. For improving undesirable soil, whether it's heavy, sticky clay or dry, dusty sand, spreading a 3- to 6-inch layer of organic material on the soil's surface and tilling or digging it into the soil will improve the soil's texture, thereby improving the health of your garden's plants.

Aged manure from herbivores like horses and cattle, compost, leaf mold, and other forms of humus (see Organic amendments for improving soil, right) are the materials of choice. In some areas, commercial mushroom compost or municipal leaf compost is also available. You may find these and other excellent organic amendments, such as composted rabbit manure or poultry manure, by checking the classified advertising in your local newspaper. They are often inexpensive or even free for hauling. Commercially available peat moss is another organic amendment. Unfortunately, peat moss, unlike compost, is not an endlessly renewable resource; some environmentalists are concerned about the harvesting of peat moss from ancient bogs.

Amending your garden's soil solves problems

Amending soil with organic materials provides several solutions to important soil problems:
- *It improves the texture:* Amended soil becomes crumbly, or friable, because the fluffy consistency of organic matter lightens compacted soil, which has little circulation of air or moisture. Amended soil also retains moisture and allows air, water, and nutrients to move through soil to roots.

ORGANIC AMENDMENTS FOR IMPROVING SOIL

The organic amendments listed below are all made from decomposing plant materials. They improve the texture, structure, and fertility of problem soils when they are mixed with it.

COMPOSTED MANURE
Composted manure is the decomposed waste from herbivores, such as horses, cows, rabbits, and chickens. It improves soil texture and drainage, and supplies low levels of plant nutrients. The pH of composted manure ranges from slightly acidic to neutral.

COMPOST
This is a blend of decomposed vegetative matter such as chopped corn stalks, straw, kitchen peelings, and grass clippings. Finished compost is usually dark brown and has the earthy smell associated with good loam. Compost improves soil texture and drainage while supplying low levels of nutrients. The pH is nearly neutral, ranging from slightly acidic to slightly alkaline.

LEAF MOLD
Compost made solely from dead leaves is called leaf mold. It is particularly favored by rose growers and woodland gardeners because these plants thrive in the slightly acidic to neutral pH of a blend of leaf mold and soil.

PEAT MOSS
This amendment is the partially decomposed remains of sphagnum moss, which is collected from ancient peat bogs. Once wetted, it retains moisture very well, but peat moss can be hard to remoisten after it has been allowed to dry out. Peat moss improves soil texture, and is an excellent acidifying agent, because its pH ranges from acidic to slightly acidic.

MUSHROOM COMPOST
This is the spent growing medium used for mushrooms. It is a blend of partially composted organic materials, including horse manure, straw, corn cobs, and peat, with added limestone and gypsum, and sometimes fertilizer. It improves soil texture and supplies low levels of nutrients. The pH ranges from slightly alkaline to neutral.

- *It improves drainage:* Water drains too slowly in clay soils and too quickly in sandy soils. Incorporating organic particles helps in both cases by loosening the soil and absorbing water like tiny sponges, releasing it slowly to lower layers of soil, giving roots time to drink in moisture as they need it.

CLAY SOIL	SANDY SOIL	LOAM SOIL
repels water, causing it to run off.	*speeds water through, losing nutrients.*	*absorbs water, keeping roots moist.*

- *It increases fertility:* Beneficial soil organisms flourish in organic soil, decomposing large bits of organic matter into nutrient-rich forms more useful to plants. As earthworms and smaller creatures move through soil, they redistribute nutrients, carrying them deeper into the root zone, and their tunnels also add beneficial air spaces (see illustration, p.322). These nutrients are held in place by the absorbent organic matter, so they are less likely to wash away.
- *It makes nutrients available:* Highly acidic or alkaline soils, which are those that register below or above a neutral pH range of 6.0 to 7.5, benefit from the neutralizing effect of incorporating organic matter, which makes previously unavailable nutrients accessible to plants. Even though some organic materials, such as fresh peat moss or pine needles, may be initially acidic, they neutralize as they turn to compost.
- *It distributes water and nutrients:* When humus, such as compost or leaf mold, is incorporated into the soil, water and the soluble nutrients that travel in it are captured and held in easy reach of plant roots by the spongelike bits of organic matter.

Nutrients build healthy plants

A plant nutrient is any element necessary for normal plant growth, including carbon, hydrogen, and oxygen, which are supplied by air. Nutrients that can be supplied by soil additives and fertilizers are divided into three groups: primary, or major, nutrients, which plants need in large amounts; secondary nutrients, which plants need in lesser amounts; and minor, or micro nutrients, which are needed in trace amounts.

Providing the essential plant nutrients listed below with synthetic fertilizers (see Reading a fertilizer label, left) or organic sources (see Organic amendments for improving soil, p.323) will prevent or reverse many plant ailments. Having your soil tested is the surest way to find out if you need to supply nutrients, and in what quantities.

Nitrogen: A primary, or major nutrient. Too little nitrogen results in abnormally pale green or yellow leaves and slow growth. Natural sources include blood meal, fishmeal, soybean meal, and cottonseed meal.

Potassium: A primary, or major nutrient. Too little potassium results in poor root development, wilting, leaf areas that turn from green to yellow, then to brown or bronze, and susceptibility to diseases. Natural sources include greensand, a pulverized rock made of clay and ancient marine deposits that is high in potassium and has many minor nutrients. Wood ash is also a rich and fast-acting form of potassium.

Phosphorous: A primary, or major nutrient. Phosphorous is vital to the development of roots, flowers, and fruits. Symptoms of deficiency include abnormally reddish leaves and poor fruit set. Natural sources include rock phosphate and steamed bone meal.

Magnesium: A major nutrient. Magnesium is necessary for seed development and photosynthesis (how plants convert sunlight into food). A shortage of magnesium results in yellowing of leaves between veins, with the yellow areas sometimes turning white. If a soil test indicates a shortage, you can supply magnesium with the natural sources of dolomitic limestone and Epsom salts.

Calcium: A secondary nutrient. Calcium is needed for vigorous growth and root formation. Deficiencies lead to problems, including weak growth, leaves yellowing and

---

READING A FERTILIZER LABEL

.Fertilizer bags contain a lot of useful information, but sometimes they have so many numbers on them that they look more like tax returns than garden products. Here is what to look for when reading the label on a fertilizer bag:

Analysis: A series of three numbers, called the guaranteed analysis, stands for the percentage of the fertilizer made up of each of the three nutrients plants need most: nitrogen, phosphorous, and potassium, in that order (also called N, P, and K). A bag listing 5-3-3, as shown, contains 5 percent nitrogen, 3 percent phosphorous, and 3 percent potassium. A fertilizer with a "balanced formula" contains an equal percentage of each primary nutrient, such as 10-10-10 (for more about nutrients, see Nutrients build healthy plants, right).

Other nutrients: Nutrients other than N, P, and K are sometimes listed on fertilizer bags. For example, a fertilizer for acid-loving plants often includes iron, which makes other soil nutrients more available.

5-3-3 — guaranteed analysis
GUARANTEED ANALYSIS

Total Nitrogen (N)	5.0%
1% ...... Water Soluble Nitrogen	
4% ..... Water Insoluble Nitrogen	
Available Phosphate (P₂O₅)	3.0%
Soluble Potash (K₂O)	3.0%
Calcium (Ca)	3.0%
Total Magnesium (Mg)	0.5%
0.3% .....Water Soluble Magnesium (Mg)	
Sulfur (S)	1.0%
1.0% ...... Combined Sulfur (S)	
Boron (B)	0.02%
Chlorine (Cl)	0.1%
Cobalt (Co)	0.0005%
Copper (Cu)	0.05%
Iron (Fe)	1.0%
Total Manganese (Mn)	0.05
0.01% ..... Water Soluble Manganese (Mn)	
Molybdenum (Mo)	0.0005%
Sodium (Na)	0.1%
Zinc (Zn)	0.05%

Potential basicity equivalent to 80 lbs. of CaCO₃ per ton.

— other nutrients

Plant-Tone is a complete plant food. It contains all the essential plant nutrients. The nutrients are derived from: Dehydrated manure, Animal tankage, Crab meal, Cocoa meal, Bone meal, Dried blood, Sunflower meal, Kelp, Greensand, Rock phosphate, and Sulfate of Potash.

— ingredients

dying, fruit rotting, a condition called blossom end rot in vegetables, and poor root growth. Other nutrients, including manganese, magnesium, and potassium must be in balance for calcium to be available to plants. If a soil test indicates a shortage, natural sources include limestone, gypsum, and crushed clam, oyster, and egg shells.

Iron: A necessary minor nutrient. Photosynthesis would be impossible without it. Too little results in yellowing between the veins of leaves. Often this and other minor nutrients are in the soil, but plants are unable to metabolize them because the balance of acidity, or pH, needs to be corrected. If a soil test indicates that iron should be added, natural sources include seaweed and seaweed extracts and iron-chelate sprays.

Boron: A minor nutrient. Boron is needed for normal growth of stems, leaves, and other plant parts. Too little results in stunted growth, thick, twisted leaves, and premature flower drop. Often this and other minor nutrients are in the soil, but plants are unable to metabolize them because the soil is too alkaline. If a soil test indicates that boron is needed, add garden sulfur to neutralize the soil or apply seaweed products or household borax.

Solving problems before planting

Whether you're beginning a new perennial garden or replanting a vegetable or annual flower garden, working in soil amendments will be easy, because you start fresh with unplanted soil each season. If you live in a cold-winter region, apply amendments and soil conditioners in the autumn so that freezing and thawing cycles can work them into the soil during the winter, sending nutrients

deeper into the ground. In mild areas, with winter rain, waiting until late winter or early spring is better because it prevents nutrients from leaching from the soil before you're ready to plant. Add organic matter and other nutrient-rich additives to soil after it has dried a bit, then wait two weeks before planting.

In either season, spread a 2- to 4-inch layer of aged manure, compost, or other decayed plant matter on top of the soil and dig it in. A rotary tiller makes short work of this job, but a shovel and garden fork will also do the trick. To prevent dry, hard clumps after tilling, avoid working wet soil. If you dig or till soil when it's wet, you'll destroy its friable texture by removing air spaces and creating clumps that dry rock hard.

Holding problems at bay

If your garden is filled with plants, you can still improve the soil by using organic mulches to amend the soil from the top down. Simply spread compost, wood chips, shredded leaves, or other organic material around existing plants, and dig it into the top 1 or 2 inches of soil with a narrow-bladed spade, trowel, or hand fork, being careful not to damage roots. This top dressing will improve your soil slowly with the help of worms and other beneficial soil creatures. They will come to the surface, then carry bits of organic matter with them down into the soil. Nutrients will also leach into the soil with rainfall and irrigation.

Any organic matter you can work into soil, even in the small spaces between plants, will add nutrients, improve water retention, and make your soil easier to work. Use a trowel to mix aged manure, compost, or decayed leaves into the soil around plants, being careful not to disturb their roots.

LET WORMS SOLVE SOIL PROBLEMS

The earthworm is a gardener's best friend. Fertile, healthy soil is full of worms that move through the earth in search of organic matter to feed on, breaking it down into nutrients that plant roots can absorb. Traveling through the soil, worms are busy creating and distributing nutrients and organic matter, and building tunnels that aerate the soil so roots can breathe. They also excrete a fertilizer of their own called castings.

To boost the worm population in your garden, surround your plants with a 2- to

3-inch-deep organic mulch, such as grass clippings, shredded bark, chopped dead leaves, old straw, aged manure, or even newspapers that you can camouflage with a topping of more natural-looking mulch. Worms will soon move in to feast on the organic matter, simultaneously doing the work of improving your soil. Renew the mulch with a new topping as it decomposes. In humid, hot climates such as the Southeast, you may need to reapply mulch every few weeks. In cooler, drier areas, twice a season may be enough.

CORRECTING PROBLEM SOILS

Soil is categorized according to the size of the particles it contains. Clay particles are the smallest, sand the largest, and silt falls between the two. These soils, unlike loam, which is an ideal blend of the three, create unique problems for gardeners and plants. You are most likely to have one of these less-than-ideal types, but the good news is that you can always improve your soil.

Plant problems caused by clay and silt soils

If you can take a handful of moist earth from your garden and form a ball that feels sticky and doesn't crumble when you poke it, your soil is mostly clay. If it does not form a ball and feels more like flour, it is mostly silt. Prevalent in the Southeast, parts of the Midwest, and in many suburban backyards where topsoil has been stripped by builders, clay and silt soils are fertile but dense and slow draining and slow to warm in spring. When dry, clay and silt are often so hard that they seem more like cement than soil.

Such a dense mass is a wonderful thing to have when you're working at a potter's wheel, but it's not a hospitable home to plants. The particles of clay and silt are jammed so closely together there's little room for air—a vital ingredient for healthy roots—and there's also less room for water and nutrients. In addition, plant roots have difficulty penetrating such heavy soil. If your garden's soil is primarily clay or silt, you will face a number of frustrating problems. Chief among them:

- *Poor drainage:* Clay and silt are slow to drain, causing them to remain wet and heavy long after rains. Their small pores inhibit air circulation, suffocating roots.
- *Winter damage:* Clay and silt soils often hold water in winter, leading to root rot, a death knell for plants that aren't naturally adapted to coping with such conditions.
- *Summer damage:* In summer the soil dries out as hard as a brick when water is scarce. This may cause the surface to crack or cause rain to run off, sometimes faster than it soaks in, which leads to drought-stressed plants, root damage, and soil erosion.
- *Hard to work:* Because clay and silt soils are so dense and heavy, they are difficult to till and plant, whether wet or dry.

Lightening up heavy clay and silt soils

Improving your clay or silt soil with organic matter goes a long way toward solving soil problems. Aged manure and compost are the best choices because they are readily available, inexpensive, and promote a lighter, more crumbly and loamy texture to soil.

Incorporating coarse sand, sold as "builder's sand," or fine gravel will improve the texture of clay and silt, but fine sand, sold as "play sand" for children's sandboxes, is likely to make matters worse, because it clogs the pores through which water, nutrients, and air circulate. Sand and gravel also have drawbacks. They dull garden tools and make it hard to slice cleanly into the earth. Also, sand and gravel are heavy and expensive to haul, and it will probably take truckloads to make any noticeable improvement.

Organic materials, such as aged manure or compost, are better choices for loosening up clay or silt soil. Organic matter improves soil fertility as well as texture, while sand and gravel provide traces of nutrients at best. Good compost made with straw, manure, and a little sand, is the best amendment of all for improving clay and silt soils.

Organic matter does double duty with clay soils. Applying a 2- to 4-inch mulch layer of grass clippings, straw, rotted hay, compost, or other organic material around your plants will keep the soil's surface from drying out in the sun. It will further improve soil by increasing earthworm activity.

Problems with sandy soil

Sandy soil is just the opposite of slippery clay: It has a gritty, sandy feel when rubbed between your fingers. Its particles are much larger than clay particles, as are the spaces between the particles. Sandy soil doesn't form clods when worked, as does clay; instead it falls apart into grains. Plant roots penetrate sandy soil easily. Sandy soil is easy to work wet or dry and can be cultivated any time of the year, except when it is frozen. If watered well and fertilized regularly, sandy soil can make good garden beds. Garden beds of dry-as-dust sandy soil, however, challenge plants in critical ways:

- *Infertility:* Sandy soil usually does not contain much organic matter, and what is there breaks down more quickly than it does in other types of soil, especially in warm climates. Soluble nutrients quickly leach out with rain and irrigation.

Raised beds are a practical solution to gardening in hard-to-till rocky, or poorly drained soils. They can be informally edged with stacked stone or bordered by wooden planks. Topping a wooden raised bed with a flat board provides a finished look and a handy seating area.

- **Poor moisture retention:** Because it retains moisture poorly, plants in sandy soil suffer from drying out too quickly, even after heavy rains.

- **Heat stress:** Sandy soil does not moderate heat as well as other soils. It heats up quickly during the day and cools rapidly at night, stressing plants and making it difficult for tender seedlings to thrive.

Solving sandy-soil problems

Just as with clay and silt soils, the key to improving sandy soil is the addition of organic matter. A 3- to 6-inch-thick layer of compost, aged manure, leaf mold, and other kinds of humus worked into the soil acts like a sponge, enabling sandy soil to hold water and soluble nutrients long enough for plants to use them, so the fertilizer you put in the soil will stay there longer. Incorporating organic matter also improves the texture of sandy soil, making it more crumbly and loamy.

After amending sandy soil, apply a 2- to 3-inch layer of organic mulch under plantings and on bare ground to conserve soil moisture and encourage the activity of earthworms and other garden-friendly soil dwellers. To maintain the healthy balance, top dress your garden each season with a fresh layer of compost.

Doing hard time with rocky soil

If your soil seems to grow more rocks than plants, you may find that even routine gardening tasks like planting are impossibly difficult. Make it easier on yourself by choosing and using the right tools for rocky soil.

Replace your traditional wide shovel with a narrow-bladed spade, sometimes called a poacher's spade, so that you can focus your attention on a smaller area and avoid hitting rocks. A pointed hoe is good in rocky soil, too, because you can use it to lever out small rocks as you work. Garden with hand tools as much as possible to focus your efforts on small areas. Get in the habit of picking up a few loose rocks every time you stroll through your garden, and you may find that soon you have enough to build a stacked-stone edging (see photograph, above), an appealing frame for a garden bed.

Rising above adversity

If you prefer not to deal with rocks and poor soil, build raised beds. Beds of loam framed by landscape timbers are fine places to grow most vegetables, flowers, and herbs. Or you can pile loam into an unframed mound, called a berm, atop your poor soil for a more natural-looking and obstacle-free garden bed.

Most vegetables, flowers, and herbs have fine, short roots that rarely penetrate the soil below a depth of 6 inches, but if you make raised beds at least 12 inches deep, you'll be able to plant deeper-rooting perennials and woody plants sold in gallon-sized nursery containers, which are about a foot tall, without having to excavate into the rocky ground beneath the raised bed. If your rocky soil drains well, plant roots will have no problem navigating around rocks below the raised bed. If your soil is impervious, you'll need to make raised beds 18 inches deep, or garden in large, deep tubs and containers.

WISE CHOICES

PLANTS FOR SANDY OR ROCKY SOILS

Trees	Zone
Ash	3–9
Birch	2–6
Hackberry	2–9
Hawthorn	3–7
White pine	3–7

Shrubs	Zone
Barberry	4–8
Butterfly bush	5–9
Five leaf aralia	4–8
Japanese kerria	4–9
Juniper	3–9
Smoke bush	4–8

Flowers	Zone
Artemisia	3–8
Butterfly weed	3–9
Daylily	4–9
English lavender	5–9
Hosta	3–9
Purple coneflower	3–9
Sedum	4–9
Tickseed	4–9
Yarrow	3–9

THE MANY ADVANTAGES OF RAISED BEDS

Raised beds are a great way to get your plants up and out of rocky soil, but that's only one advantage. Here are some others:

- The sun warms raised beds quickly, so that you can plant earlier in the spring.

- The soil stays loose in raised beds because you don't walk on it.

- You can plant closely, use space better, and you can increase your yields. There's no need for rows between plants because you can reach all the plants from the sides.

- There's less weeding. The closely placed plants shade the ground around them, stunting weed growth.

- Because you work at a higher level, the awkward kneeling and bending associated with traditional gardening is a thing of the past.

MAKING A RAISED BED

Building raised beds is a simple job. You can use pressure-treated wood for ornamental-plant beds, but it's best to avoid treated wood around vegetables. Naturally rot-resistant cedar or redwood is a good, though expensive, choice. Lumberyard pine or, better, Douglas fir will eventually rot, but beds are cheap and easy to replace.

MATERIALS

- three 2x10's, 8 ft. long, for sides and ends
- two 2x4's, 10 ft. long, for stakes
- 36 galvanized deck screws, 2½ in. long
- 16 galvanized deck screws, 3 in. long

BUILDING A RAISED BED

Here's how to make a raised bed:
1. A raised bed should be no more than 4 feet wide so that you can reach the middle; so make the end pieces by cutting an 8-foot 2x10 in half. Use two 8-foot 2x10's for the sides.
2. Before assembling the bed, drill four ⅛-inch-diameter pilot holes at one end of each board. The holes prevent the boards from splitting when you screw them together.
3. Position the boards in the garden and attach them with 3-inch galvanized deck screws. Make sure the corners are square.
4. Cut twelve 2x4 stakes, each about 20 inches long, to hold the bed in place. Trim one end of each stake to a point so that you can drive it into the ground.
5. Position the stakes in the corners and in the middle of each board as shown. Drive them to an inch below the tops of the sides. Then drill pilot holes and drive three 2½-inch galvanized deck screws through each stake into the boards.

LOCATING RAISED BEDS

If you have high-growing plants, position a bed with a long side facing west so that the plants get the maximum amount of sunlight. If you mix high- and low-growing plants, plant the lower ones on the bed's south side, where the high plants won't block the sun reaching them. If you're planting only low-growing plants, face a long side south so that all the plants are equally exposed.

To make it easy to get around your raised beds, leave a space between them. Leave 3 feet or so for a wheelbarrow or other wide equipment and as little as 1 foot if all you need is a footpath. Unless you're mulching the paths, however, don't make them narrower than your lawn mower.

CORRECTING SOIL CHEMISTRY PROBLEMS

The acidity or alkalinity of soil is measured on the pH scale, which runs from 0 for the most acidic to 14 for the most alkaline. A pH of 7 is neutral. The microorganisms that provide the nutrients your plants need are most active when the soil is neither too acidic nor too alkaline, a level ranging from 6.0 to 7.5 on the pH scale. If the soil pH isn't suitable, plants can't take up vital nutrients such as phosphorus and potassium even if the soil contains large amounts. Likewise, the availability of some minerals such as manganese, rises to toxic levels if the soil is too acidic.

Many plants can thrive in a pH ranging from an acidic 5.5 to a slightly alkaline 7.5. Vegetables produce the biggest yields in slightly acidic to neutral soil, but they, too, are accepting of a less-than-ideal pH. For any garden, keeping the soil well stocked with organic matter will improve all plants' ability to tolerate a less-than-ideal pH. But if your plants show troubling signs, such as slower-than-normal growth, unnaturally pale leaves, yellowing leaves, fruits spoiling before maturity, or evergreen needles turning yellow, it's a good time to test and correct your soil's pH.

Some plants prefer extremes of alkalinity or acidity (see Wise Choices, p.330 and p.331) and are ideal candidates for extreme soils like those of the Southwest, where alkaline soil is the norm, or parts of the Northeast, where acid rain creates acidic soil, or where it is impractical to amend the soil.

A pH test can be done with an electronic meter that provides instant results, or with a liquid that changes color when soil is added. To get your soil's pH value from a liquid soil test, you compare the color in a vial of soil mixed with test liquid to a range of color

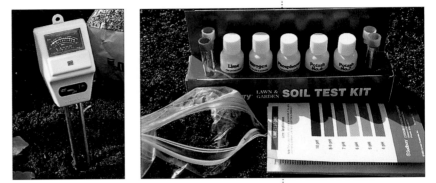

strips on a provided chart. Either testing method is inexpensive and available at garden centers and home improvement centers. You can also gather soil samples from several parts of your bed, mix them together in a small plastic bag, and mail it to a commercial testing laboratory. The laboratory will mail a report back, revealing the pH rating as well as a list of soil nutrients that are lacking. The report will also recommend the proper amount of amendments needed to correct

Most garden plants grow best in soil that is neither too acidic nor too alkaline. You can test your soil's pH, using an electronic meter (left) or a liquid soil test (right). Both are inexpensive and available at garden centers.

AMENDMENTS FOR NEUTRALIZING ACIDIC SOIL

Listed here are the best and easiest-to-use amendments for raising your soil's pH. Check the pH yearly and add amendments as needed, because it is difficult to maintain an altered pH.

GROUND LIMESTONE
Limestone (a rock composed chiefly of calcium carbonate) is ground into powder or pressed into pellets. Limestone pellets are easier to measure accurately and raise soil pH more predictably than the powdered form.

COMPOSTED MANURE
Composted manure from herbivores has a neutralizing effect on all types of soil. Make sure it is well composted to reduce the concentration of nitrogen compounds, found in fresh manure, that damage or burn plants.

MUSHROOM COMPOST
This mostly organic, spent medium used to grow mushrooms contains many ingredients,

including composted horse and chicken manure, soybean and cottonseed meal, and some fertilizers. Its slightly alkaline pH raises soil pH and helps stabilize the altered pH.

CRUSHED OYSTER AND CLAM SHELLS
The alkaline nature of shells raises soil pH, and the calcium in the shells is a nutrient, making these a useful addition to vegetable gardens, where calcium deficiency causes a condition called blossom end rot.

WOOD ASHES
The ash collected from wood-burning fireplaces and wood stoves raises soil pH and is also a source of calcium, potassium, and minor nutrients.

your soil. You can locate a laboratory with help of a garden center, or find listings in the business pages of your phone directory.

Problems created by acidic soil

Acidic soil is often found where annual rainfall and humidity are high. The eastern half of the continent, the Northwest, and some of the mountainous areas of the West have acidic soil. Areas in these regions, which once held bogs, are often highly acidic. Abundant rainfall leaches away minerals, such as calcium, that help neutralize soil pH. In many humid regions of the country, the pH of soil can be as low as 5.0.

Soil below 5.5 on the pH scale can inhibit plants' ability to absorb and metabolize some nutrients. This results in a number of symptoms that appear most often on the leaves, stems, and flowers. These symptoms include:

- Plants with abnormally dark blue-green leaves, or reddish leaves and stems, slower-than-normal growth, and few flowers and fruit, signaling a phosphorous deficiency.
- Pale green leaves over the entire plant and new leaves smaller than normal, with slow growth, signaling a nitrogen deficiency.
- Browning leaves and fruit that begins to rot at the end opposite the stem, a condition called blossom end rot, are common signs of a calcium deficiency. This condition frequently occurs in sandy, acidic soils.
- When older leaves on plants are covered with yellow blotches and vegetables and fruits are poor tasting, acidic soil is causing a magnesium deficiency.
- If older leaves turn yellow and have scorched leaf tips and thinner-than-normal stems, a plant could be suffering from potassium deficiency in acidic soil.

Solving acid soil problems

Neutralizing overly acidic soil is a simple fix for soil nutrient deficiencies. All you need is limestone, also called garden lime, which is available at garden centers. This mineral is sold as fine powder or pellets. Simply spread either over the surface of the soil in amounts recommended on the package label, and rake it lightly into the soil for rapid results. Wood ash is also fast acting and easy to get if you have a stove or fireplace, but sprinkle ashes over the ground sparingly and avoid contact with plants because ashes are caustic and can damage plant tissue on contact. Crushed eggshells and pulverized oyster and clamshells are good, slow-release neutralizing agents for acidic soils and can sometimes be had for free from food-processing plants. You won't see results right away because they require pro-

Lime that leaches from concrete walks and foundations can create alkaline-soil problems for nearby plants.

AMENDMENTS FOR NEUTRALIZING ALKALINE SOIL

Incorporating the mineral supplements listed here, along with materials listed in Organic amendments for improving soil on page 323, into your soil will help neutralize your soil's pH.

GARDEN SULFUR
A fast-acting form of elemental sulfur, usually a powder, used to lower soil pH.

PEAT MOSS (UNCOMPOSTED)
The acidic, partially decomposed remains of moss harvested from peat bogs. Peat moss becomes more neutral as it decomposes.

PINE NEEDLES (UNCOMPOSTED)
The dried foliage of conifers belonging to the genus *Pinus*. Pine needles become more neutral as they decompose.

OAK LEAVES (UNCOMPOSTED)
The acidic dried leaves from the genus *Quercus*. They neutralize as they decompose.

cessing by soil microorganisms, but within a year, your soil will be less acid, and the shells will continue to work as they break down over several seasons. Adding the universal curative organic material to your soil each season will also gradually neutralize the pH, and will add easily absorbed nutrients to help correct the imbalance. Mushroom compost, which is now sold bagged at discount garden centers as well in bulk near mushroom-growing areas, is usually slightly alkaline and makes a good amendment or top dressing for acid soils.

Problems created by alkaline soil

Pockets of alkaline soil can develop in any yard near cement foundations, walkways, or driveways, when lime leaches from the cement into the surrounding soil. But many areas of the Midwest and Southwest have naturally alkaline soil due in part to low annual rainfall and to the minerals that occur there. Sparse rainfall keeps these materials from leaching out of the soil. In such arid regions, the pH of the soil usually ranges between 7.0 and 9.0, making extreme soil alkalinity a fact of gardening life. To find garden plants that will thrive in your naturally alkaline soil, explore native plants and plants that can adapt to your conditions at local nurseries and through native plant societies.

Mild to moderate levels of alkalinity won't interfere with gardening because most plants are somewhat tolerant. But extremes (above 7.5) cause imbalances of soil chemistry and are revealed by such telltale symptoms as:

- *Leaves or needles are discolored:* Leaves on deciduous plants and broad-leaved evergreens turn yellow, but stay green along larger veins. On conifers, needles yellow.
- *Roots are weakened:* Roots are underdeveloped, and small plants are easily uprooted.

Solving alkaline soil problems

Altering alkaline soil can take time to initiate since most acidifying amendments take a season or more to have a neutralizing effect. Garden sulfur is a fast-acting amendment, but it can still take a full season to alter the pH of a planting bed. And because the leaching action of rain and irrigation can wash acidifiers out of the soil and bring in soluble alkaline elements, modifying the pH of a planting bed usually requires yearly treatments.

Start by spreading a 2-inch layer of acidic organic material, such as uncomposted pine needles, peat moss, or chopped oak leaves on planting beds. Work it into the soil around plants or till it into new beds before planting. Alternatively, you can apply elemental sulfur and gypsum (available at garden centers) at the amounts recommended on product labels. Test your soil's pH yearly to monitor progress and continue to amend as needed. In existing beds, work amendments carefully into soil surrounding plants, and mulch with pine needles or oak leaves.

CORRECTING SOIL DRAINAGE PROBLEMS

Water, water everywhere—or nowhere? When the deluge comes, it's comforting to know that your soil can handle it, channeling runoff where you want it, absorbing enough to nourish thirsty plants, and retaining some moisture for later use.

Drainage problems, which generally boil down to "too fast," or "too slow," are usually caused by less-than-ideal soil or terrain. After making the improvements listed here, your garden will welcome rain whenever it comes.

PLANTS FOR WET PLACES

Let these fabulous flowers and out-of-the-ordinary foliage plants turn a wet spot into an eye-catching oasis. But before you plant, consider how wet that spot really is. If it has standing water at least an inch deep for months at a time, select the water-loving plants below. If it is muddy most of the time but doesn't have standing water, or if it is seasonally wet in winter and early spring, select the moisture-loving plants listed.

If your wet area is big enough, you may want to add some water-tolerant trees and shrubs to the flowering and foliage plants. Willows (*Salix* spp.), pussywillow (*Salix caprea*), bald cypress (*Taxodium distichum*), and red maple (*Acer rubrum*) are adaptable choices that thrive in both waterlogged and seasonally wet soils.

PLANT	ZONE	MOISTURE-LOVING	WATER-LOVING
Arrowhead	4–10	✴	✴
Banded bullrush	7–9	✴	✴
Bowles' golden sedge	5–9	✴	
Cardinal flower	5–8	✴	
Great blue lobelia	4–8	✴	✴
Japanese iris	4–10	✴	✴
Marsh marigold	2–8	✴	✴
Monkey flower	6–9	✴	✴
Soft rush	4–9	✴	✴
Sweet flag	4–10	✴	
Yellow flag	4–10	✴	✴

Improving soil drainage

Water that fails to soak into the soil within an hour or so after a rain is one of the most exasperating problems gardeners face. It is commonly caused by heavy clay or silt soil that naturally drains slowly, a topography problem that impedes the flow of water from the yard, compacted soil (soil compressed by excess traffic), or hardpan (a layer of hardened soil beneath the surface). In arid regions, a type of hardpan made of rock-hard calcium can form at or below the soil's surface.

Identifying the cause and solving the drainage problem

If the top inch or two of soil is hard, plants are stunted or grow slowly, water drains sluggishly and pools near plants, and root growth is poor, then you are faced with compacted soil. This is often caused by working or tilling clay or silt soils when they are wet, or walking or moving equipment over soil, especially when it is wet. To remedy problems in small areas, use a hand rake to cultivate around your plants. Gently break the surface and follow with a top dressing of a 2- to 3-inch thick layer of organic mulch, such as shredded bark. The mulch will absorb rain or water from your hose, releasing it slowly, giving the water time to gradually soak into the loosened soil. The mulch also cushions the soil, making it less likely to become compacted, and attracts earthworms, which break up compacted soil as they feed on the organic mulch, and carry bits of it into their tunnels.

When the surface of your soil stays wet long after a rain, plant growth is slow, leaves turn yellow, and root growth is poor, these symptoms may signal a more challenging problem called hardpan. To determine whether hardpan is the problem, dig down to a depth of at least 18 inches and see if your shovel hits an impervious layer of soil along the way. Shallow hardpans (those occurring a few inches below the surface) can often be broken up with a broad fork. This tool looks like a giant version of a garden fork. Its long tines can break up hardpan without breaking your back.

Once the hardpan is broken, lay down a 3-inch-thick, or thicker, layer of organic matter, such as compost or leaf mold, and work it into the soil to reduce future compaction. After planting, be sure to spread a 2- to 3-inch-thick layer of organic mulch over planted areas to cushion the soil, reduce moisture evaporation, and to feed earthworms.

If your hardpan is very thick, it's best to forget about

A garden fork (top) is best for loosening ordinary garden soil, but a long-tined broad fork (bottom) is the tool of choice for breaking up compacted soil, or hardpan.

improving the soil. Instead, build a raised bed over the area to give plants room to grow. The total soil depth in a raised bed built above hardpan should be 18 inches to accommodate the roots of most herbaceous plants and shrubs (for more on raised beds, see Rising above adversity, p.327).

If you live in the Southwest, where soil is often alkaline, you'll be familiar with the stunted plants that show symptoms of nutrient deficiencies. Caliche (pronounced kuh-LEE-chee), a Spanish word for "flake of lime," is the cause. This impenetrable deposit of calcium carbonate, more familiarly known as lime, forms beneath, or sometimes on, the surface of the soil.

If you suspect you have caliche in your garden, dig to analyze the depth at which the layer occurs. If the layer is 18 inches or more below the surface, till the soil to a depth of 12 inches and work in a 4- to 6-inch layer of organic matter (see Organic amendments for improving soil, p.323). If the caliche layer is less than 18 inches from the surface, build a raised bed (see Making a raised bed, p.328), or a simple mound of earth called a berm, at least 18 inches deep. This depth allows most herbaceous plants room to root above the impervious layer. Amend the soil in the raised beds with plenty of fertility-building, moisture-retaining organic matter, such as aged manure or compost so that plant roots don't need to run deep to seek moisture or nutrients.

Making the most of waterlogged soil and standing water

If an area of your yard or garden stays wet most of the time or has standing water in winter, you may be better off not fighting nature and turning the area into a wetland garden with plants such as those listed in Plants for wet places on the facing page.

Or install a small, preformed pool or flexible pond liner so that the area holds water year-round. Make your new pool the centerpiece of the garden, featuring water plants such as American lotus (*Nelumbo lutea*) and water lilies (*Nymphaea* spp.). If mosquitoes and other insect pests are attracted to your pool, add colorful insect-eating fish, such as koi or goldfish, to control the problem.

If the wet area is due to undrained runoff, channeling the water elsewhere is another easy solution. The fastest way to accomplish this is by building a swale, an ornamental yet utilitarian feature that resembles a gravel-lined streambed when water isn't flowing. The swale will direct the water where you want it to go—to the street, a storm sewer, or elsewhere in your yard.

Preventing erosion

Just about everywhere it rains there is soil erosion. Erosion is damaging because rain most often washes away the topsoil—the most fertile layer of soil—from the garden. And with

Wet or boggy sites in your yard can easily be turned from an eyesore into an asset by planting them with colorful, moisture-loving plants, or turning them into a garden pond, complete with water lilies and brilliant goldfish or koi to consume mosquitoes and other insect pests.

WISE CHOICES

GROUNDCOVERS TO PREVENT EROSION

PLANT	ZONE
Ajuga	3–8
Bearberry	2–6
Creeping juniper	3–9
Forsythia	5–8
Ice plant	10
Pachysandra	4–8
Sedum	4–9
Spreading cotoneaster	4–7
Vinca	4–8

erosion comes loss of fertility, as raindrops loosen nutrient-rich organic particles, which are then picked up and carried away as the rain water flows downhill.

Controlling erosion

Slopes of bare soil are prone to erosion with every heavy rain. A layer of stone or rock, overlaid with a deep mulch of coarse wood chips or bark, will slow the flow of water and help to prevent gullies from forming if the slope is not too steep. On sharply sloped hillsides, such a plan won't be effective because torrential rains will wash the mulch down the hill and create gullies around the rocks. For a permanent, reliable solution, plant fast-spreading groundcovers. Their leaves will break the force of even the worst downpour, keeping it from hitting the soil directly. At the same time, the groundcovers' far-spreading roots will knit together to form a net that holds the soil in place. For steep slopes, select evergreen or woody groundcovers, such as periwinkle or creeping junipers, which will provide protection for the soil's surface all winter long. Apply a 2-inch layer of long-lasting mulch, such as bark or wood chips, around newly planted groundcover plants to keep the soil moist and hospitable for their developing roots and to suppress weeds until the planting is established.

COMPOST: THE UNIVERSAL CURE

Understanding how soil nourishes your plants is the first step toward building a healthy garden. And investing in your soil's improvement by working in soil amendments will pay off in a harvest of bigger and better fruits and vegetables and a yard full of strong, vigorous perennials, shrubs, and trees. The capital for investing in your soil and creating a healthier garden is already within your reach. A few handfuls of kitchen peelings, the weeds you pulled from your flower beds, the grass clippings you'd otherwise put on the curb for trash pickup, even the newspaper you just finished reading, put together in the right combination can be transformed into a nutrient-rich garden treasure called compost.

The one and only soil amendment you can create from materials at hand is compost. It can improve soil and help to correct any soil problem you have. Compost—a dark, crumbly substance that's nearly soil—is the cure for many garden ills. It improves the texture of your garden soil, making it crumbly and easy to work, and encourages a thriving community of vital soil organisms and earthworms, which boost the natural disease-fighting abilities of soil. Once you learn how to make compost, you'll soon discover one more thing: You can never have enough of it. Compost can solve problems anywhere you use soil—work it into beds as a soil conditioner, pile it around plants as a mulch, mix it with other materials as the basis for healthy potting soil, and even make a disease-fighting spray called compost tea—so make lots.

Creating perfect compost

Think of the raw materials for your pile as "brown," or high-carbon materials, and "green," or high-nitrogen materials. Brown materials turn into soil-building, pH-neutralizing humus, while the green materials supply the nitrogen needed by microbes to do their decomposing work. Most of your pile should be made of brown materials. These are the things that were plants long ago: straw, dry hay, dried (chopped) cornstalks, fall leaves, newspapers, brown paper bags, and dried grass. Green materials include fresh grass clippings, hedge trimmings, weeds before they have gone to seed, fresh kitchen vegetable and fruit scraps—anything that's moist and usually, well, green. The exception to the color rule is manure: though brown in color, it counts as green material when it is moist and relatively fresh because it's such a rich source of nitrogen. Fresh manure also supplies lots of good compost-activating microorganisms.

When building a compost pile, layer it like an ice-cream parfait: a thick layer of brown

Successful compost is made by alternating 4-inch layers of dried, brown plant material (left) with 1-inch layers of fresh green plant trimmings and fruit and vegetable scraps (right).

materials such as chopped dried leaves mixed with soil from your garden followed by a thin layer of green kitchen scraps, another thick layer of brown material, such as straw, topped by a thin green layer of spent flowers, leaves, and stems from your week's garden cleanup, for example. Make the high-carbon (brown) layers 4 or more inches thick, topped by a thin, 1-inch-thick layer of green (high-nitrogen) material. Moisten each layer with water as you assemble; otherwise, the dry material won't break down, and rain won't be able to penetrate the pile. To quick-start the

WHAT TO COMPOST

Build a rich compost by combining these green (high-nitrogen) materials with these brown (high-carbon) materials:

GREEN MATERIALS:
(high-nitrogen)
- Coffee grounds
- Fresh manure: horse, cow, sheep, goat, poultry, and rabbit
- Grass clippings
- Kitchen vegetable and fruit scraps
- Leftover salad
- Plant trimmings
- Soybean meal
- Weeds before they go to seed

BROWN MATERIALS:
(high-carbon)
- Aged manure
- Buckwheat hulls
- Chopped cornstalks
- Dry hay
- Dry leaves
- Egg shells
- Leftover plain pasta
- Newspaper, shredded
- Sawdust
- Stale bread
- Stems and twigs, shredded
- Straw

A CALL TO COMPOST

If you don't yet compost, here are some good reasons to start.

Finished compost is mostly humus, which, when added to soil, makes it more moisture retentive, offers a bounty of food for soil-improving microorganisms, and improves soil texture by creating spaces for air, water, and nutrients to circulate.

Finished compost is nearly neutral in pH, and helps to stabilize the balance of acidity and alkalinity of the soil, when added to it.

Compost supplies varying amounts of the major and secondary plant nutrients plus many essential minor nutrients to keep plants and soil microorganisms thriving.

With careful management, composting provides a convenient way to dispose of plant debris, which, if not composted, can become a breeding ground for everything from mold spores to mice. When you cut plants down at the end of their useful life and add them to the compost heap, they no longer invite garden problems.

Compost improves the disease resistance of garden plants because some of the organisms that break down plant material into compost produce natural antibiotics. Its disease-fighting ability also discourage the growth of soilborne fungal diseases. Used as a mulch, compost keeps disease-carrying soil from splashing onto plants during irrigation and rainfall. Steeping a few inches of compost in a bucket of water overnight or longer yields a concentrated "tea" that, when diluted to the color of weak tea and sprayed on plant leaves, discourages some fungal diseases, including powdery mildew.

WHAT NOT TO COMPOST

Avoid composting problems such as attracting animal pests, introducing disease pathogens, or creating unpleasant odors by steering clear of these materials:

- Aggressive, spreading weeds
- Animal products
- Bones
- Chunks of wood
- Dairy products
- Diseased plants or fruits
- Eggs (but do compost eggshells)
- Manure of meat-eating animals
- Oils
- Seashells, unless crushed

decomposition process, make sure the bottom of the pile is in contact with the ground and use a compost activator. Activators—also known as starters—introduce microorganisms that excel at breaking down organic matter. There are commercially available compost activators sold at garden centers. Several excellent compost activators may already be available in your garden: finished compost from a previous batch, any fresh herbivore manure, strips of sod, or good garden soil.

Because the amount of carbon and nitrogen in organic materials varies, composting is not an exact science. Like many gardening pursuits, it's something you'll get a feel for the more you do it. Generally, the rule is to use one part green (high-nitrogen) material for every four parts brown (high-carbon) material. Translated to compost-pile building, this means that for every 1-inch-thick layer of fresh weeds or other green material you add to your pile, you should top it with a 4-inch layer of straw or other brown material. Keep your layers relatively thin, about 1 to 4 inches, when you add material to the pile. This helps keep materials from matting down. During the height of the growing season, you'll probably have more green materials than brown at the ready. If you run short, buy a bale of straw from a garden center or nearby farm, or tear newspapers into thin strips or crumple them to make a layer of high-carbon material. Or stockpile dried leaves every fall, placing them in a heap next to your compost pile, where they will be handy for summer use.

Enhancing the mix

Many gardeners like to enhance compost by adding a sprinkling of mineral-rich materials to their pile, such as calcium-rich crushed eggshells or potassium-rich wood ashes, to boost the nutrient content of their finished mix. A little of these goes a long way, so use a light sprinkling of these ingredients to avoid introducing excess minerals that could interfere with the activity of composting microorganisms.

Aid composting by adding water and air

A moist, not wet, compost pile decomposes much more quickly than does a dry pile. As you add new materials, sprinkle each layer with a garden hose. If rain is scarce, spray your heap until it's moist but not soaking wet. Making it the consistency of a rung-out sponge is ideal. If rains are frequent in your region, round the top of your pile so extra water won't soak in, or shield the pile from getting sopping wet by covering it with a tarp. In drier climates, build the top with a depression in the middle to collect precious rainwater. Be careful not to make your pile too wet. If the ingredients are soggy or dripping when you turn the pile, add more dry brown material to absorb excess moisture.

Air circulating through a compost pile keeps fast-acting compost organisms working at top speed. Whether you plan to turn the pile or not, be sure to include bulky brown materials, such as straw and cornstalks, that don't pack down quickly to keep your pile well-aerated throughout. Avoid thick layers of grass clippings or unchopped leaves; these settle into solid mats that prevent the flow of air through the pile. Instead, apply these materials in shallow layers or mix them with fluffier materials before adding them. Turning the

Water your compost after each addition of new material, wetting the layers until they are as moist as a rung-out sponge. For the speediest composting, water as often as needed to maintain proper moisture.

SIZED FOR SUCCESS

The size of a compost pile has a lot to do with how fast things decompose. Piles that are too small don't heat up enough. Piles that are too large can get too hot and have too little air in their centers. A pile that is 3 to 4 feet high, 3 feet wide, and 3 feet long should cook just right.

As you build your compost pile, alternate a layer of brown plant material with a layer of green plant material. Use thin layers of greenery, such as grass clippings, and layers four times thicker of once-living, brown plant material, such as straw and whole dried leaves.

pile with a garden fork at least once a week will keep things cooking. If your muscles don't like the thought of frequent turning, simply jab a garden fork into your pile and wiggle it back and forth to let in more air.

Fast or slow cooking?

The best thing about composting is that organic material will decompose even if you do nothing to it. Passive compost piles work if you merely heap the stuff in a discreet corner of your yard and harvest the finished compost from the bottom of the pile in a year or two. The decomposing will be done by earthworms that work slower than the heat-loving microbes in an active pile, but the result is still great compost.

You can place your compost pile in sun or shade, but in cooler climates the warmth of the sun will help speed up the process. The sun's rays will warm the outside of the pile but not nearly to the temperature inside the pile. The inside may reach 140°F or higher due to microorganism activity, not the sun's heat. If the only place you have to put your compost pile is in a shaded area, don't worry: The internal temperature of a well-managed pile will climb no matter where it's located. If you live in a cold-winter climate, however, be aware that in spring a compost pile located in sun will heat up and get cooking sooner than one that's still holding winter's chill in the

shade. A sunny site will also allow you to collect finished compost earlier in the spring because snow melts faster in the sun, and the compost also thaws sooner.

Speeding up slow decomposition

Even though anticipation is a big part of gardening—first red tomato, anyone?—gardeners are also an impatient bunch. We want our compost, and we want it now! If you're diligently caring for a large, well-layered, hot compost pile, you can expect to collect finished compost in as little as six weeks. In a passive pile that's turned infrequently, or one that's in a bin smaller than 3 cubic feet, a year or two is more like it.

As long as the temperature within the pile measures 140°F or higher, things are working at the speed they should. If your pile is cooler than that, you can speed the process by heating it up with more frequent turning, spritzing it with water when it's dry, adding some green material, or increasing its size.

Keep in mind that microorganism activity, and thus the making of compost, slows when the weather cools in the fall. A slowdown in your compost production in fall is natural and unavoidable unless you live in a mild-winter climate, where compost cooks all year. To extend the compost season in colder areas, surround your pile with a snug wall of stacked straw or hay bales for insulation in the fall.

BACKYARD COMPOSTING

Compost is big business, with plastic bags of the finished product stacked into pyramids at every gardening center. But a simple backyard setup will give you the convenience of having compost ready whenever you need it, plus the satisfaction of home-cooking your own special blend—and it's a great way to make your yard waste disappear.

Garden centers are chock-full of all manner of composting containers: wire enclosures, rotating drums, and even big plastic balls that you roll around with the help of a couple of strong friends. Choose your composting enclosure or container based on your needs and preferences. A simple open pile works just fine, but a three-sided enclosure keeps things looking neater and still allows easy access. Barrel-shaped compost tumblers are a popular alternative. It is easier to turn a pile by rolling one of these compost tumblers than it is to turn a traditional pile with a garden fork. And although compost happens even if you don't turn the pile, the more often you turn it, the faster it will turn into compost, with some of the tumbler manufacturers promising compost in as little as three to six weeks, as opposed to six weeks or more when turning a traditional pile or a year or two in an un-turned pile. The biggest drawback to many commercial composters is their small size. Avoid those that hold less than 3 cubic feet. Keep in mind that the smaller the unit, the more often you'll need to empty and refill it.

Keeping compost operations neat

A compost pile may be worth its weight in gold, but you won't want it to be a focal point in your yard. Most gardeners choose a convenient but discreet location, often close to the vegetable garden, which generates a lot of raw compost material. Practice good housekeeping by raking up any debris that spills on its way to the heap. If you—or your neighbors—prefer a tidier look than a mounded, open pile, you can keep your compost in a simple home-built, three-sided enclosure of wire fencing and stakes. Or you can use enclosed containers, such as a rotating drum, to keep your composting material entirely out of sight.

Avoiding and solving compost-making problems

Fast-cooking compost operates at temperatures high enough to kill most weed seeds and disease organisms. But just to be on the safe side, ward off the possibility of contamination by never adding potentially diseased or gone-to-seed plants to the pile. Here are some simple solutions to a few common problems you might encounter when composting.

COMPOSTERS COME IN ALL SHAPES, SIZES, AND STYLES TO FIT EVERY GARDENER'S NEEDS

Although composting can be as simple as a pile of decomposing plant material, most gardeners require something more manageable in size, and, if you live in a suburban area, looks are just as important. These simple composters range from inexpensive, easy-to-make enclosures to more advanced commercial models available from garden centers and specialty catalogs.

This composter is a classic homemade design, made of boards nailed to posts, or old shipping palettes.

This simple compost bin is constructed of fence wire wrapped around four corner posts driven into the ground.

Solving odor problems

A well-balanced, well-aerated compost pile has no disagreeable odor—it smells delightfully earthy, like a freshly plowed field. If your pile smells bad, correction is usually fast and easy. Compost odor problems are a common occurrence experienced by novices, or when adding organic materials that you haven't used before. It takes a certain amount of experience to judge the moisture content of various materials and to see how they behave when added to the mix. But, by being alert to the first whiff of trouble brewing, you can quickly adjust your pile and restore its agreeable fragrance. The solution amounts to adjusting the proportion of high-carbon contents to high-nitrogen contents in the pile.

- **Eliminating sour smells:** An ammonia odor indicates that your pile is too heavy on green materials. When there isn't enough carbon present, bacteria break down green plants into ammonia, a form of nitrogen that easily evaporates and fills the air with a decidedly barnyard smell. To encourage microbes to produce less smelly forms of nitrogen (which are also more useful to plants), give them a more balanced diet by forking in more brown material. Turn the pile to mix the pockets of decomposing green materials with the new additions and to let in lots of air.

  Ammonia smell is a common complaint during lawn-mowing season, when there's a

temptation to dump thick layers of grass clippings onto the pile. Keep a bale of straw or a stack of newspapers handy, and add a 3- to 4-inch layer of straw, shredded newspapers, or other brown materials between 1-inch layers of grass. Or mix grass clippings with about twice their volume of straw, newspapers, or last year's chopped leaves on top of the compost pile or in a wheelbarrow before adding them to the compost pile.

- **Eliminating decaying odors:** Nobody wants to hold their nose when they stroll past the composting end of your yard, so keep your pile smelling sweet by avoiding the addition of trouble-making materials. Don't add

Spills are inevitable in the composting area as you add to and work the pile. Keep the area looking neat by putting a perimeter of wood chip mulch around the pile, to help disguise stray bits and pieces.

A composter using two posts to support a circle of fencing comes in handy for temporarily holding piles of leaves.

A popular commercial composter uses an easy-to-rotate plastic barrel to mix and turn the ingredients.

Another commercial composter features a rain-collecting lid and a door for easy removal of finished compost.

Plants that get their start in compost are often more vigorous than those grown in the garden. Who knows? You may win a prize for the fruits of that rampant squash vine spreading across your pile of gardener's gold.

Use a compost thermometer like the one at right to probe the center of your pile. When the temperature reaches 113° to 158° F, it's done.

COMPOSTING ORGANISMS DEFINED

Psychrophiles: These are compost-making bacteria that like it cool. They start the decomposing process and begin to generate heat as they turn plant material into compost. Because they like it cool, when the pile heats up to about room temperature, they slow down and make room for other organisms to work.

Mesophiles: These bacteria and fungi work best in temperatures that seem more comfortable to us, from about room temperature to around 110°F. As they work, they also generate heat, paving the way for organisms that like it hot.

Thermophiles: These microbes flourish in temperatures ranging from 113°F to 158°F. They live and grow in the hottest part of the pile. When they have done their work, the pile begins to cool down, and the compost is ready to use.

meats, oils, or dairy products to the pile. Animal products smell bad when they decay, and can attract rodents and other pests. Cover vegetative kitchen scraps with a layer of brown material, such as chopped leaves or straw, instead of leaving them exposed atop the pile. If your pile is smelly, turn it to bury any stinkers deeper within, where decomposition will accelerate the composting process. Increase the heat in the pile by sprinkling it with water if needed, giving it a good aerating with the garden fork, or tumbling it well if it's in a barrel composter.

Eradicate weed seeds or unwanted plants

If an application of finished compost yields a bumper crop of weeds, that's an indication that your pile was a slow cooker. Avoid future occurrences by not adding weeds or plants with seed heads. Turn and water your pile more frequently to increase the heat inside to at least 140°F to kill pesky seeds that may have inadvertently been added. An inexpensive compost thermometer lets you quickly check the temperature inside the pile.

Do not add weeds to your pile that spread aggressively by roots or rhizomes. Roots and rhizomes of Johnson's grass, Jerusalem artichokes, couch grass, and goutweed often stay alive and well even in a hot pile, ready to spring into new growth as soon as the compost is applied to your garden. Dispose of noxious weeds like these in the trash.

What to do with plants that sprout in compost

This is not a problem. Because compost is mainly used as a soil conditioner, you don't have to worry about plant roots robbing your compost of nutrients. Let that cherry tomato grow, transplant those perennial and annual seedlings to the garden, or pass the unexpected bounty on to friends. If you prefer not to see volunteer plants in your pile, be more diligent about not adding seed heads or fruits with seeds to the compost heap in the future.

Keeping rodents and other animal pests away

Remember to use only plant-derived kitchen scraps in your compost, and you'll avoid attracting rodents and other animal pests. Acceptable additives include peelings, leaves, stems, soft cores, or other unwanted parts of fruits and vegetables (but not fruit pits). If you put the scraps from last night's chicken dinner on your pile, every cat, raccoon, and dog in the neighborhood will soon come calling, not to mention smaller opportunists such as mice and chipmunks. Keep meats, oils, dairy products, and eggs out of the compost to avoid such problems. Bury suspected tempting foodstuffs, such as overripe fruit, beneath a thick layer of other material instead of leaving them as an open-air buffet. A 6-inch layer of straw or other brown material over the top of recent food-scrap additions should discourage most pests and contribute to a healthy balance of ingredients. If scavengers still rummage through the pile, fence it in and cover it with hardware cloth, chicken wire, or bird netting.

Controlling insects, slugs, and soil-dwelling invaders

It's natural for your compost pile to have a healthy population of beetles, sowbugs, snails, slugs, and other insects that dine on organic matter or on minute creatures lower in the food chain. Peskier insects such as wasps, bees, and creepy crawlies like grubs and flies may also be attracted to the decomposing fruits, vegetables, and kitchen scraps. Again, burying these additions beneath a 4- to 6-inch layer of brown material will discourage visiting pest insects. But do take time to enjoy visits from occasional insects and butterflies as interesting additions to your compost-pile ecology. They don't eat much. And insects, snails, and other small creatures attract song birds, which will visit your pile to feast on the abundance.

Camouflaging the compost pile

When you learn how to compost and see its results in the garden, you probably won't be able to stop making the stuff. This activity is wonderful for the well-being of a garden, but compost piles aren't the most attractive things in the world, and you may want to improve on the look of yours. Because a compost pile of some sort is always in the yard, a permanent solution is best.

You can transform your compost pile into a neighbor-friendly work of art by surrounding it on three sides with a screen of attractive plants, such as tall flowers or evergreens like arborvitae (*Thuja occidentalis*), hemlock (*Tsuga canadensis*), or yew (*Taxus* spp.). An added touch of color can be attained by allowing flowering vines like clematis (*Clematis* spp.) or fast-growing annual vines like morning glory to weave their way through the trees.

Catching the composting bug

Harvesting your first wheelbarrow load of rich, crumbly, fragrant compost will make you an instant convert to the habit of composting. Composting makes sense in so many ways that it's a literal waste not to start your own compost pile. When you can so easily and inexpensively improve your soil, feed your plants, reduce disease, invite beneficial soil organisms, and recycle garden trash that would otherwise be trucked away, the benefits to your garden—and to the earth—are obvious. So much good for your garden comes from such unlikely raw materials.

Once you begin routinely composting, you'll find that you begin to look at potential raw materials a little differently—with a covetous eye. Whether it's a handful of apple peelings or a wheelbarrow heaped with fall leaves, plant debris will no longer be something to leave in a trash bag on the curb. Seeing how your plants thrive in a garden of compost-improved soil, you'll discover that incorporating compost to improve soil texture and fertility is a task as satisfying as planting a flat of flowers. Using compost to improve the potential of your soil is an investment that will always pay off. It is the beginning of a better garden and also the solution to many garden problems.

When composting becomes a healthy fact of gardening life, look for ways to keep one or more piles tucked out of sight, but within arm reach of your vegetable and flower beds.

CHAPTER NINE

LAWNS

A LUSH, GREEN SWATH OF MOWED lawn has the power to make all the other elements in a landscape look even better. Lawns also provide a delightful setting for relaxation, entertainment, and family activities.

Whether you are starting a lawn from scratch, endeavoring to revive an ailing lawn, or looking for a low-maintenance lawn alternative, you can turn to this chapter to ensure your success. Here you will find tips for choosing and planting grass that will thrive in your climate and soil, learn about disease-resistant and shade-tolerant varieties, and more.

And when problems do arise, a troubleshooting section will help you deal with common lawn ailments, from weeds and pests to brown spots. As a rule, when you discover unwanted visitors or the signs of disease, take the most environmentally friendly approaches, as we list them, first. For more on careful use of organic and chemical treatments, see page 9 and pages 390 to 399.

CREATING A HEALTHY LAWN

A healthy, long-lived lawn is the result of good planning and preparation. The millions of individual plants that make up your lawn have the same needs as other plants. Tough by nature, lawn grasses will flourish if you take the time to improve the soil, select the right varieties, and plant with care. A good beginning encourages strong, healthy growth that fends off pests and diseases.

Starting a new lawn

Preparing the soil is vital for a healthy lawn. Test soil pH and nutrient levels (see Correcting soil chemistry problems, p.329), amend with plenty of organic matter, such as compost, and add nutrients as called for in the test. Improve drainage if necessary (see Dealing with poor drainage, p.349).

In northern areas, cool-season grasses that become green in spring and turn brown in winter are the grasses of choice. In mild-winter areas, warm-season grasses are best; they can withstand the long, hot, and often dry summers. They typically turn brown at first frost and become green again in late spring. To provide year-round lushness, they're often sown over each fall with cool-season grasses, which grow well in mild winter months. The process is called overseeding. Check with your local garden center for the cool-season grass varieties most suited to your area.

Seeds are the most inexpensive way to start a new lawn. In the North, sow in early spring or in fall, at least six weeks before first frost, so that the grass has time to start growing before being stressed by summer heat or winter cold. In the South and other mild-winter climates, sow warm-season grasses in late spring to early summer. Or, if you are sowing seed over existing grass for winter green, sow cool-season grasses in late summer to early fall. Keep the soil moist until the seeds sprout. After sowing, scatter a light layer of straw over the area to keep rain from washing away the seeds. Let the straw decompose.

Some grasses, such as zoysiagrass, improved Bermuda, and St. Augustine, are difficult to grow from seeds. Sprigs and plugs are less costly alternatives to sod, and work well for difficult-to-start grasses, but like seeds, they can take up to two years to fill in. Plant the sprigs or plugs in small holes or shallow furrows in tilled soil. And expect to do a lot of fussy, time-consuming initial planting and weeding. With sod, you get an instant new lawn, but it's more expensive than sprigs or plugs and awkward to handle. Selection of grasses is limited with sod, but if you buy locally, it should thrive in your yard. Lay sod (below) in early spring or fall in cold-winter

LAYING A SOD LAWN

Sod gives you an instant carpet, one ready for foot traffic in only two or three weeks. Although sod costs about twice as much as seed—and more if you hire a professional—it is a fast, durable solution for heavy-traffic areas.

Sod, grass that is measured, cut in strips, and rolled with roots and a layer of soil attached, is a convenient and fast way to lay an entire lawn or patch worn spots in existing lawns.

To lay sod, unroll a strip on soil that has been stripped of existing soil and tilled to make it easy for the sod roots to penetrate. Firm the sod by pressing it against the soil.

Stagger sod pieces so that the seams are not continuous. Water well and often until the pieces knit together.

climates, and in spring in mild-winter climates. Water as needed to give your new lawn an inch (see Weed and water now to prevent problems later, p.384) every 7 to 10 days until it is established (when you gently tug on a plant and it does not pull free of the soil, its roots are established) in two to three weeks. Avoid walking on it during this time to protect the developing roots.

Blending seeds solves problems

If your yard has a mix of sun and shade, your lawn will look better if you use two seed mixes—one blended for sun and the other for shade—rather than an all-purpose blend. It pays to invest in an improved named variety, such as the naturally low-growing, handsome, dark-green bluegrass 'Adelphi,' rather than a product simply labeled bluegrass or ryegrass. Improved varieties hold up better to drought, disease, insects, and traffic (see Trouble-free lawn grasses, p.346).

If you're planting a new lawn in part to full shade, choose a grass mix containing several species that tolerate shade. Shade stresses lawn grass, and a variety of species gives the most protection against disease, because if one or two species succumb, others in the mix may remain healthy and spread to fill in bare spots. You can improve the shade tolerance of existing lawns by overseeding them with a mix of seeds blended for shade, following the

seeding rates on the package. In general, fine fescues, St. Augustine, and zoysiagrass are the most tolerant of shade; check with your local garden center for varieties recommended for your area. Improved varieties of some grasses, even those not traditionally recommended for shade, such as fine fescues 'Alta', 'Houndog', 'Rebel', 'Reliant', 'Scaldis', and 'Nugget', as well as the Kentucky bluegrass varieties 'Bristol', 'Benson', and 'Glade' tolerate dim light.

For a quick fix, or in the dry shade under trees, where perennials grasses can't grow, plant fast-growing annual ryegrass for a summer lawn; resow as often as needed to keep a spot of green grass growing in the shade. An area of moist soil that's shaded is particularly challenging. For these spots plant the species grass rough bluegrass (*Poa trivialis*).

Caring for a lawn

Keeping an established lawn looking its best requires that you give it regular care, but you don't have to go overboard. To start, make sure you fertilize the soil, not just the grass. An annual 3-inch topping of fine-textured compost or aged manure adds organic matter to nourish beneficial soil organisms. These in turn break down thatch, the layer of dead and matted grass that accumulates on the soil's surface. In the process, nutrients are released and made available to grass roots over a long period of time. Adding organic matter also

SOWING GRASS SEED

Seed is economical but slower to fill in than sod. Sow seed evenly to avoid gaps in the lawn. Even a mild wind scatters seeds, so mix barely damp, clean sand with the seeds before sowing to help them fall straight down.

When sowing seed, work back and forth across the whole lawn from left to right, then turn and repeat the process at a right angle to the first pass. That way you'll eliminate gaps and surpluses in your spreading.

After sowing seeds, give the soil an initial deep watering. To keep the soil from drying out, spread a thin straw mulch, then water lightly every day. Let the straw decompose.

Don't walk or mow the grass until its roots are well established, usually two to three months.

promotes soil aeration and drainage and helps counteract compaction. Synthetic fertilizers with high-nitrogen formulas provide green color quickly, but except for the timed-release formulas, they don't last long or contribute to a lawn's long-term health or disease resistance. Organic fertilizer blends release more kinds of nutrients slowly over a longer time, making grass healthy and green.

Most northern lawns need fertilizing once a year, or less, depending on the condition of the soil. In the Southeast, where frequent rains leach nutrients from the soil, and grass grows quickly, two or three frequent, small applications a year will keep a lawn thriving.

Fertilize cool-season grasses in fall—October, in most areas. This promotes thick, healthy turf, by letting the roots build up nutrient reserves before going dormant. If you want or need to fertilize a lawn again, wait until early summer—late June—once spring growth has slowed. Fertilizing earlier causes grass to expend needed energy on leaf growth. This can stress plants, prevent thick turf, and increases how often you need to mow.

Fertilize warm-season grasses twice a year, once in June and again in August. Or, if you water regularly, apply half-strength fertilizer four times—in May, June, July, and August—to promote even growth.

For all grasses, use a fertilizer that contains at least some of its nitrogen in organic or synthetic slow-release form, so that it will be released over a long period. Organic and slow-release fertilizers are less apt to burn your lawn and be washed out of the soil by rain and irrigation. Organic fertilizers supply important minor nutrients not found in many synthetic fertilizers, and they have the added benefit of feeding beneficial soil organisms.

Apply fertilizer when the grass is dry. If the grass is wet, a strong concentration can cling to the blades and burn them. For even distribution, use a lawn spreader, a hand-held crank spreader, or use a hose-end sprayer for liquid fertilizers. Water afterward to work the fertilizer into the soil.

Good lawn care includes regular mowing. Set your mower to a height appropriate for your grass type. Keep warm-season Bermuda grass and zoysiagrass short (1¼ to 2 inches) and cool-season grasses at a medium height (3 inches). Keep warm-season bahia and St. Augustine, as well as cool-season tall fescue, on the long side (3 to 3½ inches). Mow higher in summer, when grasses are more likely to suffer from heat and drought and are slower to bounce back after cutting.

COOL-SEASON GRASSES

■ **FINE FESCUES** (*Festuca* spp.)
Medium green with deep roots. Tolerates shade, heat, heavy foot traffic, and drought; requires little fertilizer; and is not prone to thatch buildup. Creeping red fescue (*F. rubra*) spreads by rhizomes, rapidly filling in bare spots; other fescues grow more slowly, in clumps. Slender creeping red fescue (*F. r.* var. *trichophylla*) grows well in poor, acidic soils and resists drought, making it an excellent low-maintenance grass. 'Barcrown' is disease resistant and very durable. Sheep's fescue (*Festuca ovina* var. *tenuifolia*) grows well in shade, resists drought and disease. 'Bartok' needs little or no fertilizing.

Tall fescue (*F. elatior*) is a coarse, clumping turf grass. In mild areas it stays green year-round except during severe drought. Fescues are often included in seed mixes; tall fescues in mixes for heavy traffic or minimal upkeep. Best in Northern U.S. and Canada, mountain areas, Pacific Northwest.

Varieties: 'Austin', 'Bonsai', 'Crewcut', 'Crossfire', and 'Pixie' are dwarf tall fescues that need less mowing. 'Shenandoa', 'Tempo', and 'Tribute' resist pests. 'Phoenix' produces uniform lawns. 'Water Saver' has deep, drought-resistant roots. 'Vegas' is low growing, disease resistant, and durable.

■ **KENTUCKY BLUEGRASS** (*Poa pratensis*)
Rich, deep green color with a hint of blue on medium- to fine-textured blades. Not drought or shade tolerant. Tolerates average foot traffic. Best in Northeast, Northwest, mountain areas, cooler areas of South.

Varieties: 'Adelphi' is highly disease resistant and tolerates some shade and heat. 'Bartitia' resists rust and powdery mildew, is vigorous and drought tolerant. 'Barzan' wears bet-

Trouble-free Lawn Grasses

ter than others and is vigorous. 'Eclipse' is shade tolerant and disease resistant. 'Bristol' and 'Glade' tolerate shade and resist powdery mildew.

■ RYEGRASSES
(*Lolium multiflorum; L. perenne*)

Annual ryegrass (*L. multiflorum*) is a coarse-textured, clumping grass that gives almost instant green and is often used for overseeding and inexpensive fast cover. Perennial ryegrass (*L. perenne*) is a medium-textured, deep green grass with shallow roots, often mixed with bluegrass and fescues, because it establishes quickly and holds up well to traffic. It is not drought tolerant and suffers from heat or cold; some varieties tolerate shade. Grows in all cool-season areas, but performs best in year-round-mild coastal areas.

Varieties: 'Fiesta II', 'Yorktown II', and 'Manhattan II' tolerate shade, heat, and cold, and resist some diseases. 'SR 4200' and 'Regal' resist pests. 'Pebble Beach' can give your lawn a fairway feel.

WARM-SEASON GRASSES

■ BAHIA GRASS
(*Paspalum notatum*)

Coarse grass with deep roots and vigorous runners. Shade tolerant. Somewhat tolerant of traffic and drought. Needs less fertilizer and stays green longer than many warm-season grasses. Minimal thatch buildup. Requires frequent mowing to keep it from sending up seed stalks. Susceptible to insect and disease damage. Best for the Southeast.

Varieties: 'Argentine', 'Pensacola', and 'Paraguay' have finer texture; 'Argentine' is disease resistant.

■ BERMUDA GRASS
(*Cynodon dactylon*)

Medium to coarse texture with deep roots and aggressive runners; use deep barrier strips to keep it out of ornamental beds. Tolerates heat, drought, and traffic; is disease resistant but it is not shade tolerant. Hybrid (improved) Bermudas have a finer texture and are greener. Needs fertilizing and frequent mowing to look good. Prone to thatch buildup. Best in Southwest, Southeast, and West.

Varieties: 'Santa Ana' withstands smog or salty winds. 'Tiflawn' is durable, has good texture and color. 'Tifway' is durable and needs less fertilizer and mowing.

■ BLUE GRAMAGRASS
(*Bouteloua gracilis*)

A fine-textured, grayish green Great Plains native useful in dry, high-altitude climates. Needs full sun but tolerates heat, cold, and can survive dry spells with no irrigation (though it will brown). Grows in alkaline soil. Often mixed with buffalo grass for better coverage. Best in Rockies and High Plains.

Varieties: 'Alma', 'Hachita', and 'Lovington' are improved varieties.

■ BUFFALO GRASS
(*Buchloe dactyloides*)

A fine-textured, low-growing gray-green American native for full sun. Outstanding drought tolerance, traffic tolerance, and minimal mowing needs. Matures to about 4 inches tall but has an uneven surface. Growth from seeds is slow, but once established, spreads rapidly by runners. Will grow without irrigation in areas with at least 10 inches of annual rainfall. Good for poor and alkaline soils.

Varieties: 'Prairie' and 'Texoca' have denser growth. '609' is a further improvement, with better color and denser growth than other varieties. Blends of buffalo grass and blue gramagrass produce a thick, low-maintenance lawn that is very drought and disease resistant.

■ CENTIPEDE GRASS
(*Eremochloa ophiuroides*)

Medium texture, light green grass, with shallow roots and creeping stolons (underground stems). Not tolerant of salt or traffic. Somewhat shade tolerant. Needs minimal fertilizer but regular watering; turns brown in hot, dry weather and at onset of winter. Grows well in moderately acidic soils. Slow to spread and fill in. Best in Southeast.

Varieties: 'Oaklawn' has good pest and disease resistance. 'Centiseed' can be grown from seed. 'Centennial' is a popular choice.

■ ST. AUGUSTINE GRASS
(*Stenotaphrum secundatum*)

Coarse-textured grass that spreads aggressively by sending out runners. Excellent tolerance for humid heat, shade, and salt. Tolerates moderate traffic. Good in alkaline soils. Long dormant (brown) season and prone to thatch buildup. Best from Southeast to Southwest.

Varieties: 'Seville', 'Tamlawn', 'Floratam', and 'Raleigh' resist SADV (St. Augustine decline virus, a problem with older varieties). 'Floratine' is shade tolerant. 'Seville' stays green longer. 'Raleigh' has good pest resistance, color, and shade tolerance.

■ ZOYSIAGRASS (*Zoysia* spp.)

Dark green, medium to fine texture. Older varieties are wiry and hard on bare feet. Newer varieties overcome zoysia's tendency to turn brown early and green late. Tolerates shade, salt, heat, drought, and heavy traffic. Slow to establish. Best for southern California, coastal and upper South.

Varieties: 'Victoria' and 'De Anza' have a shorter than usual dormancy. 'Meyer' has a softer texture, resists drought and cold, but has a long dormancy. 'El Toro' is fast growing and produces less thatch. 'Z52' (super zoysia) is cold tolerant and moderately fast growing.

SOLVING LAWN PROBLEMS

Monitor your grass for signs of trouble, and act quickly to correct a problem before it affects a large area. Here's how to identify and solve common lawn problems.

Improving poor growth

Signs of poor growth, such as yellowing, wilting, or patchy spots, usually mean it's time to take a look at your nutrition program or growing conditions and make some adjustments.

Grass grows weakly or leaf tips yellow

If your grass has thin, spindly growth or shows yellowing at the tips, poor nutrition is often to blame. Test the soil (see Correcting soil chemistry problems, p.329) to find out exactly what your grass needs, and apply the recommended nutrient according to test results. Grasses vary widely in their fertilizer needs. Buffalo grass and centipede grass need little or no supplemental fertilizing, while Kentucky bluegrass needs as much as a pound of actual nitrogen per month during the growing season. Fertilize cool-season grasses in fall, and if desired, again in early summer. Fertilize warm-season grasses in late spring to early summer and again in late summer.

Grass grows poorly, but soil test shows no nutrient deficiencies

If your soil test shows no nutrient deficiencies, your lawn's poor growth may be caused by physical problems that prevent grass roots from absorbing water, nutrients, and air. Suspect compacted soil if there are bare patches or if the area receives heavy foot traffic. To improve growth in compacted areas, aerate the soil in the growing season when the soil isn't wet. For best results, rent a machine called a core aerator, which punches out small cylinders of grass and soil, opening passages for better air circulation. Water and fertilize afterward to encourage root growth.

You can also aerate soil with a pitchfork or V-bar (a pitchforklike device designed for aerating), but it takes longer and is more labor intensive than a core aerator; save this technique for small areas that need aeration, such as frequently traveled lawn paths and areas where puddles often form.

Grass grows poorly, with thick layer of dead grass on top of soil

The tightly interwoven layer of living and dead grass stems, crowns, and roots just above the soil line, called thatch, is a natural part of a living lawn. It is not caused by leaving grass clippings on the lawn; in healthy lawns, those nitrogen-rich leafy blade bits are broken down quickly by soil organisms. Excessive thatch is promoted by the overuse of fast-acting synthetic fertilizers, which suppress soil organisms while increasing grass growth.

A layer of thatch ½ inch thick or less is good: it feeds soil organisms and earthworms and acts as a mulch, conserving moisture and shading grass roots. But too much thatch encourages diseased, shallow roots and keeps water from soaking into the soil. Thatch can develop in any lawn, but it builds up faster in grasses that spread by creeping stems, especially St. Augustine, zoysiagrass, and bluegrass. It is also encouraged by overly acid soil.

To promote better growth, rake out thatch over ½ inch thick, using a dethatching rake, a manually operated tool whose knifelike tines slice through and lift out the debris, or rent a gas-powered dethatching machine, which looks something like a lawn mower, but is equipped with a row of vertical, disc-shaped blades that throw up thatch as they slice rows of narrow grooves into the lawn. Set the blades so that they barely penetrate the soil. The object is to slice up thatch, not tear up roots as a rototiller does. Dethatch any time of the year if your winters are mild. In cold climates, dethatch from spring to summer, so the lawn has time to grow new roots before winter. When finished, rake off and compost the thatch. Scatter grass seeds on any areas that were scraped bare.

To prevent future buildup, sprinkle the lawn with a thin layer of fine compost annually to restore soil organisms, switch to a slow-release fertilizer, and consider using a mulching-type lawn mower.

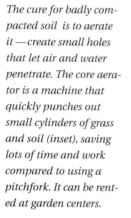

The cure for badly compacted soil is to aerate it — create small holes that let air and water penetrate. The core aerator is a machine that quickly punches out small cylinders of grass and soil (inset), saving lots of time and work compared to using a pitchfork. It can be rented at garden centers.

Grass grows poorly under trees or on the north side of buildings

Grass grows best in full sun or light shade. Deep shade, such as that beneath maples or other dense-canopied trees, lowers light levels to a point where grass turns pale and dies.

Raise the mower blade to at least 3 inches for grass in shaded areas. Mowing higher than usual allows more leaf surface for food manufacturing and encourages deep rooting.

Consider pruning trees. Removing a branch here and there to let light filter through the canopy improves the look and health of your trees as well as alleviating shade problems beneath them.

When planting a new lawn in shade, select grasses that will do well there (see Trouble-free lawn grasses, p.346). Or switch to shade-tolerant ground covers (see Wise choices, p.358) or consider turning your shady nook into a shady perennial garden.

Dealing with poor drainage

Lawn grasses thrive in well-drained soil. If your soil is constantly soggy or puddled after a rain, grass will grow poorly even if it's well fertilized and mowed.

Make improvements from the ground up. Aerate the soil to reduce compaction and follow with a ½-inch-thick top dressing of fine compost for mild drainage difficulties, such as paths that hold rainwater in shallow puddles. Fill low spots with sandy, fast-draining topsoil.

For more pervasive problems, lighten the soil texture in your yard by rototilling in topsoil, compost, and other organic matter; then smooth the prepared soil and lay sod or

reseed the problem area. If the problem is severe, consult a professional or try other measures (see Correcting soil drainage problems, p.331). Or consider replacing the lawn grass with ornamental moisture-loving plants (see Plants for wet places, p.332).

Coping with bare or brown spots

Among the most vexing ailments of a lawn, brown spots can indicate insect damage, disease, or other problems. Gauge the size and number of spots, and take a close look at the grass within and along the edges, then match it to the symptoms described below.

Many brown spots 6 to 8 inches in diameter

White grubs, the larval form of beetles including Japanese beetles, June beetles, and May beetles, live in the soil and dine on grass roots and other organic matter. When populations are high in fall and spring, the root-eating grubs can cause an outbreak of dead spots in your lawn. Pull up a handful of dead grass, and you'll find it separates easily from the severed roots. Lift a spadeful of soil and crumble it with your hands to see if you can find the brown-headed, white-bodied larvae. More than five to eight grubs per square foot of soil means it's time for action. If your lawn is heavily infested, it may attract moles, skunks, starlings, or armadillos, who will devour the grubs but further damage the lawn by digging or burrowing to reach their prey.

- Treat affected lawn areas in late summer to early fall, when grubs are active, with beneficial nematodes (see p.126), which prey on grubs, or with the botanical insecticide pyrethrum, which poisons the grubs. Follow label directions carefully.
- On summer nights, newly hatched adults are attracted to porch lights and lighted windows. Collect and destroy as many adults as possible to prevent them from mating and laying eggs in the soil.
- If your region is infested with Japanese beetles, use a lawn spreader to apply milky spore disease, a biological control, in spring.

Creating a lush green carpet of grass under the stifling shade of trees (far left) is difficult but not impossible. Plant grasses that tolerate shade, such as fine fescues and zoysiagrass. To encourage grass growth, thin the tree canopies to let more sun through and raise your mower blade so that there's more leaf surface to absorb light.

It may take several years to show results, as the bacteria spores gradually multiply in the soil and infect the grubs every spring, but you have to apply it only once, and it is a very effective control.

- As a last resort, consider a synthetic insecticide registered for lawn grass that contains the active ingredient diazinon to control grubs. Follow label directions carefully.

Grass turns brown after a drought

If your grass shows dead-looking brown patches after a prolonged absence of rain, it is probably resting rather than dead. Many grasses go dormant and turn brown when water is scarce, conserving energy until it rains again.

- To revive drought-dormant grass, soak it with at least an inch of water, then repeat a few days later. Continue adding an inch of water weekly until the grass turns green and the drought is over. Unless your lawn is made up of drought-resistant grasses, it will need an inch of water every 10 days when actively growing (see Weed and water now to prevent problems later, p.383).
- Setting your mower to a higher setting (1½ to 2½ inches is an average range) will encourage your grass to develop deeper roots to support the increased vegetation above ground—and those deep roots will help find soil moisture when the top layer dries out. Deep, infrequent watering also promotes deep, drought-resistant roots; shallow watering makes grass more susceptible to damage from drought.
- If you regularly need to supplement your natural rainfall, consider replacing your grass with varieties better suited to your climate. Warm-season grasses are generally more drought tolerant than cool-season grasses. Among the warm-season types, hybrid Bermuda, zoysiagrass, and buffalo grasses are most drought tolerant. Tall fescues and fine fescues need the least moisture of the cool-season grasses, but they don't come close to the drought tolerance of these warm-season grasses. These grasses spread rapidly from runners, and if you don't want to tear up an entire lawn to replace it, consider planting rooted cuttings called plugs. In time they will spread to fill in bare spots and overtake weakened lawns.

Small bare patches of loose, crumbly soil

FIRE ANTS

While most ant mounds are of no concern, the same cannot be said for those built by fire ants. There are a number of species, but the most dangerous is the red imported fire ant, found throughout the Southeast.

Fire ants are usually red to blackish red and range from about ⅛ inch to ½ inch long. The insects have a stinger and a nasty disposition. Each sting produces searing pain and a whitish, very itchy welt. Fire-ant mounds are typically about 1 foot high and twice as wide, although they can be much larger. In sandy soils the nests are irregularly shaped, while in clay soils they are symmetrical and larger than those made in other soils.

You can control fire ants by using insecticidal baits and garden techniques.

Scatter a synthetic insecticidal bait containing the active ingredient abamectin across the area where control is desired. Follow label directions carefully. Abamectin is a growth regulator that stops the queen ant from laying eggs. Three to five days after the bait has been applied, slowly pour 3 gallons of boiling water into the central hole in the ant hill. Repeat in five days if ants reappear from the mound.

To keep fire ants away, apply baits twice a year, in spring and fall, and scatter shredded orange rind on the area as a repellent.

Mounds or spots of fine- to medium-textured crumbly soil, usually with a small hole in the center, indicate an ant colony. These insects carry the soil from their tunnels to the surface, piling it on top of the grass. The spots are usually about 4 inches in diameter, although some species create mounds a foot or more in diameter. Though unsightly, ant colonies cause no real harm and actually do some good by aerating small areas. If ant hills appear in out-of-the-way spots, you can just ignore them.

- Use a fine-tined rake, sturdy broom, or strong stream of water from a hose to disperse the loose soil. Be alert for disturbed ants, who may rush to the attack during this operation. To avoid bites, pull your socks up over the bottoms of your pant legs and wear boots, or spray insect repellent on your shoes and legs. Then pour a kettle of boiling water into the entrance hole to kill the colony. Scatter grass seeds on the bare spot, or patch with sod.

Patches of dead and dying grass appear as snow melts in spring

If your winters are long and snowy, your lawn may show the effects of snow molds, two fungal diseases that occur as the snow melts in spring. These often appear in areas where snow is last to disappear. Look for patches of grayish to brown dead grass as snow melts. Gray snow mold causes fuzzy gray edges around the patches; pink snow mold has pinkish edges around the dead spots.

- As soon as snow melts, rake the affected area to remove infected grass and fertilize lightly with a granular lawn fertilizer. If the damage is more extensive, overseed with a grass variety resistant to snow mold, such as 'Dormie' or 'Park' Kentucky bluegrass or 'Arctared' fescue.
- Lush, long grass growth late in the season makes grass susceptible to snow molds. If molds are an annual problem, avoid fertilizing your lawn after late summer, especially with fertilizers high in phosphorus, so that

TIME-TESTED TECHNIQUES

PATCHING A LAWN SPOT

To fix a damaged spot in your lawn, use a sharp, straight-edged spade to remove a rectangle that includes all the affected grass, slicing through roots to separate the damaged area from healthy lawn. Scratch the soil surface with a hand cultivator, mix in an inch-thick layer of compost, and set a piece of healthy sod into the area. Water regularly, and avoid walking on the patch for a month or so until it has knitted together with the surrounding grass.

grass will be less succulent as it heads into winter. Give the lawn a late mowing before snow falls to keep grass short.

- Compacted soil also contributes to the problem by depriving roots of oxygen; try aerating your lawn (see photograph, p.348). If snow molds have been a problem, avoid walking on snow-covered grass, which forces the air out of the snow cover.

Grass dies in silver-dollar-sized spots

Scattered small, dead patches appear during summer and early fall. The spots may spread into larger, darker areas, indicating dollar spot disease. The dying leaf blades may show red or purplish marks at their tips. Wet grass is an open invitation to this fungal disease, which is encouraged by heavy dew or by late-day watering that leaves water on grass overnight. Dollar spot disease often occurs in fall, when cool nights combine with warm days to produce heavy dew. Thatch buildup, which holds moisture, can contribute to the problem.

- To help your lawn recover after an outbreak, rake out and dispose of accumulated thatch, then aerate (see photograph, p.348) and fertilize (see Caring for a lawn, p.345). The resulting vigorous grass growth can often outgrow the disease.
- Alkaline soil encourages dollar spot disease. Test your soil pH (see Correcting soil chemistry problems, p.329). If it is alkaline, apply a top dressing of garden sulfur to make it more acidic.
- To prevent the disease, water your lawn in the morning so that it has time to dry out before nightfall. Avoid overfertilizing, which promotes thatch buildup.
- Choose resistant cool-season grasses if you reseed part of your yard, or overseed to add resistant grasses to a lawn. These include Kentucky bluegrasses 'America', 'Adelphi', 'Eclipse', 'Primo', 'Somerset'; fine fescues 'Reliant' and 'Tournament'; and perennial ryegrasses 'Barry', 'Dasher', and 'Venlona'.

Small or large circular brown patches

Brown patch is a common, troublesome fungal disease in the Southeast and other humid areas. It attacks the grass in circular spots that range from a few inches to several feet across. The clue to identifying this disease is the grass at the edges of the brown spot: it looks water-soaked, but dries out as the patch expands. Grass inside the patch may recover even as the patch expands, so that you see a spot of green grass within a brown ring. Brown patch appears when the weather is hot and humid.

- Grass usually recovers on its own from this disease, so you do not need to replace sod. Reseed areas to help them recover; 'Manhattan II' and 'Yorktown II' ryegrass varieties resist this disease.
- To prevent brown patch, aerate the soil and avoid watering in the afternoon, so that as much air as possible can reach the roots.

Avoid fertilizing your lawn in late spring, which creates tender, succulent, disease-susceptible new growth just in time for summer humidity.

- Test the soil for deficiencies of calcium, phosphorus, and potassium, which can contribute to the problem; spread lime or a fertilizer that is high in phosphorus or potassium if indicated by the test results.

Solving problems caused by animals

Neighborhood animals and domestic pets, especially dogs, can be tough on a lawn.

Light digging in newly seeded areas

Cats rarely damage existing lawns, but they may be a problem around newly seeded areas, taking the loose, crumbly soil for a litter box.

- Cover the newly seeded areas with a knit fabric, such as a floating row cover or shade cloth, weighting the edges with rocks.

A series of holes dug in the lawn

Many dogs have a favorite digging area, producing deep holes in one section of a lawn. Behavioral training is usually the best way to deal with digging problems. Fill in any holes your dog digs, and reseed or patch with sod.

- Consider conceding the area to the dogs and camouflage it with a shrub or two.
- Give your dog a sandbox and bury treats in it to redirect the pet's digging.
- Restrict your dog's access to the area with an invisible or traditional fence.
- Run a sprinkler in the spot for a couple of days to discourage canine visits.

Brown spots a foot or less in diameter, with a ring of darker green grass

If the spots are a foot or less in diameter with a ring of darker green grass, man's best friend is the prime suspect. Dead spots of this size are usually the result of ammonia-intense urine. Around the edges, urine may be diluted to a level that supplies nitrogen to create a ring of darker green grass. Because dogs usually return to the same area, there may be a series of spots close together.

- Hose the area thoroughly and overseed. Or dig out the grass with 6 inches of soil beneath it, and reseed or patch with sod.
- Set up a sprinkler for a couple of days to flush the soil and to discourage visits.
- If all else fails, spray the area with a dog repellent, available at home and garden centers. Spray again after a heavy rain.

Raised ridges in lawn, with mounds of soil

Burrowing moles and gophers are enemies of lawn lovers. They tunnel through the soil, slice through grass roots, cause grass to brown, and create ankle-turning hazards with their hollow ridges that sink beneath your step.

- To reduce ankle-twisting and make mowing easier, crush the tunnels with your feet or a lawn roller.
- Consider calling a licensed exterminator to rid your yard of moles.
- Traps are available. If you use live traps, you may be able to relocate the animals to wild areas, but in some states this is illegal.
- As a long-term deterrent, control the moles' favorite food, grubs (see Many brown spots 6 to 8 inches in diameter, p.349).

Combating weeds

A lawn is usually a limited environment, or monoculture, of one species of thickly growing grass plants. When weeds invade the grass garden, they interrupt the flowing sameness of the lawn—not necessarily an undesirable result, because some weeds, such as dainty white English daisies and even dandelion blossoms, can add a touch of interesting diversity and textural contrast. However, weeds grow at different rates and heights than the grass, which can lead to a jungle of dandelion stems rising above your fescue.

If your lawn is beset by weeds, you need to improve your lawn-care practices as well as remove the weeds. A flourishing lawn that gets plenty of water, good nutrition, and has aerated soil is usually not subjected to weed woes. Weeds have a hard time getting a grip in such a healthy lawn, because the thick turf will shade or crowd out weed seedlings.

Annual or perennial weeds?

Weeds may be perennial plagues that persist year after year, or annuals that live and die in a single growing season. Some annual weeds, such as crabgrass, thrive in summer; others, such as chickweed and henbit, are winter

WEED-PREVENTION STRATEGIES

To discourage weeds, maintain a thick, dense turf, and avoid cutting the grass too short.

- Mow at the recommended height for your grass (usually 3 inches). If you're not sure what kind of grass you have, set your blade higher than you've been mowing, so that grass will prevent sunlight from reaching weed seeds and seedlings.

- Mow as often as needed to keep weeds from setting seed. Mow dandelions when they're butter yellow to limit them. If you slice them off when they're puffs of seed, you'll sow hundreds of new headaches.

- Monitor the water your lawn gets: at least 1 inch every 10 days encourages good root growth and a thick, weed-resistant turf.

- Fertilize in late spring with a sprinkling of compost or aged manure to boost the vitality of your grass.

Annual roots
Chickweed has the shallow roots typical of annual weeds. Luckily, these roots are easy to pull up by hand.

Perennial roots
A taproot, shown here on a dandelion, anchors many perennial weeds deep in the ground. You need a tool (p.354) to dig out such roots completely.

growers that fade when hot weather arrives. Annual weeds usually have shallow, fibrous roots, but some may produce creeping stems that grow roots as they spread. Perennial weeds, including the ubiquitous dandelion, usually have deep taproots, although a few, such as broad-leaved plantain, have fibrous roots, and some, such as Bermuda grass, have roots and stems that creep far afield, rooting as they go. The most pernicious weeds cover ground quickly by rooting either along above-ground horizontal stems (such as the annuals crabgrass and purslane and the perennials Bermuda grass and ground ivy), or from below-ground horizontal roots (including Johnson grass, goutweed, and mints). It's difficult to control these weeds by hand pulling, because any broken-off, overlooked piece of stem or root can sprout a new plant.

Most annuals are easy to pull by hand. Weeding tools, such as hand hoes or cultivators, make it easier to get all the roots, though. A bit of leverage can make weeding tougher-rooted perennials an easier chore. Use a dandelion fork—a hand tool with a long, skinny, forked blade—to remove stubborn weeds. Thrust the digger deep into the soil at the root of the plant, grasp the weed's top, and pull with a twisting motion while angling upward with the digger to pry the root free.

Combine a twist-and-pull hand motion with the thrusting leverage of a dandelion fork to pop out deep-rooted weeds.

Using herbicides on lawns

If hand pulling, good maintenance, and developing tolerance for a less-than-perfect lawn don't solve your weed problems, it may be time to turn to herbicides. Identify your weeds, then select a product that targets your particular weeds. Read labels to find out the best time to apply the product. Repeated applications of herbicides may be necessary for some deep-rooted weeds.

Herbicides fall into two general classes—pre-emergent and post-emergent. Pre-emergents prevent germinating seeds of annual grass and many broad-leaved weeds from growing. Most won't kill established weeds and lawn grasses. Pre-emergents can be based on corn gluten, a natural by-product of corn-syrup production, or they can be synthetic. Both are effective against crabgrass, dandelions, and other weeds, yet are otherwise non-

BEFORE YOU SPRAY

Always follow the label directions carefully when you apply an herbicide. Here are some general guidelines to keep in mind:

- Check the weather forecast. The label of the herbicide may advise not spraying before a rain, which can wash leaves before the chemicals have had a chance to work. On the other hand, it's good to apply some soil-drench herbicides just before it rains; the rain helps them soak into the soil and reach weed roots.

- Dress to protect your skin from contact with chemicals (see How to use pesticides safely, p.9).

- Apply most herbicides when it's around 70°F. Weeds are actively growing and will quickly absorb the chemical. But check the label; some advise against spraying when

the temperature rises to 80°F or above.

- Apply herbicide to weeds as soon as you notice them. Young, actively growing weeds are easier to kill than older ones.

- Spray before mowing to expose maximum weed tissue to treatment. The more foliage that you spray, the less chance that a weed will recover.

- Wind-borne spray, or drift, can harm other plants. Spray on a calm, breezeless day.

- Don't mulch with treated clippings. Herbicide residues can harm ornamental plants or contaminate vegetables.

- Store all pesticides out of reach of children and pets. A high, locked cabinet in a garage or shed is best (see How to use pesticides safely, p.9).

toxic. Both are available at garden centers.

Post-emergent herbicides, including those containing the active ingredients mecoprop and glyphosate, kill weeds that are already growing. Post-emergent herbicides may be selective or non-selective. Selective products are designed to kill some plants while not harming others; for example, broadleaf herbicides are selective products that kill only weeds (and garden plants) with broad leaves while not harming narrow-bladed grasses. Nonselective herbicides kill everything; weeds, grass, and garden plants.

Post-emergents are used to kill weeds that have emerged from the soil and are growing. Some kill plants upon contact with the foliage, while others are applied to the soil where they are taken up through plant roots. Be careful when applying nonselective post-emergent herbicides, such as glyphosate, which kill everything they touch, including lawn grass. Keep broadleaf herbicides away from flower beds and shrubs, and don't spray herbicides on a windy day when they can drift into neighboring areas (see Before you spray, facing page).

Mushrooms in lawn, often in ring

Fairy rings—mushrooms in circular bands of dark green grass—usually develop from the remains of an old tree or other woody organic matter. They can appear anytime during the growing season. Sometimes a ring of darker grass is visible before any mushrooms emerge. Several species of fungi produce fairy rings,

which may form single or double circles.
- Handpick or rake up any mushrooms as soon as you spot them, and dispose of them to prevent spreading spores.
- Water and fertilize the affected spot to encourage quick regrowth. Scatter new grass seeds along any dead spots.
- To eliminate a fairy ring permanently, remove the grass and soil to a depth of 1 foot and a width of 1 foot on both sides of the ring. Refill with fresh soil and reseed.

Moss in lawn

Patches of unwanted moss in your lawn can indicate several problems that make conditions difficult for grass to grow. Compacted soil, poor drainage, low fertility, shade, acidic soil, and mowing too low can all contribute to the growth of moss. Remove the moss by peeling it off by hand or with a hoe, and then start your detective work.
- If the area is holding water, making the soil constantly moist, you have a drainage or compaction problem. Aerating the soil (see photograph, p.348), followed by topdressing may correct the problem. If not, rechannel the water runoff (you may want the assistance of a landscape professional for this) or replace the lawn grass with ornamental plants that will thrive in moist conditions (see Plants for wet places, p.332).
- If there are no apparent drainage or compacted soil conditions, and you've been mowing your grass short, raise the mower blade to 3 or 3½ inches above ground and see what happens after several weeks.
- If the grass doesn't begin to fill in when it's allowed to grow longer, test the soil (see Correcting soil chemistry problems, p.329). If it is acidic, apply lime at the recommended rate to elevate the pH level to 6 or 7.
- If shade is the culprit, remove lower limbs from trees, and replace or overseed existing grass with one of the new grass varieties that performs well in shade (see Trouble-free grasses, p.346).

Common Lawn Weeds

Bermuda grass

Bluegrass, annual

Chickweed

Crabgrass

BERMUDA GRASS
(*Cynodon dactylon*)

A warm-season grass that is green in hot weather. In cool weather, it is brown and unattractive. While a welcome turf grass in warm climates, in cool areas it chokes preferred grasses, leaving lawns brown from fall to spring. Perennial; most troublesome in the West.

Root: Fast-traveling, tough, wiry rooting stems called rhizomes can grow 8 inches deep or more. Resprouts from any small pieces of stem left in soil.

Solution: Apply a systemic, nonselective herbicide during the hottest part of the summer (July or August). This is when Bermuda grass grows rapidly and will absorb the most herbicide. Repeat application twice more at two-week intervals. After the Bermuda grass is dead, rework the soil in fall and sow cool-season grasses.

BLUEGRASS, ANNUAL
(*Poa annua*)

This annual grass sprouts in fall, lives into winter until cold weather, then goes dormant and becomes green again in spring. It dies out in summer, leaving bare patches. Whitish seed heads in spring give the lawn a speckled look.

Root: Shallow, fibrous.

Solution: Mow frequently to eliminate seed heads before they mature. Dig it out with a trowel. Mow higher to shade it out; avoid overwatering and overfertilizing. Apply a pre-emergent herbicide containing the active ingredient benefin, bensulide, or DCPA in late summer, before seeds sprout.

CHICKWEED
(*Stellaria media*)

Dense, branching mats of small green leaves with tiny white flowers from late winter through spring; spreads by long-lived seeds. Annual; sprouts in fall, grows through winter and spring, self-sows, then dies in summer.

Root: Shallow, fibrous roots.

Solution: Hand dig or hoe out plants before they form seeds. Tops easily break off from roots, so try to dig up as much of the roots as you can. Spray with the systemic herbicide 2,4-D. Or if plants have gone to seed, use the pre-emergent herbicide DCPA. Use a formulation registered for chickweed, and follow label directions carefully.

CRABGRASS (*Digitaria* spp.)

Spreading clumps of coarse grassy leaves flatten out along the ground. This annual grows from summer through fall, when it sets seeds and then dies.

Root: Fibrous roots.

Solution: Hand pull before plants form seeds. Crabgrass thrives in poor, acidic soil, so fertilize and water the lawn as needed to promote a thick, dense turf that crowds out crabgrass. Crabgrass thrives where soil has a low soil pH. Have your soil tested, and apply ground limestone to raise the pH to a nearly neutral 6.5. When mowing, set the mower higher to shade out seedlings. Apply a pre-emergent herbicide that contains the active ingredient benefin, bensulide, oxadiazon, or pendimethalin in the spring. Spot-treat any surviving crabgrass plants with a post-emergent herbicide that contains the active ingredient MSMA. Use formulations registered for crabgrass, and follow label directions carefully.

CURLY DOCK
(*Rumex crispus*)

Rosettes of long, coarse, wavy-edged, dark green leaves. Perennial.

Root: Deep taproot.

Solution: Dig up with a dandelion fork. Use a synthetic herbicide registered for curly dock that contains the active ingredient 2,4-D and MCPP. Follow label directions carefully.

DAISY, ENGLISH
(*Bellis perennis*)

Low rosettes of narrow leaves topped with a cluster of small, short-stemmed white or pink-tinged flowers. Perennial; spreads rapidly and can grow year-round in mild climates.

Curly dock

Daisy, English

Root: Fibrous roots.

Solution: Hand pull. Apply a post-emergent, broadleaf herbicide containing the active ingredient dicamba, MCPP, or 2,4-D, and avoid compacting soil. Use a formulation that is registered for English daisy, and follow label directions carefully.

DANDELION
(*Taraxacum officinale*)

Rosettes of long, thin, toothed leaves and sunny yellow flowers followed by white puffs of seeds. Perennial.

Root: Deep, tenacious taproot.

Solution: Dig up with dandelion fork, ideally while blooming; try to get the entire root. Mow before seed heads appear. Spray a post-emergent, broadleaf herbicide with the active ingredient MCPP or 2,4-D, or spot treat with the post-emergent, systemic herbicide glyphosate. Use a formulation registered for dandelion, and follow label directions carefully.

GARLIC, WILD
(*Allium vineale*)

Long, narrow, round, blue-green to gray-green leaves with papery bulb-shaped buds that open to clusters of purplish or white flowers in summer. The leaves have a strong garlic or onion smell when crushed. Perennial.

Root: Fibrous roots beneath small white bulbs.

Solution: Dig up clumps with a trowel or spade. Dispose of bulbs. Be sure to remove even tiny bulblets from soil or they will resprout. Apply a synthetic

post-emergent herbicide with the active ingredient 2,4-D or MCPA. Use a formulation that is registered for wild garlic, and follow label directions carefully.

GROUND IVY
(*Glechoma hederacea*)

Creeping stems of small, dark green, scalloped leaves that root where they touch the ground. Dark blue-purple flowers appear in spring. It thrives in the sun or shade and prefers moist soil. Perennial.

Root: Fibrous roots; can resprout from bits of stem that are left in or on the soil.

Solution: Spot-treat with a post-emergent herbicide containing the active ingredient glyphosate, 2,4-D, or MCPP. Use a formulation that is registered for ground ivy, and follow label directions carefully. Repeatedly hand pull; mow close to the ground and rake up and remove runners.

KNOTWEED, PROSTRATE
(*Polygonum aviculare*)

Mats of ground-hugging stems with small, pointed, blue-green leaves that turn reddish after frost. Annual.

Root: Deep, narrow taproot with many fibrous roots.

Solution: Hoe out or hand-pull the roots, and apply a synthetic pre-emergent herbicide containing the active ingredient benefin. Apply the herbicide before the weed sprouts to prevent a new crop of seeds. Post-emergent herbicides containing the active ingredient glyphosate or 2,4-D are also effective. Use

a formulation that is registered for prostrate knotweed, and follow label directions carefully. Aerate soil (see p.348), especially in areas that are compacted from heavy traffic.

NUTSEDGE
(*Cyperus esculentus*)

Coarse, grasslike, yellowish green leaves and clusters of golden brown, branched flowers atop a three-sided stem. Perennial.

Root: Spreading fibrous roots with small tubers along them.

Solution: Spot-treat with a synthetic pre-emergent herbicide containing the active ingredient glyphosate or basagran. Use a formulation that is registered for nutsedge, and follow label directions carefully. You can discourage the growth and spread of this moisture-loving weed by improving soil drainage (see p.349). Reduce watering.

PLANTAIN
(*Plantago major* and *P. rugelii*)

Smooth, wide, oval leaves growing in ground-hugging rosettes. Perennial; produces narrow spikes of tiny green flowers in summer and fall.

Root: Short taproot plus tough, fibrous roots.

Solution: Hand-pull when young; lift established plants with a dandelion fork (see p.354). Plantain thrives in compacted soil, so encourage grass growth. Spot treat with a synthetic herbicide containing the active ingredient glyphosate, following label directions carefully.

Plantain

Nutsedge

Knotweed, prostrate

Ground ivy

Dandelion

Garlic, wild

SOLVING PROBLEMS WITH GROUNDCOVERS

Groundcovers can solve all kinds of garden dilemmas. Many fill in fast, creating a dense mass that suppresses weeds. Once established, groundcovers rarely need supplemental watering or fertilizer. By substituting these easy-care plants for lawn grass, you can cut mowing while keeping your yard lush and green. Instead of struggling to mow a slope, you can enjoy a hillside of minimal-care groundcovers, such as tawny daylily (*Hemerocallis fulva*) or heather (*Calluna vulgaris*).

If you want all-year cover, select evergreen groundcovers, such as the eternally popular periwinkle (*Vinca minor*), English ivy (*Hedera* spp.), or pachysandra (*Pachysandra* spp.), or silver-colored evergreen perennials, such as snow-in-summer (*Cerastium tomentosum*). If off-season coverage isn't a consideration, you can choose from many adaptable deciduous plants that disappear over winter, then come roaring back in spring, such as hosta (*Hosta* spp.) and sweet woodruff (*Asperula odorata*).

Planting groundcovers

Plant groundcovers in spring or early fall, when the roots have enough time to become established before the extreme cold of winter

Heather in bloom, used as a groundcover, creates a luscious carpet of color. Later it will offer a green backdrop for other flowering plants in the yard.

weather. Prepare the bed as you would for any other ornamental plants—loosening the soil, adding amendments, and leveling the surface. Popular groundcovers are sold in multiplant flats; others are sold in pots or plastic packs.

To figure out how many plants you need, measure the intended area and calculate the number of square feet you need to cover. Typically, groundcover plants spread quickly; in about two years they should cover the space, then grow denser as they mature. For fastest

*A year-round, green groundcover of periwinkle (*Vinca minor*) is a dotted-blue backdrop in spring for hostas, in foreground, and a lovely red-leafed Japanese maple (*Acer palmatum*).*

A mix of groundcovers—red ajuga, gold euonymus, blue juniper, and pink heather, among others—fill in between a lawn and a backdrop of evergreens (right). In a shady area (right, below) a variety of hostas and astilbes offer a spectrum of colors and shades.

coverage, figure on 1 foot of space between each plant of the vining type, such as periwinkle or ivy. Keep in mind that all groundcovers don't grow at the same rate, so check with your local garden center if you want a plant that will grow quickly. For flowering plants or shrubs, check the spacing recommendation on the label and then subtract about a third of that distance so that plants overlap. (For example, if the recommended spacing for heather as a garden plant is 2 feet, space your groundcover heathers 16 inches apart.) Mix and match groundcovers for a livelier planting if you like, combining plants with similar needs, but be aware that groundcover plants vary in their aggressiveness. Your careful composition may take on a life of its own as plants mature and the less vigorous growers are shouldered aside.

Planting on slopes

If you intend to use groundcovers to prevent erosion on a steep slope, use fast-growing plants or shrubby evergreens, and space them closely together with spaces filled with mulch. Begin planting at the bottom of the slope and work uphill. Then cover the area with a 2- to 4-inch layer of long-lasting mulch, such as wood chips or shredded bark. If you can't plant until several days or more after you prepare the soil, apply the mulch and then add plants when you're ready.

Weed by hand as necessary until the plants fill in, or apply mulch to smother weeds. If winter weather is eroding the slope, and channels of water are running down and washing away mulch, you can interplant a

bed of deciduous groundcover with vigorous evergreen plants, such as spreading evergreen junipers, that will hold the soil in place during winter storms.

Groundcover maintenance

Groundcovers are the ultimate low-maintenance planting. Once they're established, they live for years with little additional care beyond an annual application of fertilizer. A yearly once-over with a string trimmer at the end of the growing season will keep flowering perennial groundcovers looking tidy by removing spent flower stems and old foliage.

WISE CHOICES

GROUND COVERS IN FULL SUN

Evergreen	Zone
Artemisia	3–9
Dwarf juniper	3–9
Heather	4–6
Hen-and-chickens	5–9
Prostrate rosemary	8–11
Snow-in-summer	2–11

Deciduous	Zone
Ajuga	3–8
Algerian ivy	9–11
Allegheny pachysandra	5–9
Bearberry	2–7
Cotoneaster	4–8
English ivy	5–9
Japanese pachysandra	4–8
Memorial rose	5–8
Periwinkle	3–9
Persian ivy	6–9
Roman chamomile	4–8
Showy evening primrose	5–9
Veronica	3–8

To keep groundcover beds tidy, pull weeds and tree seedlings when you notice them.

Some shrubby, twiggy groundcovers, such as cotoneaster, may trap bits of paper and other windblown trash. Simply handpick the debris, use a leaf blower, or rake beneath the shrubs occasionally to remove it. A narrow, long-tined rake makes it easier to reach into twiggy crannies. The rake, which looks like a small leaf rake, is sold by many mail-order catalogs or a well-stocked garden center.

GROUNDCOVERS FOR PROBLEM SITES

Among paving stones

Ajuga
Cotoneaster (with conifers)
Creeping thyme
Memorial rose
Roman chamomile
Showy evening primrose
Snow-in-summer
Sweet woodruff
Veronica

Beneath trees and shrubs

Allegheny foamflower
Bearberry (acidic soil)
Cotoneaster (with conifers)
European wild ginger
Hay-scented fern
Hosta
Ivy
Pachysandra
Periwinkle
Sweet woodruff
Wintergreen
Yellow corydalis

In small spaces

Bearberry
Hen-and-chickens
Ivy
Roman chamomile
Snow-in-summer
Sweet woodruff
Veronica

Where quick cover is needed

Ajuga
Hay-scented fern
Periwinkle
Showy evening primrose
Yellow corydalis

On slopes

Cotoneaster
Dwarf junipers
Hay-scented fern
Heather
Ivy
Memorial rose
Pachysandra
Periwinkle
Prostrate rosemary
Showy evening primrose

On rock walls

Snow-in-summer
Cotoneaster
Yellow corydalis

For fall or winter interest

Allegheny foamflower
Artemisia
Bearberry
Cotoneaster
Showy evening primrose
Wintergreen

In a low-maintenance garden

Allegheny foamflower
Lungwort
Pachysandra
Veronica

For fragrance

Artemisia
Hay-scented fern
Memorial rose
Prostrate rosemary
Roman chamomile
Sweet woodruff
Wintergreen

ALTERNATIVES TO LAWNS

How much green do you need? Take a realistic look at where you and your children relax and play, and the space you will require in the coming years. You may wish to start shaving off extra lawn, turning it into easy-care groundcovers, paved areas, or beds.

Reducing lawns reduces problems

Unless you live in an area where water is so precious that lawn grass is an extravagance, or where shade is so dense that grass won't grow, you'll probably want to keep a stretch of lawn. About 600 to 800 square feet of lawn area, a space about 20 by 30 or 20 by 40 feet, is spacious enough for a gathering of friends; about 3,600 square feet is what you'll need for a rollicking game of volleyball. Consider that, according to industry figures, the average lawn is 7,000 square feet or more, and you'll see there's plenty of room for trimming.

Try these tricks to limit the size of your lawn:

- Plant low-maintenance groundcover plants, such as Russian cypress (*Microbiota decussata*) or periwinkle (*Vinca minor*), on slopes, beneath trees, or between paving.
- Practice meadow gardening, letting a part of your yard go "wild" with guided plantings of perennial flowers and grasses.
- Replace grassy paths or sitting areas with paving, such as flagstones.
- Surround trees and shrubs with thick beds of wood chips or other durable mulch.
- Replace patchy, shady areas of lawn grass with shade-tolerant evergreen groundcovers, such as English ivy (*Hedera helix*) or pachysandra (*Pachysandra terminalis*).
- Create a bird sanctuary by filling an area of your yard with groups of fruiting shrubs and evergreens and red flowers to attract hummingbirds. Blanket the remaining lawn between them with wood chips.
- Replace lawn with a small garden pool surrounded by an edging of attractive pebbles or gravel. Rake the stones into attractive patterns and dot with a Japanese maple and ornamental grasses.
- Border your yard with a wide mixed bed of shrubs, small trees, perennials, and annuals, surrounded by a durable mulch, such as wood chips.

- Focus attention on a circle or oval of green lawn grass at the far end of your yard, using a path of lawn grass to lead the eye to it. Border the grass path with groundcovers and shrubs or other plantings.
- Use a thick layer of shredded bark instead of grass beneath children's playground equipment. Grass is a surprisingly unforgiving landing surface and is not a good choice of surface beneath play equipment.
- Consider a nongrass lawn of naturally low-growing, fine-textured, dense-growth groundcover. Wild thyme (*Thymus serpyllum*) and Roman chamomile (*Anthemis nobile*) will weave into a springy, delightfully fragrant turf that holds up to light foot traffic. Use stepping stones to save wear and tear on the plants.
- Replace lawn areas with brick or other paving, especially where you plan to place benches or other seats. Not only will you reduce mowing, you won't have to lift furniture out of the way in order to trim the grass beneath it.
- Turn a sunny spot of lawn into a meadow of perennial and self-sowing annual wildflowers and native or ornamental grasses.
- If your lawn area is shady enough to grow moss, turn it into a garden of shade-loving perennials, ferns, or groundcovers.
- Extend your beds one small step at a time by spreading mulch 12 inches farther outward each time you reapply it.
- Eliminate fussy mowing chores by planting groundcovers or using mulch to tie together isolated shrubs or trees.
- If rapid mowing is your goal, make the front edges of your beds straight, and curve the corners into a concave shape that's easy to maneuver the mower around.
- Edge your flower beds with a flat mowing strip, such as bricks or concrete pavers placed flush with the soil (see photograph, left) so that two wheels of the mower can travel on them, and use short, erect plants instead of sprawling plants along the front of the bed. You'll be able to zip right along the edge without painstakingly lifting or cutting around protruding plants.

Paving stones and pebbles mixed informally with potted plants and low-growing groundcovers create a charming, easy-care, lawn-free setting.

A sturdy weather-resistant bench—either stone (left, above) or teak (left)— can create a calm and soothing nook from which you can enjoy the rest of the garden. A bench sited on an area covered with gravel, paving, or groundcover doesn't need to be moved to trim grass.

CHAPTER TEN

IN THE LANDSCAPE

A YARD TAKES MORE THAN TREES, shrubs, vines, and flowers to make it a beautiful landscape. A thoughtful design underlays any successful outdoor landscape. This chapter shows you how to study your property and make the most of its assets while minimizing or camouflaging its faults. You'll discover such tricks as dividing your yard into spaces that your eyes—and your feet—can travel through with expectation and delight, ways to lay out a path to make your home's entry welcoming, how to choose foundation plantings with flair, and a wealth of other ideas. If your yard is small, you'll find strategies here for growing more plants in less space and tips for expanding small spaces visually.

And because every yard has an eyesore or awkward spot, whether it's a neighbor's garage or a tree that has outgrown its space, this chapter offers ingenious ideas for dealing with these problem areas and many others.

SOLUTIONS FOR LANDSCAPE PROBLEMS

The biggest secret to successful landscaping is knowing what a plant needs and matching those needs to the location. If you select plants that suit your climate and your growing conditions, you will be rewarded with vigorous plants that beautify your yard with minimal maintenance.

Creating such a happy balance is often no more complicated than visiting a garden center for advice or perusing plant catalogs,

Problem-free land-scaping entails selecting plants that thrive on your site and comple-ment the style of your house. Here, shade trees, evergreens, ornamental grasses, and perennials combine to create a vibrant, low-mainte-nance planting with all-season interest.

which routinely provide this information. For solutions to problems of pests, diseases, and nutrient deficiencies, see plant entries and troubleshooting guides in Part One of this book. For help solving vexing problems, including plants that make the most of dry sites, low spots where frost collects, and slopes where soil erodes—as well as how to capitalize on a borrowed view, screen a bad one, or cre-ate inviting foundation plantings, you have come to the right place.

In this chapter, you'll find problems typi-cal to many sites and solutions to help you achieve a healthy, beautiful landscape.

Foundation plantings

Foundation plantings serve several purposes. From a practical standpoint, they conceal an exposed, and sometimes unattractive, house foundation; create a transition from the con-structed to the natural environment; serve as a welcome sign for your home; and enhance its value. A foundation planting also presents unique problems you won't encounter else-where in the landscape and requires extra care in selecting plants.

● *Exposure:* Each side of a house is exposed to a different level of heat, sunlight, moisture, and wind. A wall facing east or west, for example, receives light for only part of the day, while a north-facing wall is in almost full sun for most of the day. One side may be buf-feted by wind and wind-driven rain, while another remains dry. Although foundation plants should complement one another and create a harmonious whole, the most impor-tant consideration is to select specimens that will thrive in the given growing conditions (for lists of plants suitable for various expo-sures, see Wise choices, pp.366 and 370).

Also keep in mind that areas directly next to the house and beneath a roof overhang are dry and should not be irrigated, to keep water from seeping into the adjacent foundation or basement. The simplest solution is to cover the soil with a fabric or plastic weed barrier topped by a layer of gravel or bark chips. If an overhang does not have a gutter, mulch the area below with gravel to promote drainage and prevent soil from washing away or splat-tering the house. If you like the look of plants near the foundation, plant one or more drought-tolerant groundcovers, like creeping juniper or sedum. Plant their roots out from under the eve and allow their branches to spread over the surface of the mulch (for more on dry-soil plants, see Wise choices, p.366).

● *Space:* A foundation garden has a built-in limitation along one side, where it abuts a house wall. In an attempt to create instant fullness, the urge is to place foundation plants too close to each other or to the house—and the plants quickly outgrow their allotted spaces. Such overcrowded plants not only look unattractive but also grow poorly.

If you have an overgrown foundation planting, remove plants that cannot be severe-ly pruned and those that have died on the side next to the house. Replace them with compact-growing shrubs and trim the remain-ing ones. When buying plants, choose vari-eties whose mature size will not overwhelm the given area and space them so that they will fill the spot at maturity. Generally speak-ing, this means planting them at least as far apart as they will spread at maturity. In the

meantime, plug the gaps between the plants with fast-growing perennials and ground-covers that you can remove as the permanent plants mature and shade them out.

Plant spread is not the only space issue with foundation plants. Pay attention to a plant's ultimate height as well, choosing naturally low-growing varieties for under windows or porches. Also think about underground growth. Trees with strong, far-reaching roots can penetrate foundations and invade the lawn (for trees suited to planting by foundations or driveways, see Wise choices, p.271).

● **Location:** Foundation plants are subject to hazards from above, below, and even from the side. A heavy load of snow, large icicles, or a torrent of rainwater can fall from the roof, seriously damaging plants beneath—even

those not directly under the eaves. Prune plants that are near the roof overhang into a natural-looking pyramid shape, or trim the top so that it is narrower than the bottom to help it shed snow or rain. Plants with rounded or flat tops are more likely to be crushed or split apart by snow accumulation or a strong downpour. In areas with heavy snowfall, you may need to provide extra protection. Cover shrubs over winter with a sandwich board made of two rectangles of plywood that are taller than the plant and hinged at the top to form a peaked shelter.

Watch for branches that rub against the roof, house wall, or each other. Friction can tear bark and create wounds that become entry points for insects or diseases. Weakened branches are also more likely to break in a storm. Prune off such branches in late winter, when the plants are dormant.

Foundation plants that touch the lawn are vulnerable to damage from lawn mowers and trimmers. The best protection is to install a flat edging of bricks or paving stones set flush with the soil between the foundation garden and lawn; when cutting the grass, run the mower wheels on the edging. These mowing strips eliminate the need for a trimmer and keep the mower from nicking roots or bumping into the top growth of foundation plants.

Mowing strips do, however, add a formal element to a foundation planting. If you prefer a less formal look, place plants at least 1 foot from the lawn edge of the bed and spread an ornamental organic mulch, such as bark chips or compost, between the plants and grass. Avoid using gravel mulch near grass: gravel can become dangerous projectiles if picked up and thrown by mower blades.

•**Design:** It is easy to fall into a foundation planting with a matched set of evergreens at the house entry, trees at the corners, and

Select foundation plants with regard to their mature height to avoid obscuring windows and doors (above, left) as they grow. Naturally low-growing plants, or those that tolerate frequent pruning, such as boxwood (above, right), are better choices for a foundation garden beneath windows.

Fill temporary gaps between young foundation plants with flowering and leafy perennials.

WISE CHOICES

PLANTS FOR DRY SHADE

Groundcovers	Zone
Ajuga	3–9
Bear's-breeches	8–11
Epimedium	5–9
Periwinkle	4–8

Flowers	Zone
Gladwin iris	6–9
Lady's mantle	4–8
Maiden pink	3–9
Sweet violet	4–8

Shrubs	Zone
Barberry	4–8
English yew	5–7
Heavenly bamboo	6–9
Skimmia	7–9
Tea	7–9

clipped shrubs in between. To give your foundation planting variety while also making it appropriate, take a good look at your house. If the foundation is attractive, or little of it is exposed above ground, a simple edging of groundcover, such as bishop's hat (*Epimedium* spp.), which tolerates dry shade, and a trellis at one corner with a climbing plant, such as a clematis (*Clematis* spp.) or climbing rose (*Rosa* spp.), may be sufficient.

For a dramatic look, contrast foliage or flowers with the color of your house, using hot colors—red, orange, and yellow—against cool ones, such as blue, purple, and green. For example, a red-leaved Japanese maple (*Acer palmatum*) is striking in front of a blue-gray house with red shutters, whereas it would be lost in front of a brick house, which would be better suited to plants with blue-green foliage, such as boxwood (*Buxus* spp.) or creeping juniper (*Juniperus horizontalis*).

For a quiet color scheme, harmonize the colors of plants with your house, such as teaming cool, blue-and-green-foliaged, and pastel-flowered plants with a gray, white, or tan house.

To further help foundation plantings accent a house, match them to the shape and scale of the building. Although it is desirable to have a mix of plant sizes and shapes, the shape of the dominant plants should echo the shape of the house. A soaring hemlock (*Tsuga* spp.) is appropriate in front of a tall, peak-roofed Tudor house, while a line of ground-hugging shrubs would echo and enhance the low, horizontal lines of a one-story ranch or contemporary house.

Formal, two-storied styles, such as Colonials, call for balanced plantings. Trees and clipped shrubs that are arranged in a mirror image on either side of a centered walk echo the matched windows on either side of a centered door. On the other hand, Tudor houses, contemporary styles, and ranch houses, often have off-center doors and windows of varying sizes. Asymmetrical planting schemes that combine unclipped plants of various sizes, shapes, and species show off the architecture of such informal houses.

Because a foundation garden must perform year-round, look for plants that provide interest in more than one season. In addition to needled and broad-leaved evergreens, which form a permanent framework of foliage, include deciduous plants like dogwood (*Cornus* spp.) and birch (*Betula* spp.), which have berries in fall, attractive bark and an interesting silhouette in winter, flowers in spring, and leaves that change color from spring to summer or summer to fall.

Growing plants under trees

Specimen trees growing in the lawn often look best with nothing more than a ring of ornamental mulch beneath them. And some trees, such as maples and beeches, have such shallow feeder roots and dense canopies that little can be grown beneath them. But trees that are incorporated into foundation plantings or landscape beds look best underplanted with annuals, perennials, bulbs, ground covers, or even small shrubs. These understory plants must tolerate shade and compete well with tree roots for moisture and nutrients.

When planting under trees, look for plants that thrive in dry shade (see Wise choices, facing page). Apply an organic mulch, such as bark chips or cocoa hulls, to retain soil moisture. However, spread the mulch no deeper than 3 inches, so that oxygen can reach the tree's shallow feeder roots, and keep the mulch at least 6 inches from the tree trunk, to protect the bark from fungal rot diseases that moist mulch could encourage.

Monitor the plants carefully for signs of insufficient water or nutrients. You may want to run a soaker hose around plants during the growing season and cover the hose with mulch. This is not only a convenient method of delivering water directly to roots that may need frequent irrigation, but it also keeps foliage dry, which discourages fungal disease. Water deeply when the soil is dry 1 inch beneath the surface.

Growing plants against walls

A garden bed along a house wall or a tall fence is a great place to grow heat-loving plants that thrive in the reflected sun and windless warmth that collects there. Climbing

ALL-SEASON COLOR WITH EVERGREENS

Evergreens are not always green, as their name suggests. They may be shades of red, gold, blue, silver, or gray, and may change with the seasons and as foliage matures. Combine different plants for year-round variety in foundation plantings, screens, and garden beds.

Gold-needled evergreens include American arborvitae (*Thuja occidentalis*) 'Aurea' and 'Rhein-gold', Hinoki cypress (*Chamaecyparis obtusa*) 'Nana Aurea' and 'Fernspray Gold', Sawara cypress (*C. pisifera*) 'Filifera Aurea', and Chinese juniper (*Juniperus chinensis*) 'Pfitzeriana Aurea' and 'Saybrook Gold'. Wintergreen barberry (*Berberis julianae*) has young copper foliage.

Evergreens may also be blue-green, such as the Meserve hollies (*Ilex* × *meserveae*) 'Blue Girl', 'Blue Prince', and Stallion'; blue-gray, such as Colorado blue spruce (*Picea pungens*) 'Globosa'; gray-green, such as Eastern red cedar (*Juniperus virginiana*) 'Skyrocket'; or silver-blue, such as Colorado blue spruce (*P. pungens*) 'Hoopsii' and 'Argentea'.

roses (*Rosa* spp.) and bouganvillia (*Bouganvillia* spp.) are two of the best flowering plants for walls. This is also a practical solution to limited space, making it possible to grow fruiting plants, from grape vines to pear and apple trees, by pruning them to grow flat against a wall, without reducing their yields. As with a foundation garden, the first consideration in selecting plants for a wall is exposure, or how much light, heat, water, and wind the area receives. An east-facing wall is good for plants that are sensitive to sun, such as clematis

Mirror-image plantings, such as these roses and evergreens (below, left), echo the formality of a Colonial-style house. A contemporary house (below, right) lends itself to informal, asymmetrical foundation plantings.

A fan is an easy-to-maintain shape for plants trained against a wall. Branches of this yew have been pruned and tied to wires to create the effect. In late winter, the shrub and a border of tulips beneath it bask in the sun's warmth reflected from the wall.

ing climbing hydrangea (*Hydrangea anomala* ssp. *petiolaris*) or Boston ivy (*Parthenocissus tricuspidata*), which cling to stone, masonry, or wood with rootlike structures called holdfasts. You may need to install vine holders, which are nails with flexible hooks, or a permanent lattice for securing or tying roses or other plants that have heavy stems and can't cling.

For plants with twining stems or tendrils, such as wisteria (*Wisteria* spp.), clematis (*Clematis* spp.), and annual vines, you will need to hang a trellis. Make sure the support is sturdy enough to hold the weight of mature wisteria stems, or thin enough for the delicate stems of clematis and tendrils of annual vines to coil around.

You can grow fruit trees and other plants with pliable stems (see Wise choices, facing page) against a wall using a decorative training technique called espalier. To create an espalier, site the plant about 9 inches from the wall and wire new stems along horizontal or diagonal wires secured to the wall with screw eyes (available at hardware stores). Prune and tie new growth to the supports to create a geometric, two-dimensional shape, such as a fan (see left), diamond, or candelabra.

Growing plants in wet sites

If an area of soil in your garden is constantly wet, you have two choices: correct the drainage (see Correcting soil drainage problems, p.331) or select plants suited to moist soil. Creating a bog garden is the easiest, most attractive solution.

Many flowers, shrubs, and trees flourish in moist to waterlogged soil. Some of the best flowering perennials are Japanese iris and yellow flag iris (*Iris ensata* and *I. pseudocorus*), astilbe (*Astilbe* spp.), bee balm (*Monarda didyma*), foxglove (*Digitalis* spp.), and ligularia (*Ligularia* spp.). Shrubs that like a wet location include swamp azalea (*Rhododendron viscosum*), rosebay rhododendron (*R. maximum*), red-twig dogwood (*Cornus stolonifera*), and winterberry (*Ilex verticillata*). Among moisture-loving trees there are willows (*Salix* spp.) and bald cypress (*Taxodium distichum* var. *distichum*). (See also Making the most of waterlogged soil and standing water, p.333.)

Growing plants on windy sites

Wind dries and erodes soil, dries out and tears leaves, and snaps plant stems. If your property is exposed, select sturdy plants that can withstand wind, such as red oak (*Quercus rubra*), euonymus (*Euonymus* spp.), and ornamental

(*Clematis* spp.) and roses (*Rosa* spp.), because morning light is cooler than that in the afternoon. Plants that crave sun and heat, such as lavender and other herbs native to the Mediterranean, do best against a wall that faces south or west. A south-facing wall provides a warm, sheltered environment, where plants that are marginally hardy in your area will be protected in winter, and early-spring-flowering plants, such as tulips and daffodils will bloom sooner. Early-flowering trees may benefit from a north-facing wall, where their blossoms will be spared late frosts.

Plants located on the side of a wall that faces the opposite direction the wind is blowing will be protected from strong wind, heavy rain, and drying out in winter, but the soil there will be drier than that of other exposures. Plants on the side that faces into the blowing wind will receive more moisture but must be able to withstand damaging wind (for tough plants, see Wise choices, p.370).

The easiest plants to grow against a wall are self-clinging vines, such as the shade-lov-

grasses. Avoid plants with large or thin leaves, such as catalpa (*Catalpa* spp.) and rhododendron (*Rhododendron* spp.), or brittle, easily broken wood, including silver maple (*Acer saccharinum*), poplar (*Populus* spp.), and ornamental pear (*Pyrus calleryana* 'Bradford').

You can also minimize the effects of wind with shelters and windbreaks. To shield a shrub or small group of plants, drive three stakes into the ground on the side from which the wind blows and staple a sheet of burlap to them. Leave the shelter in place until the plants' roots are well established. To stabilize a tree, brace it with wire cables running from the tree to stakes pounded in the ground at the outer reaches of its branches, called the drip line. Cushion the wire where it wraps around branches by running it through lengths of old garden hose to prevent bark damage. Leave the wires a bit slack, so that the tree can bend a bit in the wind. Also prune deciduous trees, removing small interior stems, so that wind can pass more easily through the canopy.

Windbreaks, which are tall hedges, are the best solution for shielding a large site. Unlike a solid wall, which merely creates wind turbulence, a windbreak allows air to pass through, but breaks its force. A windbreak protects a distance 10 times its height, so a 5-foot-tall hedge, for example, will protect plants up to 50 feet away from harsh winds. Select dense, tall trees for a windbreak (see Wise choices,

p.373) and stagger them in the row for a naturalistic look. You can place flowering shrubs, such as hydrangea (*Hydrangea* spp.) or lilac (*Syringia* spp.), in front to add color and soften the look (see A tapestry hedge, p.372).

Growing plants on slopes

Slopes present a range of problems. They are difficult and dangerous to mow, subject to erosion, and awkward to maintain. The easiest and least expensive solution is to cover the slope with tough groundcover plants, which hold the soil, suppress weeds, reduce mowing, and require minimal care once established. For a sunny site, select sun rose (*Helianthemum nummularium*), basket-of-gold (*Alyssum saxatile*), daylily (*Hemerocallis* spp.), or heather (*Calluna vulgaris*). On a sunny, sandy slope, try spring heath (*Erica carnea*), an evergreen related to heather, or rugosa roses (*Rosa rugosa*), which are also salt-tolerant, making them good choices for the shore or a streetside slope in cold-winter areas.

On a shady slope, grow lily-of-the-valley (*Convallaria majalis*), sweet woodruff (*Galium odoratum*), or hardy geranium (*Geranium* spp.). Brighten dark spots with a variegated ground cover, such as the white-margined forms of vinca (*Vinca major* 'Variegata' and *V. minor* 'Variegata') or gold-splotched English ivy (*Hedera helix* 'Gold Heart'). In moist conditions, try low-growing varieties of forsythia (*Forsythia*

Permanent groundcover plantings hold a hillside in place and require little maintenance and no mowing. Rugosa rose (inset) is a hardy, disease-resistant, salt-tolerant, and beautiful hillside plant.

Streetside plants like these must be resilient enough to tolerate limited rooting space, dry soil, reflected heat, air pollution, and winter road-salt spray.

COPING WITH SLOPES

Hillsides can easily become a stage for displaying plants. Below are some design strategies for making the most of this unique gardening opportunity.

- Create terraces. A series of terraces, each defined by a low retaining wall, will divide a slope into distinct spaces with easy-care, flat profiles that can be planted to suit the exposure, such as growing herbs in a sunny area or woodland flowers in shade.

- Build a rock garden. On a gradual slope, set stones of various sizes and plant between them with soil-retaining, low-growing, groundcovers, bulbs, perennials, and shrubs. The plants will knit together nicely as they spread between the stones.

- Make a serpentine path. A sinuous path can descend a slope gradually, breaking the force of rain, and with each bend the path can encircle a garden bed.

- Add steps. On steep slopes, install steps of stone or landscape timbers, and soften their edges with ferns and creeping groundcovers.

spp.), such as 'Happy Centennial' and 'Bronxensis', or rugosa rose (*R. rugosa*), with its generous fragrance, long season of bloom, and autumn profusion of scarlet fruits, called hips.

For a large sunny slope, a meadow or prairie planting is a good option. Select wildflowers and ornamental grasses that self-sow or spread by creeping roots, and the slope will renew itself year after year with little intervention. You can either blend a variety of seeds yourself or purchase a meadow seed mix from a nursery or mail-order source. Look for tough plants that naturalize readily and can withstand heat and drought, such as fountain

grass (*Pennisetum alopecuroides*), yarrow (*Achillea millefolium*), lance-leaf coreopsis (*Coreopsis lanceolata*), purple coneflower (*Echinacea purpurea*) and sneezeweed (*Helenium autumnale*).

Shrubs can be used to retain and cover a slope, providing they are relatively low and spreading. Creeping juniper (*Juniperus horizontalis*), bearberry (*Arctostaphylos uva-ursi*), and rockspray cotoneaster (*Cotoneaster horizontalis*) are long-time favorites. Also try Carmel creeper (*Ceanothus griseus* var. *horizontalis*) and rock rose (*Cistus* spp.). Ground-cover types of shrub roses, such as *Rosa* 'Max Graf', form a low-growing, naturalistic, but prickly and unpenetrable barrier.

Growing plants at streetside and seaside

Life on the street is tough on plants, which must survive exhaust fumes, heat and light reflected from pavement, cramped roots, and road salt in winter. Seaside plants face similar challenges, including poor soil, salt spray, and wind. While certain plants can tolerate such stressors naturally, all plants in such unfriendly conditions benefit from coddling.

To conserve soil moisture and protect roots, spread a 3-inch-thick layer of organic mulch, such as wood chips, around the base of plants. Keep it 6 inches away from tree trunks and replenish it as it begins to break down. Water deeply if a week passes without rain. Also hose off the foliage to remove dust, soot, and salt, being sure to spray both leaf surfaces. In early spring and fall, fertilize plants with 1 inch of compost or aged manure, covering it over with mulch, or apply a balanced, slow-release fertilizer, such as 10-10-10 (p.324).

SOLVING LANDSCAPE DESIGN PROBLEMS

Sometimes you don't have problems with individual plants or with the growing conditions in your yard, but rather with unfavorable design situations. Whether your yard has an unattractive view, lackluster terrain, or an overgrown tree, you can use plants plus design principles to provide fresh ways to make the most of what you have.

Hiding eyesores

In an ideal world, there would not be an air-conditioning unit hulking beside the house or a woodpile covered with a bright blue tarp next door. But in the real world, eyesores seem to pop up everywhere. Fortunately, plant screens can make unappealing sites disappear.

The easiest way to block a view is to install a row of tall-growing evergreens, which are effective year-round. Select from broadleaf types, such as holly (*Ilex* spp.) and rhododendron (*Rhododendron* spp.), or needled evergreens, including cypress (*Cupressus* spp.), fir (*Abies* spp.), Japanese cedar (*Cryptomeria japonica*), pine (*Pinus* spp.), and spruce (*Picea* spp.).

Alternatively, you can erect a lattice screen or fence and let a climbing vine or rose cover it. Use either a fast-growing, flowering annual vine, such as morning glory (*Ipomoea purpurea*) or hyacinth bean (*Lablab purpureus*), or a long-

The intertwining branches of climbing roses, like yellow-flowered Lady Banks, conceal trash cans and other eyesores easily.

blooming perennial, such as clematis (*Clematis* spp.). Climbing roses make dense cover; *Rosa* 'American Pillar' or Lady Banks rose (*Rosa banksiae* var. *banksiae*) are good choices.

When hiding smaller eyesores, such as trash cans or a cooling unit, you can use either evergreen or deciduous shrubs. With the latter, look for specimens that have dense branching and ornamental features in more than one season, such as Japanese barberry (*Berberis thunbergii*) and high bush blueberry (*Vaccinium corymbosum*), which have vivid autumn color. Plant on no more than three sides, so that you still have access to utilities.

Hedges solve design problems

Hedges are useful for solving several design problems. They add privacy, cut the force of cold, drying winds, create intimate spaces in a large yard, and can mark a boundary. The best hedge plants (see Wise choices, p.372) are evergreen and have dense branching, which creates a thick screen. Of all the hedge plants, boxwood (*Buxus* spp.)—or the similar-looking Japanese holly (*Ilex crenata*) in cold climates— and yew (*Taxus* spp.) are perhaps the most versatile. You can almost sculpt with boxwood, trimming its dense foliage into a low, tidy edging for an herb garden, carving it into a tall hedge, or interweaving it with the darker

Low hedges of densely foliaged boxwood or Japanese holly make ideal edgings for herb gardens.

A TAPESTRY HEDGE

Like a tapestry, in which different colored yarns form a design, a tapestry hedge is a blend of foliage and flowering plants with various colors and textures. A tapestry hedge is an informal, naturalistic hedge that offers year-round color and requires minimum pruning. Depending on the plants you select, a tapestry hedge can become a habitat for birds and butterflies.

Keep the scheme simple, mixing two or three different plants that have similar cultural requirements. For example, alternate purple- with green-leafed varieties of European beech (*Fagus sylvatica*). Or blend green varieties of Sawara cypress

(*Chamaecyparis pisifera*), such as 'Plumosa', with gold ones, such as 'Filifera Aurea' and 'Plumosa Flavescens', or blue ones, like 'Squarrosa' and 'Boulevard'.

To make a tapestry hedge that attracts wildlife, combine flowering and fruiting plants. A shrubby dogwood, such as gray dogwood (*Cornus racemosa*), mixed with winterberry holly (*Ilex verticillata*), American cranberry bush (*Viburnum trilobum*), or winged euonymus (*Euonymus alata*) would provide spring and summer flowers, fall foliage color, and a bountiful feast for birds in the form of colorful berries.

green of yew to edge a knot garden. Yet many hedge plants, including boxwood, grow slowly, and older, larger specimens can be very costly. An economical solution is to plant a hedge of young evergreens spaced far enough apart so that they will overlap slightly when mature. Then install a second row of inexpensive, fast-growing plants in front of the first and stagger the plants to fill gaps in the hedge. Ornamental grasses or shrubs with spring flowers and fall color, such as chaste tree (*Vitex* spp.), butterfly bush (*Buddleia* spp.), forsythia (*Forsythia* spp.), or spirea (*Spirea* spp.), will fill in quickly and can easily be moved to other spots in the yard when the permanent hedge has matured. Such a hedge of mixed plants is called a tapestry hedge (for more information, see A tapestry hedge, above).

Overcoming problems with trees

Trees are inspiring landscape elements, giving a sense of permanence and dignity to any yard, and offering gifts of fruit, flowers, foliage, and shade. They have their own set of problems, however, ranging from outgrowing their space to littering the yard with peeling bark, fallen fruits, and leaf debris, as well as having pests and diseases (see Chapter 6,

pp.230–285, for specific tree problems). To make the most of their potential, select, site, and maintain trees carefully.

If a tree has outgrown it's site, you can use a visual trick, called stepping down, to help it blend into its surroundings. Plant several smaller trees and shrubs near the large tree, so that when you look at it, your eye moves upward in stages from the shortest shrubs to the small trees and finally to the tall tree. Underplant all with a bed of groundcover to unify the planting. Thinning branches from a large tree to create windows in the canopy is another way to make a big tree less imposing and to admit light.

Shade from trees, however, can make gardening and outdoor living easier in hot summer climates. If you want shade in an open yard, select a deciduous tree with a dense canopy, such as a maple (*Acer* spp.) or beech (*Fagus* spp.). Shade trees can also cool the house: place one so that it shades the southern or western facade. For lighter, dappled shade—on a terrace or in a border where you want light for plants—choose a tree with open branches and small leaves, such as a birch (*Betula* spp.), weeping cherry (*Prunus subhirtella* 'Pendula'), honey locust (*Gleditsia triacanthos*), or crape myrtle (*Lagerstroemia indica*).

To call attention away from the height of a tree, use a technique called stepping down. Surround the tree with medium and short plants, and unite the grouping by underplanting it with groundcover.

WISE CHOICES

SMALL TREES

	Zone
Carolina silverbell	5–8
Crab apple	5–8
European fan palm	8–11
Dogwood	5–9
Oriental cherry	5–8
Palo verde	8–11
Redbud	4–9
Serviceberry	4–9
Silk tree	6–9
Snowbell	5–8
Star magnolia	5–9
Washington hawthorn	3–8

TREES FOR WINDBREAKS

	Zone
American arborvitae	2–8
Eastern hemlock	3–8
Eastern red cedar 'Skyrocket'	3–8
European beech 'Dawyckii'	4–7
Italian cypress 'Stricta'	7–9
Norway spruce	2–7
Pin oak	4–9
Rocky Mountain juniper 'Moonglow'	4–7
White pine	3–8

Trees that grow exceptionally fast, such as willow (*Salix* spp.), Bradford pear (*Pyrus calleryana* 'Bradford'), poplar (*Populus* spp.), and empress tree (*Paulownia tomentosa*), can be a quick fix for a bare yard, but they produce brittle, open-grained wood that is easily broken in wind or ice storms. Locate these trees far enough from the house and driveway so that falling branches won't cause damage to these or other structures.

If you own a tree that drops pods or fruits, you can minimize cleanup by surrounding it with a wide-bed groundcover, such as pachysandra (*Pachysandra terminalis*) or periwinkle (*Vinca minor*). The fruits or seeds that fall into it will be out of sight, but will be found and relished by birds and small wildlife. To avoid future problems, select fruitless varieties, such as white mulberry (*Morus alba*) 'Kingan' and 'Chaparral'.

Paths are the practical solution to many landscape problems

Deciding where to put the paths in your yard, and whether to make them straight or curving, is the first step to creating a satisfying landscape. Different types of paths have different purposes.

● **Shape:** Straight paths direct you to a specific destination or a visual focal point. They subdivide the garden into formal sections that beg to have similar plants in each section to balance the scene. Straight paths are a no-nonsense way to go from the driveway to the door or from the house to the mailbox. So make necessary, frequently traveled paths straight and wide enough for two people to walk side by side or to pull trash cans along.

Every garden should also hold some secrets. Use your creativity to create curving paths that extend your stroll through the garden. Plant shrubs at the bends of the paths to conceal something interesting, such as a bird bath or statue, or a bench with an intriguing view to be discovered.

The width of the path determines how quickly slowly it's traveled, and if you want to to make a short path look longer, and a small garden look bigger, taper the path, making it wider at the front, narrowing the path gradually until it's quite narrow at the farthest end.

To lay out a straight path, use stakes and string, and make intersecting paths at right angles to the main path, or axis. To mark a curving path, lay out a flexible garden hose and sprinkle white flour along the hose to mark the outline on the ground.

A curved path (top) lends a sense of mystery to a garden, beckoning visitors to meander and explore what lies beyond the bend. A straight path (bottom) is the best choice for easy garden access.

● **Surface:** The primary consideration in selecting a paving material for a path is safety. No matter how attractive a path is, it must first and foremost provide secure footing. A rough surface, such as stone, is less likely to turn slippery when wet than a smooth one, such as tile. Heavily trafficked areas should be flat and level, while a strolling path can be made from stepping stones, gravel, bark chips, or other uneven material. Mixing materials adds visual interest and is an economical choice for limited budgets. Instead of a solid stone path, for instance, you can surround stepping stones with wood chips or groundcover plants; instead of a brick path, use brick as an edging to a path made of gravel or inexpensive concrete pavers.

The choice of paving material should also complement the architectural style of your house and garden. Brick and flagstone suit a formal brick or stone house; volcanic rock is a better choice for a stucco house; while gravel or slabs of a native stone are casual and naturalistic, as are wood chips.

Improving flat terrain

Changes in elevation make a yard more interest than a flat landscape, and they can also provide a precious spot of privacy by blocking views of neighboring houses or the street. You can create changes in elevation to add interest, block a view, and increase privacy. The most common location for a berm is along property lines. A dump-truck load of topsoil provides enough material to build a series of low mounds, called berms. Rake the soil into long berms that overlap for a natural shape that echoes that of mountain ranges. Top the berms with small trees and sizable shrubs to increase privacy, and landscape the remaining surface area with shorter shrubs and perennials surrounded by groundcover.

MAKING THE MOST OF SMALL SPACES

One of the most common landscaping problems is finding the space to garden and using it to best advantage. No matter what size your property, it is often difficult to envision room to grow the plants you desire.

Fooling the eye is what making the most of small spaces is all about. You can't add more square feet, but you can make an area seem larger by inviting the eye to travel around corners, up trellises, and down vistas, even before you take one step along a path, simply by using the following design principles to create the illusion of greater space.

Fooling the eye

One of the most effective ways to make a small space seem larger is to create garden rooms, or clearly defined areas that have different plantings and purposes. For example, you can divide a 20-foot-square plot into four distinct rooms: a paved sitting area shaded by an ornamental tree, a kitchen garden planted with herbs and vegetables, a rose garden, and a service area for trash cans or a compost pile hidden behind a plant screen.

In a large garden, rooms are traditionally divided with tall hedges and fences or framed with swaths of lawn. In a small area, use a scaled-down version of the same technique: divide the rooms with a low stone wall, a clipped hedge of boxwood (*Buxus* spp.) or European privet (*Ligustrum vulgare*) or a row of low-growing flowering shrubs, such as azalea (*Rhododendron* spp.). If your property slopes, consider constructing a low retaining wall to create an upper and a lower room.

Another space-expanding trick uses color. The eye is attracted first to light, bright, hot colors, such as red, orange, yellow, and even white. Plant flowers and shrubs with these colors near the house and at the front of the garden. Cool colors, such as blue, purple, and mauve shades of pink, recede. Place flowers and foliage plants with these hues at the far end of the garden to make it appear more distant. Conversely, to make a big space feel cozier, reverse the order, putting cool colors at the front and hot ones at the back.

You can also use tricks with perspective to help expand space. Small trees planted in the distance seem farther away and make the space seem bigger. If you already have a standard-sized shade tree, apple or evergreen, in the middle of your yard, plant dwarf varieties beyond it to give the illusion of even greater distance. And you can reverse the effect to make a deep yard seem more intimate by putting large trees in the distance and planting dwarf trees near the house.

Using focal points is another way to fool the eye. If a neighboring building seems to press in on your yard and can't be screened, create a distraction. Install a fountain, bench, or other interesting object in another part of the yard, for example, to draw attention away from the building.

Selecting plants

In a small garden, it is best to limit the number of species. Otherwise, the space can look jumbled and disorganized. In addition to several trees, choose just a few kinds of shrubs and herbaceous plants that are right for the site. Plant them in generous numbers to create unity and a feeling of mass that will make the space seem bigger.

Strive to balance flowering and foliage plants. Greenery provides a refreshing rest for the eye and a foil for color. Look for plants with distinctive leaves, such as bergenia (*Bergenia* spp.) and hosta (*Hosta* spp.), and for ones whose foliage stays attractive after the blooms fade, such as azalea and rhododendron (*Rhododendron* spp.), iris (*Iris* spp.), rose (*Rosa* spp.), and jasmine (*Jasminum officinale*).

Woody plants bring permanence, structure, and variation to the garden and need to be in proportion to the site. Pay attention not only to the plant's mature height and spread but also to the size of its foliage. Plants with delicate leaves, such as cut-leaf Japanese maple (*Acer palmatum* var. *dissectum*) or golden-rain tree (*Koelreuteria paniculata*), are better choices than trees with outsized leaves, like catalpa (*Catalpa* spp.).

In a confined space, it is even more important to have hard-working plants than in a large garden. Be sure to include a number of species that offer more than just pretty flowers. Look for plants that also offer ornamental fruits or seed pods, fall color, attractive bark, or an interesting shape. Good choices include Japanese stewartia (*Stewartia pseudocamellia*), a small tree with colorful fall foliage and flaking bark; any crab apple with long-lasting fruits, such as Sargeant crab apple (*Malus sargentii*) or *M.* 'Winter Gold'; red- or yellow-twig dogwood (*Cornus stolonifera* and *C. s.* 'Flaviramea'), which have brightly colored stems in winter; and ornamental grasses, whose seedheads persist through fall and winter.

A change in elevation and a mix of paved and planted areas give this compact garden (above) a spacious, open feeling.

Vertical gardening

You can't expand your garden outward, but you can always grow it upward. By using vertical accents, you not only gain more growing space but can also disguise a wall, create a contrasting backdrop for other plants, and screen views, like that of a utility pole, to create the illusion of distance.

You can grow self-climbing plants directly on a wall or erect a trellis, arch, pergola, or arbor for plants that need support. Another type of vertical planter is a *tuteur*, a free-standing plant frame in an ornamental shape that is good for adding height to a plant bed.

Not all vertical features need to be planted. A beautiful bird house or weather vane perched on a pole, a sculpture, or a tall urn can provide a striking accent in any-sized space.

Climbing plants draw the eye upward, making a small garden space appear more spacious.

PROBLEM-FREE CONTAINER PLANTS

Containers of ornamental and edible plants are delightful additions to the landscape, bringing beauty to entryways, terraces, steps, and where it may otherwise not be possible to grow plants. Yet, because containers are artificial homes for plants, they create problems, from drying out quickly to overheated or frozen roots, that you won't encounter in the garden. But, when understood, they are nonetheless easy to remedy.

Tricks for trouble-free containers

The two most common types of containers are clay and plastic. Plastic pots retain moisture longer than clay, but unlike clay, lack healthy air and water exchange through pot walls.

This, combined with overwatering, can lead to root rot. Avoid black plastic pots, which soak up the sun's heat and can cook plant roots.

Whether you use clay or plastic pots, or convert found objects into planters, frequent watering will leach nutrients from the soil, which will need to be replaced with frequent fertilizing. The most convenient type of fertilizer for container plants is a commercial, slow-release type, which supplies nutrients over many months. For an organic alternative, top the soil with a 2-inch layer of compost in spring. When setting up a container planting, make sure containers have drainage holes and that pots are elevated on bricks to allow water to drain freely out the bottom.

Types of soil

In general, soil for containers must be lighter than average garden soil, allowing air and water to pass through easily. While peat-based potting mixes are inexpensive and lightweight, soil-based mixes are a better choice, especially for plants that will remain in a pot for a long time. They have more nutrients and retain moisture better than peat mixes, which are difficult to remoisten if allowed to dry out. Soil-based mixes are also heavier, making it harder for pots to blow over.

When making your own, incorporate about one-third to one-half perlite, a lightweight expanded mineral, into soil for plastic pots. For clay pots, incorporate one-third compost into potting soil to help retain moisture. Increase the compost to one-half for moisture-loving plants like ferns.

Keeping container plants healthy

Soil in pots dries out more readily than in a garden bed, because the volume is less. Containers on a paved surface are subjected to reflected heat and light, which causes even faster moisture loss. This means that you must be vigilant in caring for container plants.

While moisture needs vary from plant to plant, most should be watered when the soil is dry 1 inch below the surface. Stick your finger in the soil to test. You should always water a plant before it wilts. After several wiltings, a plant may no longer recover, and will become susceptible to disease and insect attack.

When irrigating containers, moisten all the soil. In winter, water plants that are left outdoors. Even though they are dormant, they are living and growing, and the soil should be lightly moistened once a month.

Using containers year-round

While containers are often used as seasonal homes for annuals, containers the size of a

Containers are a way to bring a delightful array of plants to areas, such as decks (below), where it would otherwise be impossible to garden. By combining different plants in a container—coleus, ornamental sweet potato, and croton (right)—you can create colorful minigardens for sun or shade.

half whiskey barrel or larger can become permanent gardens for perennials and bulbs, as well as for slow-growing and dwarf shrubs and trees (see Wise choices, right).

If you plan to leave the container outdoors in a cold climate, make sure the pot itself can withstand winter temperatures without cracking; pots of plastic, fiberglass, or resin hold up better than clay pots. In a cold climate, choose plants that are rated hardy in two or more zones colder than your own, and a wooden or foam-resin pot, which offers some insulation. If you have container plants that are marginally hardy in your area, store them in a garage, basement, or unheated porch over the winter.

Repotting container plants

Some trees and shrubs, even dwarf varieties, can outgrow their containers and need to be repotted, either in the same or a large container. This should be done about every three to five years. To remove the plant, run a long, strong knife around the inside of the pot, loosening the soil from the pot walls. Invert the pot and gently pull its rootball out. Lay the plant on its side and cut off the bottom third of the root ball with a knife or a saw. Set the plant upright and shave off 2 inches of soil from the sides of the root mass. Untangle roots as best you can.

To replant, add to the container enough fresh soil to bring the plant back to the same level in the pot as before. Set in the plant's rootball and fill around it with with fresh soil. Firm the soil gently, water the plant well, and place it in partial shade for a week or two while it recovers. If a container is too large to repot, scoop out the top several inches of soil and replenish with new soil every spring.

LANDSCAPING FOR LIMITED ACCESS

Creaky knees, a sore back, and a limited reach don't need to restrict your gardening activities. There are a number of tricks and tools available to help gardeners with physical limitations continue to enjoy their hobby.

Making the garden accessible

If bending, stretching, and getting down to ground level are difficult, the solution may be no farther away than a local garden center or mail-order catalog. More than ever, manufac-turers are offering simple, inexpensive garden aids. Kneeling pads and stools are available with sturdy handles to make weeding and other chores more comfortable and to help you get up afterward.

For a permanent, no-bend solution, build raised beds, using inexpensive stock lumber (see Making a raised bed, p.328), decorative, easy-to-stack concrete blocks, or a commercial raised-bed kit. Make the bed no wider than 40 inches across so you can reach plants in the center of the bed. If you garden from a chair or wheelchair, build the bed no higher than the distance from the ground to your lap, plus 4 inches, to reduce the strain of reaching.

If you use a walker or wheelchair, have paved paths built between the house and garden and around the beds. Paths and ramps should be wide, level, and smooth. Make ramps from a nonskid material, such as textured concrete or decking covered with a nonslip rubber or gritty material. If you have steps in the garden, cover the treads with a nonslip rubber surface and provide railings with rounded tops on both sides.

Selecting trouble-free tools

The right tools make gardening chores a lot easier. Long-handled tools minimize bending, and well-made children's rakes and forks will extend your reach into a raised bed from a seated position. Look in garden centers and catalogs for specially designed ergonomic tools with curved handles, cushioned grips, and other features that put less strain on muscles and joints.

You can also adapt your favorite garden tools to make them more comfortable and substitute easy-to-grip household utensils for garden tools. Pad tool handles with self-adhesive foam, available at a hardware store, or the rubber hand grips sold in drug stores for crutches to make handles easier to grip.

If you don't have a water source near the garden, you can eliminate the need to lug water or walk back and forth to the faucet by using a shut-off valve, sold by home centers. With the valve in place at the nozzle end of the hose, you can leave the water temporarily turned on at the house. Simply turn the valve off instead of the spigot faucet if you want to stop watering to pull a few weeds or if you want to exchange a nozzle for a sprinkler.

With these simple ideas and aids and other labor-saving tips gleaned from gardening friends and acquaintances, you can ease your creaky knees and aching back while still enjoying your garden.

WISE CHOICES

PLANTS FOR CONTAINERS

Annuals
- *African daisy
- *Desert marigold
- *Plains coreopsis
- *Plectranthus
- *Portulaca

Perennials	Zone
*Artemesia	3–9
Fuchsia	9–10
*Sedum	4–10

Shrubs	Zone
Boxwood	6–9
Camellia	7–9
Japanese holly	5–8
Lantana	9–11

Trees	Zone
Dwarf Alberta spruce	2–6
European fan palm	9–11
Japanese black pine 'Pygmaea'	5–7
Japanese maple	5–8
Mountain pine	2–7

*Tolerates drought

CHAPTER ELEVEN

MAINTENANCE

A DAILY WALK THROUGH THE garden allows you to recognize problems while they are still small and easy to treat. With good planning and the proper techniques, you can easily keep a step ahead of small maintenance problems before they get out of hand. An early-spring spraying of dormant oil on shrubs and trees, for example, smothers overwintering insects and prevents their emergence in summer. Dividing overcrowded perennials and snipping off dead flowers throughout the growing season discourages fungal diseases. But perhaps even more importantly, a daily tour allows you to follow the subtle seasonal changes that make a living landscape endlessly rewarding.

This chapter will help you avoid many problems and tell you how to manage others. For safe use of commercial treatments in the landscape, see page 9 and pages 390 to 399.

PREVENTIVE MAINTENANCE

The best way to solve garden problems is to prevent them by practicing good garden sanitation, otherwise known as preventive maintenance. A yard of healthy, problem-free flowers, vegetables, shrubs, trees, and lawn grass can be yours. The trick is to stay one step ahead of small maintenance headaches so that they won't become full-blown maintenance migraines.

Maintenance eliminates garden problems before they start

If one thing is certain, it's that there's always trouble in paradise, but by tending to your yard on a regular basis, you'll recognize problems early, while they are still easily fixed. By simply making it a habit to walk around the garden and lawn as often as you can, you'll spot problems when they are minor. Also you'll learn to recognize the subtle, seasonal changes that call for different kinds of maintenance, from nipping off fading flowers in summer to raking up plant debris in fall. The way to prevent problems or solve problems while they're still small is to do preventive maintenance at the right time. Here is a schedule of what to do when.

LATE WINTER

When the weather is cold in waning days of winter, it is the ideal time to deal with plant problems, such as insects and diseases. It is easy to spot clusters of insect eggs and disease damage when leaves have fallen. And because pests and diseases are dormant in winter, you can control them before they have a chance to spread.

Clear up problems exposed by winter weather

Look for dead, damaged, or rotten branches. Prune stems or foliage, affliction and all, and discard them in the trash. Don't compost them; the compost may return these problems. Make a clean cut with pruners; use a pruning saw if a branch is more than 3 inches in diameter. Late winter is also a good time to prune fruit trees (see Pruning fruit and nut trees, p.293). In cold regions, prune on a warm day to avoid cutting frozen wood. If you detect insect eggs or overwintering pupae, spray the plant with dormant oil to smother the insects before warm weather causes them to hatch.

This is the time of year that four-footed pests, such as rabbits and deer, are at their boldest, often coming into backyards to feast on plants. Protect the bark of young trees and the succulent foliage of evergreen shrubs by surrounding them with wire fencing.

To guard a tender young shrub or tree against hungry four-footed pests, encircle it with a wire fence.

PRUNING TREE BRANCHES

To keep a tree healthy, prune dead or broken branches when you see them, and cut live branches in winter, while the tree is dormant. Prune according to these steps to encourage pruning wounds to heal rapidly.

1. To prevent splitting, cut halfway through the underside of the branch, 1 ft. from the trunk.

2. A few inches out from the first cut, saw halfway through the branch, from the top downward.

3. Cut the branch stub flush with the rounded area at the base of the branch, called a collar, taking care not to wound the collar.

4. The branch collar will generate healthy new tissue that will cover the wound, sealing out insects and diseases.

For earlier and better crops, start seeds indoors

The case for starting some seeds indoors is persuasive. Vegetable plants, such as Brussels sprouts, and flowers, such as annual geraniums, take three months or more from sprouting to crop. And, depending on how short your summer is, many plants that require more than 70 days to reach maturity, such as sweet onions, will fail without being given a good head start indoors.

Don't sow seeds inside too early, however. If you do, they can become potbound or tall and spindly; both conditions are hard for plants to bounce back from. Instead, use the last frost date as a target date for planting outside, and count backward if you're starting seeds indoors. It is safe to sow most seeds indoors 4 to 6 weeks before the last frost. So, if your last frost date is May 15, plan to start seeds indoors between April 2 and April 17, following seed-package recommendations. It's important to know what conditions a plant needs to grow best. Different plants behave differently—for example, some seeds need darkness to germinate, while others need light. For information on starting an individual crop, check the seed-package instructions.

In general, the method for sowing and growing most seeds is the same. To prepare individual containers or manufactured flats, which hold anywhere from 6 to 24 compartments, sterilize them by dipping into a solution of household bleach and water (see Home remedies, p.392). Rinse and air dry. Fill dried containers with a sterilized, commercial seed-starting mix, which contains no diseases that can harm vulnerable young seedlings. Water the mix with tepid water and let it

WATCH YOUR STEP

Avoid walking on your garden beds as the soil thaws in spring. In late winter and early spring, the soil is likely to be soggy, and the weight of your footfalls will compact it, making it hard to dig and plant when it dries.

If you must roam around the garden, protect the soil by laying down boards, which will distribute your weight more evenly. Use them to walk and kneel on as you set out transplants. Leave the planks as paths in the vegetable garden to remind your family not to trample young plants and seedlings.

SOWING SEEDS INDOORS

Sowing seeds indoors during winter is an inexpensive and easy way to get a head start on the growing season outdoors. Follow these steps for flawless, healthy seedlings.

1. Seed-starting gear includes sterile seed-starting mix, pots, flats, labels, and, of course, seeds.

2. Fill clean pots with sterile seeding mix and moisten a tray of warm water. Label each pot.

3. Drop two or three seeds into each pot, and cover with a thin layer of mix if directed to do so by the package label.

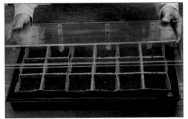

4. Cover planted pots with plastic wrap or commercial dome; keep the mix moist. When seedlings emerge, snip off weak seedlings.

drain so that it's damp. Sow and space the seeds, following the seed packet directions. To avoid problems of mistaken identity, label each container. To raise the humidity and help seedlings grow, cover the container with a molded, clear plastic lid (available at garden centers) or plastic food wrap propped up by stakes an inch or more above the soil.

Place the planted containers in a place where the soil will remain at room temperature, because seeds sprout best in warm soil. The top of a refrigerator or the top of a water heater works well for seeds that need darkness to germinate. A table near a window in a warm room is best for seeds that need light. After the seeds sprout, open the plastic covering for a few minutes daily to let in fresh air. Remove the covering when the seedlings are about ½ inch tall.

To get plants off to a fast, sure start indoors, you can use artificial lighting set on simple lamp timers to simulate the long daylight hours of spring. The lights can be placed anywhere you have the room to start seeds (for more on using artificial lights, see Grow lights, p.382). If you choose to raise seedlings in a cool place, like a basement, you may want to invest in waterproof soil-heating mats sold at garden centers and through catalogs. Placed under flats, these will keep the soil at the optimum sprouting temperature of 70°F.

Once the seedlings emerge, use a technique called bottom-watering to keep the soil in the containers moist. Set a planted seed flat in a pan of lukewarm water to soak up moisture. Remove the flat from the pan when the soil is completely moistened. This technique keeps seedling leaves dry, helping to prevent the spread of fungal diseases like damping off, which can quickly kill seedlings. Circulating the air near seedlings with a fan set on its slowest speed also fends off fungal diseases.

GROW LIGHTS

To get plants off to a fast start indoors, many gardeners rely on artificial lighting.

A homemade grow-light system may be as simple as a standard shop light fixture containing two 48-inch cool-white fluorescent tubes (one warm white and one cool white are best for coaxing house plants to flower, but green seedlings benefit most from the spectrum in inexpensive cool-white tubes). Make sure any system you get has a reflective hood to direct light to the plants, and a chain attachment for raising and lowering the fixture.

When growing plants under artificial lights, keep the tubes about 4 to 6 inches above the tops of the uppermost leaves. Plug the lights into an inexpensive lamp timer and set it for 16 or 18-hour days to simulate spring growing conditions. As the plants grow, use the chain to raise the light fixture to the proper height. If plants stretch toward the lights, lower the lights to promote strong, stocky growth. If plant leaves curl under, they're receiving too much light, and you should raise the lights by an inch or more. Keep the plants well watered to protect their tender leaves from wilting.

Replace the tubes with new ones after six months of use for maximum light output. The used tubes, which still put out light, can be used for household lighting, especially in areas like basements and garages.

EARLY SPRING

Before breaking new ground, have a good idea of what and how many plants you want to grow. Know where you want to grow them and plan to keep your garden to a size you can handle. Also, bear in mind how much sun they will require (it's listed on the seed packets). Vegetables, herbs, and many flowers need at least six to eight hours a day during the summer. In early spring before trees grow leaves, you might be fooled into setting up a bed in a place that receives too much shade later on. To solve this potential problem, observe a planting spot in various seasons and at different times of day, noting the intensity and duration of sunlight it receives before breaking ground.

Prepare seedbeds in the garden and sow hardy vegetables

Wait until the soil has thawed, drained, and truly warmed up before digging. Working in cold, sodden soil is unpleasant, and digging or tilling too early compacts the soil, which ruins its texture and drainage (for more on compaction see Dealing with poor drainage, p.349). Allow two to four weeks between breaking soil and planting. In average soil, this is a three-part process: till the soil at least 8 inches deep, work in a 4- to 6-inch layer of compost or other composted organic material, and smooth the new bed with a rake, crumbling clods of soil in your hands, as needed.

If your soil has a lot of sand or clay, you may want to test it before amending so that you can add any minerals or other nutrients that may be indicated by the results. A soil testing kit with instructions is available for a small fee from your local Cooperative Extension Service office (affiliated with a land-grant university; see your telephone book) as well as university and private testing laboratories. Typically, you mail an envelope containing several ounces of your soil. For most accurate results, take scoops of soil from a variety of locations in the intended planting area, mix in a bucket, then extract the amount of soil specified by the test instructions.

Depending on the laboratory you use and the details you request, the report can contain information on the amount of nutrients, soil acidity, or pH, and on the level of microbial activity. This information is followed by recommendations to help you correct any problems (see Correcting problem soils, p.326).

WHEN TO GET A SOIL TEST

- You plan to grow edibles (berries, fruit trees, vegetables).

- You have just broken ground for a new bed (removed a section of lawn, cleared away brush).

- This is a new yard for you, and you are unsure about the quality of its soil.

- Your plants aren't growing well.

Irrigate whenever the soil is dry 1 inch beneath the surface (above, left). Check the soil for moisture when a week passes without rain. Plant garden seeds outdoors (above) when the soil no longer feels chilly to the touch.

A fresh, new bed needs a resting period of several weeks for amendments to blend in and the soil to settle. It's a good time to get rid of weeds, which are hosts to insect pests and plant diseases. Once your bed is ready, sow seeds for hardy, early vegetables, such as radishes, carrots, spinach, and other leafy greens, directly into the soil, according to seed package directions.

Prune summer-blooming shrubs

Early spring is a good time to prune many shrubs, especially those that will bloom during the summer months, like roses and mock oranges. The idea is to get at the plants early, just as they are surging back to life, and inspire fresh new flowering growth before they set buds.

A neglected plant becomes dense and tangled and produces fewer flowers, at the top or outer branches, each season. A well-pruned shrub, on the other hand, has a neater, healthier appearance and produces flowers throughout the shrub. Proper and thorough pruning makes these plants more attractive and will even rejuvenate them—they'll look healthier and be stronger, longer-lived plants.

Weed and water now to prevent problems later

Early spring weeding entails pulling small weeds as soon as you see them. They're easier to extract—even ones with a long taproot like dandelions—while still small, especially if they are growing in damp ground. If a whole patch has emerged, slice them off at soil level with a sharp hoe, and continue to do so until they stop sprouting. Or, smother them under black plastic sheeting or newspaper, several sheets thick (black print only), and then apply an attractive mulch over it. If you want to plant in that area, you can remove the mulching material later.

Don't assume that spring rainfall will keep your garden adequately watered. As a rule, plants should be watered as often as necessary to equal an inch of water (see Spring watering and weeding, p.386) per week. Be especially attentive to young plants you set out last fall or this spring, as their shallow roots dry out rapidly.

When pruning shrubs and trees, clear out branches that rub against each other to prevent torn bark, an entry point for pests and diseases. For most plants, the best time to prune is early spring.

AVOIDING WEED INVASIONS

A completed bed, all tilled and neatly raked over, is a temporary joy to behold. Turning the soil usually brings weed seeds and weed-root fragments to the surface.

After you prepare the soil, wait at least a week before planting. If weeds are present, they will germinate by then. If there are too many to pull, attack them with a good, sharp hoe to slice through weeds, killing the weed crop before it gets a grip on your garden. Handle a hoe as you would a broom, using a light, sweeping motion to avoid disturbing the soil and exposing more weed seeds. If you can, wait another 7 to 10 days and repeat the procedure before planting.

When your garden seedlings emerge, mulch the ground around them as soon as possible with a 2-inch layer of fine-textured organic covering, such as compost or grass clippings. As the plants grow, apply a 3-inch layer of a substantial mulch, such as straw or wood chips, to smother weeds for the rest of the season.

Dig a corner of a hoe into the soil behind a weed and pull upward.

To spot-treat with an herbicide, protect surrounding plants: cover a weed with a homemade funnel and spray carefully.

Boiling water is a safe and effective alternative to chemical weed killers.

You can protect seedlings from unexpected frosts in late spring by covering them with clear plastic sheeting supported by simple wire hoops. Lift the cover on warm afternoons to let fresh air reach the young plants.

MID-SPRING

Mid-spring is a busy, exciting time, when it seems like everything is happening all at once in the yard and garden. It's the time to set new plants outdoors, divide and replant overgrown plants, and begin a routine of ongoing garden sanitation that will ensure healthy plants for the entire growing season.

Plant and protect hardy seedlings

Mid-spring is the time to plant the hardiest seedlings that you started indoors. But be sure to harden them off before planting them outside. Hardening off is the simple process of acclimatizing seedlings from a life indoors to one outdoors. Depending on the coolness of the weather and the type of plant, you can start hardening off seedlings two to four weeks before the last expected frost date. Simply set the flats or pots of small plants outdoors for a few hours each day. Choose a spot sheltered from direct sun and stiff breezes, such as a porch, along a wall or fence, or on a table under a shady tree. Let the plants stay out a few more hours each day until the lowest night temperature remains well above freezing and you feel it's safe to leave them out overnight. Then you can plant them in the garden. After planting, apply compost as a soil-moisture conserving, weed-suppressing mulch—warmer, drier weather is ahead.

If left unchecked, insect pests can undergo a population explosion over the course of the season. Anything you do in spring to reduce their numbers will mitigate future woes. Light, protective covering sheets, known as floating row covers, available from garden centers and catalogs, are made of finely spun synthetic fabric. They keep the plants 4 or more degrees warmer than the surrounding air, but aside from frost protection, their main benefit is to keep pests, such as insects and birds, away from seedlings. (For more protection from cold weather, use clear plastic sheeting; see photograph, left.)

The protective row covers are called floating

because they are lightweight and can lie directly on top of the plants, although most people prefer to drape them over a framework, such as hoops of wire or flexible plastic tubing, and tuck the edges under loose soil to keep pests out. In windy places, anchor the edges with rocks.

Monitor plants under a floating row cover closely. Pull the covering away on warm afternoons to give the plants some fresh air. When flower buds appear, remove the covering so that bees and other pollinators can do their work. If the cover is still in good condition, store it for future use.

Insect egg masses, grubs, or caterpillars on plant stems, on or under leaves, or even in the soil may be precursors to future pest onslaughts. Handpick beetles and caterpillars early in the morning, when they are cool and sluggish and easier to catch. Hunt for slugs and snails after dark, beginning about an hour after sundown, using a flashlight. Remove boards, bricks, and rocks that might provide shelter for unfriendly crawlers, such as slugs. And begin good garden sanitation by removing dead or damaged leaves and flowers to make conditions unfavorable for plant diseases throughout the upcoming season.

Divide and move plants

It's better to divide plants when they are just entering fresh growth in spring and are able to bounce back quickly than to wait until the heat of summer stresses them. When you divide perennials in spring, they will have the entire summer to generate strong new roots. This is important in cold-winter climates, because waiting will send the plants into winter without a strong root system, leaving them vulnerable to frost damage.

Undertaking this project in spring is also easier on the gardener than doing it in fall. The plants, just sprouting after their winter's rest, are a manageable size, and you can dig them from the damp ground easily. But in mild-winter climates, perennials can safely be divided in late summer. Dividing at this time will allow plants a month or two to grow new roots before winter dormancy (for details on dividing perennials, see Time-tested techniques p.29).

Spring is also an excellent time to rectify last year's design problems, because it's the best time to take out or move plants you weren't happy with last season. If you are moving a plant to a new spot, dig the hole big enough to let you extract as much of its root system as possible. Keep the root ball moist and out of the sun until you can set it into prepared soil in its new home. Tidy up the top growth by trimming away any dead or diseased stems, or stems that grow toward the interior of a shrub or rub against each other (see photograph, p.383). Remove dead or damaged roots and divide the plant if necessary before replanting. Dig a hole the size of the root ball and plant it at the same depth at which it grew previously.

Start watering regularly

If spring rains have tapered off, now's the time to begin watering your garden regularly. If you are growing plants in the ground under shady trees or at the base of shrubs, the trees, now fully leafed, may shield the plants below from rainfall or greedily suck up ground moisture—another reason to water. If watering by hand becomes too much of a chore, consider installing soaker hoses (which release water gradually), a drip irrigation system, or sprinklers. Soaker hoses and drip irrigation apply water to the roots rather than wasting it on the foliage, where it evaporates, and keeping the leaves dry also discourages the spread of fungal and bacterial diseases that travel from plant to plant in splashing water.

LATE SPRING

As spring flows into summer, seasonal tasks begin to overlap. You'll find yourself pruning the early flowering shrubs to ensure a good crop of flowers for next spring, while also planting more seeds and tender plants in the garden. And it's time to begin looking after the health of emerging plants.

Plant seeds and seedlings of heat-loving plants in warm soil

Tender or heat-loving seedlings and plants that have been waiting indoors for warm weather, such as tomatoes, peppers, or tuberous begonias, can go outside in late spring. The soil, less soggy and well warmed up, is ready to receive them.

Spend a few days or a week hardening off frost-sensitive plants. Even after they are in the ground, it's a good idea to shield the new arrivals from hot sun and drying winds with a super-lightweight floating row cover. As soon as you spot a few new leaves or flower buds, you can safely assume they are fine and remove the protection.

STAKING TIPS

- Don't put a stake in too close to a plant. Your plant is sure to get taller and broader.

- Sink a stake in as deeply and securely as you are able, so that it will be able to support the eventual weight of the plant without bending or leaning.

- If ties are necessary, choose something soft and nearly invisible (like pantyhose or yarn) and form loops around the stake and around the stem—this allows for movement and minimizes abrasion. In time, the plant's growth ought to hide these supports.

An inexpensive rain gauge will help you know when to water your plants. Water when it registers less than an inch of rain in a week. Irrigate enough to raise the level to the 1-in. mark on the gauge.

Some crops, including corn and many root crops, such as beets, grow best when the seeds are direct sown, that is, put directly into the ground outdoors rather than being started early indoors. Warm soil, 75°F or warmer, is the key to problem-free heat-loving plants, which simply won't germinate well in damp, cool soil, but will rot or delay growth.

Stake your plants

Stake plants early in the season before they become tall, floppy, unwieldy, and laden with flowers or fruits. Also take care to put the stake—metal, wood, or even a plastic stake— far enough from a plant to keep from damaging its roots. It also helps, when staking vegetables such as tomatoes, to place the stakes in the ground at the same time you put the plants in the garden. If you are staking a tall, weak-stemmed, or floppy plant, consider creating a cage for it by placing three stakes in a triangular arrangement around it and winding unobtrusive green or brown twine around the stakes to hold the plant in place without putting undue pressure on its stems. When the wind blows, the plant will be able to sway without snapping tightly tied stems.

Spring watering and weeding

In many areas, rainfall tapers off as summer approaches. Well-established plants will often take this in stride. Younger plants, and thirsty plants that wilt easily, will need supplemental watering. A general rule is to irrigate as needed to make sure your garden receives about an inch of water a week. To do this, either buy an inexpensive commercial rain gauge marked off in inches, or make one by setting a shallow container, such as an empty tuna can, near your plants. Sprinkle them until 1 inch of water collects in the rain gauge or the can.

By late spring, weeds that have escaped your notice will begin to flower. Get rid of the weed flowers, and hopefully the plants, before they go to seed. Many weeds spread by stems or roots. Just removing the flowers of these plants won't halt them. To get the problem under control early, weed often and well.

Late spring is the last, best chance to mulch your garden. If you cut your lawn regularly, the clippings may be the easiest choice. Otherwise, lay down a 3-inch layer of mulch —bark chips around new roses, straw or compost in the vegetable patch, cocoa hulls around the perennials—before a new generation of weeds pops up. The mulch will also help retain soil moisture, so you'll have to

water less often, and it will protect plants against soilborne diseases that can splash onto them with rain or irrigation.

Prune spring-blooming shrubs

Shrubs and trees that bloom in spring should not be pruned in early spring, because you would cut off the flower buds before they open. These early bloomers include popular flowering shrubs, like quince and lilac in cold climates and jasmine in California and the South.

Prune these plants immediately after their flowers brown, fade, and begin to fall to the ground. At the same time, take out deadwood, excess branches, and suckers (new sprouts). The plant will respond by generating new stems and branches on which next year's flower buds will form. If the shrub is hopelessly overgrown, you can cut it to within 1 foot of the ground. This drastic treatment will cause it to skip a season of flowering, but you can then prune as directed above in following years and be rewarded with profuse flowers every season.

SUMMER

The pests of summer range from marauding deer, rabbits, and groundhogs to ravenous slugs, snails, and Japanese beetles. You'll often see the damage before you spot the pest. If you're not sure of the culprit, go into the garden at night with a flashlight, because many plant pests are nocturnal feeders. You can collect and show the mystery caterpillar or a piece of the eaten plant to a more experienced gardener or someone at the local nursery for identification and recommended treatments.

Thwarting garden pests

Your first thought may be to spray a pesticide, but there are simpler, safer alternatives. Fence your garden or plants against rodents and deer, or set catch-and-release traps for small, furry troublemakers. Include impatiens and coleus, which rabbits don't like, in your garden. Inspect your plants often and carefully. Early morning is the best time, because insects will be sluggish and easy to catch. Knock aphids and other small insects off stems and leaves with a blast of water from a hose. Pick off and dispose of egg masses on leaf undersides. Sprinkle gritty diatomaceous earth, a commercial product made of ground crustaceans, on leaves and the ground to discourage a broad range of pests from slugs to ants (see individual plant entries in Part I for specific problems and solutions).

If infestations are large enough to warrant spraying, identify the pest and buy the appropriate product. Read the label to find out if the plant and the pest are listed on the product label, how to spray safely, and when in the creature's life cycle the product will be most effective (see pp.9 and 390 for more on safe pesticide use).

Keep plants well watered

Shallow-rooted plants, such as annual flowers and lawn grass, are vulnerable to drought at this time of year, because the soil surface dries out quickly. Allowing plants to wilt causes cells to die, weakening and setting them up for disease and insect infestations. As the summer wears on, container plants may need watering once or twice a day (see Keeping container plants healthy, p.376). But if your geraniums begin to yellow from overwatering, reduce watering to once every two weeks.

Keep lawns and shrubs healthy by watering for long periods less often. Deep soakings once or twice a week are more beneficial than daily sprinklings, because grass roots are encouraged to grow downward toward the water table, where they will find moisture even in dry times. But if rhododendron or azalea leaves yellow in moist conditions, let the soil dry between waterings or move the plants to a raised bed or well-drained soil.

Late summer is the best time to fertilize lawns. Use a high-nitrogen lawn fertilizer and apply it according to the label. Afterward, water enough to wash fertilizer into the soil and keep fertilizer buildup from causing brown spots on the grass.

Grooming plants discourages pests and diseases

Clipping, trimming, and deadheading (removing faded flowers) not only keeps your garden looking tidy but helps prevent insect and disease invasions by getting rid of dead and dying vegetation and plant debris that can harbor pests now and over winter, creating headaches in next year's garden.

Constant snipping also has a desirable effect on most plants' growth. If you allow faded flowers to remain on the plant after being pollinated, the plant's energy goes into producing seeds or fruit rather than into producing new flowers. Conversely, when you remove a faded flower, the plant will pump out more flowers. When you remove branch tips or outer leaves, you promote a lusher, thicker, more compact, and attractive plant.

Place bird netting over vulnerable crops

If your blueberry bushes or cherry trees are preparing a harvest, now's the time to protect them before the birds move in. Use a special lightweight plastic bird netting (available at garden centers and from catalogs) that allows moisture and sun to reach the plants, but thwarts hungry birds. Drape it over the plants and anchor the sides if necessary. If you want to attract birds to your garden, and your fruiting bushes or trees are tall, you can drape netting over the portion you can reach easily and allow the birds to feast on fruits that grow on the upper branches.

Four-footed pests can wreak havoc in your garden. Several strands of wire strung at a diagonal 4 ft. from the fence (left, above) will keep deer from jumping a fence. Burying small-mesh wire (left, below) at least 3 ft. deep around a bed will thwart digging groundhogs. Commercial tree wrap (above) will protect young trees from gnawing rodents.

Promptly remove faded flowers. Cut them off cleanly ¼ in. above a developing bud to inspire the plants to bloom longer.

FALL

Fall is perhaps the most important time of year for garden problem prevention. Now's the time to cut back fading stalks, leaves, and weeds, and to clean up the garden before winter. Spent foliage, left to flop over or fall off on its own, and decomposing plant debris left on the ground, can harbor overwintering pests and diseases. Removing debris reduces the likelihood of future problems. In addition, a well-trimmed garden looks neater, and you'll have less grooming to do in spring, when new shoots are trying to poke their way up.

Cleaning up the lawn and garden go hand-in-hand in fall. As you rake up dried leaves, use them to mulch your garden paths. This is also an ideal time to top beds with a 3- or 4-in. layer of compost. Winter rains will wash its nutrients into the soil within reach of the roots of next spring's crops.

Garden cleanup and soil preparation prevents future problems

Fall is when weeds go to seed—pods and seed cases spring open to release them. If you don't have time to rake up crab apples, try collecting them with a shop vacuum. If there's no time to pull plants up by the roots, chop or clip off their heads before the seeds are released. Discard all seed heads in the trash pile, not on the compost heap. If you have a large weed patch, smother it over winter by covering it with a large sheet of black plastic weighted down by bricks or rocks.

Every once in awhile, a garden plant finds legs and begins to spread and take over the garden. By fall, it will have long worn out its welcome—whether it's Japanese knotweed invading a shrub border or forget-me-nots running rampant through perennial beds. Dig or pull intruders out completely and dispose of them. Or spot treat them with an herbicide. Follow label precautions regarding when and

how to spray. And be careful not to overspray and affect innocent plants nearby.

After you remove all garden debris, weeds, and invasive plants, it's easy to prepare beds for spring. There are advantages to testing the soil and amending it in fall. You'll have plenty of time to add needed amendments to the soil before cold weather sets in. The cool weather makes autumn a nice time to break new ground. Top beds off with a 3- or 4-inch layer of compost and leave it. Winter rains will leach nutrients into the soil to give your plants a head start in the spring, and when you prepare the soil, the topping will be easy to work into the soil at planting time.

Dividing perennials now ensures a trouble-free spring

Fall is a good time to divide perennials for gardeners in most parts of the country. The plants are going dormant at this time and won't be shocked by cutting, chopping, or transplanting. And the weather conditions are congenial—the soil is still warm, and autumn rains will supply a steady supply of water to the transplants. In the spring, they'll repay your efforts with a fresh, vigorous start (for more on dividing perennials, see Time-tested techniques p.29). Spring is better for division in freezing climates (zones 5 and colder), where winter temperatures are hard on transplants.

Fertilize the lawn

Fertilizing is generally not recommended for plants heading into the winter, because it causes new growth that can be damaged by cold. But lawns are an exception and should be fertilized in fall. If you live in a mild climate and your grass has just endured a long, hot summer, fertilize it in mid-fall. In cool regions, fertilize in late summer or early fall with a lawn fertilizer especially made for fall fertilizing. The bagged lawn food intended for fall use stimulates root growth, better enabling grass to withstand winter. It also lets the grass store food that will get it off to a good start next year (for more on lawn care see Chapter 9, Lawns, p.342).

Plant spring-blooming bulbs

Autumn is the right time to plant hardy, spring-blooming bulbs. Don't put it off too late; if the ground gets drenched by rains or freezes, the project will be difficult or doomed. Buy large, firm bulbs, and plant them at the depth recommended by the vendor for your area. A rule of thumb is to sink them to a depth of two or three times their diameter. If you have a problem with rodents digging up your bulbs, sprinkle gritty gravel into the planting hole or encase your bulbs in hardware cloth before planting. Straw is an attractive nesting material for rodents; don't use it as a mulch around bulbs.

Dig and store tender bulbs and corms

In cold-climate areas, fall is the time to rescue the bulbs and corms of tender, summer plants such as caladiums, cannas, and dahlias, which will freeze and die if left in the ground over the winter. Dig them up as the foliage turns brown in early fall, trim off the remaining foliage or flower stalks, let them air dry for a week, and then layer them in paper bags filled with peat moss or vermiculite. Store the bags in a cool, dark place, such as a basement or cool closet. If the storage area is humid, dust the bulbs with the organic fungicide sulfur before bagging them and slit the bags for better ventilation. Check the bulbs monthly; discard any that look soft and sprinkle water on those that look shriveled.

Water and protect vulnerable plants from winter stress

Contrary to what you may think, winter dormancy is not always a blessing to garden plants. Frozen ground locks up water, creating a drought situation, which can injure or kill plants. So give your plants, from perennials to trees, a good, long soaking before the soil freezes in late fall.

In cold climates where the ground freezes, a heavy, 4- to 8-inch organic mulch is wise—mandatory in the case of plants of borderline hardiness. A winter mulch serves as a blanket, protecting the plants from freezing winds and frost-heaving, moderating soil temperatures, and conserving moisture. If you get consistently deep snow cover, the need for a mulch is less dire, but it's still a good idea to apply one after the first hard freeze. Also, it is a good practice to place some evergreen boughs or loose hay over low-growing plants, such as groundcovers, to protect them from snow damage without smothering them.

If your winters are bitter or if you have shrubs or roses of doubtful hardiness, there are a number of things you can do to protect them. Wrap them loosely in burlap, form

To prepare tender bulbs for winter storage, air-dry them for a week and remove dead leaves and soil (far left). Put the bulbs into a bag and dust with antifungal sulfur (near left). Then put them in into a clean paper bag filled with vermiculite and store them in a cool, dry place.

hinged, plywood sandwich board tents over them, or make a fence-wire cage around them and stuff it with dried leaves or straw. If your winter is windy, apply a waxy leaf coating, called an antidesiccant spray (available from garden centers and catalogs) as well as a burlap screen to evergreens. Antidesiccants have the added advantage of making evergreens less appetizing to deer.

⚘ TIME-TESTED TECHNIQUES ⚘

TAKE CARE OF YOUR TOOLS

After the growing season ends, get your tools ready for next year.

- Clean your tools, using soapy water. To remove stubborn muck, soak the tool, then scrub with a stiff brush.

- Rub off rust with very fine sandpaper or with fine steel wool dipped into kerosene.

- Dry the tools with an absorbent rag or paper towels. Dampness can lead to rust and spoil moving parts.

- Sharpen cutting edges with a file or a whetstone. If an edge is hopelessly dull, have it professionally sharpened.

- Wipe metal surfaces with an oiled cloth (vegetable oil is fine). Or store metal tool ends in a bucket filled with coarse sand soaked in motor oil.

- To keep wooden handles from drying out, apply a light coat of boiled linseed oil, and buff.

- Tighten screws and dab a drop or two of light machine oil on moving parts.

- Store tools out of reach of children in a cool, dry spot. Winter is an excellent time to make an organized pegboard or other storage system for your tools.

To sharpen a tool blade, file from the outer edge to the center. Use downward strokes; hold the file at an angle.

APPENDIX

UNDERSTANDING PESTICIDES

Like rakes or trowels, pesticides are garden tools, ones used to control weeds, insects or diseases. To ensure that these tools perform safely and effectively, learn to use them responsibly.

What Is a Pesticide?

Many substances—from kitchen cleansers to pet flea collars—are considered pesticides. They are divided into groups, based on the type of organism they are registered to control.

The U.S. Environmental Protection Agency (EPA) defines a pesticide as any substance or mixture "intended to prevent, destroy, or mitigate any insects, rodents, nematodes, fungi, or weeds, or other forms of life declared to be pests and any substance or mixture of substances intended for use as a plant regulator, defoliant, or desiccant."

The groups of interest to gardeners are:

- *Bactericides* to control bacterial diseases
- *Disinfectants* to kill or neutralize disease-causing organisms
- *Fungicides* kill or control fungi
- *Growth regulators* to alter the growth of plants or pests such as insects
- *Herbicides* to kill plants
- *Insecticides* to kill or control insects
- *Miticides* to kill or control mites
- *Molluscicide* to kill or control slugs and snails
- *Nematicides* to kill or control the microscopic worms called nematodes
- *Repellents* to keep pests away from a plant or area

Choosing a Pesticide

The first step in choosing is to identify the problem. Then read pesticide labels to see which ones are registered to treat the problem of the plant in question. When choosing, check the "signal word" (p.8) and pick the least toxic product. Also read the label for clothing requirements.

In this book, pesticides are divided into two categories: organic and synthetic treatments. Those described as organic are composed of or derived from naturally occurring minerals and organisms (or are widely accepted as organic treatments). The synthetics are manmade.

While organic products are generally considered more environmentally friendly than synthetic ones, be aware that all pesticides are poisons. Both can be effective against garden problems, and both can have a negative impact on the environment.

Reading the Labels

Pesticide labels carry important information for consumers. In addition to the brand name, the manufacturer's name and address, and the product's EPA registration numbers, the following items are found on pesticide labels.

- *Ingredient statement* lists the names and amounts of active ingredients.
- *Registered use statement* lists the types of pests the product is registered to control and on which plants, animals, or surfaces the product may be legally applied.
- *Precautionary statement* warns of special hazards or concerns the product may pose. For example, a statement may warn that the product is toxic to honeybees and should not be used near them.
- *First aid information* outlines antidotes and other first aid treatments to use in the event of poisoning.
- *Directions for use* describe how, according to federal law, the product should be applied—how much, how often, where, how much time must pass after application until it is safe to reenter the area or harvest fruits and vegetables, and what type of protective equipment is needed for safe application.
- *Signal words* rank the product's toxicity: CAUTION, WARNING, or DANGER (p.8).
- *Storage and disposal information* describes how to safely store and dispose of any unused portion of the product.

Applying Pesticides

Pesticides can be applied in various ways, depending on whether the product is liquid or solid and whether spot treatment or broader coverage is required. Some of the most common methods for applying pesticides include:

- *Pressurized aerosol cans.* Premixed pesticides can be pointed and sprayed to spot-treat minor problems.
- *Hose-end sprayers.* These inexpensive devices fit on the end of a garden hose and mix pesticides with water coming from the hose. They work best with liquid concentrates (wettable powders will clog them) and are convenient for treating large areas. Choose a model with an antisiphon feature that prevents pesticides from flowing back into the water supply.
- *Pressure sprayers.* Both cannister and backpack models are hand-pumped to deliver a solution of liquid concentrates or wettable powders and water. Depending on the nozzle, these sprayers can be adjusted for spot application or broad coverage.
- *Dusters.* Containers fitted with a shaker top sprinkle the pesticide over a small area.
- *Mechanical spreaders.* These rolled or hand-operated spreaders apply granules over large areas.

Different Types of Pesticides

There are a confusing number of pesticides available. Below are guidelines to help you select the proper type for your needs.

- **Biological pesticides.** A catch-all category for products that use living organisms, such as the bacteria BT (*Bacillus thuringiensis*), or are derived from living organisms, such as diatomaceous earth. Because they employ natural defenses, biological pesticides tend to be specific in the types of pests they control. They are generally of low toxicity to people, pets, and beneficial organisms.
  Caution: For many biological pesticides to work effectively, they must be applied at the proper season or growth cycle of the pest.

- **Botanical pesticides.** These pesticides are derived from plants and include such products as pyrethrin and rotenone. As a group, they work and degrade quickly, leaving little or no residue, so they are not effective in preventive treatments.
  Caution: Although derived from organic sources, these pesticides can hurt the environment. Rotenone, for example, is extremely toxic to fish.

- **Horticultural oils.** Refined petroleum products used to control scales, aphids, adelgids, and mites, these contact pesticides are safe for most plants and are of low toxicity to people and pets. Once dry, they are harmless and provide no preventive control.
  Summer oils, or refined horticultural oils, are superfine and can be used on plants during the growing season. Dormant oils are heavier and must be applied to the plant during its dormant period.

Caution: Horticultural oils should not be applied when the temperature is expected to drop below freezing or rise above 85°F. They can damage foliage if plants are sprayed while under stress, such as during droughts. Don't use horticultural oils on maples, azaleas, beeches, and many conifers.

- **Insecticidal soaps.** Made from the potassium or sodium salts of certain fatty acids, insecticidal soaps are of low toxicity to people, pets, and beneficial insects while wet, and are harmless once dry. They provide satisfactory control of many soft-bodied pests, but no preventative protection. Insecticidal soap spray must come in contact with an insect to kill it, so the spray must cover all surfaces of an infested plant.
  Caution: Insecticidal soaps can damage the leaves of plants under stress from drought, disease, or recent transplanting. Don't use on azaleas, fuchsias, Japanese maples, gardenias, horse chestnuts, bleeding heart, nasturtiums, and some lilies and ferns.
  Mix insecticidal soap concentrate with soft water (distilled water is fine); the minerals in hard water make the product less effective. Don't mix insecticidal soaps with the botanical insecticide rotenone, the fungicide lime-sulfur, or any fungicide containing copper.

- **Mineral pesticides.** Derived from such minerals as copper and sulfur, mineral pesticides are most often used as fungicides and applied as dusts or sprays.
  Caution: Some plants are sensitive to mineral pesticides. Avoid applying them to plants under the stress of drought or disease, or when temperatures rise above 85°F.

- **Synthetic pesticides.** These manufactured chemicals, sometimes synthetic forms of naturally occurring botanical substances, such as pyrethroids, are usually fast-acting and can have long-lasting residual activity.
  Caution: While many synthetic pesticides are relatively benign, others are extremely poisonous. Read the product label carefully and follow the directions exactly.

When Accidents Happen

Pesticide poisoning, which occurs through ingestion, inhalation, or skin contact, can be extremely serious. Symptoms include nausea, headache, blurred vision, and weakness. If you suspect pesticide poisoning, consult the product label for appropriate first aid action. Call 911, a doctor, or a poison-control center (the number is in the front of your telephone book) immediately. Have the pesticide product label handy so that you can read the active ingredients to the medical personnel.

To clean up minor pesticide spills in the garden or on the lawn, dig up and dispose of contaminated soil as local ordinances specify. For spills on paved surfaces, cover the pesticide with clean kitty litter, sweep it up, and dispose of it as the ordinances require. If you have concerns about how to clean up a pesticide spill, call a regional pesticide regulatory agency.

HOME REMEDIES

Home remedies have been used for generations to control garden pests and diseases. These treatments are generally harmless to people, pets, plants, and the environment, but it is best to use them with caution. Always test a remedy before using it: Spray a single leaf on an ailing plant and wait a few hours to see if the solution causes damage. As a rule, apply home remedies in the morning; high temperatures and midday sunlight can damage foliage. Because these preparations contain no preservatives, make only as much of a remedy as you need. Discard the leftovers.

BAKING-SODA SOLUTION

A solution of baking soda and water is used to control fungal diseases; the vegetable oil in this recipe helps the solution cling to foliage. You can spray it on infected foliage to discourage the spread of fungal diseases, but because this remedy is most effective as a preventative, apply it once a week to susceptible plants before disease symptoms appear. Spray each plant completely, covering all leaf surfaces.

INGREDIENTS:

2 tablespoons baking soda

1 tablespoon vegetable oil

1 cup plus 1 gallon warm water

DIRECTIONS:

1 Mix baking soda and oil in 1 cup of warm water. Stir until baking soda dissolves completely.

2 Add the solution to 1 gallon of warm water and mix thoroughly.

3 Pour solution into a clean sprayer.

BEER BAIT FOR SLUGS AND SNAILS

Slugs and snails are attracted to the sweet, yeasty combination of sugar and beer. When you place shallow containers of this mixture in the garden, slugs and snails will climb into them and drown.

INGREDIENTS:

6 ounces stale beer

A pinch of sugar

DIRECTIONS:

1 Stir the sugar into the beer.

2 Pour the mixture into shallow containers, until it is 1 inch deep. Empty tuna cans or plastic margarine tubs work well.

3 Sink the containers into soil with the rims at ground level throughout the garden.

4 Empty and refill the containers with a fresh mixture every two days.

CHAMOMILE TEA

Chamomile tea is an effective preventative against various fungal diseases; when sprayed on infected plants, it discourages the spread of disease. Sprayed on seedlings, it helps ward off damping-off disease. For plants prone to powdery mildew, such as rosemary or bee balm, weekly applications of chamomile tea are suggested to guard against infection.

INGREDIENTS:

4 chamomile tea bags or 1 tablespoon dried chamomile flowers

2 cups hot, but not boiling, water

DIRECTIONS:

1 Place chamomile in a container.

2 Add the water and let the mixture cool to room temperature.

3 Strain into a clean sprayer.

CITRUS SPRAY

The rinds of lemons and other citrus fruits contain citrus oil, a sweet-smelling substance that is harmless to humans and pets, but repels many insects. Because some plants are sensitive to citrus oil, be sure to test first by spraying a leaf with this recipe, then wait to see if damage occurs. In place of the lemons, you can substitute 4 limes, 2 or 3 tangerines, 1 large orange, or 1 grapefruit.

INGREDIENTS:

2 lemons

1 quart water

DIRECTIONS:

1 Grate the lemon rind and set aside.

2 Bring the water to a full boil.

3 Add the rind to the water and remove from heat.

4 Cover and let stand at room temperature for 24 hours.

5 Strain into a clean sprayer.

COMPOST TEA

Compost tea, which is a source of plant nutrients and disease-fighting soil organisms, is used as both a fertilizer and a preventative against most plant diseases. It can be applied as a soil drench or sprayed on foliage. For best results on ornamental plants, use compost that has been made with some aged manure. Do not use tea containing manure on edible plants, as it may contain harmful bacteria. Apply tea either at full strength as a periodic fertilizer or as a disease treatment. To use as a fertilizer with every watering, dilute the tea with water to the color of weak tea and water plants regularly.

INGREDIENTS:

2 gallons of compost (measure dry in a bucket or 1-gallon can)

4½ gallons warm water

DIRECTIONS:

1 After measuring, place compost into an old pillowcase or burlap sack, and tie the bag tightly with a length of twine.

2 Pour the water into a 10-gallon pail or other large container.

3 Immerse the sack in the water and swirl it gently for a few minutes.

4 Leave the sack in the water, cover the pail, and let stand in a shady place for a week.

5 Pour the solution into a watering can fitted with a sprinkler head to apply full strength, or dilute to the color of weak tea, as needed.

HOT-PEPPER AND GARLIC SPRAY

While garlic and pepper are popular seasonings for human food, insects find them distasteful. They can be used to make a spray that can be applied as often as needed to repel pests. Always handle hot-pepper spray very carefully and never use it to repel animals, because capsaicin, the active ingredient in pepper, is a powerful eye and skin irritant.

INGREDIENTS:

6 to 8 cloves garlic, unpeeled and crushed

1 tablespoon powdered cayenne pepper

1 quart warm water

DIRECTIONS:

1 Place the prepared garlic and pepper into a 2-quart container.

2 Add the water to the container.

3 Stir vigorously for a minute. Cover the container, set the container in a place out of direct sunlight and let it stand for two days.

4 Strain the solution into a clean sprayer.

HOT WATER DIP FOR BULBS

Bulbs infested with bulb mites can rot or transmit the pests to other bulbs in storage. This dip will kill mites on otherwise healthy bulbs. Do not dip diseased bulbs to prevent the spread of disease. Use this treatment for the bulbs of ornamental plants only, not edible tubers.

INGREDIENT:

water

DIRECTIONS:

1 Fill a container with enough water to hold the number of bulbs you wish to store.

2 Heat the water to 120°F.

3 Dip the bulbs into the heated water for three minutes.

4 Air dry bulbs and store in a cool, dry location.

HOUSEHOLD BLEACH DISINFECTANT

This solution is used to sterilize garden tools. If used between pruning cuts, it halts the spread of diseases from plant to plant by contaminated tools. Be sure to dry all metal parts thoroughly after disinfecting to prevent rust.

INGREDIENTS:

1 part household bleach (5% sodium hypochlorite)

9 parts water

DIRECTIONS:

1 Dilute bleach in water in a plastic container.

2 Soak tools in the solution for 20 minutes.

3 Shake off excess moisture and dry tools with a clean cloth.

YELLOW OR RED STICKY TRAPS

Sticky traps are used both to kill small flying insects and monitor for their presence, to help time the application of pesticides. Pests are attracted to the bright color and become entangled in the sticky coating. The traps can be used indoors for houseplants, in a greenhouse, or outdoors. Use yellow sticky strips for ornamental plants and red sticky spheres for fruit trees.

MATERIALS:

1 yellow plastic strip per plant, about 4 inches by 6 inches

or

1 red, apple-sized sphere per dwarf tree; 2 spheres per large tree

petroleum jelly

DIRECTIONS:

1 Punch a hole in one end of the strip or fasten a string or wire tie to a red sphere.

2 Smear petroleum jelly on all surfaces.

3 Hang strip by a string above the plant or fasten it with a twist tie to a stake and place it in the ground near the plant. Hang one or two red spheres to a tree, depending on its size.

4 When the trap is covered with pests, wipe off the coating. Recoat the trap to continue using as needed.

ORGANIC TREATMENTS

A **AGROBACTERIUM RADIOBACTER**
Type: Biological insecticide: bacterium
Signal word: WARNING
Use: For crown gall disease
Formulations: Emulsifiable concentrate
Health concerns: None recognized.
Environmental concerns: None recognized.

B **BT** (*Bacillus thuringiensis*) and varieties
    BTA (*B. t.* var. *aizawai*)
    BTI (*B. t.* var. *israeliensis*)
    BTK (*B. t.* var. *kurstaki*)
    BTSD (*B. t.* var. *san diego*)
    BTT (*B. t.* var. *tenebrionsis*):
Type: Biological insecticides: bacteria
Signal word: CAUTION
Use: For the larval stage of many insects
Formulations: Powder or concentrate
Health concerns: May irritate eyes.
Environmental concerns: None recognized.

BACILLUS POPILLIAE and **BACILLUS LENTIMORBUS**
See Milky spore disease.

BEAUVERIA BASSIANA (strain GHA)
Type: Biological insecticide, miticide: fungus
Signal word: CAUTION
Use: For a narrow range of mites, insects, including grasshoppers and beetles
Formulations: Wettable powder, flowable concentrate
Health concerns: None recognized.
Environmental concerns: None recognized.

BENEFICIAL NEMATODE
    (*Steinernema* spp.)
Type: Insect parasite: microscopic worm
Use: For many insects, including beetles
Health concerns: None recognized.
Environmental concerns: None recognized.

BENEFICIAL WASP
See Trichogramma wasp and Braconid wasp.

BORDEAUX MIXTURE
See Copper compounds.

BRACONID WASP
Type: Insect parasite: minute wasp
Use: For caterpillars, including tomato hornworms and corn borers
Health concerns: None recognized.
Environmental concerns: None recognized.

C **CAPSAICIN**
    (Includes hot pepper wax)
Type: Botanical repellent: *Capsicum annuum*
Signal word: CAUTION
Use: For repelling insects and animals
Formulations: Soluble concentrate, dust, liquid
Health concerns: Can irritate eyes and skin of people and animals.
Environmental concerns: None recognized.

COPPER COMPOUNDS
    (Including Bordeaux mixture, copper chloride, copper hydroxide, copper oxychloride sulfate, and copper sulfate)
Type: Fungicide, bactericide, herbicide, molluscicide, algicide: mineral
Signal word: CAUTION, WARNING, or DANGER, depending on formulation
Use: For primarily fungal, bacterial diseases
Formulations: Dust, wettable powder, concentrate
Health concerns: Poisoning is most frequently caused by ingestion. Symptoms include vomiting, severe stomach pain and nausea, sweating, shock, and headache. Poisoning may result in brain damage as well as injury to other internal organs, including liver, heart, and kidneys. Individuals may experience skin irritation after contact.
Environmental concerns: Extremely toxic to fish and aquatic life. Beneficial insects, including bees, are often killed by application of copper compounds on plants. Avoid spraying when beneficial insects are active, usually in daylight. Toxic to many soil organisms, including earthworms.

CORN GLUTEN
Type: Botanical herbicide: corn plant
Signal word: CAUTION
Use: Pre-emergent herbicide for use on established lawns to control crabgrass, foxtail grass, dandelions, lamb's-quarters, and other weeds
Formulations: Powder, granules
Health concerns: None recognized.
Environmental concerns: None recognized.

G **GARLIC OIL**
Type: Botanical repellent: *Allium sativum*
Signal word: CAUTION
Use: For repelling insects, mollusks, some vertebrates

Formulations: Granules, dust, soluble concentrate
Health concerns: None recognized.
Environmental concerns: None recognized.

H **HOT PEPPER WAX** *See* Capsaicin.

I **INSECTICIDAL SOAP**
Type: Botanical insecticide: vegetable oil, fatty acids
Signal word: CAUTION
Use: For many insects, including aphids
Formulations: Emulsifiable concentrate, ready-to-use spray
Health concerns: None recognized.
Environmental concerns: None recognized.

INSECTICIDAL SOAP and **NEEM**
Type: Botanical insecticide: vegetable oil, fatty acids; *Azadirachta indica*
Signal word: DANGER
Use: For insects and some fungal diseases
Formulations: Emulsifiable concentrate, ready-to-use spray
Health concerns: Can irritate skin.
Environmental concerns: None recognized.

L **LACEWING, GREEN LACEWING**
    (*Chrysoperla* spp.)
Type: Insect predator: flying insect
Use: For a wide variety of insects, including aphids, mealybugs, leafhoppers, scales, thrips, and whiteflies
Health concerns: None recognized.
Environmental concerns: None recognized.

LADY BEETLE, LADYBUG
    (*Hippodamia* spp.)
Type: Insect predator: beetle
Use: For many insects, including aphids, chinch bugs, mites, Colorado potato beetles, and whiteflies
Health concerns: None recognized.
Environmental concerns: None recognized.

LIME-SULFUR (Calcium polysulfide)
Type: Fungicide, insecticide, miticide: mineral
Signal word: CAUTION, WARNING, or DANGER, depending on formulation
Use: For many pests, including insects, mites, and fungal diseases
Formulations: Soluble and emulsifiable concentrates
Health concerns: None recognized.
Environmental concerns: None recognized.

M MEALYBUG DESTROYER
(*Cryptolaemus montrouzieri*)
Type: Insect predator: beetle
Use: For mealybugs, aphids, soft scale
Health concerns: None recognized.
Environmental concerns: None recognized.

MILKY SPORE DISEASE
(*Bacillus popilliae* and
B. lentimorbus)
Type: Biological insecticide: bacteria
Signal word: CAUTION
Use: For the larval stage of some insects, most notably Japanese beetles
Formulations: Granular, dust, wettable powder
Health concerns: None recognized.
Environmental concerns: None recognized.

N NEEM (Azadirachtin)
Type: Botanical insecticide, fungicide: *Azadirachta indica*
Signal word: CAUTION
Use: For many insects and some fungal diseases
Formulations: Emulsifiable and soluble concentrates
Health concerns: Can irritate skin.
Environmental concerns: None recognized.

O OIL EMULSION
Type: Insecticide, miticide: refined petroleum product
Chemical class: Unsulfonated hydrocarbon
Signal word: CAUTION or WARNING, depending on formulation
Use: For whiteflies, lace bugs, scale insects, and mites
Formulations: Emulsifiable concentrate, ready-to-use form
Mode of action: Interferes with normal metabolism.
Health concerns: Not available.
Environmental concerns: Not available.

P PARASITIC WASP
See Trichogramma wasp and Braconid wasp.

PREDATORY WASP
(*Hymenoptera* spp.)
Type: Insect predator: wasp
Use: For a wide range of insects

Health concerns: Stings from predatory wasps are painful and can be life-threatening to sensitive individuals.
Environmental concerns: None recognized.

PYRETHRIN
Type: Botanical insecticide: *Tanacetum* spp.
Signal word: CAUTION
Use: For many types of insects
Formulations: Emulsifiable concentrate, ready-to-use form
Health concerns: Can produce skin irritation, especially in sunlight. Acute exposure can result in tremors, salivation, behavioral changes, and can damage the central nervous system and immune system.
Environmental concerns: Extremely toxic to fish and other aquatic organisms and is toxic to beneficial insects.

PYRETHRIN and ROTENONE
Type: Botanical insecticide: *Tanacetum* spp.; *Lonchocarpus* spp.
Signal word: WARNING
Use: For many types of insects
Formulations: Mostly as emulsifiable concentrate
Health concerns: Can produce skin, eye, and throat irritation, especially in sunlight. Chronic exposure can produce conjunctivitis, dermatitis, sore throat, and congestion. Acute exposure can result in tremors, salivation, increased respiration followed by respiratory depression, convulsions, behavioral changes, and damage to the central nervous and immune systems. Symptoms of poisoning from ingestion include vomiting, convulsions, and breathing difficulty.
Environmental concerns: Pyrethrin and rotenone are extremely toxic to fish and other aquatic organisms, beneficial insects, and pigs.

R ROTENONE
Type: Botanical insecticide: *Lonchocarpus* spp.
Signal word: CAUTION, DANGER, depending on formulation
Use: For a wide range of insects
Formulations: Mostly as a dust and an emulsifiable concentrate

Health concerns: Very irritating to the eyes, throat, and skin. Can produce such symptoms as conjunctivitis, dermatitis, sore throat, and congestion. Inhalation can cause increased respiration, followed by respiratory depression and convulsions. Symptoms of poisoning from ingestion include vomiting, convulsions, and difficulty breathing.
Environmental concerns: Extremely toxic to fish and many forms of aquatic life. It is also highly toxic to pigs.

S STREPTOMYCIN
(Including streptomycin sulfate)
Type: Biological fungicide, bactericide, algicide: antibiotic
Signal word: CAUTION
Use: For a number of fungal and bacterial diseases
Formulations: Mostly available as a water-soluble powder and an emulsifiable concentrate
Health concerns: Streptomycin can produce skin irritations. In people allergic to it, it causes headaches, low blood pressure, skin rashes, and vomiting.
Environmental concerns: Streptomycin is very toxic to algae. When applied to some plants, such as grapes, pears, peaches, and corn, it may cause leaves to turn yellow.

SULFUR
Type: Fungicide: mineral
Signal word: CAUTION
Use: For a wide range of fungal diseases
Formulations: Mostly dust or suspension
Health concerns: May cause eye, skin irritation.
Environmental concerns: None serious. Application during hot weather can result in damage to plants. Some plants, including cucurbits and apricots, are sensitive to sulfur at any time.

T TRICHOGRAMMA WASP
(*Trichogramma* spp.)
Type: Insect parasite: wasp
Use: For a number of insects, including webworms, borers, cutworms, fruit-worms, and armyworms
Health concerns: None recognized.
Environmental concerns: None recognized.

SYNTHETIC TREATMENTS

A **ACEPHATE**
Type: Insecticide
Chemical class: Organophosphate
Signal word: CAUTION, WARNING, or DANGER, depending on formulation
Use: For chewing and sucking insects
Formulations: Granules, aerosol spray, wettable powder
Mode of action: Impairs nervous system.
Health concerns: Poisoning symptoms include eye pain, irregular heartbeat, breathing difficulty, coughing, heartburn, and abdominal cramps.
Environmental concerns: Very toxic to bees and other beneficial insects.

ABAMECTIN (Avermectin B1)
Type: Insecticide, miticide
Chemical class: Antibiotic
Signal word: CAUTION, WARNING, or DANGER, depending on formulation
Use: For mites and insects; fire ants
Formulations: Emulsifiable concentrate, granules
Mode of action: Impairs nervous system.
Health concerns: Can irritate eyes and skin.
Environmental concerns: Extremely toxic to many aquatic organisms and beneficial insects, including honeybees.

B **BASAGRAN** (*See* Bentazon).

BENDIOCARB
Type: Insecticide
Chemical class: Carbamate
Signal word: WARNING
Use: For many insects
Formulations: Dust, granules, wettable powder
Mode of action: Inhibits nerve function.
Health concerns: Poisoning symptoms include suppression of the respiratory and central nervous systems, dizziness, abdominal cramps, diarrhea, convulsions, and blurred vision.
Environmental concerns: Very toxic to birds, fish, bees, and earthworms.

BENEFIN
Type: Herbicide
Chemical class: Dinitroaniline
Signal word: CAUTION or WARNING, depending on formulation
Use: For broadleaf weeds, annual grasses
Formulations: Granules; flowable and emulsifiable concentrates
Mode of action: Disrupts cell division.

Health concerns: Slight to moderate eye, skin, and mucous-membrane irritation.
Environmental concerns: None recognized.

BENOMYL
Type: Fungicide
Chemical class: Benzimidazole
Signal word: CAUTION
Use: For many fungal diseases
Formulations: Wettable powder
Mode of action: Interrupts cell growth.
Health concerns: None serious.
Environmental concerns: Very toxic to fish, some aquatic life, and earthworms; moderately toxic to some birds.

BENSULIDE
Type: Herbicide
Chemical class: Organophosphate
Signal word: CAUTION
Use: For broadleaf weeds, annual grasses
Formulations: Emulsifiable concentrate, granules
Mode of action: Disrupts cell division.
Health concerns: Extended exposure can cause convulsions, nausea, weakness, abdominal cramps, difficulty breathing, and vomiting.
Environmental concerns: Very toxic to beneficial insects; moderately toxic to fish and other aquatic life.

BENTAZON
Type: Herbicide
Chemical class: Benzothidiazole
Signal word: CAUTION
Use: For broadleaf and narrowleaf weeds
Formulations: Flowable and soluble concentrates
Mode of action: Impairs photosynthesis.
Health concerns: Can irritate eyes, throat, skin, and lungs. Prolonged exposure can cause tremors, vomiting, diarrhea.
Environmental concerns: None recognized.

BIFENTHRIN
Type: Insecticide, miticide
Chemical class: Pyrethroid
Signal word: WARNING
Use: For many insects
Formulations: Emulsifiable concentrate, wettable powder
Mode of action: Impairs nervous system.
Health concerns: Poisoning symptoms include incoordination, tremors, salivation, diarrhea, and vomiting.
Environmental concerns: Very toxic to

fish, other aquatic life, and honeybees; moderately toxic to birds.

C **CAPTAN**
Type: Fungicide
Chemical class: Phthalimide
Signal word: CAUTION
Use: For many fungal diseases
Formulations: Emulsifiable concentrate, wettable powder, flowable formulas
Mode of action: None available
Health concerns: Concentrated form or repeated exposure can irritate eyes and skin. May be carcinogenic.
Environmental concerns: Very toxic to fish.

CARBARYL
Type: Insecticide
Chemical class: Carbamate
Signal word: CAUTION, WARNING, or DANGER, depending on formulation
Use: For many insects
Formulations: Dust, wettable powder, bait, granules, suspension
Mode of action: Impairs nervous system.
Health concerns: Poisoning symptoms include suppression of respiratory and central nervous systems, dizziness, stomach cramps, diarrhea, blurred vision, and convulsions.
Environmental concerns: Extremely toxic to honeybees, earthworms; toxic to fish.

CARBARYL and **MALATHION**
Type: Insecticide, miticide
Chemical class: Carbamate and organophosphate
Signal word: CAUTION, WARNING, or DANGER, depending on formulation
Use: For many insects and mites
Formulations: Dust, wettable powder, bait, granules, and suspension
Mode of action: Impairs nervous system.
Health concerns: Poisoning symptoms include suppression of respiratory and central nervous systems, dizziness, headache, nausea, tremors, numbness, cramps, diarrhea, blurred vision, tingling sensations, sweating, slow heartbeat, and convulsions. People with immune system disorders or on low-protein diets may be at increased risk.
Environmental concerns: Extremely toxic to some fish, earthworms, honeybees.

CARBENDAZIM
Type: Fungicide
Chemical class: Benzimidazole

Signal word: CAUTION
Use: For many fungal diseases
Formulations: Injection; best administered by a professional
Mode of action: Interrupts cell growth.
Health concerns: Can cause mild-to-severe temporary eye injury. Prolonged or frequent exposure can irritate skin in sensitive individuals.
Environmental concerns: Toxic to fish.

CHLORPYRIFOS

Type: Insecticide
Chemical class: Organophosphate
Signal word: CAUTION, WARNING, or DANGER, depending on formulation
Use: For many insects
Formulations: Granules, wettable powder, dust, emulsifiable concentrate
Mode of action: Impairs nervous system.
Health concerns: People with respiratory or liver disorders or with cholinesterase abnormalities are at greater risk. Poisoning symptoms include dizziness, headache, nausea, tremors, numbness, tingling sensations, abdominal cramps, blurred vision, sweating, slow heartbeat, and difficulty breathing.
Environmental concerns: Very toxic to birds, honeybees, and other beneficial insects; highly toxic to fish and aquatic invertebrates; serious hazard to wildlife.

CYFLUTHRIN

Type: Insecticide
Chemical class: Pyrethroid
Signal word: WARNING or DANGER, depending on formulation
Use: For many insects
Formulations: Emulsifiable concentrate, wettable powder, emulsion, sprays
Mode of action: Impairs nervous system.
Health concerns: Poisoning can produce vomiting, diarrhea, convulsions, paralysis, bloody tears, and nausea.
Environmental concerns: Toxic to fish and beneficial insects.

D ## DCPA

Type: Herbicide
Chemical class: Phthalate
Signal word: CAUTION
Use: For annual grasses, broadleaf weeds
Formulations: Wettable powder, suspension, granules
Mode of action: Inhibits germination.
Health concerns: May irritate skin
Environmental concerns: Slightly toxic to some birds and fish. Has been detected in some groundwater supplies.

DIAZINON

Type: Insecticide, miticide
Chemical class: Organophosphate

Signal word: CAUTION or WARNING, depending on formulation
Use: For many insects, especially grubs
Formulations: Granules, dust, wettable powder, emulsifiable concentrate
Mode of action: Impairs nervous system.
Health concerns: Poisoning can cause cramps, blurred vision, sweating, breathing difficulty and chest tightness, vomiting, and diarrhea.
Environmental concerns: Very toxic to birds, fish, and honeybees. Has been detected in some groundwater.

DICAMBA

Type: Herbicide
Chemical class: Benzoic acid
Signal word: WARNING
Use: For weeds before and after sprouting
Formulations: Granules; ready-to-use formulas; soluble and emulsifiable concentrates
Mode of action: Impairs growth.
Health concerns: Eye and skin irritation.
Environmental concerns: None recognized.

DIMETHOATE

Type: Insecticide, miticide
Chemical class: Organophosphate
Signal word: WARNING
Use: For many insects and mites
Formulations: Aerosol spray, dust, emulsifiable concentrate, ultra low volume (ULV) liquid
Mode of action: Impairs nervous system.
Health concerns: People with respiratory or liver disorders or cholinesterase abnormalities are at greater risk. Poisoning can cause dizziness, headache, nausea, tremors, numbness, tingling sensations, abdominal cramps, blurred vision, sweating, slow heartbeat, and difficulty breathing. Chronic exposure can cause flulike symptoms.
Environmental concerns: Very toxic to birds and bees; fairly toxic to fish.

DODINE

Type: Fungicide, bacteriacide
Chemical class: Acetate
Signal word: DANGER
Use: For scab, other plant diseases
Formulations: Wettable powder, soluble concentrate
Mode of action: Damages cell walls.
Health concerns: May irritate eyes.
Environmental concerns: Toxic to fish.

E ## ENDOSULFAN

Type: Fungicide
Chemical class: Chlorinated hydrocarbon
Signal word: CAUTION or WARNING, depending on formulation
Use: For many insects

Formulations: Dust, emulsifiable concentrate
Mode of action: Impairs nervous system.
Health concerns: Poisoning can cause difficulty breathing and swallowing, vomiting, convulsions, and diarrhea.
Environmental concerns: Toxic to birds, fish, and beneficial insects. Has been found in surface water and seafood.

ESFENVALERATE

Type: Insecticide
Chemical class: Pyrethroid
Signal word: WARNING
Use: For many insects
Formulations: Emulsifiable concentrate, ready-to-use formulas
Mode of action: Impairs nervous system.
Health concerns: Poisoning symptoms include dizziness, blurred vision, tearing eyes, burning, and itching. Minimal exposure can produce eye irritation.
Environmental concerns: Very toxic to honeybees and fish.

F ## FERBAM

Type: Fungicide
Chemical class: Dithiocarbamate
Signal word: CAUTION
Use: For many fungal diseases
Formulations: Wettable powder, dust
Mode of action: Interferes with enzymes.
Health concerns: Exposure can cause loss of muscular control, drowsiness, confusion, headache, reduced reflexes, slowed breathing, vomiting, and diarrhea. May irritate skin and eyes.
Environmental concerns: Toxic to some fish and aquatic life.

FLUAZIFOP

Type: Herbicide
Chemical class: Phenoxy
Signal word: CAUTION
Use: For many grasses, broadleaf weeds
Formulations: Emulsifiable concentrate
Mode of action: Disrupts cell metabolism.
Health concerns: May irritate eyes and skin. Very large doses can produce abdominal pain, dizziness, and central nervous system disorders.
Environmental concerns: Toxic to some fish.

G ## GLYPHOSATE

Type: Herbicide
Chemical class: Phosphoric acid compound
Signal word: CAUTION, WARNING, or DANGER, depending on formulation
Use: For many broadleaf weeds
Formulations: Powder, soluble concentrate
Mode of action: Absorbed into the plant, killing leaves, stems and roots by inhibiting amino acid synthesis.
Health concerns: Ingestion can cause skin

and eye irritation, nausea, dizziness, abdominal pain, low blood pressure, and vomiting.
Environmental concerns: Slightly toxic to fish

IMIDACLOPRID
Type: Insecticide
Chemical class: Chloronicotinyl
Signal word: CAUTION or WARNING, depending on formulation
Use: For sucking insects
Formulations: Wettable powder, dust, soluble concentrate
Mode of action: Disrupts nerve function.
Health concerns: Poisoning can produce fatigue, cramps, and muscle twitches.
Environmental concerns: Toxic to many birds and beneficial insects.

MALATHION
Type: Insecticide, miticide
Chemical class: Organophosphate
Signal word: CAUTION
Use: For insects and mites
Formulations: Wettable powder, dust, emulsifiable concentrate, ultra low volume (ULV) liquid
Mode of action: Impairs nervous system.
Health concerns: People with immune disorders or on low-protein diets may be at increased exposure risk. Poisoning symptoms include dizziness, headache, nausea, tremors, numbness, tingling sensations, abdominal cramps, blurred vision, sweating, slow heartbeat, and difficulty breathing.
Environmental concerns: Extremely toxic to honeybees and some fish.

MANCOZEB
Type: Fungicide
Chemical class: Ethylene dithiocarbamate
Signal word: CAUTION
Use: For many fungal diseases
Formulations: Dust, wettable powder
Mode of action: Interferes with enzymes.
Health concerns: Poisoning symptoms include loss of muscular control, drowsiness, confusion, headache, reduced reflexes, slowed breathing, vomiting, and diarrhea. Mild exposure may irritate skin and eyes.
Environmental concerns: Highly toxic to some fish and aquatic invertebrates.

MANEB
Type: Fungicide
Chemical class: Ethylene dithiocarbamate
Signal word: CAUTION
Use: For many fungal diseases
Formulations: Wettable powder, granules, flowable concentrate

Mode of action: Interferes with enzymes.
Health concerns: Poisoning can cause loss of muscular control, drowsiness, confusion, headache, reduced reflexes, slowed breathing, vomiting, and diarrhea. Mild exposure may irritate skin and eyes.
Environmental concerns: Toxic to fish and aquatic organisms. Do not spray on areas where animals graze or browse.

MCPP (mecoprop)
Type: Herbicide
Chemical class: Phenoxy
Signal word: CAUTION or WARNING, depending on formulation
Use: For many broadleaf weeds
Formulations: Granules, liquid concentrate
Mode of action: Interferes with enzymes.
Health concerns: Eye and skin irritation.
Environmental concerns: None recognized.

MESUROL (*See* Methiocarb).

METALAXYL
Type: Fungicide
Chemical class: Benezoid
Signal word: CAUTION
Use: For many fungal diseases
Formulations: Emulsifiable concentrate, granules, wettable powder
Mode of action: Not available.
Health concerns: Affects liver in high doses.
Environmental concerns: Low toxicity to birds, fish, and beneficial insects. Has been detected in some groundwater.

METALDEHYDE
Type: Molluscicide
Chemical class: Aldehyde
Signal word: CAUTION or WARNING, depending on formulation
Use: For slugs and snails
Formulations: Bait, dust, granules
Mode of action: Acts as stomach poison.
Health concerns: Poisoning can produce abdominal pain, nausea, vomiting, diarrhea, fever, and convulsions.
Environmental concerns: Toxic to some birds and mammals, including pets.

METHIOCARB
Type: Molluscicide
Chemical class: Carbamate
Signal word: CAUTION or WARNING, depending on formulation
Use: For snails and slugs
Formulations: Granules, dust, pellets, wettable powder, soluble concentrate
Mode of action: Interferes with enzymes.
Health concerns: Poisoning symptoms include loss of muscular control, drowsiness, confusion, headache,

reduced reflexes, slowed breathing, vomiting, and diarrhea. Mild exposure may irritate skin and eyes.
Environmental concerns: Toxic to invertebrates, fish, other aquatic life.

METHOXYCHLOR
Type: Insecticide
Chemical class: Organochlorine
Signal word: CAUTION
Use: For many insects
Formulations: Wettable powder, dust, spray, granules, emulsifiable concentrate
Mode of action: Impairs nervous system.
Health concerns: People with respiratory or liver disorders or cholinesterase abnormalities are at greater risk from exposure. Poisoning symptoms include dizziness, headache, nausea, tremors, numbness, tingling sensations, cramps, blurred vision, sweating, slow heartbeat, diarrhea, and difficulty breathing.
Environmental concerns: Very toxic to fish and shrimp. Very persistent in soil. May be an estrogen mimic.

MSMA
Type: Herbicide
Chemical class: Organic arsenical
Signal word: CAUTION or WARNING, depending on formulation
Use: For many grassy weeds
Formulations: Emulsifiable, flowable, or soluble concentrate; granules
Mode of action: Kills with arsenic.
Health concerns: Ingestion can injure central nervous system, liver, kidneys, and blood vessels. Poisoning symptoms include strong garlic breath odor; inflammation of mouth, throat, and esophagus; abdominal pain; thirst; bloody diarrhea.
Environmental concerns: Moderately toxic to fish and honeybees.

MYCLOBUTANIL
Type: Fungicide
Chemical class: Conazole
Signal word: CAUTION, WARNING, or DANGER, depending on formulation
Use: For many fungal diseases
Formulations: Wettable powders, granules
Mode of action: Inhibits protective sterol compounds.
Health concerns: Not available.
Environmental concerns: Not available.

OXADIAZON
Type: Herbicide
Chemical class: Oxadiazole
Signal word: WARNING

Use: For annual grasses, broadleaf weeds
Formulations: Emulsifiable concentrate, granules, wettable powder
Mode of action: Disrupts photosynthesis.
Health concerns: Chronic exposure may produce liver damage.
Environmental concerns: Toxic to fish and beneficial insects.

P PCNB
Type: Fungicide
Chemical class: Organochlorine
Signal word: CAUTION
Use: For many fungal diseases
Formulations: Seed treatment, emulsifiable concentrate, wettable powder
Mode of action: Not available.
Health concerns: Repeated exposure can damage liver and red blood cells and irritate skin. Also irritates eyes.
Environmental concerns: Highly toxic to fish and aquatic invertebrates. Persistent in soil; low concentrations have been found in some groundwater.

PENDIMETHALIN
Type: Herbicide
Chemical class: Dinitroaniline
Signal word: CAUTION, WARNING, depending on formulation
Use: For many grasses
Formulations: Wettable powder, emulsifiable concentrate, granules
Mode of action: Inhibits cell division.
Health concerns: May irritate skin and eyes.
Environmental concerns: Toxic to fish; may be toxic to some birds.

PHOSMET
Type: Insecticide, miticide
Chemical class: Organophosphate
Signal word: WARNING
Use: For many insects
Formulations: Wettable powder
Mode of action: Impairs nervous system.
Health concerns: Poisoning symptoms include dizziness, numbness, blurred vision, cramps, nausea, slowed heartbeat, and difficulty breathing.
Environmental concerns: Very toxic to some songbirds, most aquatic life.

PROPICONAZOLE
Type: Fungicide
Chemical class: Triazole
Signal word: WARNING
Use: For many fungal diseases
Formulations: Emulsifiable concentrate, wettable powder

Mode of action: Inhibits cell division.
Health concerns: Can irritate skin and eyes. Prolonged exposure may result in dizziness, headache, and nausea. Ingestion can cause difficulty breathing, diarrhea, and abdominal pain.
Environmental concerns: Toxic to some fish and aquatic life.

T TEBUTHIURON
Type: Herbicide
Chemical class: Urea
Signal word: CAUTION
Use: For woody and herbaceous plants
Formulations: Granules
Mode of action: Disrupts photosynthesis.
Health concerns: Irritates eyes and skin. Chronic exposure may damage pancreas.
Environmental concerns: May damage nontarget plants.

THIOPHANATE-METHYL
Type: Fungicide
Chemical class: Carbamate
Signal word: CAUTION
Use: For fungal diseases
Formulations: Emulsifiable and flowable concentrates; wettable powder
Mode of action: Disrupts cell division.
Health concerns: Eye irritation; damage to thyroid gland.
Environmental concerns: Toxic to earthworms and some fish, including catfish.

THIRAM
Type: Fungicide
Chemical class: Dithiocarbamate
Signal word: CAUTION
Use: For fungal diseases; seed protectant
Formulations: Wettable powder, dust, flowable concentrate, granules
Mode of action: Nonspecific.
Health concerns: Easily absorbed through skin; prolonged exposure can cause dizziness, nausea, fatigue, and difficulty breathing. Also irritates eyes and skin.
Environmental concerns: Very toxic to fish.

TRIADIMEFON
Type: Fungicide
Chemical class: Triazole
Signal word: CAUTION or WARNING, depending on formulation
Use: For many fungal diseases
Formulations: Wettable powder, emulsifiable concentrate
Mode of action: Is absorbed into seeds or foliage, where it kills fungi and protects against reinfection by inhibiting protective sterol compounds of fungi.

Health concerns: Poisoning symptoms include tremors, behavioral changes. Possible kidney and liver damage.
Environmental concerns: Low toxicity to birds, fish, aquatic life, and insects.

TRIFLUMIZOLE
Type: Fungicide
Chemical class: Triazole
Signal word: CAUTION or DANGER, depending on formulation
Use: For many fungal diseases
Formulations: Wettable powder
Mode of action: None available.
Health concerns: Slight eye irritation.
Environmental concerns: Slightly toxic to fish.

2,4-D
Type: Herbicide
Chemical class: Phenoxy compound
Signal word: CAUTION, WARNING, or DANGER, depending on formulation
Use: For many broadleaf weeds
Formulations: Emulsion, solution, dry compound
Mode of action: Interferes with growth.
Health concerns: Overexposure may cause coughing, dizziness, and fatigue. Repeated exposure may cause liver damage.
Environmental concerns: Some products are very toxic to fish and other aquatic organisms; moderately toxic to some birds. Found in some groundwater.

V VINCLOZOLIN
Type: Fungicide
Chemical class: Dicarboximide
Signal word: CAUTION
Use: For many fungal diseases
Formulations: Wettable powder, dust
Mode of action: Inhibits germination.
Health concerns: None serious.
Environmental concerns: Slightly toxic to fish.

Z ZIRAM
Type: Fungicide
Chemical class: Dithiocarbamate
Signal word: DANGER
Use: For many diseases; repels rodents
Formulations: Granules, wettable powder
Mode of action: Not available.
Health concerns: Can irritate eyes, skin, and throat. Repeated exposure can cause thyroid gland changes. Undetermined if carcinogenic.
Environmental concerns: Moderately toxic to some birds and aquatic organisms.

GLOSSARY

A

Acclimatization The adaptation of a plant to a site or to a change in climate.

Acidic soil Soil with a pH value less than 7.0, also called "sour" soil. *See* pH, pH scale.

Aeration Supplying oxygen to the soil by digging; or, for a lawn, by using a spiked tool to punch holes in the sod and thatch.

Alkaline soil Soil with a pH value more than 7.0, also called "sweet" soil. *See* pH, pH scale.

Amendment A material that is used to improve the soil, usually an organic or mineral material (compost, sand, limestone).

Annual A plant that completes its life cycle (germinates, matures, and dies) in one growing season.

Antitranspirant A waxy material applied to foliage that temporarily prevents water loss.

B

Bacteria Microorganisms that live in soil, water, plants, and other organic matter; bacteria can cause disease.

Beneficial insects Insects, such as predatory wasps, that prey on pest insects without harming plants.

Berm An earthen mound that is higher than the surrounding ground.

Biennial A plant that completes its life cycle in two growing seasons.

Biological control Living organisms that help control pests. Examples are BP (for controlling Japanese beetles), BT (for cabbage worms, caterpillars, and gypsy moths), BTK (for armyworms), beneficial nematodes (for insect larvae), Beauveriana bassiana (for beetles), and milky spore disease (for beetle larvae).

Blight A disease that causes plants to wither and die without rotting.

Bolting When a plant flowers and sets seed prematurely.

Borax A household product containing the plant nutrient boron.

Bordeaux mixture A substance prepared from copper sulfate and hydrated lime that is used primarily as a fungicide.

BP, BT, BTK *See* Biological control.

Bulb A swollen, modified bud with a short stem that serves as a food-storage organ for plants.

C

Caliche A hard, alkaline soil or soil crust containing white calcium carbonate; common in arid regions.

Canker A lesion of usually sunken, decayed tissue found most often on plant stems or branches.

Canopy The uppermost crown of leaves in a tree. *See* Crown.

Chelated iron A water-soluble form of iron used to treat plants with iron deficiency. *See* Chlorosis.

Chlorosis An unseasonable yellowing of leaves generally caused by disease, nutrient deficiency, or pH imbalance. *See* pH.

Clay soil Soil composed of very small particles that make it sticky, heavy, and hard to work.

Compaction Soil that has become so dense that air and water cannot penetrate; usually caused by foot or vehicular traffic.

Compost Organic matter that has decomposed; used as a fertilizer, soil conditioner, and disease inhibitor.

Compost tea A solution made by soaking compost in water, which is used as a fertilizer and disease inhibitor.

Conifer A cone-bearing tree or shrub; usually evergreen.

Contact pesticide A pesticide that kills insects or other pests on contact.

Corm An underground bulblike stem that bears roots and nourishes a young plant.

D

Crop rotation Growing a different crop on the same piece of land each year to reduce soilborne diseases and to vary the nutrient uptake of plants.

Crown The base of a plant, where the roots and stem meet, or the canopy of a tree. *See* Canopy.

Cultivar A contraction of cultivated variety, which refers to a cultivated plant whose characteristics are perpetuated by controlled propagation.

D

Damping off A fungal disease that most often attacks seedlings, causing them to collapse and die.

Deadheading The removal of spent flowers.

Deciduous Describing a plant that sheds its foliage seasonally.

Defoliate To cause a plant to lose its leaves, especially prematurely.

Diatomaceous earth Abrasive powder made of the ground, fossilized shells of aquatic diatoms that damages soft-bodied pests, such as snails and slugs, when they crawl over it.

Dieback The death of stems beginning at the tip; caused by disease, damage, or stress.

Direct seeding To sow seeds in the soil outdoors where they will sprout.

Division Propagation of a plant by separating its roots, crown, rhizomes.

Dolomite A mineral consisting of limestone and magnesium used to make soil more alkaline.

Dormancy A period when a plant temporarily stops growing, usually in winter or in dry weather.

Dormant oil A refined petroleum product sprayed on dormant plants primarily as a pesticide.

Double flower A blossom with more than the usual number of petals.

Drip irrigation A network of small hoses with many drip heads that provide water directly and efficiently to plant roots.

E

Earthworm A term referring to several types of beneficial worms that burrow into the ground, loosening the soil, aerating it, and adding nutrients.

Epsom salts A compound composed of a magnesium sulfate that is used to treat plants for magnesium deficiency.

Espalier A plant trained to grow flat against a support, such as wall.

Evergreen Plant that retains its foliage year round.

Exposure A description of the variation, intensity, and duration of sunlight, wind, and temperature of a site.

Eye A growth bud, such as the eye of a potato, or the center of a flower.

F

Foundation planting A plant border located adjacent to a building foundation.

Frass Waste, sometimes sawdustlike, excreted by insects, especially larvae.

Friable Describes soil with a crumbly texture that is easy for roots to penetrate.

Fruiting bodies The structures on flowerless plants, such as fungi and ferns, that produce spores.

Fungicide A substance that controls or destroys fungi.

Fungus A plant organism without chlorophyll that reproduces by spores and can cause disease.

G

Genus A group of plant species similar in flower form, appearance, and growth habit. The first word of the botanical name usually denotes the genus.

Germination The initial growth period of a seed.

Greensand A pulverized rock powder of sandy clay that is used to supply potassium, magnesium, and trace minerals to plants.

Grafting A method of plant propagation in which a bud or shoot from one plant is joined to the roots or a shoot of another. *See* Graft union, Rootstock, Scion.

Graft union The place on a grafted plant where the bud or shoot and rootstock join. *See* Grafting, Rootstock, Scion.

Groundcover A low-growing plant that spreads quickly to form dense colonies; often used to prevent soil erosion or cover shaded areas.

Gypsum A mineral composed of calcium sulfate that is added to the soil to improve drainage and aeration and to supply calcium.

H

Habit The characteristic growth pattern of a plant.

Hardening off The process of acclimatizing a plant that has been grown indoors to the outdoors. *See* Acclimatization.

Hardiness The ability of a plant to survive over a range of hot or cold climactic conditions.

Herbicide A chemical used to control or destroy plants.

Honeydew A viscous liquid excreted by aphids and other sucking insects that is a growth medium for certain molds and a food source for ants.

Horticultural oil A refined oil that, when mixed with water, is used as a pesticidal spray.

Humus Decayed or partially decayed organic matter derived from plants.

Hybrid The offspring of genetically dissimilar plant parents.

I

Inorganic fertilizer A synthetic fertilizer that provides nutrients to encourage plant growth.

Inorganic mulch A mulch made from an inorganic substance, such as plastic or gravel. See Mulch.

Insecticidal soap An insecticide made from salt and fatty acids mixed with water and alcohol.

Integrated pest management (IPM) An environmentally conscious approach to pest control that uses treatments from least toxic to most.

Invasive plant A plant that spreads quickly, either by seeds or roots, and chokes out other plants.

L

Larva The immature, often wormlike, life stage that emerges from the eggs of certain insects.

Limestone A sedimentary rock composed largely of calcium carbonate that is used in powdered form to provide calcium, a plant nutrient, and make soil more alkaline.

Loam A fertile, well-drained soil that consists of a balance of sand, silt, and clay; most plants thrive in it.

M

Microclimate A small area where the climate differs from that of the surrounding area.

Mulch An organic or inorganic soil covering used to conserve soil moisture, suppress weeds, and regulate soil temperature.

N

Naturalized Refers to a plant that grows well in a region to which it is not native.

Nematode A microscopic worm that lives in soil, plants, or water; some are beneficial to plants, others are harmful plant pests.

Neutral soil Soil with a pH value of 7.0. See pH.

Nitrogen A major nutrient essential for plant growth.

Node The point, usually slightly swollen, on a stem where leaves or buds form.

NPK Chemical symbols for nitrogen, phosphorous, and potassium, the three major nutrients in fertilizer.

Nutrient Any element necessary for plant growth.

O

Organic fertilizer Any substance of plant or animal origin used as a fertilizer (manure, compost); also includes mineral-based fertilizers.

Organic matter Any substance derived from plant and animal material.

Organic mulch A mulch made from an organic plant material, such as shredded bark. *See* Mulch.

Overwinter To live through winter, usually in a dormant state.

P

Peat moss Partially decayed mosses collected from boggy areas; used as a soil amendment.

Perennial Plant that lives for three or more growing seasons.

Pesticide A substance used to control and destroy insects, fungi, bacteria, mites, weeds, and other pests.

Petal A nonreproductive part of a flower—a modified leaf that is usually the showiest, most colorful part of a flower to attract pollinating insects.

pH (potential hydrogen) The measure of hydrogen ions in solution, used to indicate acidity or alkalinity. In soil, pH that is too high or too low can impede the absorption of soluble nutrients by plant roots.

pH scale A scale graded from 0 (pure acid) to 14 (pure lye) used to measure acidity or alkalinity. From the neutral point (7.0) the numbers increase or decrease geometrically; thus pH 5 is 10 times more acid that pH 6; pH 4 is 100 times more acid.

Pheromone trap A device that lures insects with a synthetic form of the chemical produced by them to attract mating partners.

Pinching The removal of a stem's soft growing tip to promote production of side shoots or flowers.

Pollination The transfer of pollen from a plant's male to the female part of the same or a different plant.

Post-emergent herbicide An herbicide used to control or destroy established plants.

Pre-emergent herbicide An herbicide that acts to control plants before or during germination.

Predatory mites Beneficial mites that prey on plant pests.

Propagate To increase the number of a plant through reproduction.

Prune To cut back the growth of a plant to maintain its vigor, retain its shape, or encourage new growth.

R

Resistant Referring to a plant that is not likely to be affected by a specific stressor, such as diseases, insects, pests, or drought.

Rhizome A thickened stem either on or under the ground that serves as a food-storage organ.

Rootstock A plant, usually of superior hardiness, used to provide roots for a grafted plant.

Rot A disease caused by fungi or bacteria that precipitates the decay of plant tissue.

Runner A spreading, slender stem that grows along the ground and roots to produce a new plant.

Rust Refers to several fungal diseases that cause rusty-looking spots on stems or leaves, especially in cool, damp weather.

S

Scab Fungal diseases that create rough raised spots on a plant's leaves or on its fruits.

Scale Soft-bodied insects that suck sap. As adults, they attach themselves to the plant and form hard, waxy protective shields.

Scarify To scratch the outer shell of a seed to encourage germination.

Scion A shoot or bud taken from one plant and grafted onto the rootstock of another. *See* Grafting.

Scorch Browning of the leaves, along the veins or the edges, due to hot weather, too much or too little fertilizer, or damage from pesticides.

Self-sow When a plant drops seeds that will produce seedlings without any assistance.

Side dressing An application of fertilizer to the soil surface but away from the plant stem.

Solarization A method that uses the sun's heat to kill soil insects, diseases, and weeds. Layers of clear plastic cover the ground for four to six weeks, heating the soil and killing organisms within the top few inches.

Species A group of very similar plants that can freely interbreed and are signified by the second word of the botanical name. *See* Genus.

Spore The separate reproductive structure produced by flowerless plants, such as ferns, mosses, and fungi, instead of seeds.

Sticky trap A pest-control device—consisting of a piece of usually colorful material coated with a sticky substance—that is used to attract and trap insect pests.

Stolon A spreading stem that grows along or under the ground and roots at the tip to produce a new plant.

Stratify To store seeds in a cool, dark, moist place for a certain period of time to promote germination.

Stress Any environmental or other factor that weakens a plant, such as drought, insects, or diseases.

Sucker A shoot arising from roots, underground stems, or the rootstock of a grafted plant.

Summer oil A refined petroleum product applied to growing plants to control and destroy insects.

Systemic pesticide An insecticide that is absorbed into the tissues of a plant and kills the insects that feed on the plant.

T

Taproot The main, downward-growing root, usually long and fleshy, that anchors a plant in the soil.

Tender Referring to a plant that is susceptible to damage from cold.

Thatch Undecomposed plant material that accumulates at the base of lawn grass.

Thinning For seedlings, this is the removal of weak or excess plants when they develop two or three true leaves. For perennials, it is removing plants or pruning plants to encourage increased air circulation.

Tolerant Referring to a plant that can endure stressors, such as droughts, diseases, pests, or cold.

Top dress To apply fertilizer to the surface of the soil.

Tuber A short, thickened, usually underground stem or root that serves as a food-storage organ for plants.

V

Virus A primitive microorganism that infects living cells and can cause disease, usually incurable.

INDEX

Page numbers in **bold type** indicate an illustration along with the text.

Page numbers in **bold type** indicate an illustration along with the text.

408 *Index*

Page numbers in **bold type** indicate an illustration along with the text.

410 *Index*

Page numbers in **bold type** indicate an illustration along with the text.

412 *Index*

Page numbers in **bold type** indicate an illustration along with the text.

CREDITS

PHOTOGRAPHS

Abbreviations

ALD Alan and Linda Detrick
ARC A. R. Chase
BJ Bill Johnson
CC Crandall & Crandall
CU Department of Plant Pathology, Cornell University
DC David Cavagnaro
DF Derek Fell
DG David Goldberg
GH Gerald Holmes
GPL Garden Picture Library
GS Gary Simone
HS Holt Studios International
JD James F. Dill
JG John Glover
JH Jerry Howard/Positive Images
JP Jerry Pavia
MD Margery Daughtrey
MDA Michael Dodge & Associates
MG Marge Garfield
NC Nigel Cattlin/Holt Studios International
OSU David Shetlar/Ohio State University
PI Positive Images
PP Pam Peirce
PR Photo Researchers
PSU Gary Moorman, Department of Plant Pathology, Pennsylvania State University
RS Richard Shiell
RW Ron West
SCI Storey Communications, Inc.
SG Stanton Gill
SH Saxon Holt
SR Susan Roth
TZ Thomas Zitter

The disease or pest shown in a photograph does not necessarily appear on the plant being discussed.

Pages: 2–3 Clive Nichols. 5 DG. 12–13 ALD. 14 *left column top to bottom:* CC, DG; *right column top to bottom:* GH, SCI, NC, GH. 15 *left column top to bottom:* ALD/PR, MG, GH; *right column top to bottom:* DC, RS, ALD, NC. 16 *left column top to bottom:* ARC, NC, SCI, DF, Jurgen Dielenschneider/HS/PR; *right column top to bottom:* PP, NC, NC, Patricia Bruno/PI, RS. 17 *left column top to bottom:* NC, DC, MDA, NC, SCI; *right column top to bottom:* MDA, ARC, PP, MDA. 18 *bottom left* Brian Carter/GPL; *center* William Ferguson; *right* DC. 19 *left* Pam Spaulding/PI; *center* DG; *right* MDA. 20 *left* BJ; *center* ALD/PR; *right* GH. 21 *left* Alan Detrick; *center* DF, *right* SCI. 22 *top left* DF; *bottom left* Casey Hoy/Ohio State Univeristy; *right* MD. 23 *left* DG; *center* MD; *right* DG. 24 PP. 25 *center* Casey Hoy/Ohio State Univeristy; *right* DG. 26 *left* MDA; *center* SCI; *top right* RS; *bottom right* NC. 27 *left* MD; *center* William Ferguson; *right* David McDonald/PhotoGarden, Inc. 28 *left* DG; *center* RS; *right* MG. 30 *top* Neil Holmes/GPL, *center top* ARC; *center bottom* RW; *right* Christine Dupuis. 31 *left* RS; *center* NC; *right*

MDA; 32 *top left* MD; *bottom left* PSU; *right* HS/PR. 33 *left* RS; *center* ARC; *right* SCI. 34 *left* DG; *center* RS; *right* MDA. 35 *top left* ARC; *bottom left* SCI; *center* RS; *right* BJ. 36 *left* Cheryl Hogue/Britstock; *top right* ARC; *bottom right* PP. 37 *left* ARC; *center* JD; *right* DG. 38 *left* DG; *center* MD; *right* RS. 39 *left* RS; *top center* MDA; *bottom center* BJ; *right* SCI. 40 *left* Mayer/Le Scanff/GPL; *center* SG. 41 *left* GH; *center* NC; *right* SR. 42 *right* NC. 43 *left* NC; *right* NC. 44 *left* DG; *center* MG; *right* Patricia Bruno/PI. 45 *left* BJ; *center* Howard Rice/GPL. 46 SCI. 47 *top left* RW; *bottom left* SG; *right* Roger Foley. 48 *left* David McDonald/Photo-Garden, Inc; *top right* MD; *bottom right* NC. 49 JD. 50 *left* JG; *center* DF; *top right* Jurgen Dielenschneider/HS/PR; *bottom right* SCI. 51 *left* DG; *center* William Ferguson; *right* DG. 52 *left* Geoff Bryant/PR; *center* SG; *top right* RS; *bottom right* GH. 53 *left* Bob Gibbons/HS; *top center* SG; *bottom center* DF; *right* All-America Selections. 54 *left* MDA; *center* CC; *top right* BJ; *bottom right* SCI. 55 *left* DG; *top center* DC; *bottom center* RS; *right* MDA. 56 *center* NC; *top right* GH; *bottom right* JD. 57 *left* PP; *center* MG; *right* RS. 58 *left* MD; *right* SCI. 59 *left* NC; *bottom left* GH; *center* NC; *right* SCI. 60 *left* Nancy Palubniak; *center* RW; *top right* Ralph Byther; *bottom right* SCI. 61 *top* Joseph Strauch; *bottom* SG. 62 DC. 63 *left* GS; *top center* NC; *bottom center* NC; *right* SCI. 64 *left* Rex Butcher/GPL; *center* Howard Rice/GPL; *top right* BJ; *bottom right* MD. 65 *left* GS; *right* SCI. 66 *left* RS; *top right* GH; *bottom right* RS. 67 *left* DF; *center* RS; *right* RS. 68 *left* SCI; *center* RS; *top right* CC; *bottom right* MG. 69 *left* MG; *center* SH; *right* Terry Wild. 70 *left* NC; *right* Steve Healey. 71 *left* RS; *top center* MDA; *bottom center* RS; *right* SCI. 72 *left* SCI; *center* DC; *top right* MD; *bottom right* MDA. 73 *left* NC; *center* NC; *right* Howard Rice/GPL. 74 *left* MG; *right* NC. 75 *left* BJ; *center* SCI; *right* Terry Wild. 76 *left* ALD; *center* ARC; *top right* CC; *bottom right* ARC. 77 *left* MDA; *top center* RS; *bottom center* SCI; *right* DC. 78 *left* Primrose Peacock/HS; *center* MDA; *top right* MDA; *bottom right* RS. 79 *left* GS; *top center* MDA; *bottom center* NC; *right* Bonnie Sue/PR. 80 *left* RS; *center* SG; *right* NC. 81 *center* NC; *right* SR. 82 *left* NC; *right* HS/PR. 83 *left* SG; *center* CC; *right* MDA. 84 *left* ALD; *center* DC; *top right* PP; *bottom right* RS. 85 *left* DF; *top center* DF; *bottom center* MDA; *right* MDA. 86–87 SR. 88 *left column top to bottom:* Steve Healey, RW, Kathy Merrifield/PR; *right column top to bottom:* Steven Koike, RW, DF, JD. 89 *left column top to bottom:* CC, GH, JD, DG, Christine Dupuis; *right column top to bottom:* RW, William D. Adams, William D. Adams, GH, RW. 90 *left column top to bottom:* DG, NC, NC, GH; *right column top to bottom:* RW, GH, RW, Bob Kennett/HS, DC. 91 *left column top to bottom:* ALD, CC, DC, PP. *right column top to bottom:* SCI, TZ, PP, MG. 92 *left* DG; *center* NC; *top right* NC; *bottom right* CC. 93 *left* ALD; *center* TZ; *top right* Pam Spaulding/PI. 94 *left* JD; *right* NC/PR. 95 *left* NC; *top center* NC;

bottom center TZ; *right* Terry Wild. 96 *left* Steven Needham/Envision; *center* Marge Garfiield; *right* RW. 97 *left* SCI; *right* Howard Rice/GPL. 98 *left* DG; *center* PP; *right* NC. 99 *left* DF; *center* RW; *right* JP. 100 *top left* JD; *bottom left* Steven Koike; *right* Steven Koike. 101 *left* NC; *right* TZ. 102 *left* DG; *center* DC; *right* GH. 103 *left* PP; *right* DC. 104 *left* NC; *center* Charles Averre/NCSU/GH; *top right* NC; *bottom right* Lee Lockwood/PI. 105 *left* DC; *center* CC; *right* SCI. 106 *left* Alan L. Detrick; *right* JD. 107 *left* SCI; *center* NC; *right* JP. 108 *left* TZ; *right* DF. 109 *left* JD; *top center* DC; *bottom center* TZ; *right* NC. 110 *left* Steven Koike; *top right* PP; *bottom right* Steven Koike. 111 *left* GH; *right* PP; *bottom* JP. 112 *left* DC; *center* GH; *right* TZ. 113 *left* GS/GS; *right* CC. 114 *left* DC; *center* P. Karunakaran/HS; *right* GH. 116 *top left* DG; *center left* Zeva Oelbaum/Envision; *bottom left* DC; *center* GH; *top right* NC; *bottom right* DG. 117 *left* NC. 118 *left* Terry Wild; *center* Richard Anthony/HS; *right* NC. 119 *left* NC; *top center* NC; *bottom center* NC; *right* ALD. 120 *left* PP; *right* Biological Photography. 121 *left* NC; *center* JD; *right* DC. 122 *top left* RW; *bottom left* NC; *right* Bob Kennett/HS. 123 RW. 124 *left* Biological Photography; *right* DG. 125 *left* RW; *center* JD; *bottom right* JP. 126 JD. 127 *top left* Christine Dupuis; *bottom left* JD; *center* DG; *right* Steven Needham/Envision. 128 *left* DG; *center* DF; *top right* Alvin E. Staffan/PR; *bottom right* DC. 129 *top left* TZ; *bottom left* TZ; *center* GH; *right* SR. 130 *left* DG; *top right* NC; *bottom right* DF. 131 *left* Inga Spence/HS; *right* DC. 132 *left* NC; *right* GH. 133 *left* Ken Sorensen; *top center* NC; *bottom center* GH; *bottom right* Osentoski & Zoda/Envision; *bottom right* Steven Needham/Envision. 134 *left* Inga Spence/HS; *center* Biological Photography; *top right* RW; *bottom right* SCI. 135 *left* PP; *right* ALD. 136 *top left* NC; *bottom left* DF; *right* ALD. 137 *left* William D. Adams; *center* GH; *right* DG. 138 *left* GS; *right* GS. 139 *left* GS; *right* DG. 140–141 Rosalind Creasy. 142 *left column top to bottom:* RW, Steve Healey, MDA; *right column top to bottom:* NC, MDA, MDA, SCI. 143 *left column top to bottom:* Joseph Strauch, MDA, NC, PP, Steven Koike; *right column top to bottom:* SCI, MDA, Steven Koike, Jurgen Dielenschneider/HS/PR, DG. 144 *left* DG; *center* MDA; *top right* PP; *bottom right* SCI. 145 *left* NC; *center* NC; *right* MDA. 146 *left* DG; *right* MDA. 147 *left* MDA; *center* Richard Anthony/HS; *right* Rosalind Creasy. 148 *left* DG; *center* SCI, *top right* MDA; *bottom right* MDA. 149 *left* NC; *center* ALD; *right* ALD. 150 *left* ALD; *center* RW; *top right* DC; *bottom right* DG. 151 *top left* Steven Koike; *bottom left* Steven Koike; *center* PP; *right* DG. 152 *left* DG; *center* NC; *top right* NC; *bottom right* MDA. 153 *left* MDA; *top center* MDA; *bottom center* MDA; *right* DG. 154 *left* MDA; *center* MDA; *top right* MDA; *bottom right* MDA. 155 *left* SCI; *top center* Joseph Strauch; *bottom center* DF; *right* DG. 156 *left* DG; *center* William Ferguson; *right* PSU. 157 *left* DG; *center* PP; *right* MDA.

158 *left* MDA; *right* Grace Davies/Omni-Photo. **159** *left* PP; *top center* PP; *bottom center* MDA; *right* DG. **160** *left* SCI; *center* MDA; *top right* MDA; *bottom right* MDA. **161** *left* SCI; *center* Joseph Strauch; *right* DG. **162** *left* DG; *center* Steve Healey; *right* GH. **163** *left* MDA; *center* Karen Bussolini/PI; *right* DG. **164–165** Clive Nichols. **166** *left column top to bottom:* DF, RS, SCI; *right column top to bottom:* NC, CU, MDA, PSU. **167** *left column top to bottom:* GS, SG, PP, ARC, DF; *right column top to bottom:* SG, GS, William E. Ferguson, GS. **168** *top left* MDA; *center* NC; *top right* CU; *bottom right* DF. **169** *left* Charles Marden Fitch; *top center* Rosie Mayer/HS; *bottom center* PSU. **170** *left* DF; *center* SCI; *right* SCI. **171** *left* MDA; *center* NC; *right* ALD/PR. **173** *top left* PP; *bottom left* GS; *center* RS; *right* SR. **174** *left* DF; *center* GS; *top right* GS; *bottom right* MDA. **175** *left* SG; *center* SCI; *right* DC. **176** *bottom left* SR; *center* PSU; *top right* ARC; *bottom right* CU. **177** *left* William E. Ferguson; *center* GS; *right* Howard Rice/GPL. **178** *bottom left* DC; *center* DF; *right* SCI. **179** *top left* SG; *bottom left* MD; *center* Steve Healey; *right* DG. **180–181** Clive Nichols. **182** *left column top to bottom:* Grace Davies/ Omni-Photo, PP, GS, NC; *right column top to bottom:* MDA, Joseph Strauch, NC, NC. **183** *left column top to bottom:* RS, NC, MG, HS/PR, CU; *right column top to bottom:* OSU, NC, GS, DF, NC. **184** *left* PSU; *right* CC. **185** *left* MG; *center* Tomomi Saito/ Dunq/PR. **186** *left* RS; *center* SCI; *top right* GS; *bottom right* Kathy Merrifield/PR. **187** *left* DF; *right* CU. **188** *left* Neil Holmes/GPL; *right* Grace Davies/Omni-Photo. **189** *top left* NC; *bottom left* NC; *center* GS; *right* J. S. Sira/GPL. **190** *top left* GS; *bottom left* GS; *right* PP. **191** *left* MD; *right* Brigitte Thomas/GPL. **192** NC. **193** *top left* NC; *bottom left* NC; *center* JD; *right* Kathy Charlton/GPL. **194** *left* MG; *top right* DF; *bottom right* JD. **195** *left* PSU; *top center* OSU; *bottom center* OSU; *right* SR. **196** *top* MDA; *bottom* NC. **197** *left* PSU; *center* NC; *right* ALD. **198** *left* Alan Detrick/E. R. Degginger; *top right* PSU; *bottom right* MDA. **199** *left* CC; *center* GS; *right* Rex Butcher/GPL. **200** *left* DC; *center* JD; *right* NC; **201** *left* RW; *top center* MG; *bottom center* CU; *right* ALD. **202** *left* NC; *right* JD. **203** *left* MDA; *right* JG. **204** *bottom left* RS; *center* CC; *bottom right* Joseph Strauch. **205** *left* Steven Healey; *right* Joseph Strauch. **206** *left* Geoff Bryant/PR; *center* MDA; *right* RW. **207** *top* NC; *bottom* MD. **208** *left* JG, *center* NC; *right* CU; **209** *left* NC; *center* CU; *right* RS. **210** *left* NC; *right* CU. **211** *top* PSU; *top center* SCI; *bottom center* GS; *right* JG. **212** *left* CU; *center* top MDA; *bottom right* William E. Ferguson. **213** *left* NC; *center* Joseph Strauch; *right* Clive Nichols. **214** *left* NC; *top right* NC; *bottom right* NC. **215** *left* GS; *right* NC. **216** *left* JG; *center* NC; *top right* NC; *bottom right* RW. **217** *top center* RS; *bottom center* NC; *right* JG. **218** *left* NC/PR; *top right* JG; *bottom right* RW. **220** *left* ALD; *top right* BJ; *bottom right* BJ. **221** *left* E. R. Degginger; *center* HS/PR; *right* Geoff Bryant/ PR. **222** *left* NC; *right* BJ. **223** *left* John Bova/ PR; *center* RW; *right* MDA. **224** *left* JG; *center* William E. Ferguson; *right* RW. **225** *left* BJ; *top center* NC; *bottom center* RS; *right* Dency Kane. **226** *left* NC; *right* GS. **227** *left* GS; *center* HS/PR; *right* MDA. **228** JD. **229** *left* DF; *center* JD; *right* Brigitte Thomas/GPL. **230–231** SR.

232 *left column top to bottom:* JG, William Ferguson, RS, RW; *right column top to bottom:* E.R. Degginger, CU, CU, CU. **233** *left column top to bottom:* RW, PP, CU, RS, CU; *right column top to bottom:* RS, RS, SCI, Primrose Peacock/HS, DF. **234** *left* RS; *center* CU; *top right* PSU; *bottom right* CU; **235** *left* CU; *top center* DF; *bottom center* DF; *right* SCI. **236** *left* Terry Wild, *center* CU; *top right* SCI; *bottom right* PSU. **237** *left* DF; *center* Willaim J. Jahoda/PR; *top and right* Clive Nichols. **238** *left* DF; *top right* BJ; *bottom right* CU. **239** *left* Alan L. Detrick/E. R. Degginger; *top center* John Bova/PR; *bottom center* CU; *right* DF. **240** *left* Guy and Edith Sternberg; *right* CU. **241** *left* CU; *right* Geoff Bryant/PR. **242** *top* RS; *bottom* Jim Steinberg/PR. **243** *left* CU; *right* SCI. **244** DF. **245** *left* BJ; *center* ALD; *right* SR. **246** *left* PSU; *top right* CU; *bottom right* SCI. **247** *left* Kathy Merrifield/PR; *right* Noble Proctor/PR. **248** *top left* RW; *bottom left* CU; *right* Liz Ball/PI. **249** *left* RW; *center* RW; *right* JG/GPL. **250** *bottom left* David McDonald/PhotoGarden, Inc; *center* Primrose Peacock/HS; *right* DF. **251** *left* NC; *center* NC; *right* Brigitte Thomas/GPL. **252** RS. **253** *left* CU; *right* RS. **254** *left* CU; *right* E.R. Degginger; *bottom right* CU. **255** *left* RS; *center* BJ; *right* George E. Jones III/PR. **256** *top left* Ken Brate/PR; *center* OSU; *right* OSU. **257** *left* OSU; *right* CU. **258** *left* Michael Gadomski/PR; *center* CU; *right* CU. **259** *top left* CU; *bottom left* CU; *center* CU; *right* SCI. **260** *left* DF; *top right* SCI; *bottom right* DF. **261** *center* CU; *top right* RS. **262** *left* JP; *center* RW; *right* GS. **263** *left* GS; *top right* CU; *bottom right* JG. **264** *left* PSU; *right* CU. **265** *left* MDA; *center* CU; *bottom right* Clive Nichols. **266** *left* Joseph Strauch; *right* Andy Morant/HS. **267** *left* DF; *right* OSU. **268** *left* CU; *right* ALD. **269** *top left* DF; *bottom left* NC; *center* BJ; *top right* Michael Gadomski/PR. **270** *left* RS, *center* GS; *right* CU; **271** *top* NC; *bottom* Charles Marden Fitch. **272** *top left* Guy Sternberg; *bottom left* PP; *right* PSU. **274** *top left* Geoff Bryant/PR. *top center* RS; *bottom center* RS; *right* Guy and Edith Sternberg; **275** *top left* NC; *bottom left* PP; *top right* RS; *bottom right* CU. **276** *left* Carleton Ray/PR; *right* RW. **277** *top left* GS; *bottom left* GS; *center* GS; *right* RS. **278** *left* CU; *top right* DF; *bottom right* MDA. **279** *left* OSU; *center* RW; *right* JG. **280** *left* OSU; *top right* NC; *bottom right* OSU. **281** *left* OSU; *right* NC. **282** *left* DF; *center* OSU; *top right* PSU; *bottom right* William J. Jahoda/PR. **283** *left* OSU; *top* right OSU; *bottom right* DF. **284** *left* Terry Wild; *center* DC; *top right* Steven Koike; *bottom right* Steven Koike. **285** *center* William Ferguson; *right* JG. **286–287** Mayer/Le Scanff/GPL. **288** *left column top to bottom:* Phil Degginger/E.R. Degginger, DF, NC, JD; *right column top to bottom:* Inga Spence/HS, William D. Adams, Len McLeod/HS/PR, Kathy Merrifield/PR. **289** *left column top to bottom:* NC, DG, NC, NC, DF; *right column top to bottom:* JD, RS, Christopher Fairweather/GPL, CU, NC. **290** *left* Mayer/Le Scanff/GPL; *center* DF; *top right* DF; *bottom right* DF. **291** NC. **292** *top left* NC; *bottom left* PP; *right* DG. **294** *left* JD; *right* NC. **295** *left* JD; *center* JD; *right* ALD/PR. **296** *left* DC; *center* DC; *top right* DF; *right* CC. **297** *left* NC; *right* JD. **298** *left* DC; *center* NC; *top right* Inga Spence/HS; *bottom right* JD. **299** *left* PP; *center* NC; *right* Howard Rice/GPL. **300** *top left* Primrose Peacock/HS;

bottom left PP; *right* RW. **301** *left* NC; *right* Joyce Photographics/PR. **302** *top left* JH/PI; *center* Kathy Merrifield/PR; *right* NC. **303** *left* Len McLeod/HS/PR; *center* RS; *right* F. Stuart Westmorland/PR. **304** *left* Len McLeod/HS/PR; *right* NC. **305** *top left* DF; *bottom left* HS/PR; *right* NC. **306** *left* Phil Degginger/E. R. Degginger; *top right* DF; *bottom right* JD. **307** *left* NC; *right* Christopher Gallagher/GPL. **308** *top left* Phil Degginger/E. R. Degginger; *bottom left* RS; *right* William D. Adams. **309** *left* NC; *center* NC; *right* Mayer/Le Scanff/GPL **310** *left* NC; *right* DC. **311** *left* RW; *top center* Ben Phillips/PI; *bottom center* J. H. Robinson; *right* DF. **312** NC **313** *left* Christopher Fairweather/ GPL; *center* JD; *right* NC/PR. **314** *left* DC; *right* RW. **315** *left* Kathy Merrifield/PR; *center* DF; *right* DC. **316** *top left* NC; *bottom left* NC/PR; *right* NC. **317** *top left* NC; *bottom left* JD; *right* HS/PR. **318** *left* RW; *right* Guy & Edith Sternberg. **319** *left* JD; *center* RW; *right* Inga Spence/HS. **320–21** SH. **324** *left* ALD; *right* ALD. **325** SH. **327** *left* Ron Evans/GPL *right* DG. **329** *left* SH; *right* CC. **330** *top* Lee Lockwood/PI; *bottom* Patricia Bruno/PI. **332** *top* NC; *bottom* ALD. **333** *left* JG; *right* Pam Spaulding/PI. **334** Dency Kane. **335** *left* DC; *right* DC. **336** DF. **338** *left* SR; *right* DF. **339** *top* JH; *bottom left* ALD/PR; *bottom center* CC; *bottom right* DF; **340** *top* MG; *bottom* ALD. **341** SH. **342–343** JH. **344** *left* SH; *center* JG; *right* CC. **345** *left* SH; *center* CC; *right* JG. **346–347** Gordon Smith/PR. **348** *left* SH; *right* SH. **349** *left* Margaret Hengel/PI; *right* NC. **350** *left* Gordon Roberts/HS; *right* CC. **351** *left* BJ; *top center* CC; *top right* SH; *bottom* NC. **352** *left* ALD; *right* Jerry Koontz/Index Stock/ Picture Cube Division. **353** *top* RS; *bottom* NC. **354** *left* SH; *right* ALD, **355** *top left* MDA; *bottom left* Gilbert Grant/PR; *right* PP. **356** *left column top to bottom* NC, RS, PP, DC; *center* PP; *right* PP. **357** *left* ALD; *center* ALD; *right column from top to bottom* DC, BJ, DC, Joseph Strauch. **358** *top* SH. **359** *top* Ron Evans/ GPL; *bottom* DC. **361** ; *top left* DG; *bottom left* SH; *right* JG. **362–363** Clive Nichols; **364** CC. **365** *top left* Roger Foley; *top right* JH; *bottom* JG. **366** Janet Loughrey. **367** *top* Roger Foley; *bottom left* JH; *bottom right* Horticultural Photographs. **368** MG. **369** *top* MG; *right* JH. **370** JH/PI. **371** *top* RS; *bottom* SH. **372** Rosemary Mayer/HS **373** Janet Loughrey.**374** *top* David McDonald/PhotoGarden, Inc; *bottom* Roger Foley. **375** *top* MG; *bottom* Bob Gibbons/HS. **376** *top* Mick Hales/GreenWorld Pictures; *bottom* Mick Hales/GreenWorld Pictures. **378–379** The Image Bank. **380** *top left* SH; *top center* SH; *bottom left* SH; *bottom center* SH; *right* ALD. **381** *top left* ALD; *top right* ALD; *bottom left* ALD; *bottom right* ALD. **382** ALD. **383** *top left* Aaron Haupt/PR; *top right* CC; *bottom* Harry Haralambou/PI. **384** *top* CC; *center left* CC; *center right* DG; *bottom* CC. **386** Alan Detrick/PR. **387** *top left* NC; *bottom left* PP; *top right* ALD; *bottom right* CC. **388** JH. **389** *top left* CC; *top right* CC; *bottom* CC.

Front cover *top row left to right:* Richard Heinzen/SuperStock, Rosalind Creasy, DK Publishing, Inc., Pamela Grafe; *bottom row left to right:* DF, RS, W. Atlee Burpee & Co., DF. **Back cover** *top* DF; *bottom* RS.

Picture research by Carousel Research, Inc.

U.S. Climate Zone Map

Published by the U.S. Department of Agriculture, the map below divides the United States into eleven hardiness zones based on the average minimum winter temperature of each region. If a plant is described as being "hardy to USDA hardiness zone 7," that means that it has survived the winter temperatures in this map's zone 7, where (on average) the lows range from 0° to 10°F.

This system for rating hardiness has obvious limitations. Microclimates are likely to make a particular garden warmer or colder than temperatures in the surrounding area, and so your yard may not entirely agree with the zone assigned to it by this map. In addition, this map doesn't take into account the threat that summer heat and humidity may pose to a plant's survival in the southern states. To remedy that, this book lists both the coldest and the warmest zone suitable for each plant.

This method of rating plant hardiness does provide a simple and fairly reliable guide to the adaptation of plants to your climate. Because the USDA map has been accepted as the standard hardiness index by the U.S. nursery industry, it is also a convenient shopping guide; you'll generally find the zone of hardiness listed for each plant in the nursery catalogs.

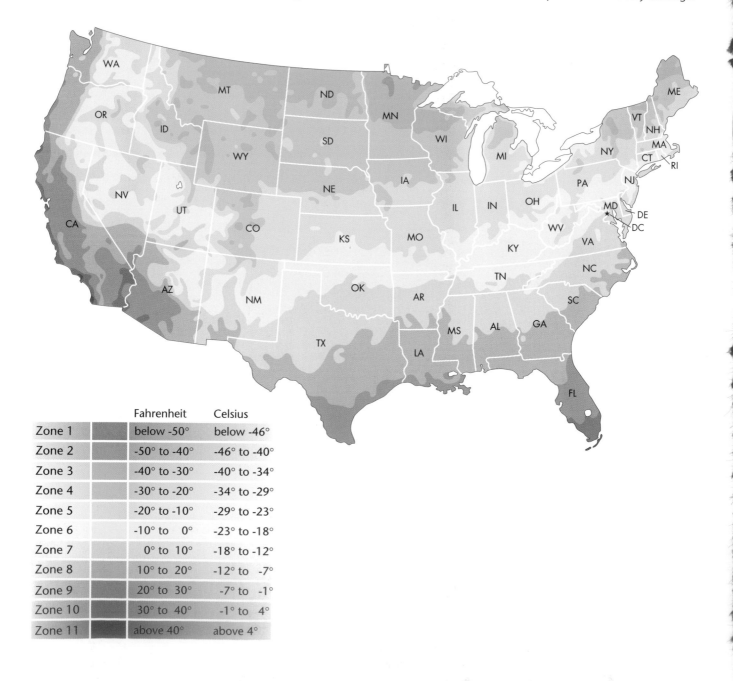

		Fahrenheit	Celsius
Zone 1		below -50°	below -46°
Zone 2		-50° to -40°	-46° to -40°
Zone 3		-40° to -30°	-40° to -34°
Zone 4		-30° to -20°	-34° to -29°
Zone 5		-20° to -10°	-29° to -23°
Zone 6		-10° to 0°	-23° to -18°
Zone 7		0° to 10°	-18° to -12°
Zone 8		10° to 20°	-12° to -7°
Zone 9		20° to 30°	-7° to -1°
Zone 10		30° to 40°	-1° to 4°
Zone 11		above 40°	above 4°